Point Lookout Prison Camp and Hospital

The North's Largest Civil War Prison

By

Richard H. Triebe

First published by Smokey River Publishing
All Rights Reserved.

ISBN—13: 978-0-9798965-3-8
ISBN—10: 0-9798965-3-3

Cover photograph: This picture of Point Lookout is from a 1864 lithograph by E. Sachse & Co., Baltimore, Md.

All photographs in this book are from the author's collection unless otherwise noted.

Other books by this author:

Confederate Fort Fisher, ISBN 1484032497
Fort Fisher to Elmira, ISBN 145368736X
On A Rising Tide, ISBN 1-4208-7849-2
Point Lookout Prison Camp and Hospital,
        Paperback, ISBN—10: 1495310140
Port Royal, ISBN 0-9798-9650-9

Printed in the United States of America

This book is printed on acid-free paper.

Contact Information:
Email: richardtriebe@aol.com

Printed in the United States of America

Smokey River Publishing

Special Dedication

This book would not have been possible without the help and support of my lovely wife Barbara Triebe. Barbara went with me to Point Lookout State Park and Museum and to the Confederate cemetery and monuments. She took numerous photographs and many of them appear in this book. Barbara did a hundred other things during the trip that I would have forgotten to do. I would truly be lost without her.

I love you Barbara for making me feel special every day of my life. Without your encouragement *Point Lookout Prison Camp and Hospital* would still be a dream.

Acknowledgments

I wish to thank all the people who assisted me at Point Lookout Museum and National Park.

There are many people I would like to thank for editing my manuscript. Everyone had something unique to offer and you all helped make my story exceptional. I want to thank Wanda Canada, Nan Graham, Virginia Kuhn, Paul Paolicelli and my lovely wife Barbara Triebe. Bless you all!

Table of Contents

__Dedication__

This book was written to honor all the soldiers who were sent to Point Lookout Prison Camp. It is hoped that in some small way this text will help to keep alive the memory of the Confederate soldiers, Sailors and Marines who perished there.

Introduction

Although it has been nearly 150 years since the end of the War Between the States, only one in depth study of the Union prisoner of war camp at Point Lookout, Maryland, has been written. Edwin W. Bietzell's book *Point Lookout Prison Camp for Confederates* will stand forever as a classic look at the North's largest prisoner of war camp. I hope to expand on his 1972 work. During my research I was fortunate to find over fifty prisoner accounts detailing their experiences at Point Lookout. Whenever possible I try to let the Confederate prisoners tell their stories in their own words. These men tell horror stories about prisoners not getting enough to eat and then wasting away with disease before they die. They also mention the awful water they had to drink which caused a deadly form of diarrhea. The men remembered the frigid winter winds that would howl in from the Chesapeake Bay and coat the prison camp with a blanket of snow and ice, making it too cold to go outside the tent. Many times they had no fire inside their tents to keep warm and some men lacked blankets, overcoats and shoes. After an unusually cold night quite often the prisoners would discover men frozen to death the following morning. The prisoners talk about dreadful diseases such as smallpox, pneumonia and typhoid fever which ravaged the prison camp and caused over four thousand deaths in less than two years. The sad fact is that the Federal government was fully aware of what was happening at their prisoner of war camps, but did little to relieve the men's suffering. The North had an abundance of food and clothing, but due to cruel decisions in high places these materials were not adequately distributed.

The largest part of my book is a detailed roster of all the Confederate prisoners who died at Point Lookout. This information was obtained by searching the Confederate soldier's records at the National Archives. During this search I discovered many soldiers who died at Point Lookout, but were never included on the Federal monument. I am not talking about a few names or even several dozen. My research has found hundreds of men who have been sadly forgotten. I have added 470 names to the roster in this book. I intend to add more names as new ones are found.

Some people may ask why I started a book about Point Lookout prison camp with a chapter named *Lincoln and the Border States*. The reason I had for discussing this was not only to show the early Civil War history of the Point Lookout area, but to illustrate how the Lincoln administration was not above breaking the law to achieve its purposes. This being said, it is easy to imagine these same men would also bend the rules of the Exchange Cartel in regards to prisoners. Not only were these rules bent, but legal and moral laws were broken as well.

Richard H. Triebe

Chapter 1

Abraham Lincoln and the Border States

The Border State of Maryland

President Abraham Lincoln found himself on dangerous ground shortly after he took office in 1861. Virginia, which had seceded from the Union, lay across the Potomac River, practically within view of the White House. To make matters worse, Washington D. C. was surrounded on three sides by Maryland, a border-state known for its Southern sympathies. Lincoln could not allow Maryland to secede from the Union. To do so would place the Nation's capital inside the enemy camp. In addition, all telegraph and rail links to the other Northern states would be severed.

Maryland, a slave-holding border state, was deeply divided over the issues of States Rights and whether slavery should be permitted in the Union. The conflict arose because of the diversity of Maryland's counties. The areas around the southeastern portion of the state were largely agricultural and their plantations prospered because of slave labor. Most people in these southern counties believed Maryland should join her sister states and secede. The northern parts of the state were pro-Union since they had small farms and closer economic ties with the North.

On April 19th, barely a week after Fort Sumter had fallen, the 6th Massachusetts Militia was ordered south to protect the capital. There was great concern over this movement in Maryland. The Federal troops had to switch trains at Baltimore, a hotbed of secessionist activity. When the citizens saw armed soldiers from another state marching through the streets like an invading army, they surrounded the troops and began throwing bricks and stones. Panicking, several soldiers fired randomly into the crowd, and chaos erupted. The officers tried to regain control and ordered their men to break off the engagement and proceed to the railroad station. When the gun smoke had cleared twelve citizens and four soldiers lay dead. This was the first bloodshed of the War Between the States.

The powers of the presidency did not give Lincoln the authority he needed to keep Maryland from seceding. The solution to this dilemma seemed obvious to Lincoln. Suspend the writ of habeas corpus and incarcerate anyone who had expressed Southern sympathies, particularly newspaper editors and legislators who disagreed with his point of view. These people would never be charged with a crime and they could be jailed indefinitely.[1]

Abraham Lincoln in 1860

1

In April of 1861 Baltimore citizens rioted when Union troops march through their city.

Although Article One, Section Nine of the United States Constitution provided for suspending the writ of habeas corpus during a rebellion or invasion, it also required that the impending legislation had to be approved by Congress. Lincoln doubted if he could get enough votes to pass this bill. In the election of 1860 the President failed to get any electoral votes from Maryland. If Lincoln wanted the writ suspended, he would have to act alone and face the consequences. On April 27, 1861, he suspended the writ of habeas corpus. This allowed the military to arrest anyone who disagreed with the government policies concerning the conduct of the war. In all, he shut down more than 300 newspapers across the nation and arrested 14,000 political prisoners. The writ's suspension would stay in effect until President Andrew Johnson revoked it on December 1, 1865.[2]

One of the newspaper editors arrested was Francis Key Howard of the Baltimore *Daily Exchange*. Howard was taken into custody on September 13, 1861, by United States Major General Nathaniel Banks enforcing the policy of President Abraham Lincoln. What was his crime? Howard wrote a critical editorial about Lincoln's suspension of the writ of habeas corpus. The article also mentioned that the Lincoln administration had declared martial law in Baltimore and imprisoned without due process George William Brown the mayor of Baltimore, Congressman Henry May, the police commissioners of Baltimore and the entire city council.[3]

In an ironic twist, Francis Key Howard was imprisoned at Fort McHenry near Baltimore Harbor. This is the very same fort that was under British bombardment on September 13, 1814. Francis Scott Key, Howard's grandfather, was being held prisoner on an enemy ship in the harbor and witnessed the countless shells burst around the fort. Key was so inspired when he saw the American flag still flying over Fort McHenry that he began to compose the poem called *The Defense of Fort McHenry*. This poem would later be put to music, renamed *The Star-Spangled Banner*, and go on to become the United States' national anthem.[4]

During the next fourteen months Howard was confined at Fort McHenry, Fortress Monroe, Fort La Fayette and Fort Warren. In each prison the cells were cold and overcrowded with political prisoners. Some of the men arrested were in their sixties and seventies and in delicate health. Several of these men contracted pneumonia and remained in their cells with no medical attention. Prisoner Charles D. Hinks was suffering with a high fever, had no bed and slept on a few blankets on the cold floor. When General Nathaniel Banks was informed of this by Hinks doctor he wrote to General Scott warning, "His death in prison would make an unpleasant public impression . . . I would respectfully recommend that authority be given to release him." Not wanting to be blamed for the man's death, Union authorities sent him to a hospital on Staten Island where he recovered.[5]

When the political prisoners complained of their harsh treatment things only got worse. The few small windows they had were closed with shutters. Iron bars were installed and padlocked so the shutters could not be opened. Now the cells were dark indeed. The prisoners did not have enough light to read even on the sunniest days.[6] In addition to being kept in dungeon like conditions, the men were not allowed any visits by family or friends. Political prisoners were also warned by the Lincoln administration not to seek legal assistance. The *Baltimore Sun* printed this article on February 6, 1862.

> *To the Political Prisoners in Fort Lafayette:*
> *I am instructed by the Secretary of State to inform you that the Department of State of the United States will not recognize anyone as an attorney for political prisoners, and will look with distrust upon all applications for release through such channels; and that such applications will be regarded as additional reasons for declining to release the prisoners.*
> *Seth C. Hawley*[7]

Chief Judge of the United States Supreme Court Roger B. Taney

Another noteworthy case is that of a farmer from Baltimore County. John Merryman was arrested for suspicion of burning railroad bridges to prevent some Pennsylvania troops from traveling through Baltimore to reinforce the Capitol. He was imprisoned at Fort McHenry on May 25th. What makes this case standout from the others is not so much what Merryman was accused of, but what President Lincoln did that made this legal action noteworthy. Merryman petitioned for a writ of habeas corpus, which was granted by Chief Judge of the Supreme Court Roger B. Taney. A writ of habeas corpus requires a person under arrest to be brought before a judge and formally accused of a crime. Taney ruled that the President does not have the power to suspend the writ of habeas corpus, even in time of rebellion. Thus, the arrest and detention of John Merryman was illegal. The writ was disobeyed by General George Cadwallader, the commanding officer at Fort McHenry, under orders from President Lincoln. Judge Taney cited Cadwallader for contempt but the general refused to appear in court. Generally the Federal Marshall's office would place the suspect under arrest, but they were not powerful enough to oppose the United States military. The Lincoln administration never bothered to appeal Taney's decision and instead chose to ignore it. The military continued to lock up anyone suspected of disloyal thoughts, words, or actions without showing just cause for charging them with an offense.[8]

On May 28, 1861, Justice Taney read a speech in court announcing his decision in the Merryman case and gave reasons why the legislative branch and not the executive branch had the powers to interpret the United States Constitution. He maintained that the President had usurped the power to suspend the writ of habeas corpus from congress. And even if the writ was suspended by congress there would still be no authority to hold a man indefinitely without trial. Taney reminded Lincoln that the constitution guarantees a speedy trial by an impartial jury. Also the defendant should be informed of the nature of the charges against him. What bothered Taney more than anything was the flagrant manner in which the action was carried out. Taney wrote, "If a writ of habeas corpus can be disregarded and suspended, [by] force of arms, then the people of the United States are no longer living under a government of laws, but every citizen holds life, liberty and property at the will and pleasure of the army officer in whose military district he may happen to be found."[9] Taney ordered that his opinion be filed in the Circuit Court of the United States and a copy be delivered to President Lincoln so there would be no mistake of him receiving it.[10]

President Abraham Lincoln was irritated that someone would question his authority. It has come to light in recent years that Lincoln did the unthinkable when he had an arrest warrant issued for Chief Judge Roger B. Taney. In his book, *When In the Course of Human Events*, Charles Adams wrote:

THE FEDERAL PHŒNIX.

Lincoln cartoon in which the president is rising like a phoenix from the fire he has set to the Free Press, the right to a Writ of Habeas Corpus, States Rights and The United States Constitution. The cartoon appeared December 3, 1864 in the *London Charvani.*

"To Lincoln, the Supreme Court was as much a threat as the Maryland legislators. According to the Federal Marshal, Ward Hill Lamon, after "due consideration the administration was determined to arrest the Chief Justice." They were getting ready to arrest members of the Maryland legislature who had been less than supportive of the Republican administration and its zeal for war on the Confederacy, so why not the justices of the Supreme Court? Lincoln issued an arrest warrant for Taney, but "then arose the question of making service." Who should make the arrest, and where should the Chief Justice be imprisoned?"

Lamon recalled, "It was finally determined to place the order of arrest in the hands of the United States Marshal for the District of Columbia." Lincoln personally gave the warrant to Marshal Lamon, instructing the marshal to "use his own discretion about making the arrest unless he should receive further orders." Lamon wisely decided to not serve the warrant unless specifically ordered to do so."

Thus the arrest never occurred. Perhaps Lamon had no desire to arrest the eighty-four year-old justice and throw him into a cold, damp prison cell.[11] John Merryman was indicted for treason, charging he had helped to burn six bridges on the Harrisburg Railroad and cut telegraph lines along "with a great multitude of persons . . . to the number of five hundred persons and upwards, armed . . . with guns, pistols, dirks, clubs and stones, and other warlike weapons . . . [did] traitorously join and assemble" against the United States of America. Merryman was released from Fort McHenry prison on bail July 13, 1861. Apparently the district attorney did not have enough evidence to convict Merryman because he was never brought to trial and the charges were eventually dropped.[12]

New York Attorney George Templeton Strong wrote about the arrests in his diary. "Not one of the many hundreds illegally arrested and locked up for months has been publicly charged with any crime or brought to the notice of a Grand Jury. They have all been capriciously arrested, so far as we can see . . . locked up for months without legal authority and without legal acquittal. All this is very bad— imbecile, dangerous, unjustifiable."[13]

Intimidation was another tool used effectively by the Lincoln administration. After citizens saw their friends and neighbors being hauled off to jail, they were afraid to speak out for fear they too would be arrested. The government wanted to be certain only loyal Union men would replace the mayor and delegates who had been seized. Maryland's fall election of 1861 was conducted in a frightening atmosphere. General John A. Dix warned the judges of election not to allow the ballot box to be "polluted by treasonable votes." He also issued orders to General Nathaniel Banks to "arrest and hold in confinement till after the election all disunionists . . . who show themselves at the polls." According to historian Dean Sprague, "Posters were put up at all the polling places in Baltimore inviting citizens to point out to the judges of election and the police anyone who took part on the 19th of April riot, in opposing the march of United States troops through Baltimore." Federal troops were stationed at polling places and often required the voters to take the Oath of Allegiance to the United States to prove their loyalty. If people refused, they were arrested as being a traitor. In an attempt to stuff the ballot boxes, Union soldiers in the field were given furloughs so they could vote, even though they were not residents of Maryland.

This article about the election appeared in the November 7, 1861 issue of the *Baltimore Sun*.

Local Matters

The Election Yesterday—Arrests—The state election for magistrate, constables and surveyor, took place yesterday, but after a short time there was no interest manifested by the democratic voters. Throughout the city, as soon as the polls were opened, the Federal police began to make arrests, and continued until all the police stations were filled to repletion. The charges upon which they were arrested were disorderly conduct, holding treasonable tickets near the polls, using treasonable language, and attempting to vote treasonable (democratic) tickets, while a few were charged with having been concerned in the affray of the 19th of April last, and others with having subsequent to that time taken up arms to prevent the passage of Federal troops through the city . . . . Large numbers of soldiers were about the city all day, with sidearms . . . . After authorities commenced making arrests about noon the polls were generally deserted by the voters of the opposite party.[14]

It's difficult to believe this ironhanded form of government existed in the United States in 1861, but such was the case. If someone lived in a Border State there was no more freedom of speech, in newspapers or otherwise, and no honest elections. America was no longer governed by a democracy if you had Southern sympathies. Tyranny and fear would rule the Border States of Kentucky, Maryland and Missouri for the next four years.

The Border State of Missouri

Like Maryland, Missouri also suffered under the aggressive Lincoln administration. The state government wished to remain neutral during the war and requested that both sides of the conflict keep their troops out of their state. Governor Claiborne Jackson also issued a statement that Missouri would furnish no supplies or troops to either side. To this end a military bill was introduced in the legislature that would grant Jackson the money and power to expand the state militia to enforce this neutrality. Union men in the Missouri legislature considered this armed neutrality as a thinly veiled attempt at secession. After all, they argued, what objection could be made against having the protection of Federal troops if their state was indeed loyal. Although the Union lawmakers were in a minority, they managed to tie up the bill in legislation until the Federal government stepped in.

May of 1861 saw a portion of the Missouri Volunteer Militia setup Camp Jackson at Lindell's Grove in St. Louis. The militia had been mobilized for annual training by Brigadier General Daniel M. Frost. Secessionist men had been gathering at the camp in anticipation of the military bill being passed. The new troops had no resemblance to an army since they had no arms or uniforms.

Union General Nathaniel Lyon

Fearing the militia was going to attack the St. Louis Federal Arsenal to seize the 39,000 rifles stored there, Secretary of War Simon Cameron ordered 21,000 of the weapons moved across the river to Alton, Illinois. Cameron also sent several regiments to reinforce the arsenal with more troops. In the meantime, General Nathaniel Lyon began enlisting and arming St. Louis Unionist volunteers.

Frost had heard rumors of Union General Nathaniel Lyon planning to attack Camp Jackson. On the morning of May 10th Frost sent word to Lyon that he had no intention of capturing the St. Louis Arsenal. Frost said, "I am greatly at a loss to know what could justify you in attacking citizens of the United States who are in the lawful performance of duties devolving upon them under the Constitution in organizing and instructing the militia of the state."[15]

Lyon paid no attention to General Frost and marched his 6,000 Union soldiers to Camp Jackson and surrounded the 800 militia gathered there. Lyon sent a note to Frost demanding his surrender and gave him a half hour to reply. When Frost sent back a message requesting more time, Lyon answered, "If you do not surrender within ten minutes, I will order my troops to open fire."[16]

General Frost had no choice but to surrender his command. His troops were ordered to lay down their arms, and the Union soldiers moved in to take charge of the prisoners. A large crowd of civilians had gathered to protest the capture of the Missouri Militia. During the march back to the arsenal violence flared between the angry mob and the Union troops. Pushing and shoving occurred, and then shots were fired. When the violence ended twenty-eight civilians and two soldiers were killed and over a hundred people were injured including a woman and a girl. Who fired first isn't clear. Some claimed that the Union soldiers fired first, while others said the soldiers shot in self-defense.[17]

All communications from Secretary of War Cameron to General Lyon were defensive in nature. The Secretary's orders were to recruit loyal citizens to build up the ranks of the garrison at the St. Louis Arsenal. That's all. There were no orders telling General Lyon to take the initiative. The Secretary assumed that Lyon would remain at the arsenal and not take offensive action as this would jeopardize the fragile peace in Missouri. Apparently the rumors of an impending assault by the Missouri Militia prompted General Lyon to capture Camp Jackson. If Lyon had done as his superiors had ordered, violence in Missouri might have been avoided. It is difficult to say for how long this uneasy peace could have been maintained, but certainly it was worth trying to preserve.

Union General Nathaniel Lyon's troops attack citizens in St. Louis streets.

When Governor Jackson heard about the surrender of the militia, he authorized the formation of a Missouri State Guard with General Sterling Price as its commander. Price was told not to let the Union army advance any farther into the state than St. Louis. A meeting was arranged between Union General Lyon and Governor Jackson to try and prevent further bloodshed. Jackson again stated his demands about keeping Federal troops out of Missouri. General Lyon refused to do this stating that Missouri was Federal territory and that no state leader could ever forbid Union forces from going wherever they were needed. He also told Governor Jackson rather than concede to these demands, "I would [prefer to] see you, and you, and you, and you, and every man, woman and child in this state, dead and buried." Lyon warned Governor Jackson that if he continued on this dangerous course it would mean war.[18]

Governor Jackson took a train to Jefferson City and arrived there in the early morning of June 12th. In order to prevent the Union army from following them, General Price ordered the bridges on the main rail lines burned.

General Lyon set out after Governor Jackson with 1,700 troops and a battery of artillery. Lyon's goal was to capture the capital at Jefferson City and destroy the State Guard.

The battles of Booneville and Carthage followed. Finally on August 10, 1861, General Lyon attacked Confederate General Benjamin McCulloch's forces near Springfield, Missouri. The battle of Wilson's Creek was important for several reasons. It was the first time the Missouri State Guard troops fought alongside the Confederate army. It was also the first major battle in the west with over 2,500 casualties. One of those killed was Federal General Nathaniel Lyon. The Federal army retreated to Springfield while the Confederate victory buoyed Southern sympathies in Missouri.

The Republican ruled Missouri State Convention voted to replace the governor, lieutenant governor and all the seats in the legislature because of their Southern loyalties. A strong Union man, Hamilton R.

7

Gamble, was appointed governor to replace Claiborne Jackson who was in exile.[19] In the fall Jackson's government set up a provisional capital and convened in the town of Neosho, Missouri. On October 28, the legislature voted on a bill for Missouri's secession from the Union, citing various outrages committed against the state and the overthrow of its government by General Lyon. The bill was passed on October 30, and on October 31, it was signed by Governor Jackson. Thus, Missouri had two governments for the rest of the war. One was loyal to the Union, while the other was a staunch supporter of the Confederacy.

The Border State of Kentucky

President Abraham Lincoln considered the Border State of Kentucky as the key to keeping Maryland and Missouri from seceding. In a September 1861 letter to Senator Orville Browning, Lincoln wrote "I think to lose Kentucky is nearly the same as to lose the whole game. Kentucky gone, we cannot hold Missouri, nor, as I think, Maryland."[20] According to Lincoln's war strategy, he needed to keep Kentucky in the Union so he would be able to move troops through the state and occupy major cities like Paducah, Frankfurt and Lexington. The problem was that Kentucky, stretching 400 miles across the center of the nation, could act as a roadblock to Lincoln's plans if she declared herself neutral and told Union troops to keep out.

Lincoln's proclamation calling for 75,000 troops from each state in the Union was met with opposition from Kentucky's governor. On April 15, 1861, Secretary of War Simon Cameron sent a telegram to all United States governors relating Lincoln's request for 75,000 troops from each state. Kentucky Governor Beriah Magoffin sent Cameron a terse reply, "Your dispatch is received. In answer I say emphatically Kentucky will furnish no troops for the wicked purpose of subduing her sister Southern states." Magoffin, who had Southern sympathies, was a firm believer the South had the right to secede because their rights have been violated.[21]

Although the Kentucky legislature did not vote to secede, it did pass a resolution of armed neutrality demanding that both Northern and Southern troops must stay out of their state. During the May election for delegates to the Border State convention it became apparent the Union candidates would win, so the Southern Rights candidates boycotted the election.[22] The Union candidates went on to score a great victory receiving 110,000 votes. With this victory Kentucky left no doubt it would remain in the Union. However, both the pro-Union and the secessionist faction were opposed to war. In the state elections, Unionists won enough additional seats to keep the Southern minded Governor Magoffin in check.

Kentucky Governor Beriah Magoffin

Kentucky nervously watched the Border States on either side of her struggling to maintain armed neutrality and wondered if she could succeed where they had failed. To the east Maryland had tried to remain neutral, but President Lincoln intervened by suspending the writ of habeas corpus and jailing hundreds of political prisoners thus forcing her to stay in the Union. To the West lay Missouri in the throes of the same situation.

In the summer of 1861, Confederate General Leonidas Polk broke Kentucky's neutrality by having his army march to Columbus and occupy the city. The Unionist legislature passed a resolution directing Governor Magoffin to demand General Polk's evacuation from Kentucky soil. The governor vetoed the resolution, but the legislature overrode his veto. When Union General Ulysses S. Grant also broke the

8

neutrality by marching troops to Paducah, Unionists in the state claimed this movement was in response to Confederate General Polk entering Kentucky first. The Legislature also appointed Union General Thomas L. Crittenden command of Kentucky forces which incensed the Southerners further.

To ensure the Southern Rights faction would not gain too much power within the state, the legislature passed an act to disenfranchise citizens who enlisted in the Confederate states Army. People who become disenfranchised not only lose their rights as a citizen of that state, but also forfeit their right to vote in state elections.[23]

Kentucky Governor Thomas E. Bramlette had Union leanings until it was suggested he should enlist Negros in the State Militia.

Not satisfied with the Unionist government, Kentucky organized a party known as the Russellville Convention. This group met for the purpose of forming a Confederate government in Kentucky. Over 100 delegates representing 68 counties elected to depose the current government, and create a provisional government loyal to Kentucky's new Confederate Governor George W. Johnson. This government was recognized by the Confederacy and on November 20, 1861, Kentucky became the 13th state admitted to the Confederacy. Even though Governor Magoffin had Southern sympathies, he refused to recognize the state's Confederate government under Johnson. He also continued to claim Kentucky's neutrality despite there being Union and Confederate troops in the state. Magoffin eventually became fed up with the deadlock of the state government and resigned as governor in 1862.[24]

Governor, and sometimes Confederate General, Johnson was killed at the battle of Shiloh in April of 1862. The provisional government elected Richard Hawes to replace Johnson and he served throughout the remainder of the war.

Kentucky had several Civil War governors which were recognized by the United States government. The most interesting governor was Thomas E. Bramlette. At the beginning of the War Between the States he accepted a commission as a Colonel in the Union Army. In violation of Kentucky's agreement to remain neutral in the Civil War, he raised and commanded the Union's 3rd Kentucky infantry. Bramlette resigned his military commission on July 13, 1862 and returned to Louisville to accept President Abraham Lincoln's offer to become the United States District Attorney for Kentucky. Union Democrats were searching for a candidate for governor and chose Bramlette to represent them. During the election, Union forces intimidated and jailed supporters of Bramlette's opponent, former governor Charles A. Wickliffe. Union General William Boyle interfered in the local election by issuing an order that threatened arrest on the charge of treason for any candidate whose opinions were hostile to the United States government. As a result, Bramlette carried the election by a margin of nearly 4 to 1.[25]

In January Governor Bramlette proclaimed that rebel sympathizers would be held responsible for all guerrilla raids in the state and promised there would be fines and imprisonment for anyone found to be aiding the guerrillas.[26] Although Bramlette was once a staunch supporter of the Union cause, within a year he issued a proclamation that he would "bloodily baptized the state into the Confederacy". The reasons for Bramlette's reversal were many. He didn't agree with General Stephen Burbridge's decision to enlist Negroes from Kentucky for military service.[27] The situation became worse on July 5, 1864, when President Lincoln suspended the writ of habeas corpus for citizens of the state.[28]

For the remainder of the war Kentucky and Missouri both had two state governments and each had Union and Confederate armies in the field. The Battle of Richmond, Kentucky, fought August 29–30, 1862, was a stunning Confederate victory when General Kirby Smith captured over 4,300 Union troops under Union Major General William Nelson. It was the first major battle in the Kentucky Campaign. The Battle of Perryville, fought on October 8, 1862, was considered a strategic Union victory since Confederate General Braxton Bragg withdrew to Tennessee. The Union remained in control of Kentucky for the remainder of the war.

Battle of Perryville, Kentucky, October 8, 1862.

Chapter 2

<u>Point Lookout Hospital</u>

Located at the southern-most tip of Maryland, Point Lookout is a peninsula bordered on the east by the Chesapeake Bay and on the southwest by the Potomac River. Its sandy shores promise a wonderful time whether it is a dip in the bay or taking out a boat to go sailing or fishing. Little wonder it became a popular vacation spot in the 1850's with a hundred beach cottages, a hotel and light house. Some of these summer homes must have been lavish indeed because they belonged to wealthy men like Cyrus B. McCormick, who invented the mechanical reaper, and Supreme Court Chief Justice Roger B. Taney. Point Lookout was a virtual paradise until the War Between the States intervened.[1]

Wanting to cash in on this rare opportunity to build a seaside resort, William Cost Johnson bought 400 acres of land at Point Lookout in 1857. Unfortunately he fell into financial difficulty when activity on the point declined. The Civil War turned people's attention away from recreation to the more serious crisis facing the nation. Just when Johnson thought nobody was interested in this property, William C. Allen made an offer to buy it. What Allen knew that Johnson didn't was the United States Army was considering the land to build a

Cyrus B. McCormick was a land owner at Point Lookout.

hospital and maybe a prison. Allen, a sharp businessman, hoped to make a quick profit by offering it to the Federal government for a military hospital in July of 1862. Johnson mortgaged the land to Allen and considered himself lucky for unloading it.[2]

With the war well into its second year, and casualties mounting, the North had an urgent need for a new military hospital. The Point Lookout area was considered ideal because of its location and the healthful sea breezes unique to the peninsula. Surgeon General William A. Hammond had the property inspected and wrote to General Montgomery C. Meigs on June 5, 1862 that the structures already there could accommodate 1,500 men with ease and the property had plenty of room to construct additional buildings.[3]

Construction of Hammond Military Hospital was begun under the supervision of Captain L. C. Edwards. The hospital had a revolutionary design aimed at giving patients the benefits of its open air construction. The building resembled the spokes of a wagon wheel and had sixteen wards radiating out from the center. All of the wards had thirty-six feet of open space between them and were exposed to the healthful air and sunshine. The hospital contained 1,400 beds for wounded Union soldiers and gravely ill Confederate prisoners. People in the 19th century had a tremendous fear of fire because all the buildings were made of wood. Hammond hospital dealt with this fear by having a centrally located 20,000 gallon water reservoir which could flood the structure in the event of a fire.

11

Hammond General Hospital at Point Lookout from 1864 lithograph by E. Sachse & Co., Baltimore, Md.

The wards were connected by a circular corridor near the center that measured eight feet wide by one hundred feet in circumference. In the middle were four buildings in the shape of a cross which shared a chapel, half-diet kitchen, library and a knapsack and baggage room.[4] A complex of over fifty buildings was constructed to support the hospital. These included the surgeon's quarters, the smallpox hospital, the commandant's residence, the provost marshal's office, the laundry, bakery and more. Although Hammond Military Hospital wasn't completed yet, it received its first patients as early as August 17, 1862.

In 1862 twenty-five Sisters of Charity came from Baltimore to help out at Hammond General Hospital. The Sisters learned early how dangerous caring for sick soldiers and prisoners could be when after only two weeks a member of their group died from typhoid fever. The procedure for soldiers and prisoners was to be buried with only a sheet wrapped around them. The soldiers wouldn't hear of this and made a special blemish free coffin of white pine for her. Doctors and officers deemed it to be a privilege to be a pallbearer at her funeral. A procession of the elite at Point Lookout walked to her gravesite on the banks of the Potomac River while the drum corps played a solemn death-march. She was buried there under the shade of the trees with full military honors and the respect of every man at Point Lookout.

Construction of Point Lookout Prisoner of War Camp

Several factors influenced the Federal government's decision to build a prisoner of war camp at Point Lookout. The most pressing need came after the battle of Gettysburg. The North had captured over 18,000 prisoners and the prison camps they had were overcrowded. Another reason for building a prison was the fact that the North wanted to end the prisoner exchange and needed more room to accommodate the extra men. In early 1863 Secretary of War Edwin M. Stanton directed General Henry Halleck to drastically reduce the number of exchanges. On May 20th Stanton ordered Colonel Hoffman to halt the prisoner exchanges, giving no reason for the abrupt stop.[5] Historians differ on the motivation behind Stanton's order. The most popular theory suggests the Federal government halted the prisoner exchanges because the Confederate authorities refused to exchange black soldiers. It is true the South would not exchange the black troops who had been captured. The Confederates maintained that these Negro soldiers were escaped slaves and were therefore recaptured property. Judge Robert Ould, the Confederate Commissioner of Exchange, said these soldiers would be returned to where they had been captured so they could be dealt with according to the laws of that state. He also added the South was willing to make an exception and exchange free blacks.[6] However, the Confederates refused to exchange white officers who had been captured in command of black troops. The South claimed these men were guilty of inciting servile insurrection and would either be put to death or otherwise punished at the discretion of the courts.

Union General Benjamin F. Butler's actions infuriated the South.

The question arises, was the Federal government's concern over the plight of the black prisoners genuine or was it merely a tool to confuse the issue so the exchange could be halted? According to the evidence found it appears that the government was more concerned about violations of the cartel than anything else. The alleged violations include paroled Confederate soldiers returning to their regiments before they were formally exchanged. In February 1863 General William S. Rosecrans wrote to Secretary of War Stanton that the rebels were violating the cartel by paroling prisoners in the field.[7]

The South agitated the North further by declaring General Benjamin F. Butler a criminal for a number of things he did while in command of New Orleans. Mr. William B. Mumford, a Confederate citizen, was one of a group of men who hauled down the American flag from the United States Mint, then tore it to pieces. Mumford was the only one caught and Butler ordered him to be hanged for his crime. On the evening before her husband was to be executed, Mrs. Mumford and her small children went to see General Butler. "Mrs. Mumford wept bitterly, as did the children, who fell about my knees," Butler remembered. The Union General remained stoic, despite her tearful pleas, and refused to pardon Mumford, saying, "Let him in the few hours he has to live look to God for his pardon."[8]

Shortly after this an incident occurred in New Orleans where Admiral David D. Farragut had a chamber pot poured on his head by a woman in a second story window. Outraged, General Butler issued the infamous General Order 28 which declared any woman who insulted an officer or soldier of the United States should be treated as a prostitute. When Confederate President Jefferson Davis learned of this he declared no Federal officers would be exchanged until General Benjamin F. Butler was executed for his crimes.[9]

Union Major General John Pope and officers of his command were charged by Confederate President Jefferson Davis with seizing Southern citizens and taking them past the Northern picket lines. The people were then released and warned not to return or they would be considered Southern spies and shot.[10] Union Major General David Hunter had also been declared a criminal for arming slaves and trying to start a servile war. After the Battle of Fort Pulaski, Georgia, Hunter began enlisting ex-slaves as soldiers in the occupied districts of South Carolina and formed the 1st South Carolina Regiment of African Descent. He also issued General Order No. 11, which states that the Negroes in Georgia, Florida and South Carolina were free. Hunter did this, however, without the permission of the Federal government. This action incensed Border State slave holders which in turn upset President Lincoln. Lincoln was trying his best to keep the Border States calm so they would not secede from the Union. The President was so concerned that he issued a proclamation on May 19, 1862. "I, Abraham Lincoln, President of the United States, proclaim and declare that the government of the United States had no knowledge, information, or belief of an intention on the part of General Hunter to issue such a proclamation. Neither General Hunter nor any other commander or person has been authorized by the government of the United States to make a proclamation declaring the slaves of any state free, and that the supposed proclamation is altogether void."[11]

Union Brigadier General August Steinwehr was also accused of arresting peaceful citizens and holding them hostage. These hostages were threatened to be killed if the Union army was attacked by Southern bushwhackers.[12] Not every incident mentioned was a violation of the Prisoner Exchange Cartel, but they all played an important part in impeding its progress.

Although the Second Confiscation and Militia Act of July 17, 1862, allowed military service for persons of African descent, the President did not authorize the use of black soldiers in combat until the Emancipation Proclamation was

Union General David Hunter was declared a criminal by the Confederacy for arming South Carolina slaves.

officially issued on January 1, 1863. Introducing black soldiers to the Northern army did not go as smoothly as Lincoln had hoped. Officers were reluctant to use colored troops in combat because they thought their fighting ability was inferior to white soldiers. In other instances, the colored troops were kept away from the front lines because it was thought that the Confederate soldiers would fight harder when they saw armed blacks facing them.[13]

It appears the crux of the issue, whether the exchanges were halted because the Confederacy refused to exchange black prisoners, depends on how many Negro soldiers had become prisoners during the six month period between January 1st and Secretary of War Stanton's May 20th order to halt the exchanges. Certainly there weren't many. The only fighting during this period where there was a sizable force of black troops on the front lines was at the battles of Port Hudson, Louisiana, and Milliken's Bend, Mississippi. At the May 26th battle of Port Hudson the 1st and 3rd Louisiana Native Guards, which were both black regiments, suffered nearly two-hundred casualties, but no soldiers were captured. The battle of Milliken's Bend occurred on the Mississippi River and involved several regiments of the Louisiana Native Guards and the white soldiers of the 23rd Iowa. The Confederate forces under General McCulloch fought a vicious, sometimes hand-to-hand fight with the entrenched Federals. McCulloch's Texas brigade inflicted 452 casualties; among these were 226 captured Union soldiers. The *Official Records* do not state if the captured troops were black or white.[14] However, neither battle would have influenced Secretary of War Stanton because they occurred several weeks after the prisoner exchange had already been halted.

Picture of Point Lookout enlisted men's prison from 1864 lithograph by E. Sachse & Co., Baltimore, Md. Seven mess halls can be seen on the left of the prison.

According to the *Official Records of the Union and Confederate Armies* the first mention of captured black soldiers is when Colonel William H. Ludlow, the Union agent for exchange, says in a June 14th letter to Confederate Judge Robert Ould, "I now give you formal notice that the United States Government will throw its protection around all its officers and men without regard to color, and will promptly retaliate for all cases violating the cartel, or the laws." The Union Government's claim that the exchanges were halted because of the Confederates refusal to exchange black prisoners of war does not hold up if you examine the dates involved. The fact remains that Secretary of War Stanton halted the Prisoner Exchange Cartel May 20th, twenty-five days before the Confederates received notice about this violation. So what was the real reason for Secretary Stanton ending the prisoner exchanges?[15]

It appears Major General Ulysses S. Grant may have provided the reason why the prisoner exchange was halted in a letter he had written to General Benjamin F. Butler. He suspected the Confederate government was violating the exchange cartel's rules by allowing paroled prisoners to rejoin the military before they were formally exchanged.[16] Grant wrote: "It is hard on our men held in Southern prisons not to exchange them, but it is humanity to those left in the ranks to fight our battles. Every man we hold, when released on parole or otherwise, becomes an active soldier against us at once either directly or indirectly. If we commence a system of exchange which liberates all prisoners taken, we will have to fight on until the whole South is exterminated." Then Grant wrote these hauntingly, prophetic words. "If we hold those caught they amount to no more than dead men." Surely he did not mean that literally, but thousands of men in both armies would ultimately die because the prisoner exchange had ended. Unfortunately Grant did not realize this was a double edged sword that cut both ways. Halting the prisoner exchange would keep thousands of Federal prisoners in Southern prisons where they would

15

ultimately die. Because of this decision Civil War prisons evolved from temporary detention facilities to long-term concentration camps and a few would become the closest thing to death camps the North had ever seen.[17]

Both Secretary of War Edwin M. Stanton and Major General Ulysses S. Grant agreed that ending the prisoner exchange would weaken the Southern army and bring the war to an earlier conclusion. For the next twenty-two months, from May 1863 until nearly the end of the war, general exchanges became nonexistent. Special exchanges for sick and wounded prisoners still occurred from time to time, but always at the urging of the South.[18]

Private Berry Benson, 1st S. C., was captured at Spotsylvania, Va., and sent to Point Lookout. Benson was one of the few men to escape from the prison.

Former Andersonville prisoner Melvin Grigsby wrote, "If there had been any considerable number of Negro soldiers in the prisons suffering with the others, then there would have been a vital principle of justice as well as honor at stake, and the white prisoners themselves would've been the last man in the world to have sacrificed that principle in order to secure their own liberty and lives. There was not a Negro soldier in Andersonville or any other prison for any considerable time. When he was captured they were either sent back to their old masters to be put to work on rebel fortifications, and they were not starved and did not suffer. Their condition as prisoners was little worse than it had been before the war. They were property in the eyes of the Confederates, and as such were taken care of. Their condition as prisoners was little worse than it had been before the war."[19]

The reason I had for discussing Lincoln and the Border States in the first chapter was not only to show the early Civil War history of the Point Lookout area, but to illustrate how the Lincoln administration was not above breaking the law to achieve its purposes. That being said, it is easy to imagine these same men would also bend the rules of the Exchange Cartel in regards to prisoners. Not only were these rules bent, but legal and moral laws were broken as well. These actions had far-reaching effects that hit close to home for Northerners. Many Union prisoners felt they were merely pawns in achieving President Lincoln's lofty goals.

President Lincoln's Refusal to See Union Prisoners from Andersonville

In early August, 1864, Union prisoners at Andersonville, Georgia, held a conference to see if they could help reestablish the prisoner exchange. The men signed a petition and planned to give it to President Lincoln, asking him not to abandon them and to reinstate the prisoner exchange. They wanted to let him know that 38,000 Union prisoners at Andersonville were sick and dying at an alarming rate. The Union prisoners approached the prison commandant, Colonel Henry Wirz, and asked if they might present this petition to President Lincoln. The Confederacy had tried everything to get the prisoner exchange reestablished so Jefferson Davis agreed to help. He gave a delegation of four Unions sergeants a temporary pardon to go and see President Lincoln with the stipulation that when negotiations were over these men would return to prison. The Union sergeants all agreed.

Lincoln not only did not meet these men, it seems he was nowhere to be found. What business did the President have that was so important that he could not listen to these men who risked their lives to preserve the Union? Was he too embarrassed to see them? Would it be too painful for him to gaze at these anxious men, look them in the eye and say, "I'm sorry, but I can't help you. My hands are tied."

Instead, Lincoln let Secretary of War Edwin M. Stanton meet with the prisoners August 23rd. Stanton told them there was nothing that he could do for them because the Union would be exchanging healthy prisoners, who would return to the Confederate ranks, while they would get sick, broken men in return.

Disheartened, Sergeant Edward Wellington Boate said after the affair, "It distresses me to state that the representatives of 38,000 Union prisoners were treated with silent contempt, the President declining to see them or have any communication with them!

"A policy like this is the quintessence of inhumanity, a disgrace to the administration which carried it out, and a blot upon the country. You rulers who make the charge that the rebels intentionally killed off our men, when I can honestly swear they were doing everything in their power to sustain us, do not lay this unflattering unction to your souls. You abandon your brave men in the hour of their cruelest need. They fought for the Union, and you reached no hand out to save the old faithful, loyal, and devoted servants of the country. You may try to shift the blame from your own shoulders, but posterity will saddle the responsibility were it justly belongs."[20]

Former Andersonville prisoner John W. Urban wrote, "Men who had cheerfully faced death on many battlefields, lay down and died brokenhearted as the terrible suspicion forced itself and their minds that the government they love so well, and fought so hard to save, was indifferent to their sad fate."[21]

Before the prisoner delegation left the north, they contacted the *New York Times* and the *New York Evening Post* and told them what had happened. The *New York Evening Post* printed the entire petition the prisoners had brought for Lincoln in its August 23rd issue.

The Confederacy was still eager to continue the prisoner exchanges. The most important reason why they wanted the exchanges to be resumed was for the sake of humanity. Prisoners were needlessly suffering because the Lincoln administration had declared certain medicines contraband of war. This occurred when the Northern blockade was initiated in 1861. As a result of this, the Confederacy had no morphine, opium, calomel or quinine to treat Northern prisoners.

When the North refused again to exchange prisoners in the summer of 1864 the Confederate Commissioner of Exchange, Judge Robert Ould, contacted Northern authorities and offered to pay gold, cotton or tobacco for medicine to be used exclusively for Union prisoners. Ould never received a reply to his offer. Ould thought perhaps Union officials did not trust the Confederate government to do this, so he told them they could send their own surgeons with medicine to treat Federal prisoners. Again the North ignored Ould's proposal.[22]

Confederate Commissioner of Exchange Judge Robert Ould

Another reason the Confederacy wanted the exchange to continue was because they did not have the food and supplies needed to provide for the men they had captured. Sending Union prisoners North would relieve the Confederacy from the burden of having to provide for these men. This was substantial because there was not enough food to give the Confederate soldiers in the field let alone Federal prisoners.

During the summer of 1864, Judge Robert Ould wrote to Union General John E. Mulford, the Assistant Agent of Exchange, and offered to send 13,000 sick and wounded Federal prisoners to Savannah, Georgia, without requiring the North to exchange any Southern prisoners. Ould urged Mulford to respond quickly because of the terrible mortality at Andersonville prison. For some unknown reason the Federal authorities did not respond to this offer until November. Even though Judge Ould did not request any prisoners in return, he was glad to see 3,208 Confederate prisoners step off the flag-of-truce boat at Savannah. Unfortunately, the Confederate prisoners were so ill that 292 of them died during the two-day voyage.[23] How could such a terrible thing happen? Union prison commandants had been told by

Colonel Hoffman to medically inspect the men to be exchanged so they would be healthy enough to survive the trip.[24]

Richard H. Dribrell, a member of the ambulance committee, was in Savannah to receive the Confederate prisoners and stated, "I have never seen a set of men in worse condition. They were so enfeebled and emaciated that we lifted them like little children. Many of them were like living skeletons. Indeed, there was one poor boy, about 17 years old, who presented the most distressing and deplorable appearance I ever saw. He was nothing but skin and bone, and besides this, he was literally eaten up with vermin. He died in the hospital in a few days after being removed, notwithstanding the kindest treatment and the use of the most judicious nourishment. Our men were in so reduced a condition that on more than one trip up on the short passage of 10 miles from the city, as many as five died. The clothing of the privates was in a wretched state of tatters and filth."[25]

New York Times
August 24, 1864

Union Prisoners at Andersonville

A delegation, consisting of four Union prisoners just released from Andersonville, Ga., will have an early interview with the President, for the purpose of presenting the case of the thirty-five thousand Union soldiers now penned up at that place as prisoners of war. The statement which these men are prepared to lay before the President is horrifying to a degree far beyond what the experience of this war has brought hitherto. In an inclosed field of thirty acres of ground, exposed to the heat of an all but tropical sun, fed upon a daily ration for each man of three-quarters of a pound of dirty corn bread and two ounces of rancid swine flesh, and supplied with water from a stagnant ditch, which forms the receptacle of the excrement of the camp, are thirty-five thousand of our bravest soldiers -- the men who were the foremost in the hard-fought field, and the most daring in the final grapple and crisis of battle. There they swelter and rot, or go raving mad, or find an end to it by crossing the "dead line," where the friendly rifle of the sentinel brings them final release without the aid of cartel or Commissioner. A seething, reeking pen, surcharged with horrors unimaginable. Pestilence in every form of deadly fever, scurvy and nameless disease raging with undisputed sway; and death making its daily harvest of half a hundred.

Such is military prison life in rebeldom. And yet we hesitate to make a general exchange, until we shall see whether the rebels shall gain a few hundred more able-bodied men than ourselves by the transaction. Able bodied men forsooth! How many score of our brave fellows will there remain in this soldier's pound before another moon has passed, either to return to the field or to bear witness to the atrocities of Southern despotism or repeat the story of their wrong? Raise an army strong enough to affect their release, says the chief scribe of the stoics, who is quite as eager to join such an army as to exchange places with a Union soldier at Andersonville.

The duty of the military authorities is surely clear. Exchange the white prisoners man for man at least; if no better can be done for the negro troops now, their time will come again, unless the South is to have a monopoly of the capture of prisoners. It is doubtless true that the maddening tortures and exposures our men have to endure form parts of the rebel scheme to compel us to make an exchange. What if it is so? They will have the odds in their favor in any case, in all that is most savage in this war. But let our authorities see to the release of our brave and patriotic soldiers.

18

Point Lookout Prisoner of War Camp

Although officially named Camp Hoffman the new prison camp in Maryland was almost always referred to as Point Lookout. It was the largest prisoner of war camp in the North and would eventually house 52,000 Confederates, 301 political and four female prisoners. By the third week in August, 1862, Commissary General of Prisoners, Colonel William Hoffman, sent 1,300 Confederate and political prisoners to Point Lookout. When this group arrived the wooden fence had not been completed yet, so the guards, with bayonets on their rifles, gathered along the perimeter of the camp, forming a living wall. Even so, there were a few escape attempts, but these were doomed to failure with several prisoners losing their lives.[26]

Union Secretary of War Edwin M. Stanton

On October 8, 1863 Point Lookout Prison Commandant Brigadier General Gilman Marston sent plans and a cost estimate for construction of prisoner's barracks to Colonel William Hoffman. Hoffman agreed with Marston's assessment that wooden barracks should be built before the cold weather settled in. He promised to give these plans to Secretary of War Edwin M. Stanton along with his recommendation that they be built as soon as possible.[27] Unfortunately, the Secretary of War refused to build the barracks because he did not believe they were a necessity. Stanton instead ordered that the prisoners were to be put into tents. These were not ordinary tents, though. They were cast-offs that the United States army could no longer use. During an inspection of the prison in October, Provost Marshall Allen G. Brady complained to his superior, General James Barnes, that 1/3 of the tents the prisoners had were unfit for use. Thus it was that Point Lookout prison camp became the only Northern Civil War prison to use tents for shelter year round.[28] Other Federal prisons utilized tents, but these were only temporary structures until permanent barracks could be built.

What possible reason did Secretary of War Stanton have for denying shelter for the Confederate prisoners at Point Lookout? Certainly it wasn't the cost. These structures would cost the United States government nothing since the materials would be purchased with the prisoner's fund and all labor would be provided by the prisoners. The fund was established by Colonel Hoffman in July, 1862, when he reduced the prisoner's rations and sold the uneaten food back to the commissary.[29] The money saved could then be used to pay for things that were not provided by the government. The Point Lookout prison's fund grew to a staggering amount, but authorization to use it was rarely granted. At the end of the war Hoffman returned $544,556 to the United States government from Point Lookout prison camp alone. The prison fund for all Union prisons combined amounted to 1.8 million dollars.[30]

So what was Stanton's motivation? The only logical explanation is that Stanton sought retaliation against the Confederate prisoners for alleged abuses suffered by Union prisoners of war. These stories of abuse did not originate in the Confederate prison in Andersonville, Georgia. Andersonville prison camp would not be built until the following year. These stories came from places like Belle Isle and Libby prisons in Richmond, Virginia, Salisbury prison in North Carolina and others. It must be remembered that Civil War prisons did not become horrid death traps until after the exchanges halted. There was no excuse for this form of retaliation other than Stanton's vindictive nature. By denying thousands of helpless prisoner's adequate shelter, the Secretary of War condemned them to a slow, painful death by disease, frostbite and gangrene. As General-in-Chief of all U. S. armies Henry Halleck was familiar with Stanton's moods. "My chief is narrow minded," he confided, "full of prejudices, exceedingly violent, reckless of the rights and feelings of others. He is coarse in his use of language, and his dislikes are mere prejudices—not founded upon any proper knowledge."[31]

Point Lookout prisoner B. T. Holliday remembered the worn out tents they called home, "We were put in Sibley tents, which were round with a pole extending from the top to an iron tripod, the pole fitting in the top of the tripod. These tents had been used by the army and had seen so much service that they would leak and we spent a very uncomfortable time." Sibley tents were large conical tents which were designed to house 12 Union soldiers. Former Point Lookout prisoner James T. Wells recalls, "Our tents were miserable affairs, being full of holes and very rotten. They were of the Sibley pattern and into each one of these 16 men were crowded. In order to lay (sic) down at night, the men were compelled to lay so close together as to exclude sleep."[32]

Sibley Tent

At Point Lookout prison camp these 18' tents were overcrowded and had as many as 18 men living in them. Holliday also noted the tents were so crowded that, "We were packed like sardines in a box. When we wanted to turn over in the night, the signal was given to turn, and all made the turn from necessity."[33]

When Charles T. Loehr addressed the George Picket Camp Confederate Veterans in 1890, he made this statement about his arrival at Point Lookout. "When we came there the prison was already full, and the small tents were totally insufficient to accommodate us. Many were without shelter of any kind, and exposed to the bad weather which prevailed for the greater part of our stay. We had but a few blankets and most of us had to lie (sic) on the bare ground; so when it rained our situation became truly deplorable."[34]

Former prisoner George M. Jones recalled how the men would keep warm on a cold night. "While we had no feather beds to lie on, we had the frozen ground. We would upon retiring form a circle into what we call 'spooning' to keep warm."[35]

Arrival at Point Lookout Prisoner of War Camp

When Confederate prisoners arrived at Point Lookout by steamer, they were lined up on the pier and searched by Federal sergeants. The guards were looking for anything that was considered contraband. This included weapons, money, jewelry, anything valuable and everything with a U. S. on it. There were several reasons for turning over money and valuables to the prison officials. With nothing of value the prisoners could not bribe the guards. Also, thievery was rampant in the prison population and locking up valuables was for the men's protection. The reason for not allowing the prisoners anything with a U. S. on it stems from the fear that prisoners might use these things to trick the guards into thinking they were United States soldiers. Also, if they did manage to escape, the prisoners could use these items to fool the citizens and make good their escape.

Former Point Lookout prisoner Corporal Dillon D. Baldwin, 18th N. C., was captured at Petersburg, Va. Baldwin took the Oath of Allegiance June 24, 1865. *Photo courtesy of North Carolina State Troops and Volunteers, Volume I.*

George M. Neese recalled the search in his book *Three Years In the Confederate Horse Artillery.* "After we disembarked we were subjected to another thorough search. This time we were formed in a hollow square and told to unwrap, spread out, and disgorge everything we had. After everything was on exhibition and ready for examination, the great chief of the searching board made a little speech, with well measured and distinctly spoken words: 'Now, men, if you have anything valuable about your person or effects in the way of watches, jewelry, or money, we give you an opportunity to turn it over to us, and we will put your name on it and deposit it at the Provost Marshall's office and give you a certificate of deposit; and when you leave this prison, either on exchange or release, and present your certificate, we will return the goods left in our charge. But if you fail or refuse to comply with these regulations submitted in good faith, we will search you thoroughly right now, and if we find anything of the kind mentioned it will be confiscated for all time to come."

Former prisoner Marcus B. Toney commented in his book *The Privatizations of a Private,* "Money was contraband of war, for a fellow might bribe his way out (of prison). Therefore, whenever a letter with money came to a prisoner it was turned over to the settler, who opened an account with the owner, and he could purchase all he wished so long as the funds held out; but when money went, a prisoner's credit was nonexistent." [36]

Former prisoner Charles T. Loehr remembered the day when he arrived at Point Lookout. "Landing at the wharf we were formed in open line for inspection; that is, we had to empty our pockets and lay our baggage on the ground before us, while the Federal sergeants amused themselves by kicking overcoats, blankets, oilcloths, canteens, and everything that had a U. S. on it, into the bay. This left us in a sad condition, for there was very little in our possession that had not been the property of the United States, at one time or another, and became ours by the many victories and captures we had helped to gain." [37]

Prisoner James T. Wells of the 2nd South Carolina infantry remembers how valuables taken in the search were never returned. "This camp had but recently been established, and there was not many prisoners here. They [the prisoners] yelled to us 'Grab your pocketbooks,' as we came into sight. They referred to the strict search in which the newcomers were subjected, in which everything, even to a few Confederate dollars, was taken from you. It was labeled and put away, to be returned to you when you were leaving; but the valuables were never returned, as they could not be found." [38]

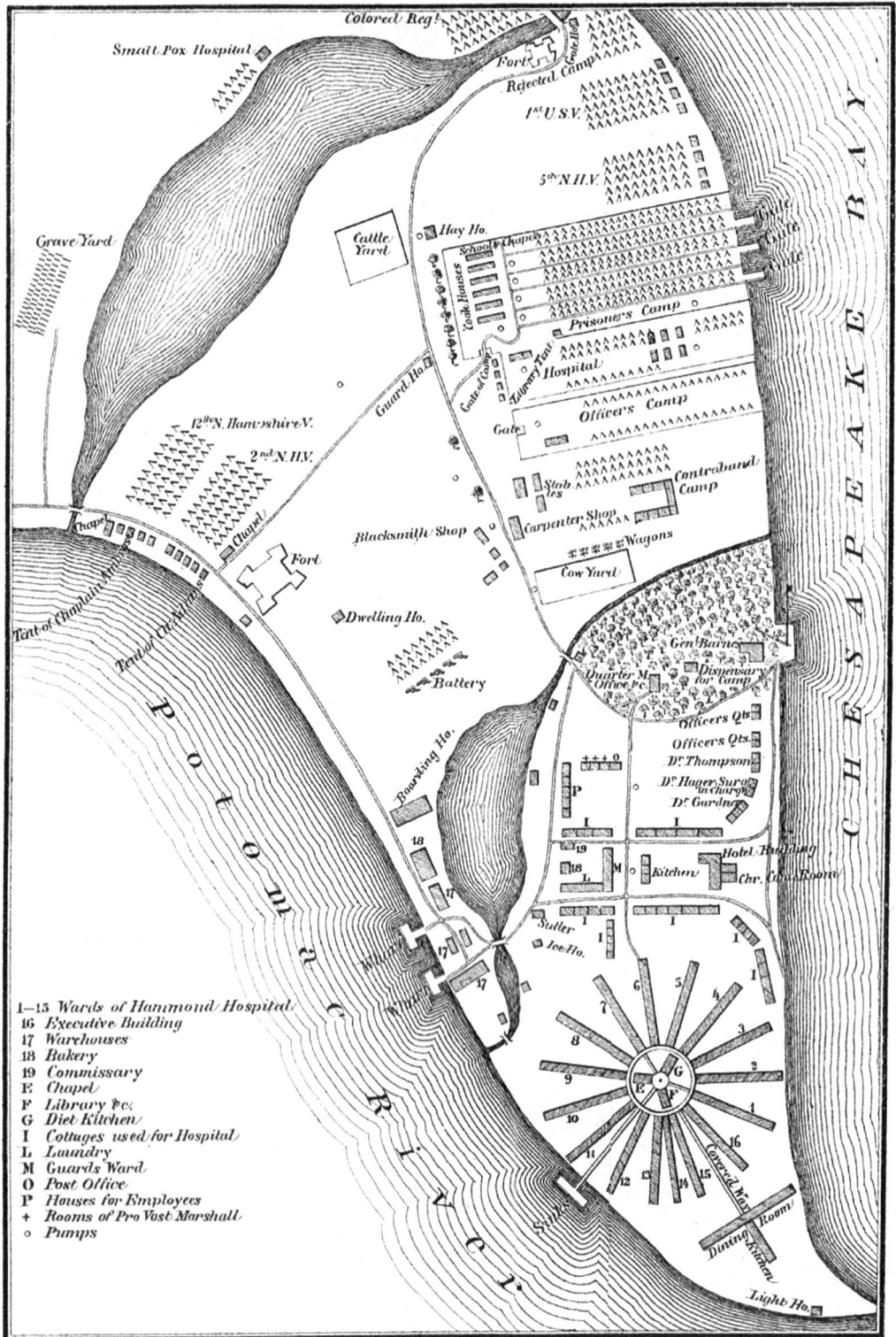

Point Lookout prison Lithograph by A. Hoan & Co., Baltimore

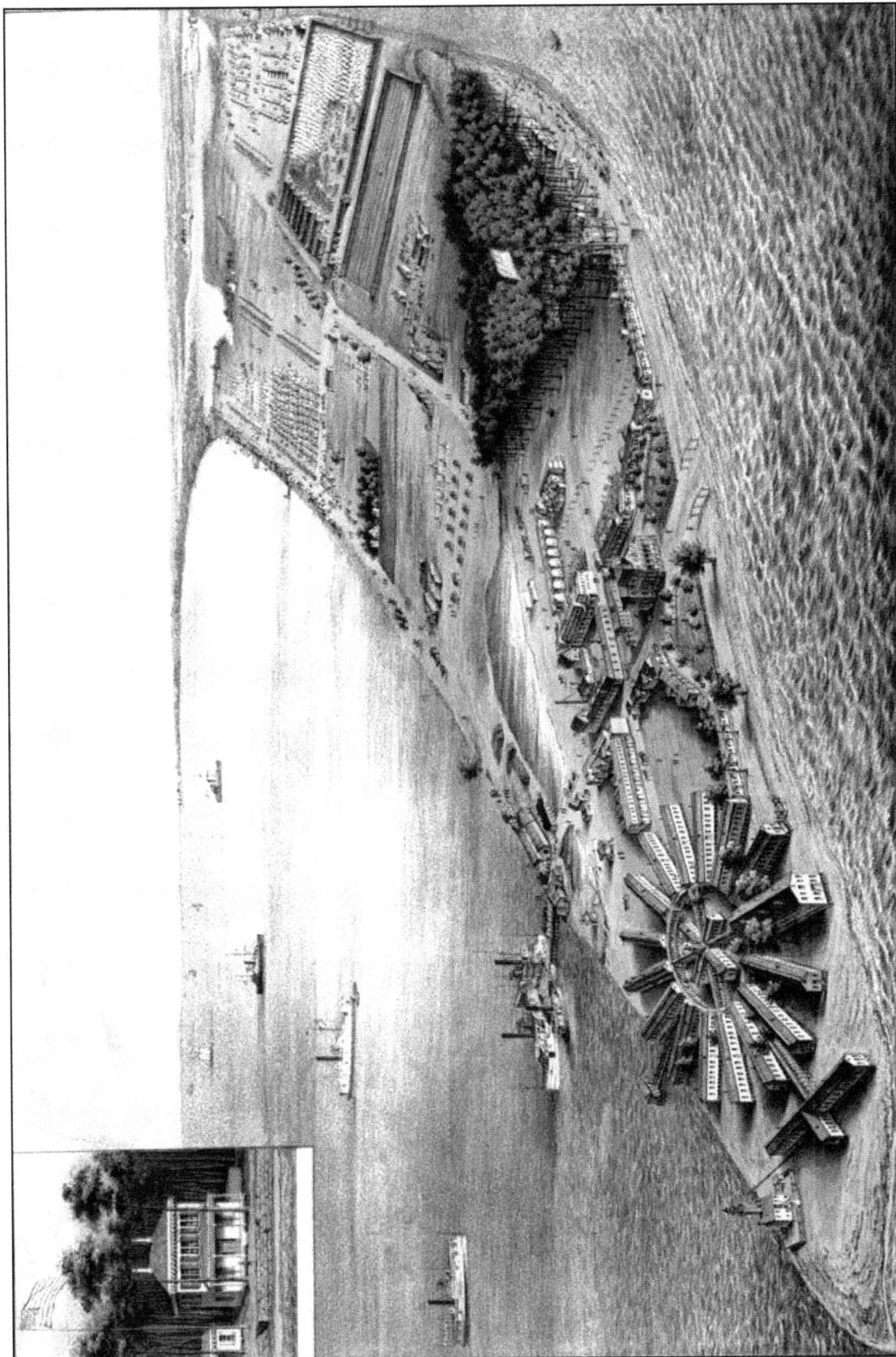

1864 lithograph by E. Sachse & Co., Baltimore, Md.

Description of Point Lookout Prisoner of War Camp

The prison camp at Point Lookout was actually two prisons. The largest one was for the enlisted men and was approximately twenty acres in size. Tents of every description made up this area of the prison. Most of them were the conical Sibley tents, Wall tents that housed twelve men, Wedge tents that housed five men, and Shelter tents which had three men living in them.[39] To the south of this was an area which housed eighteen hospital tents for the prisoners. Beyond that was a ten-acre prison for officers from the rank of lieutenant to captain. This prison only existed from August, 1863, until June, 1864. After that date officers were no longer sent to Point Lookout, and went to Fort Delaware, De. instead. The land they vacated was quickly absorbed by more hospital tents.[40] The prison camp was surrounded by a twelve foot tall fence made of two-inch planks which were buried several feet below ground.[41] On the outside of the fence, about three feet from the top, was a platform for the guards to walk on. The guards were stationed forty feet apart and every hundred feet or so was a shelter in case of rain.[42]

The prison camp was laid off into ten streets, twenty feet wide, and rows of tents were placed back to back on either side of the road. The prison population was made of ten divisions with ten companies to a division. There were a thousand men in each division and one hundred in each company. When the prisoner exchanges halted the number of prisoners at Point Lookout swelled to 20,000. When this happened a new division of a thousand men was created. Thus, there were twenty streets to accommodate all these prisoners.[43] There was one Federal sergeant in charge of a division and two Confederate sergeants assigned to each company. The Company Sergeant called the roll and made sure the prisoners kept their tents orderly. This sergeant also reported any men who were in the hospital and were otherwise missing from their company. The other was a Sick Sergeant. After morning roll call his duty was to report which prisoners were sick and draw their rations if the men were too ill to walk to the cook house.

Private James C. Elliott, 56th North Carolina Infantry, was captured at the battle of Fort Stedman, outside Petersburg, on March 25, 1864. Elliott took the Oath of Allegiance June 12, 1865. Fortunately James C. Elliott wrote a book called *The Southern Soldier Boy* about his wartime experiences, including his time at Point Lookout prison camp.

Guards Shooting Prisoners

Once Confederate soldiers were in prison and away from the battlefield, you would think that they did not have to worry about being shot. Unfortunately that was not the case. Quite often Point Lookout guards would fire on unsuspecting prisoners. We know this from the many diaries and manuscripts the prisoners left behind. In the fifty or so accounts I have read, the prisoners reported fourteen men killed and thirty-two wounded. It is difficult to get an exact number as several prisoners may refer to the same incident so. It is not easy to tell if they are talking about the same event since some of the sources do not give the date and the number of men shot is different in each account. Seventy-two percent of the shootings occurred between a Negro guard and white prisoners. This is odd since colored troops were only on duty every third day. It would seem logical that white guards would have shot twice as many prisoners since they were on guard duty most of the time. However, this was not the case. Virtually all of the shootings were unprovoked according to the prisoners. This is not to say that all colored troops had a grudge against white prisoners. According to some of the Point Lookout prisoners most Negro soldiers were very respectful and treated them well. The majority of the prisoners said the exact opposite. They said the Negro guards were seeking revenge against their former masters. The truth is probably somewhere in-between. However, it is difficult to deny so many prisoner accounts of the shootings at the prison.

Former prisoner Walter D. Addison wrote, "During my entire confinement at Point Lookout were under guard of Negro soldiers whose conduct and treatment of the prisoners was infamously cruel and in many instances they conducted themselves in a savage manner. I have witnessed them fire their muskets indiscriminately into crowded masses of prisoners, shooting two or three men at a single shot, and such outrages were tolerated by the white officers, and they were never punished nor their cases investigated. This repeatedly happened at Point Lookout, and I never heard that one was even reprimanded."[44]

Former prisoner John R. King wrote, "A tragedy took place at the cookhouse near our tent one day. A Negro [guard] stood near the gate leading to headquarters and one of our prison comrades smuggled a watch into the prison which he tried to sell to this Negro. He said to him: 'Don't you want to buy a watch?' The Negro replied, 'Yes, let me see it.' Handing the watch to him, the Negro leveled his gun, saying: 'If you don't get away from here, I will shoot you.' The man ran and reported to the white officers; a few days later the officers compelled him [Negro guard] to return the watch. This made the Negro very angry and on guard a few days later, he saw the owner of the watch going to the cookhouse with a hundred or more prisoners marching four ranks deep, so he fired at the man. Missing the rank he was in, he fired at every man in the rank next to him, two (prisoners) were shot through the body, one in the arm and one in the hand. The two who were shot through the body died, the other two lived. One was Joe Bridge of our regiment who was cared for in a hospital tent near us."[45]

Private Alfred Perkins wrote, "Several of the Negro soldiers guarding them were once slaves of some of the prisoners, and have been recognized as such. Some of them are still respectful, and call their young owners 'master' and declare they were forced to enlist. A majority of them, however, inflated by their so-called freedom, are very insolent and very overbearing. They frequently fire into the midst of the prisoners, upon the slightest provocation."[46]

Corporal John Frazier, Co. D, 57th N. C., was captured at Winchester, Va. Frazier died of disease February 1, 1865. *Photograph courtesy of Point Lookout Museum.*

The following letter from Confederate Master Sergeant William H. Laird can be found in the *Official Records* and illustrates the matter of guards shooting prisoners was a legitimate concern. Also included is a note from Captain William A. Crafts, Assistant Provost Marshall, as to Laird's character.

Colonel William Hoffman,   *June 20, 1864*
Commissary General of Prisoners, Washington, D. C.:

Colonel:

Respectfully forwarded.
From what I can learn I have every reason to believe that the within statement of Mr. Laird, who has been acting a Sgt. Maj. at this camp for a long time, is correct.
Very respectfully,

> *W. A. Crafts,*
> *Captain and Assistant Provost Marshall*

(enclosure 1)

> *Prisoner's camp, Point Lookout, April 19, 1864*

Captain W. A. Crafts, Commanding Camp:

Sir: I respectfully submit a report of the shooting case near my tent last night, and beg leave to express the hope that the case will be investigated and steps taken to preserve us against the vindictiveness of certain of the colored troops who guard us, and our lives be given all the protection consistent with good discipline. About two months ago Captain Patterson ordered that each company should have a tub, to be used at night for sink (latrine) purposes, and I obtained one for my tent and those standing near it. This tub has been used almost every night since it has been there, and was put out conspicuously in front expressly to prevent accident. Last night when the man who was shot came out of his camp tent the guard was just in front of it, and, I imagine, must have an seen the man preparing to sit down, for between the man's coming out of his tent and being shot the guard did not walk more than 20 or 30 paces. The man had scarcely sat down when, without a word, the guard turned and fired. The animus (prejudice) of the guard is manifest from his having two bullets in his gun. This statement can be substantiated by full testimony. I beg leave to extend this report that you may know what steps to take toward that protection which I ask in the name of the camp. Both the conduct and conversation of the colored man is evidence that there is a sort of rivalry among them to distinguish themselves by shooting some of us. The one who does so gains an eclat (praise) which the others envy; and animated frequently by the vindictive feelings, they make pretexts to vent them. The existence of this latter motive is sufficiently proven by the fact that the patrols often make men who leave their tents for imperative reasons come to them, and keep them sometime, tantalizing them with threats. I respectfully suggest that the protection we so solicit can only be secured by denying these men discretionary powers and confining them imperatively within their orders. I feel it my duty to say thus much.

I am, Sir, very respectfully, your obedient servant,

> *William H. Laird,*
> *Sergeant Major of camp*

(Enclosure 2)

> *Point Lookout, April 22, 1864*

Captain W. A. Crafts,
Assistant Provost Marshall, Commanding Prisoners of War Camp:

Sir: I respectfully submit a report of the conduct of the patrols of the camp last night, feeling impelled to it by the exigency (urgency) of the case. What the causes of firing were I am not able to ascertain, but the disposition of the patrols may be evidenced by the following facts, which can be substantiated, viz: In Company H, Fifth Division, one of the men lying in this tent remarked to a comrade, "You are pulling the covers off me," whereupon he was ordered out of the tent, and

26

compelled to come out by threats to shoot into the tents in case of noncompliance. Having come out he was made to double quick from the center ditch to the bay fence and back. A similar case occurred and Company E, Fourth Division, for the remark, "I have not been asleep for two hours." In company H, Fifth Division, a man while lying in this tent was struck slightly on the foot, the ball having before entering his tent passed through the one next above it. In Company H, Fourth Division, a man was very painfully wounded in the foot while lying in this tent. All of those occurrences at or about 12 PM.

Very respectfully, your obedient servant,

William H. Laird,
Sergeant Major of Camp[47]

The following table lists all the prisoners shot by Point Lookout guards that were uncovered in my research. When the guard is described as White or Negro I have included that information. Six prisoners were shot by nondescript guards totaling 13%. Seven were shot by White guards for a total of 15%. Thirty-four were shot by Negro guards for an additional 72%.

Date	Shooting Information
11/16/1863	Guard shot prisoner for looking through fence. Report of Joseph M. Kerns.
1/12/1864	Silas Douglas shot by guard. Report of Charles W. Hutt.
3/20/1864	White Sergeant Edward Young shoots and kills Lawrence Payton for sassing him. Reported by Bartlett Y. Malone.
3/22/1864	White Sergeant Edward Young shoots and kills Lawrence Payton for sassing him. Reported by Charles W. Hutt.
4/18/1864	Negro guard shot and wounded a prisoner. Reported by Bartlett Y. Malone
4/21/1864	Negro shot into tent wounding two men. Reported by Bartlett Y. Malone. May be same report as James T. Wells and N. F. Harman's, neither has a date. According to Sergeant Major William II. Laird two prisoners were shot in the foot during the same night.
5/23/1864	Negro guard shoots and kills man who accidentally stepped over the deadline near the mess hall. Wounds four other prisoners. One man later dies. Report of L. Leon and Joseph M. Kerns.
5/24/1864	Negro guard shot and killed one prisoner and wounded three more. Reported by Bartlett Y. Malone.
8/7/1864	Negro guard shot and killed a prisoner for no reason. Report of Charles W. Hutt and Joseph M. Kerns. May be same report as Bartlett Y. Malone of the same date.
8/7/1864	Negro guard shot and killed a prisoner for no reason. Report of Bartlett Y. Malone. May be same report as Charles W. Hutt of the same date.
8/15/1864	White guard shoots at a prisoner, misses him, severly wounds prisoner in tent. Report of Joseph M. Kerns.
8/28/1864	Guard shot and wounded prisoner. Report of Bartlett Y. Malone.
11/29/1864	Guard shot prisoner for looking through fence. Report of Bartlett Y. Malone.
12/7/1864	Negro guard shot and wounded a feeble prisoner for walking too slowly away from the latrine. Report of Alfred Perkins.
12/16/1864	White officer shot men crowding prison gate. One prisoner is killed and four were wounded. Report of Bartlett Y. Malone and Joseph M. Kerns.
1/22/1865	Negro guard shoots and kills prisoner during the night. Report of Bartlett Y. Malone.

The following table lists the prisoners shot by guards which have no date recorded in the report.

Date	Shooting Information
Unknown	Negro guard shot two men outside their tents at night using the latrine. Report of Walter D. Addison.
Unknown	Negro guard shot several prisoners over several days for being at the water pump. Report of a Confederate officer. May be same report task J. B. Stamp.
Unknown	Negro guard shooting into tent at night killing two prisoners. Report of N. F. Harman. May be same report as James T. Wells.
Unknown	Negro guard shoots and kills two prisoners and wounds another two over a watch. Report of John R. King.
Unknown	Guard shoots and kills man for whittling on gate. Report of Charles T. Loehr.
Unknown	Negro guard shot at one prisoner, missing him, but wounded three more at water pump near hospital. Report of J. B. Stamp.
Unknown	Guard wounded two prisoners crowding the deadline near the gate. Report of Marcus B. Toney.
Unknown	Negro guard shot into tent killing two men and wounding 2 to 3 more. Report of James T. Wells.

The Infamous Deadline

The Point Lookout Prison Camp deadline was a shallow, six-inch trench dug around the prison camp about 15 feet from the fence. The penalty for stepping over this was being shot to death. Guards were required to warn a prisoner before shooting, but this did not always happen. If there was a warning issued, it was not always heard. One thing that Point Lookout had in common with other Northern prisons was a deadline. The reason this chapter is called *The Infamous Deadline* is because Northern prison authorities denied a deadline ever existed. Over fifty first-hand accounts from former Point Lookout prisoners were examined and most of them mentioned a deadline. I have no doubt that this deadline was very real and the consequence for stepping over this line was death.[48]

Former prisoner Lewis Leon wrote about the time an unfortunate prisoner accidentally crossed the deadline. "May 23rd. We are not allowed to cross a certain line, call the deadline, but as many as 500 men go at one time to meals, of course near the door there is always a rush. Today one of our men accidentally crossed the line. He was pushed over by the crowd, when a black devil shot and killed him, and wounded two others."[49]

Private Marcus B. Toney explained another incident where a prisoner was shot for accidentally crossing the deadline. "One evening a squad which had been on detail outside entered the prison and quite a crowd rushed up to them to hear the (outside) news, and some of them were crowded over the deadline. Without hesitation the guard fired into the group, severely wounding two of our prisoners. Our ears were

Private James Madison Ragland, 46th North Carolina, was captured at Hatcher's Run, Va., and sent to Point Lookout in 1865 where he took the Oath of Allegiance. Photograph courtesy of North Carolina State Troops and Volunteers, Volume I.

frequently greeted with the expression from the colored guards. 'The bottom rail is on top; my gun wants to smoke.'"[50]

__Taps or Lights Out__

Most prisoners dreaded the nights when the Negro guards patrolled the prison. Men had been harassed, humiliated or shot when going to the latrine at night. Many prisoners were sick with diarrhea and needed to go to the sinks several times during the night. The situation became so bad that many prisoners, afraid to venture too far from their tent, chose to relieve themselves at the first opportunity. Too often this was on the ground beside the tent. For health reasons the Union officers instructed the guards to make sure the prisoners used the latrines. If the prisoner refused after being warned, it was at the discretion of the guard whether or not to use deadly force. Unfortunately this led to more shootings and death if the men did not promptly respond to the guard's orders. Some of the sickly prisoners were feeble and could barely walk. On a dark night an ill prisoner could easy be construed as being insolent when nothing of the kind had taken place. Former Point Lookout prisoner Alfred Perkins wrote, "One Negro sentinel, a few days ago, shot a prisoner as he walked slowly from sheer debility away from the foul sinks to his tent, simply because he did not and could not obey his imperative order to 'move on faster dar.' Instead of being court-martialed and punished for the wanton murder, the villain was seen a few days afterwards exalting in his promotion to a corporalcy, and posting a relief guard. This employment of former slaves to guard their masters is intended to insult and degrade the latter."

Private James H. Price, Co. B, 1st Md. Cavalry, was captured at Monterey Springs, Md. Price was exchanged December 25, 1863. Photograph courtesy of Point Lookout Museum.

Former prisoner Marcus B. Toney recalls, "At nine o'clock at night the bugle was sounded for taps or lights out, and everyone had to be in his tent at that hour with lights out. The colored soldiers patrolled along the avenues between the tents with six shooters in their hands; and if they heard any noise in a tent, they would shoot into it. Therefore, after 9 PM, Point lookout, with its army of 10,000 men, was nearly as quiet as a cemetery."[52]

Anthony M. Keiley had this to say about the Point Lookout guards at night. "A patrol made the rounds constantly from taps, the last horn at night, to reveille. They were usually armed with pistols for greater convenience, and as they are shielded from scrutiny by the darkness, the indignities and cruelties they sometimes inflicted on prisoners, who for any cause might be out of their tents between those hours, especially when the patrols were black, were outrageous. Many of these were of a character which could not by any paraphrase be decently expressed, they were, however, precisely the acts which a set of vulgar brutes, suddenly invested with a responsible authority, might be expected to take delight in."[53]

Chesapeake Bay Beach

Point Lookout was blessed with something the other prisons could only dream of. The prisoners had access to the Chesapeake Bay beach during daytime hours. The guards opened two large gates to the beach every day at sunrise and closed them again at sunset. The beach was about 100 feet wide and many of the prisoners would gather there to either work or leisurely spend the day. The prisoners could sun themselves on the sand or go for a swim in the water and dive for oysters and crabs or perhaps wash their clothes. In fact, the beach became so popular only limited numbers of prisoners were allowed on it at one time.[54]

Washermen would gather on the beach early in the morning and set up their cast iron boilers near the shore. After building a fire and boiling some water the washerman was ready for business. The reason this became a thriving concern is that all of the prisoners were infested with graybacks or body lice. The only sure way to get rid of the lice was to boil your clothing and then take a bath in the saltwater of the bay. This being the case, there is little wonder why the washermen at Point Lookout had plenty of business.

Former prisoner J. B. Stamp recalls, "The laundry business, was extensively carried on, and for one or two crackers, or a small piece of tobacco, an article of clothing would be washed, but as they were not prepared for ironing, it would be returned in a rough state."[55]

Private George Q. Peyton remembers what it was like on laundry day. After washing his clothes, he would hang them on his tent to dry. Peyton recalls there was one last chore that needed to be done. "I had to watch my clothes until they got dry to keep them from being stolen."[56]

Prisoner John R. King wrote, "Bathing in the bay was a source of pleasure granted us and we certainly took advantage of it. It was thick with bathers every day and it was a great relief to stand on the beach and watch the ships and small craft pass. Some men with a line and net waded into the water waist deep and caught big crabs. I went to the bottom where the water was ten feet deep and found a few oysters to eat, but they were poor and tough. When the tide was coming in the water was delightful, at the deadline we sat on the posts until the waves were highest, then we rode them to shore."[57]

Former prisoner Thad J. Walker remembers going to the beach at Point Lookout. "There were about 12,000 Confederates in the prison at the time from all parts of the South, and the beach fronting on the Chesapeake Bay, where we were allowed to go in limited numbers during the day, presented quite an animated appearance with the graybacks (prisoners) sunning themselves, some washing their clothing, some bathing, some making bricks for the chimneys of little crackerbox prison houses, and others fishing and crabbing."[58]

Sergeant Marquis D. Herring, Co. D, 1st North Carolina Infantry, was captured at Fisher's Hill, Va., September 22, 1864. Herring was exchanged March 17, 1865.

Private Anthony M. Keiley explained that, "The most numerous occupants (at the beach were) gamblers, who, under hastily constructed booths, which they erected every morning, and slept on every night, carried on every game of cards at which money is staked, from aristocratic Faro to cutthroat Monte. Here the dice rattled, and the cards were shuffled from morning till night; everything representing value, from a hardtack up, being freely offered and accepted as legitimate currency."[59]

30

Not everything was fun at the beach. A deadline two or three hundred yards out into the water was made by driving small logs into the mud with a pile-driver, their ends showed above the water at low tide. These served as a warning to prisoners not to go beyond that line or they would be shot.[60] There also were three wooden wharves that extended out over the water and ended at box-like structures called sinks. These sinks or latrines were built out over the water because the tide would efficiently carry away any waste.

Clothing for All Except Confederate Prisoners

Nothing proves the Confederate claim of willful prisoner abuse better than the lack of clothing issued at Northern prison camps. This cannot be hidden as easily as withholding rations. The deliberate system of refusing clothing to needy prisoners can be readily seen both on the men and also in the *Official Records of the Union and Confederate Armies*. Many of Colonel William Hoffman orders reveal his harsh measures regarding clothing issued to the prisoners. Hoffman rarely acted alone and always had the full knowledge and consent of Secretary of War Edwin M. Stanton.

Private Wright B. Batchelor, 47th North Carolina, died of disease at Point Lookout. Batchelor is one of hundreds of soldiers whose name does not appear on the Confederate Memorial. *Photo courtesy of North Carolina State Troops and Volunteers, Volume I.*

On August 12, 1863, Hoffman issued an order that will forever show his cruelty to prisoners. "You will issue no clothing of any kind except in cases of utmost necessity. So long as a prisoner has clothing upon him, however much torn, you must issue nothing to him, nor must you allow him to receive clothing from any but members of his immediate family, and only when they are in absolute want."[61]

In early November of 1863 Dr. William F. Swalm, of the Sanitary Commission, conducted an inspection of Point Lookout prison and sent a report to his superior Dr. J. H. Douglas. His report was very critical and mentioned unsanitary conditions at the prison camp and hospital.[62] The reason why Dr. Swalm's report is so important is that he was not only a doctor, but a Northerner as well. Because Swalm was familiar with disease he did not see the prisoners as the hated enemy, but pitiful men in need of medical attention. Being a doctor he was familiar with disease, its causes and prevention. Dr. Swalm appraised the prison and hospital honestly, all the time keeping in mind the safety of the prisoners. It appears he noticed many dangerous situations that the prison officials and guards did not.

Dr. Swalm wrote, "Of the 1,208 sick in the hospital last week there were 46 deaths and the mortality was slightly on the increase. They receive 30 (prisoners) per day from the (tent) hospital within the encampment and in the very worst condition. At the postmortem examinations the doctor said nearly all of those who died of diarrhea also had pneumonia. The disease did not show itself during life, probably from the extreme weak condition of the patient."[63]

After seeing Dr. Swalm's report, prison commandant General Gilman Marston wrote Colonel William Hoffman, the Commandant General of Prisoners, and said that his account was full of errors.

Hoffman would not let the Sanitary Commission conduct anymore inspections of Federal Civil War prisons. When asked by Frederick N. Knapp if he would let the Commission inspect other prisons, Hoffman responded by saying, "I beg to say that medical inspectors of the army make frequent inspections of the camps referred to, and is therefore not thought necessary to impose this labor on the Sanitary Commission."[64]

Surgeon Augustus M. Clark, Medical Inspector of Prisoners of War, was sent to Point Lookout in December of 1863. Clark did a thorough investigation and on December 22nd he sent his findings to Colonel Hoffman. He stated there were many deficiencies corrected that Dr. Swalm had mentioned, but a few still remained. Doctor Clark mentioned there were 1,037 patients in Hammond General Hospital for the month of November. Of this number 532 were Confederate patients and 505 were Union sick and wounded. During this month he stated there were 145 deaths. Doctor Clark found it interesting only one Federal soldier died during this time and the remaining were all Confederates. This seems to suggest the Federal doctors waited until a Confederate prisoner was deathly ill before putting them in the hospital. Whether this was a form of retaliation, or just a poor system of administering medical attention to the prisoners remains to be determined.[65]

Doctor Clark also reported the hospital had a very good latrine system. The sinks were built over the west side of the Potomac River and the waste was carried away by the tide.[66]

Doctor William F. Swalm of the Sanitary Commission described the Point Lookout prisoners in his report. "They are ragged and dirty and very thinly clad; that is, the very great majority. Occasionally you will find one the fortunate possessor of an overcoat, either a citizen's or the light blue ones used by our infantry, and these serve as coverings for the rags beneath. Others, are well supplied as regards underclothing, especially those who are from Baltimore, being sent to them by friends. But the great mass are in a pitiable condition, destitute of nearly everything, which, with their filthy condition, makes them really objects of commiseration. Some are without shirts, or what were once shirts are now hanging in shreds from the shoulders. In others the entire back or front will be gone, while again in some you will see a futile attempt at patching."[67]

Captain Julian P. Lee, Mosby's Rangers, was captured in Prince William County, Va. Lee was a prisoner at Point Lookout in 1863 until he took the Oath of Allegiance on June 24, 1864.

Former prisoner Charles T. Loehr remembers, "Great as the sufferings of the men were from want of sufficient food and medicines, they were much increased from want of clothing. Some were nearly naked, only one ragged shirt to wear, and this covered with vermin (lice)."[68]

Private Albert S. Caison wrote about his lack of clothes at Point Lookout. "We had been here 15 months before we got any clothing. My jacket and trousers were in strings. I had had no shirt for months, and was barefooted. When we were called out to get some clothes I had to stand two hours on the frozen ground before my turn came."[69]

An Unusual Clothing Practice

Point Lookout Prison Camp had several unusual practices concerning clothing. One involved clothing that was sent to prisoners by relatives or friends. In order to claim these articles a prisoner had to turn in an old, worn-out set of clothing. If he did not, he failed to receive the package. Former prisoner Anthony M. Keiley wrote about this bizarre practice. "In the matter of clothing, the management at Point

Lookout was simply infamous. You could receive nothing in the way of clothing without giving up the corresponding article which you might chance to possess; and so rigid was his regulation, that men who came there barefoot had been compelled to beg or buy a pair of worn-out shoes to carry to the office in lieu of a pair sent them by their friends, before they could receive the latter. To what end this plundering was committed, I could never ascertain."[70]

Another unusual practice involved searches during the weekly inspections conducted at Point Lookout. While the men were outside at roll call their tents were ransacked by guards looking for anything that was considered contraband. One of the forbidden items they were searching for was extra blankets. If there were 16 men living in a tent, only 16 blankets were allowed and the extra items were taken. What is difficult to understand is why these men were searching when many of the prisoners did not have even one blanket, let alone two.

Former prisoner George M. Neese wrote about his sleeping accommodations in his book, *Three Years in the Confederate Horse Artillery*. "Many of the prisoners are thinly clad and all of them scantily fed. I slept on the damp sand for two months without any sign of a blanket or bedding under me, and nothing but my shoe for a pillow."

Dr. Montrose A. Pallen urged the Federal government to allow him to give aid to Confederate prisoners. Government officials had Pallen arrested before he was able to help anyone.

Commenting about the weekly inspections, former prisoner Anthony M. Keeley said, "A Yankee inspected each man, taking away his extra blanket, if he had one, and appropriating any other he might chance to possess, and this accomplished, he visited the tents and seized everything therein under, the convenient nomenclature of the Federals was catalogued as 'contraband'-- blankets, boots, hats, anything. The only way to avoid this was by judicious use of greenbacks—and a trifle with suffice—it being true, with honorable exceptions, of course, that Yankee soldiers are very much like ships: to move them, you must 'slush the ways.'"[71]

Dr. Swalm, of the Sanitary Commission, wrote, "They are poorly supplied with blankets and they must have suffered severely from the cold, for it is a very bleak place. Generally they have one blanket to three men, but a great many are entirely without."[72]

It seems ludicrous for us to believe the Federal government could not afford to buy a supply of blankets for these cold, starving men who were forced to spend all winter in a tent with very little wood to make a fire. What about the Prison Fund? This is the very reason why the fund was established. This quote is from General Order 67: "With this fund will be purchased all such articles as may be necessary for the health and comfort of the prisoners and which would otherwise have to be purchased by the government." Apparently these words had little meaning to prison officials. Or was there a more sinister reason for this. Maybe such words were thought to lead the public astray while retaliation was carried out against Confederate prisoners. Little wonder the Confederacy didn't have any faith in what the Northern authoritys said.[73]

Doctor Montrose A. Pallen's Letter

In December of 1863 Dr. Montrose A. Pallen learned Confederate prisoners of war were suffering because they did not have sufficient clothing to keep them from freezing to death. On the 14th he wrote to Secretary of War Edwin M. Stanton and told him, "Many of these men are without the necessary clothing to even hide their nakedness, and during the late cold-weather several absolutely froze to death at Point Lookout, where they are living in tents, and more than half of the 9,000 confined there have not even a single blanket for covering or bedding and sleep on the bare ground, which you well know is certainly productive of an immense amount of disease and suffering." Pallen stated that he wished to travel to Richmond to acquire the funds and clothing necessary to relieve the suffering of the Confederate prisoners. He pointed out that the United States government had been allowed to provide supplies to its prisoners confined in Richmond and asked that they return the kindness. Pallen ended his letter by listing references of Major-General's such as Ulysses S Grant, William T. Sherman and others. He also promised not to divulge anything detrimental about the United States concerning the war.

It is unknown whether Secretary of War Stanton ever replied to Pallen's letter. There is no evidence that he did. Shortly after this, Dr. Pallen was captured while trying to go to Richmond on his errand of mercy. As a result, the Confederate prisoners never received the clothing that he had intended to send them and they continued to suffer during the harsh winter of 1864-65.[74]

An Uninvited Guest: Lice

One nuisance that affected all the prisoners at Point Lookout was body lice. The annoying insects were everywhere. You could not get away from them because everyone had them to some degree. They thrived in crowded environments where personal hygiene and sanitation were lacking. In prison they were often referred to as graybacks or vermin. Lice are tiny parasites, 3/16 of an inch long, which infest the victim and feed on their blood through a fine tube-like mouth. Bites from lice create small itchy spots that may result in secondary infections. Some lice can transmit typhus, which is characterized by high fever, muscle aches, mental confusion and red spots that cover the body. Under epidemic conditions, the disease may be fatal in most cases.[75]

Different methods were employed by prisoners to try and rid themselves of the pests. Many soldiers could be found picking through their clothing any time of day employing a technique they called skirmishing.

Former prisoner B. T. Holliday recalls, "Time hangs heavy on one's hands when in prison. The only diversion was card playing and waging war on graybacks, which was a daily duty for they multiplied by hundreds during the night, and no one was immune to them."[76]

George Q. Peyton wrote about the difficulty of getting rid of the pests. "Although I change my underclothes every week, the lice were on you all the time. I reckon they are in the houses and have gotten in the cracks and you can't get them out. They bother me very much and make you feel mean all the time. I could get rid of them on me, but Ellis and Hodges (Peyton's tent mates) have no change of clothes, so they can't get rid of them. Our blankets are full of them."[77]

Private John D. Huskey, Co. C, 6th N. C., was captured at Rappahannock Station, Va. Huskey was sent to Point Lookout Prison Camp and exchanged March 6, 1864. *Photo courtesy of North Carolina State Troops and Volunteers, Volume I.*

Boiling your blanket and clothing were the only sure way to get rid of the pests. However, this was only a temporary fix because a prisoner's neighbors or tent mates were literally covered with lice.

The Severe Winters of 1864 and 1865

As if coping with rotten tents, short rations and very little clothing was not enough, the prisoners had to endure the harsh northern winters of 1863, 64 and 65. The freezing weather lowered the men's resistance to disease and many of them became sick and died. The winter of 1864 was the coldest in decades and many Northern newspapers noted its low temperatures and blizzard like conditions.

Former prisoner George Q. Peyton wrote in his diary November 5, 1864, "It is a cold, disagreeable day with high winds and showers of rain. My feet almost freeze with no fire. We ran around the camp to try and warm up."[78]

Later that month Peyton made another entry in his diary about the freezing weather. "Today it is awfully cold. The ditches are frozen over, and a cold icy wind blew all day. We have no fire. God help us when winter comes if it is this cold already."[79]

James T. Wells noted in his diary on the 9th of November, 1863, "Snow fell and there was not a stick of wood in camp. The day was bitter cold, most of us were poorly clad, and very few of us had shoes of any description. We were compelled to stand in our damp tents and mark time (march in place) to keep from freezing."[80]

Former prisoner David Holt wrote, "That night a cold north wind sprang up and my thin clothes did not stop it a bit. It seemed to blow through my bones. We could not make a fire. I had one worn-out blanket and wrapped that around me and, with both hats and shoes on, lay down to suffer but not to sleep."[81]

Here is an entry from Bartlett Y. Malone's diary. "The 17th (of January) it was so coal (sic) that we all had to lye (sic) down and rap (sic) up in our blankets to keep from freezing for we had no wood to make us a fire.

The 18th it was so coal (sic) that a man's breath would freeze on his beard going from the tent to the cookhouse. Oh, it was so coal (sic) the 18th."[82]

Private Joseph M. Kerns recalled some prisoners freezing to death on January 29, 1865. "During last night several prisoners froze to death; the weather has been intensely cold for some time. One of the men, having but one blanket, got very cold and went to one of his tent mates, late in the night and asked to turn in with him. He was refused, and he again laid down by himself and in the morning was found a corpse."

Former prisoner the Reverend J. B. Traywick noted, "The prisoners being so poorly clad, and the Point so exposed to cold, it caused them great suffering. Every intensely cold night from four to seven prisoners would freeze to death. Almost no wood was furnished. About a cord of green pine to one thousand men for five days. It was a mockery."[83]

Prison Rations—Starving In a Land of Plenty

One of the most effective forms of retaliation was to withhold prisoner rations. This not only puts the prisoners in instant pain, both mentally and physically, but it also makes them more susceptible to disease by lowering their ability to fight infection. Many men went into such a deep depression that their weakened immune system made them easy prey for deadly diseases such as smallpox, typhoid fever, pneumonia, chronic diarrhea and dysentery. This type of retaliation began on July 7, 1862, with Colonel William Hoffman's creation of the Prisoner Fund. The fund was created by cutting prisoners rations and selling the uneaten food back to the commissary. Later, Hoffman's suggestion of May 19, 1864, to Secretary of War Edwin M. Stanton said, "I have the honor to suggest that the ration as now issued to prisoners of war may be considerably reduced without depriving them of the food necessary to keep them in health."[84] Stanton, who was in favor of retaliation, thought this was a wonderful idea and gave this his hearty approval. This was such a successful form of retaliation that the prisoner rations were lowered once again in the following months. What made this so popular with Stanton was that it was so easily carried out and the public

Hardtack, a cracker made from flour, water and salt, was a staple of the prisoner's diet.

was not aware of the abuse taking place. Hoffman, who was frugal by nature, loved the idea that the food withheld could be sold back to the commissary and the money put into a prison fund. The reasoning behind this fund allowed the individual prisons to purchase items that the United States government did not provide. This idea looked good on paper, but had many flaws. The fund's money accumulated fairly quickly, thanks to repeated reductions of prisoner's rations, but Hoffman was reluctant to spend any of the money on the prisoners. It seemed this fund's sole purpose was to make Hoffman look good to his superiors when he returned millions of dollars to the Federal government at the end of the war. What the fund did instead was to point an incriminating finger at him and Secretary of War Stanton as the worst offenders in the Civil War prison system.[85]

Dr. William F. Swalm of the Sanitary Commission wrote, "In being shown a (daily) ration, I do not think they received half the amount of meat they were entitled to. The ration to the well man is 3 ounces of pork, 4 ounces of beef, 10 ounces of hardtack, and 1 pint of coffee. Soup is also given once a week, potatoes and beans every five days, and soft bread once a week." The USDA Dietary Guidelines state the daily requirement of protein for an adult male is 56 grams or 7 ounces of meat. It appears Dr. Swalm was correct in his assessment that the prisoners were only receiving half of their meal allowance.[86]

Former prisoner George M. Neese recalls, "A day's rations all told is 4 ounces of meat, 14 ounces of bread, and 1 pint of bean water. The rations we get are all good in quality, but much too diminutive in quantity; I have been hungry ever since I was captured. Twice a week we get fresh beef, and sometimes we get pickled beef, and that is salty enough to make a hound yell by biting into it."[87]

Former Point Lookout prisoner William Pleasant, 4th North Carolina Cavalry, was captured near Madison Courthouse, Virginia. Pleasant joined the U. S. service January 25, 1864 in the 1st U. S. Volunteers. He died of consumption July 25, 1864. *Photo courtesy of North Carolina State Troops and Volunteers, Volume I.*

The Reverend Malachi Bowden recalled the fateful day he came to Point Lookout and heard about the rations from friends. "Upon entering the prison I discovered several men of my company who had been captured before I was. They inform me that I could not live on the rations we drew there. I found our food to be a small cup of soup, with a stray Yankee bean in it here and there, and a piece of fat pickled pork as large as your hand. This together with two or three cuts of loaf bread issued twice a day, completed our menu."[88]

Former prisoner George W. Jones recalls, "Some (prisoners) would consume a whole day's ration at one meal, and the more prudent would divide it into two or three meals. I have seen men eat anything they could lay their hands on. On one occasion when the tide on the bay was high it brought ashore an old seagull which had been dead a month or more. It was picked up by a hungry rebel and devoured with gusto that would have made a modern epicure more than ashamed of himself. I, with others who were willing to get a meal, gave my pocket knife for a pie which had been seasoned with skimming's from the slop tubs at the cookhouse, mixed with anything else that could be gotten, and for which I sorrowfully repented, for it gave me a spell of sickness which came very near sending me to the 'Peach Orchard' (cemetery) where many of the boys had gone."[89]

Private Charles Loehr remembers, "Our rations were just such as to keep us perpetually on the point of starvation, causing a painful feeling of hunger to us helpless, half-starved prisoners. Four small crackers, or a small loaf of bread per day, and a cup full of dishwater, called pea soup, horrible to taste, and a small piece of rancid salt meat, was our daily fare. So hungry were the men that they would eat almost anything they could pick up outside from the sewers; potato peelings, cabbage stalks, or most any kind of refuse that hardly the cattle would eat, was greedily devoured. The scurvy, brought on by this wretched diet, was prevalent in the most awful form."[90]

Former prisoner James T. Wells recalls, "Shortly after cutting off the coffee supply, our rations were reduced in other respects. Bread was issued in the afternoon. The men would eat it as soon as they received it. It does not take much time to consume 8 ounces of soft bread. They would then, of course, be without bread until the following afternoon. About 2 or 3 ounces of meat was given for breakfast, and a cup of greasy water for dinner. Hitherto the subtler had been allowed to sell provisions in limited quantities to those who had the money with which to purchase. This privilege was also abolished, and we were compelled to rely upon the government rations."[91]

Former prisoner David Holt recalls, "Today we march to the cookhouse and received a cup of thin bean soup and a small piece of Baker's bread and a small slice of pickled pork. The rations never changed; how they could be so rotten was not understood. Many contracted scurvy. The sick were carried to the hospital, and we never heard from them again.[92]

If men in quarters were too sick to go to the mess-hall, the company Sick Sergeant would get their rations from the kitchen and bring them back to the prisoner. The daily ration for an ill prisoner in quarters was 3 ounces of vinegar; this was the Union Army's cure for scurvy, 5 ounces of potatoes, one quarter of a pint of rice and one quarter of a pint of molasses. Doctor Swalm reported, "If the man grows worse, he was taken to the hospital tents. When sick prisoners in these tents became more ill they were admitted to Hammond General Hospital."[93]

The ration for Hammond General Hospital was as follows: Breakfast: 8 ounces bread, 1 ounce butter, 2 ounces Indian meal and 0.32 of a Gill of molasses. (A Gill is equal to one quarter of a pint.) Dinner: 6 ounces fresh beef, three boiled potatoes, two thick slices of bread with butter and 1 pint of soup with vegetables. Supper consists of 1 pint of coffee, 5 ounces of bread, 2 ounces of cheese and 1 ounce of butter.[94]

Rats Were Part of the Prison Diet

Private S. N. Bosworth recalled visiting his brother's tent during lunch time. "Doctor Snow, Ed Hall, and Elam Corder, all of my brother's company, live together, and one day when I went to see them they were eating fried rats. I remember now how good they smelled. They did not offer me any, however. Long after the war I met Corder in Elkins, and we got to talking of war times. I spoke of the rats, and asked if it was a scarcity of manners that kept him from offering me a share, and he replied that it was a scarcity of rats."[95]

Former prisoner George M. Neese wrote about a very unusual item on their menu. "Right now as I'm writing these words there is a rat vender going along the street carrying three large rats by the tail, and every few steps I hear him cry: 'Here are your rats, fresh and fat! I just now caught them at the commissary department, and I warrant them to be in fine order. Three for five cents, cheap! Here are your rats!' Talk about the heathen Chinese eating dogs, here men buy and eat rats to satisfy craving hunger right under the shadow of the proud Star-Spangled Banner and in a so-called Christian country and in a land of plenty. I have been hungry for six months now, and I could and would eat a rat or snake on toast if I had it. Only he who has been hungry for a long period knows what hunger is. I saw a man fish a scrap of beef from the slop barrel and devoured as if it were a morsel from a king's table."

Neese goes on to tell us about another unusual item he ate. "One day I drew for my meat ration the upper part of a sheep's head, his

Private John B. Swan, Co. F, 49th N. C., was captured at Petersburg, Va, and sent to Point Lookout. He was paroled June 20, 1865.

eyes still holding their old position and the eyelids decorated with cleanly washed hair like wool, cleansed nicely by boiling the meat. I shaved off the wool and ate the eyes, lids and all; the eyes were certainly delicious."[96]

Prison Coffee

One of the simple pleasures in life was taken away by the vindictive Edwin M. Stanton. On June 1, 1864, the Secretary of War issued an order saying that coffee and sugar will only be given to the sick and wounded prisoners on the recommendation of the surgeon in charge. Therefore, prisoners who were not in the hospital would not receive any coffee. The reasoning behind this new policy was that Stanton did not want the Confederate prisoners enjoying a cup of coffee while Union prisoners were suffering. Apparently Union prisoners had complained that their coffee had been halted. The Confederates always had trouble shipping coffee through the Union blockade. As the war progressed the blockade became more efficient until it was almost impossible to get anything through. This being the case, there is little wonder the Federal prisoner's coffee was halted. I have conducted a search of the *Official Records of the Army* and have found no reference to the Confederate Army stopping the use of coffee for Union prisoners. Since no records were found, it seems that individual Confederate prisons might have halted the prisoner's coffee instead of the government.

Sergeant William M. Seay, Co. E, 11th Virginia, was captured at Milford Station, Va., and sent to Point Lookout. Seay was exchanged March 14, 1865.

On June 28, 1864 Chief Surgeon of the Army C. T. Alexander wrote Colonel Hoffman saying that cutting off coffee to the Confederate prisoners seemed to increase the number of sick men in prison hospitals. Surgeon Alexander recommended that the coffee ration be reinstated because daily coffee was a necessity for prisoners. No Federal order has been found rescinding Stanton's command about halting the prisoner's coffee.[97]

Former prisoner George W. Jones recalls the time in prison when rumors spread around camp saying Union officials would stop the flow of prisoner's coffee. "There were all kinds of rumors circulating in camp, one of which was true--that our ration of coffee would be cut off because the Confederate government had cut off coffee in the prison of Andersonville. This was thought to be a great hardship, but I presume it was done on account of the Confederacy not having the coffee. So we had to put our wits together to get some coffee from somewhere. I was on detail very soon afterward outside the camp whitewashing the hospital department and I noticed a large pile of coffee grounds that had been used for the sick. The hospital was just outside the main prison camp where there were 8,000 sick prisoners and of course they were furnished with a good article of coffee. So the time came for me to act. I found an old coffee sack and made my way close to the wall, stopping close to the deadline and wary of a trench which ran under the fence. I examined the trench to see if it was sufficiently large for me to crawl through. Then, taking advantage of the guard on his beat when his back was towards me, I ran across the deadline and through the hole without being seen. I filled my sack with coffee grounds and, making my arrangements to return, had to catch my opportunity when the guard was again going from me. So I made the venture and succeeded in evading the guard, returning to the camp the proudest rebel there. With my stock of coffee grounds I would have a kettle full every morning. I would stand on the street in front of my tent and cry, 'Here's your hot coffee! A cup for a cracker!' And you could see the boys coming from every direction with a cup in one hand and a cracker in the other. So I made enough crackers to have a feast three times a day, besides having all I could use for myself, so I grew fat and greasy."[98]

Private James T. Wells remembers what happened as a result of General Butler's visit to the prison in December. "In accordance with General Butler's promise to give us more rations, our meager supply of coffee was cut off. This was not as much of a deprivation to us as might be supposed, for the coffee was slop water in every respect. Some of the prisoners went as far as to say that the commissary actually shook a small bag of coffee at each kettle (about 40 gallons of water). This was a grim joke, but it had much the appearance of truth. Shortly after cutting off the coffee supply, our rations were reduced in other respects."[99]

Freeman W. Jones remembers a prison substitute for coffee. "Bread crust coffee was a favorite drink, made simply from parched or burnt bread. It was a healthful drink to say the least of it—the best substitute we could get for coffee."[100]

Major General Benjamin F. Butler's Interview

In late December, 1863, Major General Benjamin F. Butler visited Point Lookout and conducted an interview with six Confederate sergeants assigned to the cookhouses. When questioned about rations all of the men admitted there was a good deal of grumbling about the scarcity of food. The sergeants also noted there was a great complaint about a lack of blankets. During the interview Sergeant C. P. Mooring of the 22nd Virginia infantry stated, "I have drawn no blankets in my house. I have got none myself; I have never had one."[101]

As one begins to dig deeper into the facts surrounding this interview several things begin to emerge. The interview was conducted about five months after Point Lookout had opened its gates. This is before the reductions in rations that were to occur the next year. On May 19, 1864, Colonel William Hoffman, Commissary General of Prisoners, wrote Secretary of War Stanton, and suggested a 25% reduction of the already skimpy prisoner rations. Stanton thought this was an excellent idea and agreed that it should be implemented at once. By the time this food filtered through the chain-of-command the prisoners were lucky to get half the rations that the government issued.

Butler was satisfied with the results of his interview, but his choosing cookhouse sergeants to talk to is suspicious. Being a cook was a highly sought after position in prison. Were these men truthful or were they afraid they might lose their jobs after this interview? Losing a job as a cook meant losing the extra rations the men needed to survive. Former prisoner George M. Neese wrote, "To be a cook here is a position of considerable distinction. I would rather be a cook than the company sergeant for the simple fact the cook has warm quarters to sleep and stay in, and they take good care of number one

Private Lewis Leon, Co. B, 53rd North Carolina, was captured at the battle of the Wilderness, May 5, 1864. He was sent to Point Lookout and took the Oath of Allegiance February 7, 1865.

and help themselves to all the rations they can devour. I can tell a cook in camp anywhere I see him. They are all fat and greasy, and some of them are even a little saucy, and seem to be satisfied with prison life."[102]

Sweet Letters from Home

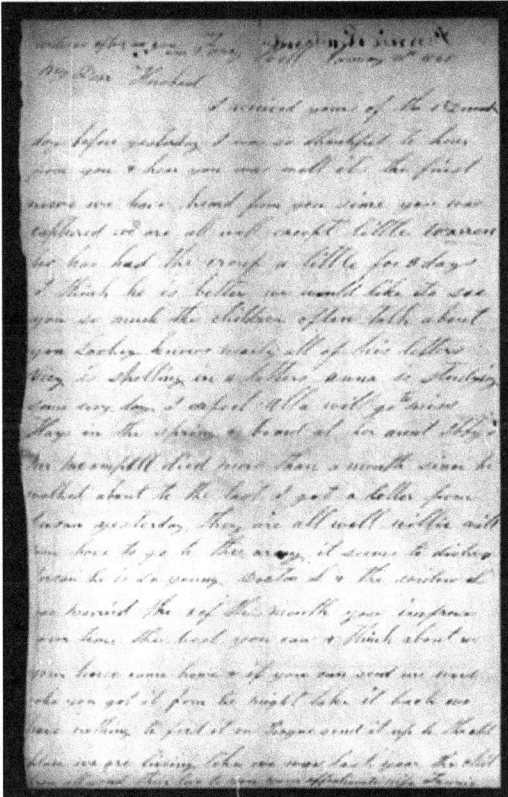

One of the most enjoyable pastimes for prisoners was reading letters from loved ones. These letters from home were extremely important for the men's morale and they provided a brief respite from the woes of prison life. Packages were especially looked forward to. Many times the prisoners would receive money or clothing which was intercepted by the prison censors. When mail for a prisoner was received the censor would open it and see if they contained anything that was contraband. All uniform clothing, boots, or equipment of any kind for military service, weapons of all kinds and intoxicating liquors, are among the contraband articles. The material for outer clothing was required to be gray or some dark mixed color. Any excess of clothing over what the prison required was also considered contraband. What this means is if a prisoner had more than one set of clothing another was not allowed. All money prisoners received was taken charge of by the Provost Marshall, who gave a receipt for it. These funds are recorded in a ledger by the camp sutler, and the prisoner was given credit for any purchases made in the sutler's store. When prisoners are paroled their money was returned to them.[103]

Former prisoner John R. King remembers there were strict rules about what the prisoner were allowed to write. "The people at home never knew how we suffered in prison. If we attempted to tell it in our letters, the censors saw that they were not mailed."[104]

In Marcus B. Tony's book, *The Privations of a Private*, he explained the rules for writing a letter. "In writing a letter you could use only one side of the sheet, as all letters had to be examined and approved before mailing, and you had to be careful and not write anything contraband. The envelopes were stamped: Prisoner's Letter, Examined and Approved."[105]

This is Private Robert M. Rowland's first prison letter from his wife Fannie. Rowland would die from disease before ever reading this letter.

Former prisoner Anthony M. Keiley recalled there were ways to send a letter longer than one page. "Some geniuses were in the habit of writing their letters at the usual long length, then sending them by detail (separate envelopes). Others cultivated a microscopic penmanship."[106]

The paragraph below is the text of Fannie Rowland's letter to her husband Robert. Robert died on May 29, 1865.

Point Lookout Prison
January 27th 1865

My Dear Husband,

I received yours of the 18th December day before yesterday. I was so thankful to hear from you & hear you was well. It's the first news we have heard from you since you was captured. We are all well except little Warren; he has had the croup a little for three days. I think he is better and would like to see you so much. The children often talk about you. Lackey knows nearly all his letters. Nancy is spelling in 4 letters. Anna is studying some every day at school. Alla will go to Miss Hays in the spring and will board at her aunt Abby's. Ivor McCampbell died more than a month since. He walked about to the last. I got a letter from Susan yesterday. They are all well. Willy will have to go to the Army. It seems so distressing, he is so young. Doctor S. & the widow S. were married on the 5th of this month. You improve your time the best you can & think about us. Your horse came home & if you can send me word who you got it from he might take it back. We have nothing to feed it on. (Illegible) sent it up to the (illegible) place. We are living like last year. The children all send their love to you. Your affectionate, Fannie
Write as often as you can, Fannie

Prisoner's Letters from Point Lookout Prison Camp

This is the text of a letter from Point Lookout prisoner Private Frederick Griffith, Company C, 9thVirginia cavalry, to his wife. Griffith was captured near Petersburg, Virginia, September 23, 1864. This long letter, which was prohibited in prison, somehow made it past the censors. Griffith comments on the gloomy accounts of the war printed by the Northern newspapers. He also states that he believes that this is no longer a war for the Union, but a war of Northern conquest and revenge.

Prison Camp Point Lookout, March 1, 1865

My Darling Wife,

Your letter of January 18th by Capt. M. of the steamer "Cour de Lion" has just been received & I don't know how I can employ my time more profitably or pleasantly than by answering it. The exchange is still going on but I fear will be several weeks yet before I will be permitted to go south as they are now taking the prisoners out according to their date of capture commencing at the oldest. I am waiting patiently though, eager for that day to arrive for I long more and more each day. I live to be free from bondage and above all to see my wife and child once more, as well as the dear ones who were so kind to you both in my absence. How truly grateful I feel that all my family are so fortunately situated when I am so perfectly unable to help them. You speak of sending me money. If you have sent me any, I have not received it and I must insist on you're not sending me anymore. My clothing I must confess are in a rather dilapidated condition though. I have not suffered in the least from cold since my capture. Mrs. Phelps sent me a very nice woolen over shirt that is all the clothing that I have gotten from the North of any description but Warren Hutt very kindly let me have a jacket and I got some underclothing from some rebs who had a surplus. The pants I now have on are made of a fine blanket and fit me well. You will be surprised when I tell you they are a monument to my industry and the work of my hand. So you see, Dear, that though I am not attired in the latest fashions of the day, I am warmly clad and comfortable and so you have been making yourself unreasonably uneasy about me. Providence has truly provided for me in time of need and it seems that your prayers have been granted. The suffering among some of the prisoners here this winter has been terrible and the mortality has been very great. Silas P. Douglas, of my old infantry company, died here last week. You can inform his friends of the fact. You say your father and mother have gone to the cottage to see Joe Chinn. What is the matter with Joe? Is he dangerously sick? Warren Hutt was exchanged not long since, he promised me that he would certainly go to see you and tell you about me. I sent Molly, Nelly, sister and yourself each a ring to remember me by. Our little son must pardon me for not sending him a present but a rattle would be the only thing that would be appropriate and could not be obtained. The newspapers give us gloomy accounts of the proceedings down south. I fear a sad and wonderful change may take place among our people since my imprisonment. Had the people remained undivided and true to themselves, Sherman instead of being the haughty conqueror that he is would now be humbled in the dust. But alas our own people, who fought desperately and nobly, have not been sustained and that too by states which first seceded and poor old Virginia whose breast bears the scars of many battles and who has been in invincible barrier to the hosts of soldiers thrown against her still stands like a Gibraltar bidding defiance to the last. God grant that she may not be overwhelmed by numbers. But the prospect presents a gloomy aspect to a prisoner and I must acknowledge that I greatly fear the result of the next campaign. Many prisoners here will take the oath rather than be exchanged. I would give anything just to know what our own people think of the present state of affairs for I know they are true to a cause they believe to be right. This is a cold, raw disagreeable evening and I should enjoy above all things spending a social quiet twilight with that happy family circle at Wilton, but I must not indulge in such hope at present for the contrast is really painful, but I must be patient and the time I pray is not far distant when my fondest hopes will be realized. I have formed many most agreeable acquaintances since from my imprisonment and I am now staying in the tent with Dr. J. N. Jones of Isle of Wright, a most elegant old gentleman, he was a citizen when captured and is kept here simply because the Yanks have it in their power to imprison him.

Private Melville D. Lang, Co. E, 62nd Va. Mounted Infantry, was captured at Fisher's Hill, Va., September 22, 1864. Lang took the Oath of Allegiance June 28, 1865.

You don't know how much I have regretted not having your daguerreotype since my capture. So you see, Darling, you should have listened to my entreaties in the summer of 62, when you had the opportunity. Where is Col. B---now and what does he do? Is B. B. In the Army now? Give my love to the family at Tappahannock and Col. B----'s. Also to all at Linden and Buena Vista. Are mother and sister in good spirits? I feel truly sorry for them in their present loathsome condition. Mary Hoxton writes me that she hears sister is to be married, but as I could give her no information on the subject, I referred her to sister who will undoubtedly be highly amused at hearing it. Poor sister I am deeply grieved at the loss of her colt, not so much for the sake of the animal, but because she was so much attached to it. I can't help feeling very uneasy about our dear little son, do let me know how he is and all about him. Good night March 2nd,

My Darling wife, I must finish my letter this morning as the prisoners may leave this evening. You are constantly on my mind and I am never so happy as when writing to you. I suppose when I get home I shall find the same sweet wife that you used to be. But our little son will be so much changed that I shall not know him. As for myself, I can't help feeling that a change has taken place in me. Things that used to be pleasant are no longer pleasures to me. I feel older (not physically) by far than when I left home, and I long each day more and more to be with my wife and child. I feel and know too well that I have never been useful to my little family and though I can't blame myself, I can't help lamenting the present helpless condition to which I am reduced. I earnestly pray that peace may soon dawn, that we may be returned to each other in peace once more. True it is, that our pecuniary circumstances are greatly changed, but with peace why should we not be happy. But tis idle to speculate upon an uncertain future. Present signs prognosticate nothing but unrelenting war. It is no longer a war for the Union but one of conquest and revenge. My opinion of Yankee characters always been anything else than exalted, but I've seen so much meanness among them since my capture that I wish I could never see one again. It is rumored that the Negroes are to be armed and emancipated in the South. I hope it may be so. The alternative is a humiliating one, but anything rather than subjugation.

I've acquired considerable experience in my profession since a prisoner and in that respect, and that alone, I've been benefited by my capture. Indeed had it not been for my profession which entitles me to the position which I occupy, I believe I should not be numbered with the living for I could never stand the hardships which the prisoners of camp are exposed. Many of the prisoners die of scurvy, a most horrible disease. I believe Dr. Thompson U. S. Surgeon in charge of the camp, does all in his power to alleviate their sufferings, but he is furnished with neither a proper diet or a sufficiency of medicine to correct the malady. I am too happy to tell you that I am quite good health and only weak from confinement. Each day that I live I chafe more and more for freedom. But I expect once more soon to be free. God has certainly been merciful to us in our affliction, but compared to others our burden has been light. How many are now captive or have been killed, whose wives and little ones are this day suffering for bread. So we have no reason to be despondent, but it benefits us rather to offer up prayers which protected us. My paper warns me, Darling, that I must close. Give my best to all the dear ones at L Farm, and Wilton. Tell them I love them more than I ever did. I feel I want to return to live among them never to be separated (while life lasts) again. Do tell some of them to write me. I suppose Johnny's little nephew is now almost large enough to play with him. Give many kisses to the dear little boy for pop. Continue your prayers for me, my Darling, for you are ever in mind. May God bless you and finally restore us to each other is the fervent prayer of your dear husband.

F. Griffith

P. S. Ask David, Blake and Colville if they ever think of me.

Point Lookout
March 4, 1864

My Dear Sister,

*   Your very kind letter of the 23rd came to hand yesterday—it is the first line I have received since my imprisonment. I have been very unwell ever since my capture suffering all the time from cola, but I feel today much better. We have been at this place one month today. This is I think a very healthy prison. I received the underclothes mother sent me a short time after my capture but*

none since. I shall do very well in respect to clothes except a hat and shoes. There is no difficulty in the way of sending money here and that gentleman that has mine can send it at any time.
 Love to all,

P. W. Carper

Brian Hummer & Pettingall are well.
P. S. We are only allowed to write one page so you must excuse brevity direct Company B, 7th Division, Prisoners Camp Point Lookout

Dear Mother,
    I have written several letters lately but cannot hear from you however I trust this may fill its mission. Cousin Robert Aldridge is still very weak and sick, being unable to walk. He is in the hospital and has the best attention possible at this place. He says tell his mother to come see him if possible. I have been quite unwell for several weeks

Private Philip W. Carper, 35th Battalion, Virginia Cavalry, was wounded at Brandy Station, Va., and sent to Point Lookout. Carper was later exchanged February 13, 1865. These are several letters Carper wrote while in prison.

suffering from some kind of fever, but I feel much better at present and soon to be entirely well. I wrote you a few weeks since to send me some eatables—such as honey (?) bread, onions, potatoes or any kind of vegetable or anything that will keep until it arrives here. Don't fail to send plenty of butter and some honey and pickles. Mr. J. W. Sexton says tell his wife a lik box. If you send me any money, which you may do if convenient, direct it to me as usual. Enclosed in another envelope directed to A. G. Brady Provost Marshall Point Lookout, Maryland, company B, 7th Division, Prison Camp Point Lookout, Maryland.
                    Sincerely and affectionately,
                        Your son,
                          P. W. Carper

Prison Hospital Tents

    Dr. William F. Swalm of the Sanitary Commission inspected the prison in September, 1863, and sent a report to his superior, Dr. J. H. Douglas. He reported that there were 18 hospital tents at Point Lookout containing about 100 of the less seriously ill prisoners. Each patient slept on a cot and was furnished with one blanket and a mattress. The hospital tents had no stoves and the men complained greatly of the cold. Only one of the tents had a wooden floor, which the doctor considered a must. The most prevalent diseases were diarrhea, scurvy, and the itch, which was probably caused by lice. A patient usually remained in this hospital until he was either healed or became worse and was then sent to Hammond General Hospital. The doctor reported 20 to 30 men went to Hammond Hospital every day. He described the dispensary as a poor excuse for one, having little or no medicine available. Swalm reported finding only half a dram of opium, 1/2 pounds of sulphether and cerate on hand to treat a hundred patients per day.

Private Charles T. Loehr recalled when he became sick and was sent to a crowded hospital tent. "The (Hammond) hospital could only accommodate about 1,200 sick, and there were no less than 6,000 sick and dying men lying within the main building and the tents surrounding it. Being assigned to a tent where there was room for 16 men, but which had no less than 40 in it, I was placed on the damp ground, only one thin blanket given me. The two nights I spent there were simply horrible. The praying, crying, and the fearful struggles of the dying during the dark night, lit up by a single small lantern, was awful. The first night about five or six died, and the next morning found me lying next to dead comrades. The second night was a repetition of the first; and that day I asked the Federal surgeon to allow me to return to camp, which he at once granted, thinking I might just as well die there as anywhere else. But I got better, how I cannot explain; perhaps it was my determination not to die there in spite of them that kept me alive."[107]

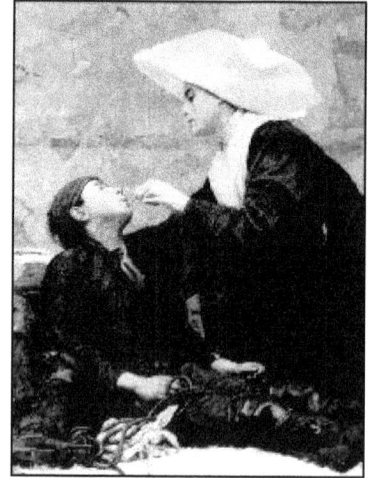

Sisters of Charity from Baltimore, Md, cared for the sick soldiers in Hammond General Hospital at Point Lookout.

Former prisoner Luther Hopkins remembers his fear about occupying a dead man's bed. "The hospitals were long tents, each holding about 30 cots. As soon as the patient died, he was taken out to the dead house, the sheets changed, and another brought in. When I was first taken there I remarked to my neighbor that I did not think that was very prudent (meaning the placing of a new patient at once on the bed that was still warm from the body that had just been removed). He replied that the bed that I was on had been occupied by a smallpox patient, and I was put on it a few minutes after the patient was taken out. However, there was a separate hospital for contagious diseases and the patient had been removed as soon as the disease developed. Most of those who went to the hospital died. The dead were all carried at once to the dead house on stretchers, and once a day a two horse wagon came in, and their bodies were laid in it like so much cordwood, taken out and buried in long trenches. The trenches were 7 feet wide and 3 feet deep, and the bodies were laid across the trench side-by-side and covered with earth.

Former prisoner Joseph H. Whitehead recalls seeing the death wagon picking up the bodies of the Confederate prisoners. "I have seen the dead hauled out by the four horse wagonload, and two wagons at a time sometimes. On one occasion there was a wagon going out loaded with the dead, and they were piled so high that one of them fell off the wagon and the coffin burst open."[108]

Smallpox Hospital Tent

An overcrowded prison environment where the men have a poor diet and live in filthy conditions is a breeding ground for deadly diseases such as smallpox. This highly contagious disease is so severe 75% of the individuals who become infected do not survive. Since the smallpox virus can live on clothing and blankets for up to 18 months, it spread with a vengeance inside the prison.[109]

A half-mile north of the prison, across Point Lookout Creek and among the pine trees and shrubs, was the smallpox hospital. The sick were put in wedge tents, three to a tent, lying on straw on the ground, with a blanket and a half to each man. Their ration was the same as the tent hospital.

A prisoner with smallpox becomes covered with scabs or pustules as the disease develops. The majority also have scurvy and highly contagious scabies which are caused by a small female mite which burrows into the skin.[110]

Private James T. Wells remembers the awful sickness in camp. "The health of the men began to fail rapidly, as soon as the prisoner's hospital was crowded. Fever in every shape abounded, and smallpox was epidemic. Nearly every tent contained one or two cases of this loathsome disease. The hospital could not accommodate all the sick, and they were left in their tents, many of them with a blanket only to protect them from the damp ground, and entirely destitute of proper nourishment. Men who were seen in the morning, apparently in health, were taken to the dead house in the afternoon, and some have been known to drop in the street, and died before they could be carried to the tents. Notwithstanding the enforcement of the most rigid sanitary policies, diseases of all kinds continued to spread with an alarming rapidity. Add to this the short rations which were meted out to us, together with

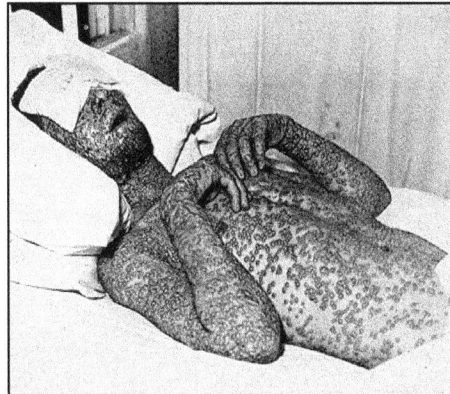

Smallpox victim

their miserable quality and the cruel treatment which we received at the hands of the Negro soldiers, and you have but a faint idea of the suffering to which we were now subjected."[111]

The disease of smallpox was indeed deadly. Nearly all of the men who became infected with the smallpox virus died from the disease. Fortunately this epidemic at Point Lookout only lasted four months. Ninety-eight percent of the smallpox cases occurred from November of 1863 to the end of February 1864. During this four month period smallpox claimed 219 lives at Point Lookout making it the fourth most deadly disease at Point Lookout prison camp. During this time many of the soldier's records never listed a cause of death. It is probable that many of these deaths were caused by smallpox.

Other Deadly Diseases

The most common diseases that preyed upon the Point Lookout prisoners were: chronic or acute diarrhea, chronic dysentery, erysipelas, pneumonia, scurvy, smallpox and typhoid fever. These diseases are listed in alphabetical order and are not in order according to their rank.

The prison camp's officers did their best in trying to keep Point Lookout clean, but sickness still plagued the camp especially during the last year when the prison was grossly overcrowded. Every prisoner who came to Point Lookout was immediately vaccinated. If someone was suspected of having smallpox, the prisoner was put in the Contagious Diseases hospital until he either died or became well.[112]

Former prisoner Walter D. Addison wrote about the horrors of 19th century vaccinations in *The Southern Historical Collection of the North Carolina* at Chapel Hill. "The courageous manner in which men were vaccinated excelled anything I have ever witnessed even surpassing the acts of savages. The modus operandi was to assemble the men in long lines with coats off and arms bared; then the butchering began by illiterate and irresponsible men. They would take hold of a thick piece of flesh, dip a lancet into the diluted virus, and then thrust it entirely through the pinched up flesh. The spurious virus soon produced such fearfully disastrous results that it became necessary to construct gangrene hospitals, from which arose a dreadful stench. Scores died from the effects; others losing arms. I have seen the sickening effects of their villainous vaccinations. There are many who can verify the above."[113]

Diarrhea

Chronic diarrhea was the leading cause of death at all military prisons during the Civil War. Diarrhea is a bacterial disease with severe abdominal discomfort, cramping and causes a violent defecation which produces a liquid stool. One of the harmful effects of diarrhea is severe depletion of body fluids leading to an electrolyte imbalance. Electrolytes are essential minerals in your body that are necessary for nerve and muscle function and other critical processes. Ignorant of germs, men in prison shared eating utensils which helped the disease to spread. Diarrhea claimed 1,039 lives making it number one on the list of Point Lookout's most deadly diseases.[114]

Reverend I. W. K. Handy, of the Presbyterian Church of Virginia, remembers what a difficult time men who suffered with chronic diarrhea had. "Sick men, perfectly emaciated from diarrhea, have been obliged to stagger through their quarters to the outhouse on the bank of the river, with filth streaming upon their legs; and then, unable to help themselves, they have fallen upon the pathway, and have been found dead in the morning. Barefooted, bareheaded and ragged men, tottering with disease, have been left to suffer long for the necessary clothing or medicines, which might have been abundantly supplied."[115]

"I was in the hospital myself a month with (diarrhea). Weakness and starvation had caused me to lose my sight, consequently often times when wandering some distance from our ward spots appeared before my eyes that I was dependent upon some kind comrade to lead me home. The blindness left me as I grew stronger. Others suffered the same way. Many times a poor fellow staggered along until his old shaky legs fail to support him, then he staggered until he was on his feet again with a ghastly smile trying to bear it bravely. It was touching to see the poor, ragged gaunt, half famished, much abused, noble fellows trying to be cheerful through it all."

Former prisoner Anthony M. Keiley wrote that diarrhea was so common that the disease affected everyone. "Visited all my comrades today, and, with one exception, found them all suffering like myself from exhausting diarrhea, induced by the poisonous water."[116]

Dysentery

Many prisoners died of chronic dysentery, but not at the alarming rate of diarrhea. Dysentery is a bacterial infection whose symptoms are intestinal inflammation, a high fever, chills, abdominal cramping, and foul-smelling, bloody diarrhea. The stool is commonly infused with pus and mucus. Although often confused with diarrhea, this disease is caused by a different type of bacteria. Dysentery was spread by malnourished prisoners who shared eating utensils and water. Dysentery claimed 232 lives making it number three on the list of Point Lookout's most deadly diseases.[117]

Erysipelas

Also known as St. Anthony's fire, erysipelas is a disease of the skin which produces reddened, swollen, raised lesions on the face and scalp. The victim's skin has a bumpy texture which gives it the appearance of an orange peel. Its symptoms are stinging and itching lesions, vomiting, fever, headache and sore throat. Erysipelas claimed twenty-five lives making it number eight on the list of Point Lookout's most deadly diseases.

Former prisoner Charles T. Loehr remembers the time when he almost died at Point Lookout. "I was never sick during the whole war, but was taken down with erysipelas at Point Lookout. It was a bad case, so the Federal surgeon said who examined me. 'Entirely too late to do anything for him; neck and face swollen black and green.' Those who did the packing up, that is placing the dead bodies in rough boxes, seeing me, one of them said, 'There goes a fellow we will have to box up tomorrow.' I was removed to the hospital pen, and with two of my company, Alexander Moss and John Harris, both of whom I saw stretched out in the dead house on the following day."[118]

Intermittent Fever

Intermittent fever, or sometimes referred to as remittent fever, is a malarial fever in which feverish periods last a few hours then alternate with periods in which the temperature is normal. Intermittent fever claimed the lives of thirty-five men making it the eighth most deadly disease at Point Lookout.

Measles

Measles is a mildly contagious, viral disease that produces a distinctive, three-day rash, low-grade fever and swollen lymph nodes. Often considered to be an early childhood disease it usually infected the younger soldiers and could possibly be deadly. In this disease is caused by the rubella virus and is transmitted through contact with blood, urine, stools or infected persons. Forty-four prisoners died with measles making it number seven on the list of Point Lookout's most deadly diseases.

Pneumonia

Civil War soldiers were under tremendous stress when captured because they were worried about what would become of them and their families. The men heard many horror stories from other soldiers who had been in prison and it was understandable they were frightened. A prisoner's ability to fight disease was weakened by stress, worry, a poor diet, inadequate water and shelter. Given all these things it was now possible for a simple cold to develop into pneumonia.

Pneumonia is a severe bacterial infection of the lungs which often impairs gas exchange. This disease is characterized by a persistent cough, sharp chest pain, shortness of breath and a high fever. With 299 deaths Pneumonia is second on the list of Point Lookout's deadly diseases.[119]

Scurvy

Hundreds of years ago sailors at sea were commonly affected by a disease that attacked the gums and teeth. Doctors quickly diagnosed the problem as a lack of fresh fruit and vegetables containing vitamin C. By the time of the American Civil War scurvy was a well-known disease which could be easily prevented. There was absolutely no reason for the appearance of this disease in civil war prisons. The existence of scurvy was due to a callous disregard by prison officials for a captured soldier's nutritional needs. Scurvy claimed 165 lives making it number five on the list of Point Lookout's most deadly diseases.

All prison officials were either consciously or unconsciously guilty of promoting disease; whether this was due to overcrowding, which led to water pollution, or merely ignoring sick prisoners until they were too ill to save. Either way, they shared responsibility for diseases in their prison. Scurvy, however, is unlike other diseases since it can be traced directly to prisoner's diet. Colonel William Hoffman, the Commissary General of Prisoners, insisted on controlling every aspect of a prisoner's life; whether it was shelter, clothing or diet. This being the case, the men's food was his responsibility. Hoffman could not plead ignorance of scurvy because

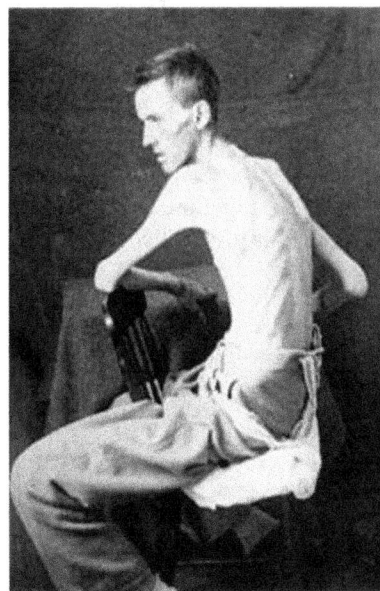

Civil War scurvy victim.

49

he had been warned many times by prison commandants and surgeons about the presence of the disease. In early November of 1863 Dr. William F. Swalm, of the Sanitary Commission, conducted an inspection of Point Lookout prison and noted that he had found scurvy to be the number one ailment both in the prisoner's tent hospital and also the smallpox hospital.[120] On November 6, 1863 General Gilman Marston, Point Lookout prison commandant, wrote to Colonel Hoffman, "The surgeon in charge of the rebel camp informs me that many of the prisoners are affected with scurvy, and he advises that vegetables be furnished to them. I thought it might be advisable to purchase a schooner load of beets, carrots, turnips, cabbages, and the like, and pay for the same out of the fund arising from the savings from their rations. It would probably not add to the actual cost of their food." Hoffman wrote back on November 9th and told Marston that this was agreeable with him. However, scurvy continued to be a problem at Point Lookout. If you look at General Marston's list there are only vegetables on it, no fruit at all. While these vegetables did have some vitamin C, they were not as high as fruit would have been. However, given the time of year fruit may not have been available.[121]

A person suffering from scurvy has a serious lack of vitamin C in his system which is essential for the production of collagen, a substance that binds teeth and bones. Symptoms include weakness, swollen and bleeding gums, loose teeth, poor wound healing and depression.[122]

Private B. T. Holliday recorded this entry in his diary for February, 1865. "I began to feel the effects of my long imprisonment. My limbs paining me; I had no appetite and I was forced to give up and go to the hospital. I was put to bed; the Dr. said I have scurvy, produced by lack of a vegetable diet. My gums sloughed away from my teeth. With my fingers I could've removed any tooth from my mouth without pain, for they were ready to drop out. A great many prisoners have scurvy. I spent several months in the hospital and witnessed many distressing scenes. One morning I awoke to find to patients dead, one on either side of me."[123]

Trying to combat scurvy the Federals introduced vinegar to the prisoner's diet. Since vinegar was made from fermented apple juice the liquid contained some vitamin C.

Former prisoner Luther Hopkins remembers the vinegar on his meals. "The dinners consisted of a tin cup of soup (generally bean or other vegetable), a small piece of meat on a tin plate, on which a little vinegar was poured to prevent scurvy."[124]

Another prisoner, Private Malachi Bowden remembers the Yankee antidote for scurvy. "They (prison officials) did allow us to draw a copious supply of vinegar. I ate this with my diet, and drank it with water, hoping that it might help to keep down the disease." Scurvy is number four on the list of Point Lookout's deadly diseases.[125]

Private Ambrose C. Wyckoff, 35th Battalion Virginia Cavalry, was captured at Cedar Creek, 10/5/1864, and sent to Point Lookout prison. Wyckoff took the Oath of Allegiance 6/2/1865. This photograph is courtesy of the Point Lookout Museum.

Smallpox

Smallpox is discussed on pages 40-41.

Typhoid Fever

Typhoid fever is a bacterial disease, often referred to as remittent fever. Its symptoms include abdominal tenderness headache, sweating, cough, high fever of 104°, bloody stool, confusion delirium and severe fatigue or weakness. This disease is caused by eating contaminated or undercooked meats, especially eggs, chicken, turkey and duck. Proper cooking reduces the risk of contracting this disease, but doesn't eliminate it. It is spread through contaminated food or water or by contact with the victim's moist lesions. One hundred twenty-five men died of Typhoid fever making it number six on the list of Point Lookout's deadly diseases. Typhoid fever claimed 125 lives making it number six on the list of Point Lookout's most deadly diseases. [126]

Point Lookout Prison Camp Deaths

Point Lookout Prison Population and Deaths by Month

Figures Obtained from *War of the Rebellion, Official Records of the Union and Confederate Armies*, Series II, Volume 8, pages 991-1002

Month and Year	Prison Population	Official Records Death Figures	Death Figures Discovered by Author
August, 1863	1,827	0	5
September, 1863	3,942	14	13
October, 1863	7,585	33	61
November, 1863	9,371	119	253
December, 1863	9,153	158	247
January, 1864	8,621	138	226
February, 1864	8,678	128	163
March, 1964	8,480	82	92
April, 1864	6,268	43	48
May, 1864	12,617	24	36
June, 1864	15,500	105	101
July, 1864	14,747	204	174
August, 1864	11,419	211	188
September, 1864	8,691	110	101
October, 1864	13,811	111	104
November, 1864	11,104	52	56
December, 1864	10,702	86	92
January, 1865	11,860	161	161
February, 1865	12,231	223	257
March, 1965	11,332	175	184
April, 1865	20,110	203	216
May, 1865	19,818	324	325
June, 1865	18,836	256	251
July, 1865	Unknown	Unknown	40
August, 1865	Unknown	Unknown	4
Total Deaths		2,960	3,397

This list was prepared using the *Official Records* and the data from the author's roster. While there were 3,826 Confederate dead on my roster you will note that on this table the total deaths are 3,397. This difference is because some of the soldiers did not have a date of death in their records or because their records could not be located. The months where the report in the *Official Records* is higher than my figure is probably due to the prisoners who do not have a date of death documented in their records. It is interesting that only 2,960 prisoner deaths were mentioned in the *Official Records* while my research provided 437 additional men. The figure on the Federal monument was later adjusted to 3,384, but even this figure falls short of the real number of deaths. An interesting aspect of this table is that it gives the prison population as well as the deaths. Even though May of 1865 had the most deaths this is fact is offset by the increase in population to 20,000. November of 1863 was actually a more deadly time at Point Lookout prison camp. It had 253 deaths but the population was less than half of what it was in May of 1865.

At least 3,731 Prisoners Died Between August 1863 and July 1865. Four hundred thirty-two prisoner deaths have been found that do not appear on the bronze tablets on the Confederate memorial. Causes of death in the table appear in order of deadliness.

	Deaths by Unknown Causes	1,075
1.	Diarrhea Deaths	1,039
2.	Pneumonia Deaths	299
3.	Dysentery Deaths	232
4.	Smallpox Deaths	219
5.	Scurvy Deaths	165
6.	Typhoid Fever Deaths	126
7.	Measles Deaths	44
8.	Died of Wounds Deaths	38
9.	Intermittent Fever Deaths	35
10.	Erysipelas Deaths	25

Confederate Deaths at Point Lookout Prison Camp by State

State	Maryland Monument Figures	Author's Figures
North Carolina	962	1,475
Virginia	640	933
Georgia	249	428
South Carolina	248	339
Tennessee	63	150
Alabama	75	149
Mississippi	42	70
Louisiana	38	58
Arkansas	4	38
Florida	31	37
Kentucky	18	22
Confederate States Cavalry	0	20
Confederate States Navy	0	20
Missouri	4	19
Maryland	6	12
Texas	6	9
Confederate States Marines	0	5
Confederate States Army	0	1
Confederate States Undesignated	618	0
Totals	3,004	3,784

Depression Can Be Deadly

It has been shown there is a strong link between depression and illness. All prisoners become depressed to a degree. However, some men dwell so much on their horrendous circumstances they become stripped of hope and consequently are more susceptible to disease. Most of these men never came home and populate the cemetery at Point Lookout.

Former prisoner George M. Neese recalled the dark cloud of gloom which had settled over him in prison at Point Lookout. "The true aspects, experiences, and characteristics of prison life in general can never be described, even by the most impressive writer, so that he who has never experienced its realities cannot form the faintest conception of the melancholy gloom that settles down like eternal night on the spirit of the man and crushes hope to the dark recesses of its lowest stage, so that life itself becomes a burden that may be dragged, but too wearisome to bear. No painter's palette ever held the color black enough to truthfully delineate the shadows that constantly hang around a prisoner of war in these United States."[127]

Neese goes on to say, "There are about 10,000 prisoners in our pen, and in that crowd I have not seen one man's smile or heard a hearty laugh since I've been here. Everyone moves around in almost sullen silence, with a sad countenance, and the whole crew looks as if they had just returned from a big funeral."[128]

An unknown Confederate officer had been corresponding with a lady in Richmond when he was a prisoner at Point Lookout. Reflecting on his plight, he wrote, "All looked dark, dismal—and the thought I might remain there for months came nearer to making my heart sink in despair than ever before. I thought that must be surely the darkest hour of my existence."[129]

Former prisoner Charles W. Hutt made this entry in his diary for April 29, 1864. "Clear and beautiful. There is nothing to disturb the monotony of such a life. I am exceedingly low spirited and cannot hear anything to dispel the dark cloud of despair which hangs over me."[130]

Private Joseph Mull, Co. K, 35th N. C., was captured at Five Forks, Va., and sent to Point Lookout Prison Camp. Mull took the Oath of Allegiance June 29, 1865.

On December 25, 1864 George Q. Peyton wrote, "A dismal and sorrowful Christmas, but we still have many things to be thankful for. We are still living and the Lord has not called us to judgment for our sins. There are hundreds in the camp or worse off than we are. Some of them have no fire at all."

Peyton wrote a few days later of the depressing prospect of greeting another year in prison. "The old year went out in silence and gloom. Our hearts are too full of the things that are happening at home to be elated at the coming of a new year. We had no Christmas and came near to having no bread as the flour gave out. The Lord be with me now. I need him."[131]

Former prisoner John R. King remembered how the men died at Point Lookout. "The poor fellows died rapidly, despondent, homesick, hungry and wretched. I have stood day after day watching the wagons carry the dead outside to be buried and each day for several weeks 16 dead men were taken through the gate."[132]

54

Moon Blindness Affected Most Prisoners

Former prisoner James T. Wells recalls there was a peculiar illness that affected prisoners at Point Lookout. "Summer was now fairly upon us, and we began to feel its effects most severely. There was not a shade tree in the camp, and the only shelter we had from the scorching rays of the sun was our dilapidated tents. The glare of the sun upon the white ground and tents soon produced what is known as 'moon blindness.' This is a disease which affects one only at night. Then one half of the camp, at least, were totally blind, and had to be led by those were more fortunate. Their fear that this might terminate in total and permanent blindness was a source of extreme anxiety to most of the men, and began to tell most fearfully upon their health and spirits. Nothing was done by the authorities (if, indeed, anything could have been done) except the issuing of green shades for the eyes, and planting some small spots with oats, rye, etc., so that the eye might have a green spots look upon."

Mess Halls and Cookhouses

Directly to the west of the prisoner's tents stood six wooden buildings that served as dining-rooms or mess halls. These wooden buildings were 160 feet in length with 20 feet used for the kitchens. Each kitchen had four 50 to 60 gallon cauldrons for preparing the prisoner's food. The prisoners were given two meals per day. Breakfast was at 8 A. M. and dinner was served at 2 P. M. Dr. Swalm wrote, "Here the rations are cooked, and I was told that they were served the meat ration all at dinner, not being enough to make two meals. Breakfast relied upon hardtack tea or coffee."[133]

Feeding 10,000 men was not an easy task, so the mess halls had the following schedule. After morning roll call the Company Sergeant would form his men into double ranks and march them to the cookhouse. When the company arrived at the cookhouse the Company Sergeant and a sergeant from the cookhouse, one on each side of the door, would count the men as they go in. This was done to make sure that no prisoners are trying to sneak in and get extra food. The dining rooms contained three tables, and each house would feed 1,500 men, 500 at a time. Each table was a long hollow rectangle, with a few cooks scattered in the hollow to watch the prisoners so they would not steal food that does not belong to them. On the table were about 100 tin plates, placed about 2 feet apart with a piece of meat on them. The prisoners marched along the table and were not allowed to touch a ration of meat until the cooks or table managers had assigned each man to a plate. When everyone was standing before a plate the signal was given and the men grab the 4 ounce ration of meat and then marched out of the dining room.[134]

Private Jesse Choplin, Co. H, 5th N. C. Cavalry, was captured near Madison Court House, Va., and was sent to Point Lookout Prison Camp. Choplin died of disease April 17, 1864.

Like all forms of society people with money fare better than those without. So it was the same with the prisoners of Point Lookout. A few prisoners were fortunate enough to have friends and relatives send them money to make life easier in prison. Yet ninety percent of the men either did not receive any money or very little and had to rely on what the United States government furnished them. Sadly, this was never enough. Many prisoners' immune systems were weakened by a lack of food.

The men who could afford them built the warmer cracker box houses. All of the cracker-box houses were located on a street called "cracker-box row". Permission was required from the Provost Marshall to build one of these homes.[135] Crackers or hardtack were shipped to the prison in sturdy 50-pound wooden boxes made of white pine. These boxes measured 32 inches long by 20 inches wide and 12 inches deep. Prisoners could buy boxes from the commissary for 10 to 15 cents, according to the demand. The boxes were carefully taken apart and the nails were saved for later use. Some longer pieces of wood were needed for the frame and ridge pole and could be gotten from outside prison by the men who were on work details. Once the 8' x 10' frame was built, then the pine boards were nailed to it. When the structure was 2 1/2 to 3 feet tall an "A-tent" was stretched across the ridge pole in the center to form the roof. A fireplace was then made of sun-dried bricks about four or five feet tall and surmounted by a flour barrel. The barrel acted as a chimney and provided the proper draft so the fire would burn more efficiently. Men could either buy the bricks from other prisoners for three cents apiece or make them themselves. The recipe is to mix sand and clay with a little water. Shape them into bricks and let the sun bake them until they were hard.[136]

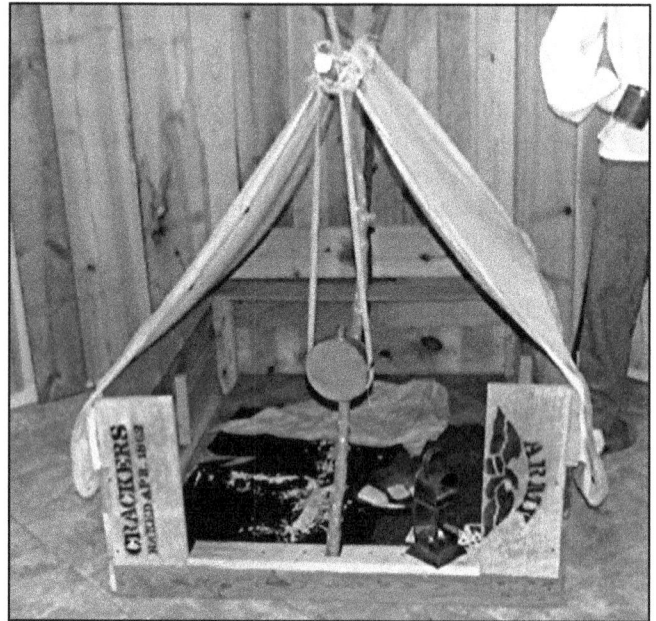

Cracker box tent is displayed at the Point Lookout Museum. Prisoners would build up the sides of their tent with boards from the cracker boxes and wallpaper the walls with pictures from *Harper's Weekly Illustrated Magazine*.

The benefits of money extended to the mess hall as well. Wealthy prisoners like Charles W. Hutt did not have to go to the mess hall to get their government issued rations. Instead, he and his mess mates pooled their money and had a designated cook prepare their meals. The cook, or his helper, would shop for items either at the sutler's store or the many prison stands that sold food. The cook would return to their tent or house and cook the food over a stove or campfire. Many prisoners credited such a diet with saving their life while they were in prison.[137] However, on August 10, 1864, Colonel Hoffman issued Circular 4 which prohibited the sutler from selling food to the prisoners. Now a major food source was closed to the men. Although they still had the food shops run by the prisoners themselves, many men were forced to eat at the government mess hall.

Water—Water Everywhere but Nary a Drop to Drink

Water is one of the most fundamental elements needed to sustain life, but it can also be one of the most deadly. Point Lookout prison camp had approximately six shallow-surface wells available for drinking water, but only two of these had water fit to drink. The others had water impregnated with iron sulfate which turned clothes yellow and left a scum on the surface of the water. Doctor Augustus M. Clark inspected the prison in December, 1863, and wrote, "(The well water is) impregnated with ferruginous and alkaline salts, giving rise to digestive and intestinal derangements. One of the good wells next to Hammond hospital was closely guarded and was used for the patients."[138]

Anthony M. Keiley wrote, "The supply of water is getting very scant, and the quality very infamous. Guards been placed over some of the pumps to prevent waste, and this being Negroes, it is necessary in order to get a drop, to ask permission in respectful terms.[139]

Private James T. Wells remembers when the water became scarce at Point Lookout. "In May, large numbers of the wounded from Grant's Army were brought into the hospital which is situated on the point outside. This water was used to wash their wounds, and gangrene made its appearance. They were compelled to send to Baltimore for water and it was brought in in casks."[140]

Former prisoner Freeman W. Jones recalled many of the prisoners found it difficult to get good water to drink. "The worse suffering we endured was for water. There were some four or five wells in camp, but in only two cases was the water fit to drink. Of course everyone wanted water from those two wells, and the consequence was they were soon in such a condition that you could not get much water from them. The water from the other wells was simply horrid. They had a sweet taste being impregnated with Copperas (iron sulfate), and after standing a while there was always a deposit on the surface upon which you could write your name. I believe this water produced more sickness and suffering than any other cause in the prison."[141]

Former prisoner George M. Neese swore that not drinking the contaminated well water saved his life. "The water is not fit to drink, as it produces a diarrhea which sticks closer than a brother, and has already killed hundreds of our prisoners. The second day after I arrived here the water made me sick with a violent diarrhea that clung to me like a leech for several days, but I learned to do without drinking a drop of water, and by that means alone I survived the evil effects of its unwholesomeness."[142]

Private Robert Jennings, 18th Va, was taken prisoner at Gettysburg. He survived Point Lookout and was paroled February 18, 1865.

Private Luther Hopkins recalled, "The water was brackish and unpleasant to the taste. The only water we had was from pumps scattered about over the camp, and during the four months that I was there the pumps were always surrounded by a thirsty crowd of from 40 to 50 prisoners, each with his tin cup, trying to wedge his way in, that he might quench his thirst.[143]

One of the benefits of going on work details is that prisoners could drink their fill of good water. This reason alone caused many men to volunteer for these details. Former prisoner George Q. Peyton recalls, "The best (thing about work details is) we get is good water. The water in the camp is impregnated with copper, and is hardly fit to drink. It will turn a white shirt yellow. There is one good well at the gate and we have a permit to get our water out of that well." Apparently the prison personnel used wells with good water and let the prisoners drink from the bad wells. This one fact probably explains why chronic diarrhea was the number one killer at Point Lookout.

Prison Camp Latrines

Properly located and maintained latrines or sinks were important health issues at Point Lookout. Once disease was introduced to the overcrowded prison camp it spread like wildfire because of the men's unsanitary practices. The most useful latrines were the ones built at the end of long piers over the Chesapeake Bay. The tide proved to be a wonderful source for washing the waste away. These were used by the prisoners during the day until the gates to the beach were closed for the night. Each company had a tub to relieve themselves in during the night.

Due to there being not enough tubs or sinks in the camp it was common to find the prisoner had relieved himself in the streets during the night. In the men's defense it must be remembered that more than half of the prison population suffered with diarrhea. It is reasonable to imagine the men were on their way to the tubs or sinks when they were suddenly stuck with a bad case of diarrhea. Men relieving themselves in the streets was a big health concern in an overcrowded prison environment. Disease was rampant and the officers and medical staff tried to reduce the number of deaths. Every month the Union prisons were required to send prisoner statistics to Colonel William Hoffman, the Commissary General of Prisoners. These reports listed the number of prisoners, how many came into the prison, and how many were exchanged or paroled. They also listed how many prisoners were admitted to the hospital and the number that died. It's ironic that Secretary of War Stanton and Colonel Hoffman would do everything they could to punish the prisoners by reducing their rations, withholding clothing, firewood and shelter and yet the officers at the prison tried their best to keep the deaths under control.

The United States Sanitary Commission sent inspector surgeon William F. Swalm to Point Lookout Prison Camp in early November of 1863. When Swalm had completed his examination, he sent his report to Colonel Hoffman and mentioned his concern about the sinks. Here is an excerpt from his report to Colonel Hoffman regarding the condition of the sinks. "Filth is gradually accumulating, and the sinks are not at all thought of, requiring a little extra exertion to walk to them. [Prisoners] void their excrement in the most convenient place to them, regardless of the comfort of others." Swalm later goes on to say, "Sinks have been prepared for them, but little or no attention is paid to them, unless they should be in close proximity when they desire to answer the calls of nature. Some of the sinks are filled and have not been covered, and not a particle of chloride of lime has been used in the encampment for a long time."[144]

Private John M. Hastings, Co. A, 17th Tenn., was captured at Fort Harrison, Va., and sent to Point Lookout Prison. He took the Oath of Allegiance March 8, 1865.

General Gilman Marston, the prison commandant at Point Lookout, was disturbed when he saw Swalm's report. He quickly sent a letter to Colonel Hoffman protesting the results of the inspection by the Sanitary Commission. Hoffman thought an army medical inspector might give him a better report, so he issued orders to have the prison inspected again.

Army medical inspector Augustus M. Clark conducted an inspection of Point Lookout in December of 1863. Clark reported the above water latrines were superior to the excavated sinks, for the tide promptly washed the offal away. However he wrote the night sinks were insufficient in number and were not promptly emptied in the morning. He also noted that during the night prisoners would often relieve themselves in the streets rather than the sinks.[145]

Prison Guards

In the early days of the prison camp the men of the 2nd, 5th and 12th Regiments of New Hampshire Volunteers shared the guard duties. On February 25, 1864, the 24th and 36th Regiments of Colored Troops were sent to Point Lookout.

The white prisoners were frustrated to see these Negro guards march into the camp. James T. Wells recalls, "On the 25 of February (1864) they (36th Colored Troops) arrived, accoutered in their military glory. They were quite a curiosity to many, as they had never, previous to this time, seen any colored troops. The first day they came on guard will be remembered by every prisoner of the camp. At the usual hour, they marched in with knapsack, haversack and canteen, equipped as for a march. The main street, along which they were stationed, was crowded with prisoners, all anxious to see the 'monkey show.' We knew their intense hatred for us, and we were well aware that the slightest demonstration on our part would be used as pretext for firing into us."[146]

Former prisoner B. T. Holliday remembers his anger at the time, "It was a bitter pill for Southern men to swallow and we felt the insult very keenly. They were impudent and tyrannical and the prisoners had to submit to many indignities."[147]

John R. King wrote about the caliber of Negro guards in his book, *My Experience in the Confederate Army and In Northern Prisons.* "Please do not think that I dislike the Negro's as a race. Many of them are my friends, but the Negros who guarded us were not accustomed to having authority over white people and the defenseless prisoners suffered at their hands. The Negro guard were very insolent and delighted in tantalizing the prisoners, for some trifle affair, we were often accused of disobedience and they would say, 'Look out, white man, the bottom rail is on top now, so you had better be careful for my gun has been wanting to smoke at you all day!' Often their threats came true. Many times during the night, when they quarreled with some poor fellow who had displeased them, we in our tent hugged the ground very closely expecting to hear a bullet sing at any moment."[148]

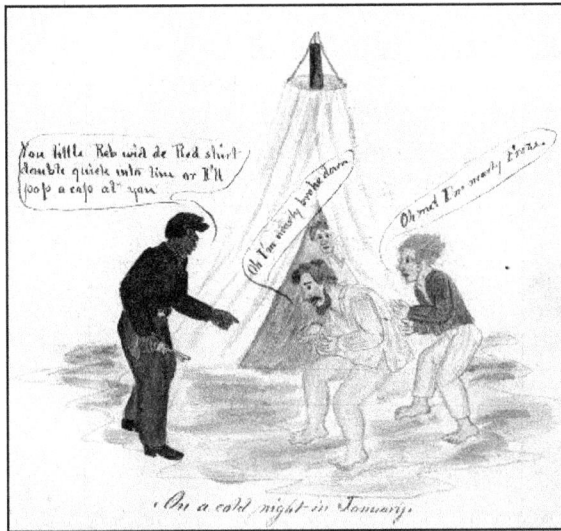

Drawing from former Point Lookout prisoner John J. Omenhauser's Sketch Book shows harassment by Negro guards at Point Lookout.

Former prisoner Charles Loehr remembers the difficulty they had with Negro guards at night. "There were hundreds of sick in camp, cases of violent diarrhea reducing the men to skeletons. As these men were compelled to frequent (sink) boxes, the Negros would often compel them at the point of the bayonet to march around in double quick time, to carry them on their backs, to kneel and pray for Abe Lincoln, and force them to submit to a variety of their brutal jokes, some of which decency would not permit me to mention."[149]

Private N. F. Harman recalls the Negro night patrols at Point Lookout with anger. "I know of these Negro patrols calling men out of their tents and chasing them up and down the streets until they were exhausted. One night two of these Negro patrols, after running one poor fellow until he could hardly move, ordered him to his tent; but before he reached it one of them called out: 'Hold on Dar, hold on. Come back here!' He then said to the prisoner,' What your sister's name and whar she lib? I want to write to her.'

Private Harman goes on to say, "One night one of these patrols shot into a tent and killed two men. When the officer came running in to see what was the matter, the Negro said he shot into the tent to make the prisoners stop talking. The fact was, all the men in this tent were asleep, but nothing was ever done to this Negro patrol for the murder of two men who were asleep when shot."[150]

B. T. Holliday recalled, "Ludicrous things happened. A Negro soldier recognized his former master, who advanced towards the fence to speak to the Negro, when the Negro accosted him after this manner. "Howd'ye Massa Robert. Mighty glad to see you but the white folks say you mussen come across that line".[151] The line Holliday referred to was the deadline.

Former Prisoner John R. King recalled the treatment of the white guards. "It has often been said that the northern people treated their prisoners well. I wish it were true, but during my imprisonment, which was more than the year, I never saw any of the good treatment, except from the old veterans, the men who would had been to the front and had seen service in the army were kind."

Was Firewood Issued at Point Lookout?

There seems to be some confusion over whether firewood was issued to the prisoners. Some men say they were never given firewood while at Point Lookout and others say they were, but it was never enough. It appears the time of the year had a bearing on the prisoner's experience. Eight months of the year, beginning in March, the prisoners were not given any firewood. If prisoners wanted to have a fire to cook their meals or to keep warm on chilly mornings they had to do one of two things. Either they bought firewood from fellow prisoners for thirty cents a bundle or they volunteered for a work detail outside of the fort so they might pick up a few scraps of wood. In his book, *Stonewall Jackson's Foot Cavalry,* former prisoner George Q. Peyton wrote, "The men on detail generally pick up coal and wood to keep them warm. Those who do not go on detail must freeze." Work details were very popular among the prisoners and not everyone who reported for work in the morning actually got it. Although firewood was issued to prisoners from November 14th, 1864 through February of 1865, there were still several problems.[152] The firewood issued was one cord a day for a division of 1,000 prisoners. A cord of wood measures four feet by four feet by eight feet. This amount may have been enough to keep one hundred men moderately warm, but not one thousand. There was also a catch. In order to build a fire in your tent you needed to have a stove or fireplace. This was something the Federal government did not provide for the prisoners. It was necessary for the men to use sun dried bricks to construct a fireplace.[153] Alfred Jefferson Smith made an entry in his diary for October 30, 1864. This was written before the firewood was issued in November. "No wood allowed to make fires. All shiver for want of clothes, blankets and rations, suffering is general and keen."[154]

Private John M. Coleman, Co. C, 7th KY Cavalry, was captured at Buffington, Ohio. Coleman was exchanged March 2, 1865.

Just because firewood was issued to prisoners in the winter months does not mean that the wood was distributed every day. George Q. Peyton remembers on December 11, 1864, "Yankees did not give us any wood today. The supply is small and the Yankees have the first grab at it." The following morning two men were found frozen to death. He goes on later to say, "Got no wood today, although it was very cold. Yankees don't care if we freeze."[155]

Private William Haigh kept a diary and recorded the events surrounding the four months he spent at the prison. "We were put into an old rickety tent without fire or fuel to pass the night on the damp ground, with no covering but a blanket and nothing to protect us from the ground."[156]

60

Former prisoner James T. Wells remembers, "The 2nd, 5th and 12th New Hampshire constituted the guard, with two batteries of artillery and a squadron of cavalry. These troops were housed in comfortable tents, and as we saw the smoke rising from the innumerable stovepipes projecting from their tents, we could not but indulge in bitter thoughts of their cruelty."[157]

George M. Neese also complained about the quality and quantity of the wood issued. "Even wood seems to be a scarce commodity in Uncle Sam's vast realm, as we get a very scanty supply, and that is mostly green pine, which never fails to make more smoke than fire. The wood allowed each tent is not enough to keep a little fire more than a day in a week, and actually I have not seen nor felt a good fire this whole winter."[159]

Tobacco and Hardtack Were Used as Money

Since money was not allowed at Point Lookout the prisoners needed some form of exchange for goods. Tobacco proved to be the ideal substitute since it could easily be divided and was readily available. One pound of tobacco was worth about a dollar. The pound was usually divided into twenty squares or quids. These were often referred to as chews. The value of each quid was five cents. This system of trade made it possible to have a thriving marketplace.

Former prisoner Berry Benson wrote, "Tobacco I found to be the medium of trade, the currency, and the chew was the unit thereof. But tobacco and hardtack had the same value. One cracker equals one chew. A user of tobacco, feeling that he must have a chew, saves a cracker from his dinner (ill can he spare it!), walks up to an exchange table, deposits his cracker and takes up a chew, saying never a word, the relative value is so well-established."[160]

At Point Lookout gambling tables seemed to spring up everywhere, and men with nothing to do frequently visit these tables. Private James Elliott noticed that, "Tobacco was the most common medium of exchange. All the smaller gambling concerns used pieces of tobacco cut up into chews, the larger cuts passing for five or ten chews."[161]

Apparently nothing was wasted in prison. Not even tobacco after it had been chewed. Former prisoner Thad Walker recalled, "Tobacco was a very scarce and valuable article at Point Lookout, and happy was the individual fortunate enough to secure any. I have often seen men following a lucky chewer and waiting for him to finish his chew and beg it for himself. The poor fellows would daily hunt for discarded chews and consider themselves lucky if they found one."[162]

Private Marcus B. Toney, 1st Tennessee Infantry, was captured May 12, 1864 at Spotsylvania Court House, Virginia. Toney was sent to Point Lookout and took the Oath of Allegiance June 14, 1865. Toney wrote of his wartime experiences in the book *The Privations of a Private*. Such books and diaries by Civil War soldiers are highly sought after by researchers.

Former prisoner George M. Neese remembers, "I have seen men walking along the streets gathering up chewed cud's of tobacco for smoking purposes. They picked the little ground-up quids to pieces and spread them in the sunshine until dried, then smoked the debris."[163]

Confederate Colonel John S. Mosby poses with his men. Mosby is seated in the center, third from the right. Some of Mosby's cavalry troopers were captured and sent to Point Lookout prison camp.

Trades Flourished at Point Lookout

Many men in prison chose to make the best of their situation by attending church, learning to read and write or by joining a debating society. Others practiced a trade or learned a new one. The benefits of having a trade were many. First, it kept the inmate occupied and made the time go by faster. Second, he earned a wage which allowed him to purchase items that would make life in prison more comfortable. Food and clothing were the most sought after things because it was nearly impossible to live on what the government issued the prisoners.

All that was needed for creative prisoners to setup shop was to hang the appropriate sign outside his tent, and display his wares on a cracker-box table. These items could range from rings, watch fobs, fans, artwork, clocks and many more. Other men performed a service. There were barbers, tailors, shoemakers and laundry men. There was practically no end to the possibilities if a prisoner had the desire to succeed and set his mind to it.

Former prisoner B. T. Holliday recalls the many shops inside prison. "Some prisoners of a mechanical turn made trinkets, such as rings, putting settings of German silver in them. These trinkets they would sell to northern visitors who came to look us over to see if we had horns."[164]

Berry Benson wrote about the different trades that flourished at Point Lookout. "It was a curious sight to see, different trades being plied, such as cobbling, perhaps some kind of small carpenters work."[165]

Private David Holt remembers being awed by the creativity of the prisoners. "Something of interest was always going on in prison. Some men put up a miniature rope factory, where all the machinery was made of scraps of wood, iron, and bone as could be picked up around the place. Another fellow was making clocks, with works of bone and frames of Yankee canteens. The springs he made out of barrel hoops cut to the right size and tempered. In our tent we had a barber. Every man who had a trade or profession was trying to follow his calling. As I had neither, I followed my nose and roamed around like a roaring lion."[166]

Former prisoner James T. Wells wrote about the unique things the prisoners made. "The first engine made in camp excited much curiosity and wonder among the prisoners, and was visited by a large number of them. It was indeed a curiosity, and a description of it may not be out of place. The boiler was made from an old camp kettle, the mouth of which was plugged up with wood. The pistons and connecting rods were made of wood, and the valves and heads were contrived from old mustard boxes. It does not seem possible that this could be done, yet it was, and the machines were of sufficient power to drive turning lathes, from which pen handles, bodkins, etc., were turned out. The first of these wonderful machines was made by a Georgian, who could neither read nor write. In a short while there were seven of them in different parts of the camp, and as they would whistle every morning previous to commencing work, it reminded one of the machine shops in large cities."[167]

Private Anderson T. Mayo, 26th Miss, was captured at Hather's Run, Va., and sent to Point Lookout prison. Mayo took the Oath of Allegiance June 29, 1865. *Photo courtesy of Point Lookout Museum.*

Tent Cutters

Any time you have a large number of men with very few possessions you will also find crime. Stealing from your neighbor was almost a way of life in prison at Point Lookout. One type of criminal was the tent cutter. These men would prowl about the camps, and if they saw something inside a tent they wanted they would remember its position and come back later when no one was around. Instead of going into the tent through the door they cut a slit in the approximate location and reached in and took what they wanted.

Former prisoner Bartlett Y. Malone wrote about the prison tent cutters. "There were some men in camp who had been going about and cutting (tents) and slipping men's hats, boots, and sometimes (sic), would get some money. They cut into ours and got money and cloathen (sic) all amounting to $100. One nite (sic) the Negros on gard (sic) caught them. They was then placed under guard and made to wear a barrel shirt (and marched) up and down the streets with large letters on them. The letters read the 'Tent Cutters'."[168]

George Q. Peyton wrote, "You can't leave anything out a minute before it is stolen. The thief will come in to see if there is anything near the side of the tent, then go outside and cut a hole in the canvas and pull it through. A man grabbed a thief's hand and got badly cut by him."[169]

Point Lookout Punishments

Maintaining discipline in prison can be difficult when there are 10,000 men who believe they can do as they please. A violation of the prison's rules was met with several types of punishment. Some were as simple as digging latrines or filling old ones. Other punishments were meant for showing the rest of the prisoners that that person was a thief, a tent cutter, or perhaps a dog eater. Men who were dog eaters would lure an officer's pet into a trap where the animal is caught by fellow prisoners and then eaten.

Former prisoner John R. King wrote about such an account in his book. "Captain Whiton, the boss of the cookhouse, had a fat dog which was very friendly and one day was missing. So the captain found upon investigation that two hungry fellows had killed his dog. Enraged with anger he had the two men taken to headquarters, barrel shirt put on them and dog eater painted on the (sign)."[170]

A favorite punishment was the barrel shirt. One end of a barrel was knocked out then turned over and a hole was cut in the other side through which the head passed. The barrel was then placed over a prisoner and he was required to walk around for several hours, twice a day, in the hot sun wearing a sign announcing his crime. In another punishment prisoners were lashed to an eight foot tall wooden horse where the seat had been sharpened into a thin edge. The prisoner then had to sit for several hours with his hands tied behind his back, while he squirmed, trying to find a less painful position.

Former prisoner Luther Hopkins wrote about a particularly brutal punishment. "The punishment for trying to escape was cruel. Those who were caught at it were strung up to a pole by the thumbs, with the tips of their toes just touching the ground. Sometimes the men would faint, and had to be cut down."

One of the punishments at Point Lookout was wearing a barrel shirt and walking around the camp. Courtesy of *Hardtack and Coffee.*

Private Marcus B. Toney wrote in his diary, "This has been another dark day for us. About eight o'clock in the morning the news flashed through the prison: 'President Abraham Lincoln assassinated by a rebel.' Immediately after hearing this one indiscreet prisoner yelled out: "It is a good thing; old Abe ought to have been killed long ago." The guards immediately rushed on him, and I thought that he would get the bayonet; but they trotted him to the headquarters of Colonel Beall, who ordered him tied up by the thumbs. This is a very cruel mode of punishment. A man is tied up by the thumbs and pulled up until he is on his tip toes, and there is no way to relieve the pressure. If he tries to relieve his thumbs, the toes get it; and if the toes are relieved, the thumbs are in trouble. In a very short time he will faint, and is then cut down."[171]

Former prisoner Walter D. Addison wrote about another cruel punishment the prisoners had to endure. "A most horrible instrument of torture used in prison was called a sweat box. For trivial offenses men were therein confined for hours, in the scorching suns of July and August, without food or water and removed in many cases only when the victim was more dead than alive. I vividly recollect when one man dropped with rigid limbs swollen and almost paralyzed, and died in a few days from the effects. This instrument of torture consisted of a narrow upright box, about 7 feet high, and wide enough to fit an ordinary sized man. It stood in a perpendicular position with its victim without ventilation, and the poor victim left to sweat to death.[172]

Women Were Not Excluded From Point Lookout

It seems the fairer sex was not immune to being thrown into Point Lookout prison. It is difficult to believe this happened, but apparently four women were arrested. Perhaps the reason for Kath Davidson and Mary E. C. Gilliam's incarceration at Point Lookout was because of the prison camps close proximity to Leonardtown, Md., where the April 15, 1864 arrests were made. Both ladies were being held for suspicion of blockade-running. Little more is known about these women except that they were not kept at Point Lookout very long.

Another woman who was held prisoner at Point Lookout is Mrs. Hunter Davidson. All we know about her is she was captured in January of 1864 for an unknown offense in Annapolis, Md. What her offense was could never be determined.

Mrs. Jane A. Perkins was a school teacher from Danville Virginia. When her husband Patrick joined Captain B. Z. Price's company of the Danville Virginia artillery, she cropped her hair short and joined him. It appears Mrs. Perkins never really enlisted in the Confederate Army because there are no records for her under that name. The only soldiers named Perkins' in that regiment are Private Anderson M. Perkins and William M. Perkins. Her husband Patrick may have joined a different regiment. Jane was reported to have been captured May 27, 1864 at the battle of North Anna in Virginia and sent to Point Lookout prison camp.[173]

When asked by Provost Marshall A. G. Brady why she was in prison, Mrs. Perkins told him, "I can straddle a horse, jump a fence, and kill a Yankee as well as any Rebel." Major Brady frowned and then commented that she was where she belonged.[174]

It is reported that Mrs. Perkins was six and half months pregnant when she was captured and gave birth

Woman disguised as male Civil War soldier.

to a baby boy. On July 12th, 1864, Jane A. Perkins was transferred to Old Capitol Prison in Washington D. C.

Former prisoner Anthony Keilly noted, "I must not forget to mention that among the convicts was a woman! She was captured in the Valley of Virginia, I was informed, while acting as a member of an artillery company, and her sex discovered, probably, on the usual search for valuables. Common civilities suggested a conversation with her; and one day as I was passing the little tent which was assigned to her exclusively, I approached her for the purpose of making some inquiries, as well as letting her know that we were disposed to serve her in any way possible to prisoners. She seemed, however, indisposed to converse, and I was compelled to give up the chase. Why the Yanks detain women I can't imagine."[175]

Federal Surgeon C. T. Alexander mentions a Sarah Jane Perkins being held a prisoner at Point Lookout prison camp. It is assumed he meant Jane A. Perkins. On July 9, 1864, Alexander wrote Colonel William Hoffman, "Among the prisoners is a woman, Sarah Jane Perkins, whose removal is desirable."[176] Apparently Alexander thought that having a woman in prison was too much of a distraction for the men.

Work Details

Work details provided many advantages for Point Lookout prisoners and consequently they were highly sought after. The most common benefit was that these details would provide the men with an extra ration of food or a small piece of tobacco. It also gave prisoners a chance to get good, clean water which was not available in prison. Another reason they were highly sought after was they afforded the prisoners a chance to scavenge pieces of wood to bring back to the prison so they could build a fire. Some men volunteered unloading cargo ships in hopes of stealing some of the cargo of rations. Going outside the prison gates provided the opportunity for freedom from the confines of the prison walls and a chance to hear some news from the front. Work details in the winter provided a chance for prisoners to warm up through physical activity. Last but not least, sometimes a journey outside the prison gates would provide the opportunity to escape.

Private William Scarborough, 15th Ga, was captured July 4th at Gettysburg. Scarborough was transferred for exchange while he was in the hospital.

Former prisoner Anthony M. Keiley wrote, "There is quite a contention for the privilege of working [details]. Almost every day there is some description of labor to be performed outside the pen, for which volunteers are sought and easily obtained among the prisoners. Those selected for the work are mustered into a company, their names taken down, and under Yankee guards they are carried outside to the scene of their work. This consists principally in the unloading of vessels at the wharf, in building hospitals, commissary storerooms, stables, etc.[177]

Marcus Toney recalls the many times he labored on work details. "All the commissaries, wood, etc., was unloaded by details of prisoners; and many of them were anxious to get on this detail, as it gave them a day outside of prison walls, and also sometimes an opportunity to appropriate some extra rations, and they could hear what they called Grapevine news. Newspapers were not allowed in the prison, and our chance to hear anything from the front was very limited."[178]

Former prisoner George W. Jones recalls, "The prisoners were allowed to go outside the camp on details to cut wood, whitewash buildings and unload boats, and when a requisition was made for certain number of men to go outside 1,000 men would rush to the gate, all eager to get extra rations for their work. On one occasion I was on the detail of 100 to help unload a large boat loaded with rations for the prisoners which were hardtack, pickled pork, sugar and coffee, beans, vegetables for dried soup, pickled beef, etc. Of course they were always guards to watch our maneuvers. The provisions had been carried from the boat to the commissary, a distance of 300 to 400 yards. The prisoners took advantage of it by going into a cracker box or opening a barrel of sugar and coffee, and anything else they could do. Everything was working lovely, as we thought, and every rebel had his britches and pockets full like a frog eating shot, too heavy to move. All things were merry with bright anticipations of the feast when we went back to camp. But when the time came for us to march, they formed us into two ranks and marched us within 20 paces of the gate. The column was halted with the command, right face! The officer of the day rode up and down the line, drew his sword and gave the command to 'shake rags.' Silence reigned supreme for a few minutes and then the captain gave the same command, the prisoners still remained perfectly silent. Finally, with a broad smile on his face, he gave the order, 'Take off your trousers and disgorge', which we proceeded to do according to the command, each man in rotation. That was done by turning our trousers upside down in order that what was in the pockets and legs would tumble out.

Now imagine the result. There was in one pile a mass of every article that was unloaded from the boat, making a heap as big as a hogshead, at which the boys looked very wistfully and with many regrets. So we marched back into camp, sadder but wiser specimens of human nature and disappointed ragamuffins."[179]

Federal Raids into Northern Virginia

Federal cavalry

Between the months of January and September of 1864 Federal Colonel Alonzo G. Draper and the 36th Colored Troops stationed at Point Lookout prison camp conducted a series of five raids on the Northern Neck of Virginia. Three of these raids were documented in the Official Records. Little is known about the other actions except for their dates. At least one of these raids was highly questionable because of the articles confiscated.

The first documented raid took place April 12th and was conducted by 300 men of the 36th Colored Troops and 50 men of the U. S. Cavalry. The soldiers boarded the steamer *Long Branch* and crossed over the Potomac River to Westmoreland County, Virginia. General Edward W. Hinks wrote of the raid, "I proceeded from this district to the Virginia shore in search of contraband goods and to break up blockading establishments."[180]

"On Wednesday morning I affected a landing on the right bank of lower Machodoc Creek, and sent a boat expedition in charge of Colonel Draper across the creek to scour the peninsula between it and the Nomini River, to search for contraband goods, which resulted in seizing 177 boxes of superior Gravely tobacco, probably worth $40,000 U. S. currency. Mr. Joseph H. Maddox, who claimed to own the tobacco, and to be an emissary of the Federal government, was taken as a prisoner."

"The object of the expedition having been accomplished, I returned to this point with the tobacco seized and about 50 contraband's (slaves), and without any loss of men or material."

This question begs to be answered: Why did General Hinks confiscate that tobacco? Did he really believe taking it would help the war effort or was Hinks eager to share in the spoils of war?

Another raid took place May 11th and lasted three days. The purpose of this expedition was to destroy Confederate torpedoes on the Rappahannock River. Colonel Alonzo G. Draper wrote, "The expedition accomplished the destruction or capture of nine torpedoes, burnt one mill, killed five of the enemy, captured five, including two acting masters in the rebel Navy, captured 33 head of cattle, 22 horses and mules, and quite a number of vehicles of various descriptions. Our total loss was one man killed, two seriously and one slightly wounded."[181] This raid was sound because it had a useful military objective in mind.

There was very little Confederate resistance to this Federal invasion of Northern Virginia except for a few minor skirmishes. The results of the first action have already been discussed, but another confrontation proved embarrassing for the Federal raiders. The next day these same soldiers made up for their cowardice by standing their ground in a skirmish against Confederates forces. Fortunately we have Colonel Alonso G. Draper's account of the June 11th raid in the official records.

"Sir: I have the honor to report that on the evening of the 11th (June) I embarked on the steam transports *Georgia, Charleston, Long Branch*, and *Favorite* with 475 men of the 36th U. S. Colored Troops and 49 men of the 2nd and 5th U. S. Cavalry, under command of first Lieutenant J. C. Denney. The 5th U. S. Cavalry proceeded to Pope's Creek, Virginia, on the Potomac River for the purpose of procuring horses for the quartermaster's department, and farming implements, transportation, etc., for the contraband settlement on the Patuxent River.

On the morning of the 12th we landed at Pope's Creek and divided into two detachments, 300 men under Captain Hart of the 36th, taking the road running by a northerly course to Smith's Wharf, and thence along the Rappahannock to Warsaw, where all detachments were to meet on the evening of the 13th.

On the 16th 2nd Lieutenant O'Brien permitted three men of his company to leave the battalion and go to a house about a mile distant, notwithstanding my orders that no man should be allowed to leave the column. In all other respects Lieutenant O'Brien performed his duties in a very acceptable manner. Of these three men from O'Brien's company only one returned, of the other two one was murdered by the rebel cavalry and the other wounded and probably killed, as he crawled into the woods and could not afterward be found.

Hearing the firing of the afternoon of the 16th, I rode out with about 40 of the cavalry to ascertain the cause. Emerging from the woods about a mile from Union Wharf, we perceived a body of rebel cavalry about a mile ahead, at a point of woods where the road forks. Sending forward three men as an advance guard, we advanced upon them. The advance guard reported 200 cavalry in the rebel column; but subsequent information showed their force to be much smaller. At a suitable distance I ordered a charge, directly after which the enemy opened fire upon us. After riding to within sixty yards of the rebel position, I found myself alone, only my assistant adjutant-general and a few

1st Lieutenant Warren G. Turner, Co. E, 6th North Carolina, was captured November 7, 1863 at Rappahannock Station, Virginia. Turner was sent to Point Lookout and exchanged March 13, 1865.

faithful orderlies remaining by me. I turned and ordered the cavalry to close up; whereupon the rebels set up their customary yell, and my escort turned their horse's heads to the rear and ran for their lives, seeing which the rebels immediately charged upon us. I tried in vain to rally my men, calling upon them a dozen times to halt and face the enemy. In this vain attempt I was seconded by Captain Gibbs, of the Fourth Rhode Island Volunteers, my acting assistant adjutant-general, and by a few men among the cavalry who repeated my orders to halt. I remained on the ground until my orderly and one other man had been captured by my side, and another dismounted man had had time to run to the rear, get over the fence, and escape. Finally, finding myself enveloped in the dust of the rebel pursuit and entirely alone, I followed the crowd. The rebels pursued 200 or 300 yards then turned back, evidently astonished at their success."

Colonel Draper goes on to say, "On the morning of 17 June, the anniversary of Bunker Hill, I thought it proper to make one more attempt to wipe out the disgrace which the cavalry had brought upon the expedition. Leaving about 300 men to load the transports, I marched with 200 men of the 36th, and 36 of the cavalry under Sergeant Cain, to the point where the road bends, which is about 1000 yards from the rebel position, where we again found them, this time in force, numbering, according to the best information, 150 men of the 9th Virginia Cavalry, and 450 infantry, who were mostly home guards; the whole under command of Lieutenant-Colonel Lewis, of the 9th Virginia Cavalry. I posted the cavalry at the bend, with 50 of the infantry concealed in the woods behind them, in such a position as to rake the roads in case our cavalry should again be repulsed.

Riding out of the woods by the right flank of the battalion, where I could observe the effect of our fire, I ordered the firing to commence by rank; desiring to reserve a portion of my fire until I could determine the strength and purposes of the enemy, to ascertain whether he had any flanking force in the woods where we lay. Our first volley had a marked effect, evidently taking the enemy by surprise, as he expected a charge. At the first fire several of the enemy were seen to fall, and heard to scream. They immediately returned our fire, apparently every man for himself. We poured in our volleys in rapid secession, and soon threw the rebels into great confusion; at every discharge crowds of them took to the woods in their rear. Perceiving that the end was near, I sent a mounted officer to show the cavalry where they could pass through the fence, and thus avoid the enemies stockade in their charge. At about the fifth volley the rebels disappeared. I immediately fired another volley and sounded the charge for the cavalry, at the same time moving the infantry forward into the open field in forming an assaulting and supporting line. The cavalry advanced at a slow trot, and afterward at a walk, the infantry being obliged to halt for them to come up. We then moved upon the rebel position which was entirely abandoned. I sent forward a portion of the cavalry to reconnoiter, but no enemy could be found for miles."

"When the expedition returned to Point Lookout, arriving early in the morning of the 21st instant. We brought in 375 head of cattle, 160 horses and mules, about 600 contraband's, including between 60 and 70 recruits for the army and navy, and a large number of plows, harrows, cultivators, wheat drills, corn-shellers, harness, carts, and carriages etc. for the use of the contraband settlement on the Patuxent."[182]

Private John Jacob Levi Yost, Co. G, 5th N. C., was captured at Gettysburg, Pa., and was sent to Point Lookout Prison Camp. Yost died of disease August 23, 1864.

These raids did not go unnoticed by the men in prison. Former prisoner Anthony M. Keiley devotes two pages in his book to these raids. Keeley writes, "Thursday, June 16, Last night the Negro Regiment, which constitutes part of our guard, and which has been raiding over in Westmoreland and the adjacent counties, returned with great beating of drums and blowing of fife's. The captives of these brave soldiers of the Republic consisted of 100 head of cattle--- principally poor women's cows--several ploughs, buggies, primeval sulkies, harrows, beds, chairs, etc., and from twenty to thirty decrepit citizens! This is the service in which these demons are regularly employed every month, and sometimes more frequently than once in thirty days, they are sent across the river on a plundering tour. The Yankees are too much ashamed of this to fill their newspapers with the doings of these valiant swashbucklers, but they are glad of the means of keeping alive, by this promise of stated plundering, the martial ardor and fidelity of their black brethren, and, of course, are not unwilling to share the spoils. These raids, which were usually made in a country entirely devoid of Confederate soldiers, are, of course, without any earthly justification or purpose, except to gratify the malignity and feed the beastliness of their new allies, whose delight in the safe robberies is, as may be expected, boundless. The old men are usually kept a short time in an undisclosed camp outside, under guard of the Negroes, and then return to their homes."[183]

Escape from Point Lookout Prison Camp

The horrible conditions at Point Lookout prison camp made escape attempts inevitable. Although many men tried to break out from the prison only 50 were successful. The low, sandy peninsula made tunneling out of the prison an impossible task. With this popular avenue of escape closed, the prisoners needed to find something else to take its place. The Chesapeake Bay provided the men with that opportunity.

Former prisoner Luther Hopkins wrote, "Occasionally prisoners made their escape. One ingenious method that baffled our guards for a long time was the following: The prisoners were allowed to go outside of the enclosure on the beach to bathe. And if an empty barrel or box happened to be floating on the water, a prisoner in bathing would watch his opportunity, slip his head under the barrel or box, and then as the tide drifted up the river, would follow it, keeping as near the shore as necessary until he got beyond the reach of the guards, and then take to the woods."

Former prisoner George Jones remembers, "All kinds of plans were devised for escape. There were prisoners who got together cracker boxes to make a small sailboat, and by some means evaded the guard and made their escape across Chesapeake Bay. After that our camp was regularly inspected and we were kept under the closest surveillance."[184]

Private Anthony M. Keiley wrote of another escape attempt with two boats. "The [cracker-box house] occupants, an ingenious party with considerable mechanical skill, had contrived to accumulate cracker-box lumber in large quantities without exciting suspicion, under pretense of building a larger house; and by watching their opportunities, had fashioned their material into two canoes, each capable of containing two or three men. These boats could be carried under the arm, the various parts disjointed, without exciting suspicion; and could be readily fitted together even in the dark, for those who were familiar with their construction. Everything promised success, and they were awaiting a night of favoring darkness, having made the necessary arrangements for getting outside the inclosure—that is to say, bribe the guard. In their frail boats they had resolved to trust themselves, for love of sweet liberty, to the mercy of the river, which at its mouth is exceedingly rough, when unfortunately the Yanks got wind of the daring project. They sent a guard to the house, found the canoes, made a bonfire of them and then razed their castle to the ground, leaving not a bit of it standing."[185]

Luther B. Lake and four other prisoners managed to escape Point Lookout prison camp by wading into the Chesapeake Bay to bathe and keeping an eye on the guard. When his back was turned, and he was walking his post in the other direction, they waded out 250 yards to a sandbar that ran parallel to the shore. They were not discovered and followed the sandbar 2 1/2 miles until they were well clear of the prison. By this time it was dark

General Robert E. Lee formulated a plan to rescue the prisoner at Point Lookout.

and they waded back to shore. Many people they met helped them escape by giving the ragged prisoners food and clothing.[186]

Former prisoner Luther Hopkins noted that prisoners who were caught trying to escape were strung up to a pole by the thumbs, with the tips of their toes just touching the ground. Punishing a prisoner for attempting to escape was strictly forbidden by General Order's numbers 49 and 100 which can be found in the *Official Records*. "A prisoner of war who escapes may be shot or otherwise killed in his flight; but neither death nor any other punishment shall be inflicted upon him simply for his attempt to escape which the law of war does not consider a crime."[187]

General Lee's Rescue Plan for the Prisoners at Point Lookout

In late 1863 Confederate General Robert E. Lee conceived a plan to relieve the Union Army's pressure on the Richmond and Petersburg area and also rescue the prisoners at Point Lookout. If Lee sent a large force up the Shenandoah Valley to attack Washington, D. C., General Grant would be forced to take troops away from Richmond and Point Lookout to defend the nation's capital. A Confederate cavalry brigade under General Bradley T. Johnson would leave Early's force at Washington and attack the prison camp from the mainland. While this was happening Confederate Commander John Taylor Wood was to run the Union blockade off Wilmington, North Carolina, with several naval vessels and sail to

Point Lookout, Maryland. The plan called for him to land 800 soldiers and attack the prison camp. The plan called for the released prisoners to join in the attack of Washington if practicable, otherwise they were to cross the Potomac River and head south. General Lee figured if he was able to capture Washington, it would have an adverse effect on Northern morale and improve the South's bargaining position for a negotiated cease-fire. However, the conditions proved unfavorable in the fall of 1863, so General Lee waited until the proper time to put his plan into action.[188]

Due to the Union's aggressive spring campaign of 1864, General Ulysses S. Grant's army suffered a staggering 40,000 casualties in the battles of Cold Harbor and the Wilderness. Consequently Grant stripped troops from places such as Washington D. C. and Point Lookout prison camp to replace his losses. Lee, noticing General Grant was moving Federal troops away from Washington to build up his depleted forces around Richmond, saw this as the ideal time to threaten the Capitol and rescue the prisoners at Point Lookout.

Confederate Commodore John Taylor Wood (on the left) and his brother Robert pose for the camera. John was assigned the task of liberating the Point Lookout prisoners.

General Lee created the Army of the Valley and ordered Lieutenant General Jubal Early to sweep the Union troops from the Shenandoah Valley and then march on Washington. Early's army advanced into the Shenandoah and joined forces with General John Breckenridge, General John D. Imboden and General John C. Vaughn. This added 5,000 cavalry to Early's 14,000 man army. Early's Confederates met a smaller Union army under Major General David Hunter on June 18, 1864 at Lynchburg, Md. Early's army easily routed the Federals and sent them fleeing back to Baltimore. Early's force then crossed the Potomac River, creating panic in the North. The only Union army between Early's Confederates and Washington was 6,000 men under General Lew Wallace. On July 9th General Early met Wallace's Federal army at Monocacy Junction outside of Frederick, Md.. After repeated attacks, the larger Confederate army forced Wallace's men from the field inflicting 1,294 casualties. General Wallace, however, achieved his objective by delaying Early's army for a day, giving the Union forces around Washington more time to build their defenses and obtain reinforcements.[189]

On July 11th General Early's Confederates marched to the outskirts of Washington, D. C. but the arrival of more than 20,000 Union soldiers prevented a full-scale assault. General Early then turned his attention to Fort Stevens. As the Confederate army advanced on the fort, heavy rifle fire broke out along the whole front. Earlier, President Lincoln and his wife Mary rode out to observe the attack from the safety of the Fort. Lincoln and several officers were standing on the parapet when a Confederate sharpshooter wounded the man next to the President. Lincoln was immediately ordered to take cover and was whisked away from the area.

Before the assault on Fort Stevens had taken place, Early gave orders to General Bradley T. Johnson to cut the communications and rail lines around Baltimore, and then head south to assist Commodore Wood's attack on Point Lookout prison camp. According to Johnson his cavalry raid of 300 miles would be the longest cavalry ride of the war taking only three and a half days to complete. Johnson's cavalry cut the telegraph lines from Baltimore to Washington D. C., and burned bridges and railroad cars, then start his fifty-mile hell-for-leather dash to Point Lookout. Johnson warned General Early before he began his ride that, "horseflesh could not do it, but I would do whatever man and horse could do."[190] Johnson later explained how he was able to accomplish this feat by, "Keeping out flankers on each side of my column, who sent all the horses they could get, which were led to the rear of the column and when a man's horse

71

gave out, he fell out and waited on the roadside until the rear and fresh horses came up, when he remounted, turning his own horse on the roadside and rejoining his command. The horses left were well bred horses from Southwest Virginia and far better than the overfed, fat, pudgy horses that we got, these last could not stand over 20 miles March."[191] To General Johnson's dismay, he was ordered to turn back because the plan had been cancelled.

After meeting with General Lee about his plans to rescue the Point Lookout prisoners, Commodore John Taylor Wood traveled to Wilmington North Carolina to gather men for the attack. Wood assembled a fleet of five gunboats, 800 men and 20,000 rifles to give to the liberated prisoners. On July 9th Wood telegraphed General Lee and said that he would try and leave Wilmington that night.[192]

Apparently there was a breach of security because President Jefferson Davis mentioned to Lee that word of the plan was common knowledge on the streets of Richmond. Lee responded by saying that his Army also knew of the plan to rescue the Point Lookout prisoners. On July 10th Davis telegraphed Commodore Wood with this message. "The object and destination of your expedition have somehow become so generally known that I fear your operations will meet unexpected obstacles. General Lee has communicated with you, and left your actions to your discretion."[193] However, President Davis changed his mind later and told Commodore Wood that he decided against the idea. This proved to be the death-knell for the plan to rescue the Point Lookout prisoners.[194]

Private Franklin W. Waters, Co. F, 3rd N. C. Cavalry, was captured near Plymouth, N. C., and was sent to Point Lookout Prison Camp. Waters took the Oath of Allegiance May 14, 1865.

The Union forces around Point Lookout prison camp were not idle while this was going on. They increased their naval presence by sending the 46-gun *USS Minnesota* to guard the mouth of the Chesapeake Bay and warning her captain to be vigilant against an attack by the Southern Navy on Point Lookout prison camp. She was later joined by the *USS Fort Jackson, USS Monticello* and the *USS Santiago de Cuba*. Gideon Wells, the United States Secretary of the Navy, warned Rear-Admiral S. P. Lee, "It is stated by refugees to the senior military officer at Point Lookout that Lieutenant Wood and 800 men have left Richmond for Wilmington to take two armed vessels and attempt the release of the prisoners at Point Lookout." "Great vigilance is therefore necessary."[195]

Later in July the Army constructed several stockades and field works on the neck of land that separated Point Lookout from the mainland. These fortifications had a moat which was 20 feet across and 15 feet deep. The dirt from the ditch was used to create a mound, which was flat on top and mounted four guns which could be trained in any direction. Fort Lincoln was also constructed on the Potomac side of the camp in case the Confederate Navy attempted a landing. Most of these preparations were not completed until the end of the month which was several weeks after the planned attack.[196]

It has been said that Point Lookout had very few prisoners because of the threat. This is incorrect. According to Colonel William Hoffman's telegram of July 27, 1864, prison officials were just beginning to remove half of the prisoners to Elmira, New York.[197] At the time of the planned attack Point Lookout prison camp contained around 15,000 prisoners.

It appears that even the prisoners at Point Lookout prison camp may have known about Lee's rescue attempt. Private Bartlett Yancey Malone wrote about the attack in his Point Lookout diary. "The 13th day of July it was reported that General Ewel was fiting (sic) at Washington, and that our cavalry was in 4 miles of this plaice (sic) the Yanks was hurried up sent in all detailes (sic) at two o'clock in the eavning (sic) and run thir (sic) artillery out in frunt (sic) of the block house and plaised (sic) it in position."

Former prisoner B. T. Holiday wrote, "During my imprisonment, there were many rumors of an exchange of prisoners, which raised our hopes, only to be dashed to the ground. At the time of General Early's advance on Washington City, in July of 1864, there was a rumor that he would make an effort to release us, but he was unable to accomplish it. Had he succeeded in doing so, he would have augmented his Army by 20,000 men. After his raid, 10,000 prisoners were sent from Point Lookout to Elmira, N. Y."[198]

Northern Pressure to Take the Oath of Allegiance

One of the ways to weaken the Confederate army was to take away its fighting men. An effective way to do this was to entice the Southern prisoners to take the Oath of Allegiance to the Union. Many prisoners felt that the abuses they endured were a cruel attempt by Union officials to get them to take the Oath of Allegiance. The following prisoner's statements show how they were coerced into taking the oath.

"As United States officers used every means to induce the prisoners to take the oath, it is fair to presume that 'the best government the sun never shown upon' was now reduced to the policy of starving men into allegiance to it."[199]

Former prisoner James T. Wells recalls the tactics the Union army used to convince prisoners to take the oath. "The cruelty of the United States officials towards us seemed to know no bounds. Every day or two fresh orders were issued forbidding some privileges and abridging others. It would be a very difficult matter to describe our sufferings and privatizations during this terrible winter. Hunger and cold forced many to forswear allegiance to the 'stars and bars' and enlist under the flag of the enemy. All who did so were formed in a regiment of cavalry and sent of the Western frontier, and very many of them, as soon as an opportunity presented itself, deserted and returned to their native land."

Wells goes on to say, "Fears of death, either by disease or the hands of Negroes, forced many true

Private David A. Brown of Alexander's Battalion Light Artillery was captured April 6, 1865, at Harper's Farm, Virginia. Brown took the Oath of Allegiance June 23, 1865.

Southern soldiers to think of taking the oath. This could readily be done, by application to the proper authorities, and release obtained—only, however, to be drafted in the United States Army. An opportunity to take the oath, and go into the United States Army, was now freely extended to all the prisoners, as the officials gave notice that a 'drawing for hostages in retaliation for the Fort Pillow massacre was to take place at some early day. Preparations were accordingly made, and finally the 20th of May was announced as a day upon which to determine the fate of many men. The ruse took remarkably well, and some hundred or so flocked to the gate, to swear fealty (intense fidelity) to 'Uncle Sam.' "[200]

"There are 7,000 of our prisoners at this point. Most of them have been in prison 12 months and have suffered many indignities, and have been subjected to the most galling ordeal of sacrifice and hardship, which none but themselves can realize. The Yankees, with characteristic malignity, use the most cowardly means and inducements to cause our men to desert that country which they love so well.

Our rations are curtailed, our blankets taken from us, no wood furnished; our men are shot down in cold blood.

"Then comes the comedy. The officials, in the livery of the United States government, with faces radiant with smiles, ride through our prison. The Oath of Allegiance to the United States is offered us, and our men are entreated to leave the 'so-called Confederacy' and fight under the glorious 'stars & stripes', and be relieved from the horrors and suffering of prison life. These are only a few of the means employed. Everything that Yankee ingenuity and malice can suggest is used to accomplish this purpose.

"But, thank God! These southern patriots, though tortured and persecuted by the representatives of 'the best government the world ever saw', still remain true and faithful to the cause which they have espouse; they reject with indignation and contempt the offers of our magnanimous Yankee philanthropists, and anxiously, hopefully look forward to the future, when they shall once more, with musket in hand, be under the folds of that banner which on more than a hundred fields has waved triumphantly in the face of the United States Army.

"We are told every day by our guards that Richmond has fallen, that our armies are beaten and demoralized, that our people are discontented and starving, that our troops are deserting, and that we are in a last-ditch, etc. Of course such rumors and reports have no other effect upon us than to make us more determined, if ever the opportunity offers, to revenge these base calumnies (false statements) and insulting taunts. The worst feature of our imprisonment is being guarded by Negro soldiers—our own slaves stolen from us by our magnanimous 'Northern brethren'. The southern spirit is invincible, it will surmount all obstacles; and overcome all hardships, and endure all privatizations to secure our people a separate nationality, distinct from this modern monocular city that established Washington."[201]

Although the prisoners formed a committee to try and persuade men not to take the oath, some men still volunteered to join the Union Army. When reasoning with these men did not succeed, harsher methods were used on these galvanized Yankees.

Former prisoner James T. Wells remembers what happened to men who were going to take the oath. "Whenever it was known that a prisoner intended taking the oath (and it was very difficult to conceal the matter from his tent mates), a party would proceed to his tent the night previous, call him out and administer a severe flogging. They even went so far as to clip off the ears of one. Of course the parties who did this work were completely disguised. Thus it will be seen that the Kuklux existed at Point Lookout before it did in South Carolina. The enforcement of these harsh measures decreased the number of oath takers materially, and the United States was compelled to seek elsewhere for recruits."[202]

Oath of Allegiance

When the war ended April 9, 1865, the prisoners at Point Lookout looked forward to being paroled. According to their way of thinking, the gates to the prison would automatically swing open and they would walk out free men. When this didn't happen the prisoners grew more anxious with each passing day. Rumors flourish in prison and spread like wildfire. One of these rumors said that the reason for the delay in releasing prisoners was due to retaliation for President Lincoln's assassination. The Confederate prisoners had every right to be concerned about their release. Dozens of men were dying every day. Which one of them would be next?

Former prisoner George M. Neese wrote this entry in his diary. "May 3rd—The whole camp registered today for the purpose of taking the Oath of Allegiance to the United States. It seems that the war is over outside of the prison, but we are kept here and treated just as we have been before the war closed; it looks a little like as if the Yanks are afraid to turn us loose.

"Death is still swinging that fatal scythe with a deadlier stroke in this patch than it does beyond the prison gates, and many a man in here today will go through the prison gate dressed in a coffin before we get out."[203]

Private B. T. Holiday wrote, "The booming of the Canon in April told us of Gen'l Lee's surrender. We knew our day of deliverance was at hand. In a few days came the appalling intelligence of President

Prisoners at Point Lookout Prison Camp gather beneath a United States flag to take the Oath of Allegiance.

Lincoln's assassination. We were filled with horror at the dastardly act and realized the serious consequences that could result from it. A change in the demeanor of the officials towards us was noticeable. We felt that it would deter our release, which it did, for we were not released until the middle of June two months after the war was over."[204]

Former prisoner James C. Elliott describes what it was like after Lincoln had been shot. "The death of the President probably delayed our release. After the Confederacy went down we were aliens without governmental protection in our native land. The proposition to take the Oath of Allegiance with full rights of citizenship under the old flag of our fathers seemed as good as we could expect, and we were soon anxious to do so and return home. About the 6th of June they began to discharge us."[205]

Private John P. Murphy wrote this in his diary for May 11, 1865, "No boddy [sic] leaves the prison. All of the men seem to be despondent. No rumors afloat. The day was very dark overhead.

Monday, June 12th, 1865. All things looked dark and gloomy. I visited camps, the boys seem to be in low spirits."[206]

Private B. T. Holliday remembers taking the oath as well. "There is an end to all earthly things at last the good news came that we were to leave this place of sorrow and torture and go back to dear old Virginia again. Virginians were to be called first. How glad I was that I was a Virginian. We were taken to an adjoining enclosure, where we remain for several days, our names were being enrolled in the books, and we signed our parole not to take up arms until exchanged. There was a platform, over the top of which was stretched a large U. S. flag. This platform held standing room for 16 men, and that number was called up at a time. And the oath administered to them. How fortunate we knew nothing concerning 'germs' in those days for thousands of dirty men kissed the same Bible. The work of paroling was slow, for they were particular to get our names, age, state, county, company, regiment, height, color of eyes and hair, all of which was recorded in large books, which I suppose are in the archives in Washington. What a difficult task they would have in identifying us old, gray-headed, wrinkled men of today.

The large steamer *City of New York* was at the wharf waiting for us. As we left the prison enclosure or the boat we remembered Lot's wife and never looked back."[207]

Former Point Lookout prisoner George M. Neese remembers, "After we were through with the oath taking we were turned loose on a green, grassy sward (turf) outside of the prison gate, and the men were so wild with joy that old veterans playfully tumbled and rolled on the grass like young schoolboys."[208]

Oath of Allegiance of Private Wesley Hensley

Private Charles T. Loehr addressed the Pickett Camp Confederate Veterans, October 10, 1890, and said, "Could a picture been taken of the men who arrived in Richmond from the prison pens during those days, it would not be believed that the men who walked from the boat at Rockets in June, 1865, were the proud soldier boys that left here in April, 1861. Silent, friendless, and sorrowful each went his own way. No welcome, no cheer awaited their return to the city and to their homes. Oh how few could boast of having homes! Nothing but ruins everywhere; but the man who was a good soldier generally proved himself to be a good citizen. The ruins are gone, war and desolation have passed away—may it never return."[209]

Former prisoner Albert S. Caison, a native of Fayetteville, North Carolina, recalls how prison had changed him. "I had been in prison twenty months, three and a half at Fort Delaware, and seventeen at Point Lookout. We were paroled in March, 1865, and a pitiful set of men we were. I weighed barely 90 pounds, was almost a skeleton, and so weak I could barely walk. But I was free, and going home and that was the best tonic I could have."[210]

Former prisoner B. T. Holliday recalled an incident that happened when he came home. "I reached home, my sister was sitting on the front porch and when I reached the porch and stood before her, she did not recognize me. Why should she? My appearance had changed. I weighed 160 pounds when captured and my weight now was 95 pounds."[211]

Private J. P. Traywick wrote about leaving prison. "I was paroled, and left Point Lookout February 18, 1865. While free from any special sickness, I was reduced to 65 pounds in weight, purely for want of sufficient food. What I have written is in no spirit of vindictiveness, but merely to preserve the facts of history."[212]

Men Were Forever Changed by Prison

Most Civil War soldiers were changed forever by the war. However, the prisoners at Point Lookout were changed in a much different way. Some bore physical scars while other scars were emotional. Many men would find it difficult to smile again after experiencing man's cruelty to his fellow man. These men were hardened in a way that only months or years of abuse can produce. Some men lost limbs to frostbite, or gangrene, while others were robbed of something more precious—their health. Many men refused to die in a Yankee prison and came home to pass away weeks or months later simply because they wanted to be buried in Southern soil. There are numerous accounts of former prisoners dying within days of their release.

These soldiers bore the brunt of the worst the Civil War had to offer. It is difficult to imagine the hell these men went through. Indeed, it is impossible! All of these men did their patriotic duty and deserve our deepest gratitude and respect.

A Tribute to the Men of Point Lookout Prison Camp

Former prisoner B. T. Holliday recalled that several years after the war he met a gentleman who lived in St. Mary's County, Maryland, where Lookout Point is located. Holliday recorded what the man had to say about the brave Confederate soldiers at the prison:

A TYPICAL CONFEDERATE SOLDIER.

"No one knows the suffering of body and mind those ragged, sick and hungry Confederate prisoners, on a desolate barren neck of land, hot in summer and cold in winter; these brave men went through the tortures of hell itself. Poorly clad and starved almost to the verge of skeletons, they bore their unfortunate lot with fortitude and submission, so characteristic of the Confederate soldiers. These men could have passed this cup from them by taking the Oath of Allegiance to the United States. They would have been released at once, but rather than become traitors to the cause for which they fought, they suffered imprisonment and torture, hunger, even death, spurning the offer that was made to them so frequently to take the oath, and be at liberty once more. Has the world ever witnessed a greater spectacle than the loyalty and patriotism of these gallant Southern boys."[213]

Chapter 3

Early Prisoner Exchange

The American Civil War has often been thought of as the first modern war. Certainly, it saw many warfare firsts: the first use of extensive trench warfare; the first use of rifled weapons; the first bombardment of civilian areas like Atlanta, Charleston and Vicksburg. It was also the first time mines and hand grenades were used. Unfortunately these destructive ideas extended to the prison system as well.

As the war dragged on and feelings became more bitter, the prisons became less of a temporary detention center and more like long-term concentration camps. During the last year of the war, prison camps ultimately evolved into retaliatory prisons or death camps.[1]

An unwritten policy prescribed that high ranking Union officials were to give the Confederate prisoners the same sort of treatment that the Union prisoners were receiving in the South. All of these things along with an unhealthy environment, an inadequate diet, and lack of proper clothing, shelter and medical attention contributed to Point Lookout prison's death toll.

When the Civil War began there was an orderly system of prisoner exchange that allowed the soldiers to go home after a brief period of captivity usually lasting 30 days or less. Many times commanding generals exchanged prisoners on the battlefield using only a gentleman's agreement. President Abraham Lincoln did not condone these exchanges because to do so he would have to recognize the Confederate government as a legitimate, sovereign power. Therefore, no general exchanges could be permitted. Secretary of War Edwin M. Stanton told Major General George B. McClellan, "*It is not deemed proper for officers bearing flags of truce in respect to the exchange of prisoners to hold any conference with the rebel officers upon the general subject of the existing contest or upon any other subject than what relates to the exchange of prisoners.*" The battlefield exchanges, which worked quite well, now ceased to exist.[2]

Private Francis Ostwalt, Co. E, 11th North Carolina, was captured July 3, 1863, at Gettysburg, Pa. Ostwalt was sent to Point Lookout prison camp where he died of smallpox December 30, 1863.

Mounting pressure from politicians, newspapers, petitions, forced congress to act. On December 12, 1861, congress passed a joint-resolution that said, "*Resolved, by the Senate and House of Representatives of the United States of America in Congress assembled, that the President of the United States be requested to inaugurate systematic measures for the exchange of prisoners in the present rebellion.*"[3] Now President Lincoln had no choice but to renew the prisoner exchange. After much debate the Dix-Hill Cartel was created and introduced July 22, 1862. Several important points of the new exchange policy were that prisoners should be exchanged within 10 days of capture and paroled prisoners could not rejoin the military until their enemy counterpart had reached his own lines.[4]

The typical prisoner exchange went this way. The official points of exchange were City Point in the East and Vicksburg in the West. Commissioners of exchange were appointed by each government, the men exchanged lists and then figured how many on each side were to be exchanged. A specific number of enlisted men were exchanged for an equal number of prisoners on the other side. A sergeant was exchanged for 2 privates, a lieutenant for 4 privates, a captain for 6 privates, a major for 8 privates, a colonel for 15 privates, and a general for 60 privates. If one side still had prisoners left after the other side had exhausted its supply of prisoners by exchange, those excess prisoners would be released on parole. Paroled prisoners were returned to their side, but were prohibited by an oath of honor from taking up arms until they were properly exchanged. Generally each side maintained parole camps where their paroled soldiers were kept while they awaited exchange, but in other cases the parolee was allowed to return home until exchanged.[5]

The prisoner exchange cartel was extremely fragile because of distrust and hostility on both sides. Finally the cartel broke down because Confederate President Jefferson Davis suspended the parole of Union officers following the execution of William Mumford, charged with destroying a United States flag, by Union General Benjamin F. Butler earlier that year. In reaction, Union Secretary of War Edwin M. Stanton ordered a halt to all exchanges of commissioned officers.

Joint Resolution 97

Federal Master Sergeant Washington S. Toland of the 83rd New York had been a prisoner in Confederate Belle Isle and Libby prisons in Richmond, Virginia, until he was exchanged in March of 1864. Upon his release Toland wrote a letter to the editor of the *New York Times* where he described "prison cruelties" as lack of adequate food, clothing and shelter. The newspaper printed his story in April, 1864, under the title of "Prison Life at Richmond—Its Cruelties." Lonnie Speer's book, *Portals of Hell: Military Prisons of the Civil War,* lists Libby prison as having only twenty deaths at the end of the war and Belle Isle, 300 deaths. To put this into perspective, Belle Isle had as many prisoners as Elmira did but only 1/10 as many deaths.[6]

Secretary of War Edwin Stanton received a copy of Master Sergeant Toland's letter. About the same time Stanton also heard from the Commissary General of Prisoners, Colonel William Hoffman, who wrote, "I respectfully suggest, as a means of compelling the rebels to adopt a less barbarous policy toward the prisoners in their hands that the rebel officers at Johnson's Island be allowed only half rations; that their clothing be reduced to what is only sufficient to cover their nakedness, and that they be denied the privilege of purchasing the articles allowed to other prisoners."[7]

On May 3rd Colonel Hoffman filed a report of his observation of Union prisoners who had been returned from Richmond. The returning prisoners were so mentally and physically deteriorated that Hoffman became convinced that Union prisoners of war were being deliberately starved to death. Again Hoffman urged that retaliatory measures be put in place.

Secretary of War Stanton had always suspected that Union prisoners were receiving poor treatment from the Confederates. Now, with the aid of Colonel

38TH CONGRESS.
2D SESSION.

S. R. 97.

IN THE SENATE OF THE UNITED STATES.

JANUARY 26, 1865.

Ordered to be printed.

Mr. WADE submitted the following amendment:

JOINT RESOLUTION

Advising retaliation for the cruel treatment of prisoners by the insurgents.

Whereas it has come to the knowledge of Congress that great numbers of our soldiers who have fallen as prisoners of war into the hands of the insurgents, have been subjected to treatment unexampled for cruelty in the history of civilized war, and finding its parallels only in the conduct of savage tribes; a treatment resulting in the death of multitudes by the slow but designed process of starvation and by mortal diseases occasioned by insufficient and unhealthy food, by wanton exposure of their persons to the inclemency of the weather and by deliberate assassination of innocent and unoffending men; and the murder in cold blood of prisoners after surrender; and whereas a continuance of these barbarities, in contempt of the laws of war and in disregard of the remonstrances of the national authorities, has presented to us the alternative of suffering our brave soldiers thus to be destroyed, or to apply the principle of retaliation for their protection: Therefore,

Senate Joint Resolution 97 which calls for retaliation on Confederate prisoners was read on the floor of the United States Senate in January 1865.

Hoffman and the *New York Times*, he urged a retaliation bill. On May 5th Stanton wrote President Lincoln, telling him of the abuses suffered by Union prisoners of war. The Secretary of War then proposed that "precisely the same rations and treatment be henceforth practiced to the whole number of rebel officers remaining in our hands that are practiced against either soldiers or officers in our service held by the rebels."[8]

On May 4th Stanton wrote Senator Benjamin Wade, "The enormity of the crime committed by the rebels towards our prisoners for the last several months is not known or realized by our own people, and cannot but fill with horror the civilized world when the facts are revealed. There appears to have been a deliberate system of savage and barbarous treatment and starvation."[9]

Senator Wade then wrote *Resolution 97* and read it on the floor of the Senate on January 26, 1865. This joint resolution would have the full effect of a law if passed by both houses of Congress and signed by the chief executive. Congress passed it, but to his credit President Lincoln did not sign it. The first part of the resolution is included here to show the mindset of the Northern politicians at the time.

Joint resolution 97 read:

S.R. 97
Mr. Wade submitted the following amendment.
JOINT RESOLUTION
Advising retaliation for the cruel treatment of prisoners by the insurgents.

"Whereas it has come to the knowledge of Congress that great numbers of our soldiers who have fallen as prisoners of war into the hands of the insurgents, have been subjected to treatment unexampled for cruelty in the history of civilized war, and finding its parallels only in the conduct of savage tribes; a treatment resulting in the death of multitudes by the slow but designed process of starvation and by mortal diseases occasioned by insufficient and unhealthy food, by wanton exposure of their persons to the inclemency of the weather and by deliberate assassination of innocent and unoffending men; and the murder in cold blood of prisoners after surrender; and whereas a continuance of these barbarities, in contempt of the laws of war and in disregard of the remonstrance's of the national authorities, has presented to us the alternative of suffering our brave soldiers thus to be destroyed, or to apply the principle of retaliation for their protection: Therefore, resolved by the Senate and House of Representatives of the United States of America in Congress assembled, That in the judgment of Congress, it has become justifiable and necessary that the President should, in order to prevent the continuance and recurrence of such barbarities, and to insure the observance by the insurgents of the laws of civilized war, resort at once to measures of retaliation."[10]

Articles favoring retaliation frequently appeared in the Northern newspapers that autumn. The *New York Times* spoke of how the inhumane treatment of Union prisoners of war had *"stained and sullied the vesture of Southern chivalry. No such disgrace, thank God, touches the North! Everything that our own soldiers are allowed by law is cheerfully given to our prisoners. Such clothing, such food as the poor Southron never enjoyed at home, is heaped before him when in our hands. . . . None suffer from want."* The *Times* then proclaimed: *"We believe that the most active measures should be undertaken to insure corresponding treatment of our own brave soldiers. We urge that rebel prisoners should no longer live in luxury while ours are dying of starvation and neglect."*[11]

Ever the politician, President Abraham Lincoln did not want anything to reflect badly on his administration. In his book, *The Lincoln Nobody Knows*, Historian Richard N. Current wrote that the President had an arrangement with Secretary Stanton: "Such apparently was the division of labor between Lincoln and Stanton, between lenity and the law. If a life was spared, Lincoln could get the credit. If not, Stanton with would take the blame." Lincoln himself admitted, "I want to oblige everybody whenever I can and Stanton and I have an understanding that if I send an order to him which cannot be consistently granted, he is to refuse it." One thing was certain: Stanton was a major decision maker in Lincoln's scheme of things.[12]

England's Attempt to Help Confederate Prisoners

In April of 1876 *The Southern Historical Society Papers* reported that the Honorable A. J. Beresford Hope wrote Secretary Stanton for permission to raise money in England to alleviate the status of prisoners in Northern prisons. Stanton said, "Almighty God! No! The government of the United States is rich enough to provide for its prisoners and needs no foreign help."[13]

Judge Robert Ould, the Confederate agent of prisoner exchange, wrote a letter in October to Major John E. Mulford, his Federal counterpart. Ould pointed out that thousands of prisoners of war would be held through the winter of 1864-65. Ould proposed a plan to ease the suffering of the Confederate prisoners. If the North would send a ship to Mobile, Alabama, 1,000 bales of cotton would be loaded aboard and sent to New York City. The cotton would be sold and the money collected would be used to purchase clothing, blankets, and other necessities for the Confederate soldiers being held in Northern prisons. General Grant was receptive to the idea.

Historian Michael Horigan wrote, "The simplicity of the plan raised hopes for success of the operation. However, a series of delays orchestrated by Secretary of War Stanton all but eliminated any possibility of the clothing and blankets arriving in Northern prison camps before the beginning of the winter season."[14]

Private John P. Greenlee, Co. K, 22th N. C., was captured at Petersburg, Va. and sent to Point Lookout Prison Camp. Greenlee took the Oath of Allegiance June 27, 1865.

In December the U.S. Transport *Atlanta*, under a flag of truce, sailed into the harbor at Mobile. The delays began when Secretary Stanton objected to the Confederate officer who was to sell the cotton in New York. Judge Ould wanted Major General Isaac R. Trimble to handle matters in New York. It took Stanton three weeks to find a suitable replacement in Confederate General William N. R. Beall. Beall had just been paroled from Fort Warren and was in the custody of Union General Halbert E. Paine. Due to further delays in transferring the cotton the *Atlanta* did not dock in New York Harbor until January 24th. Unfortunately due to the rapidly declining cotton market the cargo yielded less than 50 percent of its value from November.

Chapter 4

The Confederate Prison Camp at Andersonville, Georgia

A great number of Northern citizens felt the Confederacy was guilty of brutal behavior in its treatment of Union prisoners of war because of retaliatory articles in the Union newspapers. The truth is the South was hard-pressed to provide food and medicine for their own people, let alone prisoners of war. The devastating impact of three years of war had seriously depleted the region's agricultural production. General Sherman's March to the Sea and up through the Carolinas carried out a scorched earth policy and burned public buildings, many homes and centers of transportation. In 1863 General Philip Sheridan's Army followed a similar course by burning the crops and farms in the fertile Shenandoah Valley. These things not only stopped the Confederates from receiving supplies but seriously impaired any attempt to properly feed Union prisoners of war at places such as Andersonville.

Did Major-General Sherman really intend to free the Union prisoners at Andersonville?

Most people in the North were unaware that their own government was partly responsible for the mistreatment of Union prisoners. The Northern blockade of Southern ports slowed to a trickle the foods and medicine that might have helped Union prisoners. Every time the prisoner of war exchanges were halted it was done by the North. The Confederacy wanted to relieve itself of the burden of caring for thousands of Union prisoners and tried repeatedly to re-establish the exchange, but all too often their appeals fell on deaf ears.

It has been shown that leaving Union prisoners in the South was a strategy used by the North. Secretary of War Edwin M. Stanton and General Ulysses S Grant did not want to exchange Union prisoners because it was felt these men would take resources away from the Confederacy and drain its strength further by having to care for thousands of Union prisoners. It was also felt the exchanged Confederate prisoners would be healthy enough to go right back into the Army while the North would only receive sick and broken men in return.[1]

Andersonville prisoner Second Lieutenant James M. Page wrote, "The report was brought to us by the incoming prisoners that the authorities had shut down on exchanging prisoners. About August 1st, we heard the cold-blooded and atrocious news [proclamation by the government] from Edward M. Stanton, that the exchange of prisoners was at an end. 'We will not exchange able-bodied men for skeletons,' and 'we do not propose to reinforce the rebel army by exchanging prisoners.'"

Lieutenant Page continued, "Now it was a certainty. We realize that we were forsaken by our government. The war office at Washington preferred to let us die rather than exchange us! The refusal upon the part of our government to exchange prisoners was now an assured fact. The sick lost hope and died. Those in better condition physically became disheartened and sick. It is no wonder that during August nearly 3000 prisoners died at Andersonville."[2]

How badly did General William T. Sherman want to rescue the thousands of prisoners at Camp Oglethorpe at Macon and Andersonville prison camp, Georgia? He had a 72,000 man Army less than 100 miles from the prisons and yet he didn't capture them. General George Stoneman urged Sherman to permit him take 2,500 cavalry and liberate the Union prisoners. Sherman finally agreed to this ill-fated rescue attempt, but his effort was halfhearted at best. If Sherman seriously intended to free those Union prisoners, he would have sent a larger force that contained infantry and wagons to carry the released men to Savannah where they could be shipped home. He did none of these things. This is a force a commander might send out on a raid. Certainly this small number of troops would not be enough to rescue tens of thousands of sick prisoners.

It was clear General Sherman never intended to free the prisoners at Andersonville. He did not want to slow his advance by having to care for thousands of sick and feeble men who badly needed medical attention. Sherman did not have the food needed for these extra men or the transportation, and it would be dangerous to slow his army to a crawl in enemy territory. Confederate General Joe Wheeler's cavalry was constantly nipping at his heels,

Union General George Stoneman led an ill-fated attempt to free the prisoners at Andersonville.

and Generals Hood and Johnston were out there waiting for an opportunity to strike.

On July 27, 1864, General George Stoneman began his march to tear up the railroads between Atlanta and Macon, Georgia, and to free the Union prisoners at several Confederate prison camps. Stoneman's force of 2,500 cavalry was well mounted having abandoned their broken down horses and seizing fresh mounts that they found along the route. Confederate General Alfred Iversen Jr. overtook Stoneman's troopers on Hillsboro Road, south of the town of Round Oak and near a small church named ironically named Sunshine Church. Confederate General Armstrong's cavalry assaulted Stoneman's flanks and rear, while Iversen's cavalry attacked the front of his force, effectively surrounding him.

Seeing no way out, Stoneman, along with 500 troopers, fought a rear-guard action while the rest of his command attacked the weakest point on the Confederate line. The Union cavalry fought their way out, but General Stoneman and his men were captured. The Union lost 1,000 men and three cannon in this unsuccessful raid. In retrospect, it is believed General Sherman sent this force to rescue the Union prisoners at Andersonville, not because he believed it would be successful, but to show that he made an attempt to free the prisoners.[3]

Sherman's army was able to move deep into enemy territory because it was self-sufficient and did not have to worry about lines of supply. Soldiers called bummers went out ahead of the Army and scoured the countryside for miles around in search of food. The forage not only consisted of foodstuff, but horses and mules, cows, sheep, and pigs as well. Union Captain Charles E. Belknap commanded such a detail and commented, "If a rich find was made, the men were loaded with all they could carry, and the torch did away with the balance to the great distress of the inhabitants."[4]

Sherman realized that remaining in one spot for too long was hazardous because the bummers needed new land to provide the food and horses his men required. The swath of land they had moved through had been stripped bare and could no longer support them. In essence, Sherman's Army needed to move forward to stay alive. If he attempted to rescue the Union prisoners at Andersonville it might mean capture or death for him and his men. Sherman would not allow this. He would have never permitted his grand design of marching to the sea to be ruined by a few thousand prisoners.

Several years after the war Federal Major-General Benjamin F. Butler wrote about the starving Confederate soldiers and reasoned they could only give a small amount of food and clothing to prisoners.

"While I do not mean to apologize for the manner in which our prisoners were treated, I feel bound to say that from careful examinations of the subject, I do not believe that either the people or the higher authorities of the Confederacy were in so great degree responsible as they have been accused. In the matter of starvation the fact is incontestable that a soldier of our army would have quite easily starved on the rations which in the latter days of the war were served out to the Confederate soldiers before Petersburg. I examined the haversacks of many Confederate soldiers captured on picket during the summer of 1864 and found therein, as their rations for three days, scarcely more than a pint of kernels of corn, parched or blacken by the fire, a long piece of meat, most frequently bacon, some three inches long by an inch and a half wide and less than a half an inch thick. Now, no Northern soldier could have lived three days upon that, and the lank, emaciated condition of the (Confederate) prisoner fully testified to the meagerness of his means of sustenance.

Butler goes on to say, "With regard to clothing, it was simply impossible for the Confederates at that time to have any sufficient clothing upon the bodies of their soldiers, and many passed the winters barefoot. Necessity, therefore, would seem to have compelled the condition of food and clothing given by them to the Federal prisoners, for it was not possible for authorities to supply it without taking the clothing from their soldiers in the field."[5]

TREASURE SEEKERS.

General Sherman's bummers and looters did a disservice to the Union army because their cruel acts would never be forgotten by the Southern people.

Where Are All the Deaths?

While compiling the prisoner roster for this book, I found it curious that only two Point Lookout death certificates listed frostbite as the official cause of death. I also wondered why only one prisoner had been listed as being shot to death by a guard when it has been shown that at least 20 men had been killed. The officials at Point Lookout were unable to determine what had caused a prisoner's death in 30% of the cases which leaves a lot of room for speculation as to what caused these deaths. In virtually all of the instances where the cause of death was unknown, no official death certificate was ever found. Instead there would be a notation on the prisoner's record that he died on a particular date. This lack of an official death certificates makes one wonder if these documents were purposely destroyed to conceal the real reason for the prisoner's death.

I did some investigation into the prisoner's deaths and may have found an answer. On April 18, 1864, Paul Thoroughgood of the 4th North Carolina Cavalry was asleep in this tent when he was shot twice by a Negro guard. One bullet struck the right side of his chest, fracturing a rib, but not hitting any vital organs. The other ball grazed the skin, creating a three-inch wound. I searched the prisoner's military records and found that he died April 26, 1864, of pneumonia. Nothing on his record indicated that he was shot by a guard. When looking further, I discovered a letter by Point Lookout Surgeon James H. Thompson in which he mentions treating two gunshot wounds on Paul Thoroughgood. Another letter addressed to Surgeon Thompson by Doctor W. A. Harvey says the prisoner had died. Harvey, the medical examiner at Thoroughgood's autopsy, mentions finding a secondary infection of pneumonia. Unfortunately when the prisoner's death report was filled out they forgot to mention Thoroughgood was shot twice by a guard. Instead, they list the cause of death as pneumonia. Upon seeing this report, someone would have no way of knowing he had been shot by a prison guard unless they took the time to read the doctor's letters. Apparently this was how the undesirable deaths at Point Lookout were concealed.

At first glance it seems Private Paul Thouroughgood, 4th N. C. Cavalry, died of pneumonia. The author discovered two letters from different doctors that state he had been shot twice by a guard several days before his death.

Another questionable death is that of Private George P. Wallace of the 10th Regiment Virginia Cavalry. Wallace's records at the National Archives say only that he, "Died 1/27/1864". Upon further investigation of the *Virginia Regimental History Series* it was determined Private George P. Wallace died from being shot by a guard at Point Lookout. The roster of prisoners who died list 960 deaths attributed to unknown causes. One has to wonder how many of these deaths were the result of freezing to death or being shot by prison guards.

PRISONERS OF WAR CAMP HOSPITAL,
Point Lookout, Md., April 19, 1864.

Major Weymouth,
First U.S. Volunteers and Provost Marshal:

MAJOR: I have the honor to report having received into this hospital and dressed the wounds of Paul Thoroughgood, Company C, Fourth North Carolina Cavalry, prisoner of war, said to have been wounded by the guard at about 9.30 last p.m. The missiles consisted, judging from the character of the wounds, of two balls or slugs. One entered right side at anterior border of axilla, passing obliquely downward and emerging at right side of spinous processes on a plane four inches below that of entrance. Distance between point of entrance and that of exit, eight inches. Cavity of thorax not opened and no bone injured. Second ball grazed and wounded the skin at a distance of three inches. Patient at this time doing well.

Very respectfully, your obedient servant,

JAMES H. THOMPSON,

Surgeon, U.S. Volunteers, in Charge.[6]

Headquarters Medical Department
Prisoner of War Camp & Hospital
Point Lookout, Md.
April 26th 1864

Surgeon James H. Thompson,
U. S. Volunteers,
In Charge,

Sir,

I have the honor to report the death and postmortem appearances of pris. P. Thoroughgood, Co. C, 4th N. C. Cav. shot by the guard April 18, 9:30 PM. The ball fractured the eighth rib at its angle without entering the cavity of the thorax. The right lung was in a state of hepalization and pustulant infiltration. [The right lung was infected by pneumonia, bruised from the trauma of the gunshot and consequently did not have the proper blood flow.] The remaining organs exhibited no particular lesions except such as occur as a secondary result or evidence of pneumonia. From the above mentioned postmortem appearances, we conclude that although the wound may have contributed somewhat to the fatal result, it did not constitute the first cause. And we are unable to say whether or not the man would have recovered had his preexistent disease not been increased and intensified by the wound.

Very Respectfully,
W. A. Harvey

No. 1.

RECORD OF DEATH AND INTERMENT.

Name and number of person interred. *Justice S,*

Number and locality of the grave . *1259 In Pris of War Grave Yard*

Hospital number of the deceased . . *7220*

Regiment, rank, and company . . *Co K 3 N Ce Res a Private*

Residence before enlistment . . . .

Conjugal condition, (and if married,)
the residence of the widow) . . }

Cause of death . . . . }   *Frost Bite*

Age of the deceased . . . . . .

Nativity . . . .

References and remarks . . . . }

Date of death and burial . . . .   *March 10 , 186 5*

Duplicates sent to the Adjutant General of the United States Army, and to the Sexton of the Cemetery.

da:

This is the death certificate of Private Solomon Justice, 3rd N. C. Junior Reserves. Justice was only 15 years old when he was captured at Fort Fisher in December, 1864. He was sent to Point Lookout prison camp where he died of frost bite two and a half months later.

Did President Lincoln Have Knowledge of Prisoner Abuse?

President Abraham Lincoln was the consummate politician. After his first tumultuous year in office Lincoln learned how to avoid controversy and remain unscathed. Sometimes the job of president means making unpopular decisions. Since Lincoln did not want to tarnish his image, he needed someone with authority to carry out his more controversial policies. The man for the job was Secretary of War Edwin M. Stanton. In November 1861 Stanton, who was then Attorney General, urged Secretary of War Cameron to issue a report arguing that slaves should be armed to fight against the Confederacy. Therefore it was no surprise to learn about Stanton's negative attitude regarding the South, so his retaliatory orders, such as reducing rations for the Confederate prisoners did not shock anyone. Stanton became the perfect hatchet man for Lincoln. It must be remembered that all the orders Stanton issued had the approval of President Lincoln. Therefore it can be assumed Lincoln gave tacit permission for these orders to be carried out. If they proved unpopular, Stanton knew how to take the blame so nothing would touch the President.[7]

In April of 1861 President Abraham Lincoln declared a blockade of Southern ports and took an unprecedented step by designating certain medicines as contraband of war. This was something unheard of prior to the War Between the States. Denying your enemy access to medicine was considered cruel and uncivilized because to do so would inflict more pain and suffering on the sick and wounded. Medicines like morphine, opium, calomel and quinine were crucial in the treatment of disease and wounds. These badly needed medical items became increasingly scarce in the South. As a result, the Federal blockade caused suffering among Union prisoners as well as Southern soldiers and citizens.

Union Army Surgeon William H. Gardner spoke at the 1863 American Medical Association Convention in Chicago and petitioned the United States government to lift some of the restrictions on medicines and surgical appliances that were considered contraband. Gardner argued that banning such items affected their own soldiers, many of whom were prisoners in the hands of the Confederates. Doctor Gardner also stated that banning medical items was heartless and worthy of the "Dark Ages". Instead of agreeing with him, the learned medical men of the North forgot their noble and unselfish profession of helping their fellow man and hissed and booed Gardner from the stage.[8]

President Lincoln was a hands-on president who knew everything concerning the war and the movement of his armies. When the North was doing poorly during the first few years of the conflict, it was Lincoln who changed commanding generals of the army six times until he found someone who could at least sometimes fight Robert E. Lee to a draw. It was well known that Lincoln would go daily to the War Department's telegraph-room and anxiously follow the army's movements via telegraph. In fact, he was able to communicate to his generals and became the first United States president to become actively involved to the battles. When major battles were being waged it was not unusual for Lincoln to stay in the telegraph office all night. This can be documented according to the time on the dispatches he sent. President Lincoln therefore knew just about everything concerning his army.

President Lincoln also received many requests from prisoner's families who described the horrendous conditions in the prisons. It is known Lincoln read at least some of these letters because he did grant a few paroles. To believe he knew nothing of the prisoner's situation would be naive.[9] This knowledge coupled with Lincoln's refusal to see the prisoner delegation from Andersonville in August of 1864 raises suspicions that the President not only know about the brutal conditions that prisoners live under, but tends to make him appear insensitive to their desperate situation. These men were living under horrendous conditions that saw 29% of their fellow prisoners died from disease. The prisoner exchange had been halted during the summer of 1863 by the vindictive Secretary of War Stanton and it only needed President Lincoln to step in to reestablish the prisoner exchange, but he refused to do it. It is for these reasons that I believe President Lincoln had full knowledge of prison brutality, but did nothing to alleviate it.

This is a note from President Lincoln asking for the release of Union 1st Lt. Edward P. Brooks.

The most damning piece of evidence against Lincoln was his decision to ignore the Union prisoners who traveled from Andersonville, Georgia, to meet him in Washington, D. C. If Lincoln was truly unaware of the horrors the prisoners faced he would have gladly seen these men so they could discuss their situation and try to improve it. However, the President chose not to see them. Why would he do such a cruel thing? Could it be that Lincoln already knew what the prisoners were going to tell him, and he had no suitable reply to give them? One thing regarding the prisoners is certain though. The President would never allow the government's policy of halting the prisoner exchanges to be jeopardized by a few Union prisoners. Lincoln's decision is difficult to understand in light of the fact that the North was winning the war when the Andersonville prisoners came to see him in August of 1864.[10]

Confederate Cemetery and Monuments

In 1867 the United States government sent Quartermaster Department agent E. Edward Gilbert to Point Lookout to survey the land and consolidate the scattered graveyards in preparation for building a national cemetery. Five cemeteries contained the bodies of Confederate prisoners, Union soldiers and contrabands that died during the last two years of the war. Soon after the conflict the military transferred the Union remains to Arlington National Cemetery outside of Washington, D. C. A lot of maintenance was needed as the graveyard's wooden headboards had been covered by weeds and shifting sand. So much so, it was difficult to locate some of the graves. Gilbert wrote Lt. Colonel E. E. Camp that he had problems digging in the loose sand and gravel as it had a tendency to fall back into the hole. Because of this extra work, he was forced to bury two bodies in one grave.

The burial sites at Point Lookout would be moved several times in the next 50 years. One of the largest prisoner's cemeteries was located just north of the enlisted men's prison camp until 1870, but due to erosion it was moved farther inland to Tanner's Creek. The cemetery stayed there until 1910 and then it was moved again. The final resting place for the prisoners is located a short distance north of the prison camp on Maryland Route 5 near Scotland. The state of Maryland and the Federal government erected two monuments for the Confederate soldiers and civilians who died at Point Lookout. Due to the frequent moving of the cemetery, it was difficult to identify the soldiers so they were buried in a mass grave. The cemetery is beautifully maintained by the Veterans Administration.

Sgt. Barlett Y. Malone, Co. H, 6th N. C., was captured at Rappahannock Station, Va., and sent to Point Lookout. He was exchanged February 24, 1865. Fortunately Malone and many others have left behind his diary recounting his prison life which many researchers use today.

The smaller monument was erected by the people of St. Mary's County in Maryland along with the help of Calvert and Charles counties. The monument is an obelisk of white marble, about 25 feet in height and has inscriptions on all four sides. The south face reads:

"At the call of patriotism and duty they encountered the perils of the field, endured the trials of a prison, and were faithful, even unto death."

The east face lists the number of deaths for each state in the Confederacy.

Virginia 640.	Mississippi 42.
North Carolina 962.	Florida 31.
South Carolina 248.	Kentucky 18.
Georgia 249.	Texas 6.
Alabama 75.	Maryland 6.
Tennessee 63.	Arkansas 4.
Louisiana 38.	Missouri 4, 2386.

Confederate States Not Designated 618.
Total 3004

The north face has a bronze tablet that reads:
Colonel Wm. Elliott,
General Wm. C. Oates
And
Gov. James H. Berry
Being US Commissioners to Mark Confederate Graves,
The State of Maryland Having Ceded to the Federal
Government the Cemetery to Which the Bodies of
The Confederates Who Died Prisoners of War at
Point Lookout Military Prison Had Been Removed,
The War Department Granted Permission to Have the
State Monument Removed and Re-Erected at This,
The Original Prison Burying Ground.
A D 1910-1911

Below this tablet is engraved: "Dulce et decorum est pro Patria Mori. [Latin for: "It is right and proper to die for one's country."] When the federal government sold the property this monument was on, it was moved again in 1938 to its original position. The West face of the monument reads:

1876
Erected
By the
State of Maryland
In memory of
The Confederate Soldiers
Who Died Prisoners of War
At Point Lookout, From
March 1st 1864 to June 30, 1865

In 1910 the state transferred ownership of the cemetery to the federal government. The government erected an 85 foot-high granite obelisk which has 12 bronze tablets listing the names and commands of the Confederate dead. The tablets were placed in each side of the monument and set around the earthen mound beneath it. These name plates list 3,382 known Confederate soldiers, sailors, marines and civilians who died at Point Lookout. Further research by the author located over 400 names of Confederate soldiers who also died at Point Lookout prison camp. These names have been added to the roster in this book.

The bronze tablet on the face of this monument reads:

ERECTED BY
THE

UNITED STATES

TO MARK THE BURIAL PLACE
OF

CONFEDERATE

SOLDIERS AND SAILORS

WHO DIED AT POINT LOOKOUT, MD.
WHILE PRISONERS OF WAR AND WERE THERE
BURIED TO THE NUMBER OF 3,384. BUT WHOSE
REMAINS WERE SUBSEQUENTLY MOVED
EITHER TO THEIR RESPECTIVE HOMES OR TO
THIS CEMETERY WHERE THE INDIVIDUAL GRAVES
CANNOT NOW BE IDENTIFIED.

Prisoner Deaths That Do Not Appear on the Confederate Memorial

All Confederate prisoner deaths from Point Lookout Prison Camp should be found on bronze tablets surrounding the Confederate Memorial. In my research I have discovered over four hundred soldiers who died in prison and whose names do not appear on these tablets. Why they were forgotten is hard to say. Was this due to sloppy bookkeeping or a deliberate attempt to minimize the deaths at the prison? It must be remembered that the North was enraged by the thousands of deaths at Andersonville, Georgia. In an attempt to seek vengeance Andersonville prison Commandant Captain Henry Wirz was tried, convicted and executed for war crimes that happened during the Civil War. Could it be possible the Union was deliberately keeping deaths down to make their prisoner of war camps appear so much better than the Southern prisons?

I find it amazing that I was able to find over four hundred prisoner's deaths which do not appear on the Federal monument's tablets. If a 21th century author like me was able to find these deaths 150 years after the war had ended, what does it say about the prison officials at Point Lookout Prison Camp?

The Federal Monument

This sign is on the fence to the Confederate cemetery.

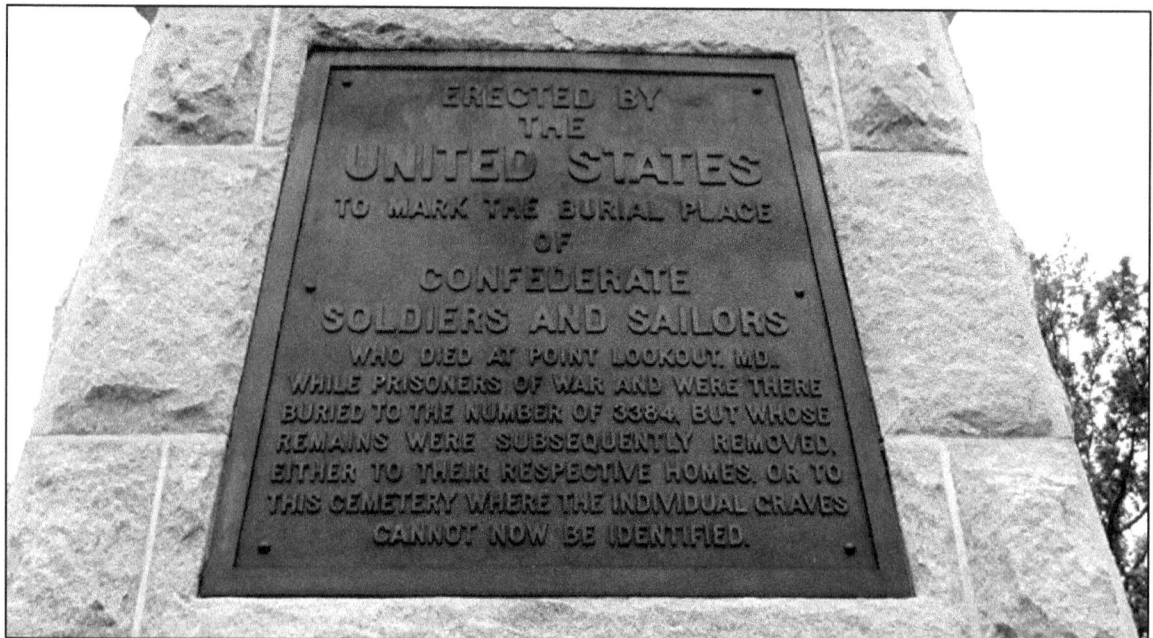

ERECTED BY
THE
UNITED STATES
TO MARK THE BURIAL PLACE
OF
CONFEDERATE
SOLDIERS AND SAILORS
WHO DIED AT POINT LOOKOUT, MD.
WHILE PRISONERS OF WAR AND WERE THERE
BURIED TO THE NUMBER OF 3384, BUT WHOSE
REMAINS WERE SUBSEQUENTLY REMOVED.
EITHER TO THEIR RESPECTIVE HOMES, OR TO
THIS CEMETERY WHERE THE INDIVIDUAL GRAVES
CANNOT NOW BE IDENTIFIED.

Constructed in May, 1911, the 85 foot Federal monument to the Confederate dead at Point Lookout Prison Camp is an impressive and beautiful structure made of white granite. The 12 bronze tablets on the sides list most of the names of the prisoners.

The Federal monument is surrounded by bronze name plates of the Confederate dead.

This is one of the bronze tablets which list the Confederate dead.

<u>Maryland State Confederate Monument</u>

The Maryland State Confederate monument was the original marker for the cemetery at Point Lookout. It was erected in 1876.

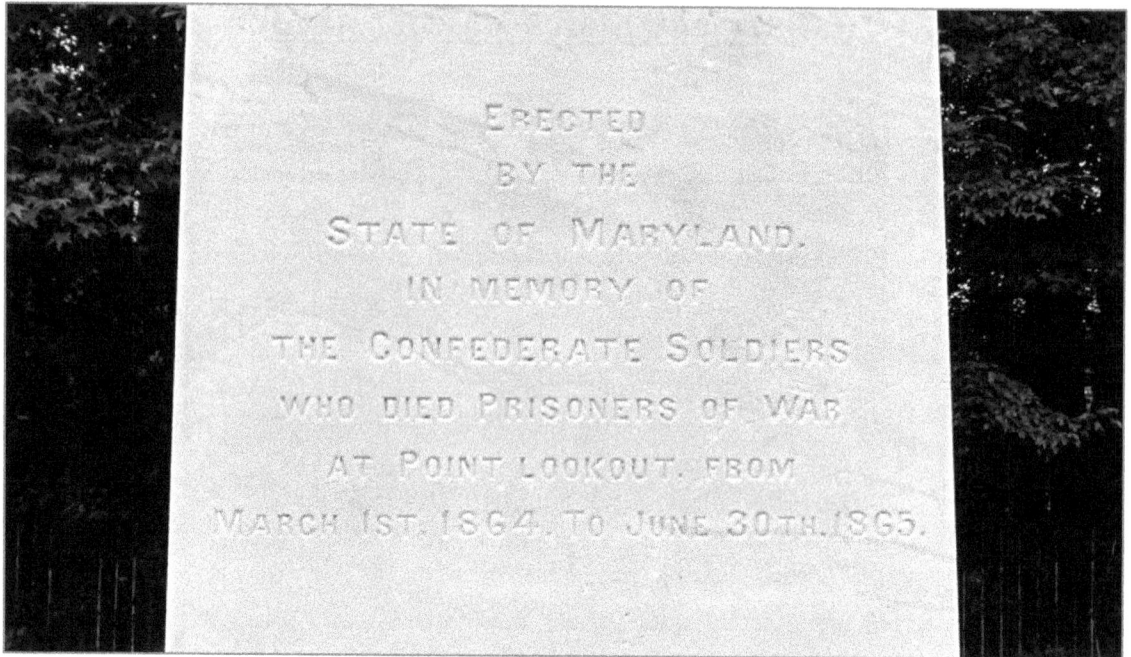

Inscription on the state of Maryland's Confederate monument.

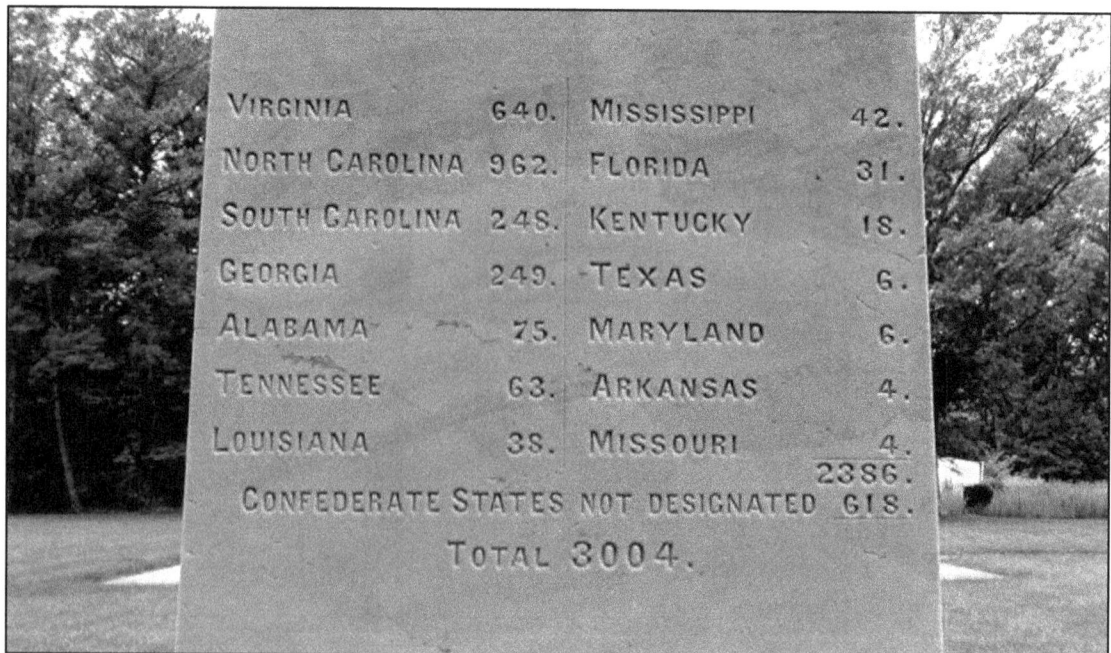

The Maryland monument lists the number of Confederate prisoners who died from each state.

<u>Confederate Memorial Park</u>

Confederate Memorial Park was built September 6, 2008 by the Point Lookout Descendants Organization. It is a beautiful park and has many plaques containing Confederate prisoners' statements about the prison.

Confederate Memorial Park has a bronze statue of a barefoot prisoner wearing an old torn shirt and trousers which have been mended. This is an accurate representation of the how the Point Lookout prisoner's dressed. Many of the men imprisoned here say their clothing was tattered rags and some of the men did not have shoes to wear even in cold weather.

100

n W. Harper 14th NC Reg ed Pt. Lookout	Andrew J. Keister Co. K, 62 nd VA Inf. Survived Pt. Lookout	Francis M. Davenport E Hamptons Legion SC Survived Pt. Lookout	Hillary M. Callaham Co.C, 11th VA Inf. Survived Pt. Lookout	Joel McDaniel Price Co.A, 18th VA Inf. d Pt. Lookout
wis B. Creech 17th SC Inf. Pt. Lookout	Lt. Thomas O. Moss Co.G, 23rd VA Inf. Survived Pt. Lookout	Pvt. Dewitt C. Isler Co.C, 5th FL Inf. Died at Pt. Lookout	Nimrod Shoe Co. C, 45th NC Inf. Died at Pt. Lookout	Lovey Ivey Co.A, 30th NC Inf. Died at Pt. Lookou
bs Jones 3rd NC Inf. Pt. Lookout	Joshua W. Poole Co A 10 Bn NC Hy Art Died at Pt. Lookout	Benjamin F. Keith 2 Arty, 36 NC Troops Survived Pt. Lookout	George W. Nuckles Co. B, 49th VA Inf. Survived Pt. Lookout	Anderson R. Thom Co.I, 57th NC In Survived Pt. Look
n Schacht th VA Inf t. Lookout	James P. Emerson Co E, 26th NC Inf. Survived Pt. Lookout	John Thomas Ballard Co. I, 60th AL Inf. Died at Pt. Lookout	Lindsay F. Austin Co.A, 48th NC Inf. Survived Pt. Lookout	John L. Austi Co.D, 37th NC Died at Pt. Loo
orter TX Cav. ookout	Jonas Edwards Co.D, 3rd NC Lt Arty Survived Pt. Lookout	John T. Rochelle Co.D, 3rd NC Inf. Survived Pt. Lookout	Ransom H. Idol Co.K, 45th NC Inf. Survived Pt. Lookout	Pvt. Lemuel Co.E, 61st N Survived Pt. L
ee	Sgt. James W. Buster	Alexander A. Saain	W H P	Francis Mario

At Confederate Memorial Park prisoner's relatives can purchase a brick in their great grandfather's name which lists his company and regiment and is then placed beneath the Confederate statue.

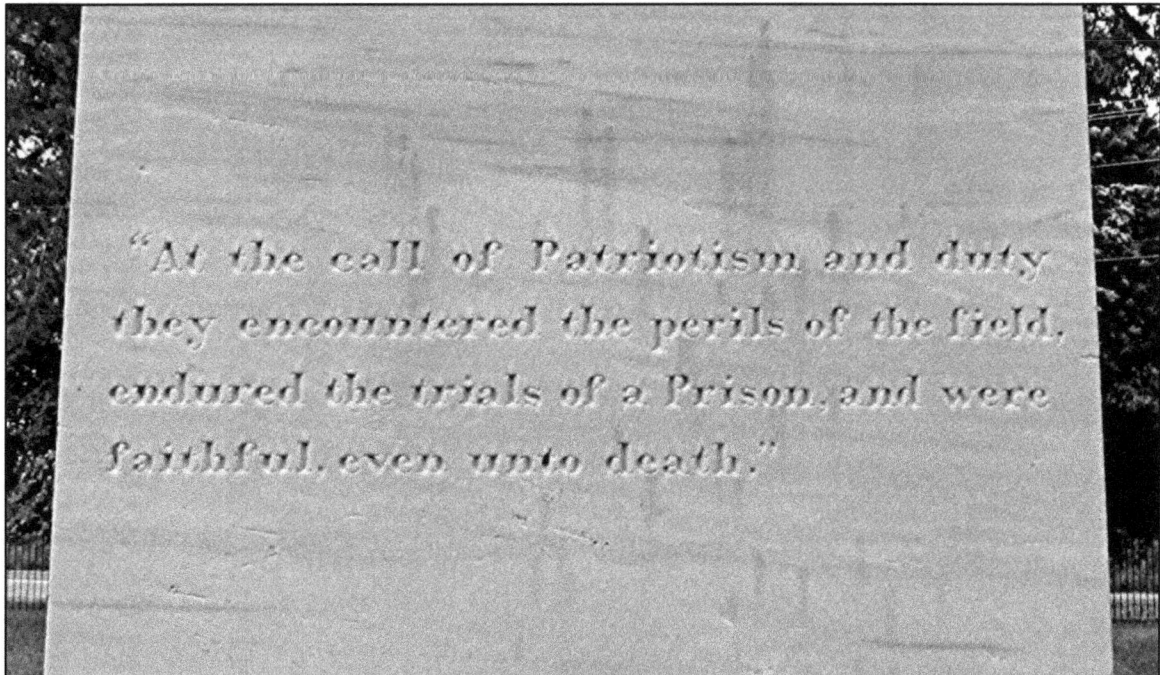

"At the call of Patriotism and duty they encountered the perils of the field, endured the trials of a Prison, and were faithful, even unto death."

Beautiful inscription on the Maryland monument honors all Confederate soldiers who became prisoners.

Fort Lincoln

Fort Lincoln was located on the Potomac River, across from the prison. The fort's guard house and many other building were recreated for the public to enjoy.

Fort Lincoln's officer's quarters and barracks. The entire fort is surrounded by earthworks.

Barracks interior at Fort Lincoln.

Point Lookout Museum

No trip to Point Lookout prison would be complete without visiting the museum. The building is shared with the Maryland Marshland Nature Center and a gift shop. The museum tells the history of the Point Lookout area as well as the prison. They have displays showing a cracker-box tent, a typical hospital scene complete with a nurse, a guard shack, artifacts found at the prison camp and a wall that displays numerous photographs of the Point Lookout prisoners. There is also a 3-D display of Fort Lincoln which was one of the forts that guarded the prison. This display gives you an idea of how the original Fort Lincoln appeared. There is a recreation of the Fort you can visit, but the earthen walls are not as extensive as they used to be.

The park is at the southern tip of St. Mary's County, at the junction of the Potomac River and the Chesapeake Bay. It can be reached via Maryland Route 5. The museum is open May through October, on Saturday and Sunday from 9 AM - 5 PM so plan your trip accordingly. The telephone number of the museum is 301-872-5688.

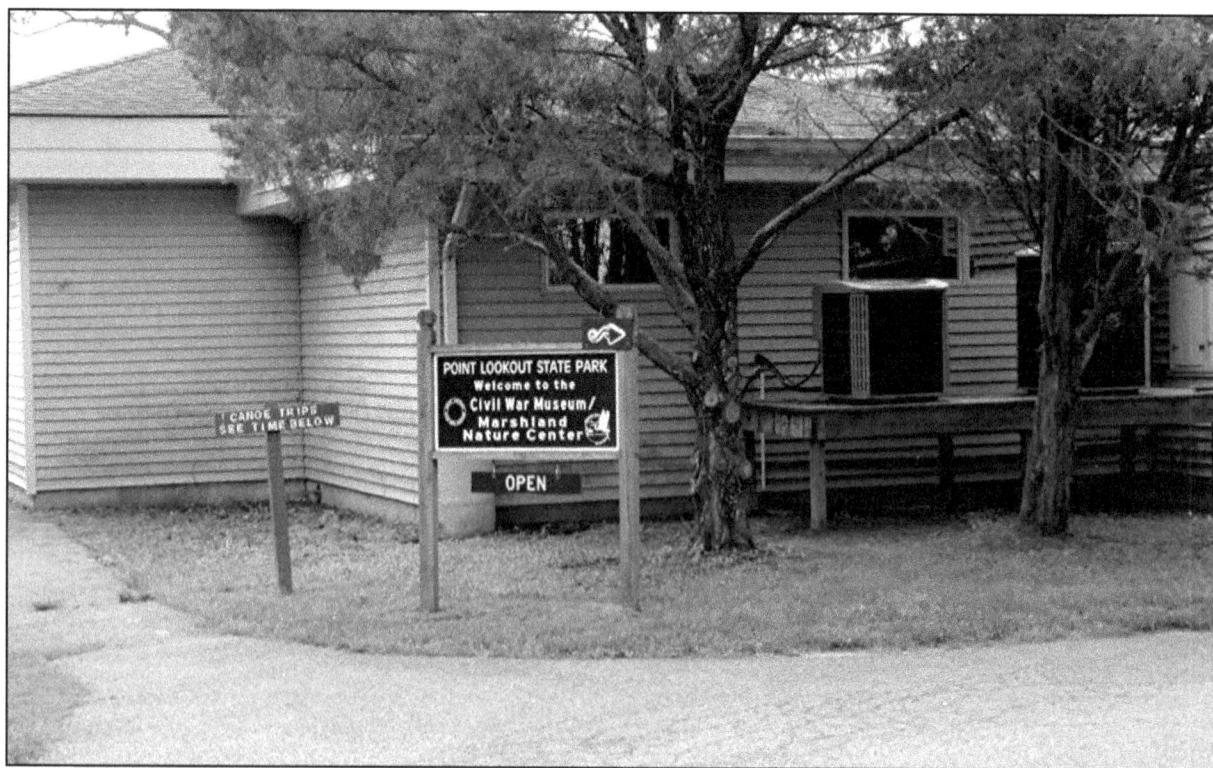

Civil War Museum and Marshland Nature Center

Point Lookout Museum has many displays of prison life. This tent was constructed by using cracker-boxes.

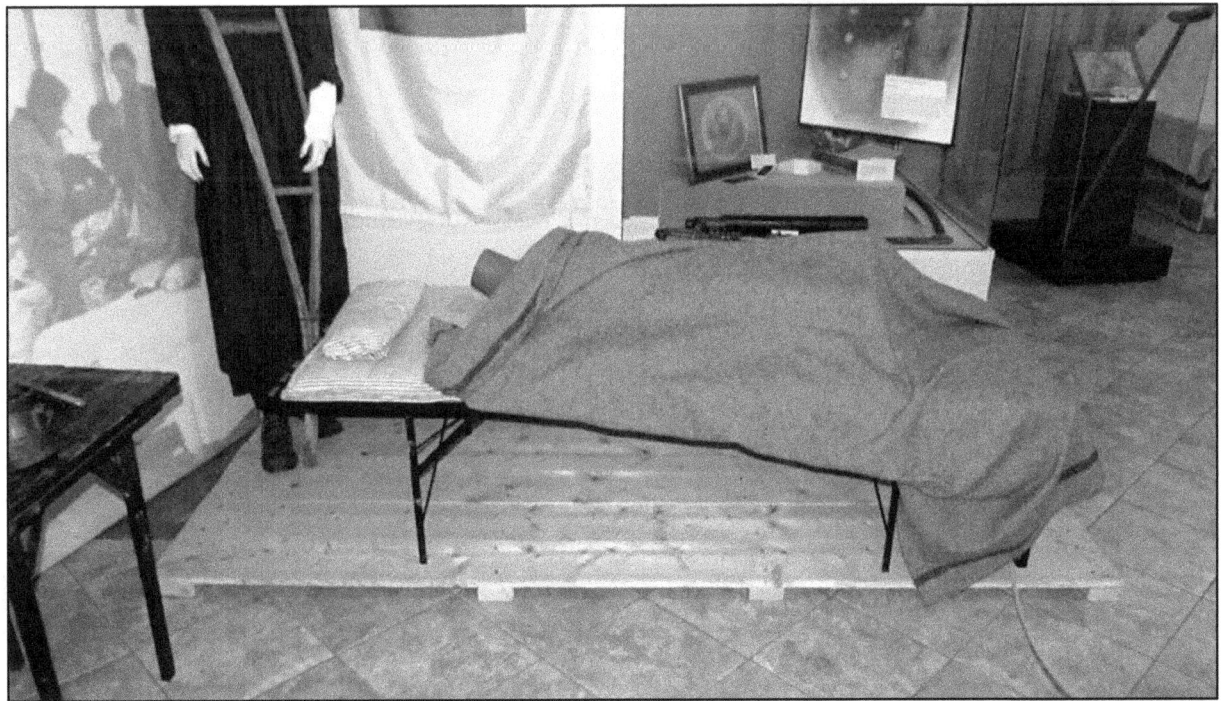

Hospital display at Point Lookout

Point Lookout prisoner photographs are displayed at the museum.

3D model on Fort Lincoln

Political Prisoners Who Died at Point Lookout

The author has come into procession of an old government document listing all of the prisoners who died at Point Lookout Prison Camp. What is extraordinary about this list is it contains the names of over 38 civilians that also died at the prison. To my knowledge this is the first time this list has ever appeared in print. The name of this document is *List of Confederate soldier and sailors who, while prisoners of war, died at Point Lookout, Maryland.* In the following table this document will be referred to as LCSS.

	Name	Residence	Date of Death	Remarks
A	Unknown			
B	Banks, William

Political Prisoner | Citizen of Middlesex County, Virginia | 2/23/1865, Buried at Point Lookout Old Confederate Cemetery | Reference: LCSS, Page 533 |
| | Blasingame, John

Political Prisoner | Unknown | 11/5/1864, Buried at Point Lookout Old Confederate Cemetery | Reference: LCSS, page 536 |
| **C** | Calhoun, D.

Political Prisoner | Citizen of Bertie County, North Carolina | 5/8/1864, Buried at Point Lookout Old Confederate Cemetery | Reference: LCSS, page 540 |
| | Carter, J. J.

Political Prisoner | Citizen of Bowling Green, Kentucky | 3/22/1865, Buried at Point Lookout Old Confederate Cemetery | Reference: LCSS, page 542 |
| | Chamlers, James

Political Prisoner | Unknown, Captured on Blockade Runner | 3/13/1865, Buried at Point Lookout Old Confederate Cemetery | Reference: LCSS, page 542 |

	Name	Residence	Date of Death	Remarks
	Cheatham, F. T. Political Prisoner	Citizen of Bermuda Hundred, Virginia	3/23/1865, Buried at Point Lookout Old Confederate Cemetery	Reference: LCSS, page 543
	Clark, Munford Political Prisoner	Citizen of Charles City Court House, State Unknown	9/16/1864, Buried at Point Lookout Old Confederate Cemetery	Reference: LCSS, page 543
	Cocke, J. B. Political Prisoner	Citizen of Virginia	11/24/1864, Buried at Point Lookout Old Confederate Cemetery	Reference: LCSS, page 544
	Coghill, J. O. Political Prisoner	Citizen of Chesterfield County, Virginia	8/26/1864, Buried at Point Lookout Old Confederate Cemetery	Reference: LCSS, page 544
	Cramp, Lemuel Political Prisoner	Unknown	12/25/1864, Buried at Point Lookout Old Confederate Cemetery Reference: LCSS, page 546	
D	Deagle, William H. Political Prisoner	Citizen of Middlesex County, Virginia	11/11/1863, Buried at Point Lookout Old Confederate Cemetery	6/22/1864, Middlesex County, Virginia, Received From US Gunboat Jacob Bell. Reference: LCSS, Page 548
	Deda, William T. Political Prisoner	Citizen of Louden County, Virginia	7/22/1864, Buried at Point Lookout Old Confederate Cemetery	Reference: LCSS, Page 549
F	Unknown			

	Name	Residence	Date of Death	Remarks
G	George, J. M. Political Prisoner	Citizen of Lancaster County, Virginia	4/26/1864, Buried at Point Lookout Old Confederate Cemetery	Reference: LCSS, Page 556
	Gelham, Marcus Political Prisoner	Citizen of Prince George County, Virginia	7/28/1864, Buried at Point Lookout Old Confederate Cemetery	Reference: LCSS, Page 556
	Giles, Anthony Political Prisoner	Citizen of Amelia County, Virginia	5/9/1865, Buried at Point Lookout Old Confederate Cemetery	Reference: LCSS, Page 557
H	Humphrey, William F. Political Prisoner	Citizen of Culpepper County, Virginia	8/21/1864, Buried at Point Lookout Old Confederate Cemetery	Reference: LCSS, Page 566
I	Unknown			
J	Jennings, James Political Prisoner	Citizen of Chesterfield County, Virginia	8/23/1864, Buried at Point Lookout Old Confederate Cemetery	Reference: LCSS, Page 568
	Jones, G. Political Prisoner	Citizen of Spotsylvania, Virginia	9/16/1864, Buried at Point Lookout Old Confederate Cemetery	Reference: LCSS, Page 569
	Jones, Jerry Political Prisoner	Citizen of Virginia	11/9/1864, Buried at Point Lookout Old Confederate Cemetery	Reference: LCSS, Page 569

	Name	Residence	Date of Death	Remarks
K	Unknown			
L	Laughlin, Seth Political Prisoner	Citizen of Randolph, State Unknown	8/2/1864, Buried at Point Lookout Old Confederate Cemetery	Reference: LCSS, Page 572
M	McDonald, John Political Prisoner	Citizen of Montgomery County, North Carolina	1/11/1865, Buried at Point Lookout Old Confederate Cemetery	Reference: LCSS, Page 576
	McGuire, F. W. Political Prisoner	Citizen of Westmoreland County, Virginia	10/19/1864, Buried at Point Lookout Old Confederate Cemetery	Reference: LCSS, Page 576
	Miller, Philip Political Prisoner	Citizen of Virginia	5/21/1865, Buried at Point Lookout Old Confederate Cemetery	Reference: LCSS, Page 579
	Monroe, Henry Political Prisoner	Citizen of Fairfax County, Virginia	8/11/1864, Buried at Point Lookout Old Confederate Cemetery	Reference: LCSS, Page 580
N	Noel, E. G. Political Prisoner	Citizen of Chesterfield County, Virginia	8/16/1864, Buried at Point Lookout Old Confederate Cemetery	Reference: LCSS, Page 582
O	Unknown			

	Name	Residence	Date of Death	Remarks
P	Parr, James Political Prisoner	Citizen of Isle of Wight County, Virginia	11/10/1864, Buried at Point Lookout Old Confederate Cemetery	Reference: LCSS, Page 584
	Porter, A. G. Political Prisoner	Citizen of Effingham County, Georgia	2/7/1865, Buried at Point Lookout Old Confederate Cemetery	Reference: LCSS, Page 587
Q	Unknown			
R	Rivers, Drew Political Prisoner	Citizen of Chesterfield District, South Carolina	5/8/65, Buried at Point Lookout Old Confederate Cemetery	Reference: LCSS, Page 591
	Roberts, Isaac Political Prisoner	Citizen of Bullock County, Georgia	3/6/1865, Buried at Point Lookout Old Confederate Cemetery	Reference: LCSS, Page 591
S	Sewall, John C. Political Prisoner	Citizen of Fairfax County, Virginia	1/6/1865, Buried at Point Lookout Old Confederate Cemetery	Reference: LCSS, Page 594
	Shirley, James D. Political Prisoner	Citizen of Prince William County, Virginia	7/22/1864, Buried at Point Lookout Old Confederate Cemetery	Reference: LCSS, Page 595
	Southard, J. M. Political Prisoner	Citizen of Prince William County, Virginia	5/12/1865, Buried at Point Lookout Old Confederate Cemetery	Reference: LCSS, Page 597

	Name	Residence	Date of Death	Remarks
T	Throgdon, Isaac Political Prisoner	Citizen of Randolph County, North Carolina	10/10/1864, Buried at Point Lookout Old Confederate Cemetery	Reference: LCSS, Page 602
U	Unknown			
V	Vaidon, M. F. Political Prisoner	Citizen of Virginia	11/18/1864, Buried at Point Lookout Old Confederate Cemetery	Reference: LCSS, Page 604
	Vaughn, V. Political Prisoner	Citizen of Middlesex County, Virginia	10/12/1864, Buried at Point Lookout Old Confederate Cemetery	Reference: LCSS, Page 604
W	Weedon, W. A. Political Prisoner	Citizen, Unknown	6/20/1864, Buried at Point Lookout Old Confederate Cemetery	Reference: LCSS, Page 607
	White, Joseph L. Political Prisoner	Citizen of Sumner County, Tennessee	6/6/1865, Buried at Point Lookout Old Confederate Cemetery	Reference: LCSS, Page 608
	Woodyard, James Political Prisoner 1.	Citizen of Fairfax County, Virginia	8/17/1864, Buried at Point Lookout Old Confederate Cemetery	Reference: LCSS, Page 611
X	Unknown			
Y	Unknown			
Z	Unknown			

A Roster of the Confederate Dead at Point Lookout

"At the call of patriotism and duty they encountered the perils of the field, endured the trial of a prison and were faithful even unto death."
Confederate Memorial at Point Lookout, Maryland

This roster was compiled by Richard H. Triebe. The original roster is from the bronze tablets on the Point Lookout Prison Camp monument. The information I used to make this roster was found at the National Archives and Records Administration. My roster lists 3,826 Confederate prisoners and gives ten pieces of information about each soldier. There are a few soldiers which I have been unable to locate. This is probably due to misspelling of the soldier's name or it might result from having the wrong regiment or even the wrong state. Many of the captured soldiers were wounded, but it was never recorded in their files. If a soldier had been captured at the battle of Gettysburg and his records show he was taken prisoner on July 4th or 5th, it is very likely he was wounded or sick. Many of these men would have been arrested in field hospitals and therefore were not taken into custody until after the battle. This roster also includes 470 prisoners who died at Point Lookout Prison Camp, but were never included on the bronze tablets of the Federal monument. If the reader has any information regarding these men please email me at richardtriebe@aol.com. Only information that is backed up by historical documents will be included in this roster. Such items as published regimental histories or the soldier's records from the National Archives may be submitted as proof of service.

Name	Age	Enlisted	Residence	Unit	Captured	Date and Cause of Death
Aaron, John W. Private	Unk	8/11/1862, Tuscaloosa, Alabama	Tuscaloosa County, Alabama	Co. G, 51st Alabama Infantry	6/27/1863, Shelbyville, Tennessee	Died of Chronic Diarrhea 11/10/1863
Abercrombie, A. Private	Unk	5/1/1862, Camp Tripp, Virginia	Unknown	Co. B, 1st South Carolina Cavalry	Virginia, 9/22/1863, Near Madison Court House, Virginia	Died of Unknown Causes, 1/29/1864
Abernathy, Robert T. Private Name Not On Monument	32	5/3/1863 Nashville, Nash County, North Carolina, Volunteer	Nash County, North Carolina	Co. A, 47th North Carolina Infantry	10/27/1864 Burgess' Mill, Near Petersburg, Virginia	Died of Chronic Diarrhea and Scurvy, 2/3/1865
Abrams, C. G. Private	Unk	3/31/1862, Fort Lowery, Virginia	Essex County, Virginia	Co. K, 55th Virginia Infantry	8/6/1863, Glouster Point, Virginia	Died of Chronic Diarrhea, 2/17/1865

Name	Age	Enlisted	Residence	Unit	Captured	Date and Cause of Death
Abshire, Robert T. Private	Unk	5/23/1861, Lynchburg, Virginia	Franklin County, Virginia	Co. B, 24th Virginia Infantry	7/3/1863, Gettysburg, Pennsylvania	Died of Unknown Causes, 2/12/1864
Abread, B. A. Private	Unk	Unknown	Unknown	Co. B, 3rd North Carolina Junior Reserves	12/25/1864, Fort Fisher, North Carolina	Died of Rubeola, (Measles), 2/4/1865
Actor, John A. Private Name Not On Monument	Unk	Unknown	Unknown	Co. K, 6th North Carolina Infantry	5/30/1864 Mechanicsville, Virginia	Died of Inflammation of the Bowels, 7/0/1864
Adams, Alfred H. Private Name Not On Monument	Unk	10/15/1861 Hawley's Store, Georgia	Unknown	Co. E, 38th Georgia Infantry	7/5/1863 Waterloo, Pennsylvania	Died of Acute Diarrhea, 8/27/1864
Adams, C. K. Private	19	11/1/1863, Raleigh, North Carolina	Wake County, North Carolina	Co. H, 21st North Carolina Infantry	9/19/1864, Winchester, Virginia, Gunshot Wound of Head	Cause of Death, Apoplexy (stroke), Date Unknown
Adams, Edward L. Private	31	5/25/1861, Halifax County Court House, Virginia	Halifax County, Virginia, Farmer	Co. H, 3rd Virginia Cavalry	7/3/1863, Gettysburg, Pennsylvania	Died of Chronic Diarrhea, 1/19/1864
Adams, Homer Private	Unk	2/1863, Unknown	Unknown	Co. A, 13th Alabama Infantry	7/3/1863, Gettysburg, Pennsylvania	Died of Unknown Causes, 12/23/1863
Adams, J. S. Private	Unk	Unknown	Unknown	Georgia Reserve Infantry	Unknown	Unable to Locate
Adams, Joshua J. Private	19	3/27/1862, Surry County, North Carolina	Surry County, North Carolina	Co. B, 53rd North Carolina Infantry	7/11/1864, Near Washington, DC	Died of Chronic Diarrhea, 10/26/1864,

Name	Age	Enlisted	Residence	Unit	Captured	Date and Cause of Death
Adams, Samuel Lee Sergeant	22	11/2/1861, Alexander County, North Carolina	Alexander County, North Carolina	Co. G, 38th North Carolina Infantry	5/23/184, North Anna River, Virginia	Died of Chronic Diarrhea, 4/20/1865
Adams, W. M. Private	Unk	3/11/1863, Hartwell, Georgia	Hart County, Georgia	Co. C, 16th Georgia Infantry	6/1/1864, Gaines mill or Farm, Virginia	Date and Cause of Death Unknown
Adcock, Thomas A. Private	Unk	3/10/1862, Buckingham County, Virginia	Buckingham County, Virginia	Co. A, 57th Virginia Infantry	7/3/1863, Gettysburg, Pennsylvania	Died of Unknown Causes, 2/24/1864
Adderton, William Stokes Private Name Not On Monument	24	7/16/1862 Raleigh, North Carolina	Davidson County, North Carolina	Co. D, 14th North Carolina Infantry	5/17/1864 Spotsylvania Court House, Virginia	Died of Unknown Causes, 10/30/1864
Addison, W. S. Private	Unk	Unknown	Unknown	Co. B, 14th South Carolina Infantry	Unknown	Unable to Locate
Adkins, Richard E. Private Name Not On Monument	Unk	6/4/1861 Collands, Virginia	Unknown	Co. A, 38th Virginia Infantry	7/4/1863, Gettysburg, Pennsylvania, Wounded	Date and Cause of Death Unknown
Akers, Joseph H. Private	Unk	3/1/1864, Orange Court House, Virginia	Amherst County, Virginia	Co. E, 2nd Virginia Cavalry	10/19/1864, Cedar Creek or Strasburg, Virginia	Died of Typhoid Fever, 12/19/1864
Albritton, James M. Private	Unk	3/4/1862, Georgetown, Georgia	Quitman County, Georgia	Co. G, 51st Georgia Infantry	7/3/1863, Gettysburg, Pennsylvania	Died of Variola (Smallpox), 12/24/1863
Albritton, Thomas J. Private	Unk	8/15/1862, Dale County, Alabama	Dale County, Alabama	Co. K, 15th Alabama Infantry	7/3/1863, Gettysburg, Pennsylvania	Died of Variola (Smallpox), 11/14/1863
Albritton, William C. Sergeant	Unk	4/5/1863, Macon, Georgia	Bibb County, Georgia	Co. H, 64th Georgia Infantry	8/16/1864, Deep Bottom, Virginia	Died of Typhoid Fever, 1/5/1865
Aldrick, R. M. Private	Unk	Unknown	Unknown	Co. B, 35th Battalion, Virginia Cavalry	9/14/1863, Loudon County, Virginia	Died Unknown Causes, 8/17/1864

Name	Age	Enlisted	Residence	Unit	Captured	Date and Cause of Death
Aldrid, M. J. Private Name Not On Monument	Unk	12/3/1863 Randolph County, North Carolina	Rockingham County, North Carolina	Co. I, 13th North Carolina Infantry	5/6/1864 Wilderness or Mine Run, Virginia	Died of Acute Dysentery, 7/1/1864
Alexander, Basil Private	23	4/23/1861, Fairfax County Court House, Virginia	Fairfax County, Virginia	Co. F, 11th Virginia Cavalry	11/30/1863, Mountsville, Virginia	Died of Unknown Causes, 8/18/1864
Alexander, George W. Sergeant	Unk	7/15/1861, Elberton, Georgia	Unknown	Co. F, 15th Georgia Infantry	Unknown	Died of Chronic Dysentery, 11/19/1864
Alexander, J. N. Corporal	28	2/1/1862, Charlotte, North Carolina, Volunteer	Mecklenburg County, North Carolina	Co. A, 11th North Carolina Infantry	Unknown	Died of Chronic Diarrhea, 11/7/1863
Alexander, John Private	Unk	7/13/1861, Mount Gilead, Virginia	Loudoun County, Virginia	Co. E, 8th Virginia Infantry	Unknown, 10/20/1863	Died of Chronic Diarrhea, 8/29/1864
Alexander, S. M. Private	Unk	Date Unknown, Craven County, North Carolina	Tyrell County, North Carolina	Co. B, 67th North Carolina Infantry	8/10/1863, New Bern, North Carolina	Died of Unknown Causes, 8/27/1864
Alexander, Thomas S. Private	Unk	5/14/1862, Forsyth, Georgia	Monroe County, Georgia	Co. D, 31st Georgia Infantry	7/7/1863, Washington County, Maryland	Died of Variola (Smallpox), 11/7/1863
Alexander, William Private Name Not On Monument	Unk	7/13/1861, Mount Gilead, Virginia	Loudoun County, Virginia	Co. I, 8th Virginia Infantry	11/20/1863 Mountsville, Virginia	Died of Chronic Diarrhea, 8/28/1864
Alford, Julius Private	Unk	Unknown	Unknown	Co. F, 19th Georgia Infantry	8/21/1864, Globe Tavern, Near Weldon Railroad, Virginia	Died of Acute Diarrhea, 10/26/1864
Allen, Bennett Private	Unk	5/2/1862, Camp Moore, Louisiana	Orleans Parish, Louisiana	Co. G, 9th Louisiana Infantry	7/5/1863, South Mountain, Maryland	Died of Variola (Smallpox), 1/3/1864
Allen, E. J. Private	Unk	Unknown	Unknown	Anderson's Brigade	Unknown	Unable to Locate

117

Name	Age	Enlisted	Residence	Unit	Captured	Date and Cause of Death
Allen, George W. Private	36	10/1/1862, Newport, Tennessee	Cocke County, Tennessee	Co. I, 60th Tennessee Mounted Infantry	5/17/ 1863, Big Black Bridge, Near Vicksburg, Mississippi	Date and Cause of Death Unknown
Allen, G. W. Private	Unk	3/4/1862, Starkville, Lee County, Georgia	Lee County, Georgia	Co. B, 51st Georgia Infantry	7/3/1863, Gettysburg, Pennsylvania	Died of Chronic Diarrhea, 1/5/1864
Allen, J. V. Private	Unk	Unknown	Unknown	Co. C, 5th Alabama Infantry	Unknown	Unable to Locate
Allen, James Private	Unk	Unknown	Unknown	Co. E, 59th Alabama Infantry	Unknown	Unable to Locate
Allen, John Private	25	10/3/1862, Morristown, Tennessee	Hamblen County, Tennessee	Co. C, 61st Tennessee Mounted Infantry	5/17/ 1863, Big Black Bridge, Near Vicksburg, Mississippi	Died of Unknown Causes, 10/?/1863
Allen, Joseph H. Private	Unk	5/27/1863, Place Unknown	Unknown	Co. I, 11th Virginia Infantry	5/21/1864, Milford Station, Virginia	Died of Chronic Diarrhea, 1/28/1865
Allen, Ruffin Private Name Not On Monument	33	2/1/1863 Chapel Hill, North Carolina, Volunteer	Orange County, North Carolina	Co. G, 11th North Carolina Infantry	10/14/1863, Bristoe Station, Virginia	Died of Unknown Causes, 9/3/1864
Allen, Thomas J. Private Name Not On Monument	Unk	5/10/1862 Cartersville, Georgia	Bartow County, Georgia	Co. K, 60th Georgia Infantry	5/20/1864 Spotsylvania Court House, Virginia	Died of Unknown Causes, 9/6/1864
Allen, William Private	Unk	2/22/1863, Stewart County, Georgia	Stewart County, Georgia	Co. K, 2nd Georgia Infantry	7/3/1863, Gettysburg, Pennsylvania	Died of Unknown Causes, 2/1/1864
Allen, William W. Private	Unk	10/18/1862, Taylorsburg, Tennessee	Unknown	Co. C, 26th Tennessee Infantry	5/16/1864, Near Resaca, Sugar Valley, Georgia.	Died From Inflammation of Lungs (Pneumonia), 4/25/1865

Name	Age	Enlisted	Residence	Unit	Captured	Date and Cause of Death
Alley, Richard Private	38	5/9/1862, Franklin County, North Carolina, Volunteer	Franklin County, North Carolina	Co. K, 44th North Carolina Infantry	10/27/1864, Boyton Plank Road or Burgess' Mill, Petersburg, Virginia	Died of Chronic Diarrhea, 1/4/1865
Allison, Bassell Private	Unk	9/14/1862, Salem, Virginia	Roanoke County, Virginia	Co. H, 6th Virginia Cavalry	8/20/1863, Fauquier County, Virginia	Died of Unknown Causes, 8/22/1864
Allison, Beatie J. Private Name Not On Monument	Unk	9/14/1862, Smyth County, Virginia	Unknown	Co. E, 23rd Battalion Virginia Infantry	9/19/1864, Winchester, Virginia	Died of Chronic Dysentery, 3/16/1865
Allison, Lee Private	18	6/21/1861, Alamance County, North Carolina	Orange County, North Carolina, Farmer	Co. K, 6th North Carolina	7/3/1863, Gettysburg, Pennsylvania	Died of Diphtheria, 10/31/1863
Allison, Thomas J. Private	Unk	Unknown	Unknown	9th Alabama Cavalry	6/27/1863, Shelbyville, Tennessee	Died of Chronic Diarrhea, 1/28/1864
Allison, William Private	Unk	9/14/1861, Smyth County, Virginia	Unknown	Co. E, 23rd Virginia Infantry	9/19/1864, Winchester, Virginia	Died of Pneumonia, 2/2/1865
Allmond, Nathan A. Private	21	1/15/1863, Wake County, North Carolina	Wake County, North Carolina	Co. I, 47th North Carolina Infantry	Unknown	Died of Unknown Causes, 4/4/1864
Allmond, Wiley P. Private	22	5/6/1862, Wake County, North Carolina, Volunteer	Wake County, North Carolina	Co. I, 47th North Carolina Infantry	10/14/1863, Bristoe Station, Virginia	Died of Unknown Causes, 5/3/1864
Allred, James F. Private	Unk	10/6/1863, Camp Vance, North Carolina	Burke County, North Carolina	Co. M, 16th North Carolina Infantry	5/23/1864, Jericho Ford, North Anna, Virginia	Died of Scurvy, 3/15/1865

Name	Age	Enlisted	Residence	Unit	Captured	Date and Cause of Death
Allred, Thomas M. Private	20	3/18/1862, Randolph County, North Carolina, Volunteer	Randolph County, North Carolina	Co. L, 22nd North Carolina Infantry	7/3/1863, Gettysburg, Pennsylvania	Died of Chronic Dysentery, 11/12/1864
Alman, H. G. Private	Unk	5/31/1861, Atlanta, Georgia	Heard County, Georgia	Co. G, 7th Georgia Infantry	5/22/1864, Culpeper, Virginia	Died of Unknown Causes, 8/18/1864
Allman, Leonard Private	29	3/1/1862, Cabarrus County, North Carolina, Volunteer	Cabarrus County, North Carolina	Co. B, 7th North Carolina Infantry	7/14/1863, Falling Waters, Maryland	Died of Unknown Causes, 3/8/1864
Almond, G. F. Private	Unk	Unknown	Unknown	Co. C, 5th North Carolina Infantry	7/5/1863, Gettysburg, Pennsylvania	Died of Unknown Causes, 1/9/1864
Almond, John M. Private Name Not On Monument	28	8/8/1862 Stanly County, North Carolina, Conscript	Unknown, Farmer	Co. F, 5th North Carolina Infantry	7/6/1863 Hagerstown, Pennsylvania	Died of Smallpox, 1/8/1864
Almond, Nathan Private Name Not On Monument	24	3/25/1862 Stanly County, North Carolina, Volunteer	Stanly County, North Carolina	Co. I, 52nd North Carolina Infantry	10/14/1863, Bristoe Station, Virginia	Died of Acute Diarrhea, 10/13/1864
Alphin, Calvin M. Private Name Not On Monument	30	12/24/1861 Wake County, North Carolina, Volunteer	Duplin County, North Carolina, Farmer	Co. A, 38th North Carolina Infantry	5/6/1864, Wilderness, Virginia	Died of Chronic Diarrhea, 2/27/1865
Alread, B. A. Private Name Not On Monument	Unk	Unknown	Unknown	Co. B, 2nd North Carolina Junior Reserve Infantry	12/25/1864, Fort Fisher, North Carolina	Died of Rubeola (Measles) 2/4/1865

120

Name	Age	Enlisted	Residence	Unit	Captured	Date and Cause of Death
Alread, James E. Private	Unk	3/1/1862, Camp Moore, Louisiana	Orleans Parish, Louisiana	Co. A, 12th Louisiana Infantry	5/16/1863, Champion Hill, Tennessee	Died of Unknown Causes, 12/11/1863
Alsbrook, S. C. Private	33	6/24/1863, Halifax County, North Carolina, Conscript	Halifax County, North Carolina	Co. A, 30th North Carolina Infantry	11/7/1863, Kelly's Ford, Rappahannock, Virginia	Died of Chronic Dysentery, 2/8/1864
Alson, P. Private	Unk	Unknown	Unknown	Co. I, 51st Virginia Infantry	9/19/1864, Winchester, Virginia	Died of Unknown Causes, 4/23/1865
Aman, Jesse Private Name Not On Monument	28	8/1/1862 Jacksonville, North Carolina	Onslow County, North Carolina	Co. H, 3rd North Carolina Cavalry	12/17/1863, Greenville, North Carolina	Died of Chronic Diarrhea, 3/4/1865
Aman, Starkey B. Private	Unk	5/1/1862, Onslow County, North Carolina	Onslow County, North Carolina	Co. I, 27th North Carolina Infantry	3/31/1865, Humphrey's Station, Virginia	Died of Chronic Diarrhea, 5/28/1865
Amburn, Francis M. Private	19	3/20/1862, Camp Mangum, Stokes County, North Carolina	Stokes County, North Carolina, Farmer	Co. F, 53rd North Carolina Infantry	5/19/1864, Spotsylvania Court House, Virginia	Died of Unknown Causes, 6/19/1864
Amerson, Abraham Private	Unk	10/5/1861, Columbus, Georgia	Muscogee County, Georgia	Co. B, 31st Georgia Infantry	7/3/1863, Gettysburg, Pennsylvania	Died of Intermittent Fever, 11/6/1863
Amick, James J. Private	Unk	12/20/1861, Dutch Fork, Lexington District, South Carolina	Unknown	Co. I, 15th South Carolina Infantry	8/6/1864, Halltown, Virginia	Died of Scurvy, 6/20/1865
Amos, James Private	27	4/1/1862, Camp Hampton, Charleston, South Carolina	Spartanburg District, South Carolina, Collier	Co. I, 18th South Carolina Infantry	4/2/1865, Sutherland Station, Virginia	Died of Chronic Dysentery, 6/12/1865

Name	Age	Enlisted	Residence	Unit	Captured	Date and Cause of Death
Amos, J. Thomas Private	31	9/18/1862, Lockapoka, Alabama	Lee County, Alabama	Co. I, 47th Alabama Infantry	5/6/1864, Spotsylvania Court House, Virginia	Died of Unknown Causes, 5/30/1864
Anders, Thomas J. See: Andrews, Thomas J.				Co. D, 16th North Carolina Infantry		
Anderson, Charles Moore Private	34	7/16/1861, Staunton, Virginia	Augusta County, Virginia Taylor	Co. D, 52nd Virginia Infantry	9/24/1864, Fisher's Hill, Virginia	Died of Chronic Dysentery, 1/2/1865
Anderson, Jerome B. Sergeant	30	10/14/1861, Smyth County, Virginia	Smyth County, Virginia Laborer	Co. E, 50th Virginia Infantry	9/19/1864, Winchester, Virginia	Died of Chronic Dysentery, 1/29/1865
Anderson, Noah Private	Unk	Unknown	Unknown	Co. A, 67th North Carolina Infantry	4/26/1864, Swift Creek, Virginia	Died of Chronic Dysentery, 1/26/1865
Anderton, William J. Private	Unk	7/15/1862, Raleigh, Wake County, North Carolina	Northampton County, North Carolina,	Co. H, 1st North Carolina Cavalry	9/22/1863, Madison Court House, Virginia	Died of Chronic Diarrhea, 2/23/1864
Andrews, Charles P. Private	Unk	3/14/1864, Indian Creek, Virginia	Unknown	Monroe Virginia Light Artillery Battery	9/19/1864, Winchester, Virginia	Died From Inflammation of Lungs (Pneumonia), 4/19/1865
Andrews, John H. Private Name Not On Monument	23	8/23/1861 Camp Trusdale, Tennessee	Unknown	Co. B, 23rd Tennessee Infantry	6/17/1864, Near Petersburg, Virginia	Died of Unknown Causes, 7/13/1864

Name	Age	Enlisted	Residence	Unit	Captured	Date and Cause of Death
Andrews, Thomas J. Private	26	9/27/1862, Raleigh, North Carolina, Conscript	Orange County, North Carolina	Co. D, 16th North Carolina Infantry	5/23/1864, North Anna River, Virginia	Died of Unknown Causes, 8/30/1864
Angel, John Private Name Not On Monument	26	11/6/1861 Washington, Beaufort County, North Carolina	Beaufort County, North Carolina	Co. B, 61st North Carolina Infantry	9/30/1864, Chaffin's Farm or Fort Harrison, Virginia	Died of Chronic Diarrhea and Scurvy, 2/8/1865
Angus, William Private	Unk	4/22/1862, Gordonsville, Virginia	Orange County, Virginia	Co. E, 13th Virginia Infantry	5/19/1864, Spotsylvania Court House, Virginia	Died of Unknown Causes, 8/2/1864
Ansell, John H. Private	Unk	6/20/1861, Panne County, Virginia	Panne County, Virginia	Co. F, 15th Virginia Infantry	9/14/1863, Near Culpepper, Virginia	Died of Pneumonia, 10/18/1863
Anthony, A. H. Sergeant	Unk	6/13/1861, Camp McDonald, Georgia	Bartow, Georgia	Co. H, 18th Georgia Infantry	10/19/1864, Cedar Creek or Strasburg, Virginia	Died of Congestive Intermittent Fever, 5/8/1865
Anthony, Philip S. Sergeant	Unk	6/2/1861, Cascade, Virginia	Unknown	Co. K, 38th Virginia Infantry	7/4/1863, Gettysburg, Pennsylvania	Died of Pneumonia, 2/11/1865
Apple, John A. Private	19	4/21/1862, Guilford County, North Carolina	Guilford County, North Carolina,	Co. A, 53rd North Carolina Infantry	4/2/1865, Petersburg, Virginia	Died of Pneumonia, 5/31/1865
Arant, John W. Private Name Not On Monument	Unk	12/24/1861 Orangeburg District, South Carolina	Unknown	Co. A, 5th South Carolina Cavalry	12/1/1864 Stony Creek, Virginia	Died of Pneumonia, 2/22/1865

Name	Age	Enlisted	Residence	Unit	Captured	Date and Cause of Death
Arbogast, William S. Private	Unk	4/5/1862, Camp Shenandoah, Virginia	Pendleton County, West Virginia	Co. E, 25th Virginia Infantry	7/3/1863, Chambersburg, Pennsylvania	Died of Chronic Diarrhea, 1/30/1865
Archer, Calvin Sergeant	Unk	8/6/1861, Nansemond County, Virginia	Nansemond County, Virginia	Co. E, 6th Virginia Infantry	10/27/1864, Boyton Plank Road or Burgess' Mill, Virginia	Died of Pneumonia, 4/2/1865
Ardenfield, J. Private	Unk	5/28/1863, Quincy, Florida	Dougherty, Georgia	Co. D, 64th Georgia Infantry	6/17/1864, Petersburg, Virginia	Died of Chronic Diarrhea, 9/16/1864
Ardis, J. G. Private	Unk	4/8/1861, Savanna, Georgia	Unknown	Co. C, 18th Georgia Battalion Infantry	4/6/1865, High Bridge, Virginia	Died of General Debility (Loss of Strength, Feeble), 6/23/1865
Armfield, John J. Private	Unk	Unknown	Unknown	Co. C, 30th North Carolina Infantry	4/6/1865, Farmville, Virginia	Died of Chronic Diarrhea, 6/18/1865
Armstrong, Elihu Private Name Not On Monument	23	7/4/1861 Talladega, Alabama	Talladega County, Alabama	Co. B, 5th Alabama Infantry	5/5/1864 Wilderness, Virginia	Died of Unknown Causes, 7/1/1864
Armstrong, Jared Private Name Not On Monument	19	6/11/1861 Hevener's Store, Virginia	Highland County, Virginia, Farm Hand	Co. F, 25th Virginia Infantry	4/6/1865 Farmville, Virginia	Died of Chronic Diarrhea, 6/26/1865
Armstrong, John J. Sergeant	Unk	7/5/1861, Camp Boone, Tennessee	Unknown	Co. I, 3rd Kentucky Mounted Infantry	5/17/1863, Baker's Creek, Champion Hill, Tennessee	Died of Unknown Causes, 5/1/1864
Armstrong, John Private	42	2/19/1862, Duplin County, North Carolina	Sampson County, North Carolina, Cooper	Co. B, 51st North Carolina Infantry	9/30/1864, Fort Harrison, Virginia	Died of Chronic Diarrhea, 12/10/1864

Name	Age	Enlisted	Residence	Unit	Captured	Date and Cause of Death
Arnett, Samuel M. Private	42	7/13/1861, Leesburg, Virginia	Loudoun County, Virginia	Co. A, 8th Virginia Infantry	Gettysburg, Pennsylvania 7/3/1863	Died of Unknown Causes, 1/6/1864
Arney, W. P. Private	Unk	5/26/1864, Camp Vance, North Carolina	Burke County, North Carolina	Co. G, 3rd North Carolina Junior Reserves	12/25/1864, Fort Fisher, North Carolina	Died of Pneumonia, 2/16/1865
Arnold, Julius B. D. Private	Unk	7/15/1861, Elbert County, Georgia	Elbert County, Georgia	Co. I, 15th Georgia Battalion Infantry	7/2/1863, Gettysburg, Pennsylvania	Died of Chronic Diarrhea, 5/6/1864
Arnold, Marcus Private	Unk	5/17/1863, Grace Church, Virginia	Unknown	Co. A, 6th Alabama Infantry	4/2/1865, Petersburg, Virginia	Died of Intermittent Fever, 6/2/1865
Ashford, Samuel A. Sergeant	Unk	11/10/1862, Richmond, Virginia	Henrico County, Virginia	Co. C, 25th Virginia Infantry	4/6/1865, Amelia Court House, Virginia	Died of Acute Dysentery, 6/3/1865
Ashley, Richard S. Private	24	7/20/1861, Camp Pickens, Sandy Springs, Anderson District, South Carolina	Unknown	Co. G, 1st South Carolina Rifles	7/14/1863, Falling Waters, Maryland	Died of Variola (Smallpox), 8/23/1864
Ashworth, William O. Private	Unk	8/31/1861, Mason's Hill, Virginia	Unknown	Co. C, 24th Virginia Infantry	Gettysburg, Pennsylvania, 7/3/1863	Died of Acute Bronchitis, 2/10/1864
Askew, John Private	19	8/10/1861, Warren County, North Carolina, Volunteer	Warren County, North Carolina	Co. B, 30th North Carolina Infantry	11/7/1863, Kelly's Ford, Rappahannock, Virginia	Died of Unknown Causes, 8/5/1864
Askew, Thomas P. Private	17	7/4/1861, Madison County, North Carolina, Volunteer	Madison County, North Carolina	Co. H, 2nd North Carolina Infantry	7/3/1863, Gunshot Wound of the Finger, Gettysburg, Pennsylvania	Died of Chronic Diarrhea, 2/4/1864

Name	Age	Enlisted	Residence	Unit	Captured	Date and Cause of Death
Atkin, Thomas S. Sergeant	18	3/1/1863, Buncombe County, North Carolina	Buncombe County, North Carolina	Co. K, 11th North Carolina Infantry	10/27/1864, Boyton Plank Road or Burgess' Mill, Virginia	Died of Chronic Diarrhea, 1/8/1865
Atkins, John H. Private	Unk	3/6/1862, Richmond, Virginia	Henrico County, Virginia	Co. G, 22nd Battalion Virginia Infantry	7/14/1863, Falling Waters, Maryland	Died of Chronic Diarrhea, 12/24/1864
Atkins, Samuel W. Private	28	8/19/1861, Crab Tree, Wake County, North Carolina	Wake County, North Carolina	Co. D, 26th North Carolina Infantry	7/3/1863, Gettysburg, Pennsylvania	Died of Acute Diarrhea, 10/23/1864
Atkins, William Private	26	7/4/1862, Salisbury, Alamance County, North Carolina, Volunteer	Alamance County, North Carolina	Co. I, 57th North Carolina Infantry	11/7/1863, Rappahannock Station, Virginia	Died of Unknown Causes, 2/14/1864
Atkinson, Wiley Private	Unk	2/3/1862, Shepherdsville Columbus County, North Carolina, Volunteer	Columbus County, North Carolina	Co. C, 7th North Carolina Infantry	5/6/1864, Wilderness, Virginia	Died of Intermittent Fever, 7/24/1864
Atphin, Calvin Private	30	12/24/1861, Wake County, North Carolina	Duplin County, North Carolina, Farmer	Co. A, 38th North Carolina Infantry	5/6/1864, Wilderness, Virginia	Died of Chronic Diarrhea, 2/27/1865
Attaway, T. G. Private	Unk	10/4/1861, Edgefield District, South Carolina	Unknown	Co. F, 27th South Carolina Infantry	2/20/1865, Fort Anderson, Near Town Creek, North Carolina	Died of Acute Diarrhea, 6/18/1865
Attmore, Sitgreaves Private Name Not On Monument	35	3/22/1861 Camp Holmes, North Carolina	Wake County, North Carolina	Co. K, 10th Regiment North Carolina Heavy Artillery	1/15/1865, Fort Fisher, North Carolina	Died of Chronic Diarrhea, 5/22/1865

Name	Age	Enlisted	Residence	Unit	Captured	Date and Cause of Death
Austin, David A. Private	26	4/8/1862, Lenoir County, North Carolina	Alexander County, North Carolina	Co. G, 37th North Carolina Infantry	5/23/1864, Milford, Virginia	Died of Chronic Dysentery, 3/8/1865
Austin, J. Private	18	7/16/1862, Raliegh, North Carolina, Conscript	Johnson County, North Carolina, Farmer	Co. D, 5th North Carolina Infantry	5/17/1864, Spotsylvania Court House, Virginia	Transferred to Elmira, Died of Smallpox at Elmira, 3/19/1865
Austin, James M. Private Name Not On Monument	39	6/19/1861 Buckingham Court House, Virginia	Buckingham County, Virginia	Co. E, 21st Virginia Infantry	9/25/1864 Harrisburg, Virginia	Died of Consumption 3/20/1865
Austin, John G. Sergeant Name Not On Monument	31	4/3/1862, Taylorsville, Alexander County, North Carolina, Volunteer	Burke County, North Carolina	Co. H, 55th North Carolina Infantry	7/3/1863, Gettysburg, Pennsylvania	Died of Chronic Diarrhea 11/5/1863
Austin, John L. Private	22	9/16/1861, Union County, North Carolina	Union County, North Carolina, Farmer	Co. D, 37th North Carolina Infantry	7/3/1863, Gettysburg, Pennsylvania	Died of Typhoid Fever, 11/19/1863
Austin, Joseph B. Private Name Not On Monument	27	7/8/1862 Yanceyville, North Carolina	Unknown	Co. B, 4th North Carolina Cavalry	7/19/1863 Ashby's Gap, Virginia	Died of Unknown Causes 12/15/1863
Autry, Newsome Private	26	4/16/1863, Sampson County, North Carolina	Unknown, Laborer	Co. A, 36th North Carolina Heavy Artillery	1/15/1865, Fort Fisher, North Carolina	Died of Unknown Causes, 3/2/1865

Name	Age	Enlisted	Residence	Unit	Captured	Date and Cause of Death
Avant, J. R. Sergeant	Unk	12/20/1861, Georgetown, South Carolina	Kingstree, South Carolina	Co. A, 21st South Carolina Infantry	8/21/1864, Globe Tavern, Near Weldon Railroad, North Carolina	Died of Dropsy, 1/15/1865
Avant, J. W. Private	Unk	Unknown	Unknown	Co. A, 5th South Carolina Cavalry	Unknown	Unable to Locate
Avery, Furney Private	37	4/28/1863, Wake County, North Carolina	Craven County, North Carolina	Co. E, 4th North Carolina Infantry	7/23/1863, Manassas, Virginia	Died of Chronic Diarrhea, 11/21/1863
Avery, Joseph Private	Unk	3/20/1864, Macon, Georgia	Henry County, Georgia	Co. H, 27th Georgia Infantry	3/19/1865, Bentonville, North Carolina	Died of Chronic Diarrhea, 6/24/1865
Ayers, Anderson K. Private Name Not On Monument	Unk	6/26/1863 Lewisburg, Virginia	Greenbrier County, West Virginia	Co. G, 26th Virginia Battalion Infantry	5/31/1864, Cold Harbor, Virginia	Died of Measles, 7/9/1864
Ayers, Jefferson Private	Unk	12/9/1861, Camp Hampton, South Carolina	Lancaster County, South Carolina	Co. K, 17th South Carolina Infantry	5/25/1865, Hatchers Run, Near Richmond, Virginia, Gunshot Wound Over Left Eye	Died of Chronic Diarrhea, 7/2/1865
Ayers, Nathaniel M. Private	24	4/24/1861, Fancy Grove, Virginia	Bedford County, Virginia, Farmer	Co. B, 14th Virginia Infantry	7/3/1863, Gettysburg, Pennsylvania	Died of Unknown Causes, 4/6/1864
Aylor, Thomas J. Private	Unk	4/24/1863, Madison Court House, Virginia	Madison County, Virginia	Co. C, 4th Virginia Cavalry	10/1/1864, Port Republic, Virginia	Died of Chronic Diarrhea, 2/22/1865

Name	Age	Enlisted	Residence	Unit	Captured	Date and Cause of Death
Ayres, Richard R. Private	35	2/2/1863, Culpeper Court House, Virginia	Davis Mills, Bedford County, Virginia, Farmer	Co. F, 2nd Virginia Cavalry	7/3/1863, Gettysburg, Pennsylvania	Died of Unknown Causes, 1/22/1864

Name	Age	Enlisted	Residence	Unit	Captured	Date and Cause of Death
Babb, John Private	Unk	5/10/1862, Cartersville, Georgia	Bartow County, Georgia	Co. K, 60th Georgia Infantry	7/3/1863, Gettysburg, Pennsylvania	Died of Unknown Causes, 11/16/1863
Bachelor, James N. See: Batchelor, James N.				Co. G, 35th Georgia Infantry		
Backman, Jonathan Private	23	9/27/1862, Blountsville, Tennessee	Unknown	Co. F, 61st Tennessee Mounted Infantry	5/19/1863, Big Black Bridge, Near Vicksburg, Mississippi	Died of Chronic Diarrhea and Scurvy, 1/4/1864
Badson, Calvin Private Name Not On Monument	Unk	2/25/1863 Onslow County, North Carolina	Onslow County, North Carolina	Co. E, 5th North Carolina Cavalry	9/10/1864, Petersburg, Virginia	Died of Chronic Diarrhea, 3/24/1865
Baggly, Thomas W. Private	37	7/4/1862, Statesville, Iredell County, North Carolina	Iredell County, North Carolina, Wagon Maker	Co. G, 57th North Carolina Infantry	2/6/1865, Hatcher's Run, Virginia	Died of Congestive Chills, 2/16/1865
Bailey, Andrew J. Private	Unk	6/20/1862, Mercer County, Virginia	Mercer County, Virginia	Co. D, 17th Virginia Cavalry	11/12/1864, Near Nineveh, Virginia	Died of Unknown Causes, 5/13/1865
Bailey, Jonathan S. Private	Unk	8/4/1863, Princeton, West Virginia	Mercer County, West Virginia	Co. H, 60th Virginia Infantry	9/22/1864, Fisher Hill, Virginia	Died of Acute Dysentery, 11/7/1864
Bailey, L. J. Private	Unk	9/18/1863 Illegible	Unknown	Co. H, 57th North Carolina Cavalry	9/22/1863, Near Madison Court House, Virginia	Died of Typhoid Fever, 1/7/1864

Name	Age	Enlisted	Residence	Unit	Captured	Date and Cause of Death
Bailey, Mathias Private Name Not On Monument	Unk	12/6/1863, Princeton, West Virginia	Mercer County, West Virginia	Co. H, 60th Virginia Infantry	6/5/1864, New Hope, Piedmont, Virginia	Died of Malarial Fever, 9/19/1864
Bailey, William A. Private Name Not On Monument	19	9/26/1864 Danville, Virginia	Pittsylvania County, Virginia	Co. A, 18th Virginia Infantry	4/6/1865, Harper's Farm, Virginia	Died of Chronic Diarrhea, 6/26/1865
Bailey, William W. Private	22	9/27/1862, Blountsville, Tennessee	Unknown	Co. H, 60th Tennessee Mounted Infantry	5/16/1863, Big Black Bridge, Near Vicksburg, Mississippi	Died of Unknown Causes, 12/25/1863
Baker, Cleveas Private	20	4/19/1861, Harper's Ferry, Virginia	Orange County, Virginia, Farmer	Co. C, 13th Virginia Infantry	9/19/1864, Winchester, Virginia	Died of Chronic Dysentery, 1/27/1865
Baker, Elijah Private Name Not On Monument	32	2/27/1862, Gatesville, North Carolina	Gates County, North Carolina	Co. C, 52nd North Carolina Infantry	7/5/1863, Gettysburg, Pennsylvania	Died of Erysipelas of the Face, Bacterial Infection of the Skin, 11/1/1863
Baker, Henry Private	Unk	7/15/1862, Greene County, North Carolina	Greene County, North Carolina	Co. E, 61st North Carolina Cavalry	8/19/1864, Globe Tavern, Near Weldon Railroad, Near Petersburg, Virginia	Died of Chronic Diarrhea, 2/8/1865
Baker, Henry, M. Private	18	Brunswick County, North Carolina, 1/9/1864, Volunteer	Sampson County, North Carolina, Farmer	Co. A, 36th North Carolina Heavy Artillery	1/15/1865, Fort Fisher, North Carolina	Died of Inflammation Of Lungs (Pneumonia), 4/9/1865
Baker, James G. Private Not Listed On Monument	25	5/2/1862, Wake County, North Carolina	Franklin County, North Carolina	Co. B, 47th North Carolina Infantry	7/3/1863, Gettysburg, Pennsylvania, Wounded	Died of Chronic Diarrhea, 2/2/1865

Name	Age	Enlisted	Residence	Unit	Captured	Date and Cause of Death
Baker, Jesse J. Private Name Not On Monument	17	4/7/1864 Wayne County, North Carolina	Wayne County, North Carolina	Co. D, 1st Battalion North Carolina Heavy Artillery	1/15/1865, Fort Fisher, North Carolina, Severe Gunshot Wound Left Leg	Died of Wounds and Pyaemia 2/7/1865, Left Leg Amputated
Baker, John Private	36	Fort Fisher, New Hanover County, North Carolina, 3/18/1862, Volunteer	White Pine, Gaston County, North Carolina, Blacksmith	Co. C, 36th North Carolina Heavy Artillery	1/15/1865, Fort Fisher, North Carolina	Died of Chronic Diarrhea, 1/31/1865
Baker, John G. Private	25	5/2/1862, Wake County, North Carolina, Volunteer	Franklin County, North Carolina	Co. B, 47th North Carolina Infantry	7/3/1863, Gettysburg, Pennsylvania	Died of Chronic Diarrhea, 2/2/1865
Baker, John V. Sergeant	34	7/9/1861, Cobb County, Georgia	Cobb County, Georgia	Co. D, 14th Georgia Infantry	7/4/1863, Falling Waters, Near Hagerstown, Maryland	Acute Rheumatism and Scurvy, 12/15/1863
Baker, William Private	Unk	Unknown	Unknown	Co. C, 52nd North Carolina Infantry	Unknown	Unable to Locate
Balance, Stephen Private Name Not On Monument	Unk	Unknown	Unknown	Co. B, 61st Georgia Infantry	8/19/1864, Globe Tavern, Near Weldon Railroad, Virginia	Died of Chronic Dysentery 2/14/1865
Balcom, Aaron Private	Unk	5/9/1862, Anderson Court House, South Carolina	Anderson District, South Carolina	Co. E, 20th South Carolina Infantry	2/14/1865, Sandy Run, South Carolina	Died of Chronic Diarrhea, 5/17/1865
Balderson, Manoah B. Private	Unk	11/4/1863, Richmond County, Virginia	Richmond County, Virginia	Co. D, 17th Virginia Infantry	4/2/1865, Amelia County, Virginia	Died of Unknown Causes, 5/13/1865
Baldwin, Anderson C. Private	Unk	6/1/1861, Eatonton, Georgia	Putnam County, Georgia	Co. B, 3rd Georgia Infantry	7/2/1863, Gettysburg, Pennsylvania	Died of Variola (Smallpox), 11/18/1863

131

Name	Age	Enlisted	Residence	Unit	Captured	Date and Cause of Death
Baldwin, Madison Private	31	3/8/1862, Richmond County, North Carolina	Richmond County, North Carolina, Farmer	Co. F, 52nd North Carolina Infantry	7/5/1863, Gettysburg, Pennsylvania	Died of Dysentery, Scurvy and Erysipelas of the Face, 11/1/1863
Baldwin, Robert W. Private	Unk	5/16/1861, Crimea, Virginia	Rockbridge County, Virginia	Co. G, 53rd Virginia Infantry	7/3/1863, Gettysburg, Pennsylvania	Died of Chronic Diarrhea, 11/15/1863
Baldwin, W. M. Private	Unk	Unknown	Unknown	Co. F, 55th North Carolina Infantry	Unknown	Unable to Locate
Baldwin, William H. Private	Unk	8/10/1862, Hamilton, Georgia	Harris County, Georgia	Co. K, 35th Georgia Infantry	5/24/1864, Jerico Ford, North Anna, Virginia	Died of Congestive Intermittent Fever, 2/10/1865
Balentine, D. O. S. Private	Unk	2/25/1863, South Santee, South Carolina	Unknown	Co. D, 4th South Carolina Cavalry	6/20/1864, Louisa Court House, Virginia	Died of Chronic Diarrhea, 7/23/1864
Baliff, William M. Corporal	Unk	7/24/1862, Carroll County, Virginia	Carroll County, Virginia	Co. E, 30th Virginia Infantry	9/19/1864, Winchester, Virginia	Died of Acute Dysentery, 5/10/1865
Ball, Abraham Private	29	9/27/1862, Jonesboro, Tennessee	Washington County, Tennessee	Co. G, 60th Tennessee Mounted Infantry	5/17/1863, Big Black Bridge, Near Vicksburg, Mississippi	Died of Chronic Diarrhea, 11/28/1863
Ball, J. J. Private	Unk	4/10/1863, Charleston, South Carolina	Charleston County, South Carolina	Co. D, 27th South Carolina Infantry	8/21/1864, Globe Tavern, Near Weldon Railroad, Virginia	Died of Chronic Dysentery, 12/11/1864
Ballard, C. H. Corporal	Unk	4/29/1863, White S. Springs, Virginia	Jackson County, Ohio Carpenter	Co. F, 26th Virginia Battalion	10/19/1864, Cedar Creek or Strasburg, Virginia	Date and Cause of Death Unknown
Ballard, John T. Private	Unk	5/5/1862, Fort Deposit, Alabama	Unknown	Co. I, 60th Alabama Infantry	4/3/1865, Sutherland Station, Virginia	Died of Chronic Diarrhea, 5/4/1865
Ballentine, George W. Sergeant	33	Elizabethtown, Bladen County, North Carolina, 5/6/1862,	Bladen County, North Carolina, Turpentine	Co. K, 40th North Carolina Light Artillery	1/15/1865, Fort Fisher, North Carolina, Gunshot Wound Right Calf	Died of Erysipelas (Bacterial Infection of the Skin), 4/10/1865

Name	Age	Enlisted	Residence	Unit	Captured	Date and Cause of Death
Bame, David Private	Unk	7/15/1861, Salisbury, North Carolina	Rowan County, North Carolina	Co. K, 40th North Carolina Light Artillery	4/5/1865, Amelia Court House, Virginia	Died of Chronic Diarrhea, 5/31/1865
Bane, Marcus Private Name Not On Monument	Unk	Unknown	Unknown	Co. F, 53rd Virginia Infantry	4/1/1865 Dinwiddie Court House, Virginia	Died of Pneumonia 5/4/1865
Banister, James Private	Unk	7/1/1861, Concord, Georgia	Pike County, Georgia	Co. D, 2nd North Carolina Battalion	7/4/1863, South Mountain, Maryland, Gunshot Wound of Right Leg	Died of Pleuritis, Pleurisy, Inflammation of the Lungs (Pneumonia), 1/8/1864
Banks, John Private	Unk	Unknown	Unknown	Co. B, 34th Alabama Infantry	11/25/1863, Missionary Ridge, Tennessee	Died of Chronic Diarrhea, 2/23/1865
Banner, M. V. Private	Unk	10/22/1864, Forsyth County, North Carolina	Forsyth County, North Carolina	Co. D, 21st North Carolina Infantry	2/6/1865, Hatcher's Run, Near Petersburg, Virginia	Died of Neuralgia, Nerve Damage, 2/17/1865
Barber, William Private	Unk	12/14/1862, Jacksonville, North Carolina	Onslow County, North Carolina	Co. H, 3rd Cavalry, 41st North Carolina	1/4/1854, Gaines Bridge, Greenville, North Carolina	Died of Congestive Fever, 3/1/1865
Bard, William Private	Unk	Unknown	Unknown	Co. E, 1st Virginia Reserve Infantry	4/6/1865, Harper's Farm, Virginia	Died of Pneumonia, 5/31/1865
Barger, Babel Private	28	7/7/1862, Newton, North Carolina	Catawba County, North Carolina, Laborer	Co. E, 57th North Carolina Infantry	11/7/1863, Rappahannock, Virginia	Died of Chronic Dysentery, 3/10/1865
Barger, George H. Private	37	12/17/1862, Rowan County, North Carolina	Rowan County, North Carolina	Co. K, 8th North Carolina Infantry	9/30/1864, Fort Harrison, Virginia	Died of Chronic Diarrhea, 2/16/1865

Name	Age	Enlisted	Residence	Unit	Captured	Date and Cause of Death
Barker, B. Private	Unk	Unknown	Unknown	Co. D, 3rd North Carolina Junior Reserves	12/29/1864, Fort Fisher, North Carolina	Died of Inflammation of the Brain, 1/23/1865
Barker, Moses Private	Unk	10/14/1864, Danville, Virginia	Pittsylvania County, Virginia	Co. A, 38th Virginia Infantry	4/2/1865, Dinwiddie Court House, Virginia	Died of Unknown Causes, 6/23/1865
Barnes, Abner J. Private	18	10/1/1862, Edgecombe County, North Carolina	Martin County, North Carolina	Co. H, 61st North Carolina Infantry	9/30/1864, Fort Harrison, Virginia	Died Of Rubeola (Measles), 3/27/1865
Barnes, Elias Private	29	5/1/1862, Davidson County, North Carolina	Davidson County, North Carolina	Co. A, 54th North Carolina Infantry	10/19/1864, Cedar Creek, Virginia	Died of Congestive Intermittent Fever, 11/26/1864
Barnes, James Private	25	4/2/1862, Hamilton, North Carolina	Camden County, North Carolina Farmer	Co. H, 17th North Carolina Infantry	1/26/1864, Near Plymouth, North Carolina	Died of Chronic Diarrhea, 2/16/1865
Barnes, James W. Corporal	Unk	4/25/1862, Wilson, North Carolina	Unknown	Co. H, 7th Confederate Cavalry, Partisan Rangers	9/30/1864, Near Petersburg, Virginia	Died of Chronic Diarrhea, 11/1/1864
Barnes, John W. Private Name Not On Monument	31	3/24/1864 Wilmington, North Carolina	Wilmington, New Hanover County, North Carolina, School Teacher	Co. F, 10th Battalion North Carolina Light Artillery	1/15/1865, Fort Fisher, North Carolina, Wounded Severely in Left Thigh, Fracture of Femur	Died Of Pyaemia, 2/10/1865
Barnes, Murphy Private	Unk	7/4/1862, Catawba County, North Carolina	Catawba County, North Carolina	Co. E, 57th North Carolina Infantry	11/7/1863, Rappahannock Station, Virginia	Died of Pneumonia, 1/27/1865
Barnes, Stephen J. Private	34	6/18/1863, Wilson County, North Carolina	Wilson County, North Carolina	Co. D, 2nd North Carolina Infantry	11/7/1863, Kelly's Ford, Rappahannock Station, Virginia	Died of Chronic Diarrhea, 1/31/1864
Barnes, Washington L. Sergeant	23	8/28/1861, Wilson County, North Carolina	Wilson County, North Carolina	Co. D, 2nd North Carolina Infantry	11/7/1863, Kelly's Ford, Rappahannock Station, Virginia	Died of Typhoid Fever, 5/13/1864

Name	Age	Enlisted	Residence	Unit	Captured	Date and Cause of Death
Barnes, William Private Name Not On Monument	Unk	5/16/1862 Darlington District, South Carolina	Darlington District, South Carolina	Co. B, 21st South Carolina Infantry	1/15/1865, Fort Fisher, North Carolina, Gunshot Wound of Back	Died of Wounds, 2/6/1865
Barnette, John L. Private Name Not On Monument	Unk	8/20/1861 Mobile, Alabama	Mobile County, Alabama	Co. E, 3rd Alabama Cavalry	6/27/1863, Shelbyville, Tennessee	Died of Unknown Causes, 11/23/1863
Barnhardt, Daniel C. Private	27	7/4/1862, Cabarrus County, North Carolina	Cabarrus County, North Carolina, Farmer	Co. H, 57th North Carolina Infantry	11/7/1863, Rappahannock Station, Virginia	Died of Pneumonia, 1/30/1865
Barnhardt, Tobias Private	29	3/21/1862, Cabarrus County, North Carolina	Cabarrus County, North Carolina	Co. A, 52nd North Carolina Infantry	7/3/1863, Gettysburg, Pennsylvania	Died of Chronic Diarrhea & Scurvy, 11/3/1863
Barnwell, James M. Private	Unk	Unknown	Unknown	Co. A, 34th North Carolina Infantry	3/25/1865, Fort Stedman, Near Petersburg, Virginia	Died of Rubeola (Measles) 6/8/1865
Barradall, William J. Sergeant Name Not On Monument	23	5/18/1861 Chuckatuck, Virginia	Suffolk County, Virginia	Co. F, 9th Virginia Infantry	7/3/1863, Gettysburg, Pennsylvania	Died of Chronic Diarrhea, 3/25/1864
Barrett, Alfred N. Private	Unk	3/15/1862, St. Martin, Louisiana	St. Martin's Parish, Louisiana	Co. C, 8th Louisiana Infantry	11/7/1863, Kelly's Ford, Rappahannock Station, Virginia	Died of Chronic Diarrhea, 12/19/1863
Barrett, James R. Private	21	8/15/1861, Athens, Cobb County, Georgia	Cobb County, Georgia, Farmer	Philips Cavalry Legion, Georgia Infantry	Unknown	Date and Cause of Death Unknown
Barrett, James R. Private	Unk	6/4/1861, Montgomery, Alabama	Montgomery County, Alabama	Co. H, 10th Alabama Infantry	7/3/1863, Gettysburg, Pennsylvania	Died of Variola (Smallpox), 11/6/1863

Name	Age	Enlisted	Residence	Unit	Captured	Date and Cause of Death
Barrier, John L. Private	29	3/13/1862, Cabarrus County, North Carolina	Cabarrus County, North Carolina	Co. A, 20th North Carolina Infantry	7/3/1863, Gettysburg, Pennsylvania	Died of Chronic Diarrhea, 12/25/1864
Barringer, George A. Private	30	8/13/1862, Northampton, North Carolina, Conscript	Stanley County, North Carolina, Farmer	Co. G, 5th North Carolina Infantry	9/19/1864, Winchester, Virginia, Wounded in Foot	Died of Chronic Diarrhea, 3/19/1865
Barringer, Paul D. Sergeant	29	7/4/1861, Rowan County, North Carolina	Rowan County, North Carolina	Co. G, 5th North Carolina Infantry	7/1/1863, Gettysburg, Pennsylvania	Died of Variola (Smallpox), 12/30/1864
Barron, Joseph M. Private	Unk	7/8/1861, Griffin, Georgia	Spalding County, Georgia	Co. C, 13th Georgia Infantry	7/4/1863, South Mountain, Maryland	Died of Unknown Causes, 3/25/1864
Bartlett, G. S. Private	Unk	Unknown	Unknown	Co. A, 36th Virginia Cavalry	Unknown	Unable to Locate
Bartlett, James P. Private	38	4/27/1863, Swannanoa, Buncombe County, North Carolina, Volunteer	Buncombe County, North Carolina	Co. K, 11th North Carolina Infantry	7/3/1863, Gettysburg, Pennsylvania	Died of Unknown Causes, 1/1/1864
Bartlett, William H. Private	Unk	6/4/1861, Warsaw, Virginia	Richmond County, Virginia	Co. D, 40th Virginia Infantry	7/4/1863, South Mountain, Maryland	Died of Unknown Causes, 2/9/1864
Barton, J. Private	33	9/10/1862, Union Springs, Alabama	Bullock County, Alabama	Co. D, 5th Alabama Cavalry	Unknown	Date and Cause of Death Unknown
Barton, Joseph Private	Unk	6/16/1863, Greenville, South Carolina, Conscript	Greenville District, South Carolina	Co. K, Hampton's South Carolina Legion	10/28/1864, Unknown	Died of Chronic Diarrhea, 3/13/1865
Barton, Robert A. Private	Unk	12/19/1862, McMinnville, Tennessee	Unknown	Co. E, 44th Tennessee Infantry	4/2/1865, Petersburg, Virginia	Died of Unknown Causes, 6/9/1865
Basdon, Calvin Private	Unk	2/25/1863, Onslow County, North Carolina	Onslow County, North Carolina	Co. E, 5th North Carolina Cavalry	9/15/1864, Near Petersburg, Virginia	Died of Chronic Diarrhea, 3/24/1865

Name	Age	Enlisted	Residence	Unit	Captured	Date and Cause of Death
Basley, John H. Private	Unk	Unknown	Unknown	Co. E, 18th Virginia Infantry	9/29/1864, Bridgewater, Virginia	Died of Typhoid Fever, 12/12/1864
Bass, Abel See: Boss, Abel				Co. G, 3rd Alabama Infantry		
Bass, Burton Private	23	2/26/1862, Statesville, North Carolina, Volunteer	Iredell County, North Carolina	Co. E, 11th North Carolina Infantry	10/27/1864, Boyton Plank Road or Burgess' Mill, Virginia	Died of Chronic Diarrhea, 3/10/1865
Bass, George E. Private	Unk	2/24/1862, Sparta, Georgia	Hancock County, Georgia	Co. K, 15th Georgia Infantry	7/3/1863, Gettysburg, Pennsylvania	Died of Chronic Diarrhea, 2/22/1864
Bass, Lewis U. Private	16	4/2/1862, Magnolia, Duplin County, North Carolina, Substitute	Duplin County, North Carolina	Co. A, 43rd North Carolina Infantry	7/4/1863, South Mountain, Gettysburg, Pennsylvania	Died of Unknown Causes, 3/7/1864
Bass, William T. Private	48	2/24/1862, Nash County, North Carolina	Nash County, North Carolina, Farmer	Co. A, 47th North Carolina Infantry	7/14/1863, Falling Waters, Maryland	Died of Unknown Causes, 3/28/1864
Bastabel, Granville W. Private Name Not On Monument	Unk	6/11/1863 Pocahontas County, Virginia	Upshur, Virginia, Clerk	Co. A, 47th Battalion Virginia Cavalry	7/6/1863 Weston, Lewis County, Virginia	Died of Unknown Causes, 10/?/1863
Batchelor, James E. Corporal	24	5/25/1861, Wilson County, North Carolina, Volunteer	Nash County, North Carolina, Farmer	Co. E, 7th North Carolina Infantry	5/5/1864, Wilderness, Virginia	Died of Unknown Causes, 7/31/1864
Batchelor, James N. Private	Unk	9/16/1861, Walton County, Georgia	Walton County, Georgia	Co. G, 35th Georgia Infantry	5/6/1864, Mine Run, Virginia	Died of Unknown Causes, 7/28/1864
Batchelor, Neverson A. Private	23	9/10/1861, Nash County, North Carolina	Nash County, North Carolina	Co. I, 30th North Carolina Infantry	11/7/1863, Kelly's Ford, Virginia	Died of Variola (Smallpox), 2/9/1864

Name	Age	Enlisted	Residence	Unit	Captured	Date and Cause of Death
Batchelor, Wright B. Private Name Not On Monument	Unk	7/15/1862 Camp Holmes, North Carolina	Wake County, North Carolina	Co. H, 47th North Carolina Infantry	3/25/1865, Fort Stedman, Near Petersburg, Virginia	Died of Chronic Diarrhea, 6/26/1865
Batty, Zach T. Private	Unk	Unknown	Unknown	Co. D, 2nd Virginia Reserve Infantry	Unknown	Unable to Locate
Bauch, William J. Private	Unk	2/1/1864, Richmond, Virginia	Henrico County, Virginia	Co. F, 25th Virginia Infantry	4/6/1865, Sailor's Creek, Virginia	Died of Typhoid Fever, 5/18/1865
Bayne, Marcus Private	Unk	Unknown	Unknown	Co. F, 53rd Virginia Infantry	4/5/1865, Dinwiddie Court House, Virginia	Died of Pneumonia, 5/4/1865
Beadles, Robert S. Private	Unk	6/1/1861, Bond's Store, Virginia	Unknown	King William Virginia Light Artillery Battery	7/4/1863, Gettysburg, Pennsylvania	Died of Unknown Causes, 2/22/1864
Beal, Charles Private	Unk	10/1/1864, Camp Holmes, Raleigh, North Carolina	Mecklenburg County, North Carolina	Co. E, 11th North Carolina Infantry	10/27/1864, Boyton Plank Road or Burgess' Mill, Virginia	Died of Peritonitis, Inflammation of the lining of the Abdomen, 1/2/1865
Beal, John Private	Unk	10/1/1864, Camp Holmes, Raleigh, North Carolina	Mecklenburg County, North Carolina	Co. E, 11th North Carolina Infantry	10/27/1864, Boyton Plank Road or Burgess' Mill, Virginia	Died of Catarrh, Inflammation of the Mucous Membranes, 3/9/1865
Beall, W. T. Private	Unk	Unknown	Unknown	Virginia Light Artillery	Unknown	Unable to Locate
Beam, Joshua C. Private	18	3/29/1862, Cleveland County, North Carolina	Cleveland County, North Carolina, Farmer	Co. C, 55th North Carolina Infantry	7/2/1863, Gettysburg, Pennsylvania	Died of Chronic Diarrhea, 3/25/1864
Beaman, Jesse R. Private	32	4/21/1862, Wilson County, North Carolina	Wilson County, North Carolina, Carpenter	Co. A, 55th North Carolina Infantry	7/1/1863, Gettysburg, Pennsylvania	Died of Variola (Smallpox), 12/10/1863

Name	Age	Enlisted	Residence	Unit	Captured	Date and Cause of Death
Beard, Edmond S. Private	Unk	5/14/1862, La Fayette, Walker County, Georgia	Walker County, Georgia	Co. G, 9th Georgia Infantry	7/3/1863, Gettysburg, Pennsylvania, Wounded	Died of Chronic Diarrhea, 2/26/1864
Beasley, John Private	Unk	3/7/1864 Richmond, Virginia, Conscript	Henrico County, Virginia	Co. D, 56th Virginia Infantry	4/6/1865, High Bridge, Virginia	Died of Chronic Diarrhea, 6/8/1865
Beasley, William R. Private	24	5/21/1861, Raleigh, North Carolina, Volunteer	Wake County, North Carolina, Carpenter	Co. K, 14th North Carolina Infantry	7/2/1863, Gettysburg, Pennsylvania	Died of Unknown Causes, 1/12/1864
Beaty, Junius F. Private Name Not On Monument	19	3/11/1862 Concord, North Carolina, Volunteer	Cabarrus County, North Carolina, Manufacturer	Co. A, 52nd North Carolina Infantry	10/27/1864 Burgess' Mill, Near Petersburg, Virginia	Died of Chronic Diarrhea, 3/13/1865
Bean, David Corporal	Unk	3/1/1862, Washington, Arkansas	Unknown	Co. E, 20th Arkansas Infantry	5/16/1863, Big Black Bridge, Mississippi	Died of Chronic Diarrhea, 12/21/1863
Beaver, Moses Private	Unk	10/31/1864, Iredell County, North Carolina	Iredell County, North Carolina	Co. C, 48th North Carolina Infantry	4/5/1865, Appomattox River, Virginia	Died of Typhoid Fever, 4/30/1865
Beaver, Richard Private	Unk	5/18/1861, Lenoir County, North Carolina	Lenoir County, North Carolina	Co. D, 27th North Carolina Infantry	10/14/1863, Bristow Station, Virginia	Died of Gangrene, 12/15/1864
Beckwith, F. Ansil Private Name Not On Monument	24	3/7/1862 Wake County, North Carolina	Wake County, North Carolina, Farmer	Co. H, 47th North Carolina Infantry	10/27/1864, Boyton Plank Road or Burgess' Mill, Near Petersburg, Virginia	Died of Chronic Diarrhea, 2/21/1865
Beddingfield, John C. Private	Unk	8/13/1861, Camp Moore, Louisiana	Orleans Parish, Louisiana	Co. A, 12th Louisiana Infantry	5/16/1863, Champion Hill, Virginia	Died of Chronic Diarrhea, 2/3/1864
Beirne, Andrew See: Burne, Andrew				Co. B, 14th Virginia Cavalry		

Name	Age	Enlisted	Residence	Unit	Captured	Date and Cause of Death
Bell, Andrew J. Private	Unk	3/20/1862, Rock Hill, South Carolina	Unknown	Co. H, 12th South Carolina Infantry	5/24/1864, North Anna River, Virginia	Died of Scurvy, 3/6/1865
Bell, Bythol Private	25	2/14/1862, Halifax County, North Carolina	Halifax County, North Carolina, Cabinet Maker	Co. F, 43rd North Carolina Infantry	7/5/1863, Gettysburg, Pennsylvania	Died of Unknown Causes, 2/24/1864
Bell, Elijah H. Private	Unk	3/13/1862, Fredericksburg Virginia	Spotsylvania County, Virginia	Co. M, 55th Virginia Infantry	7/14/1863, Falling Waters, Maryland	Died of Chronic Diarrhea and Scurvy, 10/29/1863
Bell, George T. Sergeant	Unk	6/22/1862, Wytheville, Virginia	Wythe County, Virginia	Co. B, 8th Virginia Cavalry	12/21/1864, Lacey Springs, Virginia	Died of Pneumonia, 3/21/1865
Bell, J. M. Captain	Unk	Unknown	Unknown	Co. H, 67th North Carolina Infantry	12/31/1864, Martin County, Virginia	Died of Intermittent Fever, 2/18/1865
Bell, J. R. Private	Unk	Unknown	Unknown	Co. F, 1st Virginia Cavalry	Unknown	Unable to Locate
Bell, John W. Private	Unk	Unknown	Unknown	Co. H, 7th Confederate Cavalry	Unknown	Unable to Locate
Bell, Samuel F. Private	31	6/13/1861, Jamestown, Virginia	Culpepper County, Virginia	Co. F, 14th Virginia Infantry	7/3/1863, Gettysburg, Pennsylvania	Died of Variola (Smallpox), 12/9/1863
Bell, Sanders W. Private	Unk	9/6/1861, Barnwell, South Carolina	Barnwell County, South Carolina	Co. A, 1st South Carolina Infantry	5/23/1864, Noel Station, North Anna River, Virginia	Died of Unknown Causes, 6/18/1864
Bell, Thomas H. Private	Unk	5/13/1861, Aldie, Virginia	Loudoun County, Virginia	Co. D, 8th Virginia Infantry	7/3/1863, Gettysburg, Pennsylvania	Died of Chronic Diarrhea, 2/10/1864

Name	Age	Enlisted	Residence	Unit	Captured	Date and Cause of Death
Bell, William H. Private	Unk	6/30/1862, Edgefield, South Carolina	Columbia, South Carolina	Co. A, 7th Battalion South Carolina Infantry	5/16/1864, Near Drewry's Bluff, Virginia	Died of Unknown Causes, 7/25/1864
Bell, William W. Private	Unk	9/22/1862, Camp Holmes, Raleigh, North Carolina	Wake County, North Carolina	Co. D, 26th North Carolina Infantry	10/27/1864, Boyton Plank Road or Burgess' Mill, Virginia	Died of Typhoid Fever, 11/28/1864
Bellinger, S. Private	Unk	Unknown	Unknown	Co. G, 57th Virginia Infantry	7/2/1863, Gettysburg, Pennsylvania	Died of Typhoid Fever and Dysentery, 3/6/1864
Bellune, J. T. Private	Unk	5/5/1864, Decatur, Georgia	DeKalb County, Georgia	Co. F, 22nd Battalion Georgia Artillery	12/13/1864, Fort McAllister, Georgia, Gunshot Wound Left Arm	Died of Pneumonia, 3/5/1865
Benifield, William Private	Unk	3/27/1864, Ray Town, Tennessee	Unknown	Co. I, 50th Georgia Infantry	6/1/1864, Gaines Farm, Virginia	Died of Pneumonia, 12/15/1864
Bennett, Alexander Private	25	10/2/1862, Wake County, North Carolina, Conscript	Union County, North Carolina	Co. F, 28th North Carolina Infantry	5/12/1864, Wilderness, Virginia, Wounded	Died of Unknown Causes, 6/6/1864
Bennett, David W. Private	Unk	4/28/1862, Madison, Florida	Madison County, Florida	Co. D, 5th Florida Infantry	7/17/1864, Spotsylvania, Virginia	Died of Unknown Causes, 7/17/1864
Bennett, Henry Private	20	9/16/1861, Union County, North Carolina	Union County, North Carolina, Farmer	Co. D, 37th North Carolina Infantry	7/5/1863, Gettysburg, Pennsylvania	Died of Unknown Causes, 4/9/1864
Bennett, James T. Private	26	9/24/1861, Montgomery, Alabama	Montgomery County, Alabama	Co. F, Jeff Davis Legion, Mississippi Cavalry	8/1/1863, Brandy Station, Virginia	Died of Unknown Causes, 6/5/1864
Bennett, Joab Private	Unk	3/10/1862, Mobile, Alabama	Mobile County, Alabama	Co. C, 3rd Alabama Cavalry	Unknown	Date and Cause of Death Unknown
Bennett, William Private	Unk	8/15/1864, Camp Holmes, Raleigh, North Carolina	Wake County, North Carolina	Co. C, 3rd North Carolina Junior Reserve	12/25/1864, Fort Fisher, North Carolina	Died of Unknown Causes, 4/5/1865

Name	Age	Enlisted	Residence	Unit	Captured	Date and Cause of Death
Bennett, William Private	Unk	7/9/1861, Troup County, Georgia	Troup County, Georgia	Co. F, 21th Georgia Infantry	7/4/1863, Gettysburg, Pennsylvania, Wounded	Died of Unknown Causes, 3/5/1864
Bennett, William F. Private	Unk	8/22/1863, Butler County, Alabama	Butler County, Alabama	Co. D, 61st Alabama Infantry	4/2/1865, Petersburg, Virginia	Died of Chronic Diarrhea, 5/16/1865
Bently, Noah J. Private	Unk	8/20/1863, Camp Hill, North Carolina Conscript	Unknown	Co. C, 18th North Carolina Infantry	5/12/1864, Spotsylvania Court House, Virginia	Died of Chronic Dysentery, 9/1/1864
Benton, John Private	Unk	8/15/1862, Fort Sumter, South Carolina	Charleston, South Carolina, Butcher	Co. G, 1st Alabama Artillery	3/1/1865, Fayetteville, North Carolina	Date and Cause of Death Unknown
Berry, Andrew J. Private	Unk	5/14/1862, Rome, Georgia	Floyd County, Georgia	Co. D, Philip's Legion, Georgia Infantry Battalion	6/2/1864, Gaines Farm, Virginia	Died of Unknown Causes, 8/6/1864
Berry, James Private	Unk	6/24/1862, Richmond County, Georgia	Richmond County, Georgia	Co. K, 10th Georgia Infantry	4/6/1865, Farmville, Virginia	Died of Unknown Causes, 6/3/1865
Berryhill, Andrew Private	30	5/13/1862, Mecklenburg County, North Carolina	Mecklenburg County, North Carolina, Miller	Co. B, 53rd North Carolina Infantry	7/5/1863, Gettysburg, Pennsylvania Gunshot Wound Right Arm	Died of Variola (Smallpox), 12/8/1863
Best, William C. Private	Unk	8/3/1864, Wayne County, North Carolina	Wayne County, North Carolina	Co. A, 55th North Carolina Infantry	4/2/1865, Hatcher's Run, Sutherland's Station, Virginia	Died of Acute Dysentery, 4/29/1865
Betenbaugh, John Private	Unk	Unknown	Unknown	Co. F, 15th South Carolina Infantry	7/12/1863, Gettysburg, Pennsylvania	Died of Scurvy, 3/24/1865, Died On March to be Exchanged
Bethune, M. Private	Unk	10/8/1864, Camp Holmes, Raleigh, North Carolina	Wake County, North Carolina	Co. E, 1st North Carolina Junior Reserves	12/25/1864, Fort Fisher, North Carolina	Died of Pneumonia, 3/12/1865
Bettis, John F. Private	Unk	9/20/1862, Jackson County, Virginia	Unknown	Co. F, 37th Battalion Virginia Cavalry	7/8/1864, Frederick, Virginia	Died of Pneumonia, 3/23/1865

Name	Age	Enlisted	Residence	Unit	Captured	Date and Cause of Death
Betts, W. H. Sergeant	16	9/8/1862, Wake County, North Carolina	Wake County, North Carolina	Co. C, 31st North Carolina Infantry	9/30/1864, Fort Harrison, Virginia	Died of Chronic Diarrhea, 1/18/1865
Beverly, John B. Private	Unk	10/1/1863, Colleton, South Carolina	Colleton County, South Carolina	Co. K, 11th South Carolina Infantry	2/28/1865, Fort Anderson, Near Town Creek, North Carolina	Died of Pneumonia, 4/22/1865
Bibbey, James Private	Unk	9/19/1863, Camp Vance, North Carolina	Burke County, North Carolina	Co. K, 16th North Carolina Infantry	5/23/1864, North Anna River, Virginia	Died of Unknown Causes, 6/12/1864
Bickley, Joseph H. Private Name Not On Monument	Unk	3/18/1862, Camp Elliott, South Carolina	Unknown	Co. I, 15th South Carolina Infantry	8/26/1864, Halltown, Virginia	Died of Chronic Diarrhea, 7/17/1865
Bicknell, Alvin L. Private	18	4/22/1862, Wilkes County, North Carolina	North Hampton County, North Carolina, Farmer	Co. F, 54th North Carolina Infantry	5/24/1864, Milford Station, Virginia	Died of Variola (Smallpox), 12/10/1864
Bigby, Benjamin F. Private	24	7/1/1861, Westville, Alabama	Dale, Alabama	Co. E, 15th Alabama Infantry	7/2/1863, Gettysburg, Pennsylvania	Date and Cause of Death Unknown
Bigg, Kenneth M. Private	20	8/27/1861, Union County, North Carolina	Lumberton, Robeson County, North Carolina	Co. F, 40th North Carolina Light Artillery	1/15/1865, Fort Fisher, North Carolina	Died of Pneumonia, 4/29/1865
Biggers, James W. Private	18	4/26/1861, Oxford, Mississippi	Toccopola, Mississippi, Student	Co. G, 11th Mississippi Infantry	7/14/1863, Falling Waters, Maryland, Gunshot Wound	Died of Chronic Diarrhea, 1/17/1864
Bigham, Elijah Private	Unk	11/12/1863, Charleston, South Carolina	Charleston County, South Carolina	Co. A, 17th South Carolina Infantry	4/4/1865, Amelia Court House, Virginia	Died of Intermittent Fever, 5/26/1865

Name	Age	Enlisted	Residence	Unit	Captured	Date and Cause of Death
Bigham, John R. Private	19	2/1/1862, Charlotte, Mecklenburg County, North Carolina, Volunteer	Mecklenburg County, North Carolina	Co. A, 11th North Carolina Infantry	7/2/1863, Gettysburg, Pennsylvania, Gunshot Wound of Buttocks and Left Thigh	Died of Unknown Causes, 8/28/1864
Billings, Joseph Private Name Not On Monument	Unk	Unknown	Unknown	Co. G, 6th North Carolina Infantry	7/4/1863, Gettysburg, Pennsylvania	Died of Unknown Causes, 3/?/1865
Billings, Martin Private	31	3/4/1862, Ellijay, Georgia	Gilmer County, Georgia	Co. K, 11th Georgia Infantry	5/6/1864, Mine Run, Wilderness, Virginia	Died of Unknown Causes, 9/8/1864
Bingham, R. W. Private	25	3/11/1862, Burke County, North Carolina	Burke County, North Carolina	Co. D, 11th North Carolina Infantry	10/14/1863, Bristoe Station, Virginia	Died of Unknown Causes, 8/12/1864
Birchfield, James Private	Unk	9/23/1861, Pocahontas, Arkansas	Randolph County, Arkansas	Co. B, 21st Arkansas Infantry	5/17/1863, Big Black Bridge Bridge, Mississippi	Died of Chronic Diarrhea and Pneumonia, 12/14/1863
Bird, Henry B. Private	Unk	3/4/1862, Johnson County, Georgia	Johnson County, Georgia	Co. F, 48th Georgia Infantry	7/1/1863, Gettysburg, Pennsylvania	Died of Chronic Diarrhea and Erysipelas (Skin Infection) 12/11/1863
Bird, William Private	Unk	3/4/1862, Swainsboro, Georgia	Emanuel County, Georgia	Co. H, 48th Georgia Infantry	7/23/1863, Manassas Gap, Virginia	Died of Variola (Smallpox), 12/30/1863
Birmingham, Joshua M. Private	Unk	2/27/1862, Enterprise, Mississippi	Clarke County, Mississippi	Co. C, 2nd Mississippi Infantry	7/1/1863, Gettysburg, Pennsylvania	Died of Chronic Diarrhea, 12/22/1863
Bishop, Larkin Private	21	3/14/1862, Wilkesboro, North Carolina	Wilkes County, North Carolina, Farmer	Co. F, 52nd North Carolina Infantry	7/14/1863, Falling Waters, Maryland	Died of Chronic Diarrhea, 11/20/1863
Bishop, M. Private	22	2/27/1862, Wake County, North Carolina	Wake County, North Carolina, Farmer	Co. C, 47th North Carolina Infantry	7/14/1863, Falling Waters, Maryland	Died of Chronic Diarrhea, 1/11/1864

Name	Age	Enlisted	Residence	Unit	Captured	Date and Cause of Death
Bissett, Jackson Private	27	4/19/1862, Stanhope, Nash County, North Carolina, Volunteer	Nash County, North Carolina, Farmer	Co. A, 47th North Carolina Infantry	7/14/1863, Falling Waters, Maryland	Died of Unknown Causes, 12/19/1863
Bivens, Peter M. Private	20	4/22/1862, Cleveland County, North Carolina, Volunteer	Catawba County, North Carolina, Farmer	Co. F, 55th North Carolina Infantry	7/1/1863, Gettysburg, Pennsylvania	Died of Unknown Causes, 2/19/1864
Black, Adam Private	23	8/12/1862, Statesville, Iredell County, North Carolina, Conscript	Gaston County, North Carolina	Co. D, 37th North Carolina Infantry	7/3/1863, Gettysburg, Pennsylvania	Died of Unknown Causes, 8/11/1864
Black, W. W. Private	Unk	10/4/1863, Camp Vance, Wake County, North Carolina	Cleveland County, North Carolina	Co. I, 15th North Carolina Infantry	5/12/1864, Spotsylvania Court House, Virginia	Died of Unknown Causes, 7/21/1864
Blackburn, J. C. Private	18	10/26/1863, Camp Holmes, Raleigh, North Carolina, Conscript	Wake County, North Carolina	Co. A, 3rd North Carolina Infantry	5/12/1864, Spotsylvania Court House, Virginia	Died of Unknown Causes, 7/28/1863
Blackburn, John H. Private	Unk	6/17/1863, Snow Hill, North Carolina	Greene County, North Carolina	Co. G, 7th Confederate Cavalry	9/30/1864, Fort Harrison, Virginia	Died of Unknown Causes, 3/8/1865
Blackburn, John E. Private	Unk	4/14/1862, Des Arc, Arkansas	Unknown	Co. B, 1st Missouri Cavalry	5/16/1863, Champion Hill, Virginia	Died of Unknown Causes, 2/5/1864
Blackburn, Robert L. Corporal	Unk	5/21/1861, Tappahannock Virginia	Essex County, Virginia	Co. A, 55th Virginia Infantry	7/14/1863, Falling Waters, Maryland	Died of Chronic Diarrhea, 1/1/1864
Blackman, Hugh G. Private	Unk	4/11/1863, Camp Tucker, South Carolina	Unknown	Co. F, 4th South Carolina Cavalry	5/30/1864, Old Church, Virginia	Died of Rubeola (Measles) 8/18/1864
Blackston, William L. Private	Unk	4/26/1861, Richmond County, Georgia	Richmond County, Georgia	Co. G, 3rd Georgia Infantry	7/3/1863, Gettysburg, Pennsylvania	Died of Variola (Smallpox), 11/17/1863

Name	Age	Enlisted	Residence	Unit	Captured	Date and Cause of Death
Blackwelder, M. W. Private	Unk	2/10/1864, Taylorsville, Virginia	Hanover County, Virginia	Co. C, 23rd North Carolina Infantry	5/12/1864, Spotsylvania Court House, Virginia	Died of Chronic Diarrhea, 10/25/1864
Blackwelder, W. Private	40	9/2/1863, Camp Holmes, Raleigh, North Carolina	Cabarrus County, North Carolina	Co. C, 30th North Carolina Infantry	11/7/1863, Kelly's Ford, Rappahannock Station, Virginia	Died of Congestive Chill, 4/16/1864
Blackwell, Johnson D. Private	35	10/1/1862, Newport, Tennessee	Cocke County, Tennessee	Co. I, 60th Tennessee Mounted Infantry	5/17/1863, Big Black Bridge, Mississippi	Died of Unknown Causes, 4/5/1864
Blair, J. H. Private	20	9/18/1862. Hillsboro, Virginia	Pocahontas County, West Virginia, Farmer	Co. D, 14th Virginia Cavalry	11/11/1864, Cedarville, Virginia	Died of Chronic Diarrhea, 1/24/1865
Blair, Lorenzo R. Private	Unk	9/3/1862, Jacksonville, Alabama	Calhoun County, Alabama	Co. G, 3rd Alabama Cavalry	6/27/1863, Shelbyville, Tennessee	Died of Variola (Smallpox), 11/11/1863
Blakely, James J. Private	18	3/1/1863, Mecklenburg County, North Carolina	Mecklenburg County, North Carolina	Co. F, 11th North Carolina Infantry	7/14/1863, Falling Waters, Maryland	Died of Pneumonia, 4/1/1865
Blain, Abner W. Corporal	35	6/18/1863, Camp No. West, Virginia	Unknown	Co. I, 20th Virginia Cavalry	9/27/1864, Harrisonburg, Virginia	Died of Congestive Intermittent Fever, 2/9/1865
Blalock, William R. Private	28	7/5/1861, Atlanta, Georgia	Fannin County, Georgia	Co. E, 11th Georgia Infantry	7/5/1863, Gettysburg, Pennsylvania, Wounded	Died of Remittent Fever, 2/18/1865
Blanchard, Eldridge S. Private	Unk	5/10/1862, Gatesville, North Carolina	Gates County, North Carolina	Co. C, 52nd North Carolina Infantry	7/3/1863, Gettysburg, Pennsylvania	Died of Chronic Hepatitis, 2/3/1865
Bland, J. P. Sergeant	21	5/7/1861, New Prospect, Virginia	King and Queen County, Virginia, Farmer	Co. C, 26th Virginia Infantry	6/17/1864, Jordan's Farm, Petersburg, Virginia	Date and Cause of Death Unknown

Name	Age	Enlisted	Residence	Unit	Captured	Date and Cause of Death
Blankenship, Washington W. Private	35	6/8/1863, Camp Vance, North Carolina, Conscript	Burke County, North Carolina	Co. B, 34th North Carolina Infantry	6/4/1864, Cold Harbor, Virginia	Died of Unknown Causes, 7/23/1864
Blanton, Charles D. Private	25	5/29/1861, Corinth, Mississippi	Alcorn County, Mississippi	Co. H, 15th Mississippi Infantry	12/17/1864, Franklin, Tennessee	Died of Chronic Diarrhea, 4/16/1865
Blaylock, Chesley H. Private	30	7/17/1862, Camp Holmes, Raleigh, North Carolina	Orange County, North Carolina	Co. G, 27th North Carolina Infantry	10/14/1863, Bristoe Station, Virginia	Died of Unknown Causes, 8/1/1864
Blaylock, William K. See: Blalock, William K.				Co. E, 11th Georgia Infantry		
Blevins, S. Private	Unk	9/1/1864, Camp Vance, North Carolina	Burke County, North Carolina	Co. K, 32nd North Carolina Infantry	9/19/1864, Winchester, Virginia	Died of Scurvy, 4/29/1865
Blocker, Thomas Private	Unk	10/1/1864, Columbus, South Carolina	Clarendon District, South Carolina	Co. K, 1st South Carolina Infantry	3/16/1865, Waynesboro, Virginia	Died of Pneumonia, 5/26/1865
Bloodworth, John D. Corporal	Unk	6/10/1861, Wilkinson County, Georgia	Wilkinson County, Georgia	Co. F, 3rd Georgia Infantry	8/16/1864, Deep Bottom Run, Virginia	Died of Debility, 3/31/1865
Bloodworth, Richard J. Private Name Not On Monument	Unk	3/4/1864 Butler, Georgia	Taylor County, Georgia	Co. E, 45th Georgia Infantry	5/23/1864, Jerico Ford, North Anna River, Virginia	Died of Unknown Causes, 7/14/1864
Blount, William H. Private	23	9/4/1861, Camp Bienville, Louisiana	Unknown	Co. C, 9th Louisiana Infantry	11/7/1863, Kelly's Ford, Rappahannock, Virginia	Died of Variola (Smallpox), 12/31/1863

Name	Age	Enlisted	Residence	Unit	Captured	Date and Cause of Death
Blunt, Charles P. Private Name Not On Monument	40	Unknown	Unknown	Co. D, 1st Virginia Cavalry	4/3/1865, Richmond, Virginia, Captured in Hospital After Lee's Surrender	Died of Chronic Diarrhea, 5/25/1865
Boatwright, Samuel O. Private	Unk	Unknown	Palmyra, Fluvanna County, Virginia	Co. C, 44th Virginia Infantry	5/12/1864, Spotsylvania Court House, Virginia	Died of Unknown Causes, 8/19/1864
Boitnett, David H. Private	Unk	6/17/1861, Rocky Mount, Franklin County, Virginia	Franklin County, Virginia	Co. C, 42nd Virginia Infantry	9/19/1864, Winchester, Virginia	Died of Pneumonia, 3/29/1865
Bolen, Kerney Private	30	10/10/1862, Raleigh, North Carolina, Conscript	Guilford County, North Carolina	Co. B, 52nd North Carolina Infantry	7/3/1863, Gettysburg, Pennsylvania	Died of Chronic Diarrhea, 1/3/1864
Boley, John W. Private	Unk	5/1/1862, White Sulphur Springs, West Virginia	Greenbrier County, West Virginia	Co. K, 22nd Virginia Infantry	9/19/1864, Winchester, Virginia	Died of Gastro Intestinitis, 2/4/1865
Bolick, Benjamin Sidney Private Name Not On Monument	20	3/17/1862 Lincolnton, North Carolina	Lincoln County, North Carolina	Co. I, 11th North Carolina Infantry	7/3/1863, Gettysburg, Pennsylvania	Died of Unknown Causes, 10/30/1863
Bollendorf, Nicholas Private	Unk	6/4/1861, Camp Moore, Louisiana	Orleans Parish, Louisiana	Co. C, 6th Louisiana Infantry	5/5/1864, Mine Run, Virginia	Died of Pneumonia, 5/31/1864
Bollinger, Theodore Private	Unk	11/19/1862, Warm Springs, Virginia	Bath County, Virginia	Co. B, 62nd Virginia Infantry	7/3/1863, Gettysburg, Pennsylvania	Died of Chronic Diarrhea, 2/5/1864
Bolton, Foster M. Private Not Listed On Monument	24	4/28/1862, Cumberland County, North Carolina	Cumberland County, North Carolina	Co. C, 54th North Carolina Infantry	7/9/1863, Williamsport, Maryland, Deserted to the Enemy	Died of Unknown Causes, 3/15/1864

Name	Age	Enlisted	Residence	Unit	Captured	Date and Cause of Death
Bolton, John R. Private	Unk	12/21/1863, Cumberland County, North Carolina	Cumberland County, North Carolina	Co. I, 51st North Carolina Infantry	3/12/1865, Fayetteville, North Carolina	Died of Catarrh, (Inflammation of Mucous Membranes) 5/1/1865
Boney, Thomas E. Private	Unk	2/1/1863, Kinston, Lenoir County, North Carolina	Lenoir County, North Carolina	Co. B, 4th North Carolina Cavalry	7/4/1863, Gettysburg, Pennsylvania, Captured During Retreat	Died of Chronic Diarrhea and Dropsy of Lungs, 10/28/1863
Bonham, J. J. Private Name Not On Monument	Unk	7/3/1861 Sandy Ridge, Alabama	Loundes County, Alabama	Co. B, 14th Alabama Infantry	6/1/1864 Mechanicsville, Virginia	Died of Unknown Causes, 7/12/1864
Booher, Jacob H. Private	Unk	3/28/1862, Goodson, Virginia	Unknown	Co. A, 37th Virginia Infantry	9/22/1864, Fisher's Hill, Virginia, Wounded in Right Thigh	Date and Cause of Death Unknown
Booker, William C. Sergeant	22	5/29/1861, Wake County, North Carolina	Wake County, North Carolina	Co. D, 26th North Carolina Infantry	10/27/1864, Boyton Plank Road or Burgess' Mill, Virginia	Died of Chronic Diarrhea, 3/30/1865
Booth, Samuel Sergeant	26	6/10/1861, Athens, Alabama	Limestone County, Georgia	Co. H, 9th Alabama Infantry	7/5/1863, Gettysburg, Pennsylvania, Gunshot Wound Right Leg	Died of Wounds, 1/11/1864
Borchers, George Sergeant	Unk	5/14/1862, Augusta, Georgia	Richmond County, Georgia	Co. F, 12th Georgia Battalion, Light Artillery	9/19/1864, Winchester, Virginia	Died of Acute Diarrhea, 10/26/1864
Borders, Stephen H. Private	Unk	3/4/1862, Camilla, Georgia	Mitchell County, Georgia	Co. F, 6th Georgia Infantry	8/19/1864, Globe Tavern, Near Weldon Railroad, Virginia	Died of Acute Diarrhea, 1/26/1865
Boren, Manchester Private Name Not On Monument	Unk	9/12/1863 Charleston, South Carolina	Charleston County, South Carolina	Co. F, 22nd South Carolina Infantry	6/2/1864 Bermuda Hundred, Virginia	Died of Unknown Causes, 7/5/1864

Name	Age	Enlisted	Residence	Unit	Captured	Date and Cause of Death
Boss, Abel Private Name Not On Monument	Unk	8/26/1862, Henry County, Alabama	Henry County, Alabama	Co. G, 3rd Alabama Infantry	10/19/1864, Cedar Creek or Strasburg, Virginia	Died of Chronic Diarrhea, 1/8/1865
Bostwick, Little B. Private	Unk	Unknown	Unknown	Co. E, 36th Georgia Infantry	12/17/1864, Nashville, Tennessee	Died of Chronic Diarrhea, 6/6/1865
Boswell, Patrick Henry Private	22	7/24/1861, Bedford County, Virginia	Bedford County, Virginia	Co. I, 58th Virginia Infantry	9/22/1864, Fisher's Hill, Virginia	Died of Chronic Diarrhea, 10/15/1864
Bouton, Daniel M. Private	26	9/27/1861, Zollicoffer, Tennessee	Unknown	Co. E, 61st Tennessee Mounted Infantry	5/16/1863, Big Black, Near Vickburg, Tennessee	Date and Cause of Death Unknown
Bowden, Rufus Private	19	4/22/1862, Franklin County, North Carolina	Franklin County, North Carolina	Co. G, 47th North Carolina Infantry	10/27/1864, Boyton Plank Road or Burgess' Mill, Virginia	Died of Chronic Dysentery, 1/20/1865
Bowen, Marquis D. Private	Unk	3/3/1862, Atlanta, Georgia	Fulton County, Georgia	Co. K, 22nd Georgia Infantry	8/16/1864, Deep Bottom, Petersburg, Virginia, Wounded	Died of Unknown Causes, 9/9/1864
Bower, William E. Private	Unk	Unknown	Unknown	Co. C, 5th Virginia Cavalry	4/1/1865, Five Forks, Virginia	Died of Typhoid Fever, 5/18/1865
Bowers, J. A. Private	Unk	3/31/1862, Place Unknown	Unknown	Co. C, 11th North Carolina Infantry	Unknown	Died of Pneumonia, 5/5/1865
Bowers, James S. Corporal	Unk	1/2/1862, Camp Hampton, South Carolina, Conscript	Lancaster County, South Carolina	Co. H, Holcombe Legion, South Carolina Infantry	4/2/1865, Five Forks, Virginia	Died of Chronic Dysentery, 6/3/1865
Bowers, John Private	28	3/4/1862, Richmond Factory, Georgia	Richmond County, Georgia	Co. I, 48th Georgia Infantry	7/3/1863, Gettysburg, Pennsylvania	Died of Erysipelas of the Face and Head, 11/5/1863

Name	Age	Enlisted	Residence	Unit	Captured	Date and Cause of Death
Bowling, B. L. Private	20	4/29/1861, Livingston, Texas	Polk County, Texas	Co. B, 1st Texas Infantry	7/4/1863, Gettysburg, Pennsylvania	Died of Unknown Causes, 8/6/1864
Bowling, Chesley Private Not Listed On Monument	35	2/25/1863, Granville County, North Carolina	Granville County, North Carolina	Co. K, 55th North Carolina Infantry	7/14/1863, Falling Waters, Maryland	Died of Chronic Diarrhea, 10/16/1863
Bowman, David H. Private	19	2/20/1863, Stokes County, North Carolina	Stokes County, North Carolina	Co. D, 52nd North Carolina Infantry	7/4/1863, Gettysburg, Pennsylvania, Gunshot Wound Right Leg	Died of Wounds, 11/18/1863
Bowman, Henry Private	Unk	6/22/1862, Wythe County, Virginia	Wythe County, Virginia	Co. B, 50th Virginia Infantry	7/3/1863, Gettysburg, Pennsylvania	Died of Variola (Smallpox), 12/3/1863
Boyd, Jesse J. Private	Unk	1/5/1862, Charlotte, Mecklenburg County, North Carolina	Mecklenburg County, North Carolina	Co. H, 11th North Carolina Infantry	4/2/1865, Petersburg, Virginia	Died of Infection of Lungs, 4/29/1865
Boyd, John H. Private	18	2/10/1863, Granville County, North Carolina	Granville County, North Carolina	Co. K, 55th North Carolina Infantry	7/1/1863, Gettysburg, Pennsylvania	Died of Variola (Smallpox), 12/6/1863
Boyett, John A. Private	17	Brunswick County, North Carolina, 12/4/1863, Volunteer	Warsaw, Duplin County, North Carolina	Co. A, 36th North Carolina Heavy Artillery	1/15/1865, Fort Fisher, North Carolina	Died of Pneumonia, 2/9/1865
Boyles, Jeff Private	Unk	2/16/1863, Orange Spring, Florida	Unknown	Co. F, 9th Florida Infantry	6/24/1864, Petersburg, Virginia	Died of Scurvy, 4/27/1865
Boyles, John W. Private	18	5/22/1861, Rockingham County, North Carolina	Rockingham County, North Carolina	Co. K, 13th North Carolina Infantry	7/1/1863, Gettysburg, Pennsylvania	Died of Chronic Diarrhea and Scurvy, 1/3/1864

Name	Age	Enlisted	Residence	Unit	Captured	Date and Cause of Death
Boyles, Lucius C. Private	Unk	5/14/1862, Camp McCarthy, Florida	Unknown	Co. B, 9th Florida Infantry	9/9/1864, Petersburg, Virginia	Died of Chronic Diarrhea, 11/2/1864
Bracy, Samuel P. Landsman	Unk	Unknown	Unknown	Confederate States Navy,	Unknown	Date and Cause of Death Unknown
Bradbury, Harrison Private	21	4/29/1861, Winchester, Tennessee	Franklin County, Tennessee	Co. C, 1st Tennessee Infantry	7/1/1863, Gettysburg, Pennsylvania	Died of Chronic Diarrhea, 12/26/1863
Bradfield, H. Private	30	5/?/1862, Prince William County, Virginia	Prince William County, Virginia	Co. R, 15th Virginia Cavalry	8/22/1863, Prince William County, Virginia	Died of Chronic Diarrhea, 12/28/1863
Bradford, Walter A. Private	18	6/6/1861, Laurens Court House, South Carolina	Laurens, South Carolina	Co. A, 3rd South Carolina Infantry	7/5/1863, Gettysburg, Pennsylvania	Died of Unknown Causes, 2/15/1864
Bradley, David P. Private	Unk	3/4/1862, Hawkinsville, Georgia	Pulaski County, Georgia	Co. F, 31st Georgia Infantry	7/5/1863, South Mountain, Maryland, Wounded	Died of Variola (Smallpox), 12/5/1863
Bradley, J. H. Private	Unk	10/17/1862, Sumter, South Carolina	Sumter County, South Carolina	Co. F, 7th South Carolina Cavalry	Unknown	Date and Cause of Death Unknown
Bradley, Joseph L. Corporal	21	3/15/1862, Marion, McDowell County, North Carolina, Volunteer	McDowell County, North Carolina	Co. K, 22nd North Carolina Infantry	5/6/1864, Wilderness, Virginia	Died of Unknown Causes, 6/2/1864
Bradley, Joseph T. 1st Sergeant	21	4/30/1861, Corinth, Mississippi	Alcorn County, Mississippi	Co. A, 12th Mississippi Infantry	8/21/1864, Globe Tavern, Near Weldon Railroad, Virginia	Died of Chronic Diarrhea, 5/28/1865
Bradshaw, Jesse Sergeant	26	11/2/1861, Alexander County, North Carolina, Volunteer	Alexander County, North Carolina, Farmer	Co. D, 38th North Carolina Infantry	7/5/1863, Gettysburg, Pennsylvania	Died of Unknown Causes, 8/11/1864

Name	Age	Enlisted	Residence	Unit	Captured	Date and Cause of Death
Bradshaw, Jonas N. Private Name Not On Monument	26	11/2/1861 Alexander County, North Carolina	Alexander County, North Carolina, Farmer	Co. G, 38th North Carolina Infantry	7/5/1863, Gettysburg, Pennsylvania	Died of Unknown Causes, 8/11/1864
Bradwell, G. M. Private	Unk	Unknown	Unknown	Co. B, 11th Georgia Infantry	7/5/1863, Gettysburg, Pennsylvania	Died of Unknown Causes, 11/10/1863
Brady, Zimri Sergeant	21	3/12/1862, Ashboro, North Carolina	Randolph County, North Carolina, Farmer	Co. H, 44th North Carolina Infantry	10/27/1864, Boyton Plank Road or Burgess' Mill, Virginia	Died of Chronic Diarrhea, 1/24/1865
Bragg, John T. B. Private	18	4/19/1861, Petersburg, Virginia	Chesterfield County, Virginia	Co. A, 12th Virginia Infantry	4/6/1863, Jetersville, Virginia	Died of Acute Diarrhea, 5/23/1865
Bragg, Joseph Private	Unk	5/1/1862, White Sulphur Springs, West Virginia	Greenbrier County, West Virginia	Co. E, 22nd Virginia Infantry	9/19/1864, Winchester, Virginia	Died of Pneumonia, 2/4/1865
Bragg, William Private	Unk	9/15/1862, Charleston, West Virginia	Kanawha County, West Virginia	Co. A, 22nd Virginia Infantry	9/19/1864, Winchester, Virginia	Died of Chronic Diarrhea, 2/8/1864
Bragg, William Private	Unk	1/8/1863, Lewisburg, Virginia	Greenbrier County, West Virginia	Co. A, 26th Battalion Virginia Infantry	6/3/1864, Gaines' Farm, Virginia	Died of Rubeola (Measles) 8/22/1864
Brakefield, Henry N. Private	27	5/10/1862, Meriwether County, Georgia	Meriwether County, Georgia	Co. A, 60th Georgia Infantry	7/3/1863, Gettysburg, Pennsylvania	Died of Chronic Diarrhea, 3/15/1864
Bramlett, J. M. Private	Unk	Unknown	Unknown	Co. E, 51st Georgia Infantry	6/27/1863, Shelbyville, Tennessee	Died of Chronic Diarrhea, 12/17/1863
Brandt, John F. Private	46	2/3/1864, Pocotaligo, Jasper County, South Carolina	Jasper County, South Carolina	Co. C, 19th South Carolina Cavalry	3/5/1865, Florence, South Carolina	Died of Unknown Causes, 5/31/1865

Name	Age	Enlisted	Residence	Unit	Captured	Date and Cause of Death
Branning, W. M. Private	Unk	Unknown	Unknown	Co. K, 57th North Carolina Infantry	Unknown	Unable to Locate
Bransdale, J. W. Private	Unk	Unknown	Unknown	Co. F, 9th Virginia Infantry	Unknown	Unable to Locate
Branson, John M. Private	Unk	8/18/1864, Raleigh, Wake County, North Carolina	Wake County, North Carolina	Co. K, 2nd Battalion North Carolina Infantry	9/19/1864, Winchester, Virginia	Died of Chronic Diarrhea, 3/17/1865
Brantley, W. H. Private Name Not On Monument	Unk	11/2/1863 Albany, Georgia	Dougherty County, Georgia	Co. K, 28th Battalion Georgia Siege Artillery	3/9/1865, Near Fayetteville, North Carolina	Died of Chronic Pneumonia, 6/26/1865
Branton, John Private	Unk	7/1/1863, Goldsboro, North Carolina	Unknown	Co. G, 10th North Carolina, Artillery	10/30/1864, Plymouth, North Carolina	Died of Pneumonia, 3/2/1865
Brassett, Henry C. Private	Unk	10/15/1861, Camp Relief, Louisiana	Unknown	Co. C, 4th Louisiana Infantry	12/16/1864, Nashville, Tennessee	Date and Cause of Death Unknown
Brassfield, James W. Private	32	2/13/1862, Wake County, North Carolina	Orange County, North Carolina	Co. D, 30th North Carolina Infantry	7/3/1863, Gettysburg, Pennsylvania	Died of Chronic Diarrhea, 2/12/1864
Braswell, Jesse Private	48	3/1/1863, Camp Near Kinston, Lenoir County, North Carolina, Substitute	Nash County, North Carolina	Co. H, 32nd North Carolina Infantry	5/10/1864, Mine Run, Virginia	Died of Unknown Causes, 9/3/1864
Braswell, Lemuel T. Private	19	2/24/1862, Nash County, North Carolina	Nash County, North Carolina, Farmer	Co. A, 47th North Carolina Infantry	7/14/1863, Falling Waters, Maryland	Died of Unknown Causes, 12/11/1863
Brattain, Absalom W. Private	Unk	10/30/1864, Stanly, County, North Carolina	Stanly County, North Carolina	Co. C, 42nd North Carolina Infantry	3/10/1865, Wise Forks, Near Kinston, North Carolina	Died of Acute Diarrhea, 5/4/1865

Name	Age	Enlisted	Residence	Unit	Captured	Date and Cause of Death
Bray, John H. Private	Unk	3/1/1862, Rockport, Arkansas	Unknown	Co. D, 12th Battalion Arkansas Sharp Shooters	5/10/1863, Champion Hill, Tennessee	Died of Variola (Smallpox), 11/27/1863
Brazelton, James R. Private	20	4/29/1861, Franklin County, Tennessee	Franklin County, Tennessee	Co. F, 1st Tennessee Infantry	10/1/1864, Petersburg, Virginia	Died of Chronic Dysentery, 3/1/1865
Brazil, Robert H.	Unk	7/3/1861, Atlanta, Georgia	Hall County, Georgia	Co. A, 11th Georgia Infantry	7/5/1863, Gettysburg, Pennsylvania	Died of Variola (Smallpox), 11/9/1863
Breece, G. W. Private	Unk	7/20/1863, Raleigh, North Carolina	Wake County, North Carolina	Co. I, 14th North Carolina Infantry	4/6/1865, Farmville, Virginia	Died of Scurvy, 4/25/1865
Breedlove, Jesse E. Private	24	6/25/1861, Buncombe County, North Carolina	Macon County, North Carolina	Co. K, 1st Carolina Cavalry	12/1/1864, Stony Creek, Virginia	Died of Pneumonia, 4/8/1865
Breedlove, Henry Newman Private	Unk	2/6/1864, Camp Holmes, Raleigh, North Carolina	Wake County, North Carolina	Co. M, 22nd North Carolina Infantry	5/23/1864, North Anna River, Virginia	Died of Chronic Diarrhea, 6/6/1865
Brewer, Elijah Private	Unk	7/15/1862, Wake County, North Carolina	Rowan County, North Carolina	Co. K, 5th North Carolina Infantry	7/5/1863, Gettysburg, Pennsylvania	Died of Variola (Smallpox), 12/23/1863
Brice, Thomas K. Private Name Not On Monument	Unk	5/5/1862 Charleston, South Carolina	Charleston County, South Carolina	Co. F, 1st South Carolina Infantry	8/14/1864, Deep Bottom, Virginia	Died of Chronic Diarrhea, 2/24/1865
Bridges, Green H. Private	Unk	2/17/1863, Charleston, South Carolina	Charleston County, South Carolina	Co. K, 27th South Carolina Infantry	6/18/1864, Petersburg, Virginia	Died of Unknown Causes, 7/26/1864
Bridges, George W. Private	27	3/4/1862, Franklin County, North Carolina	Franklin County, North Carolina, Farmer	Co. F, 47th North Carolina Infantry	10/27/1864, Boyton Plank Road or Burgess' Mill, Virginia	Died of Consumption (Tuberculosis), 1/29/1865

Name	Age	Enlisted	Residence	Unit	Captured	Date and Cause of Death
Bridgewaters, William Private	19	10/3/1862, Morristown, Tennessee	Hamblen County, Tennessee	Co. G, 61st Tennessee Mounted Infantry	5/17/1863, Big Black Bridge, Mississippi	Died of Unknown Causes, 12/28/1863
Bridwell, J. McD. Private Name Not On Monument	Unk	5/18/1861, Augusta, Georgia	Richmond County, Georgia	Co. B, 10th Georgia Infantry	7/3/1863, Gettysburg, Pennsylvania	Died of Smallpox, 11/10/1863
Bright, A. Tate Private	Unk	9/3/1861, Camp McDonald, Georgia	Murray County, Georgia	Co. D, 22nd Georgia Infantry	7/14/1863, Falling Waters, Maryland	Died of Chronic Diarrhea and Scurvy, 11/21/1863
Bright, David Private	Unk	12/3/1862, Camp Washington, Virginia	Augusta County, Virginia, Laborer	Co. G, 25th Virginia Infantry	9/19/1864, Winchester, Virginia	Died of Remittent Fever, 3/16/1865
Bright, George F. Private	30	4/30/1864, Camp Lee, Prince Edward County, Virginia	Swift Creek, Craven County, North Carolina, Farmer	Co. A, Confederate States Marine Corp	1/15/1865, Fort Fisher, North Carolina	Died of Pneumonia, 3/6/1865
Brightwell, William C. Private Name Not On Monument	Unk	10/14/1864 Danville, Virginia	Pittsylvania County, Virginia	Co. G, 38th Virginia Infantry	4/2/1865 Petersburg, Virginia	Died of Scurvy and Typhoid Fever, 7/8/1865
Brigman, John Private	44	9/16/1863, Union County, North Carolina, Conscript	Union County, North Carolina	Co. E, 30th North Carolina Infantry	5/31/1864, Old Church Tavern, Virginia	Died of Chronic Diarrhea, 10/24/1864
Brignac, Alceste Private	Unk	7/22/1861, Camp Moore, Louisiana	Orleans Parish, Louisiana	Co. H, 10th Louisiana Infantry	5/12/1864, Wilderness, Virginia	Died of Unknown Causes, 6/29/1864
Brinsfield, John Private	30	2/27/1863, Guilford County, North Carolina	Guilford County, North Carolina, Mechanic	Co. F, 54th North Carolina Infantry	11/7/1863, Rappahannock Station, Virginia	Died of Variola (Smallpox), 12/18/1863
Brisendein, Jesse R. Private	Unk	3/22/1864, Chaffin's Farm, Virginia	Unknown	Co. G, 28th Virginia Infantry	4/6/1865, Farmville, Virginia	Died of Typhoid Fever, 5/19/1865

156

Name	Age	Enlisted	Residence	Unit	Captured	Date and Cause of Death
Bristow, George F. Private Name Not On Monument	Unk	7/28/1863 Saluda, Virginia	Middlesex County, Virginia	Co. C, 55th Virginia Infantry	5/5/1864 Wilderness, Virginia	Died of Unknown Causes, 7/13/1864
Britt, Noah Private	Unk	3/11/1863, Wilmington, North Carolina	New Hanover County, North Carolina	Co. F, 10th North Carolina, Artillery	3/19/1865, Goldsboro, North Carolina	Died of Scurvy, 5/2/1865
Broach, Benjamin Private	23	6/2/1861, Centerville, Virginia	Culpepper County, Virginia, Farmer	Co. H, 26th Virginia Infantry	4/6/1865, High Bridge, Virginia	Died of Acute Dysentery, 5/2/1865
Broach, Robert Private	Unk	6/12/1861, Center Cross, Virginia	Essex County, Virginia	Co. H, 55th Virginia Infantry	7/14/1863, Falling Waters, Maryland	Died of Unknown Causes, 3/17/1864
Broaddus, Reuben Corporal	27	4/24/1861, Sparta, Virginia	Sparta, Virginia, Manager	Co. H, 30th Virginia Infantry	4/6/1865, High Bridge, Virginia	Died of Pneumonia, 5/3/1865
BroadFoot, William G. Private.	Unk	4/26/1861, Place Unknown	Unknown	Co. E, 11th Mississippi Infantry	7/14/1863, Falling Waters, Maryland	Died of Chronic Diarrhea, 1/15/1864
Brock, James M. Private Name Not On Monument	Unk	7/9/1861, Carterville, Georgia	Bartow County, Georgia	Co. K, 14th Georgia Infantry	4/2/1865 Petersburg, Virginia	Died of Dysentery, 5/3/1865
Brock, John William Corporal Name Not On Monument	26	7/5/1862, Salisbury, North Carolina, Volunteer	Davis County, North Carolina	Co. A, 57th North Carolina Infantry	7/5/1863, Gettysburg, Pennsylvania	Died of Unknown Causes, 7/13/1864
Brockwell, Lorenzo Private	Unk	3/26/1862, Jamestown, Virginia	James City County, Virginia	Co. D, 10th Battalion Virginia Artillery	4/6/1865, Archer's Farm, Harper's Ferry, Virginia	Died of Unknown Causes, 6/13/1865

157

Name	Age	Enlisted	Residence	Unit	Captured	Date and Cause of Death
Brogdon, Andrew J. Private	32	3/7/1862, Camp Mangum, North Carolina	Wake County, North Carolina, Clerk	Co. E, 47th North Carolina Infantry	7/3/1863, Gettysburg, Pennsylvania	Died of Chronic Diarrhea, 1/7/1864
Brook, John Private	Unk	Unknown	Unknown	Cabell's Battery, Virginia	Unknown	Unable to Locate
Brookman, Robert H. Private	20	6/25/1861, Wythe County, Virginia	Pulaski County, Virginia	Co. I, 50th Virginia Infantry	5/5/1864, Wilderness, Virginia	Died of Chronic Diarrhea, 6/24/1864
Brookman, S. Private	Unk	Unknown	Unknown	Co. H, 5th Virginia Infantry	Unknown	Died of Chronic Diarrhea, 8/21/1864
Brooks, Cyrus D. Private Name Not On Monument	37	3/26/1863, Chatham County, North Carolina	Goldston, Chatham County, North Carolina, Farmer	Co. G, 40th North Carolina Light Artillery	1/15/1865, Fort Fisher, North Carolina	Died of Chronic Diarrhea, 2/3/1865
Brooks, James A. Private Name Not On Monument	Unk	4/5/1862, Glascock County, Georgia	Glascock County, Georgia	Co. B, 22nd Georgia Infantry	7/23/1863, Manassas, Virginia	Died of Unknown Causes, 1/15/1864
Brooks, James O. Private	41	7/10/1863, Lake City, Florida	Columbia County, Florida	Co. G, 9th Florida Infantry	6/24/1864, Petersburg, Virginia	Died of Unknown Causes, 9/2/1864
Broom, William Private	20	2/27/1863, Union County, Massachusetts	Union County, Massachusetts	Co. A, 48th North Carolina Infantry	3/25/1865, Hatcher's Run, Virginia	Died of Chronic Diarrhea, 6/1/1865
Brothers, Wilson Private	Unk	11/1/1862, Prince George County, Virginia	Currituck County, North Carolina	Co. G, 4th North Carolina Cavalry	10/14/1863, Newler's Bridge, North Carolina	Died of Unknown Causes, 9/12/1864
Browman, G. E. Private	Unk	Unknown	Unknown	Co. F, 49th Virginia Infantry	Unknown	Unable to Locate

Name	Age	Enlisted	Residence	Unit	Captured	Date and Cause of Death
Brown, Alwyn H. Private	19	8/27/1861, Charleston, South Carolina	Charleston County, South Carolina	Co. L, 1st South Carolina Infantry	7/14/1863, Falling Waters, Maryland	Died of Chronic Diarrhea and Scurvy, 6/5/1865
Brown, A. J. Private	Unk	Unknown	Unknown	Co. F, 1st Virginia Cavalry	7/13/1863, Loudon County, Virginia, Gunshot Wound Right Thigh	Cause of Death Unknown, 2/13/1864
Brown, Amos J. Private	29	2/6/1862, New Hanover County, North Carolina	Wilmington, New Hanover County, North Carolina, Clerk	Co. D, 36th North Carolina Heavy Artillery	1/15/1865, Fort Fisher, North Carolina	Died of Chronic Diarrhea, 6/14/1865
Brown, Archibald Private	3	Wilmington, New Hanover County, North Carolina, 4/22/1862, Volunteer	Duplin County, North Carolina, Farmer,	Co. C, 36th North Carolina Heavy Artillery	1/15/1865, Fort Fisher, North Carolina	Died of Dropsy, 3/21/1865
Brown, Carlos Private	Unk	Unknown	Unknown	Co. D, 42nd Georgia Infantry	2/10/1865, Edisto River, South Carolina	Cause of Death Unknown, 5/16/1865
Brown, David Private	Unk	2/22/1864, Columbia, South Carolina	Richland County, South Carolina	Co. G, 25th South Carolina Infantry	2/20/1865, Fort Anderson, Near Town Creek, North Carolina	Died of Chronic Diarrhea, 5/8/1865
Brown, Elam Private	Unk	1/1/1864, Brevard, North Carolina	Transylvania County, North Carolina	Co. C, 6th North Carolina Cavalry	3/17/1865, Kinston, New Hope, North Carolina	Died of Scurvy, 4/24/1865
Brown, Elias Private	45	9/23/1862, Boon's Creek, Tennessee	Unknown	Co. D, 60th Tennessee Mounted Infantry	5/17/ 1863, Big Black Bridge, Near Vicksburg, Mississippi	Died of Chronic Diarrhea and Smallpox, 11/23/1863
Brown, Elijah Private	22	9/22/1862, Camp French, Near Petersburg, Virginia	Wilkes County, North Carolina	Co. F, 52nd North Carolina Infantry	10/27/1864, Burgess' Mill, Virginia	Died of Chronic Diarrhea, 12/19/1864
Brown, F. W. Private	25	12/30/1861, Columbia, South Carolina	Richland County, South Carolina	Co. D, 20th South Carolina Infantry	10/19/1864, Cedar Creek or Strasburg, Virginia	Died of Lithiasis, 5/11/1865

Name	Age	Enlisted	Residence	Unit	Captured	Date and Cause of Death
Brown, George L. Private	Unk	3/30/1864, Kinston, North Carolina	Stewart County, Georgia	Co. I, 21st Georgia Infantry	2/6/1865, Hatcher's Run, Virginia	Died of Rubeola (Measles) 4/7/1865
Brown, J. Private	Unk	7/30/1861, Marion, Virginia	Smyth County, Virginia	Co. D, 4th Virginia Infantry	7/3/1863, Gettysburg, Pennsylvania	Died of Chronic Diarrhea, 12/26/1863
Brown, J. E. Private	Unk	Unknown	Unknown	Co. C, 6th North Carolina Cavalry	Unknown	Unable to Locate
Brown, J. L. Private	Unk	2/15/1863, Adam's Store, Alabama	Unknown	Co. B, 12th Alabama Infantry	4/6/1865, Harper's Farm, Virginia	Died of Rubeola (Measles) 6/10/1865
Brown, J. W. Private	Unk	Unknown	Unknown	Co. H, 7th Tennessee Infantry	Unknown	Unable to Locate
Brown, James A. Private	Unk	3/18/1862, Place Unknown	Unknown	Co. C, 11th Virginia Infantry	5/21/1864, Milford's Station, Virginia	Died of Pneumonia-Typhoid Fever, 3/14/1865
Brown, James T. Corporal	Unk	8/26/1862, Richmond, Virginia	Henrico County, Virginia	Co. F, 2nd Battalion Maryland Infantry	8/19/1864, Globe Tavern, Near Weldon Railroad, Virginia	Died of Chronic Diarrhea, 4/23/1865
Brown, Jesse Private	Unk	1/29/1862, Columbia, South Carolina	Richland County, South Carolina	Co. E, 2nd South Carolina Infantry	8/1/1863, Brandy Station, Virginia	Died of Scorbutus (Scurvy) 11/13/1863
Brown, John L. Private	27	9/22/1862, Camp French, Near Petersburg, Virginia, Conscript	Wilkes County, North Carolina	Co. I, 52nd North Carolina Infantry	5/12/1864, Spotsylvania Court House, Virginia	Died of Unknown Causes, 7/28/1864
Brown, John C. Sergeant	29	4/4/1862, Yadkin County, North Carolina	Yadkin County, North Carolina	Co. F, 28th North Carolina Infantry	7/3/1863, Gettysburg, Pennsylvania	Died of Variola (Smallpox), 11/25/1864
Brown, John Garland Private	Unk	9/9/1864, Camp Lee, Prince Edward County, Virginia	Prince Edward County, Virginia	Co. D, 18th Virginia Infantry	4/6/1865, Sailor's Creek, Virginia	Died of Pneumonia, 5/15/1865

Name	Age	Enlisted	Residence	Unit	Captured	Date and Cause of Death
Brown, John W. Private	26	7/15/1862, Raleigh, North Carolina, Conscript	Johnston County, North Carolina	Co. C, 1st North Carolina Infantry	5/12/1864, Spotsylvania Court House, Virginia	Died of Unknown Causes, 7/31/1864
Brown Joseph T. Private	Unk	2/1/1862, Place Unknown	Unknown	Co. D, 11th Mississippi Infantry	Unknown	Died of Unknown Causes, 1/9/1864
Brown, Thomas H. Private	Unk	Unknown	Unknown	Co. D, 9th Virginia Infantry	4/1/1865, Five Forks, Virginia	Died of inflammation of Throat, 5/28/1865
Brown, William C. Sergeant	Unk	4/20/1863, Atlanta, Georgia	Fulton County, Georgia	Co. K, 64th Georgia Infantry	8/17/1864, Deep Bottom, Virginia	Died of Chronic Diarrhea, 4/14/1865
Brown, William L. Private	Unk	3/7/1862, Danville, Virginia	Pittsylvania County, Virginia	Co. L, 38th Virginia Infantry	7/3/1863, Gettysburg, Pennsylvania	Died of Chronic Diarrhea and Scurvy, 12/12/1863
Brown, William M. Private	23	9/25/1862, Fordtown, Tennessee	Unknown	Co. E, 60th Tennessee Mounted Infantry	5/17/1863, Big Black Bridge, Near Vicksburg, Mississippi	Died of Unknown Causes, 5/4/1864
Brown, William W. Private	Unk	11/13/1861, Savannah, Georgia	Stewart County, Georgia	Co. E, 31st Georgia Infantry	7/14/1863, Williamsport, Virginia	Died of Pneumonia-Typhoid Fever, 11/18/1863
Browning, James L. Private	18	4/4/1863, Alamance County, North Carolina	Unknown	Co. K, 6th North Carolina Infantry	11/7/1863, Kelly's Ford, Rappahannock Station, Virginia	Died of Congestion of the Brain, 2/18/1865
Browning, James M. Private	Unk	6/18/1861, Fort Macon, North Carolina	Caswell County, North Carolina	Co. G, 27th North Carolina Infantry	10/14/1863, Bristoe Station, Virginia	Died of Chronic Diarrhea, 1/11/1864
Browning, William Private Name Not On Monument	16	3/22/1862, Winston, North Carolina	Forsyth County, North Carolina	Co. K, 52nd North Carolina Infantry	7/14/1863, Falling Waters, Maryland	Died of Chronic Diarrhea, 5/3/1864

Name	Age	Enlisted	Residence	Unit	Captured	Date and Cause of Death
Broyles, Alfred Private	23	10/21/1862, Randolph County, North Carolina Conscript	Randolph County, North Carolina	Co. H, 47th North Carolina Infantry	7/5/1863, Gettysburg, Pennsylvania	Died of Chronic Diarrhea and Scurvy, 12/17/1863
Bruce, G. W. See: Breece, G. W.				Co. I, 14th North Carolina Infantry		
Bruce, Henley G. Private Not Listed On the Monument	Unk	2/10/1863, Floyd County, Virginia	Floyd County, Virginia	Co. F, 8th Virginia Cavalry	5/7/1864, Tazwell County, Virginia	Died of Unknown Causes On Route To Be Exchanged, 3/19/1865
Bryan, Joshua Private	27	3/12/1862, Jasper, County, Georgia	Jasper, County, Georgia	Co. C, 14th Georgia Infantry	5/24/1864, Jericho Ford, North Anna River, Virginia	Died of Scurvy, 3/17/1865
Bryan, William B. Private	Unk	7/7/1862, Trenton, North Carolina	Jones County, North Carolina	Co. A, 66th North Carolina Infantry	2/20/1864, Near Fairfield, Virginia	Died of Chronic Diarrhea, 3/12/1865
Bryant, James P. Sergeant	Unk	4/23/1861, Falmouth, Virginia	Unknown	Co. A, 47th Virginia Infantry	8/19/1864, Globe Tavern, Near Weldon Railroad, Virginia	Died of Pneumonia, 2/22/1865
Bryant, John Westley Private Not Listed On Monument	Unk	3/4/1862, Hamilton, Georgia	Harris County, Georgia	Co. K, 35th Georgia Infantry	7/3/1863, Gettysburg, Pennsylvania	Died of Chronic Diarrhea, 8/22/1864
Bryant, Michael A. Private	22	6/10/1861, Monticello, Arkansas	Unknown	Co. C, 1st North Carolina Infantry	5/12/1864, Spotsylvania Court House, Virginia	Died of Chronic Diarrhea, 6/11/1865
Bryant, Samuel Private	Unk	7/18/1861, Jackson, Virginia	Unknown	Co. K, 57th Virginia Infantry	4/1/1865, Five Forks, Virginia	Died of Chronic Diarrhea, 5/20/1865

Name	Age	Enlisted	Residence	Unit	Captured	Date and Cause of Death
Bryant, William Private	Unk	5/19/1864, Raleigh, Wake County, North Carolina	Wake County, North Carolina	Co. C, 2nd North Carolina Infantry	4/6/1865, Farmville, Virginia	Died of Chronic Diarrhea, 6/24/1865
Bryant, William N. Private	Unk	3/1/1863, Brownsburg, Virginia	Rockbridge County, Virginia	Cobb's Legion Battalion, Georgia Cavalry	9/22/1863, Jack's Shop, Near Madison Court House, Virginia	Died of Variola (Smallpox), 11/17/1863
Bryles, Alfred Private Not Listed On Monument	23	10/27/1862, Randolph County, North Carolina	Randolph County, North Carolina	Co. H, 47th North Carolina Infantry	7/5/1863, Gettysburg, Pennsylvania, Wounded	Died of Chronic Diarrhea & Pneumonia, 12/17/1863
Buchanan, P. M. Private	Unk	3/29/1861, Smythe County, Virginia	Unknown	Co. E, 23rd Battalion, Virginia	9/19/1864, Winchester, Virginia	Died of Chronic Diarrhea, 11/28/1864
Buchanan, Samuel T. Captain Not Listed On Monument	25	5/18/1861, Seven Mile Ford, Virginia	Unknown	Co. D, 48th, Virginia Infantry	5/12/1864 Near Spotsylvania Court House, Virginia	Died of Unknown Causes 7/16/1864
Buckley, Mercer M. Sergeant	26	2/26/1862, Meridian, Tennessee	Unknown	Co. I, 36th Mississippi Infantry	10/5/1864, Altoona, Georgia	Died of Apoplexy, (Bleeding From a Stroke), 5/4/1865
Budd, Lemuel G. Corporal	27	4/3/1862, Wayne County, North Carolina	Wayne County, North Carolina, Farmer	Co. G, 55th North Carolina Infantry	7/1/1863, Gettysburg, Pennsylvania	Died of Debility (Loss of Strength, Feeble), 11/28/1863
Bullis, Benjamin F. Corporal	32	6/12/1861, Wilkesboro, North Carolina, Volunteer	Wilkes County, North Carolina	Co. C, 26th North Carolina Infantry	7/3/1863, Gettysburg, Pennsylvania, Wounded	Died of Unknown Causes, 2/9/1864
Bullock, D. Private	Unk	6/6/1861, Greenville Butler County, Alabama	Butler County, Alabama	Co. G, 9th Alabama Infantry	5/6/1864, Wilderness, Virginia	Died of Unknown Causes, 7/26/1864

Name	Age	Enlisted	Residence	Unit	Captured	Date and Cause of Death
Bullock, William Private	Unk	4/20/1861, Greenville, North Carolina	Pitt County, North Carolina	Co. H, 27th North Carolina Infantry	5/24/1864, North Anna River, Hanover Junction, Virginia	Died of Unknown Causes, 8/7/1864
Bumey, John H. Corporal	Unk	Unknown	Unknown	Co. E, 42nd Virginia Cavalry	Unknown	Unable to Locate
Bumgarner, David A. Private Not Listed On Monument	18	4/19/1862, Cleveland County, North Carolina, Volunteer	Cleveland County, North Carolina, Farmer	Co. F, 55th North Carolina Infantry	7/1/1863, Gettysburg, Pennsylvania	Died of Unknown Causes, 8/20/1863
Bumgarner, Wesley L. Private	Unk	9/7/1862, Conscript	Unknown	Co. H, 18th North Carolina Infantry	5/12/1864, Spotsylvania Court House, Virginia	Died of Unknown Causes, 8/15/1864
Bumpers, Samuel Private Not Listed On Monument	37	9/8/1862, Clark County, Alabama	Clark County, Alabama	Co. I, 6th Alabama Infantry	4/15/1865, Harper's Farm, Virginia	Died of Chronic Diarrhea, 7/12/1865
Bunch, Jethro J. Private	22	5/30/1861, Weldon, North Carolina, Volunteer	Halifax County, North Carolina	Co. H, 5th North Carolina Infantry	7/13/1863, Williamsport, Gettysburg, Pennsylvania,	Died of Smallpox, 1/11/1864
Bunch, John W. Private	20	7/9/1861, Staunton, Virginia	Augusta County, Virginia	Co. A, 52nd Virginia Infantry	7/6/1863, Chambersburg, Maryland	Died of Chronic Diarrhea, 12/18/1863
Bunn, A. L. Corporal	Unk	7/2/1863, Strasburg, Virginia	Shenandoah County, Virginia	Co. K, 54th North Carolina Infantry	11/7/1863, Rappahannock Station, Virginia	Died of Unknown Causes, 4/7/1864
Burden, Z. J. Private	Unk	Unknown	Unknown	Co. F, 4th North Carolina Cavalry	Unknown	Unable to Locate
Burke, James M. Private	Unk	10/1/1862, Front Royal, Virginia	Warren County, Virginia	Co. B, 6th Virginia Infantry	5/31/1864, Cold Harbor, Virginia	Died of Acute Dysentery, 6/28/1864

Name	Age	Enlisted	Residence	Unit	Captured	Date and Cause of Death
Burke, William L. Private	21	7/8/1862, Chatham County, North Carolina	Chatham County, North Carolina, Cabinet Maker	Co. D, 61st North Carolina Infantry	8/26/1863, Battery Wagner, Morris Island, South Carolina	Died of Variola (Smallpox), 12/18/1863
Burkhalter, Bryant Private	Unk	5/9/1862, Reidsville, Georgia	Tattnall County, Georgia	Co. H, 61st Georgia Infantry	5/12/1864, Wilderness, Virginia	Died of Chronic Diarrhea, 10/22/1864
Burkhalter, James Private	Unk	Unknown	Unknown	White's Battalion, Virginia Artillery	3/19/1865, Averasboro, North Carolina	Died of Acute Diarrhea, 4/17/1865
Burne, Andrew Private	Unk	5/28/1864, Sweet Springs, Virginia	Monroe County, Virginia	Co. B, 14th Virginia Cavalry	11/12/1864, Near Nineveh, Virginia	Died of Typhoid Fever, 2/20/1865
Burnett, Burrell Private	27	2/26/1862, Perry's Mill, Franklin County, North Carolina	Franklin County, North Carolina, Farmer	Co. K, 44th North Carolina Infantry	10/14/1863, Bristoe Station, Virginia	Died of Unknown Causes, 2/1/1864
Burnett, Calvin Private	34	2/11/1862, Nash County, North Carolina	Nash County, North Carolina, Farmer	Co. A, 47th North Carolina Infantry	10/14/1863, Bristoe Station, Virginia	Died of Chronic Diarrhea, 2/13/1865
Burnett, Edwin H. Private	Unk	5/18/1861, Boydton, Virginia	Mecklenburg County, Virginia	Co. G, 38th Virginia Infantry	7/3/1863, Gettysburg, Pennsylvania, Wounded in Side	Died of Chronic Diarrhea, 3/8/1865
Burney, John H. Corporal Not Listed On Monument	Unk	1/15/1863, Camp Burney, North Carolina	Unknown	Co. E, 67th North Carolina Infantry	12/13/1863, Near Haddock's Cross Roads, Charles City Court House, Virginia	Died of Chronic Dysentery, 2/13/1865
Burney, Shipman B. Private	42	8/31/1862, Fort St. Philip, Brunswick County, North Carolina	Brunswick County, North Carolina	Co. E, 36th North Carolina Heavy Artillery	1/15/1865, Fort Fisher, North Carolina, Wounded Left Shoulder	Died of Wounds, 2/15/1865

Name	Age	Enlisted	Residence	Unit	Captured	Date and Cause of Death
Burns, Edward Fireman Not Listed On Monument	Unk	Unknown	Unknown	Blockade Runner Hope	Captured By USS Eolious at Sea Off Wilmington, North Carolina	Died of Unknown Causes, 1/7/1865
Burns, W. P. Private	Unk	5/12/1862, Macon, Georgia	Unknown	Philip's Legion, Georgia Infantry	8/1/1863, Brandy Station, Virginia	Died of Scurvy, 6/25/1865
Burrage, E. H. M. Private	29	8/8/1862, Wake County, North Carolina	Stanley County, North Carolina	Co. D, 5th North Carolina Infantry	7/3/1863, Gettysburg, Pennsylvania	Died of Variola (Smallpox), 11/25/1863
Burren, H. M. Private	Unk	Unknown	Unknown	Co. D, 7th Alabama Cavalry	Unknown	Unable to Locate
Burroughs, William C. Private	Unk	3/1/1863, Wentworth, North Carolina	Rockingham, North Carolina	Co. D, 5th North Carolina Cavalry	7/5/1863, Gettysburg, Pennsylvania	Died of Chronic Diarrhea, 12/5/1863
Burton, James M. Private Not Listed On Monument	Unk	5/12/1861, Columbia, South Carolina	Richland County, South Carolina	Co. C, 1st South Carolina Artillery	3/16/1865, Smith's Ford, North Carolina	Died of Congestive, Intermittent Fever, 4/17/1865
Burton, James W. Private	Unk	5/10/1861, Winchester, Virginia	Unknown	Co. D, 33rd Virginia Infantry	12/30/1863, St. John's Run, Virginia	Died of Chronic Diarrhea, 2/8/1865
Burton, John E. Private	Unk	Unknown	Unknown	Hood's Battalion, Virginia Reserves	6/15/1864, Petersburg, Virginia	Died of Unknown Causes, 10/7/1864
Burton, William J. Private	Unk	10/20/1864, Richmond, Virginia	Henrico County, Virginia	Co. E, 59th Virginia Infantry	4/6/1865, Farmville, Virginia	Died of Chronic Diarrhea, 5/25/1865

Name	Age	Enlisted	Residence	Unit	Captured	Date and Cause of Death
Busbin, P. J. Private	Unk	3/10/1862, Gadsden, Alabama	Etowah County, Alabama	Co. B, 4th Alabama Cavalry	6/23/1863, Shelbyville, Tennessee	Died of Scurvy, 10/31/1863
Buster, James W. Private	Unk	12/9/1861, Osage River, Missouri	Bloomington, Macon County, Missouri, Farmer	Co. B, 5th Missouri Infantry	5/16/1863, Champion Hill, Tennessee	Date and Cause of Death Unknown
Butler, Bentley B. Private	Unk	3/13/1862, Fredericksburg Virginia	Spotsylvania County, Virginia	Co. M, 55th Virginia Infantry	6/10/1864, Spotsylvania Court House, Virginia	Died of Chronic Dysentery, 12/29/1864
Butler, Fountain W. Private	Unk	4/1/1862, Fair River, Mississippi	Laurence County, Mississippi	Co. C, 33rd Mississippi Infantry	5/16/1863, Champion Hill, Tennessee	Died of Chronic Diarrhea, 12/13/1863
Butler, J. Daniel Sergeant	Unk	3/14/1862, Camp Anderson, Florida	Unknown	Co. I, 5th Florida Infantry	6/12/1864, Spotsylvania Court House, Virginia	Died of Unknown Causes, 6/29/1864
Butler, Solomon D. Private	Unk	5/5/1862, Suffolk, Virginia	Isle of Wight County, Virginia	Co. A, 14th Virginia Infantry	6/16/1863, Suffolk, Virginia	Died of Chronic Diarrhea, 1/10/1864
Bynum, William L. Private	18	3/25/1862, Lincoln County, North Carolina, Volunteer	Lincoln County, North Carolina, Farmer	Co. H, 52nd North Carolina Infantry	7/5/1863, Gettysburg, Pennsylvania	Died of Unknown Causes, 1/11/1864
Bywaters, Smith Private	32	5/25/1861, Oak Shade, Virginia	Unknown, Farmer	Co. D, 4th Virginia Cavalry	7/4/1863, Gettysburg, Pennsylvania	Died of Chronic Diarrhea, 1/11/1864

Name	Age	Enlisted	Residence	Unit	Captured	Date and Cause of Death
Cage, Thomas W. Corporal	Unk	10/28/1861, Fairfax Court House, Virginia	Fairfax County, Virginia	Co. K, 3rd Virginia Infantry	4/6/1865, Farmville, Sailor's Creek, Virginia	Died of Disease, 6/21/1865

Name	Age	Enlisted	Residence	Unit	Captured	Date and Cause of Death
Cahill, J. C. Private	Unk	9/11/1863, Charles City Court House, Virginia	Unknown	Co. H, 24th Virginia Cavalry	12/13/1863, Charles City Court House, Virginia	Died of Chronic Diarrhea, 9/3/1864
Calhoon, Wilson G. Private	22	11/15/1861, Portsmouth, Virginia, Volunteer	Tyrrell County, North Carolina	Co. A, 32nd North Carolina Infantry	7/5/1863, Gettysburg, Pennsylvania	Died of Variola (Smallpox), 2/9/1864
Cain, B. F. Sergeant	Unk	7/8/1861, Griffin, Georgia	Terrell County, Georgia	Co. H, 13th Georgia Infantry	9/22/1864, Fisher's Hill, Virginia	Died of Chronic Diarrhea, 2/10/1865
Cain, Isaac Private	Unk	8/1/1862, Barbour County, West Virginia	Barbour County, West Virginia	Co. H, 62nd Virginia Mounted Infantry	7/7/1863, Williamsport, Virginia	Date and Cause of Death Unknown
Cain, S. G. Corporal	Unk	7/16/1864, Marion, South Carolina	Marion District, South Carolina	Co. C, 26th South Carolina Infantry	10/27/1864, Boyton Plank Road or Burgess' Mill, Virginia	Died of Bronchitis, 3/16/1865
Calaway, Cyrus Private	Unk	Unknown	Unknown	Co. A, 12th Alabama Infantry	4/2/1865, Petersburg, Virginia	Died of Acute Dysentery, 5/28/1865
Calaway, John Private Not Listed On Monument	24	8/12/1862, Knoxville, Tennessee	Knox County, Tennessee	Co. C, Ashby's 2nd Tennessee Cavalry	5/30/1863, Mill Springs, Kentucky	Died of Unknown Causes, 8/13/1864
Calder, J. B. See: Crowder, John				Co. I, 55th North Carolina Infantry		
Caldwell, H. G. Sergeant	Unk	12/9/1861, Camp Hampton, Columbia, South Carolina	Richland County, South Carolina	Co. K, 17th South Carolina Infantry	4/1/1865, Five Forks, Virginia	Died of Chronic Diarrhea, 5/1/1865
Caldwell, Miles P. Private	Unk	Unknown	Unknown	Co. B, 28th Virginia Infantry	Unknown	Date and Cause of Death Unknown

Name	Age	Enlisted	Residence	Unit	Captured	Date and Cause of Death
Calender, John A. Private	Unk	3/12/1862, Camp Moore, Mississippi	Orleans Parish, Louisiana	Co. K, 3rd Mississippi Infantry	12/16/1864, Nashville, Tennessee	Died of Scurvy, 4/26/1865
Calhoun, Conway O. Corporal	Unk	6/12/1861, Lafayette, Walker County, Georgia	Walker County, Georgia	Co. G, 9th Georgia Infantry	7/2/1863, Gettysburg, Pennsylvania, Gunshot Wound in Right Thigh	Died of Wounds, 4/6/1864
Calhoun, David Private Not Listed On Monument	Unk	Unknown	Unknown	Co. B, 66th North Carolina Infantry	2/20/1863, Near Fairfield, Bertie County, North Carolina	Died of Pneumonia, 5/8/1864
Calhoun, William A. Private Not Listed On Monument	Unk	10/14/1864 Danville, Virginia	Pittsylvania County, Virginia	Co. E, 38th Virginia Infantry	7/3/1865 Five Forks, Virginia	Died of Chronic Diarrhea, 7/3/1865
Calk, Fate Private	Unk	8/31/1864, Cleveland County, North Carolina	Cleveland County, North Carolina	Co. G, 49th North Carolina Infantry	4/1/1865, Five Forks, Virginia	Died of Unknown Causes, 6/14/1865
Callahan, Hezekiah L. Private	Unk	5/5/1862, Lynchburg, Virginia	Unknown	Captain George S. Davidson's Battery, Co. C, 13th Battalion, Virginia Light Artillery	4/6/1865, Farmville, Virginia	Died of Chronic Dysentery, 6/2/1865
Calloway, John Private	24	8/12/1862, Knoxville, Tennessee	Knox County, Tennessee	Co. C, 2nd Tennessee Cavalry	5/30/1863, Mill Spring, Kentucky	Died of Unknown Causes, 8/13/1864
Calwell, Jacob Private	Unk	2/17/1863, Waynesville, North Carolina	Haywood County, North Carolina	Co. E, Thomas' North Carolina Legion	9/19/1864, Winchester, Virginia	Died of Unknown Causes, 5/27/1865

Name	Age	Enlisted	Residence	Unit	Captured	Date and Cause of Death
Camack, Andrew F. Corporal	Unk	4/5/1862, Winnsboro, South Carolina	Fairfield County, South Carolina	Co. E, 15th South Carolina Infantry	8/25/1864, Harpers Ferry, Virginia	Died of Chronic Diarrhea, 5/22/1865
Cameron, Daniel T. Private	30	11/27/1861, Camp Mangum, Raleigh, North Carolina, Volunteer	Cumberland County, North Carolina, Farmer	Co. C, 35th North Carolina Infantry	5/20/1864, Between Petersburg and Richmond, Virginia	Died of Pneumonia, 1/6/1865
Cameron, L. A. Private	Unk	12/9/1861, Huntsville, Tennessee	Scott County, Tennessee	Co. D, (Forrest's) 3rd Tennessee Cavalry	6/28/1863, Decherd, Tennessee	Date and Cause of Death Unknown
Campbell, A. C. Private	Unk	Unknown	Unknown	Co. A, 38th North Carolina Infantry	Unknown	Died of Unknown Causes, 2/27/1865
Campbell, Alfred C. Private Not Listed On Monument	41	6/1/1861, Valleytown, Cherokee County, North Carolina	Cherokee County, North Carolina	Co. D, 25th North Carolina Infantry	8/21/1864, Globe Tavern, Weldon Rail Road, Virginia	Died of Chronic Diarrhea, 2/26/1865
Campbell, Isaac P. See Campbell, J. P.				Co. B, 53rd North Carolina Infantry		
Campbell, J. F. Private	Unk	Unknown	Unknown	Co. H, 44th North Carolina Infantry	Unknown	Unable to Locate
Campbell, J. M. Private	31	6/2/1862, Chesterfield, South Carolina	Chesterfield District, South Carolina	Co. D, 6th South Carolina Cavalry	12/10/1864, Armstrong Mills, Virginia	Died of Pneumonia, 4/2/1865
Campbell, J. P. Private	Unk	2/10/1864 Charlotte, North Carolina	Mecklenburg County, North Carolina	Co. B, 53rd North Carolina Infantry	7/5/1863, Gettysburg, Pennsylvania	Died of Smallpox, 1/9/1864
Campbell, James H. Private	Unk	5/14/1861, Philippi, West Virginia	Barbour County, West Virginia	Co. H, 31st Virginia Infantry	7/5/1863, Gettysburg, Pennsylvania, Wounded	Date and Cause of Death Unknown

Name	Age	Enlisted	Residence	Unit	Captured	Date and Cause of Death
Campbell, John A. Private Not Listed On Monument	19	4/2/1862, Chatham County, North Carolina, Substitute	Randolph County, North Carolina Farmer	Co. I, 53rd North Carolina Infantry	7/5/1863, Gettysburg, Pennsylvania	Died of Unknown Causes, 1/1/1864
Campbell, John L. Private	Unk	3/7/1864, Salem, Roanoke County, Virginia	Roanoke County, Virginia	Co. E, 28th Virginia Infantry	4/6/1865, Harper's Farm, Virginia	Died of Congestive Intermittent Fever, 5/7/1865
Campbell, Marius G. Sergeant	Unk	8/7/1861, West Point, Virginia	Unknown	Co. H, 53rd Virginia Infantry	7/3/1863, Gettysburg, Pennsylvania	Died of Chronic Diarrhea, 9/16/1864
Canipe, L. Private	Unk	Unknown	Unknown	Co. F, 55th North Carolina Infantry	Unknown	Unable to Locate
Cannaday, George Private	17	9/30/1862 Drewry's Bluff, Virginia, Conscript	Guilford County, North Carolina	Co. C, 45th North Carolina Infantry	7/5/1863, Gettysburg, Pennsylvania	Died of Chronic Diarrhea, 12/29/1863
Cannon, James Private	Unk	11/29/1863, Camp Holmes, Raleigh, North Carolina	Wake County, North Carolina	Co. M, 22nd North Carolina Infantry	5/24/1864, Hanover Junction, Virginia	Died of Unknown Causes, 6/28/1864
Cannon, William R. Private	Unk	5/29/1863, Tallapoosa County, Alabama	Tallapoosa County, Alabama	Co. I, 61st Alabama Infantry	5/5/1864, Spotsylvania Court House, Virginia	Died of Acute Diarrhea, 6/15/1864
Canter, John Private	Unk	1/25/1864, Wake County, North Carolina	Wake County, North Carolina	Co. G, 26th North Carolina Infantry	!0/27/64, Burgess' Mill, Virginia	Died of Scurvy, 5/7/1865
Cantrell, W. H. Private	Unk	5/18/1861, Camp Harris, Tennessee	Unknown	Co. A, 16th Tennessee Infantry	12/25/1864 Pulaski, Tennessee, Gunshot Wound Left Hip	Died of Hospital Gangrene, 5/5/1865
Cantwright, J. Private	Unk	Unknown	Unknown	Co. E, 66th North Carolina Infantry	8/8/1863, Place Unknown	Died of Unknown Causes, 2/7/1864

Name	Age	Enlisted	Residence	Unit	Captured	Date and Cause of Death
Capps, Andrew J. Sergeant	23	3/15/1861, Pinners Point, Virginia	Unknown	Co. C, 13th Virginia Cavalry	12/1/1864, Stony Creek, Virginia	Died of Chronic Diarrhea, 4/5/1865
Capps, James M. Private	25	9/7/1861, Montgomery, Alabama	Nashville, Tennessee	Co. B, 25th Alabama Infantry	12/18/1864, Franklin, Tennessee, Gunshot Wound Right Arm, Amputation of Right Arm	Died of Chronic Diarrhea, 5/27/1865
Capps, Josiah Corporal	23	5/15/1861, Churchland, Norfolk County, Virginia	Norfolk County, Virginia	Co. I, 9th Virginia Infantry	7/3/1863, Gettysburg, Pennsylvania	Died of Variola (Smallpox), 12/24/1863
Carden, Levi W. Private	Unk	5/1/1864, Raleigh, Wake County, North Carolina	Wake County, North Carolina	Co. F, 27th North Carolina Infantry	5/24/1864, Near Hanover Court House, Virginia	Died of Unknown Causes, 8/10/1864
Cardy, John Private	Unk	Unknown	Unknown	Co. C, 1st Virginia Artillery	Unknown	Unable to Locate
Carley, Elisha See Kerley, Elisha				Co. F, 32nd North Carolina Infantry		
Carneal, James B. Private	32	3/10/1862 Caroline County, Virginia	Caroline County, Virginia, Farmer	Co. K, 47th Virginia Infantry	4/6/1865, Farmville, Sailor's Creek, Virginia	Died of Acute Dysentery, 5/7/1865
Carney, David Private	Unk	7/20/1861, Amsterdam, Virginia	Botetourt County, Virginia	Co. K, 28th Virginia Infantry	8/25/1864, Howlett's House, Virginia	Died of Chronic Diarrhea, 3/15/1865
Carney, Waddy T. Private	24	6/11/1861, Camp McDonald, Cobb County, Georgia	Cobb County, Georgia	Philip's Legion, Georgia Infantry	5/23/1864, North Anna River, Virginia	Died of Scurvy, 4/26/1865
Carney, Wright Sergeant	35	1/18/1862, Tarboro, Edgecombe County, North Carolina	Edgecombe County, North Carolina, Farmer	Co. B, 44th North Carolina Infantry	10/27/1864, Burgess' Mill, Near Petersburg, Virginia	Died of Chronic Diarrhea, 4/8/1865

Name	Age	Enlisted	Residence	Unit	Captured	Date and Cause of Death
Carpenter, David Private	Unk	3/26/1862, Lincoln County, North Carolina, Volunteer	Lincoln County, North Carolina	Co. I, 11th North Carolina Infantry	7/5/1863, Gettysburg, Pennsylvania, Wounded	Died of Unknown Causes, 3/19/1864
Carpenter, Edmund L. Private	31	5/10/1862, Wadesboro, North Carolina	Anson County, North Carolina	Co. K, 26th North Carolina Infantry	7/14/1863, Falling Waters, Maryland	Died of Unknown Causes, 12/21/1863
Carpenter, Isaac Private Name Not On Monument	23	7/1/1861 Wadesboro, North Carolina, Volunteer	Anson County, North Carolina	Co. K, 26th North Carolina Infantry	7/3/1863, Gettysburg, Pennsylvania	Died of Smallpox, 12/21/1863
Carpenter, James E. Private Name Not On Monument	21	3/1/1861, Tarboro, Edgecombe County, North Carolina	Edgecombe County, North Carolina	Co. B, 6th Virginia Cavalry	1/12/1864, Rappahannock County, Virginia	Died of Unknown Causes, 7/6/1864
Carpenter, Mathew T. Private Name Not On Monument	Unk	2/10/1864, Louisa, Virginia	Louisa County, Virginia	Montgomery's Company, Virginia Light Artillery	Unknown	Died of Unknown Causes, 12/?/1864
Carpenter, Monroe Private	21	3/15/1862, Lincolnton, Lincoln County, North Carolina	Gaston County, North Carolina	Co. L, 1st North Carolina Infantry	7/3/1863, Gettysburg, Pennsylvania	Died of Chronic Dysentery, 2/21/1865
Carpenter, Peter Z. Private	19	3/29/1862, Shelby, Cleveland County, North Carolina, Volunteer	Cleveland County, North Carolina, Farmer	Co. C, 55th North Carolina Infantry	7/3/1863, Gettysburg, Pennsylvania	Died of Pneumonia, 5/27/1865
Carpenter, P. H. Private	Unk	4/9/1863, Tarboro, Edgecombe County, North Carolina	Edgecombe County, North Carolina	Co. K, 7th Virginia Infantry	5/21/1864, Milford Station, Virginia	Died of Typhoid Fever, 12/10/1864
Carr, Henry Private	Unk	7/25/1863, Tuskegee, Alabama	Macon County, Alabama	Co. H, 61st Alabama Infantry	5/19/1864, Spotsylvania Court House, Virginia	Died of Unknown Causes, 6/18/1864

Name	Age	Enlisted	Residence	Unit	Captured	Date and Cause of Death
Carr, R. B. See: Corr, Richard B.				Co. C, 55th Virginia Infantry		
Carrel, Rufus Private Not Listed On Monument	18	2/27/1862, Rockingham County, North Carolina	Rockingham County, North Carolina	Co. E, 45th North Carolina Infantry	5/10/1864, Spotsylvania Court House, Virginia	Died of Unknown Causes, 7/31/1864
Carriker, Martin A. Private	19	7/1/1861, Cabarrus County, North Carolina	Cabarrus County, North Carolina, Farmer	Co. B, 7th North Carolina Infantry	7/3/1863, Gettysburg, Pennsylvania	Died of Pneumonia, 1/15/1864
Carriker, William P. Private	21	7/4/1862, Cabarrus County, North Carolina	Cabarrus County, North Carolina	Co. E, 57th North Carolina Infantry	11/7/1863, Rappahannock Station, Virginia	Died of Smallpox, 12/23/1863
Carroll, F. M. Private	Unk	3/1/1862, Franklin County, Georgia	Pickens County, Georgia	Co. H, 24th Georgia Infantry	10/19/1864, Cedar Creek or Strasburg, Virginia	Died of Acute Dysentery, 11/28/1864
Carroll, J. B. Private	18	3/29/1862, Cleveland County, North Carolina	Cleveland County, North Carolina, Farmer	Co. C, 55th North Carolina Infantry	7/14/1863, Falling Waters, Maryland	Died of Variola (Smallpox), 11/30/1863
Carroll, Ransom Private	36	9/23/1863, Camp Holmes, Raleigh, North Carolina, Conscript	Johnston County, North Carolina	Co. E, 14th North Carolina Infantry	9/19/1864, Winchester, Virginia	Died of Chronic Diarrhea, 2/21/1865
Carson, I. O. Private	Unk	2/25/1862, Lewisville, Arkansas	Lafayette County, Arkansas	Co. A, 19th Arkansas Infantry	5/16/1863, Champion Hill, Tennessee	Died of Chronic Diarrhea, 2/1/1864
Carswell, Azor Private	Unk	10/6/1863, Morganton, Burke County, North Carolina	Burke County, North Carolina	Co. B, 54th North Carolina Infantry	11/7/1863, Rappahannock Station, Virginia	Died of Chronic Diarrhea and Pneumonia, 11/25/1863

Name	Age	Enlisted	Residence	Unit	Captured	Date and Cause of Death
Carswell, Michael H. Private	26	9/22/1862, Burke County, North Carolina, Conscript	Burke County, North Carolina	Co. F, 6th North Carolina Infantry	7/5/1863, Chambersburg, Pennsylvania, Captured in Hospital being treated for Debility	Died of Unknown Causes, 10/6/1864
Carswell, Thomas H. Private Name Not On Monument	38	1/15/1662, Burke County, North Carolina	Burke County, North Carolina	Co. B, 11th North Carolina Infantry	7/14/1863, Falling Waters, Maryland	Died of Unknown Causes, 3/10/1864
Carter, A. J. Private	18	3/12/1862, Randolph County, North Carolina, Volunteer	Randolph County, North Carolina	Co. F, 22nd North Carolina Infantry	7/14/1863, Falling Waters, Maryland	Died of Chronic Diarrhea & Scurvy, 11/5/1863
Carter, C. T. Private	Unk	Unknown	Unknown	Co. A, Mosby's Regiment of Virginia Cavalry	7/19/1863, Upperville, Virginia	Died of Typhoid Fever, 12/30/1863
Carter, Daniel L. Private	23	5/3/1861, Rockingham County, North Carolina	Rockingham County, North Carolina	Co. D, 5th North Carolina Cavalry	4/3/1865, Finity Church, Virginia	Date and Cause of Death Unknown
Carter, G. A. Private	Unk	11/1/1863, Raleigh, North Carolina	Wake County, North Carolina	Co. H, 21st North Carolina Infantry	2/3/1864, New Berne, North Carolina	Died of Scurvy, 5/17/1865
Carter, Harry Private	Unk	6/8/1861, Camp Moore, Louisiana	Orleans Parish, Louisiana	Co. A, 6th Louisiana Infantry	5/4/1864, Mine Run, Virginia	Died of Unknown Causes, 7/24/1864
Carter, James H. Private	23	6/10/1861, Dogwood Grove, Burgaw County, North Carolina	New Hanover County, North Carolina	Co. K, 3rd North Carolina Infantry	7/5/1863, Gettysburg, Pennsylvania, Wounded	Died of Unknown Causes, 10/20/1863
Carter, John S. Private	Unk	4/3/1862, Norfolk, Virginia	Chesapeake County, Virginia	Co. B, 6th Virginia Infantry	7/14/1863, Falling Waters, Maryland	Died of Infection of the Face & Smallpox, 12/26/1863,

Name	Age	Enlisted	Residence	Unit	Captured	Date and Cause of Death
Carter, John Private	Unk	Unknown	Unknown	Co. B, 25th Virginia Infantry Battalion	Unknown	Died of Smallpox, 1/4/1864
Carter, Logan C. Private	19	5/3/1862, Yadkin County, North Carolina	Yadkin County, North Carolina, Farmer	Co. A, 54th North Carolina Infantry	11/7/1863, Rappahannock Station, Virginia	Died of Variola (Smallpox), 2/26/1864
Carter, Monroe A. Private	Unk	Unknown	Unknown	Co. F, 56th Virginia Infantry	4/6/1865, Bunksville, Virginia	Died of Chronic Diarrhea, 5/5/1865
Carter, Peter K. Private	Unk	3/8/1862, Ridgeway, Virginia	Henry County, Virginia	Co. A, 42nd Virginia Infantry	5/12/1864, Spotsylvania Court House, Virginia	Died From Inflammation of Lungs (Pneumonia), 10/17/1864
Carter, S. A. Sergeant	Unk	2/15/1862, Pope County, Arkansas	Pope County, Arkansas	Co. D, 1st Battalion Arkansas Cavalry	5/17/ 1863, Big Black Bridge, Near Vicksburg, Mississippi	Died of Chronic Diarrhea, 11/27/1863
Carter, Samuel J. Private Not Listed On Monument	Unk	Unknown	Chatham County, North Carolina	Co. E, 5th North Carolina Infantry	4/3/1865 Southerland Station, Virginia	Died of Chronic Dysentery, 7/10/1865
Carter, Thomas B. Private	22	3/11/1862, Elm Grove, Rockingham County, North Carolina, Volunteer	Rockingham County, North Carolina, Farmer	Co. F, 45th North Carolina Infantry	7/5/1863, Gettysburg, Pennsylvania, Wounded	Died of Unknown Causes, 2/4/1864
Carter, Wilford Private	Unk	10/23/1863, Kenansville, Duplin County, North Carolina	Davidson County, North Carolina	Co. I, 42nd North Carolina Infantry	2/20/1865, Near Wilmington, North Carolina	Died From Inflammation of Lungs (Pneumonia), 4/12/1865
Carter, William Green Private Not Listed On Monument	Unk	2/29/1864, Richmond, Virginia, Conscript	Halifax County, Virginia	Co. K, 14th Virginia Infantry	4/1/1865, Five Forks, Virginia	Died of Unknown Causes, 7/28/1865

Name	Age	Enlisted	Residence	Unit	Captured	Date and Cause of Death
Carter, William M. Private	Unk	3/30/1862, Yadkinville, North Carolina	Yadkin County, North Carolina	Co. I, 28th North Carolina Infantry	7/3/1863, Gettysburg, Pennsylvania, Wounded	Died of Unknown Causes, 8/24/1863
Cartwright, Jesse Landsman	Unk	Unknown	Unknown	Confederate States Navy, Assigned to the CSS Albemarle, Plymouth, North Carolina, 1864	Unknown	Date and Cause of Death Unknown
Cartwright, John Private Not Listed On Monument	Unk	Unknown	Unknown	Co. E, 66th North Carolina Infantry	9/8/1863, Unknown	Died of Unknown Causes, 2/9/1864
Carvender, A. Private	Unk	Unknown	Unknown	Co. K, 26th North Carolina Infantry	Unknown	Unable to Locate
Cary, William H. Private	Unk	7/25/1861, Pine Bluff, Arkansas	Jefferson County, Arkansas	Co. F, 9th Arkansas Infantry	5/16/1863, Champion Hill, Tennessee	Died of Smallpox While Waiting to Be Exchanged 12/25/1863
Cash, James B. Private	Unk	4/21/1864, Camp Lee, Virginia	Prince Edward County, Virginia	Co. B, 14th Virginia Infantry	4/1/1865, Five Forks, Virginia	Died of Unknown Causes, 5/25/1865
Cash, S. L. Private Not Listed On Monument	23	10/1/1862, Newport, Tennessee	Cocke County, Tennessee	Co. I, 60th Tennessee Mounted Infantry	5/17/1863, Big Black Bridge, Near Vicksburg, Mississippi	Died of Unknown Causes, 2/21/1864
Casler, Charles Private	Unk	10/22/1861, Winchester, Virginia	Frederick County, Virginia	Co. A, 11th Virginia Cavalry	9/22/1863, Jack's Shop, Madison County, Virginia	Died of Unknown Causes, 7/29/1864
Cassell, Robert E. V. Private	Unk	11/14/1862, Pendleton, Virginia	Veach, Virginia	Co. C, 62nd Virginia Infantry	7/3/1863, Gettysburg, Pennsylvania	Died of Chronic Diarrhea, 2/9/1865

Name	Age	Enlisted	Residence	Unit	Captured	Date and Cause of Death
Casselman, J. D. Private	Unk	1/13/1862, Mount Pleasant, South Carolina	Charleston District, South Carolina	Co. I, 26th South Carolina Infantry	5/20/1864, Drewry's Bluff, Virginia, Gunshot Fracture of Left Femur	Died of Unknown Causes, 6/17/1864
Cast, Samuel M. Private	Unk	6/4/1861, Asheville, Alabama	St. Clair County, Alabama	Co. A, 10th Alabama Infantry	7/1/1863, Gettysburg, Pennsylvania	Died of Unknown Causes, 2/29/1864
Catchings, Seymore S. Corporal	Unk	3/4/1862, Randolph County, Georgia	Randolph County, Georgia	Co. H, 51st Georgia Infantry	4/6/1865, Farmville, Virginia	Died of Acute Dysentery, 5/4/1865
Cates, Willis J. Private	19	5/20/1862, Orange County, North Carolina	Orange County, North Carolina	Co. K, 44th North Carolina Infantry	10/27/1864, Burgess' Mill, Virginia	Died of Chronic Diarrhea, 1/31/1865
Caudill, Jefferson Private	Unk	5/3/1862, Alleghany County, North Carolina, Volunteer	Alleghany County, North Carolina	Co. I, 61st North Carolina Infantry	9/30/1864, Fort Harrison, Virginia	Died of Pneumonia, 3/8/1865
Caul, Stephen Private	Unk	6/14/1861, New Orleans, Louisiana	New Orleans, Louisiana	Co. C, Confederate States Marine Corp	1/15/1865, Fort Fisher, North Carolina	Died of Pneumonia, 3/8/1865
Cauley, Luke Private	Unk	9/3/1862, Camp McDonald, Georgia	Unknown	Co. G, 15th Georgia Infantry	7/4/1863, Gettysburg, Pennsylvania	Died of Chronic Diarrhea, 1/12/1864
Causby, D. A. Private See Cosby, D. A.				Co. B, 11th North Carolina Infantry		
Cauthen, John M. See: Coffing, John M.				Co. D, 7th, South Carolina Infantry		

Name	Age	Enlisted	Residence	Unit	Captured	Date and Cause of Death
Cavanaugh, George W. Private	21	3/3/1862, New Wilmington, Hanover County, North Carolina, Volunteer	Duplin County, North Carolina	Co. K, 30th North Carolina Infantry	10/20/1863, Warrenton, Virginia	Died of Chronic Diarrhea, 2/5/1865
Cavanaugh, Thomas Private	27	3/5/1862, New Orleans, Louisiana	New Orleans, Louisiana, Laborer	Co. I, 7th Louisiana Infantry	5/12/1864, Spotsylvania Court House, Virginia	Died of Unknown Causes, 7/27/1864
Caw, James Private	Unk	Unknown	Unknown	Co. H, 25th Virginia Infantry	Unknown	Date and Cause Unknown
Chamberlain, Haywood Private	20	2/27/1862, Reidsville, North Carolina	Rockingham County, North Carolina, Farmer	Co. E, 45th North Carolina Infantry	5/12/1864, Spotsylvania Court House, Virginia	Died of Unknown Causes, 7/31/1864
Chambers, Calvin Private	Unk	10/9/1862, Franklin County, Virginia	Franklin County, Virginia	Co. F, 59th Virginia Infantry	4/6/1865, Farmville, Virginia	Died of Chronic Dysentery, 5/14/1865
Chambers, L. H. Private	20	7/3/1861, Atlanta, Georgia	Houston County, Georgia, Farmer	Co. K, 11th Georgia Infantry	7/5/1863, Gettysburg, Pennsylvania, Wounded	Died of Unknown Causes, 2/13/1864
Chambers, Roswell Private	Unk	5/3/1861, Decatur, Tennessee	Meigs County, Tennessee	Co. I, 3rd Tennessee Mounted Infantry	5/17/1863, Big Black Bridge, Near Vicksburg, Mississippi	Died of Variola (Smallpox), 2/18/1864
Champion, John C. Private	Unk	9/1/1862, Jacksonville, Alabama	Calhoun County, Alabama	Co. G, 3rd Alabama Infantry	6/27/1863, Shelbyville, Tennessee	Died of Variola (Smallpox), 1/17/1864
Chandler, A. W. Private	Unk	Unknown	Unknown	Johnson's Militia	Unknown	Unable to Locate
Chandler, Joseph L. F. Private	Unk	9/23/1861, Place Illegible	Unknown	Co. B, 3rd Georgia Infantry	7/21/1863, Chester Gap, Virginia	Died of Unknown Causes, 9/12/1864

Name	Age	Enlisted	Residence	Unit	Captured	Date and Cause of Death
Chaney, Elisha Private	Unk	9/30/1862, Morristown, Tennessee	Hamblen County, Tennessee	Co. A, 60th Tennessee Mounted Infantry	5/17/ 1863, Big Black Bridge, Near Vicksburg, Mississippi	Died of Unknown Causes, 12/24/1863
Chaplain, R. J. 1st Sergeant	19	6/29/1861, Smithfield, Virginia	Isle of Wight County, Virginia, Clerk	Co. D, 3rd Virginia Infantry	7/3/1863, Gettysburg, Pennsylvania	Died of Unknown Causes, 7/31/1864
Chaplin, J. Private	Unk	Unknown	Unknown	Co. H, 5th North Carolina Infantry	9/23/1863, Near Madison Court House, Virginia	Died of Chronic Diarrhea, 4/16/1864
Charaeler, W. P. See Carriker, William P.				Co. H, 57th North Carolina Infantry		
Charaker, J. W. Private	Unk	5/5/1862, Zebulon, Georgia	Pike County, Georgia	Co. H, 53rd Georgia Infantry	7/4/1863, Cashtown, Pennsylvania	Died of Variola (Smallpox), 11/25/1863
Chatham, Thomas J. Private	21	3/15/1862, Roswell, Georgia	Atlanta, Georgia	Co. E, Cobb's Legion, Georgia Infantry	7/3/1863, Gettysburg, Pennsylvania	Died of Variola (Smallpox), 7/2/1863
Cheatham, Nathan F. Private	Unk	Unknown	Unknown	Co. D, 14th Virginia Infantry	Unknown	Unable to Locate
Cheek, John M. Private	Unk	5/24/1864, Bedford, Virginia	Unknown, Drummer for Regiment	Co. B, 28th Virginia Infantry	4/3/1865, Richmond, Virginia	Died of Typhoid Fever, 6/5/1865
Chesley, Boling Private	35	2/25/1863, Granville County, North Carolina	Granville County, North Carolina	Co. K, 55th North Carolina Infantry	7/14/1863, Falling Waters, Maryland	Died of Chronic Diarrhea, 10/16/1863
Chestnut, William F. Private	21	6/1/1861, Fort Macon, North Carolina, Volunteer	Wayne County, North Carolina	Co. A, 27th North Carolina Infantry	10/14/1863, Bristoe Station, Virginia	Died of Unknown Causes, 8/14/1864

Name	Age	Enlisted	Residence	Unit	Captured	Date and Cause of Death
Chewning, J. W. Private	Unk	5/9/1862, Morris Island, South Carolina	Charleston District, South Carolina	Co. I, 23rd South Carolina Infantry	4/1/1865, Petersburg, Virginia	Died of Chronic Diarrhea 6/13/1865
Childress, Charles F. Private	Unk	Unknown	Unknown	Co. I, 42nd Virginia Infantry	9/23/1864, Cedar Creek or Strasburg, Virginia,	Died of Chronic Diarrhea, 3/17/1865
Childress, James M. Private	Unk	2/20/1863, Buckingham Court House, Virginia	Buckingham County, Virginia	Co. E, 21st Virginia Infantry	7/5/1863, Gettysburg, Pennsylvania, Wounded In Knee	Died of Anasarca, Accumulation Of Fluid In Tissues, 2/24/1864
Chisenhall, Samuel Private	20	2/26/1862, Chapel Hill, North Carolina, Volunteer	Orange County, North Carolina	Co. G, 11th North Carolina Infantry	4/2/1865, Petersburg, Virginia	Died of Pneumonia, 5/8/1865
Chocalate, John See: Chocklett, John				Co. B, 18th Virginia Infantry		
Chocklett, John Private	Unk	9/1/1864, Chester, Virginia	Chesterfield County, Virginia	Co. B, 18th Virginia Infantry	4/6/1865, High Bridge, Virginia	Died of Rubeola (Measles) 6/15/1865
Chrisman, George F. Private	18	3/12/1862, Guilford County, North Carolina	Guilford County, North Carolina	Co. F, 34th North Carolina Infantry	11/7/1863, Rappahannock Station, Virginia	Died of Chronic Diarrhea, 11/29/1864
Christian, Thomas J. Private Not Listed On Monument	Unk	8/7/1862, Forsyth, Georgia	Monroe County, Georgia	Co. A, 14th Georgia Infantry	5/6/1864, Wilderness, Virginia	Died of Rubeola (Measles) 7/1/1864
Christie, Newton J. Private	Unk	7/30/1863, C. Narrows, Virginia	Giles County, Virginia	Chapman's Battery, Virginia Light Artillery	10/19/1864, Cedar Creek or Strasburg, Virginia	Died of Rubeola (Measles) 3/29/1865

Name	Age	Enlisted	Residence	Unit	Captured	Date and Cause of Death
Christin, M. Private	Unk	6/1/1862, C. Narrows, Virginia	Giles County, Virginia	Chapman's Battery, Formerly McLaughlin's Battery, Virginia Artillery	10/19/1864, Cedar Creek or Strasburg, Virginia	Died of Pneumonia, 3/1/1865
Christy, G. W. Private	Unk	4/13/1864, Hanover Junction, Virginia	Hanover County, Virginia	2nd Battery Maryland Artillery	10/9/1864, Woodstock, Virginia	Died of Scurvy, 4/1/1865
Church, Marcellus Sergeant	24	4/29/1862, Oxford, Calhoun County, Mississippi	Calhoun County, Mississippi	Co. F, 42nd Mississippi Infantry	7/5/1863, Gettysburg, Pennsylvania	Died of Chronic Diarrhea, 1/25/1864
Clardy, George T. Private	Unk	4/27/1864, Halifax County, Virginia	Halifax County, Virginia	Co. H, 14th Virginia Infantry	4/5/1865, Five Forks, Virginia	Died of Scurvy, 4/26/1865
Clark, Adam Rufus Private Not Listed On Monument	46	3/5/1863, Gaston County, North Carolina, Substitute	Gaston County, North Carolina	Co. E, 34th, North Carolina Infantry	5/23/1864, North Anna or Near Hanover Junction, Virginia	Died of Chronic Diarrhea & Scurvy, 2/16/1865
Clark, Archibald B. Private	48	9/2/1863, Camp Holmes, Raleigh, North Carolina, Substitute	Bladen County, North Carolina	Co. K, 40th, North Carolina Artillery	3/25/1865, Goldsboro, North Carolina	Died of Pneumonia, 5/9/1865
Clark, E. B. Sergeant	Unk	Unknown	Unknown	Co. B, 50th Virginia Infantry	5/12/1864, Spotsylvania Court House, Virginia	Died of Chronic Diarrhea, 9/15/1864
Clark, Edward Private	18	2/13/1862, Pitt County, North Carolina, Volunteer	Pitt County, North Carolina	Co. C, 44th, North Carolina Infantry	10/27/1864, Burgess' Mill, Near Petersburg, Virginia	Died of Ascitis, Accumulation Of Fluid In the abdominal Cavity, 1/9/1865
Clark, Maben Private	Unk	9/29/1864, Chatham County, North Carolina, Conscript	Chatham County, North Carolina	Co. F, 53rd, North Carolina Infantry	10/19/1864, Cedar Creek or Strasburg, Virginia	Died of Pneumonia, 5/19/1865

Name	Age	Enlisted	Residence	Unit	Captured	Date and Cause of Death
Clark, Noah L. Private	Unk	5/26/1864, Weldon North Carolina	Henderson County, North Carolina	Co. H, 25th, North Carolina Infantry	8/21/1864, Globe Tavern, Weldon Rail Road, Virginia	Died of Unknown Causes, 10/12/1864
Clark, Philip G. Private	Unk	10/15/1864, Camp Lee, Virginia	Prince Edward County, Virginia	Co. E, 28th Virginia Infantry	4/6/1864, Harper's Farm, Virginia	Died of Chronic Diarrhea, 5/15/1865
Clarke, Addison L. Private	Unk	5/15/1864, White Hall, Virginia	Frederick County, Virginia	Co. I, 7th Virginia Infantry	4/6/1864, Harper's Farm, Virginia	Died of Typhoid Fever, 5/28/1865
Clarke, Benjamin N. Private	Unk	8/26/1862, Calhoun, Georgia	Laurens County, Georgia	Co. G, 49th Georgia Infantry	6/29/1863, Hagerstown, Maryland	Died of Typhoid Fever, 10/31/1863
Clarke, John L. Private	Unk	2/15/1864, White Hall, Virginia	Frederick County, Virginia	Co. I, 7th Virginia Infantry	4/15/1865, Harper's Farm, Virginia	Died of Acute Dysentery, 5/17/1865
Clarke, William N. Private	Unk	7/15/1863, Camp Holmes, Raleigh, North Carolina, Conscript	Wake County, North Carolina	Co. F, 8th, North Carolina Infantry	9/30/1864, Fort Harrison, Virginia	Died of Chronic Dysentery, 2/10/1865
Claxton, Henry Private	Unk	4/22/1862, Louisville, Georgia	Jefferson County, Georgia	Co. E, 48th, Georgia Infantry	7/2/1863, Gettysburg, Pennsylvania, Gunshot Fracture of Right Clavicle	Died of Variola (Smallpox), 11/24/1863
Clayton, Daniel M. Private	Unk	1/1/1862, Monticello, Florida	Laurens County, Georgia	Co. A, 5th, Florida Infantry	5/12/1864, Spotsylvania Court House, Virginia	Died of Unknown Causes, 7/24/1864
Clements, William A. Corporal	Unk	4/23/1861, Amherst Court House, Virginia	Amherst County, Virginia	Co. I, 49th Virginia Infantry	7/3/1863, Gettysburg, Pennsylvania, Wounded	Died of Unknown Causes, 4/10/1864
Clendenon, Arglen H. Private	Unk	9/20/1862, Charleston, West Virginia	Kanawha County, West Virginia	Co. G, 22nd Virginia Infantry	9/19/1864, Winchester, Virginia	Died of Acute Bronchitis, 2/24/1865

Name	Age	Enlisted	Residence	Unit	Captured	Date and Cause of Death
Cline, John L. H. Private	18	2/18/1863, Newton, North Carolina	Catawba County, North Carolina	Co. C, 28th, North Carolina Infantry	5/12/1864, Wilderness, Virginia	Died of Unknown Causes, 6/19/1864
Clippard, Marcus Private	28	3/31/1863, Newton, North Carolina	Catawba County, North Carolina	Co. E, 32nd, North Carolina Infantry	5/10/1864, Wilderness, Virginia	Died of Unknown Causes, 9/5/1864
Cloninger, Eli A. Private	24	10/2/1862, Lincolnton, North Carolina, Conscript	Lincoln County, North Carolina	Co. H, 52nd, North Carolina Infantry	10/14/1863, Bristoe Station, Virginia	Died of Unknown Causes, 8/13/1864
Close, Robert A. Private	30	7/15/1862, Guilford County, North Carolina	Guilford County, North Carolina	Co. I, 5th, North Carolina Infantry	7/12/1863, Hagerstown, Maryland	Died of Unknown Causes, 10/?/1863
Cloutz, William L. Private	30	7/4/1862, Salisbury, North Carolina, Volunteer	Rowan County, North Carolina	Co. H, 57th, North Carolina Infantry	11/7/1863, Kelly's Ford, Rappahannock, Virginia	Died of Variola (Smallpox), 2/5/1864
Clower, Lewis B. Private	Unk	8/26/1864, Leetown, Virginia	Frederick County, Virginia	Co. C, 26th Virginia Infantry	9/19/1864, Winchester, Virginia	Died of Unknown Causes of Heart, 1/14/1865
Cloyd, W. H. Private	Unk	Unknown	Unknown	Co. H, 8th Tennessee Cavalry	1/30/1865, Robertsville, North Carolina	Died of Chronic Diarrhea, 6/24/1865
Cluff, Richard O. Private	Unk	Unknown	Unknown	Stile's Georgia Artillery	Unknown	Unable to Locate
Cobb, G. W. Private	43	8/13/181, Yorkville, York District, South Carolina	Lightwood Knot Springs (near Columbia), South Carolina	Co. B, 12th, South Carolina Infantry	7/14/1863, Falling Waters, Maryland	Died of Chronic Diarrhea, 11/25/1863
Cobb, Henry L. Private	22	7/15/1862, Guilford County, North Carolina	Guilford County, North Carolina	Co. I, 5th, North Carolina Cavalry	7/12/1863, Hagerstown, Maryland	Died of Chronic Diarrhea, 12/21/1863

Name	Age	Enlisted	Residence	Unit	Captured	Date and Cause of Death
Cobb, Larry G. Lieutenant	Unk	4/30/1862, Cuthbert, Georgia	Randolph County, Georgia	Co. A, 55th, Georgia Infantry	9/9/63, Cumberland Gap, Virginia	Died of Chronic Diarrhea, 10/6/1864
Cobb, Robert A. Corporal	20	8/23/1861, Walhalla Pickens District, South Carolina	Pickens District, South Carolina	Co. K, 12th, South Carolina Infantry	7/14/1863, Falling Waters, Maryland	Died of Chronic Diarrhea, 4/22/1864
Cobber, A. Private	Unk	Unknown	Unknown	Co. A, 43rd, North Carolina Infantry	Unknown	Unable to Locate
Coble, Alexander Private Not Listed On Monument	32	5/11/1863, Camp Holmes, North Carolina	Wake County, North Carolina, Farmer	Co. D, 3rd, Battalion North Carolina Light Artillery	1/15/1865, Fort Fisher, North Carolina, Gunshot Wound Of Right Arm	Right Arm Amputated, Died of Wounds, 2/16/1865
Coble, John M. Private	18	4/18/1864, Camp Vance, North Carolina	Burke County, North Carolina	Co. D, 54th, North Carolina Infantry	5/23/1864, Bethel Church, North Anna River, Virginia	Died of Unknown Causes, 6/17/1864
Cobler, Edmond Private	23	9/5/1862, Raleigh, North Carolina, Conscript	Rockingham County, North Carolina	Co. A, 2nd, North Carolina Infantry	11/7/1863, Kelly's Ford, Rappahannock Station, Virginia	Died of Unknown Causes, 7/31/1864
Cobler, Greenville Private	Unk	10/3/1863, Raleigh, North Carolina	Rockingham County, North Carolina	Co. A, 2nd, North Carolina Infantry	11/7/1863, Kelly's Ford, Rappahannock Station, Virginia	Died of Unknown Causes, 1/30/1864
Cochran, James Private	Unk	Unknown	Unknown	Co. A, 35th, Battalion Virginia Cavalry	11/20/1863, Near Aldie, Loudon County, Virginia	Died of Unknown Causes, 2/13/1864
Cochran, Robert W. Private	Unk	4/7/1864, Pisgah Church, Virginia, Conscript	Orange County, Virginia	Co. D, 25th, Virginia Infantry	5/12/1864, Spotsylvania Court House, Virginia	Died of Intermittent Fever, 6/17/1864

Name	Age	Enlisted	Residence	Unit	Captured	Date and Cause of Death
Cochran, William Private Not Listed On Monument	Unk	6/4/1861, Alexandria, Alabama	Calhoun County, Alabama	Co. D, 10th, Alabama Infantry	7/2/1863, Gettysburg, Pennsylvania	Died of Unknown Causes, 11/16/1863
Cockerham, Pleasant R. Private	Unk	11/13/1864, Raleigh, North Carolina	Wake County, North Carolina	Co. H, 21st, North Carolina Infantry	3/25/1865, Fort Stedman, Near Petersburg, Virginia	Died of Chronic Diarrhea, 6/12/1865
Cockrell, Samuel See: Crockrell, Samuel				Co. D, 20th, North Carolina Infantry		
Coer, S. O. Private	Unk	Unknown	Unknown	Co. K, 10th, North Carolina Infantry	Unknown	Unable to Locate
Coffey, Larkin Private	22	3/19/1862, Lenoir County, North Carolina, Volunteer	Caldwell County, North Carolina	Co. A, 22nd, North Carolina Infantry	5/23/1864, Beaver Dam, Virginia	Died of Unknown Causes, 8/4/1864
Coffing, John M. Private	Unk	3/20/1862, Kershaw, South Carolina	Kershaw District, South Carolina	Co. D, 7th, South Carolina Infantry	8/21/1864, Globe Tavern, Near Weldon Railroad, Virginia	Died of Chronic Diarrhea, 2/28/1865
Coger, J. M. Sergeant	Unk	Unknown	Unknown	Co. H, 42nd, Virginia Infantry	7/4/1863, South Mountain, Maryland	Died of Chronic Diarrhea and Smallpox, 12/14/1863
Coggin, Henry T. Sergeant	19	2/13/1862, Franklin County, North Carolina, Volunteer	Franklin County, North Carolina, Farmer	Co. F, 47th, North Carolina Infantry	7/5/1863, Gettysburg, Pennsylvania	Died of Chronic Diarrhea, 2/12/1864
Coggin, James B. Private	18	3/1/1862, Troy North Carolina, Volunteer	Montgomery County, North Carolina, Farmer	Co. F, 44th, North Carolina Infantry	10/27/1864, Boydton Plank Road, Near Petersburg, Virginia	Died of Unknown Causes, 5/27/1865
Coghill, George Private	Unk	11/24/1863, Raleigh, North Carolina	Rockingham County, North Carolina	Co. K, 13th, North Carolina Infantry	5/23/1864, North Anna or Near Hanover Junction, Virginia	Died of Unknown Causes, 6/21/1864

Name	Age	Enlisted	Residence	Unit	Captured	Date and Cause of Death
Colbert, Alexander Private	Unk	5/?/1862, Place Unknown, Virginia	Unknown	Co. H, 15th Virginia, Partisan Rangers, Cavalry	6/20/1863, Cedar Run, Occoquan Ford, Virginia	Died of Unknown Causes, 8/28/1865
Coleman, George Private	Unk	2/1/1864, Danville, Virginia, Conscript	Pittsylvania County, Virginia	Co. G, 45th, North Carolina Infantry	5/10/1864, Spotsylvania Court House, Virginia	Died of Unknown Causes, 6/26/1864
Coleman, Robert E. Private	25	2/27/1862, Reidsville, North Carolina, Volunteer	Rockingham, North Carolina, Farmer	Co. E, 45th North Carolina Infantry	7/1/1863, Gettysburg, Pennsylvania, Gunshot Wound Left Thigh, Fracture of Femur,	Died of Unknown Causes, 6/22/1864
Collier, James L. Private	Unk	7/15/1861, Norfolk, Virginia	Chesapeake County, Virginia	Co. F, 12th Virginia, Infantry	7/2/1863, Gettysburg, Pennsylvania	Died of Chronic Diarrhea, 1/19/1865
Collins, Andrew J. Private	Unk	8/14/1861, Ellaville, Georgia	Schley County, Georgia	Co. B, 17th Georgia, Infantry	7/3/1863, Gettysburg, Pennsylvania	Died of Variola (Smallpox), 11/5/1863
Collins, E. O. Private	Unk	9/7/1862, Greeneville, Columbia, South Carolina	Richland County, South Carolina	Co. F, 1st South Carolina Infantry	5/21/1864, Milford Station, Virginia	Died of Unknown Causes, 9/12/186
Collins, Jonathan Private	29	9/23/1862, Boones Creek, Tennessee	Haynesville, Tennessee	Co. D, 60th Tennessee Mounted Infantry	5/17/ 1863, Big Black Bridge, Near Vicksburg, Mississippi	Died of Chronic Diarrhea, 12/11/1863
Collins, T. Private	Unk	Unknown	Unknown	Co. B, 50th, Virginia Infantry	7/3/1863, Gettysburg, Pennsylvania	Died of Unknown Causes, 11/12/1863
Collum, James Private	Unk	5/8/1862, Gainesville, Hall County, Georgia	Hall County, Georgia	Co. K, 43rd Georgia, Infantry	5/16/1863, Champion Hill, Tennessee	Died of Chronic Diarrhea, 1/30/1864
Coltrane, Jesse H. Private	31	7/4/1862, Winston, North Carolina	Forsyth County, North Carolina	Co. D, 57th, North Carolina Infantry	2/6/1865, Near Petersburg, Virginia	Died of Chronic Diarrhea, 5/23/1865

Name	Age	Enlisted	Residence	Unit	Captured	Date and Cause of Death
Colvin, Henry H. Private	23	4/14/1861, Lynchburg, Virginia	Franklin County, Virginia	Co. E, 11th, Virginia Infantry	5/21/1864, Milford Station, Virginia	Died of Unknown Causes, 2/4/1865
Colvord, Jesse A. Private	23	2/20/1862, Jefferson, North Carolina	Wilkes County, North Carolina	Co. B, 1st, North Carolina Cavalry	7/3/1863, Gettysburg, Pennsylvania	Died of Unknown Causes, 9/12/1864
Colzer, William Private	Unk	Unknown	Unknown	Co. G, 13th Georgia, Infantry	4/6/1865, Burkesville, Virginia	Died of Unknown Causes, 5/30/1865
Combs, Wesley Private	19	6/12/1861, Wilkesboro, North Carolina	Wilkes County, North Carolina	Co. C, 26th, North Carolina Infantry	7/5/1863, Gettysburg, Pennsylvania, Wounded	Died of Unknown Causes, 1/4/1864
Conder, William Private	Unk	12/17/1862, Yorktown, Virginia	Union County, North Carolina	Co. B, 15th, North Carolina Infantry	10/14/1863, Bristoe Station, Virginia	Died of Unknown Causes, 2/19/1864
Condon, Jerome F. Private	37	8/5/1861, Pocotaligo, South Carolina	Jasper County, South Carolina	Co. F, 11th, South Carolina Infantry	5/15/1864, Sandy Creek, Virginia, Gunshot Wound Right Shoulder & Arm	Died of Wounds, 5/31/1864
Congleton, Alexander Corporal	18	3/17/1862, Pitt County, North Carolina	Pitt County, North Carolina, Coach Maker	Co. C, 44th, North Carolina Infantry	10/14/1863, Bristoe Station, Virginia	Died of Unknown Causes, 1/3/1864
Conner, Aaron W. Private	29	7/15/1862, Henderson County, North Carolina, Volunteer	Buncombe County, North Carolina	Co. H, 25th, North Carolina Infantry	2/6/1865, Near Petersburg, Virginia	Died of Chronic Diarrhea, 6/1/1865
Conner, Alfred M. Private	Unk	11/10/1861, St. Vincent, Florida	Unknown	Co. I, 4th, Florida Infantry	12/7/1864, Murfreesboro, Near Stones River, Tennessee	Died of Chronic Dysentery, 5/21/1865

Name	Age	Enlisted	Residence	Unit	Captured	Date and Cause of Death
Conner, James A. Private	41	Unknown	Unknown	Co. F, 2nd Kentucky Mounted Rifles	6/16/1863, Triplet Bridge, Kentucky	Died of Unknown Causes, 8/12/1864
Conred, James W. Corporal	Unk	7/4/1862, Newton, North Carolina, Substitute for W. Robinson	Catawba County, North Carolina	Co. E, 57th, North Carolina Infantry	11/7/1863, Kelly's Ford, Rappahannock Station, Virginia	Died of Acute Diarrhea, 3/18/1865
Cook, David Private	31	9/15/1862, Morganton, North Carolina, Conscript	Burke County, North Carolina	Co. D, 6th, North Carolina Infantry	11/7/1863, Kelly's Ford, Rappahannock, Virginia	Died of Chronic Dysentery, 5/29/1865
Cook, Edwin Seaman	Unk	Unknown	Unknown	North Carolina Naval Battery	4/6/1865, Jetersville, Virginia	Date and Cause of Death Unknown
Cook, Stephen Private	Unk	12/13/1861, Franklin, North Carolina	Macon County, North Carolina	Co. B, 66th, North Carolina Infantry	3/8/1865, Near Kinston, North Carolina	Died of Chronic Diarrhea, 5/6/1865
Cook, Thomas M. Private	25	4/24/1861, Philadelphia, Mississippi	Neshoba County, Mississippi	Co. D, 11th Mississippi Infantry	7/14/1863, Falling Waters, Maryland	Died of Chronic Diarrhea, 2/18/1864
Cook, W. J. Private	Unk	6/25/1864, Place Unknown, Conscript	Unknown	15th (Lucas) Battalion South Carolina Heavy Artillery	3/15/1865, Place Illegible, North Carolina	Died of Pneumonia, 5/16/1865
Cook, Washington Private	Unk	6/11/1861, Geneva, Georgia	Talbot County, Georgia	Co. E, 9th Georgia Infantry	7/3/1863, Gettysburg, Pennsylvania	Died of Chronic Dysentery and Pneumonia, 2/22/1864
Cook, William Private	Unk	10/24/1864, Abingdon, Virginia	Washington County, Virginia	Co. H, 37th Virginia Infantry	3/25/1865, Fort Stedman, Near Petersburg, Virginia	Died of Typhoid Fever, 6/19/1865

Name	Age	Enlisted	Residence	Unit	Captured	Date and Cause of Death
Cook, William D. Lieutenant	36	12/25/1861, Bennettsville, South Carolina	Columbia, Richland County, South Carolina	Co. F, 21st South Carolina Infantry	1/15/1865, Fort Fisher, North Carolina, Gunshot Wound Left Shoulder and Left Knee	Amputated Left Leg, Died of Wounds, 4/27/1865
Cooke, Robert Private	23	4/10/1862, Blountsville, Alabama	Blount County, Alabama	Co. F, 48th Alabama Infantry	7/2/1863, Gettysburg, Pennsylvania	Died of Chronic Diarrhea, 12/3/1863
Coon, G. W. Private	Unk	Unknown	Unknown	Co. C, 54th, North Carolina Infantry	Unknown	Unable to Locate
Cooper, James L. Sergeant	31	7/19/1862, Dualla Town, North Carolina	Jackson County, North Carolina, Farmer	1st Regiment Thomas' Legion, North Carolina Infantry	9/14/1864, Winchester, Virginia	Died From Inflammation of the Bowels, 1/25/1865
Cooper, Thomas D. Private	38	1/1/1862, Springfield, Missouri	Jackson County, Missouri, Farmer	Co. E, 6th Missouri Infantry	5/16/1863, Baker's Creek, Champion Hill, Tennessee	Date and Cause of Death Unknown
Cooper, William W. Private	Unk	6/11/1861, Lynchburg, Virginia	Franklin County, Virginia	Co. D, 24th, Virginia Infantry	4/6/1865, Burkesville, Virginia	Died of Catarrh (Inflammation of Mucus Membranes, Usually Nose and Throat), 5/3/1865
Copening, Abraham K. Private	19	8/20/1862, Camp Hill, North Carolina, Conscript	Unknown	Co. C, 18th, North Carolina Infantry	5/21/1864, Spotsylvania Court House, Virginia	Died of Unknown Causes, 9/30/1864
Corcoran, William M. Private	Unk	6/4/1861, Alexandria, Alabama	Calhoun County, Alabama	Co. D, 10th, Alabama Infantry	7/1/1863, Gettysburg, Pennsylvania	Died of Unknown Causes, 11/16/1863
Cork, Walter Private	20	4/21/1862, D. College, North Carolina	Mecklenburg County, North Carolina, Student	Co. K, 56th, North Carolina Infantry	3/25/1865, Fort Stedman, Virginia	Died of Scurvy, 5/28/1865

Name	Age	Enlisted	Residence	Unit	Captured	Date and Cause of Death
Corkern, John G. Private	18	7/7/1861, Camp Moore, Louisiana	Franklinton, Louisiana, Farmer	Co. I, 9th Louisiana Infantry	11/7/1863, Kelly's Ford, Rappahannock Station, Virginia	Died of Unknown Causes, 8/30/1864
Corr, Richard B. Private Not Listed On Monument	Unk	7/18/1861, Urbana, Virginia	Middlesex County, Virginia	Co. C, 55th Virginia Infantry	7/14/1863, Falling Waters, Maryland	Died of Chronic Diarrhea, 1/2/1864
Corran, Edgar Private Not Listed On Monument	18	3/10/1862. Barrett's Point, Virginia	Unknown	Co. I, 3rd Virginia Infantry	7/3/1863, Gettysburg, Pennsylvania	Died of Unknown Causes, 7/15/1864
Correll, William C. Sergeant	27	7/4/1862, Salisbury, North Carolina, Volunteer	Rowan County, North Carolina	Co. A, 57th, North Carolina Infantry	7/5/1863, Gettysburg, Pennsylvania	Died of Variola (Smallpox), 11/24/1863
Corum, William W. Private	23	3/3/1862, Greensboro, North Carolina	Guilford County, North Carolina, Farmer	Co. B, 45th, North Carolina Infantry	7/5/1863, South Mountain, Gettysburg, Pennsylvania	Died of Unknown Causes, 1/3/1864
Cosby, D. A. Private	38	1/15/1862, Burke County, North Carolina, Volunteer	Burke County, North Carolina	Co. D, 11th, North Carolina Infantry	7/14/1863, Falling Waters, Maryland	Died of Chronic Diarrhea, 3/10/1864
Couch, William H. Corporal	Unk	7/15/1862, Chapel Hill, North Carolina	Orange County, North Carolina	Co. G, 11th, North Carolina Infantry	10/27/1864, Boyton Plank Road or Burgess' Mill, Virginia	Died of Chronic Diarrhea, 4/24/1865
Coulter, George J. Private	32	3/5/1862, Blue Sulfur Springs, Virginia	Huntersville, Virginia, Farmer	Co. K, 14th, Virginia Cavalry	11/12/1864, Near Nineveh, Virginia	Died of Chronic Diarrhea, 4/23/1865
Council, Calvin H. Private	Unk	Unknown	Unknown	Co. D, 35th, North Carolina Infantry	6/17/1864, Near Petersburg, Virginia	Died of Unknown Causes, 8/2/1864

Name	Age	Enlisted	Residence	Unit	Captured	Date and Cause of Death
Coursey, Francis M. Private	Unk	8/25/1862, Atlanta, Georgia, Conscript	Fulton County, Georgia	Co. C, 21st, Georgia Infantry	10/19/1864, Cedar Creek, Virginia	Died of Acute Dysentery, 12/21/1864
Courtney, Basil Private	22	5/26/1861, Morrisville, Virginia	Fauquier County, Virginia, Shoemaker	Co. I, 11th, Virginia Infantry	7/3/1863, Gettysburg, Pennsylvania	Died of Chronic Diarrhea, 2/1/1864
Covington, J. Private	Unk	Unknown	Unknown	Co. B, 30th, North Carolina Infantry	Unknown	Unable to Locate
Covington, John B. Private	16	3/10/1862, Richmond County, North Carolina	Richmond County, North Carolina, Farmer	Co. F, 52nd, North Carolina Infantry	7/14/1863, Falling Waters, Maryland	Died of Variola (Smallpox), 11/28/1863
Covington, William H. Private	Unk	5/26/1861, Heathsville, Virginia	Unknown	Co. F, 40th, Virginia Infantry	7/14/1863, Falling Waters, Maryland	Died of Chronic Diarrhea, 2/14/1864
Covington, William H. Corporal	Unk	2/24/1863, Prince Edward County, Virginia	Prince Edward County, Virginia	Co. E, 18th, Virginia Infantry	3/31/1865, Hatcher's Run, Virginia	Died of Chronic Diarrhea, 5/16/1865
Cowlee, J. P. Private	Unk	Unknown	Unknown	Fry's Battery Virginia Artillery	Unknown	Unable to Locate
Cowley, Thomas J. Private	Unk	Unknown	Unknown	Co. B, 10th, Virginia Infantry	6/21/1864, Near Petersburg, Virginia	Died of Scurvy, 2/23/1865
Cox, Addison K. Private	Unk	6/4/1861, Warsaw, Virginia	Richmond County, Virginia	Co. H, 40th, Virginia Infantry	7/14/1863, Falling Waters, Maryland	Died of Unknown Causes, 1/26/1864
Cox, J. E. N. Private	Unk	3/1/1863, Chester Station, Virginia, Conscript	Unknown	Co. I, 7th, Virginia Infantry	4/6/1865, Harper's Farm, Virginia	Died of Rubeola (Measles) 6/8/1865
Cox, Morgan M. Sergeant	21	5/23/1861, Fredericksburg Virginia	Fredericksburg Virginia, Clerk	Co. C, 30th, Virginia Infantry	4/1/1865, Five Forks, Virginia	Died of Chronic Diarrhea, 5/30/1865

Name	Age	Enlisted	Residence	Unit	Captured	Date and Cause of Death
Cox, Philip Private	Unk	6/12/1861, Center Cross, Virginia	Essex County, Virginia	Co. K, 55th, Virginia Infantry	7/14/1863, Falling Waters, Maryland	Died of Unknown Causes, 2/2/1864
Cox, Samuel Private	Unk	Unknown	Unknown	Co. D, 15th, South Carolina Infantry	Unknown	Unable to Locate
Cox, Terill Private	Unk	6/4/1861, Fork of Wilson, Virginia	Unknown	Co. D, 50th, Virginia Infantry	7/5/1863, Cashtown, Pennsylvania	Died of Chronic Diarrhea, 12/3/1863
Cox, William Sergeant	Unk	9/25/1862, Ford Town, Tennessee	Unknown	Co. E, 60th Tennessee Mounted Infantry	5/17/1863, Big Black Bridge, Near Vicksburg, Mississippi	Died of Unknown Causes, 8/18/1864
Cox, William E. Private	Unk	4/20/1864, Walker's Creek, Virginia	Unknown	Jackson's Virginia Horse Artillery	9/23/1864, Cedar Creek or Strasburg, Virginia	Died of Unknown Causes, 11/5/1864
Cozart, Allen Private	18	8/28/1863, Greenville, North Carolina	Granville County, North Carolina, Farmer	Co. B, 1st North Carolina Cavalry	4/2/1865, Ford's Station, Virginia	Died of Acute Dysentery, 5/28/1865
Crabb, Joseph Private	22	11/1/1862, Bay Springs, Mississippi	Hickory Plains, Mississippi, Farmer	Co. H, 26th Mississippi Infantry	5/16/1863, Baker's Creek, Champion Hill, Tennessee	Died of Chronic Diarrhea, 11/8/1863
Crabtree, George Private Not Listed On Monument	Unk	1/20/1864, Richland, South Carolina	Unknown	Co. K, 1st, South Carolina Infantry	5/12/1864, Spotsylvania Court House, Virginia	Died of Chronic Diarrhea, 7/17/1865
Crabtree, William F. Private	23	3/14/1864, Pisgah Church, North Carolina	Unknown Farmer	Co. D, 1st, North Carolina Infantry	5/12/1864, Spotsylvania Court House, Virginia	Died of Acute Dysentery, 8/16/1864
Craft, John H. Private	Unk	6/26/1861, Lewisburg, Virginia	Alleghany County, Virginia, Boat Builder	Co. D, 60th, Virginia Infantry	10/20/1864, Woodstock, Virginia	Died of Acute Dysentery, 1/6/1865

Name	Age	Enlisted	Residence	Unit	Captured	Date and Cause of Death
Craghead, Thomas L. Private	43	3/23/1862, Richmond, Virginia	Halesford, Franklin County, Virginia	Co. K, 10th, Virginia Cavalry	9/10/1864, Petersburg, Virginia	Died of Unknown Causes, 9/23/1864
Cralle, William C. Sergeant	Unk	1/25/1862, St. John's, Virginia	Unknown	Stiles' Virginia Heavy Artillery	4/6/1865, Farmville, Virginia	Died of Scurvy, 6/18/1865
Cranford, Ezekiel Private Not Listed On Monument	Unk	7/1/1863, Chatham County, North Carolina	Chatham County, North Carolina	Co. D, 61st, North Carolina Infantry	7/27/1863, Morris Island, South Carolina	Died of Dropsy, 6/27/1865
Crawford, Benjamin F. 1st Sergeant	Unk	5/20/1863, Dickison Bay, Florida	Unknown	Co. I, 11th, Florida Infantry	4/6/1865, Burkeville, Virginia	Died of Chronic Diarrhea, 6/3/1865
Crawford, Daniel A. Private	Unk	10/29/1863, Columbia, South Carolina	Richland County, South Carolina	Co. C, 23rd, South Carolina Infantry	4/1/1865, Five Forks, Virginia	Died of Gunshot Wound, 6/18/1865
Crawford, Martin L. Private	43	5/1/1862, Wilmington, North Carolina	Pitt County, North Carolina, Farmer	Co. G, 61st, North Carolina Infantry	8/26/1863, Battery Wagner, Morris Island, South Carolina	Died of Variola (Smallpox), 12/11/1863
Crawford, P. G. Private	Unk	11/5/1863, Talladega, Alabama	Talladega County, Alabama	Jeff Davis Alabama Artillery	5/19/1864, Spotsylvania Court House, Wilderness, Virginia	Died of Unknown Causes, 6/10/1864
Creasy, Alfred L. Private	Unk	2/15/1863, Culpepper Court House, Virginia	Unknown	Co. G, 28th, Virginia Infantry	4/6/1865, Burkesville, Virginia	Died of Chronic Diarrhea, 6/4/1865
Creasy, Samuel H. Private	Unk	10/15/1864, Bedford, Virginia, Conscript	Unknown	Co. B, 28th, Virginia Infantry	4/6/1865 Farmville, Virginia	Died of Remittent Fever, 6/19/165
Creecy, James E. Corporal	23	2/15/1862, Edenton, North Carolina, Volunteer	Perquimans County, North Carolina	Co. F, 11th, North Carolina Infantry	7/14/1863, Falling Waters, Maryland	Died of Unknown Causes, 2/15/1864

Name	Age	Enlisted	Residence	Unit	Captured	Date and Cause of Death
Creed, H. Private	Unk	Unknown	Unknown	Co. B, 50th, Georgia Infantry	Unknown	Unable to Locate
Cribb, John B. Sergeant	Unk	5/5/1862, Battery Walker, Georgia	Ware County, Georgia	Co. B, 50th, Georgia Infantry	4/6/1865, Amelia Court House, Virginia	Died of Chronic Dysentery, 6/16/1865
Crichlow, John Private	Unk	5/16/1862, Bertie County, North Carolina	Unknown	Co. K, 3rd, North Carolina Cavalry	4/2/1865, Petersburg, Virginia	Died of Chronic Dysentery, 6/15/1865
Cridlin, James Christopher Corporal	Unk	4/6/1864, Camp Orange, Virginia	Unknown	Co. E, 55th, Virginia Infantry	4/6/1865, High Bridge, Virginia	Died of Pneumonia, 5/10/1865
Crickman, W. H. Private	23	7/15/1862, Raleigh, North Carolina, Conscript	Nash County, North Carolina	Co. C, 1st, North Carolina Infantry	7/3/1863, Gettysburg, Pennsylvania	Died of Scurvy, 11/23/1863
Crocker, Matthew B. Private	23	3/7/1863, Wake County, North Carolina, Volunteer	Wake County, North Carolina, Farmer	Co. H, 47th, North Carolina Infantry	7/3/1863, Gettysburg, Pennsylvania	Died of Chronic Dysentery, 11/20/1863
Crocker, William J. Private	30	8/15/1862, Iredell County, North Carolina, Conscript	Mecklenburg County, North Carolina	Co. I, 37th, North Carolina Infantry	5/12/1864, Spotsylvania Court House, Virginia	Died of Chronic Diarrhea, 11/3/1864
Crockett, William B. Private	Unk	7/2/1861, Wytheville, Virginia	Wythe County, Virginia	Co. C, 50th, Virginia Infantry	5/12/1864, Spotsylvania Court House, Virginia	Died of Unknown Causes, 8/29/1864
Crockrell, Samuel Private	28	4/26/1861, Columbus County, North Carolina, Volunteer	Johnson County, North Carolina	Co. D, 20th, North Carolina Infantry	7/1/1863, Gettysburg, Pennsylvania	Died of Unknown Causes, 4/5/1864
Cromer, John L. Private	Unk	5/14/1862, Newberry, South Carolina	Newberry County, South Carolina	Co. F, 20th, South Carolina Infantry	10/19/1864, Cedar Creek or Strasburg, Virginia	Died of Typhoid Fever, 12/21/1864

Name	Age	Enlisted	Residence	Unit	Captured	Date and Cause of Death
Cronse, David Private	29	9/23/1863, Boons Creek, Tennessee	Unknown	Co. D, 60th Tennessee Mounted Infantry	5/17/ 1863, Big Black Bridge, Near Vicksburg, Mississippi	Died of Variola (Smallpox), 12/15/1863
Cross, Isaac Private	Unk	7/10/1864, Scott County, Virginia	Scott County, Virginia	Co. H, 48th, Virginia Infantry	5/12/1864, Near Spotsylvania Court House, Virginia	Died of Chronic Diarrhea, 10/18/1864
Cross, John D. Private	Unk	2/27/1862, Graney Island, Virginia	Unknown	Co. D, 9th, Virginia Infantry	7/3/1863, Gettysburg, Pennsylvania	Died of Variola (Smallpox), 11/29/1863
Cross, John T. Private	Unk	5/24/1861, Sussex Court House, Virginia	Sussex County, Virginia	Co. A, 41st, Virginia Infantry	10/27/1864, Boyton Plank Road or Burgess' Mill, Virginia	Died of Consumption, 3/30/1865
Crouch, Robert A. Private	Unk	9/10/1861, Camp Stephens, Georgia	Mariweather County, Georgia	Co. E, 28th, Georgia Infantry	9/6/1863, Morris Island, Charleston, South Carolina	Died of Variola (Smallpox), 12/31/1863
Crouch, Samuel C. Sergeant	33	3/8/1862, Richmond County, North Carolina, Volunteer	Richmond County, North Carolina	Co. E, 52nd, North Carolina Infantry	7/5/1863, Gettysburg, Pennsylvania	Died of Unknown Causes, 8/10/1864
Crow, John W. Corporal	Unk	6/4/1861, Ashville, Georgia	Unknown	Co. A, 10th, Alabama Infantry	6/30/1864, Near Petersburg, Virginia	Died of Chronic Diarrhea, 4/22/1865
Crowder, John P. Private Not Listed On Monument	20	3/29/1862, X-Roads, Cleveland County, North Carolina, Volunteer	Cleveland County, North Carolina	Co. C, 55th, North Carolina Infantry	7/5/1863, Gettysburg, Pennsylvania	Died of Chronic Diarrhea, 10/12/1864
Crowder, William Private	Unk	5/5/1864, Petersburg, Virginia	Chesterfield County, Virginia	Co. E, 3rd (Archer's) Battalion, Virginia Reserves	6/9/1864, Rive's Farm Near the Plank Road, Petersburg, Virginia	Died of Unknown Causes, 7/31/1864
Crowson, Edward M. Sergeant	21	4/20/1861, Guilford County, North Carolina, Volunteer	Guilford County, North Carolina	Co. B, 27th, North Carolina Infantry	10/14/1863, Bristoe Station, Virginia	Died of Chronic Diarrhea, 1/16/1864

Name	Age	Enlisted	Residence	Unit	Captured	Date and Cause of Death
Crum, James W. T. Private	Unk	8/22/1862, Calhoun, Georgia	Berrien County, Georgia	Co. I, 50th, Georgia Infantry	10/19/1864, Cedar Creek or Strasburg, Virginia	Died of Chronic Diarrhea, 1/15/1865
Crumbley, Fernando Private	Unk	12/13/1862, Griffon, Georgia	Unknown	Co. G, 63rd, Georgia Infantry	11/19/1864, Henry County, Georgia	Died of Chronic Diarrhea, 2/8/1865
Crump, Lemuel Private Not Listed On Monument	Unk	Unknown	Unknown	Co. F, 3rd Virginia Cavalry	Unknown	Died of Chronic Dysentery, 12/25/1864
Cruse, Ambrose Private	20	8/6/1861, Mount Pleasant, North Carolina, Volunteer	Cabarrus County, North Carolina, Farmer	Co. H, 8th, North Carolina Infantry	9/30/1864, Fort Harrison, Virginia	Died of Chronic Dysentery, 2/28/1865
Crutchfield, Francis M. Private	Unk	5/10/1864, Mount Pelia, Tennessee	Mount Pelia, Weakley County, Tennessee	Co. H, 22nd Tennessee Cavalry	12/17/1864, Near Franklin, Tennessee	Died of Chronic Diarrhea, 6/12/1865
Crutchfield, William H. Private	Unk	5/28/1861, Cartersville, North Carolina	Duplin County, North Carolina	Co. E, 26th, North Carolina Infantry	7/4/1863, South Mountain, Maryland	Died of Variola (Smallpox), 12/23/1863
Culbreck, J. F. Private	Unk	Unknown	Unknown	Co. D, 19th, Georgia Infantry	3/8/1865, Near Kinston, North Carolina	Died of Chronic Dysentery, 5/30/1865
Cully, John T. Private	28	6/20/1861, Abingdon, Virginia	Washington County, Virginia	Co. B, 48th, Virginia Infantry	7/4/1863, South Mountain, Maryland	Died of Variola (Smallpox), 12/18/1863
Culpepper, James T. Corporal	Unk	3/4/1862, Blakely Island, Georgia	Early County, Georgia	Co. A, 51st, Georgia Infantry	7/3/1863, Gettysburg, Pennsylvania	Died of Chronic Diarrhea, 2/7/1864

Name	Age	Enlisted	Residence	Unit	Captured	Date and Cause of Death
Culpepper, M. W. Private	Unk	Unknown	Unknown	Co. A, 14th, Virginia Infantry	Unknown	Unable to Locate
Cumby, Elisha B. Private	Unk	4/24/1861, Halifax County, Virginia	Unknown	Co. A, 53rd, Virginia Infantry	7/3/1863, Gettysburg, Pennsylvania	Died of Unknown Causes, 2/3/1864
Cumby, Frank W. Private	Unk	5/24/1861, Appomattox, Virginia	Appomattox County, Virginia	Co. A, 20th, Virginia Heavy Artillery	4/6/1865, Farmville, Virginia	Died of Chronic Diarrhea, 6/21/1865
Cumby, Nathan Private	Unk	7/21/1862, Richmond County, Georgia	Troup County, Georgia	Co. B, 4th, Georgia Infantry	7/5/1863, Waterloo, Gettysburg, Pennsylvania	Died of Smallpox, 11/8/1863
Cummings, A. Jesse Private	Unk	8/15/1864, Fisher's Hill, Virginia	Unknown	Co. H, 26th, Virginia Infantry	9/19/1864, Winchester, Virginia	Died of Pleuritis, Pleurisy, Inflammation of the Lungs, 3/6/1865
Cunningham, Unknown Private	Unk	Unknown	Unknown	Powhatan Virginia Reserve Infantry	Unknown	Unable to Locate
Cunningham, H. M. Private	26	4/14/1861, Spartanburg, South Carolina	Spartanburg District, South Carolina	Co. K, 3rd, South Carolina Infantry	5/23/1864, North Anna River, Virginia	Died of Pneumonia, 1/5/1865
Currence, D. A. Private	Unk	3/2/1864, Columbia, South Carolina	Richland County, South Carolina	Co. F, 17th, South Carolina Infantry	4/5/1865, Five Forks, Virginia	Died of Chronic Dysentery, 5/8/1865
Curry, D. G. Sergeant	Unk	2/28/1862, Mobile, Alabama	Unknown	Co. F, 3rd Alabama Cavalry	6/27/1863, Shelbyville, Tennessee	Died of Unknown Causes, 2/24/1864
Curry, J. Private	Unk	Unknown	Unknown	Co. H, 57th, North Carolina Infantry	Unknown	Unable to Locate

Name	Age	Enlisted	Residence	Unit	Captured	Date and Cause of Death
Cushing, Seborne A. Private	22	3/10/1862, Martin County, North Carolina, Volunteer	Martin County, North Carolina	Co. A, 17th, North Carolina Infantry	10/2/1864, Chapin's Farm, Virginia	Died of Apoplexy (Stroke), 12/24/1864
Cutrell, Elizer Private	Unk	Unknown	Unknown	Co. ?, 66th, North Carolina Infantry	Unknown	Unable to Locate
Cutler, James N. Private	Unk	5/15/1864, South Hampton, Virginia	Unknown	Co. G, 3rd, Virginia Infantry	4/1/1865, Five Forks, Virginia	Died of Diphtheria, 5/6/1865
Cutlip, Wesley J. Private	21	6/13/1862, Conrads, Virginia	Braxton County, Virginia, Farmer	Co. G, 25th, Virginia Infantry	5/5/1864, Wilderness, Virginia	Died of Unknown Causes, 8/8/1864

Name	Age	Enlisted	Residence	Unit	Captured	Date and Cause of Death
Dabney, Robert Private	Unk	4/25/1861, Powhatan Court House, Virginia	Powhatan County, Virginia	Co. E, 4th, Virginia Cavalry	10/9/1864, Cedar Creek or Strasburg, Virginia	Died of Typhoid Fever, 2/22/1865
Dacus, Paschal H. Private	Unk	3/15/1862, Camp Bartow, Atlanta, Georgia	Dawson County, Georgia	Co. E, 38rd, Georgia Infantry	4/22/1864, Fisher's Hill, Virginia	Died of Measles, 3/10/1865
Dailey, Bartley Y. Corporal	25	9/26/1862, Wake County, North Carolina	Lincoln County, North Carolina	Co. C, 16th, North Carolina Infantry	5/6/1864, Wilderness, Virginia	Date and Cause of Death Unknown
Dailey, James T. Private	20	3/20/1862, Arkansas	Unknown	Co. E, 1st, Missouri Cavalry	5/17/1863, Big Black Bridge, Near Vicksburg, Mississippi	Died of Chronic Diarrhea, 11/3/1863
Dameron, Samuel Private	Unk	2/20/1864, Tappahannock Virginia	Essex County, Virginia	Co. E, 40th, Virginia Infantry	4/6/1865, Burkesville, Virginia	Died of Typhoid Fever, 5/9/1865
Dampeer, W. Private	Unk	5/16/1864, Quitman, Georgia	Unknown	Co. E, 1st Battalion Georgia Reserves	12/13/1864, Fort McAllister, Georgia	Died of Intermittent Fever, 2/24/1865

Name	Age	Enlisted	Residence	Unit	Captured	Date and Cause of Death
Dancy, Daniel D. Private	Unk	10/1/1863, Wilkesboro, North Carolina	Wilkes County, North Carolina	Co. G, 56th, North Carolina Infantry	3/25/1865, Fort Stedman, Near Petersburg, Virginia	Died From Inflammation of Lungs (Pneumonia), 6/1/1865
Daniel, C. P. Private	19	10/2/1862, Mossy Creek, Tennessee	Jefferson County, Tennessee	Co. F, 61st Tennessee Mounted Infantry	5/17/1863, Big Black Bridge, Near Vicksburg, Mississippi	Died of Chronic Diarrhea, 11/6/1863
Daniel, George O. Private	Unk	7/18/1861, Reese's Church, Charlotte, Virginia	Unknown	Co. I, 56th, Virginia Infantry	8/25/1864, Near Howlet's House, Virginia	Died of Chronic Diarrhea, 4/17/1865
Daniel, Isham H. Private	Unk	Date Unknown, Petersburg, Virginia	Chesterfield County, Virginia	Holcombe's South Carolina Volunteers Legion	4/1/1865, Five Forks, Virginia	Died of Unknown Causes, 6/9/1865
Daniel, Thomas K. Private	52	5/8/1862, Camp Mangum, North Carolina, Substitute	Wake County, North Carolina	Co. I, 47th, North Carolina Infantry	7/5/1863, Gettysburg, Pennsylvania	Died of Variola (Smallpox), 3/3/1865
Daniel, William H. Private	Unk	4/20/1862, Montgomery, Alabama	Montgomery County, Alabama	Co. B, 51st, Captain Thompson's Company of Alabama Cavalry	6/27/1863, Liberty Gap, Shelbyville, Tennessee	Died of Scurvy, 11/13/1863
Daniels, Edward G. Corporal	Unk	12/28/1861, Camp Hampton, Columbia, South Carolina	Richland County, South Carolina	Co. G, 7th Battalion South Carolina Infantry	8/21/1864, Globe Tavern, Weldon Rail Road, Virginia	Died of Scurvy, 4/19/1865
Daniels, Thomas S. Private	Unk	2/21/1862, Columbus, Kentucky	Hickman County, Kentucky	Co. K, 12th Louisiana Infantry	5/16/1863, Champion Hill, Tennessee	Died of Unknown Causes, 1/6/1864
Dankins, George Private	Unk	10/14/1864, Raleigh, North Carolina	Wake County, North Carolina	Co. A, 5th North Carolina Infantry	2/6/1865, Near Petersburg, Virginia	Died of Catarrh, (Inflammation of the Mucous Membranes), 2/21/1865
Darington, Robert Private	Unk	Unknown	Unknown	Virginia Reserve Infantry	Unknown	Unable to Locate

Name	Age	Enlisted	Residence	Unit	Captured	Date and Cause of Death
Darnell, William E. Private	23	4/18/1861, Warrington,	Warren County, North Carolina	Co. F, 12th, North Carolina Infantry	5/6/1864, Wilderness, Virginia	Died of Unknown Causes, 8/7/1864
Darr, James Private	Unk	Unknown	Unknown	White's 35th Battalion Virginia Cavalry	Unknown	Unable to Locate
Darr, John D. Private	17	1/30/1865, Illegible	Unknown	Stark's Battalion Light Virginia Artillery	Unknown	Died of Chronic Diarrhea, 6/9/1865
Davenport, Benjamin S. Corporal	Unk	1/28/1862, Columbia, North Carolina	Tyrrell County, North Carolina	Co. G, 1st North Carolina Infantry	7/3/1863, Gettysburg, Pennsylvania	Died of Unknown Causes, 2/19/1864
Davenport, H. Private	Unk	2/11/1863, Newberry, South Carolina	Newberry County, South Carolina	Co. E, 27th, South Carolina Infantry	6/24/1864, Near Petersburg, Virginia	Died of Chronic Dysentery, 9/10/1864
David, G. Private Not Listed On Monument	Unk	Unknown	Unknown	Co. H, 61st Georgia Infantry	Unknown	Died of Smallpox, 11/25/186?
Davidson, William F. Private	Unk	8/1/1862, Gordonsville, Virginia	Orange County, Virginia	Co. A, 22nd, Virginia Infantry	6/27/1863, Mercerville, Sharpsburg, Virginia	Died of Unknown Causes, 3/15/1864
Davis, Alexander Private	18	5/30/1863, Fort Caswell, North Carolina	Robeson County, North Carolina, Farmer	Co. E, 40th Regiment, 3rd North Carolina Light Artillery	1/15/1865, Fort Fisher, North Carolina	Died of Pneumonia, 2/13/1865
Davis, Augustus C. Private	Unk	9/1/1863, Camp Vance, North Carolina	Burke County, North Carolina	Co. A, 34th North Carolina Infantry	5/6/1864, Wilderness, Virginia	Died of Unknown Causes, 6/20/1864
Davis, B. W. Seaman	Unk	Unknown	Unknown	Confederate States Navy	Unknown	Unable to Locate

Name	Age	Enlisted	Residence	Unit	Captured	Date and Cause of Death
Davis, Benjamin J. Private	22	10/2/1863, Mossy Creek, Tennessee	Jefferson County, Tennessee	Co. F, 61st Tennessee Mounted Infantry	5/17/ 1863, Big Black Bridge, Near Vicksburg, Mississippi	Died of Chronic Diarrhea, 1/4/1864
Davis, Calvin Private	23	3/8/1862, Wilmington, North Carolina	Robeson County, North Carolina	Co. F, 3rd North Carolina Infantry	5/12/1864, Spotsylvania Court House, Virginia	Died of Unknown Causes, 7/17/1864
Davis, Dougan Private	17	12/4/1862, Randolph County, North Carolina	Randolph County, North Carolina	Co. F, 2nd Battalion North Carolina Infantry	11/8/1863, Brandy Station, Virginia	Died of Variola (Smallpox), 3/18/1864
Davis, Edwin W. Private	Unk	11/15/1861, Camp Green, Charleston, South Carolina	Clarendon District, South Carolina	Co. I, 23rd South Carolina Infantry	4/2/1865, Petersburg, Virginia	Died of Acute Diarrhea, 5/27/1865
Davis, Henry Private	25	11/3/1863, Franklin, Virginia, Conscript	Randolph County, North Carolina, Carpenter	Co. G, 52nd North Carolina Infantry	5/12/1864, Spotsylvania Court House, Virginia	Died of Unknown Causes, 8/6/1864
Davis, Henry R. Private Not Listed On Monument	30	5/2/1862, Wilson County, North Carolina	Wilson County, North Carolina	Co. A, 55th North Carolina Infantry	10/14/1863, Bristoe Station, Virginia	Died of Inflammation of Lungs (Pneumonia), 11/4/1864
Davis, Henry R. Private	20	2/28/1862, Augusta, Georgia	Richmond County, Georgia	Co. C, 48th Georgia Infantry	4/6/1865, Harper's Farm, Virginia	Died of Pneumonia, 5/7/1865
Davis, Hiram M. Corporal	22	4/8/1861, Columbia, South Carolina	Richland County, South Carolina	Co. C, 2nd South Carolina Infantry	10/19/1864, Cedar Creek or Strasburg, Virginia	Died of Typhoid Fever, 6/6/1865
Davis, Isaac Private	Unk	7/20/1861, Dunnsville, Virginia	Unknown	Co. G, 55th, Virginia Infantry	5/23/1864, Place Not Stated	Died of Remittent Fever, 3/29/1865
Davis, J. P. Private	Unk	5/1/1863, Columbia, South Carolina	Richland County, South Carolina	Co. K, Holcombe Legion, South Carolina Infantry	5/7/1864, Stony Creek, Virginia	Died of Unknown Causes, 6/6/1864

Name	Age	Enlisted	Residence	Unit	Captured	Date and Cause of Death
Davis, J. Robertson Private	Unk	6/29/1861, Darlington, South Carolina	Darlington District, South Carolina	Co. E, 6th South Carolina Infantry	5/23/1864, North Anna River, Virginia	Died of Unknown Causes, 10/16/1864
Davis, James Private	18	8/20/1863, Lenoir County, North Carolina, Conscript	Caldwell County, North Carolina	Co. F, 26th North Carolina Infantry	10/14/1863, Bristoe Station, Virginia	Died of Unknown Causes, 8/13/1864
Davis, James Private	34	6/7/1861, Camp Moore, Louisiana	Orleans Parish, Louisiana, Laborer	Co. F, 7th Louisiana Infantry	Unknown	Died of Chronic Diarrhea, 2/20/1865
Davis, James A. Private	Unk	3/17/1862, Camden, South Carolina	Kershaw District, South Carolina	Co. H, 7th South Carolina Infantry	5/30/1864, Near Old Church, Virginia	Died of Pneumonia, 6/7/1865
Davis, James M. Private	Unk	9/16/1864, Camp Holmes, Raleigh, North Carolina	Wake County, North Carolina	Co. F, 32nd North Carolina Infantry	10/19/1864, Cedar Creek or Strasburg, Virginia	Died of Frost Bite, 2/13/1865
Davis, Jesse Private	35	2/22/1862, Nash County, North Carolina, Volunteer	Hyde County, North Carolina, Farmer	Co. A, 47th North Carolina Infantry	10/14/1863, Bristoe Station, Virginia	Died of Variola (Smallpox), 3/30/1864
Davis, Jesse Private	22	9/27/1864, Raleigh, North Carolina, Conscript	Beaufort County, North Carolina	Co. B, 33rd North Carolina Infantry	4/2/1865, Petersburg, Virginia	Died of Chronic Diarrhea, 6/21/1865
Davis, John Private	Unk	4/20/1864, Orange, Virginia	Unknown	Co. E, 44th North Carolina Infantry	10/27/1865, Near Petersburg, Virginia	Died of Chronic Diarrhea, 2/24/1865
Davis, Lorenzo A. Private	18	9/2/1861, Rutherford County, North Carolina, Volunteer	Rutherford County, North Carolina, Farmer	Co. C, 34th North Carolina Infantry	8/1/1863, Culpepper Court House, Brandy Station, Virginia	Died of Chronic Diarrhea and Smallpox, 2/2/1864
Davis, Miles A. Private	Unk	8/1/1861, Decatur, Georgia	DeKalb County, Georgia	Co. D, 3rd Battalion Georgia Sharp Shooters	4/6/1865, Farmville, Virginia	Died of Chronic Dysentery, 6/13/1865

Name	Age	Enlisted	Residence	Unit	Captured	Date and Cause of Death
Davis, Temple Treman Private	Unk	6/3/1862, Near Richmond, Charlotte County, Virginia	Charlotte County, Virginia	Co. K, 18th, Virginia Infantry	7/3/1863, Gettysburg, Pennsylvania	Died of Unknown Causes, 4/7/1864
Davis, Thomas Private Not Listed On Monument	36	3/13/1863, James Island, South Carolina	Charleston District, South Carolina	Co. F, 25th South Carolina Infantry	1/15/1865, Fort Fisher, North Carolina, Gunshot Fracture of Right Leg and Knee	Amputated Right Leg, Died of Wounds, 2/9/1865
Davis, Thomas Jefferson Private	Unk	7/19/1861, Monroe, Georgia	Walton County, Georgia	Co. F, 16th, Georgia Infantry	7/5/1863, Gettysburg, Pennsylvania	Died of Chronic Dysentery, 5/28/1865
Davis, Thomas R. Corporal	19	3/22/1862, Winston, Forsyth County, North Carolina, Volunteer	Forsyth County, North Carolina, Farmer	Co. K, 52nd North Carolina Infantry	7/5/1863, Gettysburg, Pennsylvania	Died of Scurvy, 11/11/1863
Davis, W. R. Seaman	Unk	Unknown	Unknown	Confederate States Navy	Unknown	Unable to Locate
Davis, William R. Private	20	6/1/1861, Fort Macon, North Carolina, Volunteer	Wayne County, North Carolina	Co. A, 27th North Carolina Infantry	10/14/1863, Bristoe Station, Virginia	Died of Chronic Diarrhea, 2/27/1865
Dawson, Burwell Private	18	2/18/1863, Sampson County, North Carolina, Volunteer	Newton Grove, Sampson County, North Carolina	Co. A, 36th North Carolina Heavy Artillery	1/15/1865, Fort Fisher, North Carolina	Died of Pneumonia, 3/17/1865
Dawson, John Private	38	1/14/1863, New Bern, North Carolina	Craven County, North Carolina, Farmer	Co. C, 61st North Carolina Infantry	8/19/1864, Globe Tavern, Near Weldon Railroad, Virginia	Died of Unknown Causes, 2/22/1865
Dawson, William H. Private	19	5/10/1861, Sampson County, North Carolina, Volunteer	Sampson County, North Carolina, Apprentice	Co. H, 20th North Carolina Infantry	7/1/1863, Gettysburg, Pennsylvania	Died of Chronic Diarrhea and Scurvy, 1/18/1864

Name	Age	Enlisted	Residence	Unit	Captured	Date and Cause of Death
Day, A. Private	Unk	Unknown	Unknown	Co. C, 4th South Carolina Infantry	Unknown	Unable to Locate
Deagle, William H. Citizen Not Listed On Monument	Unk	Unknown	Unknown	Citizen	6/22/1864, Middlesex County, Virginia, Received From US Gunboat Jacob Bell	Died of Unknown Causes, 2/14/1865
Deal, Alfred Private	Unk	9/15/1864, Fort McRea, North Carolina	Unknown	Co. I, 47th North Carolina Infantry	10/27/1864, Burgess' Mill, Near Petersburg, Virginia	Died of Chronic Diarrhea, 3/12/1865
Deal, William S. Private	25	10/11/1863, Camp Vance, Morganton, North Carolina	Burke County, North Carolina	Co. F, 38th North Carolina Infantry	4/2/1865, Hatchers Run, Near Richmond, Virginia	Died of Remittent Fever, 5/30/1865
Deale, Theophilus N. Private	Unk	8/27/1862, Richmond, Virginia	Henrico County, Virginia	Co. A, 2nd Maryland Battalion Infantry	8/19/1864, Globe Tavern, Near Weldon Railroad, Virginia	Died of Chronic Diarrhea, 9/22/1864
Dean, Frank A. Private Not Listed On Monument	20	3/7/1863, Savannah, Georgia	Unknown	Co. E, Confederate States Marines, Guard on CSS Savannah	1/15/1865, Fort Fisher, North Carolina, Wounded, Concussion of Brain	Died of Chronic Diarrhea, 7/18/1865
Dean, James Private	Unk	Unknown	Unknown	Co. E, 56th, Virginia Infantry	4/6/1865, Amelia Court House, Virginia	Died of Acute Rheumatism, 4/25/1865
Deans, Dorsey H. Private	23	10/18/1863, Nash County, North Carolina, Conscript	Johnston County, North Carolina	Co. D, 47th North Carolina Infantry	10/14/1863, Bristoe Station, Virginia	Died of Pneumonia, 3/7/1865
Deas, William T. Private	Unk	7/15/1861, Sparta, Georgia	Hancock County, Georgia	Co. K, 15th Georgia Infantry	7/3/1863, Gettysburg, Pennsylvania	Died of Chronic Diarrhea, 4/8/1864

Name	Age	Enlisted	Residence	Unit	Captured	Date and Cause of Death
Deaver, Richard Private Not Listed On Monument	Unk	5/18/1861, Lenoir County, North Carolina, Conscript	Lenoir County, North Carolina	Co. D, 27th North Carolina Infantry	10/14/1863, Bristoe Station, Virginia	Died of Gangrene, 12/15/1864
Dedafield, Churchfield Sergeant	Unk	2/22/1863, Pine Bluff, Arkansas	Jefferson County, Arkansas	Co. A, 12th Battalion Arkansas Sharp Shooters	5/17/1863, Big Black Bridge, Near Vicksburg, Mississippi	Died of Pneumonia, 10/23/1863
Dees, Francis M. Sergeant	30	5/15/1862, Dalton, Georgia	Whitfield County, Georgia	Co. E, 12th Georgia Cavalry	6/24/1863, Middleton, Tennessee	Died of Variola (Smallpox), 1/15/1864
Dees, William Boggan Private	31	9/25/1863, Camp French, North Carolina, Conscript	Stanly County, North Carolina	Co. I, 52nd North Carolina Infantry	10/14/1863, Bristoe Station, Virginia	Died of Chronic Diarrhea, 1/19/1865
Deggerhart, J. V. Private	19	3/14/1862, Charlotte, North Carolina	Mecklenburg County, North Carolina	Co. H, 11th North Carolina Infantry	10/27/1864, Boyton Plank Road or Burgess' Mill, Virginia	Died of Acute Dysentery, 1/31/1865
Dellinger, Samuel W. Sergeant Not Listed On Monument	23	5/18/1861, Lincolnton, Lincoln County, North Carolina, Conscript	Lincoln County, North Carolina	Co. G, 57th North Carolina Infantry	7/5/1863, Gettysburg, Pennsylvania	Date and Cause of Death Unknown
DeLoach, James Private	36	6/2/1862, Coosahatchie, South Carolina	Beaufort District, South Carolina	Co. F, 11th South Carolina Infantry	1/15/1865, Fort Fisher, North Carolina	Died of Chronic Diarrhea, 7/8/1865
Delp, Granville Private	Unk	2/15/1863, Carroll County, Virginia	Unknown	Co. F, 29th, Virginia Infantry	5/8/1864, Near Petersburg, Virginia	Died of Measles, 3/11/1865
Dennard, J. Isaac Private	Unk	11/13/1861, Savannah, Georgia	Stewart County, Georgia	Co. E, 31st Georgia Infantry	7/4/1863, South Mountain, Maryland	Died of Chronic Diarrhea, 1/9/1864

Name	Age	Enlisted	Residence	Unit	Captured	Date and Cause of Death
Denning, Jesse F. Private	27	9/7/1861, Sampson County, North Carolina	Sampson County, North Carolina, Farmer	Co. H, 20th North Carolina Infantry	6/10/1864, Spotsylvania Court House, Virginia	Died of Unknown Causes, 7/17/1864
Dennison, John Private	25	9/16/1861, Knoxville, Tennessee	Knox County, Tennessee, Molder	Co. C, 37th Tennessee Infantry	6/28/1863, Fairfield, Tennessee	Date and Cause of Death Unknown
Dent, James Private	44	Unknown	Wert County, Virginia, Farmer	Co. A, 19th, Virginia Cavalry	5/19/1863, Roane County, Virginia	Died of Unknown Causes, 11/20/1863
Denton, C. C. Private	44	8/1/1863, Cleveland, Tennessee	Unknown	Co. H, 63rd Tennessee Infantry	6/17/1864, Petersburg, Virginia	Date and Cause of Death Unknown
Deramus, James M. Private	Unk	6/2/1862, Corinth, Mississippi	Unknown	Co. G, 6th Alabama Infantry	5/8/1864, Wilderness, Virginia	Died of Unknown Causes, 6/21/1864
Dewberry, J. R. See: Dubrey, John R.				Co. E, 40th Virginia Infantry		
Dewell, Hubbard Private Not Listed On Monument	Unk	5/10/1862, Petersburg, Virginia	Chesterfield County, Virginia	Co. E, 18th Battalion Virginia Heavy Artillery	4/6/1865, Archer's Farm, Virginia	Died of Chronic Diarrhea, 5/26/1865
Dewitt, William Private	26	3/17/1862, Whitlock, Virginia	Augusta County, Virginia	Co. C, 23rd Virginia Infantry	9/25/1864, Harrisonburg, Virginia	Died of Chronic Diarrhea, 12/2/1864
Dews, Edwin Sergeant	20	6/23/1861, Smithfield, Virginia	Isle of Wight County, Virginia	Co. I, 3rd Virginia Infantry	7/3/1863, Gettysburg, Pennsylvania	Died of Intermittent Fever, 9/7/1864

Name	Age	Enlisted	Residence	Unit	Captured	Date and Cause of Death
Dickens, Reuben R. Private	36	4/29/1862, Guilford County, North Carolina, Substitute For John McAdoo	Davidson, North Carolina, Miner	Co. F, 54th North Carolina Infantry	11/7/1863, Rappahannock, Virginia	Died of Unknown Causes, 8/26/1864
Dickens, Thomas Private	33	6/25/1861, Russell, Virginia	Russell County, Virginia	Co. K, 48th, Virginia Infantry	7/4/1863, South Mountain, Maryland	Died of Chronic Diarrhea, 2/15/1864
Dickerson, David C. Private	Unk	10/24/1864, Washington County, Virginia	Washington County, Virginia	Co. I, 48th, Virginia Infantry	4/6/1865, Farmville, Virginia	Died of Pneumonia, 5/26/1865
Dickson, John Private	Unk	7/14/1862, Camp Brown, Butler, Georgia	Taylor County, Georgia	Co. C, 59th, Georgia Infantry	7/4/1863, Cashtown, Pennsylvania	Died of Pneumonia, 11/8/1863
Digh, A. Crowel Private	20	3/29/1862, X-Roads, Cleveland County, North Carolina	Cleveland County, North Carolina, Farmer	Co. C, 55th North Carolina Infantry	7/1/1863, Gettysburg, Pennsylvania	Died of Chronic Diarrhea, 10/23/1863
Dillingham, Steed Private Not Listed On Monument	Unk	5/16/1861, Alisona, Tennessee	Unknown	Co. A, 17th Tennessee Infantry	6/17/1864, Petersburg, Virginia	Died of Unknown Causes, 7/15/1864
Dillion, Joseph T. Sergeant	Unk	7/3/1861, Lynchburg, Virginia	Franklin County, Virginia	Co. G, 42nd, Virginia Infantry	5/12/1864, Spotsylvania Court House, Virginia	Died of Unknown Causes, 9/9/1864
Dillion, Thad C. Private	Unk	2/18/1864, Henry County, Virginia, Conscript	Henry County, Virginia	Co. H, 42nd, Virginia Infantry	5/12/1864, Spotsylvania Court House, Virginia	Died of Unknown Causes, 6/4/1864
Dilon, Edwin L. Private	Unk	7/3/1861, Lynchburg, Virginia	Franklin County, Virginia	Co. G, 42nd, Virginia Infantry	5/12/1864, Spotsylvania Court House, Virginia	Died of Unknown Causes, 6/19/1864

Name	Age	Enlisted	Residence	Unit	Captured	Date and Cause of Death
Dingess, William M. Private	Unk	1/3/1864, Logan Court House, Virginia	Logan County, Virginia	Co. D, 36th, Virginia Infantry	9/24/1864, Winchester, Virginia	Died of Chronic Diarrhea, 3/31/1865
Dinsmore, John H. Corporal	35	9/26/1862, Henderson Mills, Green County, Tennessee	Unknown	Co. D, 61st Tennessee Mounted Infantry	5/17/1863, Big Black Bridge, Near Vicksburg, Mississippi	Died of Chronic Diarrhea, 12/20/1863
Dismukes, C. B. Private	21	2/11/1863, Pittsboro, Chatham, North Carolina, Volunteer	Chatham County, North Carolina	Co. E, 44th North Carolina Infantry	10/27/1864, Boyton Plank Road or Burgess' Mill, Virginia	Died of Unknown Causes, 12/11/1864
Dixon, Fleming B. Private	18	8/17/1861, Lightwood Knot Springs, South Carolina	Unknown	Co. G, 14th South Carolina Infantry	8/17/1864, Deep Bottom, Virginia	Died of Chronic Diarrhea, 1/27/1865
Dixon, Franklin Private Not Listed On Monument	39	Unknown	Unknown	22nd Battalion, Georgia Heavy Artillery	12/19/1864 Savannah, Georgia	Died of Acute Diarrhea, 2/14/1865
Dixon, J. M. Private	Unk	4/20/1864, Camp Holmes, Raleigh, North Carolina	Wake County, North Carolina	Co. E, 34th North Carolina Infantry	5/24/1864, Hanover Junction, Virginia	Died of Unknown Causes, 8/15/1864
Dobbs, Joseph H. Private	Unk	6/4/1861, Ashville, Alabama	St. Clair County, Alabama	Co. A, 10th Alabama Infantry	7/4/1863, Gettysburg, Pennsylvania, Wounded, Grape Shot Right Hip	Died of Unknown Causes, 11/15/1863
Dobson, J. C. Private	Unk	Unknown	Unknown	Co. D, 22nd South Carolina Infantry	Unknown	Unable to Locate
Doby, Joseph W. Private	Unk	8/6/1864, Camden, South Carolina	Kershaw District, South Carolina	Co. H, 7th South Carolina Cavalry	8/17/1864, White Oak Swamp, Virginia	Died of Erysipelas (inflammation of Skin and mucous membranes), 1/29/1865

Name	Age	Enlisted	Residence	Unit	Captured	Date and Cause of Death
Dodson, William D. Private Not Listed On Monument	39	3/12/1862, Laurel Grove, Virginia	Pittsylvania County, Virginia	Co. C, 38th Virginia Infantry	8/25/1864, Bermuda Hundred, Virginia	Died of Chronic Diarrhea, 2/20/1865
Dolinger, William Private	30	6/7/1864, Pulaski, Virginia	Pulaski County, Virginia	Co. E, 23rd, Virginia Infantry	10/19/1864, Cedar Creek or Strasburg, Virginia	Died of Chronic Diarrhea, 4/2/1865
Donaldson, James P. Sergeant	23	6/22/1861, Selma, Arkansas	Lynchburg, Arkansas	Co. D, 3rd, Arkansas Infantry	10/7/1864, Darbytown Road, Richmond, Virginia	Died of Scrofula (Tuberculosis of the Lymph Glands), 4/21/1865
Done, John Private	20	3/1/1862, Raleigh, North Carolina	Wake County, North Carolina, Laborer	Co. C, 47th North Carolina Infantry	7/3/1863, Gettysburg, Pennsylvania, Gunshot Wound of Lungs	Died of Wounds, 10/22/1863
Donnaha, John M. Private	21	6/27/1861, Camp Anderson, North Carolina, Volunteer	Iredell County, North Carolina	Co. A, 4th North Carolina Infantry	7/2/1863, Gettysburg, Pennsylvania	Died of Chronic Diarrhea, 4/17/1864
Donohoe, Lewis J. Private	Unk	5/8/1861, Haymarket, Virginia	Prince William County, Virginia	Co. C, 8th, Virginia Infantry	7/4/1863, Gettysburg, Pennsylvania	Died of Chronic Diarrhea, 1/18/1865
Dooley, J. T. Private Not Listed On Monument	Unk	12/31/1861, Lexington District, South Carolina	Lexington District, South Carolina	Co. H, 20th, South Carolina Infantry	10/19/1864, Cedar Creek or Strasburg, Virginia	Died of Chronic Diarrhea, 3/21/1865
Dooley, Ro Burwell Sergeant	23	5/28/1861, Forest Depot, Virginia	Bedford County, Virginia, Farmer	Co. G, 2nd, Virginia Cavalry	7/3/1863, Gettysburg, Pennsylvania	Died of Unknown Causes, 1/6/1864
Doughtie, John A. Private	Unk	6/4/1861, Suffolk, Virginia	Isle of Wight County, Virginia	Co. I, 13th, Virginia Cavalry	7/12/1863, Hagerstown, Maryland	Died of Chronic Diarrhea, 12/31/1863

Name	Age	Enlisted	Residence	Unit	Captured	Date and Cause of Death
Doughtie, Thomas Private	18	9/15/1862, Raleigh, North Carolina	Hertford County, North Carolina	Co. G, 31st North Carolina Infantry	6/1/1864, Cold Harbor, Virginia	Died of Chronic Diarrhea, 10/20/1864
Douglass, Daniel H. Private	37	9/15/1861, Alleghany County, North Carolina	Ashe County, North Carolina, Farmer	Co. K, 37th North Carolina Infantry	6/22/1864, Near Petersburg, Virginia	Died of Unknown Causes, 8/24/1864
Douglass, David Daniel Private	Unk	5/8/1862, Savannah, Georgia	Unknown	Co. C, 38th Georgia Infantry	7/2/1863, Gettysburg, Pennsylvania, Wounded Severely in Right Leg	Died of Unknown Causes, 3/10/1864
Douglass, N. J. Private Not Listed On Monument	Unk	3/15/1862 Charlottesville Virginia	Albemarle County, Virginia	Captain Carrington's Co. Charlottesville, Virginia Light Artillery	10/19/1864, Cedar Creek or Strasburg, Virginia	Died of Scorbutis (Scurvy), 5/1/1865
Douglass, William T. Private	Unk	6/1/1861, Bond's Store, Virginia	Unknown	Carter's Company Virginia Light Artillery	10/19/1864, Near Cedar Creek or Strasburg, Virginia	Died of Unknown Causes, 5/2/1865
Dove, Booker Private	Unk	9/24/1864, Place Unknown	Unknown	Co. I, 53rd, Virginia Infantry	4/1/1865, Five Forks, Virginia	Died of Phthisis (Wasting Away of the Body) 5/3/1865
Dowdy, Jesse Private	Unk	7/20/1861, Springfield, Virginia	Fairfax County, Virginia	Co. D, 57th, Virginia Infantry	4/3/1865, Petersburg, Virginia	Died of Acute Diarrhea, 5/10/1865
Dowdy, John D. Private	Unk	7/1/1861, Cumberland Court House, Virginia	Cumberland County, Virginia	Co. D, 21st, Virginia Infantry	7/3/1863, Gettysburg, Pennsylvania	Died of Chronic Diarrhea and Scurvy, 1/13/1864
Dowland, John J. Private	Unk	2/25/1862, Alton, Missouri	Oregon County, Missouri	Co. I, 1st & 4th Consolidated Missouri Infantry	5/16/1863, Champion Hill, Tennessee	Died of Unknown Causes, 4/9/1864
Dowman, Robert P. Sergeant	Unk	3/9/1862, Sussex Court House, Virginia	Sussex County, Virginia	Co. D, 13th, Virginia Cavalry	7/3/1863, Gettysburg, Pennsylvania	Died of Variola (Smallpox), 4/14/1864

Name	Age	Enlisted	Residence	Unit	Captured	Date and Cause of Death
Downs, James A. Private	Unk	5/8/1861, Haymarket, Virginia	Prince William County, Virginia	Co. C, 4th, Virginia Cavalry	6/20/1863, Green Springs, Virginia	Died of Chronic Diarrhea and Scurvy, 12/11/1863
Drake, Nathaniel A. Private	Unk	7/15/1862, Hendersonville North Carolina	Henderson County, North Carolina	Co. D, 6th, North Carolina Cavalry	6/22/1864, Jackson's Mills, Near Kinston, North Carolina	Died of Unknown Causes, 9/16/1864
Draper, Alexander Private	22	6/12/1861, Weldon, North Carolina, Volunteer	Yates County, North Carolina, Saddler	Co. B, 5th, North Carolina Infantry	7/3/1863, Gettysburg, Pennsylvania	Died of Chronic Diarrhea, 12/12/1863
Driggers, Joel R. Private	26	7/6/1861, Hilton Head, South Carolina	Beaufort District, South Carolina	Co. C, 11th, South Carolina Infantry	2/20/1865, Near Town Creek, North Carolina	Died of Pneumonia, 5/8/1865
Driggers, Roberson Private	40	7/6/1861, Hilton Head, South Carolina	Beaufort District, South Carolina	Co. C, 11th, South Carolina Infantry	2/20/1865, Near Town Creek, North Carolina	Died of Chronic Diarrhea, 6/19/1865
Drinkard, John N. Private	43	10/12/1864, Camp Lee, Prince Edward County, Virginia	Prince Edward County, Virginia	Co. D, 18th, Virginia Infantry	4/6/1865, Prince Edward County, Virginia	Died of Chronic Diarrhea, 4/28/1865
Driscol, Richard A. Private	Unk	10/8/1862, Paris, Virginia	Fauquier County, Virginia	Co. A, 6th, Virginia Cavalry	5/12/1864, Yellow Tavern, Hanover County, Virginia	Died of Unknown Causes, 7/24/1864
Driver, Thomas M. Private	Unk	Unknown	Unknown	Co. E, 10th, Georgia Infantry	Unknown	Unable to Locate
Druit, John W. Private	Unk	Unknown	Unknown	Co. C, 22nd North Carolina Infantry	4/6/1865, Burkesville, Virginia	Died of Unknown Causes, 6/5/1865
Dry, Thomas N. Private	18	8/8/1862, Raleigh, North Carolina, Conscript	Cabarrus County, North Carolina,	Co. B, 5th, North Carolina Infantry	7/2/1863, Gettysburg, Pennsylvania	Died of Variola (Smallpox), 1/20/1864
Dubrey, John R. Private	Unk	5/1/1862, Heathsville, Virginia	Richmond, Virginia	Co. E, 40th Virginia Infantry	7/14/1863, Falling Waters, Maryland	Died of Unknown Causes, 1/31/1864

Name	Age	Enlisted	Residence	Unit	Captured	Date and Cause of Death
Dudley, James B. Private	Unk	3/7/1863, Hamilton Crossing, Virginia	Milton County, Georgia	Co. B, 38th, Georgia Infantry	5/20/1864, Spotsylvania Court House, Virginia	Died of Acute Dysentery, 9/1/1864
Dudley, Joseph E. Private	Unk	2/15/1862, Atlanta, Georgia	Fulton County, Georgia	Co. A, 1st Battalion Confederate Infantry	4/2/1865, Hatcher's Run, Virginia	Died of Pneumonia, 4/17/1865
Dudley, Willis W. Private	Unk	1/26/1862, Plinkhorn Point, Virginia	Unknown	Co. B, 61st, Virginia Infantry	4/6/1865, Amelia Court House, Virginia	Died of Chronic Diarrhea, 6/4/1865
Duell, Herbert W. Private	Unk	Unknown	Unknown	Co. C, 18th, Georgia Infantry	Unknown	Unable to Locate
Duff, W. W. Corporal	Unk	Unknown	Unknown	Co. H, 5th, Virginia Infantry	Unknown	Unable to Locate
Duffey, James L. Sergeant	27	5/13/1862, Tallapoosa County, Alabama	Tallapoosa County, Alabama	Co. F, 47th, Alabama Infantry	5/6/1864, Spotsylvania Court House, Virginia	Died of Unknown Causes, 8/8/1864
Duke, Daniel Private	21	3/6/1862, Portsmouth, Virginia	Norfolk County, Virginia	Co. H, 61st, Virginia Infantry	7/3/1863, Gettysburg, Pennsylvania	Died of Chronic Diarrhea and Scurvy, 11/22/1863
Duke, Nash Private	47	3/4/1862, Orange County, North Carolina, Volunteer	Orange County, North Carolina	Co. B, 6th, North Carolina Infantry	11/7/1863, Kelly's Ford, Rappahannock Station, Virginia	Died of Variola (Smallpox), 6/24/1864
Duke, Ranson H. Private	42	9/10/1863, Franklin County, North Carolina, Conscript	Franklin County, North Carolina,	Co. B, 4th, North Carolina Infantry	5/12/1864, Spotsylvania Court House, Virginia	Died of Unknown Causes, 8/8/1864
Duke, William J. Sergeant Not Listed On Monument	Unk	2.20/1862, Gates County, North Carolina, Volunteer	Gates County, North Carolina	Co. B, 33rd, North Carolina Infantry	7/5/1863, Gettysburg, Pennsylvania	Died of Unknown Causes, 7/13/1864

Name	Age	Enlisted	Residence	Unit	Captured	Date and Cause of Death
Dula, William L.\n\nPrivate	Unk	4/24/1862, Wilkes County, North Carolina	Mecklenburg County, North Carolina	Co. K, 42nd, North Carolina Infantry	3/10/1865, Wise Forks, Near Kinston, North Carolina	Died of Typhoid Fever, 6/5/1865
Duley, James L.\n\nPrivate	Unk	Unknown	Unknown	Co. H, 20th, Georgia Infantry	Unknown	Unable to Locate
Dunbar, John D.\n\nPrivate	Unk	2/10/1863, Elon, Arkansas	Unknown	Co. K, 9th, Arkansas Infantry	5/16/1863, Champion Hill, Tennessee	Died of Chronic Diarrhea, 10/27/1863
Duncan, George W.\n\nPrivate	24	1/21/1863, Raleigh, North Carolina, Conscript	Halifax County, North Carolina	Co. D, 43nd, North Carolina Infantry	11/7/1863, Rapidan River, Virginia	Died of Unknown Causes, 7/31/1864
Duncan, James C.\n\nPrivate	Unk	4/15/1862, Halifax County, North Carolina	Halifax County, North Carolina	Co. B, 34th, Virginia Infantry	4/2/1865, Sutherland Station, Virginia	Died of Chronic Diarrhea, 5/25/1865
Duncan, Richard\n\nPrivate	Unk	4/3/1862, Suffolk, Virginia	Isle of Wight County, Virginia	Co. E, 14th, Virginia Infantry	7/5/1863, Gettysburg, Pennsylvania	Died of Unknown Causes, 12/24/1863
Duncan, Thomas\n\nPrivate	Unk	4/3/1862, Suffolk, Virginia	Halifax County, Virginia	Co. E, 14th, Virginia Infantry	7/5/1863, Gettysburg, Pennsylvania	Died of Variola (Smallpox), 12/5/1863
Dunigan, Edward J.\n\n3rd Engineer	Unk	Unknown	Unknown	Confederate States Navy	Unknown	Died of Unknown Causes 4/15/1865
Dunn, Bernard\n\nPrivate	23	4/28/1861, New Orleans, Louisiana	Born In Ireland, Clerk	Co. D, 1st Louisiana Infantry	7/1/1863, Gettysburg, Pennsylvania, Wounded Thighs, Fractured Femur Right Thigh	Died of Wounds, 4/13/1864
Dunn, James V.\n\nPrivate	Unk	3/3/1862, Fort Lowry, Virginia	Unknown	Co. G, 55th, Virginia Infantry	5/6/1864, Wilderness, Virginia	Died od Unknown Causes, 10/22/1864

Name	Age	Enlisted	Residence	Unit	Captured	Date and Cause of Death
Dunn, John B. Private	38	3/27/1862, Rutherford County, North Carolina	Anson County, North Carolina	Co. K, 50th, North Carolina Infantry	10/24/1864, Near Petersburg, Virginia	Died of Congestion of Brain, 3/30/1865
Dunn, William Private	30	3/20/1862, Salisbury, North Carolina	Rowan County, North Carolina, Farmer	Co. B, 46th, North Carolina Infantry	10/14/1863, Bristoe Station, Virginia	Died of Unknown Causes, 1/16/1865
Dunn, William A. Private	Unk	7/4/1861, Charleston, West Virginia	Kanawha County, West Virginia	Co. F, 22nd, Virginia Infantry	9/19/1864, Winchester, Virginia	Died of Pneumonia, 1/23/1865
Dunnegan, Lorenzo Private	Unk	5/16/1862, Hillsboro, Orange County, North Carolina	Orange County, North Carolina	Co. G, 27th, North Carolina Infantry	10/14/1863, Bristoe Station, Virginia	Died of Unknown Causes, 11/5/1863
Dunston, Fielding T. Private	Unk	7/25/1861, Camp Hodges, Jamestown Island, Virginia	Unknown	Co. D, 14th, Virginia Infantry	7/5/1863, Gettysburg, Pennsylvania	Died of Unknown Causes, 8/11/1864
Durham, Atlas P. Private	27	3/4/1862, Blakely, Georgia	Early County, Georgia	Co. A, 51st, Georgia Infantry	7/3/1863, Gettysburg, Pennsylvania	Died of Chronic Diarrhea, 10/24/1863
Durham, Daniel P. Sergeant	28	3/4/1862, Blakely, Georgia	Early County, Georgia	Co. A, 51st, Georgia Infantry	7/3/1863, Gettysburg, Pennsylvania	Died of Variola (Smallpox), 12/5/1863
Durham, Elisha Private	38	10/19/1864, Camp Holmes, Raleigh, North Carolina, Conscript	Orange County, North Carolina, Blacksmith	Co. G, 27th, North Carolina Infantry	4/7/1865, Petersburg, Virginia	Died of Unknown Causes, 6/5/1865
Durham, Eugene E. Private	Unk	10/27/1864, Petersburg, Virginia	Chesterfield County, Virginia	Captain Donald's Co., Virginia Light Artillery	4/2/1865, Petersburg, Virginia	Died of Erysipelas (Disease of the Mucus Membranes), 5/11/1865
Durham, George W. Private	18	3/4/1862, Douglass, Georgia	Coffee County, Georgia	Co. C, 50th, Georgia Infantry	10/19/1864, Cedar Creek or Strasburg, Virginia	Died of Acute Rheumatism, 2/2/1865

Name	Age	Enlisted	Residence	Unit	Captured	Date and Cause of Death
Durham, William P. Private	Unk	2/17/1862, Acworth, Georgia	Cobb County, Georgia	Co. A, 18th, Georgia Infantry	10/19/1864, Cedar Creek or Strasburg, Virginia	Died of Scurvy, 5/12/1865
Durham, William H. Private	Unk	3/4/1862, Blakely, Georgia	Early County, Georgia	Co. A, 51th, Georgia Infantry	7/3/1863, Gettysburg, Pennsylvania	Died of Acute Dysentery, 10/28/1863
Durr, John Private	Unk	2/15/1864, James Island, South Carolina	Charleston District, South Carolina	Co. G, 11th, South Carolina Infantry	6/15/1864, Near Petersburg, Virginia	Died of Unknown Causes, 8/1/1864
Durrough, Zachary G. Private	Unk	3/24/1863, Columbus, Georgia	Muscogee County, Georgia	Co. I, 64th, Georgia Infantry	4/6/1865, Burkesville, Virginia	Died of Chronic Diarrhea, 5/30/1865
Dutton, Elijah F. Private	28	5/7/1861, Gloucester Court House, Virginia	Gloucester County, Virginia Farmer	Co. A, 5th, Virginia Infantry	2/28/1864, Gloucester County, Virginia	Died of Scurvy, 4/9/1865
Duvall, Perry J. Private	22	3/10/1862, Canton, Mississippi	Canton, Mississippi, Farmer	Co. C, 18th Mississippi Infantry	7/3/1863, Gettysburg, Pennsylvania	Died of Unknown Causes, 4/13/1864
Dynum, William Lafayette Private Not Listed On Monument	18	3/25/1862, Lincoln County, North Carolina	Lincoln County, North Carolina, Farmer	Co. H, 52nd, North Carolina Infantry	7/3/1863, Gettysburg, Pennsylvania	Died of Unknown Causes, 1/11/1864
Dyson, A. S. Private	Unk	5/20/1862, Darlington, South Carolina	Darlington District, South Carolina	Co. G, 21st, South Carolina Infantry	7/10/1863, Morris Island, South Carolina	Died of Typhoid Fever, 12/23/1863

Name	Age	Enlisted	Residence	Unit	Captured	Date and Cause of Death
Eagin, Bertrand Private	Unk	3/8/1862, Athens, Alabama	Limestone County, Alabama	Co. F, 9th Alabama Infantry	7/1/1863, Gettysburg, Pennsylvania	Died of Chronic Diarrhea and Scurvy, 12/28/1863

Name	Age	Enlisted	Residence	Unit	Captured	Date and Cause of Death
Eaker, John Jr. Private	20	10/10/1861, Cleveland County, North Carolina, Volunteer	Gaston County, North Carolina, Farmer	Co. F, 34th, North Carolina Infantry	7/5/1863, Gettysburg, Pennsylvania	Died of Unknown Causes, 12/1/1863
Early, John W. Private	Unk	8/31/1861, Mason's Hill, Virginia	Unknown	Co. C, 24th, Virginia Infantry	7/3/1863, Gettysburg, Pennsylvania	Died of Chronic Dysentery, 2/4/1864
Earnhardt, William C. Private	35	4/1/1863, Charlotte, North Carolina	Mecklenburg County, North Carolina	Co. E, 11th, North Carolina Infantry	7/3/1863, Gettysburg, Pennsylvania	Died of Chronic Diarrhea, 10/23/1863
Earnhart, S. O. See: Earnheardt, S. O.				Co. A, 11th, North Carolina Infantry		
Earnhart, William P 2nd Lieutenant	20	7/7/1862, Salisbury, North Carolina, Volunteer	Rowan County, North Carolina	Co. A, 57th, North Carolina Infantry	11/7/1863, Rappahannock, Virginia	Died of Chronic Diarrhea, 6/9/1864
Earnheardt, S. O. Private.	40	4/1/1863, Charlotte, North Carolina	Mecklenburg County, North Carolina	Co. A, 11th, North Carolina Infantry	7/14/1863, Falling Waters, Maryland	Died of Chronic Diarrhea, 4/25/1864
Earp, Andrew W. Private	34	3/8/1862, Wilkes County, North Carolina, Volunteer	Wilkes County, North Carolina	Co. B, 55th, North Carolina Infantry	7/14/1863, Falling Waters, Maryland	Died of Chronic Diarrhea and Scurvy, 11/25/1863
East, George W. Private	Unk	3/21/1862, Suffolk, Virginia	Isle of Wight County, Virginia	Co. I, 53rd, Virginia Infantry	7/3/1863, Gettysburg, Pennsylvania	Died of Typhoid Fever, 2/6/1864
East, John H. Corporal	Unk	10/28/1861, Halifax Court House, Virginia	Halifax Court House, Virginia	Co. K, 3rd, Virginia Infantry	4/2/1865, Petersburg, Virginia	Died of Chronic Dysentery, 4/12/1865

Name	Age	Enlisted	Residence	Unit	Captured	Date and Cause of Death
East, Nathaniel W. Private Not Listed On Monument	Unk	7/1/1861, Pittsylvania, Virginia	Pittsylvania County, Virginia	Co. H, 21st, Virginia Infantry	5/12/1864 Spotsylvania Court House, Virginia	Died of Unknown Causes, 7/28/1864
East, William Y. Private	Unk	Unknown	Unknown	Co. K, 56th, Virginia Infantry	4/6/1865, Farmville, Virginia	Died of Pneumonia, 5/31/1865
Eastep, William Corporal	19	5/3/1862, Alleghany County, North Carolina, Volunteer	Alleghany County, North Carolina	Co. I, 61st, North Carolina Infantry	3/10/1865, Wise Forks, Near Kinston, North Carolina	Died of Acute Dysentery, 5/15/1865
Easter, Daniel Private	Unk	11/1/1864, Camp Lee, Prince Edward County, Virginia	Prince Edward County, Virginia	Co. C, 29th, Virginia Infantry	4/6/1865, Farmville, Virginia	Died of Pneumonia, 4/28/1865
Easterland, Lemuel Private	Unk	9/21/1861, Camp McDonald, Georgia	Unknown	Co. C, 22nd, Georgia Infantry	7/3/1863, Gettysburg, Pennsylvania	Died of Chronic Diarrhea, 12/25/1863
Easterling, Edward L. Sergeant	20	7/3/1861, Atlanta, Georgia	Wallen, Catoosa County, Georgia	Co. G, 11th, Georgia Infantry	7/14/1863, Falling Waters, Maryland	Died of Unknown Causes, 1/28/1864
Eaton, J. C. Private	Unk	7/15/1862, Mocksville, North Carolina	Davie County, North Carolina	Co. H, 5th, North Carolina Infantry	7/12/1863, Hagerstown, Maryland	Died of Typhoid Fever, 10/31/1863
Echols, John Private	Unk	6/2/1863, Morris Island, South Carolina	Charleston District, South Carolina	Co. I, 1st, South Carolina Artillery	7/10/1863, Morris Island, South Carolina	Died of Chronic Diarrhea, 11/6/1863
Eddins, John P. Sergeant	Unk	2/15/1862, Prairie County, Arkansas	Prairie County, Arkansas	Co. G, 21st, Arkansas Infantry	5/17/1863, Champion Hill, Tennessee	Died of Chronic Diarrhea, 11/7/1863

Name	Age	Enlisted	Residence	Unit	Captured	Date and Cause of Death
Eddleton, James Private	Unk	8/10/1861, Hanover County, Virginia	Hanover County, Virginia	Carter's Battalion Virginia Light Artillery	7/5/1863, Taken Prisoner On March From Gettysburg to Hagerstown, Maryland	Died of Chronic Diarrhea, 3/20/1864
Edens, J. H. Private	Unk	8/18/1863, Snead's Ferry, North Carolina	Onslow County, North Carolina	Co. D, 7th Confederate Cavalry	6/21/1864, Snead's Ferry, North Carolina	Died of Chronic Diarrhea, 1/8/1865
Edington, John M. Private	40	2/15/1863, Okolona, Mississippi	Pontotoc, Mississippi, Farmer	Co. G, 2nd Mississippi Infantry	7/5/1863, Gettysburg, Pennsylvania	Died of Unknown Causes, 9/28/1863
Edmonds, James A. Private Not Listed On Monument	Unk	10/14/1864, Danville, Virginia	Pittsylvania County, Virginia	Co. D, 38th, Virginia Infantry	4/1/1865, Five Forks, Virginia	Died of Chronic Diarrhea, 7/15/1865
Edmondson, John Private	Unk	9/3/1861, Brunswick, Georgia	Brooks County, Georgia	Co. C, 26th, Georgia Infantry	10/23/1864, Cedar Creek or Strasburg, Virginia	Died of Chronic Diarrhea, 4/28/1865
Edwards, Edwin C. Private	Unk	5/25/1861, Hague, Virginia	Unknown	Co. K, 40th, Virginia Infantry	7/14/1863, Falling Waters, Maryland	Died of Unknown Causes, 10/12/1863
Edwards, Henry J. Private	20	5/6/1862, North Hampton County, North Carolina	North Hampton County, North Carolina, Farmer	Co. E, 56th, North Carolina Infantry	5/22/1863, Gum Swamp, North Carolina	Died of Pneumonia, 2/9/1865
Edwards, Henry T. Private	18	8/20/1863, Fort Caswell, North Carolina	Edgecombe County, North Carolina	Co. F, 36th North Carolina Heavy Artillery	1/15/1865, Fort Fisher, North Carolina	Died of Pneumonia, 2/7/1865
Edwards, James J. Private Not Listed On Monument	21	2/25/1862, Isle of Wright Court House, Virginia	Isle of Wright County, Virginia	Co. K, 40th, Virginia Infantry	7/3/1863, Gettysburg, Pennsylvania	Died of Chronic Diarrhea & Scurvy, 2/19/1865

Name	Age	Enlisted	Residence	Unit	Captured	Date and Cause of Death
Edwards, James M. Private	24	4/26/1864, Raleigh, North Carolina	Mecklenburg County, North Carolina	Co. H, 11th, North Carolina Infantry	10/27/1864, Boyton Plank Road or Burgess' Mill, Virginia	Died of Chronic Diarrhea and Scurvy, 4/15/1865
Edwards, John D. Private	18	3/6/1862, Chatham County, North Carolina, Substitute	Chatham County, North Carolina	Co. G, 26th, North Carolina Infantry	10/27/1864, Burgess' Mill, Virginia	Died of Erysipelas of the Face, (Bacterial Infection of the Skin), 3/18/1865
Edwards, John W. Private	25	4/10/1862, Wilson County, North Carolina	Wilson County, North Carolina, Farmer	Co. F, 61st, North Carolina Infantry	9/30/1864, Fort Harrison, Virginia	Died of Pneumonia, 5/30/1865
Edwards, Lewis Private	36	8/10/1863, Orange County Court House, Virginia, Conscript	Lincoln County, North Carolina	Co. G, 52nd, North Carolina Infantry	10/14/1863, Bristoe Station, Virginia	Died of Variola (Smallpox), 1/9/1864
Edwards, Marshall Private	Unk	9/15/1864, Camp Holmes, Raleigh, North Carolina	Mecklenburg County, North Carolina	Co. E, 11th, North Carolina Infantry	10/27/1864, Boyton Plank Road or Burgess' Mill, Virginia	Died of Acute Dysentery, 12/18/1864
Edwards, Murphy Private	21	6/10/1861, Matthews, North Carolina, Volunteer	Mecklenburg County, North Carolina	Co. G, 26th, North Carolina Infantry	7/14/1863, Falling Waters, Maryland	Died of Chronic Diarrhea, 12/20/1864
Edwards, Richard Sergeant	Unk	3/13/1862, Martin's X-Roads, North Carolina	Northampton County, North Carolina, Farmer	Co. D, 54th, North Carolina Infantry	11/7/1863, Rappahannock, Virginia	Died of Unknown Causes, 8/29/1864
Edwards, Samuel Private	Unk	8/1/1864, Bedford, Virginia	Bedford County, Virginia	Co. E, 28th, Virginia Infantry	4/6/1865, Harper's Farm, Virginia	Died of Typhoid Fever, 6/4/1865
Edwards, Thomas J. Private	Unk	11/16/1863, Camp Randolph, Georgia	Unknown	Co. G, 64th, Georgia Infantry	8/17/1864, Deep Bottom, Virginia	Died of Chronic Diarrhea, 10/22/1864
Edwards, William S. Private	19	7/25/1862, Pitt County, North Carolina, Conscript	Pitt County, North Carolina	Co. E, 55th, North Carolina Infantry	7/1/1863, Gettysburg, Pennsylvania	Died of Chronic Diarrhea, 12/1/1864

Name	Age	Enlisted	Residence	Unit	Captured	Date and Cause of Death
Eidson, Barnabas L. Private Not Listed On Monument	18	1/31/1863, Statesville, North Carolina, Conscript	Iredell County, North Carolina	Co. C, 48th, North Carolina Infantry	3/25/1864, Near Petersburg, Virginia	Died of Chronic Diarrhea, 7/15/1865
Eldridge, James Private	Unk	6/22/1864, Bristol, Tennessee	Sullivan County, Tennessee	Co. I, 14th Tennessee Infantry	5/4/1864, Wilderness, Virginia	Died of Chronic Diarrhea, 11/4/1864
Eldridge, Jefferson J. Private	30	3/4/1862, Fort Gaines, Georgia	Clay County, Georgia	Co. I, 51st, Georgia Infantry	7/3/1863, Gettysburg, Pennsylvania	Died of Variola (Smallpox), 10/?/1863
Elkins, John F. J. Private Not Listed On Monument	Unk	4/19/1864, Talladega, Alabama	Talladega County, Alabama	Co. I, 14th Tennessee Infantry	5/12/1864 Spotsylvania Court House, Virginia	Died of Unknown Causes, 7/3/1864
Ellickson, Robert V. Private	22	3/1/1862, Oak Hill, North Carolina, Volunteer	Granville County, North Carolina, Farmer	Co. E, 55th, North Carolina Infantry	7/5/1863, Gettysburg, Pennsylvania	Died of Acute Diarrhea, 9/17/1864
Ellington, Charles Private	Unk	Unknown	Rockingham County, North Carolina	Co. H, 13th, North Carolina Infantry	4/2/1865, Dinwiddie Court House, Virginia	Died of Erysipelas (Bacterial Infection of the Skin), 6/25/1865
Elliott, B. D. Private	Unk	Unknown	Unknown	Co. C, 22nd Battalion Georgia Heavy Artillery	3/16/1865, Goldsboro, North Carolina	Died of Pneumonia, 5/4/1865
Elliott, Charles Whitson Private	25	5/3/1862, Troy, North Carolina, Volunteer	Montgomery County, North Carolina	Co. F, 44th, North Carolina Infantry	4/2/1865, Near Petersburg, Virginia	Died of Pneumonia, 6/8/1865
Elliott, John Private Not Listed On Monument	18	4/29/1864, Tarboro, North Carolina	Edgecombe County, North Carolina	Co. L, 17th, North Carolina Infantry	10/27/1864, Near Darbytown Road, Near Petersburg, Virginia	Died of Chronic Diarrhea, 2/22/1865

Name	Age	Enlisted	Residence	Unit	Captured	Date and Cause of Death
Ellis, Henry H. Private	26	6/29/1862, Darlington, South Carolina	Darlington District, South Carolina	Co. E, 6th, South Carolina Infantry	4/6/1865, Richmond, Virginia	Died of Typhoid Fever, 5/23/1865
Ellis, James M. Private	34	9/3/1862, Mocksville, North Carolina	Davie County, North Carolina	Co. M, 7th Confederate Cavalry	4/14/1864, Morris Mills, Virginia	Died of Unknown Causes, 8/17/1864
Ellis, James N. Sergeant	23	5/28/1862, Cartersville, Chatham County, North Carolina, Volunteer	Chatham County, North Carolina	Co. E, 26th, North Carolina Infantry	7/5/1863, Gettysburg, Pennsylvania, Wounded	Died of Unknown Causes, 1/23/1864
Ellis, John Sergeant	Unk	5/8/1864, Savannah, Georgia	Stewart County, Georgia	Co. D, 1st Battalion Georgia Reserves	12/18/1864, Fort McAllister, Georgia	Died of Chronic Diarrhea, 5/15/1865
Ellison, J. B. See: Allison, Beatie J.				Co. E, 23rd, Virginia Infantry		
Elmore, Ellis Private	25	1/14/1862, Darlington, South Carolina	Darlington District, South Carolina	Co. H, 21th, South Carolina Infantry	5/9/1864, Near Petersburg, Virginia	Died of Chronic Diarrhea, 5/14/1865
Elmore, Richard M. Private	Unk	1/21/1863, Diascund Bridge, Virginia	Brunswick County, Virginia	Co. E, 59th Virginia Infantry	5/8/1864, Nottaway Bridge, Virginia	Died of Unknown Causes, 9/6/1864
Embrey, James T. Private	Unk	4/12/1862, Louisa Court House, Virginia	Louisa County, Virginia	Co. I, 11th Virginia Infantry	7/3/1863, Gettysburg, Pennsylvania, Wounded Right Thigh	Died of Complications From Wounds, 4/14/1864
Emerson, R. D. Private	Unk	4/17/1864, Camp Lee, Prince Edward County, Virginia, Conscript	Prince Edward County, Virginia	Co. C, 5th Virginia Cavalry	9/24/1864, Luray, Virginia	Died of Unknown Causes, 5/23/1865
English, John Private	22	10/17/1861, Marlboro District, South Carolina	Marlboro District, South Carolina	Co. G, 23rd, South Carolina Infantry	3/6/1865, Bennettsville, South Carolina	Died of Unknown Causes, 5/18/1865

Name	Age	Enlisted	Residence	Unit	Captured	Date and Cause of Death
English, William Private	Unk	8/31/1861, Camp McDonald, Warren County, Georgia	Warren County, Georgia	Co. H, 22nd Georgia Infantry	7/2/1863, Gettysburg, Pennsylvania	Date and Cause of Death Unknown
Enloe, Thomas A. Private	19	5/15/1864, Baldwin, Florida	Duval County, Florida	Co. G, 18th, South Carolina Infantry	5/20/1864, Near Drury's Bluff, Virginia, Gunshot Wound of Abdomen	Died of Wounds, 6/5/1864
Ennis, J. Private	Unk	5/3/1862, Dumfries, Virginia	Jonesboro, Washington County, North Carolina	Co. E, 60th Mounted Tennessee Infantry	5/17/1863, Big Black Bridge, Near Vicksburg, Mississippi	Died of Variola (Smallpox), 3/17/1864
Epling, Henry Private	Unk	Unknown	Unknown	Co. H, 32nd, Virginia Infantry	6/6/1864, Cold Harbor, Virginia	Died of Intermittent Fever, 9/21/1864
Epperson, James E. Private	Unk	2/9/1863, Sturgeonville, Brunswick County, Virginia	Brunswick County, Virginia	Co. E, 56th, Virginia Infantry	7/3/1863, Gettysburg, Pennsylvania	Died of Unknown Causes, 12/24/1863
Eppes, Edward Private	Unk	5/6/1861, Fort Powhatan, Virginia	Unknown	Co. C, 53rd, Virginia Infantry	4/1/1865, Five Forks, Virginia	Died of Enteritis (Inflammation of Intestines), 5/24/1865
Epting, J. M. Private	20	8/28/1861, Hopes Station, Lexington District, South Carolina	Lexington District, South Carolina	Co. H, 13th, South Carolina Infantry	7/14/1863, Falling Waters, Maryland	Died of Chronic Diarrhea, 1/7/1864
Erwin, George Private	Unk	4/13/1863, Brevard, North Carolina	Transylvania County, North Carolina	Co. B, 6th, North Carolina Cavalry	6/22/1864, Jackson's Mills, Near Kinston, North Carolina	Died of Unknown Causes, 10/21/1864
Erwin, William R. Private	Unk	12/1/1862, Charlotte, North Carolina	Mecklenburg County, North Carolina	Co. F, 5th, North Carolina Cavalry	10/14/1863, Catlett's Station, Virginia	Died of Unknown Causes, 8/21/1864
Estep, William Private Not Listed On Monument	19	5/3/1862, Alleghany County, North Carolina, Volunteer	Alleghany County, North Carolina	Co. I, 61st, North Carolina Infantry	3/10/1864, Near Kinston, North Carolina	Died of Acute Dysentery, 5/15/1864

Name	Age	Enlisted	Residence	Unit	Captured	Date and Cause of Death
Ester, D. H. See: Estill, Davis H.				Co. H, 22nd, Virginia Infantry		
Estes, Samuel Private	29	9/6/1862, Morristown, Tennessee	Jefferson, Tennessee	Co. H, 60th Mounted Tennessee Infantry	7/4/1863, Vicksburg, Mississippi	Date and Cause of Death Unknown
Estill, Davis H. Private.	17	5/20/1863, Lewisburg, Virginia	Charleston, West Virginia	Co. H, 22nd, Virginia Infantry	9/19/1864, Winchester, Virginia	Died of Chronic Diarrhea, 1/5/1865
Etherridge, Samuel A. Corporal	Unk	4/18/1862, Currituck Court House, North Carolina	Currituck County, North Carolina	Co. G, 4th, North Carolina Cavalry	8/6/1863, Mountain Run, Virginia	Died of Unknown Causes, 10/?/1863
Eubanks, William W. Private	Unk	9/6/1861, Eastville, Alabama	Chilton County, Alabama	Co. E, 13th, Alabama Infantry	7/14/1863, Falling Waters, Maryland	Died of Chronic Diarrhea, 11/13/1863
Evans, Absolam Private	Unk	6/26/1861, Portsmouth, Virginia	Greene County, Georgia	Co. C, 3rd, Georgia Infantry	7/2/1863, Gettysburg, Pennsylvania, Wounded	Died of Variola (Smallpox), 11/16/1863
Evans, G. K. Private	Unk	4/27/1863, Richmond, Georgia	Henrico County, Virginia	Co. K, 4th, Virginia Cavalry	7/4/1863, Gettysburg, Pennsylvania	Died of Unknown Causes, 9/21/1863
Evans, George Private	34	9/29/1862, North Carolina	Unknown	Co. I, 55th, North Carolina Infantry	7/14/1863, Falling Waters, Maryland	Died of Pneumonia, 11/29/1863
Evans, George W. Private Not Listed On Monument	Unk	5/30/1861, Kentuck, Virginia	Pittsylvania County, Virginia	Co. A, 38th, Virginia Infantry	7/3/1863, Gettysburg, Pennsylvania	Died of Unknown Causes, 11/19/1863

Name	Age	Enlisted	Residence	Unit	Captured	Date and Cause of Death
Evans, Henry Private	29	3/8/1862, Claiborne Parish, Louisiana	Claiborne Parish, Louisiana	Co. G, 12th Louisiana Infantry	12/17/1864, Franklin, Tennessee, Gunshot Fracture of Radius in Left Arm	Died of Erysipelas (Bacterial Infection of the Skin), 5/28/1865
Evans, John W. Private	Unk	5/18/1861, Boydton, Virginia	Mecklenburg County, Virginia	Co. A, 38th, Virginia Infantry	Unknown	Date and Cause of Death Unknown
Evans, Robert Private	29	7/15/1862, Guilford County, North Carolina Conscript	Guilford County, North Carolina	Co. A, 1st, North Carolina Cavalry	7/3/1863, Gettysburg, Pennsylvania	Died of Unknown Causes, 8/30/1864
Evans, W. W. Private	19	3/8/1862, Wilmington, North Carolina	Brunswick County, North Carolina	Co. A, 1st, North Carolina Cavalry	5/12/1864, Spotsylvania Court House, Virginia	Died of Unknown Causes, 10/?/1864
Ewell, F. G. Private	Unk	Unknown	Unknown	Co. F, 66th, North Carolina Infantry	8/14/1863, Elizabeth City, Virginia	Died of Variola (Smallpox), 12/10/1863
Ewell, Isaac. A. Private	Unk	2/21/1862, Norfolk County, Virginia	Norfolk County, Virginia	Co. F, 6th, Virginia Infantry	8/16/1864, Deep Bottom, Virginia	Died of Chronic Diarrhea, 9/14/1864

Name	Age	Enlisted	Residence	Unit	Captured	Date and Cause of Death
Fair, Henry Private	22	5/1/1862, Burke County, North Carolina, Volunteer	Burke County, North Carolina	Co. D, 11th, North Carolina Infantry	10/27/1864, Burgess' Mill, Near Petersburg, Virginia	Died of Chronic Diarrhea and Scurvy, 4/18/1865
Faircloth, Barnabas Private	21	6/10/1861, Clinton, North Carolina, Volunteer	Sampson County, North Carolina	Co. I, 20th, North Carolina Infantry	7/1/1863, Gettysburg, Pennsylvania	Died of Chronic Diarrhea, 4/15/1864
Faircloth, Philip Private	Unk	11/1/1863, Orange County Court House, Virginia	Wilkes County, North Carolina	Co. C, 26th, North Carolina Infantry	10/27/1864, Boyton Plank Road or Burgess' Mill, Virginia	Died of Chronic Dysentery, 1/1/1865

Name	Age	Enlisted	Residence	Unit	Captured	Date and Cause of Death
Falconer, Joseph S. Private	45	6/26/1861, Gualey Bridge, Virginia	Fayette, Virginia, Farmer	Co. C, 60th, Virginia Infantry	5/7/1863, Tazwell County, Virginia	Died of Unknown Causes, 11/4/1863
Falkner, George C. Private	21	6/11/1862, Henderson County, North Carolina, Volunteer	Granville County, North Carolina, Farmer	Co. G, 23rd, North Carolina Infantry	7/1/1863, Gettysburg, Pennsylvania	Died of Unknown Causes, 1/16/1864
Fallin, George W. Private Not Listed On Monument	29	3/4/1862 Crawfordville, Georgia	Taliaferro County, Georgia	Co. D, 49th, Georgia Infantry	3/25/1865, Hatcher's Run, Virginia	Died of Typhoid Fever, 7/9/1865
Falls, James Private	Unk	Unknown	Unknown	Co. C, 20th, Virginia Heavy Artillery	4/6/1865, Burkesville, Virginia	Died of Acute Diarrhea, 5/30/1865
Falvey, Michael Private Not Listed On Monument	Unk	7/?/1863, Martinsburg, Virginia, Substitute	Berkeley County, Virginia	Co. B, Phillips Legion Cavalry Battalion, Georgia	8/1/1863, Brandy Station, Virginia	Died of Chronic Diarrhea, 4/18/1864
Farall, Patrick Private	Unk	11/3/1862, Jackson, Mississippi	Madison County, Mississippi	Jeff Davis Mississippi Legion Cavalry	10/27/1863, Burkes Station, Virginia	Died of Unknown Causes, 3/19/1864
Farley, Andrew T. Private	Unk	8/10/1862, White Sulphur Springs, West Virginia	Greenbrier County, West Virginia	Co. I, 60th, Virginia Infantry	9/19/1864, Winchester, Virginia	Died of Chronic Diarrhea, 1/4/1865
Farley, George H. Private	Unk	10/9/1863, Chaffin's Bluff, Virginia	Unknown	Captain Allen's Company Virginia Heavy Artillery	4/6/1865, Harper Farm, Virginia	Died of Chronic Diarrhea, 5/17/1865
Farmer, Jasper P. Private	Unk	11/2/1863, Charleston, South Carolina	Charleston County, South Carolina	Co. B, 27th, South Carolina Infantry	2/20/1865, Town Creek, Fort Anderson, North Carolina	Died of Pneumonia, 5/2/1865

Name	Age	Enlisted	Residence	Unit	Captured	Date and Cause of Death
Farmer, Moses J. Private Not Listed On Monument	16	4/12/1864, Petersburg, Virginia	Chesterfield County, Virginia	Co. K, 14th Virginia Infantry, Deserted Regiment 4/13/1864	5/14/1864, Chesterfield County, Virginia	Died of Chronic Diarrhea, 4/3/1865
Farmer, Robert B. Private	41	8/2/1861, Bowling Green, Virginia	Caroline County, Virginia	Co. G, 47th, Virginia Infantry	10/1/1864, Petersburg, Virginia	Died of Acute Dysentery, 10/17/1864
Farmer, William D. Private	Unk	9/30/1862, Pike County, Alabama	Pike County, Alabama	Co. C, 6th, Alabama Infantry	5/19/1864, Spotsylvania Court House, Virginia	Died of Unknown Causes, 6/27/1864
Farnsworth, John Private	Unk	Date Unknown, Knoxville, Tennessee	Knox County, Tennessee	Co. I, 59th, Mounted Tennessee Cavalry	10/28/1864, Jefferson County, Tennessee	Died of Acute Diarrhea, 5/4/1865
Farr, Henry Private Name Not On Monument	22	5/1/1862 Burke County, North Carolina	Burke County, North Carolina	Co. D, 11th, North Carolina Infantry	10/27/1864 Burgess' Mill, Virginia	Died of Chronic Diarrhea, 4/18/1865
Farrar, J. O. Private	Unk	5/11/1861, New Orleans, Louisiana	Orleans Parish, Louisiana	Co. K, 2nd Louisiana Infantry	5/12/1864, Wilderness, Virginia	Died of Unknown Causes, 6/1/1864
Farris, John W. Private	18	4/26/1862, Lockapoka, Alabama	Lee County, Alabama	Co. D, 47th Alabama Infantry	4/5/1865, Goodes Bridge, Richmond, Virginia	Died of Acute Diarrhea, 4/27/1865
Faughader, Joseph H. Private.	18	4/18/1861, Jefferson County Court House, Virginia	Jefferson County, Virginia	Co. A, 2nd, Virginia Infantry	5/12/1864, Near Spotsylvania Court House, Virginia	Died of Unknown Causes, 6/14/1864
Faulk, Joseph E. Private	Unk	6/26/1861, Marion District Court House, South Carolina	Marion District, South Carolina	Co. L, 7th, South Carolina Infantry	5/22/1864, North Anna River, Virginia	Died of Unknown Causes, 8/13/1864
Faulkenberry, Joseph W. Private.	22	4/24/1861, Camden, South Carolina	Kershaw District, South Carolina	Co. G, 2nd, South Carolina Infantry	7/23/1863, Hedgesville or Martinsburg, Virginia	Died of Unknown Causes, 1/18/1865

Name	Age	Enlisted	Residence	Unit	Captured	Date and Cause of Death
Faulkner, James See: Falconer, Joseph S.				Co. C, 60th, Virginia Infantry		
Fauntleroy, James H. Private	18	12/18/1861, Green County, Missouri	Buchanon, Missouri, Farmer	Co. E, 1st Missouri Cavalry	5/17/ 1863, Big Black Bridge, Near Vicksburg, Mississippi	Date and Cause of Death Unknown
Fauntleroy, Robert B. Private	Unk	12/24/1863, Richmond, Virginia	Henrico County, Virginia	Co. A, 15th, Virginia Cavalry, Transferred from 9th Virginia Infantry	2/3/1864, New Bern, North Carolina	Died of Unknown Causes, 8/26/1864
Feagle, George Private	31	8/25/1861, Dutch Fork, Lexington District, South Carolina	Lexington District, South Carolina	Co. I, 15th, South Carolina Infantry	7/4/1863, Gettysburg, Pennsylvania	Died of Pneumonia, 7/27/1864
Fears, Andrew J. Sergeant	24	4/29/1861, Corinth, Poutotoe County, Mississippi	Tupelo, Mississippi, Farmer	Co. G, 2nd Mississippi Infantry	7/3/1863, Gettysburg, Pennsylvania, Gunshot Wound Right Leg, Fracture	Died of Wounds, 1/8/1864
Feazel, William E. Private	Unk	6/16/1864, Saltville, Virginia	Smyth County, Virginia	Co. D, 45th, Virginia Infantry	9/19/1864, Winchester, Virginia	Died of Acute Dysentery, 2/5/1865
Fendall, Thomas See: Phendal, Thomas				Co. E, 52nd, Virginia Infantry		
Fentress, William W. Private	Unk	3/10/1862, Lyn Beach, Virginia	Unknown	Co. G, 15th, Virginia Cavalry	9/14/1863, Near Culpepper, Virginia	Died of Unknown Causes, 7/31/1864
Ferguson, Hays Private	Unk	10/1/1862, Bunker Hill, Virginia, Conscript	Berkeley County, Virginia	Co. K, 2nd, Virginia Infantry	5/19/1864, Spotsylvania Court House, Virginia	Died of Unknown Causes, 8/13/1864
Ferguson, S. W. Private	Unk	Unknown	Unknown	Co. I, 17th Tennessee Infantry	9/19/1864, Chickamauga, Georgia	Died of Scurvy, 4/23/1865

Name	Age	Enlisted	Residence	Unit	Captured	Date and Cause of Death
Ferrell, R. A. Private	Unk	10/4/1862, Abbeville, Alabama	Henry County, Alabama	Co. A, 6th Alabama Infantry	10/19/1864, Cedar Creek or Strasburg, Virginia	Died of Pneumonia, 3/26/1865
Ferrell, William Private Name Not On Monument	Unk	12/7/1863, Orange County, Virginia	Orange County, Virginia	Co. C, 52nd, North Carolina Infantry	5/12/1864, Spotsylvania Court House, Virginia	Died of Debility, 9/9/1864
Ferrill, Edward Private	20	6/15/1861, Alamance County, North Carolina, Volunteer	Alamance County, North Carolina	Co. D, 6th, North Carolina Infantry	11/7/1863, Rappahannock Station, Virginia	Died of Unknown Causes, 9/8/1864
Fetner, D. A. Private	Unk	11/21/1861, Columbia, North Carolina	Richland County, South Carolina	Co. D, 7th, North Carolina Cavalry	2/21/1865, Near Waynesboro, North Carolina	Died of Pneumonia, 5/3/1865
Fiddler, James H. Private	Unk	10/11/1862, Winchester, Virginia	Frederick County, Virginia	Richardson's 13th Battalion Virginia Cavalry	6/25/1863, Cartersville, Maryland	Died of Unknown Causes, 3/9/1864
Fielder, John A. Private	Unk	Unknown	Unknown	Co. K, 51st, Virginia Infantry	9/19/1864, Winchester, Virginia	Died of Rubeola (Measles), 3/9/1865
Fielding, J. B. Private	Unk	11/2/1864, Anderson, South Carolina	Anderson County, South Carolina	Co. D, Hampton's South Carolina Legion Infantry	1/25/1865, Darbytown Road, Near Richmond, Virginia	Died of Chronic Diarrhea, 6/11/1865
Fields, John C. Private	20	5/17/1861, Jefferson County, North Carolina, Volunteer	Alleghany County, North Carolina	Co. A, 26th, North Carolina Infantry	7/14/1863, Falling Waters, Maryland	Died of Chronic Dysentery, 10/18/1863
Fields, William Private	47	5/14/1862, Johnston County, North Carolina	Johnston County, North Carolina, Farmer	Co. G, 55th, North Carolina Infantry	7/14/1863, Falling Waters, Maryland	Died of Pneumonia and Typhoid Fever, 1/10/1864

Name	Age	Enlisted	Residence	Unit	Captured	Date and Cause of Death
Figg, Daniel E. Private Name Not On Monument	Unk	5/6/1862, Fort Powhatan, Virginia	Unknown	Co. D, 53rd, Virginia Infantry	6/29/1864, Near Petersburg, Virginia	Died of Typhoid Fever, 7/13/1865
Finch, John P. Private	Unk	5/1/1864, Kinston, North Carolina	Lenoir County, North Carolina	Co. A, Holcombe's South Carolina Legion Infantry	4/1/1865, Five Forks, Virginia	Died of Typhoid Fever, 5/19/1865
Finch, Jordan Private	Unk	3/15/1862, Henderson County, North Carolina, Volunteer	Granville County, North Carolina	Co. G, 23rd, North Carolina Infantry	7/1/1863, Gettysburg, Pennsylvania	Died of Unknown Causes, 1/15/1864
Finley, Sidney J. Private	Unk	12/5/1861, Columbia, South Carolina	Richland County, South Carolina	Co. A, Lauren's 3rd Battalion, South Carolina Infantry	5/23/1864, Hanover Junction, Pennsylvania	Died of Acute Diarrhea, 2/8/1865
Fish, John Private	21	Unknown	Unknown	Co. D, 7th Tennessee Infantry	4/3/1865, After Surrender, Richmond, Virginia	Died of Typhoid Fever, 6/18/1865
Fisher, H. L. Private	Unk	7/13/1861, Hart County, Georgia	Hart County, Georgia	Co. H, 15th Georgia Infantry	7/3/1863, Gettysburg, Pennsylvania	Died of Unknown Causes, 1/27/1864
Fisher, J. A. Private	Unk	10/8/1863, Mississippi, Conscript	Unknown	Co. C, 3rd, North Carolina Infantry	5/15/1864, Spotsylvania Court House, Virginia	Died of Unknown Causes, 6/17/1864
Fisher, James W. Private	19	4/18/1861, Martinsburg, Virginia	Berkeley County, Virginia	Co. D, 2nd, Virginia Infantry	5/12/1864, Near Spotsylvania Court House, Virginia	Date and Cause of Death Unknown
Fisher, P. J. Private	26	5/8/1862, Camp Hill, Stanley County, North Carolina, Conscript	Stanley County, North Carolina	Co. F, 5th, North Carolina Infantry	7/3/1863, Gettysburg, Pennsylvania, Wounded	Died of Acute Dysentery, 1/6/1864
Fitzgerald, Perry Private	35	3/4/1862, Irwinville, Georgia	Irwin County, Georgia	Co. F, 49th Georgia Infantry	7/2/1863, Gettysburg, Pennsylvania	Died From Inflammation of Lungs (Pneumonia), 2/6/1865

Name	Age	Enlisted	Residence	Unit	Captured	Date and Cause of Death
Flagg, William C. Private Name Not On Monument	30	4/17/1861, Christensburg, Virginia	Montgomery County, Virginia, Farmer	Co. D, 2nd, Virginia Infantry	5/12/1864, Near Spotsylvania Court House, Virginia	Died of Unknown Causes, 7/7/1864
Flake, Hyman Private Name Not On Monument	23	9/15/1861, Pitt County, North Carolina, Conscript	Pitt County, North Carolina	Co. G, 8th, North Carolina Infantry	6/1/1864, Cold Harbor, Virginia	Died of Unknown Causes, 7/2/1864
Fleming, John R. Private Name Not On Monument	Unk	10/15/1861, Haley's Store, Georgia	Unknown	Co. F, 38th Georgia Infantry	5/15/1864, Spotsylvania Court House, Virginia	Died of Unknown Causes, 7/15/1864
Flemister, James M. Private	20	5/9/1862, Gordon, Georgia	Wilkinson County, Georgia	Co. B, 14th Georgia Infantry	5/12/1864, Spotsylvania Court House, Virginia	Died of Unknown Causes, 7/31/1864
Fletcher, J. C. Sergeant	Unk	9/22/1862, Waynesville, Georgia	Brantley County, Georgia	Co. G, 7th Georgia Cavalry	6/11/1864, Louisa Court House, Virginia	Died of Unknown Causes, 10/21/1864
Fletcher, William H. Private	23	5/8/1864, Brassfield, North Carolina, Volunteer	Wake County, North Carolina	Co. I, 47th, North Carolina Infantry	7/5/1863, Gettysburg, Pennsylvania	Died of Chronic Diarrhea, 2/24/1864
Flinn, Marvin Private	23	7/20/1861, Camp Pickens, Anderson District, South Carolina	Anderson District, South Carolina	Co. G, Orr's 1st South Carolina Rifles Infantry	7/14/1863, Falling Waters, Maryland	Died of Chronic Diarrhea and Erysipelas, Bacterial Infection of the Skin, 11/24/1863

Name	Age	Enlisted	Residence	Unit	Captured	Date and Cause of Death
Flippen, Jesse A. Private	42	11/14/1864, Conscript Camp, North Carolina, Conscript	Unknown	Co. D, 45th, North Carolina Infantry	4/2/1865, Petersburg, Virginia	Died of Chronic Diarrhea, 6/18/1865
Flippin, Samuel J. Private	24	5/29/1861, Wytheville, Virginia	Wythe County, Virginia	Co. E, 47th, Virginia Infantry	9/19/1864, Winchester, Virginia	Died of Chronic Diarrhea, 3/8/1865
Flower, James Private	Unk	3/27/1862, Lee's Mills, Virginia	Deasonville, Mississippi, Farmer	Co. F, 18th Mississippi Infantry	7/2/1863, Gettysburg, Pennsylvania, Wounded in Right Hip and Leg	Died of Complications From Wounds, 3/16/1864
Flowers, George F. Private	16	1/16/1862, Fort Campbell, North Carolina	Unknown	Co. G, 36th North Carolina Heavy Artillery	7/25/1864, Cape Fear River, North Carolina	Died of Epilepsy, 5/23/1865
Floyd, Charles F. Private	20	4/29/1861, Warrenton, North Carolina, Volunteer	Warren County, North Carolina, Farmer	Co. F, 12th, North Carolina Infantry	7/4/1863, Gettysburg, Pennsylvania	Died of Chronic Diarrhea, 10/18/1863
Floyd, Everett Private	Unk	6/4/1864, Camp of Instruction, Columbia, South Carolina, Conscript	Richland County, South Carolina	Co. B, 1st South Carolina Artillery	3/19/1865, Goldsboro, North Carolina	Died of Pneumonia, 5/5/1865
Floyd, Henry P. Private Name Not On Monument	Unk	3/4/1862, Fulton County, Georgia	Fulton County, Georgia	Co. I, 42nd, Georgia Infantry	Unknown	Died of Unknown Causes, 3/15/1865
Floyd, John B. Private	Unk	1/20/1863, Montgomery County, Alabama	Montgomery County, Alabama	Co. C, 61st, Alabama Infantry	5/15/1864, Spotsylvania Court House, Virginia	Died of Unknown Causes, 6/25/1865
Floyd, Merideth D. Private	26	8/8/1862, Raleigh, North Carolina, Conscript	Stanly County, North Carolina	Co. B, 5th, North Carolina Infantry	7/2/1863, Gettysburg, Pennsylvania	Died of Variola (Smallpox), 11/7/1863

Name	Age	Enlisted	Residence	Unit	Captured	Date and Cause of Death
Floyd, William W. Corporal	17	7/8/1861, Bentonville, Arkansas	Benton County, Arkansas	Co. C, 15th, Arkansas Infantry	5/16/1863, Big Black Bridge, Near Vicksburg, Mississippi	Died of Chronic Diarrhea, 1/8/1864
Fogerty, A. J. Private	Unk	3/4/1862, Talbotton, Georgia	Talbot County, Georgia	Co. E, 9th, Georgia Infantry	7/3/1863, Gettysburg, Pennsylvania	Date and Cause of Death Unknown
Fogle, G. H. Private	Unk	2/26/1863, Orangeburg District, South Carolina	Orangeburg District, South Carolina	Co. I, 2nd South Carolina Artillery	3/11/1865, Fayetteville, North Carolina	Died of Chronic Diarrhea, 5/3/1865
Fogleman, Peter L. Private Name Not On Monument	20	5/19/1863, Place Unknown, Conscript	Unknown	Co. D, 7th North Carolina Infantry	7/3/1863, Gettysburg, Pennsylvania	Died of Remittent Fever, 2/24/1864
Fogleman, Tobias Private Name Not On Monument	Unk	12/28/1864, Guilford County, North Carolina, Conscript	Guilford County, North Carolina	Co. E, 67th North Carolina Infantry	4/2/1865, Petersburg, Virginia	Died of Remittent Fever, 6/26/1865
Folsom, W. J. Private	Unk	Unknown	Unknown	Co. D, 20th Battalion Georgia Cavalry	Unknown	Unable to Locate
Fontenot, Viale Private	Unk	3/6/1862, St. Landry, Louisiana	Washington, Louisiana, Farmer	Co. C, 6th Louisiana Infantry	5/5/1864, Mine Run, Virginia	Died of Unknown Causes, 6/20/1864
Forbes, Daniel Private	Unk	4/6/1863, Greenville, Georgia	Meriweather County, Georgia	Co. I, 8th Georgia Cavalry	10/4/1864, Gatesville, North Carolina	Died of Pneumonia, 5/7/1865
Ford, James Captain	28	8/12/1861, Knoxville, Tennessee	Kingston, Tennessee	Co. C, 2nd Ashby's Tennessee Cavalry	10/7/1863, Near Farmington, Tennessee	Died of Unknown Causes, 6/26/1864

Name	Age	Enlisted	Residence	Unit	Captured	Date and Cause of Death
Forehand, Berry A. Private	Unk	2/8/1864, Macon, Georgia	Richmond County, Georgia	Co. A, 22nd, Georgia Infantry	8/17/1864, Deep Bottom, Virginia	Died of Scurvy, 4/7/1865
Forest, Sylvester B. Private	Unk	1/15/1863, Camp Burney, North Carolina	Unknown	Co. E, 67th North Carolina Infantry	11/25/1863, Haddocks Crossroads, Near Greenville, North Carolina	Died of Scurvy, 2/27/1865
Forsythe, Michael Sergeant	Unk	1/1/1864, Corinth, Mississippi	Alcorn County, Mississippi	Co. A, 18th (Newsom's) Tennessee Cavalry	12/17/1864, Near Franklin, Tennessee	Died of Acute Diarrhea, 5/28/1865
Fortner, John G. Private	29	10/9/181, Taylorsville, Alexander County, North Carolina	Wilkes County, North Carolina, Farmer	Co. G, 37th North Carolina Infantry	7/3/1863, Gettysburg, Pennsylvania	Died of Chronic Diarrhea, 11/17/1863
Fortune, William Private	26	6/5/1861, Lynchburg, Virginia	Franklin County, Virginia	Co. E, 11th, Virginia Infantry	5/21/1864, Milford Station, Virginia	Died of Unknown Causes, 8/1/1864
Foster, Abner J. Private	Unk	12/16/1862, Spartanburg, South Carolina	Spartanburg District, South Carolina	Co. D, Palmetto South Carolina Sharp Shooters	4/3/1865, Richmond, Virginia	Died of Chronic Diarrhea, 4/27/1865
Foster, George H. Private	16	12/2/1864, Battery Five, Virginia	Unknown	Co. E, 19th Battalion Virginia Heavy Infantry	4/6/1865, Sailor's Creek, Virginia	Died of Pneumonia, 5/4/1865
Foster, John C. Private	43	9/27/1863, Camp Holmes, Raleigh, North Carolina, Conscript	Orange County, North Carolina	Co. I, 4th North Carolina Infantry	5/15/1864, Place Unknown	Died of Remittent Fever, /23/1865
Foster, James M. Private	25	7/4/1862, Salisbury, Alamance County, North Carolina, Volunteer	Alamance County, North Carolina	Co. I, 57th North Carolina Infantry	7/2/1863, Gettysburg, Pennsylvania	Died of Unknown Causes, 2/7/1864
Foster, J. W. Private	37	2/26/1862, Chester Station, Virginia, Conscript	Unknown	Co. C, 18th, Virginia Infantry	7/3/1863, Gettysburg, Pennsylvania	Died of Chronic Diarrhea, 1/31/1865

Name	Age	Enlisted	Residence	Unit	Captured	Date and Cause of Death
Foster, Joseph Private	Unk	3/7/1863, King and Queen Court House, Virginia	Unknown	Co. E, 24th Battalion Virginia Cavalry	5/17/1864, Hanover County, Virginia	Died of Unknown Causes, 4/12/1865
Foster, Thomas H. 1st Lieutenant	29	8/27/1861, Salem, Virginia	Roanoke County, Virginia	Co. E, 6th Battalion Virginia Cavalry	9/13/1863, Brandy Station, Virginia	Died of Chronic Diarrhea, 8/21/1864
Foster, Thomas Private	Unk	3/8/1862, Poosa County, Alabama	Poosa County, Alabama	Co. H, 13th, Alabama Infantry	7/14/1863, Falling Waters, Maryland	Died of Chronic Diarrhea, 3/29/1865
Foster, William T. Private	19	4/21/1862, Watson's, North Carolina	Alamance County, North Carolina, Farmer	Co. K, 47th North Carolina Infantry	10/27/1864, Boyton Plank Road or Burgess' Mill, Virginia	Died of Chronic Dysentery, 12/14/1864
Fountain, John H. Private	Unk	8/21/1861, Irwinton, Georgia	Wilkinson County, Georgia	Co. I, 3rd, Georgia Infantry	7/5/1863, Williamsport, Maryland	Died of Chronic Diarrhea, 12/2/1863
Fountain, Robert B. Private	Unk	10/14/1864, Danville, Virginia	Pittsylvania County, Virginia	Co. D, 38th, Virginia Infantry	4/1/1865, White Oak Road, Virginia	Died of Chronic Diarrhea, 5/22/1865
Foust, Bolling G. Private	Unk	3/10/1862, Callands, Virginia	Pittsylvania County, Virginia	Co. B, 38th, Virginia Infantry	7/3/1863, Gettysburg, Pennsylvania	Died of Variola (Smallpox), 11/17/1863
Foust, Henry Private	Unk	Unknown	Unknown	Co. H, 3rd, Alabama Infantry	4/2/1865, Petersburg, Virginia	Died of Chronic Diarrhea, 6/26/1865
Fowler, James Private	Unk	Unknown	Unknown	Co. H, 10th Georgia Cavalry	Unknown	Unable to Locate
Fowler, John Private	38	3/6/1862, Volunteer North Carolina	Wake County, North Carolina	Co. I, 47th North Carolina Infantry	10/14/1863, Bristoe Station, Virginia	Died of Pneumonia, 11/13/1863

Name	Age	Enlisted	Residence	Unit	Captured	Date and Cause of Death
Fowler, Wiley R. Private	Unk	2/19/1864, Columbia, South Carolina	Richland County, South Carolina	Co. E, 18th South Carolina Infantry	4/6/1865, Amelia Court House, Virginia	Died of Catarrh, Inflammation of the Mucous Membranes, 4/23/1865
Fox, James H. Private	Unk	Unknown	Unknown	Co. A, 19th, Virginia Infantry	Unknown	Unable to Locate
Fox, William F. Private	Unk	9/21/1862, Camp Mangum, North Carolina, Conscript	Wilkes County, North Carolina	Co. B, 26th North Carolina Infantry	7/14/1863, Falling Waters, Maryland	Died of Unknown Causes, 12/28/1863
Fraiser, James J. A. Private	Unk	8/24/1861, Hewassee, Town County, Georgia	Town County, Georgia	Co. D, 24th, Georgia Infantry	10/19/1864, Cedar Creek or Strasburg, Virginia	Died of Pneumonia, 5/19/1865
Frame, Thomas C. Private	Unk	10/4/1862, Little Birch, Braxton County, Virginia	Unknown	Co. I, 17th, Virginia Cavalry	7/17/1863, Sheppardston, Virginia	Died of Pneumonia, 11/2/1863
Franklin, Avory Private	Unk	1/9/1863, Goldsboro, North Carolina	Unknown	Co. A, 22nd South Carolina Infantry	6/2/1864, Bermuda Hundred, Virginia	Died of Typhoid Fever, 12/7/1864
Franklin, O. C. Corporal	Unk	4/15/1861, Livingston, Alabama	Unknown	Co. G, 5th, Alabama Infantry	5/5/1864, Spotsylvania Court House, Virginia	Died of Chronic Diarrhea, 2/15/1865
Franklin, Thomas H. Private	Unk	3/5/1862, Campbell Court House, Virginia	Unknown	Co. D, 20th Battalion Virginia Heavy Artillery	4/6/1865, Farmville, Virginia	Died of Intermittent Fever, 5/12/1865
Franklin, William C. Private	22	6/11/1861, Winston, North Carolina	Forsyth County, North Carolina	Co. K, 21st North Carolina Infantry	7/3/1863, Gettysburg, Pennsylvania, Wounded in Body	Died of Chronic Diarrhea, 2/21/1864

Name	Age	Enlisted	Residence	Unit	Captured	Date and Cause of Death
Franklin, William H. Private Name Not On Monument	28	7/18/1861, Mathias Point, Brooks Station, Virginia	Westmoreland, County, Virginia	Co. C, 9th, Virginia Cavalry	6/30/1863, Hanover, Pennsylvania	Date and Cause of Death Unknown
Franks, Gabriel Private	Unk	3/1/1862, Washington, Arkansas	Hempstead County, Arkansas	Co. A, 20th, Arkansas Infantry	5/17/1863, Edwards Station, Big Black Bridge, Near Vicksburg, Mississippi	Died of Unknown Causes, 10/?/1863
Frazer, James J. A. See: Fraiser, James J. A.				Co. D, 24th, Georgia Infantry		
Frazer, John L. Lieutenant	Unk	7/30/1862, Calhoun, Georgia	Berrien County, Georgia	Co. G, 61st, Georgia Infantry	5/12/1864, Spotsylvania Court House, Virginia	Died of Unknown Causes, 6/24/1864
Frazier, F. A. Private	Unk	5/21/1864, Camp Vance, North Carolina	Burke County, North Carolina	Co. E, 3rd North Carolina Junior Reserves	12/25/1864, Fort Fisher, North Carolina	Died of Typhoid Fever, 6/22/1865
Frazier, Hughie Y. Private Name Not On Monument	Unk	7/4/1862, Newton, Salisbury County, North Carolina	Catawba County, North Carolina	Co. E, 57th North Carolina Infantry	11/7/1863, Rappahannock Station, Virginia	Died of Chronic Bronchitis, 2/4/1865
Frazier, John Corporal	33	7/4/1862, Winston, North Carolina	Forsyth County, North Carolina	Co. D, 57th North Carolina Infantry	9/19/1864, Winchester, Virginia	Died of Acute Dysentery, 2/1/1865
Frazier, William Private	Unk	7/7/1862, Newton, North Carolina	Catawba County, North Carolina	Co. E, 57th North Carolina Infantry	11/7/1863, Rappahannock, Virginia	Died of Congestion of the Brain, 1/27/1865
Freeman, Isaac Private	26	3/13/1862, Carthage, North Carolina, Volunteer	Moore County, North Carolina, Farmer	Co. D, 48th North Carolina Infantry	10/14/1863, Bristoe Station, Virginia	Died of Chronic Diarrhea, 11/16/1863

Name	Age	Enlisted	Residence	Unit	Captured	Date and Cause of Death
Freeman, J. H. Private	Unk	7/15/1862, Camp Holmes, Raleigh, North Carolina	Wake County, North Carolina	Co. D, 47th North Carolina Infantry	10/27/1864, Burgess' Mill, Virginia	Died of Chronic Diarrhea, 3/12/1865
Freeman, O. P. Private	25	4/2/1862, Union Parish, Louisiana	Union Parish, Louisiana	Co. G, 6th Louisiana Infantry	5/5/1864, Mine Run, Virginia	Died of Unknown Causes, 6/25/1864
Freeman, Philip L. Private	Unk	10/22/1861, Centerville, Virginia	Culpepper County, Virginia	Co. C, 7th, Virginia Infantry	5/21/1864, Milford Station, Virginia	Died of Chronic Diarrhea, 2/24/1865
Frick, E. D. Private	Unk	2/18/1863, Lexington, South Carolina	Lexington County, South Carolina	Co. C, 20th South Carolina Infantry	10/19/1864, Cedar Creek or Strasburg, Virginia	Died of Pneumonia, 2/21/1865
Frick, John D. Private Name Not On Monument	19	4/9/1862, Walhalla, South Carolina	Pickens District, South Carolina	Co. C, 1st South Carolina Infantry	7/6/1863, Gettysburg, Pennsylvania	Died of Remittent Fever, 8/31/1863
Frierson, Augustus C. Private	Unk	4/1/1863, Pocotaligo, South Carolina	Jasper County, South Carolina	Co. K, 4th South Carolina Infantry	5/30/1864, Old Church, Virginia	Died of Unknown Causes, 7/30/1864
Friezlande, William Private	Unk	2/14/1862, Monroe, North Carolina	Union County, North Carolina	Co. B, 26th North Carolina Infantry	7/5/1863, Gettysburg, Pennsylvania	Died of Chronic Diarrhea, 1/2/1864
Frith, Henry H. Private Name Not On Monument	Unk	2/15/1863, Marion, Alabama	Perry County, Alabama	Co. K, 8th Alabama Infantry	7/2/1863, Gettysburg, Pennsylvania	Died of Typhoid/ Pneumonia, 8/28/1863
Fritts, Henry Private	28	7/15/1862, Raleigh, North Carolina, Conscript	Davidson County, North Carolina	Co. B, 49th North Carolina Infantry	4/20/1863, Bermuda Hundred, Virginia	Died of Remittent Fever, 8/22/1864

Name	Age	Enlisted	Residence	Unit	Captured	Date and Cause of Death
Fritz, Leonard Private	Unk	2/20/1862, Boston Mountain, Arkansas	Unknown	Co. C, 15th Arkansas Infantry	5/17/ 1863, Big Black Bridge, Near Vicksburg, Mississippi	Died of Chronic Diarrhea, 11/5/1863
Fry, J. G. Private	19	6/26/1864, Petersburg, Virginia	Chesterfield County, Virginia	Co. H, 20th South Carolina Infantry	9/19/1864, Winchester, Virginia	Died of Pneumonia, 3/19/1865
Fugate, Daniel Private	Unk	10/1/1862, Whitesburg, Kentucky	Letcher County, Kentucky	Co. G, 13th Kentucky Cavalry	6/6/1863, Perry County, Kentucky	Died of Unknown Causes, 7/17/1864
Fugnary, John Private	Unk	1/20/1863, Moore County, North Carolina	Moore County, North Carolina	Co. F, 50th North Carolina Cavalry	10/31/1864, Plymouth, North Carolina	Died of Unknown Causes, 3/7/1865
Fulcher, Josiah Private	Unk	11/2/1864, Camp Holmes, Raleigh, North Carolina	Wake County, North Carolina	Co. C, 3rd North Carolina Junior Reserves	12/25/1864, Fort Fisher, North Carolina	Died of Pneumonia, 1/28/1865
Fulcher, William J. Private	Unk	8/26/1864, Shepperdstown, Virginia	Jefferson County, Virginia	Co. H, 26th, Virginia Infantry	9/19/1864, Winchester, Virginia	Died of Chronic Dysentery, 1/19/1865
Fulford, Anson B. Corporal	20	6/9/1861, Newbern, North Carolina, Volunteer	Carteret County, North Carolina	Co. K, 2nd North Carolina Infantry	11/7/1863, Kelly's Ford, Rappahannock Station, Virginia	Died of Unknown Causes, 2/11/1864
Fulford, James Private	37	4/5/1862, Currituck Court House, North Carolina	Currituck Court House, North Carolina	Co. G, 4th North Carolina Cavalry	10/14/1863, Catlett's Station, Virginia	Died of Chronic Diarrhea, 12/8/1863
Fulk, Charles A. Private	26	8/29/1862, Raleigh, North Carolina, Conscript	Wake County, North Carolina	Co. K, 2nd North Carolina Infantry	11/7/1863, Rappahannock Station, Virginia	Died of Chronic Dysentery, 12/15/1864
Fulk, David E. Private	24	8/29/1862, Raleigh, North Carolina, Conscript	Wake County, North Carolina	Co. K, 2nd North Carolina Infantry	11/7/1863, Rappahannock Station, Virginia	Died of Remittent Fever, 12/7/1864

Name	Age	Enlisted	Residence	Unit	Captured	Date and Cause of Death
Fulk, John David Private	20	5/30/1861, Germantown, North Carolina, Volunteer	Stokes County, North Carolina	Co. G, 21st North Carolina Infantry	9/22/1864, Fisher's Hill, Virginia	Died of Pneumonia, 5/15/1865
Fuller, Byam Private	Unk	3/1/1862, Franklin County, Georgia	Franklin County, Georgia	Co. H, 24th, Georgia Infantry	6/3/1864, Gaine's Mill, Virginia	Died of Acute Diarrhea, 9/4/1864
Fuller, C. J. Private	Unk	3/13/1862, Greenville, Alabama	Butler County, Alabama	Co. C, 9th, Alabama Infantry	7/3/1863, Gettysburg, Pennsylvania	Died of Variola (Smallpox), 12/23/1863
Fuller, J. T. Sergeant	Unk	6/11/1861, Camp McDonald, Georgia	Gordon County, Georgia	Co. E, 18th, Georgia Infantry	5/6/1864, Mine Run, Virginia	Died of Heart Disease, 2/13/1865
Fuller, Josiah E. Sergeant	25	6/4/1861, Callands, Pittsylvania County, Virginia	Pittsylvania County, Virginia	Co. B, 38th, Virginia Infantry	7/4/1863, Gettysburg, Pennsylvania	Died of Chronic Diarrhea, 1/1/1864
Fuller, Robert S. Corporal	Unk	4/23/1861, Eatonton, Georgia	Putnam County, Georgia	Co. B, 3rd, Georgia Infantry	7/4/1863, Gettysburg, Pennsylvania, Wounded Right Ankle	Died of Unknown Causes, 3/27/1864
Fulmer, John A. Private	Unk	Unknown	Unknown	Co. C, 6th South Carolina Infantry	2/28/1865, Near Chesterfield, South Carolina	Died of Intermittent Fever, 4/5/1865
Fulp, Russell Private	Unk	8/24/1864, Camp Holmes, Raleigh, North Carolina	Wake County, North Carolina	Co. B, 3rd North Carolina Junior Reserves	12/25/1864, Fort Fisher, North Carolina	Died of Unknown Causes, 2/8/1865
Funk, Andrew J. Private	24	4/24/1861, Elk Creek, Virginia	Grayson County, Virginia	Co. F, 4th, Virginia Infantry	5/12/1864, Near Spotsylvania Court House, Virginia	Died of Unknown Causes, 10/18/1864
Fuqua, Joel B. Sergeant	Unk	7/2/1861, Bethel, Virginia	Hampton County, Virginia	Co. F, 50th, Virginia Infantry	5/12/1864, Near Spotsylvania Court House, Virginia	Died of Unknown Causes, 6/17/1864

Name	Age	Enlisted	Residence	Unit	Captured	Date and Cause of Death
Fuquay, John A. Private Not Listed On Monument	25	3/11/1862, Lillington, North Carolina	Harnett County, North Carolina, Farmer	Co. H, 50th, North Carolina Infantry	11/13/1863, Hanover County, North Carolina	Died of Chronic Dysentery, 3/7/1865
Furr, Adam M. Private	20	7/7/1862, Cabarrus County, North Carolina	Cabarrus County, North Carolina	Co. E, 4th North Carolina Cavalry	7/4/1863, South Mountain, Maryland	Died of Unknown Causes, 1/28/1864
Furr, Allison Private	23	7/3/1861, Cabarrus County, North Carolina, Volunteer	Cabarrus County, North Carolina, Farmer	Co. B, 7th North Carolina Infantry	7/3/1863, Gettysburg, Pennsylvania	Died of Unknown Causes, 1/6/1864

Name	Age	Enlisted	Residence	Unit	Captured	Date and Cause of Death
Gaines, Green B. Private	Unk	7/22/1861, Forsyth County, Georgia	Forsyth County, Georgia	Co. B, 21st North Carolina Infantry	7/4/1863, Gettysburg, Pennsylvania, Gunshot Wound Arm	Died of Chronic Diarrhea, 1/26/1864
Gaines, Henry F. Corporal	20	5/27/1861, Richmond, Virginia	Charlotte, North Carolina, Farmer	Co. K, 18th, Virginia Infantry	7/3/1863, Gettysburg, Pennsylvania	Died of Chronic Diarrhea, 1/29/1864
Gaines, J. P. Private	Unk	4/1/1862, Charleston, South Carolina	Charleston County, South Carolina	Co. A, 22nd South Carolina Infantry	6/2/1864, Near Bermuda Hundred, Virginia	Died of Chronic Diarrhea, 2/12/1865
Galbraith, Harvey Sergeant	25	9/24/1862, Mooresburg, Tennessee	Hawkins County, Tennessee	Co. C, 63rd Tennessee Infantry	4/2/1865, Petersburg, Virginia	Died of Unknown Causes, 5/31/1865
Gallop, Isaac Private	19	5/6/1862, Camden County, North Carolina, Volunteer	Camden County, North Carolina	Co. A, 56th North Carolina Infantry	5/20/1864, Near Drury's Bluff, Virginia, Gunshot Wound Left Hip	Died of Chronic Diarrhea, 2/27/1865
Gamble, S. Jack Private	Unk	9/25/1862, Clark County, Alabama	Clark County, Alabama	Co. E, 3rd Alabama Infantry	7/14/1863, Harristown, Virginia	Died of Chronic Diarrhea, 12/19/1863

Name	Age	Enlisted	Residence	Unit	Captured	Date and Cause of Death
Gardner, Alfred Corporal	28	1/27/1862, Greenville, North Carolina	Pitt County, North Carolina, Farmer	Co. I, 44st North Carolina Infantry	10/27/1864, Boyton Plank Road or Burgess' Mill, Virginia	Died of Debility (Feebleness), 4/12/1865
Gardner, Charles S. Private	18	5/3/1861, Jerusalem, Virginia	Southampton County, Virginia	Co. D, 3rd, Virginia Infantry	7/3/1863, Gettysburg, Pennsylvania	Died of Unknown Causes, 12/23/1863
Gardner, Daniel See: Garner, Daniel				Co. G, 49th North Carolina Infantry		
Gardner, Giles M. Private	34	9/17/1863, Carroll County, Virginia	Carroll County, Virginia	Co. E, 17th, Virginia Infantry	3/31/1865, Dinwiddie Court House, Virginia	Died of Unknown Causes, 5/13/1865
Gardner, John A. Private	Unk	4/11/1862, Hugar Barracks, Virginia	Unknown	Co. H, 16th, Virginia Infantry	7/4/1863, Gettysburg, Pennsylvania, Wounded	Died of Unknown Causes, 1/2/1864
Gardner, N. C. Private	Unk	Unknown	Unknown	Co. D, 21st, Arkansas Infantry	Unknown	Unable to Locate
Gardner, William Private	27	7/10/1862, Mandarin, Florida	Duval County, Florida	Co. A, 2nd, Florida Infantry	3/27/1863, St John's River, East Florida	Cause of Death Not Stated, 12/14/1863
Garland, Edward Private	Unk	9/16/1863, Georgetown, South Carolina	Georgetown County, South Carolina	Co. F, 7th South Carolina Cavalry	4/6/1865, Burkesville, Virginia	Died of Chronic Diarrhea, 5/31/1865
Garman, G. W. Private	Unk	Unknown	Unknown	Co. I, 5th North Carolina Infantry	Unknown	Unable to Locate
Garner, Daniel Private	46	3/18/1862, Shelby, North Carolina, Volunteer	Cleveland County, North Carolina	Co. G, 49th North Carolina Infantry	4/1/1865, Five Forks, Virginia	Died of Chronic Diarrhea, 6/21/1865
Garner, M. H. Private	Unk	5/8/1862, Monroeville, Alabama	Monroe County, Alabama	Co. F, 36th, Alabama Infantry	12/17/1864, Near Franklin, Tennessee	Died of Pneumonia, 4/21/1865

Name	Age	Enlisted	Residence	Unit	Captured	Date and Cause of Death
Garrett, Edward B. Private	Unk	2/15/1863, Charleston, South Carolina	Charleston County, South Carolina	Co. D, 27th South Carolina Infantry	8/21/1864, Globe Tavern, Near Weldon Railroad, Virginia	Died of Rheumatism, 2/12/1865
Garrett, Stephen Private	39	2/15/1862, Edenton, North Carolina, Volunteer	Chowan County, North Carolina	Co. F, 11th North Carolina Infantry	10/14/1863, Bristoe Station, Virginia	Died of Chronic Diarrhea, 11/6/1863
Garrett, William S. Private	Unk	10/10/1863, Buckingham Court House, Virginia	Buckingham County, Virginia	Co. E, 21st Virginia Infantry	9/19/1864, Winchester, Virginia	Died From Inflammation of Lungs (Pneumonia), 4/7/1865
Garriss, Junius H. Private	Unk	3/26/1862, Jackson, North Carolina	Northampton County, North Carolina, Farmer	Co. D, 54th North Carolina Infantry	11/7/1863, Rappahannock, Virginia	Died of Variola (Smallpox), 1/131864
Garrison, Alfred Private	Unk	10/1/1864, Camp Holmes, Raleigh, North Carolina	Mecklenburg County, North Carolina	Co. E, 11th North Carolina Infantry	10/27/1864, Boyton Plank Road or Burgess' Mill, Virginia	Died of Erysipelas (Bacterial Infection of the Skin), 3/26/1865
Garrison, J. See: Garriss, Junius H.				Co. D, 54th North Carolina Infantry		
Garry, J. W. Private	Unk	Unknown	Unknown	Stiles' Georgia Artillery	Unknown	Unable to Locate
Garter, Carrell Private	Unk	Unknown	Unknown	Co. D, 44th North Carolina Infantry	1/18/1865, Smithville, North Carolina	Died of Unknown Causes, 2/5/1865, Died Aboard Transport Northern Light
Garver, J. M. Private	20	7/8/1861, Salisbury, North Carolina, Volunteer	Rowan County, North Carolina	Co. K, 5th North Carolina Infantry	7/3/1863, Gettysburg, Pennsylvania	Died of Unknown Causes, 5/26/1864
Gary, Richard G. Private	Unk	3/10/1862, Buckingham, North Carolina	Unknown	Co. K, 4th Virginia Cavalry	7/5/1863, Gettysburg, Pennsylvania	Died of Chronic Diarrhea, 3/1/1864

Name	Age	Enlisted	Residence	Unit	Captured	Date and Cause of Death
Gary, Thomas J. Private Name Not On Monument	Unk	12/9/1864, Chaffin's Bluff, Virginia	Unknown	Pamumkey Virginia Heavy Artillery	4/6/1865, Harper's Farm, Virginia	Died of Pneumonia, 6/4/1865
Gary, Washington G. Private	43	3/20/1862, Richmond, Virginia	Chesterfield County, Virginia	Co. B, 41st Virginia Infantry	8/19/1864, Globe Tavern, Near Weldon Railroad, Virginia, Gunshot Wound Right Lung and Hand	Died of Complications of Wounds, 3/1/1865
Gash, Martin M. Sergeant	Unk	7/15/1862, Hendersonville North Carolina	Henderson County, North Carolina	Co. D, 6th North Carolina Cavalry	6/22/1864, Jackson's Mills, North Carolina	Died of Chronic Dysentery, 7/31/1864
Gaskins, P. D. Corporal	Unk	5/12/1862, Swift Creek, North Carolina	Swift Creek, North Carolina	Co. I, 44th North Carolina Infantry	10/14/1863, Bristoe Station, Virginia	Died of Variola (Smallpox), 12/6/1863
Gaston, D. L. Private	Unk	3/3/1862, Camp Arkansas, Arkansas	Unknown	Co. H, 19th Arkansas Infantry	5/16/1863, Champion Hill, Tennessee	Died of Chronic Diarrhea, 11/12/1863
Gates, David Private	Unk	4/2/1862, Mouth of Indian River, Tazewell County, Virginia	Tazewell County, Virginia	Co. H, 29th Virginia Infantry	5/8/1864, Near Petersburg, Virginia	Died of Scurvy, 3/16/1865
Gates, Solomon G. Sergeant	18	5/4/1861, Dobson, North Carolina, Volunteer	Surry County, North Carolina	Co. A, 28th North Carolina Infantry	7/3/1863, Gettysburg, Pennsylvania, Wounded	Died of Unknown Causes, 1/16/1864
Gatlin, Stewart Private	Unk	9/25/1862, Cleveland, Bradley County, Tennessee	Bradley County, Tennessee	Co. E, 62nd Tennessee Infantry	8/18/1863, Charleston, Tennessee.	Died of Chronic Diarrhea, 4/13/1865
Gay, James Private	40	3/17/1862, Shephards Town, Virginia	Jefferson County, Virginia	Co. D, 12th Virginia Cavalry	9/6/1863, Loudon County, Virginia	Died of Chronic Diarrhea, 9/19/1864

Name	Age	Enlisted	Residence	Unit	Captured	Date and Cause of Death
Gay, Thomas B. Private	30	5/6/1861, Mobile, Alabama	Mobile County, Alabama	Co. E, 8th Alabama Infantry	7/3/1863, Gettysburg, Pennsylvania, Gunshot Wound Right Arm	Died of Chronic Diarrhea and Typhoid Fever, 11/29/1863
Gentry, C. O. Private	16	3/5/1862, Camp Winder, Virginia	Unknown, Student	Co. E, 22nd Battalion Virginia Artillery	7/14/1863, Falling Waters, Maryland	Died of Unknown Causes, 8/29/1864
Gentry, John M. Private	26	5/8/1861, Marion, Alabama	Sevier, Alabama, Farmer	Co. A, 8th Alabama Infantry	7/3/1863, Gettysburg, Pennsylvania	Died of Unknown Causes, 1/10/1864
Gentry, Joseph W. Private	24	3/5/1862, New Bethel, Rockingham County, North Carolina	Stokes County, North Carolina, Farmer	Co. G, 45th North Carolina Infantry	5/24/1864, Hanover Junction, Virginia	Died of Pneumonia, 1/26/1865
George, Lewis Private	21	5/14/1862, Camp McCarthy, Putnam County, Florida	Putnam County, Florida	Co. B, 9th Florida Infantry	9/9/1864, Petersburg, Virginia	Died of Unknown Causes, 3/1/1865
Gerrity, Michael Private	32	5/10/1861, New Orleans, Louisiana	New Orleans, Louisiana Laborer, Born in Ireland	Co. G, 5th Louisiana Infantry	11/7/1863, Rappahannock Station, Virginia	Died of Chronic Diarrhea, 2/9/1864
Gerry, William B. Private Not Listed On Monument	18	2/18/1863, Camp Finagin, Florida	Unknown	Co. D, 2nd Florida Infantry	8/201863, Place of Capture Unknown	Died of Pneumonia, 8/20/1863
Ghent, Emmett M. Corporal	18	5/23/1861, Dinwiddie Court House, Virginia	Dinwiddie County, Virginia, Student	Co. C, 3rd Virginia Infantry	7/5/1863, Gettysburg, Pennsylvania	Died of Unknown Causes, 9/18/1863
Gibbs, John B. Private	Unk	Unknown	Unknown	Co. A, 66th North Carolina Infantry	2/20/1864, Near Fairfield, North Carolina	Died of Chronic Diarrhea, 2/17/1865

Name	Age	Enlisted	Residence	Unit	Captured	Date and Cause of Death
Gibbs, T. M. See: Gibson, Tandy M.				Fry's Virginia Battery		
Gibson, Flavius M. Private	Unk	5/10/1861, Lebanon, Virginia	Russell County, Virginia	Co. C, 37th Virginia Infantry	7/3/1863, Gettysburg, Pennsylvania	Died of Acute Dysentery, 8/27/1864
Gibson, Jason J. Private Not Listed On Monument	Unk	2/22/1863 Montgomery, Alabama	Montgomery County, Alabama	Co. E, 3rd Alabama Cavalry	5/13/1864 Spotsylvania Court House, Virginia	Died of Unknown Causes, 7/4/1864
Gibson, John A. Private	28	2/28/1862, Graham, North Carolina, Volunteer	Alamance County, North Carolina	Co. F, 6th North Carolina Infantry	7/2/1863, Gettysburg, Pennsylvania, Gunshot Wound Right Thigh	Died of Unknown Causes, 2/24/1864
Gibson, John S. Private	Unk	10/18/1864, Marion, South Carolina	Marion District, South Carolina	Co. L, 21st South Carolina Infantry	2/20/1865, Near Town Creek, North Carolina	Died of Chronic Diarrhea, 5/10/1865
Gibson, Nathan W. Private	Unk	2/6/1864, Chesterfield District, South Carolina	Chesterfield District, South Carolina	Co. F, 26th South Carolina Infantry	4/1/1865, South Side Railroad, Virginia	Died of Acute Dysentery and Scurvy, 4/25/1865
Gibson, Tandy M. Private	Unk	4/2/1862, Charlottesville Virginia	Albemarle County, Virginia	Captain Carrington's Co. Charlottesville Virginia Light Artillery	10/19/1864, Cedar Creek or Strasburg, Virginia	Died of Tuberculosis, 12/16/1864
Gibson, William G. Private	Unk	10/1/1864, Troy, North Carolina, Conscript	Montgomery County, North Carolina	Co. F, 44th North Carolina Infantry	10/27/1864, Boydton Plank Road, Near Petersburg, Virginia	Died of Typhoid Fever, 2/23/1865
Gilbert, George L. Private	Unk	3/7/1864, Orange County Court House, Virginia	Bartow County, Georgia	Co. K, 14th Georgia Infantry	4/2/1865, Petersburg, Virginia	Died of Chronic Diarrhea, 6/23/1865

Name	Age	Enlisted	Residence	Unit	Captured	Date and Cause of Death
Giles, Allen Private Not Listed On Monument	Unk	8/1/1861 Lorena, Alabama	Unknown	Co. K, 14th Alabama Infantry	7/5/1863 Gettysburg, Pennsylvania	Died of Chronic Diarrhea, 5/29/1865
Giles, Church V. Private	35	3/20/1862, Danville, Virginia	Pittsylvania County, Virginia	Co. C, 5th Virginia Cavalry	9/24/1864, Luray, Virginia	Died of Chronic Diarrhea, 12/10/1864
Giles, James R. Private	Unk	9/15/1862, Jacksonville, North Carolina	Onslow County, North Carolina	Co. H, 3rd North Carolina Cavalry	12/17/1863, Greenville, North Carolina	Died of Rubeola (Measles), 8/11/1864
Giles, John A. Private Not Listed On Monument	Unk	3/4/1862 Albany, Georgia	Dougherty County, Georgia	Co. K, 51st Georgia Infantry	4/6/1865, Farmville, Virginia	Died of Chronic Diarrhea, 7/2/1865
Giles, William B. Private	26	6/1/1861, Lock's Creek, North Carolina, Volunteer	Cumberland County, North Carolina	Co. E, 8th North Carolina Infantry	5/21/1864, Cold Harbor, Virginia	Died of Debility (Loss of Strength, Feeble), 4/29/1865
Giles, William W. Private	28	5/1/1862, Morgantown, North Carolina, Volunteer	Burke County, North Carolina	Co. D, 11th North Carolina Infantry	7/3/1863, Gettysburg, Pennsylvania	Died of Chronic Diarrhea, 11/27/1863
Gill, W. E. Private	Unk	10/10/1864, Richmond, Virginia	Henrico County, Virginia	Co. G, 24th Virginia Cavalry	1/28/1865, White Oak, Virginia	Died of Chronic Diarrhea, 4/28/1865
Gillespie, James R. Sergeant	Unk	3/5/1863, Henderson County, North Carolina	Henderson County, North Carolina	Co. D, 6th North Carolina Cavalry	6/3/1863, Simpson's Ford, Kentucky	Died of Unknown Causes, 5/3/1864
Gilley, William Corporal	Unk	6/8/1861, Ridgeway, Virginia	Henry County, Virginia	Co. A, 42nd Virginia Infantry	7/5/1863, Gettysburg, Pennsylvania	Died of Variola (Smallpox), 5/3/1864

Name	Age	Enlisted	Residence	Unit	Captured	Date and Cause of Death
Gilliam, F. A. Private	Unk	Unknown	Unknown	Co. B, 18th Virginia Infantry	Unknown	Died of Pneumonia, 5/9/1865
Gilliland, Thomas Private	Unk	Unknown	Unknown	Co. I, 49th North Carolina Infantry	4/1/1865, Five Forks, Virginia	Died of Paralysis, 5/20/1865
Gilmer, J. L. Private	Unk	Unknown	Unknown	Co. C, 18th Mississippi Infantry	12/19/1864, Near Savannah, Georgia	Died of Chronic Diarrhea, 2/12/1865
Gilmer, John Private	Unk	3/1/1862, Suffolk, Virginia	Jackson County, Virginia	Co. G, 16th Georgia Infantry	7/3/1863, Gettysburg, Pennsylvania	Died of Chronic Diarrhea, 1/16/1864
Givens, Texas P. Private	Unk	3/12/1862, Craig Court House, Virginia	Craig County, Virginia	Co. B, 28th Virginia Infantry	7/2/1863, Gettysburg, Pennsylvania	Died of Unknown Causes, 12/23/1863
Gladden, Silas L. Private	Unk	5/10/1862, Cartersville, Georgia	Bartow County, Georgia	Co. K, 60th Georgia Infantry	9/23/1864, Cedar Creek or Strasburg, Virginia	Died of Consumption (Tuberculosis), 3/7/1865
Glenn, Isaiah Private	Unk	8/5/1861, Monterey, Virginia	Highland County, Virginia	Co. A, 25th Virginia Infantry	5/15/1864, Wilderness, Virginia	Died of Unknown Causes, 8/1/1864
Glenn, Joseph Private Not Listed On Monument	Unk	8/1/1861, Staunton, Virginia	Rockbridge County, Virginia	Co. E, 52nd Virginia Infantry	7/21/1864, Winchester, Virginia, Wounded	Died of Typhoid Fever, 7/30/1864
Glenn, Paton S. Private	Unk	Unknown	Unknown	Co. A, 5th Missouri Infantry	5/16/1863, Champion Hill, Tennessee	Died of Unknown Causes, 1/11/1864
Glover, B. W. Private	Unk	4/18/1864, Taylorsville, North Carolina	Alexander County, North Carolina	Co. D, 5th North Carolina Infantry	10/19/1864, Cedar Creek or Strasburg, Virginia	Died of Pneumonia, 2/23/1865

Name	Age	Enlisted	Residence	Unit	Captured	Date and Cause of Death
Glover, Jacob Private	22	3/18/1862, Salisbury, North Carolina, Volunteer	Stanly County, North Carolina	Co. C, 42th North Carolina Infantry	6/18/1864, Near Petersburg, Virginia	Died of Scurvy, 4/19/1865
Gobble, Hubbard A. Private	26	7/15/1862, Raleigh, North Carolina, Conscript	Davidson County, North Carolina	Co. C, 15th North Carolina Infantry	4/2/1865, Hatcher's Run, Virginia	Died of Acute Diarrhea, 6/15/1865
Godfrey, J. W. Private	Unk	1/1/1862, Adam's Run, South Carolina	Unknown	Co. C, Holcombe's Legion South Carolina Infantry	11/6/1864, Near Petersburg, Virginia	Died of Chronic Diarrhea, 4/2/1865
Godsey, Clinton Private	28	3/2/1863, Hazard, Whitesburg, Kentucky	Perry County, Kentucky	Co. I, 13th Kentucky Cavalry	5/17/1863, Lexington, Kentucky	Died of Unknown Causes, 11/19/1863
Godwin, Daniel Private	Unk	10/18/1864, Camp Holmes, Raleigh, North Carolina	Wake County, North Carolina	Co. D, 38th North Carolina Infantry	3/30/1865, Hatcher's Run, Virginia	Died of Unknown Causes, 6/8/1865
Godwin, james Private	Unk	6/10/1861, Morgan, Georgia	Calhoun County, Georgia	Co. D, 12th Georgia Infantry	7/3/1863, Gettysburg, Pennsylvania	Died of Unknown Causes, 11/1/1863
Goforth, E. George Private	Unk	Unknown	Unknown, Farmer	Co. A, 3rd North Carolina Junior Reserves	12/25/1864, Fort Fisher, North Carolina	Died of Unknown Causes, 2/13/1865
Goings, Enoch Private	Unk	1/1/1864, Wytheville, Virginia	Wythe County, Virginia	Co. G, 22nd Virginia Cavalry	9/19/1864, Winchester, Virginia	Died of Acute Diarrhea, 10/24/1864
Gold, John M. Private	24	4/29/1861, Lexington, Virginia	Rockbridge County, Virginia	Captain Graham's Co., Rockbridge Virginia Light Artillery	7/5/1863, Gettysburg, Pennsylvania	Died of Unknown Causes, 1/14/1864
Golding, Thomas Private	20	3/17/1862, Jonesville, North Carolina	Surry County, North Carolina, Farmer	Co. H, 54th North Carolina Infantry	11/7/1863, Rappahannock, Virginia	Died of Chronic Diarrhea, 12/8/1864

Name	Age	Enlisted	Residence	Unit	Captured	Date and Cause of Death
Good, Jackson Private	17	4/25/1862, Elk Run, Virginia	Unknown	Co. D, 10th Virginia Infantry	7/5/1863, Gettysburg, Pennsylvania	Died of Variola (Smallpox), 11/18/1863
Good, John Private	Unk	7/8/1862, Morganton, North Carolina	Burke County, North Carolina	Co. H, 6th North Carolina Cavalry	6/21/1864, Jackson's Mill, North Carolina	Died of Typhoid Fever, 9/11/1864
Goodman, Pleas W. Private Not Listed On Monument	19	7/18/1863, Carrolton, Alabama	Pickens County, Alabama	Co. C, 41st Alabama Infantry	4/3/1865, Richmond, Virginia, After General Lee's Surrender	Died of Chronic Diarrhea, 5/21/1865
Goodman, Samuel C. Private Not Listed On Monument	33	8/18/1862, Statesville, Iredell County, North Carolina, Conscript	Iredell County, North Carolina	Co. D, 7th North Carolina Infantry	5/6/1864, Wilderness, Virginia	Died of Unknown Causes, 10/29/1864
Goodman, William H. Private	26	8/6/1861, Mount Pleasant, North Carolina, Volunteer	Cabarrus County, North Carolina, Farmer	Co. H, 8th North Carolina Infantry	9/30/1864, Fort Harrison, Virginia	Died of Chronic Diarrhea, 4/10/1865
Goodwin, Alexander Private	23	12/20/1861, Cheraw, Chesterfield District, South Carolina	Chesterfield District, South Carolina	Co. D, 21st South Carolina Infantry	7/10/1863, Morris Island, South Carolina	Died of Chronic Diarrhea, 10/15/1864
Goodwin, Benjamin F. Private	23	2/15/1862, Center Hill, North Carolina, Volunteer	Chowan County, North Carolina	Co. B, 11th North Carolina Infantry	7/14/1863, Falling Waters, Maryland	Died of Unknown Causes, 1/6/1864
Goodwin, R. E. Private	Unk	5/24/1864, Camp Vance, North Carolina	Burke County, North Carolina	Co. B, 3rd North Carolina Junior Reserves	12/25/1864, Fort Fisher, North Carolina	Died of Unknown Causes, 5/23/1865
Goosan, G. Private	Unk	Unknown	Unknown	Co. F, 32nd North Carolina Infantry	Unknown	Unable to Locate
Gordon, George Private	24	2/11/1864, Essex County, Virginia	Fredericksburg Virginia, Lawyer	Co. K, 9th Virginia Cavalry	5/27/1864, Mulberry Hill, Virginia	Died of Unknown Causes, 7/26/1864

Name	Age	Enlisted	Residence	Unit	Captured	Date and Cause of Death
Gordon, Obediah Private	Unk	3/19/1862, Richmond, Virginia	Henrico County, Virginia	Co. A, 24th Virginia Cavalry	5/14/1864, Fort Darling, Virginia	Died of Unknown Causes, 10/24/1864
Gordon, Robert H. Private	Unk	4/1/1862, Lee's Farm, Yorktown, Virginia	York County, Virginia	Co. D, 3rd Virginia Cavalry	1/15/1865, Near Richmond, Virginia	Died of Pneumonia, 3/16/1865
Gordon, Thomas C. Private	Unk	2/14/1863, Camp Holmes, Monroe, North Carolina, Conscript	Union County, North Carolina	Co. B, 26th North Carolina Infantry	10/27/1864, Boyton Plank Road or Burgess' Mill, Virginia	Died of Typhoid Fever, 1/20/1865
Gordy, William Private	Unk	3/24/1863, Columbia County, Georgia	Columbia County, Georgia	Co. I, 64th Georgia Infantry	4/3/1865, Richmond Hospital, Virginia	Died of Erysipelas (Bacterial Infection of the Skin), 7/2/1865
Gorred, N. See: Garrett, William S.				Co. E, 21st Virginia Infantry		
Gossett, Abraham Private	Unk	Unknown	Unknown	Co. B, 12th North Carolina Infantry	3/25/1865, Fort Stedman, Near Petersburg, Virginia	Died of Unknown Causes, 4/19/1865
Gould, Charles W. Private	Unk	1/9/1863, Fort Boggs, Georgia	Unknown	Co. B, 18th Georgia Infantry	4/6/1865, High Bridge, Virginia	Died of Acute Dysentery, 6/16/1865
Gower, James R. Private	33	3/3/1863, Camp Mangum, Raleigh, North Carolina, Volunteer	Wake County, North Carolina, Farmer	Co. E, 47th North Carolina Infantry	7/5/1863, Gettysburg, Pennsylvania	Died of Unknown Causes, 11/26/1863
Grady, Needham Private	Unk	2/15/1862, Duplin County, North Carolina, Volunteer	Duplin County, North Carolina	Co. E, 3rd North Carolina Infantry	7/3/1863, Gettysburg, Pennsylvania	Died of Pneumonia and Typhoid Fever, 12/23/1863
Gramage, H. Private	Unk	Unknown	Unknown	Co. G, 4th Virginia Infantry	5/5/1863, Wayne County, Virginia	Died of Variola (Smallpox), 12/22/1863

Name	Age	Enlisted	Residence	Unit	Captured	Date and Cause of Death
Grambling, A. M. Corporal	Unk	12/21/1862, Orangeburg District, South Carolina	Orangeburg District, South Carolina	Co. B, 20th South Carolina Infantry	10/23/1864, Cedar Creek or Strasburg, Virginia	Died of Scurvy, 3/19/1865
Granade, Andrew J. Private	20	3/4/1862, Columbia County, Georgia	Columbia County, Georgia	Co. K, 48th Georgia Infantry	7/2/1863, Gettysburg, Pennsylvania	Died of Chronic Diarrhea, 1/3/1864
Granade, Timothy Private	Unk	2/19/1862, Conyers, Georgia	Newton County, Georgia	Co. B, 35th Georgia Infantry	7/1/1863, Gettysburg, Pennsylvania	Died of Unknown Causes, 1/22/1864
Grant, James Private	Unk	9/30/1863, Camp Lee, Georgia	Unknown	Co. E, 4th Georgia Cavalry	12/10/1864, Near Savannah, Georgia	Died of Acute Diarrhea, 5/31/1865
Grant, Jordan W. Private	23	4/24/1861, Portsmouth, Virginia	Norfolk County, Virginia, Ship Carpenter	Co. G, 9th Virginia Infantry	7/3/1863, Gettysburg, Pennsylvania	Died of Chronic Diarrhea, 1/1/1864
Grant, Seaton L. Private	31	8/1/1861, Staunton, Virginia	Rockbridge County, Virginia, Farmer	Co. G, 58th Virginia Infantry	5/22/1864, North Anna River, Virginia	Died of Chronic Dysentery, 2/23/1865
Grant, Thomas J. Private	Unk	5/7/1862, Atlanta, Georgia	Fulton County, Georgia	Co. I, 59th Georgia Infantry	5/24/1864, Bull's Church, Virginia	Died of Unknown Causes, 9/1/1864
Grant, Thomas T. Sergeant	Unk	5/31/1861, Hanover Court House, Virginia	Hanover County, Virginia	Co. H, 22nd Virginia Infantry	9/19/1864, Winchester, Virginia	Died of Chronic Diarrhea, 10/8/1864
Grant, William R. Private	23	7/9/1861, Jackson, North Carolina, Volunteer	Northampton County, North Carolina	Co. H, 2nd North Carolina Cavalry	7/1/1863, Gettysburg, Pennsylvania	Died of Chronic Diarrhea, 11/6/1863
Graves, Alonzo Private	Unk	Unknown	Unknown	Co. K, 66th North Carolina Infantry	1/15/1864, Currituck County, North Carolina	Died of Acute Bronchitis, 4/4/1865

Name	Age	Enlisted	Residence	Unit	Captured	Date and Cause of Death
Graves, David P. Private	Unk	1/1/1862, Camp Trowsdale, Tennessee	Unknown	Co. H, 44th Tennessee Infantry	4/4/1865, Petersburg, Virginia, Wounded	Died of Hospital Gangrene, 5/11/1865
Graves, Francis Private	21	11/12/1861, Currick County, North Carolina, Volunteer	Currick County, North Carolina	Co. B, 8th North Carolina Infantry	9/30/1864, Chaffin's Farm, Near Fort Harrison, Virginia	Died of Pneumonia, 3/17/1865
Gravett, William J. Private	Unk	8/12/1864, Halifax, Virginia, Conscript	Halifax County, Virginia	Co. B, 1st Virginia Infantry	4/2/1865, Petersburg, Virginia	Died of Acute Diarrhea, 6/9/1865
Gray, Baswell C. Private	Unk	5/9/1862, Subligna, Georgia	Chattooga County, Georgia	Co. I, 35th Georgia Infantry	7/3/1863, Gettysburg, Pennsylvania, Wounded	Died of Unknown Causes, 1/31/1864
Gray, Edwin Private	Unk	3/10/1862, Fort Boykin, Virginia	Born Isle of Wight, Virginia	Co. E, 9th Virginia Infantry	7/3/1863, Gettysburg, Pennsylvania	Died of Chronic Diarrhea and Scurvy, 12/12/1863
Gray, John Private	22	3/21/1862, Sweetwater, Tennessee	Monroe County, Tennessee	Co. K, 31st Tennessee Infantry	5/17/1863, Big Black Bridge, Near Vicksburg, Mississippi	Died of Variola (Smallpox), 2/6/1864
Gray, John A. Corporal	21	5/9/1861, Corinth, Mississippi	Alcorn County, Mississippi	Co. I, 12th Mississippi Infantry	5/3/1863, Chancellorsville Virginia, Fractured Skull From A Piece Of Shell	Died of Unknown Causes, 2/23/1864
Gray, Seaborn A. Corporal	36	3/4/1862, Macon, Georgia	Bibb County, Georgia	Co. D, 10th Georgia Infantry	8/17/1864, Deep Bottom, Virginia	Died of Chronic Diarrhea, 10/30/1864
Gray, Solomon Private	Unk	9/22/1863, Princeton, West Virginia	Mercer County, West Virginia	Co. F, 36th Virginia Infantry	9/19/1864, Winchester, Virginia	Died of Chronic Diarrhea, 3/8/1865
Green, B. F. Private	Unk	Unknown	Unknown	Co. I, 38th Georgia Infantry	6/3/1864, Talapatomoy Creek, Bowling Green, Virginia, Deserted To the Enemy	Died of Unknown Causes, 7/24/1864

Name	Age	Enlisted	Residence	Unit	Captured	Date and Cause of Death
Green, Bartley Private	Unk	12/7/1862, Fort Boggs, Georgia	Unknown	Co. A, 18th Georgia Infantry	4/6/1865, High Bridge, Virginia	Died of Chronic Diarrhea, 6/1/1865
Green, Calvin Corporal	19	5/27/1862, Troy, North Carolina, Volunteer	Montgomery County, North Carolina	Co. C, 23rd North Carolina Infantry	7/1/1863, Gettysburg, Pennsylvania	Died of Unknown Causes, 10/17/1863
Green, George W. Corporal	37	3/1/1862, Troy, North Carolina, Volunteer	Montgomery County, North Carolina	Co. H, 44th North Carolina Infantry	10/14/1863, Bristoe Station, Virginia	Died of Pneumonia, 11/28/1863
Green, James M. Private	25	5/14/1862, Grenada, Mississippi	Arkabuta, Mississippi, Farmer	Co. B, 42nd Mississippi Infantry	7/1/1863, Gettysburg, Pennsylvania	Died of Debility From Fever, 1/15/1864
Green, Joel Private	Unk	11/5/1864, Raleigh, Wake County, North Carolina	Wake County, North Carolina	Co. E, 28th North Carolina Infantry	4/2/1865, Petersburg, Virginia	Died of Consumption (Tuberculosis), 5/31/1865
Green, John A. Private Not Listed On Monument	31	5/7/1861, Asheville, North Carolina, Volunteer	Buncombe County, North Carolina	Co. F, 16th North Carolina Infantry	7/3/1863, Gettysburg, Pennsylvania	Died of Chronic Diarrhea & Scurvy, 2/10/1865
Green, John E. Private	Unk	6/13/1861, Monroe, Georgia	Walton County, Georgia	Co. C, 9th Georgia Infantry	7/3/1863, Gettysburg, Pennsylvania	Died of Chronic Diarrhea, 10/23/1863
Green, John P. Private	28	5/12/1862, Shelby, North Carolina, Volunteer	Cleveland County, North Carolina, Farmer	Co. D, 55th North Carolina Infantry	4/3/1865, Amelia Court House, Virginia	Died of Unknown Causes, 6/9/1865
Green, Joseph Private	Unk	Unknown	Watauga, North Carolina	Co. E, 9th Virginia Infantry	4/1/1865, Five Forks, Virginia	Died of Unknown Causes, 5/28/1865
Green, Thomas Private	25	3/26/1862, Shelby, North Carolina, Volunteer	Cleveland County, North Carolina	Co. D, 55th North Carolina Infantry	4/2/1865, Hatcher's Run, Virginia	Died of Typhoid Fever, 5/31/1865

Name	Age	Enlisted	Residence	Unit	Captured	Date and Cause of Death
Green, Thomas C. Private	Unk	2/27/1862, Kentuck, Virginia	Pittsylvania County, Virginia	Co. A, 38th Virginia Infantry	7/3/1863, Gettysburg, Pennsylvania	Died of Unknown Causes, 8/11/1864
Green, Thomas J. Corporal	20	3/4/1862, Wilkinson, Georgia	Wilkinson County, Georgia	Co. A, 49th Georgia Infantry	7/2/1863, Gettysburg, Pennsylvania	Died of Typhoid Fever, 2/9/1865
Green William H. Private	23	7/10/1861, Cumb Gap, Tennessee	Claiborne County, Tennessee	Co. I, Ashby's 2nd Tennessee Cavalry	3/31/1863, Sommersett, Pulaski County, Kentucky	Died of Unknown Causes, 3/19/1864
Green, William J. Private	Unk	5/6/1862, Glasscock, Georgia	Glasscock County, Georgia	Co. B, 22nd Georgia Infantry	7/23/1863, Manassas, Virginia	Died of Smallpox, 12/23/1863
Greenway, A. Clifford Private	Unk	9/14/1862, Columbus County, North Carolina	Columbus County, North Carolina	Co. I, 54th North Carolina Infantry	11/7/1863, Kelly's Ford, Rappahannock Station, Virginia	Died of Unknown Causes, 3/6/1864
Greer, Edmund J. Private Not Listed On Monument	30	3/22/1862, Wilkes County, North Carolina	Wilkes County, North Carolina	Co. B, 55th North Carolina Infantry	7/1/1863, Gettysburg, Pennsylvania	Died of Unknown Causes, 2/13/1864
Greer, John M. Private	Unk	9/1/1862, Virginia	Unknown	Co. C, 8th Virginia Infantry	8/25/1864, Near Howlett's House, Virginia	Died of Unknown Causes, 9/14/1864
Greeson, David Private Not Listed On Monument	37	3/5/1862, Alamance County, North Carolina, Substitute	Guilford County, North Carolina	Co. F, 53rd North Carolina Infantry	7/5/1863, Gettysburg, Pennsylvania, Deserted to the Enemy	Died of Chronic Diarrhea, 11/8/1863
Gregory, Elijah Sergeant	18	5/10/1861, Sampson County, North Carolina, Volunteer	Sampson County, North Carolina, Student	Co. H, 20th North Carolina Infantry	7/1/1863, Gettysburg, Pennsylvania	Died of Unknown Causes, 8/2/1864

Name	Age	Enlisted	Residence	Unit	Captured	Date and Cause of Death
Gregory, John H. Private	Unk	3/4/1862, White County, Georgia	Hall County, Georgia	Co. G, 24th Georgia Infantry	7/3/1863, Gettysburg, Pennsylvania	Died of Variola (Smallpox), 11/28/1863
Gregory, John H. Private	Unk	Unknown	Unknown	Co. C, 8th Virginia Infantry	Unknown	Unable to locate
Gregory, John T. Private	20	3/31/1862, Bertie County, North Carolina	Bertie County, North Carolina	Co. C, 11th North Carolina Infantry	7/3/1863, Gettysburg, Pennsylvania	Died of Variola (Smallpox), 2/10/1864
Gregery, Obadiah Private	Unk	4/27/1862, Richmond, Virginia	Henrico County, Virginia	Co. K, 4th Virginia Cavalry	10/9/1864, Cedar Creek or Strasburg, Virginia	Died of Typhoid Fever, 12/15/1864
Greshsaw, D. Private	Unk	Unknown	Unknown	Co. F, 52nd North Carolina Infantry	Unknown	Unable to Locate
Grey, Alex Private	Unk	1/15/1863. Camp Burney, North Carolina	Unknown	Co. E, 67th North Carolina Whitford's Battery	11/25/1863, Near Greenville, North Carolina	Died of Anasaica (Edema or Swelling of the Legs and Ankles), 9/12/1864
Grice, John E. Private	23	8/12/1861, Camp Butler, South Carolina	Unknown	Co. D, 14th South Carolina Infantry	7/29/1864, Petersburg, Virginia	Died of Chronic Diarrhea, 11/6/1864
Grier, Alfred S. Private	Unk	5/4/1862, Savannah, Georgia	Meriweather County, Georgia	Co. B, 13th Georgia Infantry	7/5/1863, Waterloo, Gettysburg, Pennsylvania	Died of Chronic Diarrhea, 12/21/1863
Grier, E. J. Sergeant	30	3/22/1862, Wilkes County, North Carolina, Volunteer	Wilkes County, North Carolina	Co. B, 55th North Carolina Infantry	7/5/1863, Gettysburg, Pennsylvania	Died of Unknown Causes, 2/15/1864
Grier, Lawrence Private	Unk	4/15/1864, Charlotte, North Carolina	Mecklenburg County, North Carolina	Co. F, 49th North Carolina Infantry	4/1/1865, Southside Railroad, Virginia	Died of Debility (Loss of Strength, Feeble), 6/23/1865

Name	Age	Enlisted	Residence	Unit	Captured	Date and Cause of Death
Griffin, Charles P. Private	Unk	10/8/1862, Raleigh, North Carolina, Conscript	Wake County, North Carolina	Co. B, 43rd North Carolina Infantry	7/5/1863, Gettysburg, Pennsylvania	Died of Chronic Diarrhea, 10/31/1863
Griffin, F. M. Private	Unk	5/5/1864, Centerville, Alabama, Conscript	Centerville, Alabama, Farmer	Co. H, 8th Alabama Infantry	4/3/1865, Captured in Richmond, Virginia, Hospital After Lee's Surrender	Died of Chronic Diarrhea, 6/2/1865
Griffin, Farrington Private	24	2/7/1862, Monroe, North Carolina, Volunteer	Union County, North Carolina, Farmer	Co. B, 43rd North Carolina Infantry	4/2/1865, Petersburg, Virginia	Died of Scurvy, 6/2/1865
Griffin, James Thomas Private Not Listed On Monument	31	10/6/1861, Rutherford County, North Carolina, Volunteer	Rutherford County, North Carolina, Farmer	Co. I, 34th North Carolina Infantry	5/24/1864, North Anna River, Virginia	Died of Inflammation of Liver, 2/5/1865
Griffin, John T. Private	Unk	10/3/1863, Camp Holmes, Raleigh, North Carolina	Wake County, North Carolina	Co. C, 24th North Carolina Infantry	6/17/1864, Near Petersburg, Virginia	Died of Unknown Causes, 8/14/1864
Griffin, John W. Private	Unk	3/4/1862, Dawson, Georgia	Terrell County, Georgia	Co. F, 51st Georgia Infantry	4/6/1865, Farmville, Virginia	Died of Unknown Causes, 6/12/1865
Grimsley, Allen Corporal	28	7/15/1862, Green County, North Carolina, Conscript	Green County, North Carolina	Co. E, 61st North Carolina Infantry	8/26/1863, Battery Wagner, Morris Island, South Carolina	Died of Unknown Causes, 1/24/1864
Grinstead, Joseph Private	18	6/21/1863, Alamance County, North Carolina, Volunteer	Alamance County, North Carolina	Co. K, 6th North Carolina Infantry	11/7/1863, Kelly's Ford, Rappahannock, Virginia	Died of Chronic Diarrhea, 2/20/1865
Grooms, William M. C. Private	Unk	5/9/1862, Reidsville, Georgia	Tattnall County, Georgia	Co. H, 61st Georgia Infantry	11/30/1863, Rapidan River, Virginia	Died of Chronic Diarrhea, 2/16/1865
Groseclose, James Private Not Listed On Monument	Unk	5/22/1861 Rose Hill, Lee County, Virginia	Lee County, Virginia	Co. E, 37th Virginia Infantry	7/3/1863 Gettysburg, Pennsylvania	Died of Chronic Diarrhea, 3/12/1864

Name	Age	Enlisted	Residence	Unit	Captured	Date and Cause of Death
Grover, D. Private	Unk	Unknown	Unknown	Co. H, 61st Tennessee Mounted Infantry	Unknown	Unable to Locate
Grow, Milo W. Private	Unk	3/4/1862, Miller County, Georgia	Albany, Georgia, School Teacher	Co. D, 51st Georgia Infantry	7/3/1863, Gettysburg, Pennsylvania, Wounded	Died of Chronic Diarrhea, 1/24/1864
Grubb, John Private Not Listed On Monument	Unk	5/1/1862, Davidson County, North Carolina	Davidson County, North Carolina	Co. A, 42nd North Carolina Infantry	12/25/1864, Fort Fisher, North Carolina	Died of Unknown Causes, 6/27/1865
Grubbs, Thomas Private	Unk	8/25/1864, Barnwell, South Carolina, Conscript	Barnwell County, South Carolina	Co. C, 1st South Carolina Artillery	3/16/1865, Smith's Ford, Virginia	Died of Chronic Diarrhea, 6/15/1865
Gufford, Seth Private	18	2/15/1862, Kenansville, North Carolina, Volunteer	Duplin County, North Carolina	Co. C, 2nd North Carolina Infantry	11/7/1863, Kelly's Ford, Rappahannock Station, Virginia	Died of Chronic Diarrhea, 2/14/1865
Guillory, Zenon Private Not Listed On Monument	Unk	3/3/1862, St. Landry, Louisiana	St. Landry Parish, Louisiana, Farmer	Co. C, 6th Louisiana Infantry	5/5/1864, Mine Run, Virginia	Died of Intermittent Fever, 7/3/1864
Guinn, Green A. Private Not Listed On Monument	Unk	5/10/1861 Selma, Alabama	Dallas County, Alabama	Co. D, 5th Alabama Infantry	7/2/1863 Gettysburg, Pennsylvania	Died of Remittent Fever, 7/3/1864
Guinn, William Private	27	5/11/1862, Camp Mangum, North Carolina, Volunteer	Johnston County, North Carolina	Co. C, 50th North Carolina Infantry	9/29/1864, Alligator River, Tyrrell County, North Carolina	Died of Scurvy, 6/13/1865
Gullett, Joseph T. Private	16	7/7/1862, Salisbury, North Carolina, Substitute	Davie County, North Carolina	Co. H, 57th North Carolina Infantry	7/5/1863, Gettysburg, Pennsylvania	Died of Chronic Diarrhea, 1/12/1864

Name	Age	Enlisted	Residence	Unit	Captured	Date and Cause of Death
Gum, Abisha R. Private	19	6/11/1861, Hevener's Store, Virginia	Highland County, Virginia, Farm	Co. F, 25th Virginia Infantry	5/6/1864, Wilderness, Virginia	Died of Chronic Diarrhea, 10/24/1864
Gunn, David D. Private	Unk	10/31/1864, Camp Holmes, Raleigh, North Carolina	Wake County, North Carolina	Co. D, 18th North Carolina Infantry	4/2/1865, Petersburg, Virginia	Died of Pneumonia, 4/2/1865
Gunter, Joshua Private	37	3/13/1862, Greenville, Alabama	Butler County, Alabama	Co. K, 33rd Alabama Infantry	12/17/1864, Franklin, Tennessee	Died of Chronic Diarrhea, 6/26/1865
Gunter, W. Joseph Private	Unk	4/15/1861, Edge District, South Carolina	Edge District, South Carolina	Co. M, 7th South Carolina Infantry	10/19/1864, Cedar Creek or Strasburg, Virginia	Died of Chronic Diarrhea, 12/27/1864
Gurkin, James Private	Unk	9/16/1862, Martin County, North Carolina	Martin County, North Carolina	Co. K, 3rd North Carolina Cavalry	10/24/1863, Plymouth, Washington County, North Carolina	Died of Unknown Causes, 9/15/1864
Guyot, Thomas D. Private	20	6/5/1861 Norfolk, Virginia	Chesapeake County, Virginia	Captain Frank Hugar's Company Virginia Light Artillery	4/2/1865, Petersburg, Virginia	Died of Remittent Fever, 5/14/1865
Gwaltney, Benjamin L. W. Corporal Not Listed On Monument	19	6/23/1861 Smithfield, Virginia	Isle of Wight County, Virginia	Co. I, 3rd Virginia Infantry	7/4/1863, Gettysburg, Pennsylvania, Gunshot Wound Right Hand	Died of Chronic Diarrhea & Scurvy, 3/6/1865
Gwaltney, John J. Private Not Listed On Monument	Unk	8/1/1862 Macon, Georgia	Bibb County, Georgia	Co. E, 10th Battalion Georgia Infantry	8/17/1864, Deep Bottom, Virginia	Died of Scurvy, 3/7/1865
Gwinn, William See: Guinn, William				Co. C, 50th North Carolina Infantry		

Name & Rank	Age	Enlisted & Age	Residence	Unit	Captured	Date and Cause of Death
Hackett, James W. Private	44	4/25/1862 Kilmanock, Virginia, Conscript	Caroline County, Virginia, Farmer	Co. H, 40th Virginia Infantry	4/6/1865, Burkesville, Virginia	Died of Chronic Diarrhea, 5/24/1865
Haddon, A. Franklin Private	31	3/19/1862 Abbeville District, South Carolina	Abbeville District, South Carolina	Orr's Regiment 1st South Carolina Rifles	7/14/1863, Falling Waters, Maryland	Died of Typhoid Fever, 2/10/1865
Hager, Henry W. Private	Unk	4/2/1862 Mouth of Indian, Virginia	Tazewell County, Virginia	Co. I, 29th Virginia Infantry	3/8/1865 Petersburg, Virginia	Died of Chronic Diarrhea, 2/12/1865
Haines, Virgil S. Private	Unk	2/4/1864 Charlottesville Virginia	Albemarle County, Virginia	Shank's Virginia Horse Artillery	10/19/1864, Cedar Creek or Strasburg, Virginia	Died of Chronic Dysentery, 2/14/1865
Hair, James A. Private	32	7/4/1862 Salisbury, North Carolina, Volunteer	Iredell County, North Carolina	Co. B, 57th North Carolina Infantry	11/7/1863, Rappahannock Station, Virginia	Died of Chronic Diarrhea, 3/4/1864
Hale, Alison Sergeant	20	9/23/1862 Boon's Creek, Tennessee	Unknown	Co. I, 60th Tennessee Mounted Infantry	5/17/1863, Big Black Bridge, Near Vicksburg, Mississippi	Died of Unknown Causes, 2/7/1864
Hale, Creed Private	Unk	5/1/1862 Norfolk County, Virginia	Norfolk County, Virginia	Co. A, 6th Virginia Infantry	10/27/1864 Burgess' Mill, Near Petersburg, Virginia	Died of Unknown Causes, 3/25/1865
Haley, Samuel M. Private	18	4/24/1861 Charlotte Court House, Virginia	Charlotte County, Virginia Mechanic	Co. K, 18th Virginia Infantry	7/3/1863, Gettysburg, Pennsylvania	Died of Chronic Diarrhea, 2/15/1864
Haley, William H. Private	Unk	5/10/1862 Granville County, North Carolina	Granville County, North Carolina	Co. I, 55th North Carolina Infantry	7/1/1863, Gettysburg, Pennsylvania	Died of Chronic Diarrhea and Scurvy, 11/29/1863
Hall, Andrew Sergeant	Unk	11/3/1861 Dardanelle, Arkansas	Yell County, Arkansas	Co. H, 21st Arkansas Infantry	5/17/1863, Big Black Bridge, Near Vicksburg, Mississippi	Died of Chronic Diarrhea, 11/29/1863

Name & Rank	Age	Enlisted & Age	Residence	Unit	Captured	Date and Cause of Death
Hall, David Private	31	9/5/1862 Raleigh, North Carolina, Conscript	Surry County, North Carolina	Co. A, 2nd North Carolina Infantry	11/7/1863, Rappahannock, Virginia	Died of Unknown Causes, 1/31/1864
Hall, Isaac Private	Unk	12/28/1861 Pee Dee Bridge, Georgetown, South Carolina	Georgetown County, South Carolina	Co. K, 21st South Carolina Infantry	7/10/1863 Morris Island, South Carolina	Died of Unknown Causes, 1/9/1864
Hall, J. Private	Unk	Unknown	Unknown	Co. D, 2nd South Carolina Infantry	Unknown	Unable to Locate
Hall, James Private	Unk	Unknown	Unknown, Mechanic	Co. D, 9th Virginia Infantry	4/1/1865, Five Forks, Virginia	Died of Pneumonia, 5/6/1865
Hall, John Cororal	25	7/22/1861 Fort Boykin, Virginia	Unknown	Co. I, 3rd Virginia Infantry	7/3/1863, Gettysburg, Pennsylvania	Died of Unknown Causes, 2/25/1864
Hall, John A. Corporal	23	6/1/1861 Fayetteville, North Carolina	Cumberland County, North Carolina	Co. F, 24th North Carolina Infantry	6/17/1864 Petersburg, Virginia	Died of Pneumonia, 10/28/1864
Hall, L. W. Private	Unk	11/15/1863 Camp Mercer, Georgia	Unknown	Clinch's Battery, Georgia Light Artillery	12/13/1864 Fort McAllister, Georgia	Died of Chronic Diarrhea, 6/19/1865
Hall, P. J. Private	Unk	Unknown	Unknown	Co. B, 18th Georgia Infantry	8/16/1864 Front Royal, Virginia	Died of Unknown Causes, 10/25/1864
Hall, Robert Private Not Listed On Monument	Unk	10/26/1863 Camp Holmes, Raleigh, North Carolina	Wake County, North Carolina	Co. E, 33rd North Carolina Infantry	5/12/1864 Spotsylvania Court House, Virginia	Died of Unknown Causes 7/13/1864
Hall, Samuel F. Private	Unk	6/30/1861 Berkley County, Virginia	Berkley County, Virginia, Mechanic	Co. D, 27th Virginia Infantry	7/5/1863 Gettysburg, Pennsylvania	Died of Unknown Causes, 3/24/1864

Name & Rank	Age	Enlisted & Age	Residence	Unit	Captured	Date and Cause of Death
Hall, William Private	19	3/4/1862, Albany, Georgia	Johnson County, Georgia	Co. K, Bonaud's Battery, 48th Battalion Georgia Artillery	7/2/1863 Gettysburg, Pennsylvania	Died of Nephritis, 8/30/1863
Hall, William P. Private Not Listed On Monument	Unk	11/8/1863 Pocotaligo, Georgia	Pocotaligo County, Georgia	Co. N, 38th Georgia Infantry	5/21/1864, Milford Station, Virginia	Died of Unknown Causes, 7/27/1864
Halsey, Thomas Private Not Listed On Monument	21	6/28/1861, Grayson County, Virginia	Grayson County, Virginia	Co. I, 51st Virginia Infantry	7/3/1863 Gettysburg, Pennsylvania, Gunshot Wound In Left Groin	Died of Dropsy, 4/23/1865
Halstead, James H. Private	Unk	10/15/1862 Charleston, West Virginia	Kanawha County, West Virginia	Co. C, 36th Virginia Infantry	9/19/1864 Winchester, Virginia	Died of Remittent Fever, 4/4/1865
Ham, John Private	Unk	Unknown	Unknown	Co. B, 7th South Carolina Infantry	Unknown	Unable to Locate
Ham, William H. Private Not Listed On Monument	19	7/5/1861, Buffalo Gap, Virginia	Louisa County, Virginia	Co. D, 44th Virginia Infantry	5/12/1864 Spotsylvania Court House, Virginia	Died of Measles, 7/7/1864
Hamby, A. B. H. Private	Unk	7/1/1863 Charleston, South Carolina	Charleston County, South Carolina, Mechanic	Co. C, 27th South Carolina Infantry	6/24/1864, Near Petersburg, Virginia	Died of Unknown Causes, 8/19/1864
Hames, Gadbury Private	Unk	9/1/1862 Grahamville, South Carolina	Unknown	Co. G, 27th South Carolina Infantry	3/11/1865 Florence, Georgia	Died of Inflammation of Lungs, 4/9/1865
Hames, L. B. Private	Unk	2/17/1863 Charleston, South Carolina	Charleston County, South Carolina	Co. B, 27th South Carolina Infantry	8/21/1864 Globe Tavern, Near Weldon Railroad, Virginia	Died of Scurvy, 4/4/1865

Name & Rank	Age	Enlisted & Age	Residence	Unit	Captured	Date and Cause of Death
Hamilton, Archibald Private	17	1/26/1863 Port Hudson, Louisiana	Unknown	Co. C, 49th Tennessee Infantry	11/30/1864 Franklin, Tennessee	Died of Pneumonia, 5/1/1865
Hamilton, Henry Private	17	6/1/1864 Wilmington, North Carolina	Harnett County, North Carolina, Farmer	Co. H, 3rd North Carolina Junior Reserves	12/25/1864, Fort Fisher, North Carolina	Died of Scurvy, 6/22/1865
Hamilton, John F. Private	19	3/17/1862 Concord, North Carolina	Cabarrus County, North Carolina, Farmer	Co. A, 52nd North Carolina Infantry	7/3/1863 Gettysburg, Pennsylvania	Died of Unknown Causes, 5/28/1864
Hamilton, Thomas J. Sergeant	26	8/31/1861 Memphis, Tennessee	Shelby County, Tennessee	Co. F, 22nd Mississippi Infantry	12/17/1864 Franklin, Tennessee, Gunshot Wound in Left Arm	Died of Acute Dysentery, 4/25/1865
Hamilton, William H. Private	19	3/1/1863 Friar's Point, Mississippi	Unknown	Co. H, 33rd Mississippi Infantry	5/16/1863, Baker's Creek, Champion Hill, Tennessee	Died of Unknown Causes, 10/24/1864
Hamlett, John H. Private	Unk	5/17/1861 Nashville, Tennessee	Davidson County, Tennessee, Mechanic	Co. G, 3rd Tennessee Infantry	5/12/1863 Raymond, Fort Donelson, Mississippi	Dicd of Unknown Causes, 5/2/1864
Hamlett, Robert T. Private	35	3/11/1863, Person County, North Carolina	Unknown	Co. E, 35th North Carolina Infantry	4/2/1865, South Side Railroad, Virginia	Died of Acute Diarrhea, 5/31/1865
Hamlin, James L. Private	Unk	5/13/1862, Macon, Georgia	Bibb County, Georgia	Co. D, 10th Battalion Georgia Infantry	9/10/1864 Petersburg, Virginia	Died of Chronic Dysentery, 2/18/1865
Hammersley Thomas Private	Unk	Unknown	Unknown	Winder's South Carolina Artillery	Unknown	Unable to Locate
Hammock, Lewis L. Private	Unk	8/25/1863 Camp Lee, Virginia, Conscript	Prince Edward County, Virginia	Co. I, 8th Virginia Infantry	4/3/1865 Amelia Court House, Virginia	Died of Chronic Diarrhea, 5/21/1865

Name & Rank	Age	Enlisted & Age	Residence	Unit	Captured	Date and Cause of Death
Hammock, Robert H. Private Not Listed On Monument	Unk	6/11/1861, Geneva, Georgia	Talbot County, Georgia	Co. E, 9th Georgia Infantry	7/3/1863 Gettysburg, Pennsylvania, Wounded	Died of Unknown Causes, 7/15/1864
Hammonds, George Private	Unk	12/1/1863 Butler County, Alabama	Unknown	Co. E, 61st Alabama Infantry	9/19/1864 Winchester, Virginia	Died of Unknown Causes, 1/14/1865
Hamrick, Isaac Private Not Listed On Monument	23	5/12/1862 Shelby, North Carolina, Volunteer	Cleveland County, North Carolina, Farmer	Co. D, 55th North Carolina Infantry	7/14/1863, Falling Waters, Maryland	Died of Unknown Causes, 2/27/1864
Hamrick, James Private	28	5/12/1862 Shelby, North Carolina, Volunteer	Cleveland County, North Carolina	Co. D, 55th North Carolina Infantry	7/1/1863, Gettysburg, Pennsylvania	Died of Unknown Causes, 9/13/1864
Hamrick, William C. Sergeant	23	11/21/1861 Cleveland County, North Carolina, Volunteer	Rutherford County, North Carolina, Farmer	Co. I, 38th North Carolina Infantry	7/2/1863 Gettysburg, Pennsylvania	Died of Unknown Causes, 8/18/1864
Hancock, Lafayette Private Not Listed On Monument	Unk	2/27/1862 Republican Grove, Virginia	Halifax County, Virginia	Co. F, 38th Virginia Infantry	7/3/1863 Gettysburg, Pennsylvania	Died of Smallpox, 1/8/1864
Hancock, Samuel Private	Unk	2/27/1862 Republican Grove, Virginia	Halifax County, Virginia	Co. F, 38th Virginia Infantry	7/3/1863 Gettysburg, Pennsylvania	Date and Cause of Death Unknown
Hancock, William J. Private	20	4/23/1861 Clarksville, Halifax County, North Carolina	Bertie County, North Carolina	Co. G, 3rd North Carolina Cavalry	12/30/1863 Captured Below Greenville, North Carolina	Died of Billious Fever, 2/20/1865
Haney, Samuel J. Private Not Listed On Monument	Unk	5/5/1862, Union County, North Carolina	Union County, North Carolina	Co. I, 53rd North Carolina Infantry	4/2/1865, Petersburg, Virginia	Died of Remittent Fever, 6/25/1865

Name & Rank	Age	Enlisted & Age	Residence	Unit	Captured	Date and Cause of Death
Hanie, Harvey Private Not Listed On Monument	33	8/19/1863, Fort Branch, North Carolina	Wadesboro, Anson County, North Carolina	Co. G, 40th North Carolina Light Artillery	1/15/1865, Fort Fisher, North Carolina, Gunshot Wound Right Side of Chest	Died of Wounds, 3/10/1865
Hankla, Joseph W. Private Not Listed On Monument	Unk	2/11/1863, Arlington, Virginia	Unknown	Co. I, 26th Virginia Infantry	6/13/1864, Gaines Farm, Virginia	Died of Unknown Causes, 7/7/1864
Hanlan, W. H. Private Not Listed On Monument	Unk	Unknown	Unknown	Co. C, 4th Virginia Cavalry	7/3/1863, Gettysburg, Pennsylvania	Died of Unknown Causes, 12/22/1864
Harbinson, H. M. Private	Unk	5/21/1864 Camp Vance, North Carolina	Burke County, North Carolina	Co. E, 3rd North Carolina Junior Reserves	12/25/1864, Fort Fisher, North Carolina	Died of Pneumonia, 1/30/1865
Harcum, Joseph Sergeant	Unk	5/26/1861 Heathsville, Virginia	Unknown	Co. F, 40th Virginia Infantry	7/14/1863, Falling Waters, Maryland	Died of Chronic Diarrhea, 11/2/1863
Harden, Austin W. Corporal	31	7/8/1862, Salisbury, North Carolina, Volunteer	Alamance County, North Carolina, Farmer	Co. I, 57th North Carolina Infantry	7/5/1863 Gettysburg, Pennsylvania	Died of Unknown Causes, 12/22/1863
Harden, H. D. Private	Unk	3/4/1862, Miller County, Georgia	Miller County, Georgia	Co. I, 51st Georgia Infantry	7/3/1863 Emmetsburg, Gettysburg, Pennsylvania	Died of Smallpox, 2/3/1865
Hardin, John J. Private	26	7/3/1864, Iredell County, North Carolina, Volunteer	Iredell County, North Carolina	Co. B, 2nd North Carolina Cavalry	9/10/1864 Petersburg, Virginia	Died of Pneumonia, 2/19/1865
Hardison, Bates B. Private Not Listed On Monument	Unk	2/15/1862 Beaufort County, North Carolina	Beaufort County, North Carolina	Co. I, 40th Regiment, 3rd North Carolina Light Artillery	1/15/1865, Fort Fisher, North Carolina, Gunshot Wound Left Elbow	Died of Encephalitis, 6/26/1865

Name & Rank	Age	Enlisted & Age	Residence	Unit	Captured	Date and Cause of Death
Hardison, Joseph R. Private	31	5/1/1862 Williamston, North Carolina, Volunteer	Martin County, North Carolina	Co. H, 1st North Carolina Infantry	2/23/1864 Near Plymouth, North Carolina	Died of Typhoid-Pneumonia
Hardman, Francis M. Private	Unk	4/28/1862 Marietta, Cobb County, Georgia	Cobb County, Georgia	Phillip's Georgia Legion Infantry	7/3/1863 Gettysburg, Pennsylvania	Died of Unknown Causes, 3/13/1864
Hardman, William Henry Private Not Listed On Monument	Unk	5/10/1863, Camp Berry, Sutton, Virginia	Lewis County, Virginia	Co. I, 31st Virginia Infantry	3/25/1865, Fort Stedman, Near Petersburg, Virginia	Died of Typhoid Fever, 7/10/1865
Hare, Thomas D. Private	Unk	1/23/1862 Cheraw District, South Carolina	Cheraw District, South Carolina	Co. A, 1st South Carolina Infantry	9/7/1863 Morris Island, South Carolina	Died of Chronic Diarrhea, 1/11/1864
Harlow, William H. Private	Unk	4/4/1862 Madison Court House, Virginia	Madison County, Virginia	· Co. C, 4th Virginia Cavalry	7/5/1863 Greencastle, Gettysburg, Pennsylvania	Died of Unknown Causes, 12/?/1863
Harmon, Jesse Private	Unk	Unknown	Unknown	Co. B, 34 Alabama Infantry	12/16/1864 Near Nashville, Tennessee	Died of Chronic Diarrhea, 6/22/1865
Harmon, John G. Private	46	3/18/1862 Cleveland County, North Carolina	Cleveland County, North Carolina, Blacksmith	Co. G, 49th North Carolina Infantry	3/25/1865, Fort Stedman, Near Petersburg, Virginia	Died of Pneumonia, 4/11/1865
Harmon, W. S. Sergeant	Unk	1/7/1862 Camp Hampton, South Carolina	Lancaster County, South Carolina	Co. H, Holcombe's South Carolina Legion Infantry	4/1/1865, Five Forks, Virginia	Died of Unknown Causes, 5/13/1865
Harmond, Joseph G. Private	Unk	3/14/1862 Athens, Alabama	Limestone County, Alabama	Co. F, 9th Alabama Infantry	7/3/1863 Gettysburg, Pennsylvania	Died of Chronic Diarrhea, 4/3/1864
Harney, Daniel Private	Unk	8/19/1862 Richmond, Virginia	Henrico County, Virginia	Co. D, 2nd Maryland Infantry	4/2/1865 Petersburg, Virginia	Died of Chronic Diarrhea, 5/1/1865

Name & Rank	Age	Enlisted & Age	Residence	Unit	Captured	Date and Cause of Death
Harold, Daniel B. Private	Unk	5/24/1861 Lynchburg, Virginia	Franklin County, Virginia	Co. C, 24th Virginia Infantry	7/3/1863 Gettysburg, Pennsylvania, Gunshot Wounds Arm and Right Temple, Fracture Right Parietal Bone of the Skull	Died of Wounds, Date Unknown
Harold, E. Private	Unk	Unknown	Unknown	Co. G, 22nd North Carolina Infantry	Unknown	Unable to Locate
Harold, W. B. See: Harrell, William B.				Co. K, 50th Virginia Infantry		
Harp, Littleton Private	Unk	7/28/1862 Petersburg, Virginia	Chesterfield County, Virginia	Pegram's Company Virginia Light Artillery	12/11/1864 Sussex Court House, Virginia	Died of Chronic Diarrhea, 6/14/1865
Harper, Calvin T. Private	24	7/15/1862 Raleigh, North Carolina, Conscript	Chatham County, North Carolina	Co. A, 5th North Carolina Infantry	7/2/1863 Gettysburg, Pennsylvania	Died of Chronic Diarrhea, 12/7/1863
Harper, F. M. Private	Unk	5/6/1861 Grove Hill, Alabama	Clarke County, Alabama	Co. I, 5th Alabama Infantry	7/5/1863 Waterloo, Pennsylvania	Died of Chronic Diarrhea, 12/8/1864
Harper, F. M. Private Not Listed On Monument	Unk	Unknown	Unknown	Co. C, 1st North Carolina Infantry	5/12/1864, Spotsylvania Court House, Virginia	Died of Canacumoras, 5/24/1864
Harper, Higdon Private	26	3/1/1862 Nash County, North Carolina, Volunteer	Nash County, North Carolina	Co. H, 32nd North Carolina Infantry	5/10/1864, Mine Run, Virginia	Died of Unknown Causes, 5/24/1864

Name & Rank	Age	Enlisted & Age	Residence	Unit	Captured	Date and Cause of Death
Harper, James N. Private	33	2/25/1862 Sandy Creek, North Carolina	Franklin County, North Carolina, Farmer	Co. G, 47th North Carolina Infantry	4/3/1865 Deep Creek, Virginia	Died of Unknown Causes, 6/25/1865
Harper, Joel Private	Unk	3/21/1864 Orange County Court House, North Carolina	Wilson, North Carolina	Co. C, 1st North Carolina Infantry	5/12/1864 Spotsylvania Court House, Virginia	Died of Typhoid Fever 8/7/1864
Harper, John B. Private	20	3/12/1862 Asheboro, North Carolina	Chatham County, North Carolina, Farmer	Co. B, 52nd North Carolina Infantry	10/27/1864 Near Petersburg, Virginia	Died of Chronic Diarrhea, 4/12/1865
Harper, John R. Private	30	9/3/1862 Mocksville, North Carolina	Forsyth County, North Carolina Farmer	Co. G, 7th Confederate Cavalry	9/30/1864 Fort Harrison, Virginia	Died of Chronic Diarrhea, 4/3/1865
Harper, W. J. Private	Unk	3/10/1862 Cahaba, Alabama	Dallas County, Alabama	Co. F, 5th Alabama Infantry	7/2/1863 Gettysburg, Pennsylvania	Died of Chronic Diarrhea, 12/28/1863
Harrell, Ellmanser J. Private Not Listed On Monument	Unk	10/6/1863 McDowell County, North Carolina	McDowell County, North Carolina	Co. G, 22nd North Carolina Infantry	5/23/1864 Jericho Mills, Virginia	Died of Chronic Diarrhea, 1/7/1865
Harrell, John L. Private	Unk	5/30/1861 Weldon, North Carolina	Nansemond County, Virginia	Co. K, 41st Virginia Infantry	6/1/1864 Cold Harbor, Virginia	Died of Smallpox 7/21/1864
Harrell, Joseph S. Private	18	3/1/1862 Gates County, North Carolina	Gates County, North Carolina	Co. E, 33rd North Carolina Infantry	7/14/1863 Falling Waters, Maryland	Died of Chronic Diarrhea, 12/29/1863
Harrell, William B. Private	Unk	4/26/1862, Patrick County, Virginia	Patrick County, Virginia	Co. K, 50th Virginia Infantry	7/4/1863 Gettysburg, Pennsylvania	Died of Acute Diarrhea, 12/1/1864
Harrelson, William Private	Unk	Unknown	Unknown	Co. K, 1st South Carolina Artillery	Unknown	Unable to Locate

Name & Rank	Age	Enlisted & Age	Residence	Unit	Captured	Date and Cause of Death
Haroldson, Edward F. Private	Unk	Unknown	Unknown	Co. B, 1st South Carolina Infantry	4/2/1865 Burkesville, Virginia	Died of Chronic Diarrhea, 6/23/1865
Harris, Columbus R. Private Not Listed On Monument	Unk	7/3/1861, Lynchburg, Virginia	Franklin County, Virginia	Co. G, 42nd Virginia Infantry	5/12/1864 Spotsylvania Court House, Virginia	Died of Unknown Causes 7/7/1864
Harris, Francis A. Private	36	2/1/1862 Edenton, North Carolina, Volunteer	Chowan County, North Carolina	Co. A, 1st North Carolina Infantry	7/3/1863 Gettysburg, Pennsylvania	Died of Unknown Causes, 12/21/1863
Harris, Henry Private	20	10/1/1861 Marshall, Texas	Marshall, Harrison County, Texas	Co. C, 7th Texas Infantry	5/12/1863 Raymond, Mississippi Near Vicksburg	Died of Unknown Causes, 10/?/1863
Harris, J. D. Sergeant	Unk	7/29/1861 Fredonia, Alabama	Chambers County, Alabama	Co. D, 14th Alabama Infantry	7/3/1863 Gettysburg, Pennsylvania	Died of Chronic Diarrhea, 11/7/1863
Harris, J. P. Private	37	3/13/1862 Rutherford, North Carolina	Unknown	Co. G, 16th North Carolina Infantry	5/24/1864 North Anna River, Virginia	Died of Unknown Causes, 8/14/1864
Harris, James M. Private	Unk	Unknown	Unknown	Co. D, 1st Virginia Infantry	Unknown	Unable to Locate
Harris, John Private	Unk	3/4/1864 Franklin, North Carolina	Macon County, North Carolina	Co. I, 55th North Carolina Infantry	4/2/1865 Hatcher's Run, Virginia	Died of Chronic Diarrhea, 4/23/1865
Harris, John H. Sergeant	23	4/13/1861 Barnes Crossroads, Greenville, Alabama	Butler County, Alabama	Co. F, 7th Alabama Infantry	6/27/1863 Shelbyville, Tennessee	Died of Chronic Diarrhea, 1/4/1864
Harris, John N. Private	28	8/16/1861 Warren County, North Carolina, Volunteer	Warren County, North Carolina	Co. B, 30th North Carolina Infantry	11/7/1863 Kelly's Ford, Rappahannock, Virginia	Died of Unknown Causes, 8/12/1864

Name & Rank	Age	Enlisted & Age	Residence	Unit	Captured	Date and Cause of Death
Harris, Manhonel H. Private Not Listed On Monument	25	12/5/1861, Sae River, Greene County, Missouri	Unknown	Co. K, 1st Missouri Cavalry	5/17/1863, Big Black Bridge, Near Vicksburg, Mississippi	Died of Unknown Causes, 12/22/1863
Harris, Martin Private	Unk	5/1/1863 Adam's Run, South Carolina	Unknown	Co. K, Holcombe's Legion, South Carolina Infantry	4/1/1865 Five Forks, Virginia	Died of Chronic Diarrhea, 5/24/1865
Harris, Reuben Sergeant	35	3/25/1862 Albemarle, North Carolina, Volunteer	Stanly County, North Carolina, Farmer	Co. I, 52nd North Carolina Infantry	7/3/1863 Gettysburg, Pennsylvania	Died of Chronic Diarrhea, 11/11/1863
Harris, Thomas J. Private	Unk	6/11/1863 James Island, South Carolina	Charleston District, South Carolina	Co. E, 2nd South Carolina Artillery	3/10/1865 Near Goldsboro, North Carolina	Died of Pleurisy, 4/28/1865
Harris, Thomas C. Corporal	29	4/28/1862 Perquimans County, North Carolina, Volunteer	Perquimans County, North Carolina	Co. F, 11th North Carolina Infantry	10/27/1864, Near Petersburg, Virginia	Died of Unknown Causes, 1/2/1865
Harris, Thomas C. Sergeant	Unk	9/24/1861 Hall & Guinnett Counties, Georgia	Hall County, Georgia	Co. H, 35th Georgia Infantry	3/25/1865, Fort Stedman, Near Petersburg, Virginia	Died From Inflammation of Lungs (Pneumonia), 4/10/1865
Harris, Thomas F. Private	Unk	3/12/1862 Danville, Virginia	Pittsylvania County, Virginia	Co. A, 18th Virginia Infantry	7/3/1863 Gettysburg, Pennsylvania	Died of Unknown Causes, 3/11/1864
Harris, W. Private	Unk	Unknown	Unknown	Co. K, 1st Mississippi Cavalry	Unknown	Unable to Locate
Harris, William Private	27	5/13/1862 Greensboro, Guilford County, North Carolina	Guilford County, North Carolina	Co. F, 54th North Carolina Infantry	11/7/1863, Kelly's Ford, Rappahannock, Virginia	Died of Unknown Causes, 2/10/1864
Harris, William Private	Unk	11/1/1863 Germantown, North Carolina	Unknown	Co. G, 21st North Carolina Infantry	5/22/1864, North Anna River, Virginia	Died of Chronic Diarrhea, 8/20/1864

Name & Rank	Age	Enlisted & Age	Residence	Unit	Captured	Date and Cause of Death
Harris, William H. Private	34	7/15/1862 Raleigh, North Carolina, Conscript	Pitt County, North Carolina	Co. D, 3rd North Carolina Infantry	11/28/1863 Mine Run, Virginia	Died of Unknown Causes, 3/24/1865
Harrison, Alvin M. Private	39	1/20/1862 New Hope, North Carolina, Volunteer	Wake County, North Carolina, Miller	Co. I, 47th North Carolina Infantry	7/3/1863 Gettysburg, Pennsylvania	Died of Chronic Diarrhea, 12/30/1863
Harrison, Benjamin W. Private	16	9/22/1863 Petersburg, Virginia	Chesterfield County, Virginia	Co. G, 53rd Virginia Infantry	4/1/1865 Five Forks, Virginia	Died of Pneumonia, 4/25/1865
Harrison, Christopher C. Private	25	7/1/1861 Carthage, North Carolina, Volunteer	Moore County, North Carolina	Co. H, 26th North Carolina Infantry	10/27/1864 Burgess Mill, Near Petersbug, Virginia	Died of Unknown Causes, 2/14/1865
Harrison, Samuel D. Private	17	3/12/1862 Homer, Louisiana	Homer, Louisiana, Printer	Co. A, 9th Louisiana Infantry	9/22/1864 Fisher's Hill, Cedar Creek or Strasburg, Virginia	Died of Unknown Causes, 1/24/1865
Harrison, W. H. Private	Unk	Unknown	Unknown	Co. A, Mosby's Partisan Rangers, Virginia, Cavalry	8/4/1863 Rectortown, Virginia	Died of Unknown Causes, 1/6/1864
Harrison, William Private	Unk	8/18/1864 Andersonville, Georgia	Unknown	Co. G, Fannin's 1st Georgia Reserves	12/19/1864 Near Savannah, Georgia	Died of Chronic Diarrhea, 5/31/1865
Harrison, Wilson Samuel Private Not Listed On Monument	Unk	5/26/1864 Bluffton, South Carolina, Conscript	Unknown	Co. K, 1st South Carolina Artillery	3/16/1865, Near Smithville, North Carolina	Died of Pneumonia, 4/14/1865
Harriss, Charles E. Private	17	3/30/1861 Littleton, North Carolina, Volunteer	Warren County, North Carolina	Co. A, 14th North Carolina Infantry	7/14/1863 Williamsport, Maryland	Died of Unknown Causes, 2/6/1864

Name & Rank	Age	Enlisted & Age	Residence	Unit	Captured	Date and Cause of Death
Harrold, Edward F. Private Not Listed On Monument	Unk	Unknown	Unknown	Co. B, 1st South Carolina Infantry	9/2/1865, Burkeville, Virginia	Died of Chronic Diarrhea, 6/23/1865
Harrold, William B. Private Not Listed On Monument	Unk	Unknown	Unknown	Co. K, 50th Virginia Infantry	7/4/1863 Gettysburg, Pennsylvania	Died of Acute Diarrhea, 12/1/1864
Harry, John W. Private Not Listed On Monument	Unk	5/9/1861 Lynchburg, Virginia	Franklin County, Virginia	Co. D, 1st Battalion Virginia Infantry	4/6/1865, Amelia County, Virginia	Died of Unknown Causes, 5/8/1865
Hart, T. C. Sergeant	Unk	4/11/1862 Coles Island, South Carolina	Jasper County, South Carolina	Co. G, 27th South Carolina Infantry	8/21/1864 Globe Tavern, Near Weldon Railroad, Virginia	Died of Acute Diarrhea, 12/17/1864
Hart, William Private	Unk	10/21/1861 Camp Near Point Gap, Virginia	Unknown	Co. H, 5th Kentucky Mounted Infantry	Unknown	Died of Unknown Causes, 3/30/1862 on Stony Creek, Virginia
Hartgrove, Richard D. S. Private	23	2/27/1862, Charlotte, North Carolina, Volunteer	Mecklenburg County, North Carolina	Co. E, 11th North Carolina Infantry	10/27/1864 Burgess' Hill, Near Petersburg, Virginia	Died of Pneumonia, 3/19/1865
Hartless, Dabney Private	Unk	7/2/1861 Bethel, Virginia	Hampton County, Virginia	Co. F, 50th Virginia Infantry	5/12/1864 Near Spotsylvania Court House, Virginia	Died of Pneumonia, 10/29/1864
Hartly, Alexander L. Private	24	9/14/1861 Boone, North Carolina, Volunteer	Watauga, North Carolina, Farmer	Co. B, 37th North Carolina Infantry	7/3/1863 Gettysburg, Pennsylvania	Died of Chronic Diarrhea & Diphtheria, 11/7/1863

Name & Rank	Age	Enlisted & Age	Residence	Unit	Captured	Date and Cause of Death
Harvey, George W. Private	Unk	2/26/1862 Dragoon Camp, Alabama	Unknown	Co. E, 7th Mobile Dragoons Alabama Mounted Volunteers	6/27/1863 Shelbyville, Tennessee	Died of Unknown Causes, 8/9/1864
Harvey, George W. Private	Unk	1/10/1862 Columbia, South Carolina	Richland County, South Carolina	Co. D, 22nd South Carolina Infantry	6/3/1864 Near Bermuda Hundred, Virginia	Died of Scurvy, 4/1/1865
Harvey, James S. Private	Unk	5/1/1862 Snapping Shoals, Georgia	Newton County, Georgia	Co. B, 53rd Georgia Infantry	4/6/1865, Harper's Farm, Virginia	Died of Unknown Causes, 6/25/1865
Harvey, John M. Private	Unk	5/15/1862 Camp Success, Virginia	Unknown	Co. E, 4th Virginia Infantry	5/12/1864 Spotsylvania Court House, Virginia	Died of Acute Dysentery, 8/26/1864
Harvy, Joel Private	16	8/1/1864 Fort Fisher, North Carolina	Elizabethtown Bladen County, North Carolina	Co. H, 36th North Carolina Heavy Artillery	1/15/1865 Fort Fisher, North Carolina	Died of Pneumonia, 2/12/1865
Harwood, Reding Private	Unk	11/7/1863 Albemarle, North Carolina	Unknown	Co. K, 28th North Carolina Infantry	5/12/1864 Wilderness, Virginia	Died of Unknown Causes, 6/2/1864
Harwood, William H. Private	26	5/9/1861 Charles City Court House, Virginia	Charles City County, Virginia	Co. D, 3rd Virginia Cavalry	7/4/1863 Gettysburg, Pennsylvania	Died of Unknown Causes, 3/31/1864
Hash, Byronn B. Private	19	6/4/1861 Fork of Wilson, Virginia	Grayson County, Virginia, Laborer	Co. B, 50th Virginia Infantry	7/4/1863 Cashtown, Pennsylvania	Died of Smallpox, 1/26/1864
Hashbarger, George W. Private	Unk	12/27/1862 West Point, Tennessee	Unknown	Co. K, 48th Tennessee Infantry	6/23/1864 Marietta Georgia	Died of Scurvy, 5/23/1865
Haskey, James Private	Unk	Unknown	Unknown	Coleman's Virginia Battery	Unknown	Unable to Locate

Name & Rank	Age	Enlisted & Age	Residence	Unit	Captured	Date and Cause of Death
Hass, R. M. Private	Unk	9/6/1862 Statesville, North Carolina, Conscript	Catawba County, North Carolina	Co. A, 23rd North Carolina Infantry	7/1/1863 Gettysburg, Pennsylvania	Died of Smallpox, 10/21/1863
Hasty, Samuel W. Private	30	7/17/1862 Raleigh, North Carolina, Conscript	Richmond County, North Carolina	Co. G, 2nd North Carolina Infantry	4/3/1865 Richmond, Virginia, Captured After Lee's Surrender	Died of Bronchitis, 6/19/1865
Hatfield, Joshua Private	25	7/24/1861 Newland, North Carolina, Volunteer	Perquitank County, North Carolina, Laborer	Co. A, 8th North Carolina Infantry	9/30/1864 Fort Harrison, Virginia	Died of Chronic Dysentery, 2/19/1865
Hauldron, George W. Private	Unk	2/25/1862 Bedford County, Virginia	Unknown	Co. C, 20th Battalion Virginia Heavy Artillery	4/6/1865 Burkesville, Virginia	Died of Paralysis, 4/30/1865
Havens, George F. Private	Unk	8/8/1863 Tazwell County, Virginia	Unknown	Co. F, 22nd Virginia Cavalry	9/19/1864 Winchester, Virginia	Died of Consumption, 2/28/1865
Hawkins, Lewis P. Private	Unk	12/14/1863 Monroe County, Virginia	Monroe County, Virginia	Co. K, 22nd Virginia Infantry	9/22/1864 Fisher's Hill, Virginia	Died Typhoid Fever, 11/6/1864
Hawkins, Thomas Private	Unk	7/8/1862 Hillsboro, North Carolina	Unknown	Co. F, 33rd North Carolina Infantry	5/6/1864, Wilderness, Virginia	Died of Chronic Diarrhea, 10/25/1864
Hawkins, William D. Corporal	Unk	6/4/1861 Republican Grove, Virginia	Halifax County, Virginia	Co. F, 38th Virginia Infantry	7/3/1863 Gettysburg, Pennsylvania	Died of Chronic Diarrhea, 12/18/1863
Hawks, Frederick B. Private	Unk	4/30/1862 Norfolk, Virginia	Chesapeake County, Virginia	Co. H, 9th Virginia Infantry	4/1/1865, Five Forks, Virginia	Died of Typhoid Fever, 5/15/1865
Hawley, Ransom F. Private Not Listed On Monument	25	5/10/1861 Newton Grove, Sampson County, North Carolina, Volunteer	Sampson County, North Carolina, Cooper	Co. H, 20th North Carolina Infantry	5/12/1864 Near Spotsylvania Court House, Virginia	Died of Unknown Causes, 7/15/1864

Name & Rank	Age	Enlisted & Age	Residence	Unit	Captured	Date and Cause of Death
Haws, Joseph M. Private	22	11/25/1862 Rowlands, Virginia	Greenbrier County, Virginia, Farmer	Co. K, 14th Virginia Cavalry	5/1/1863 Greenbrier County, West Virginia	Died of Unknown Causes, 12/12/1863
Hawthorne, Samuel S. Private	18	7/24/1861 Abingdon, Virginia	Washington County, Virginia	Co. H, 37th Virginia Infantry	7/4/1863 Gettysburg, Pennsylvania	Died of Chronic Diarrhea, 1/5/1864
Hawthorne, Thomas M. Private	19	7/20/1861 Camp Pickens, Anderson District, South Carolina	Unknown	Co. G, Orr's Regiment 1st South Carolina Rifles	7/14/1863, Falling Waters, Maryland	Died of Chronic Diarrhea, 3/16/1864
Haydon, W. See: Herden, William				Co. K, 21st Virginia Cavalry		
Hayes, Calvin Sergeant	22	6/12/1861, Weldon, North Carolina, Volunteer	Yates County, North Carolina	Co. B, 5th North Carolina Infantry	7/2/1863 Gettysburg, Pennsylvania	Died of Smallpox, 10/21/1863
Hayes, Hayden Private	Unk	5/16/63 Hanover Court House, Virginia	Unknown	Johnson's Company, Stuart's Horse Artillery, Virginia	10/9/1864, Cedar Creek or Strasburg, Virginia	Died of Chronic Diarrhea, 5/8/1865
Hayes, Joseph Private Not Listed On Monument	Unk	6/6/1864 Petersburg, Virginia	Chesterfield County, Virginia	Co. D, 42nd North Carolina Infantry	4/?/1864 Petersburg, Virginia	Died of Unknown Causes, 7/30/1864
Haynes, Addison Private	Unk	6/12/1861, Center Cross, Virginia	Essex County, Virginia	Co. G, 55th Virginia Infantry	7/14/1863, Falling Waters, Maryland	Died of Chronic Diarrhea & Erysipelas 12/8/1863
Haynes, Virgil S. Private Not Listed On Monument	Unk	2/4/1864, Charlottesville Virginia	Albemarle County, Virginia	Johnson's Company, Stuart's Horse Artillery, Virginia	10/9/1864, Cedar Creek or Strasburg, Virginia	Died of Chronic Dysentery, 2/13/1865

Name & Rank	Age	Enlisted & Age	Residence	Unit	Captured	Date and Cause of Death
Haynie, Yarrett Private	Unk	3/8/1862 Farnham Church, Camp Lewis, Virginia	Unknown	Co. K, 9th Virginia Cavalry	7/3/1863 Gettysburg, Pennsylvania	Died of Chronic Diarrhea, 11/14/1863
Hays, Calvin Sergeant	22	6/12/1861 Weldon, North Carolina, Volunteer	Yates County, North Carolina, Farmer	Co. B, 5th North Carolina Infantry	7/2/1863 Gettysburg, Pennsylvania	Died of Smallpox, 10/21/1863
Hays, John Private	Unk	Unknown	Unknown	Co. A, 26th Virginia Infantry	Unknown	Unable to Locate
Hays, N. Private	Unk	6/6/1864 Petersburg, Virginia	Chesterfield County, Virginia	Co. H, 42nd North Carolina Infantry	6/15/1864 Petersburg, Virginia	Died of Unknown Causes, 7/30/1864
Hays, Samuel L. Private	17	1/14/1862 Springfield, Missouri	Savannah, Andrew County, Missouri, Farmer	Co. D, 3rd Battalion, Missouri Cavalry	5/17/1863, Big Black Bridge, Near Vicksburg, Mississippi	Died of Chronic Diarrhea, 12/261863
Hays, Thomas Private	Unk	Unknown	Unknown	Co. K, 30th Battalion Georgia Infantry	2/12/1865 Orangeburg, South Carolina	Died of Chronic Diarrhea, 4/6/1865
Hazlewood, Asa Private Not Listed On Monument	Unk	4/5/1864, Camp Stokes, North Carolina	Unknown	Co. I, 34th North Carolina Infantry	5/23/1864, North Anna River, Virginia	Died of Unknown Causes 7/4/1864
Healey, Albert Private	Unk	Unknown	Unknown	Co. E, 3rd Alabama Cavalry	6/27/1863, Shelbyville, Tennessee	Died of Unknown Causes, 12/3/1863
Hearn, David W. Private Not Listed On Monument	Unk	4/3/1864, Camp Holmes, Raleigh, North Carolina	Wake County, North Carolina	Co. C, 38th North Carolina Infantry	5/23/1864, Beaver Dam, North Anna River, Virginia	Died of Unknown Causes 7/4/1864

Name & Rank	Age	Enlisted & Age	Residence	Unit	Captured	Date and Cause of Death
Heart, Wyatt Private	28	6/20/1861 Alamance County, North Carolina, Volunteer	Alamance County, North Carolina	Co. K, 6th North Carolina Infantry	11/7/1863 Rappahannock Station, Virginia	Died of Unknown Causes, 4/4/1864
Heath, Richard T. Private	25	5/24/1861 Newbern, North Carolina, Substitute	Craven County, North Carolina	Co. F, 2nd North Carolina Infantry	11/7/1863, Rappahannock Station, Virginia	Died of Chronic Diarrhea, 4/24/1865
Heaton, C. T. Private	25	7/26/1861 Hilton Head, South Carolina	Beaufort District, South Carolina	Co. H, 11th South Carolina Infantry	6/18/1864, Near Petersburg, Virginia	Died of Scrofula, 12/5/1864
Hedden, John S. Private	24	5/1/1861 Tippah County, Mississippi	Unknown	Co. F, 2nd Mississippi Infantry	7/14/1863, Falling Waters, Maryland	Died of Unknown Causes, 1/7/1864
Hedgepeth, Arch B. Private	Unk	5/5/1862 Lumberton, Robeson County, North Carolina	Robeson County, North Carolina	Co. B, 50th North Carolina Infantry	3/12/1865, Fayetteville, North Carolina	Died of Chronic Diarrhea, 4/27/1865
Hedrick, Samuel Seaman	Unk	Unknown	Unknown	Naval Battalion, Confederate States Navy	Unknown	Unable to Locate
Hefner, John Marcus Private	Unk	7/7/1862 Newton, Catawba County, North Carolina	Catawba County, North Carolina	Co. E, 57th North Carolina Infantry	6/6/1864, Cold Harbor, Virginia	Died of Unknown Causes, 7/27/1864
Helton, Alfred F. Private	Unk	2/28/1863 Fredericksburg Virginia, Volunteer	Catawba County, North Carolina, Volunteer	Co. F, 23rd North Carolina Infantry	7/1/1863, Gettysburg, Pennsylvania	Died of Unknown Causes, 7/30/1864
Henderson, Ezekiel Private	30	4/27/1863 Buncombe County, North Carolina, Volunteer	Buncombe County, North Carolina	Co. K, 11th North Carolina Infantry	10/27/1864, Petersburg, Virginia, Shell Wound Left Thigh	Died of Chronic Diarrhea, 4/28/1865
Henderson, J. L. Private	Unk	Unknown	Unknown	Co. M, 6th Tennessee Infantry	Unknown	Unable to Locate

Name & Rank	Age	Enlisted & Age	Residence	Unit	Captured	Date and Cause of Death
Hazlewood, Asa Private Not Listed On Monument	Unk	4/5/1864, Camp Stokes, North Carolina	Unknown	Co. I, 34th North Carolina Infantry	5/23/1864, North Anna River, Virginia	Died of Unknown Causes 7/4/1864
Henderson, Joseph E. Private	Unk	4/16/1862 Giles County, Virginia	Giles County, Virginia	Co. I, 36th Virginia Infantry	9/19/1865 Winchester, Virginia	Died of Chronic Diarrhea, 1/29/1865
Henderson, Thomas M. Private	22	2/1/1862 Charlotte, North Carolina, Volunteer	Mecklenburg County, North Carolina	Co. A, 11th North Carolina Infantry	7/14/1863, Falling Waters, Maryland	Died of Unknown Causes, 2/9/1864
Hendrick, William W. Private	Unk	9/8/1863 Columbia, South Carolina	Richland County, South Carolina	Co. C, 22nd South Carolina Infantry	7/30/1864, Petersburg, Virginia	Died of Chronic Diarrhea, 10/26/1864
Hendricks, Eusebeous S. Private	19	3/29/1862 X-Roads, North Carolina	Cleveland County, North Carolina, Farmer	Co. C, 55th North Carolina Infantry	7/3/1863, Gettysburg, Pennsylvania	Died of Acute Rheumatism, 10/30/1863
Hendricks, James M. Private	23	9/16/1861 Mecklenburg County, North Carolina, Volunteer	Cabarrus County, North Carolina, Farmer	Co. C, 37th North Carolina Infantry	4/2/1865, Petersburg, Virginia	Died of Pneumonia, 6/12/1865
Hendricks, James W. Private Not Listed On Monument	Unk	6/10/1861, Fort Ganes, Bullock County, Georgia	Bulloch County, Georgia	Co. I, 9th Georgia Infantry	7/5/1863, Gettysburg, Pennsylvania	Died of Unknown Causes Date Unknown
Hendrix, Nathaniel Sergeant	21	5/1/1862 Winston, Forsyth County, North Carolina, Volunteer	Forsyth County, North Carolina	Co. K, 48th North Carolina Infantry	5/6/1865 Petersburg, Virginia, Deserted to the Enemy	Died of Chronic Diarrhea, 5/6/1865
Hendry, Harrison H. Sergeant	Unk	5/6/1864 Quitman, Georgia	Brooks County, Georgia	Co. E, 1st Battalion Georgia Reserves	12/13/1864 Fort McAllister, Georgia	Died of Consumption, 4/15/1865
Henning, George W. Private	Unk	5/4/1861 Charleston, South Carolina	Charleston County, South Carolina	Co. B, 15th Battalion South Carolina Heavy Artillery	3/13/1861 Fayetteville, North Carolina	Died of Acute Diarrhea, 6/17/1865

Name & Rank	Age	Enlisted & Age	Residence	Unit	Captured	Date and Cause of Death
Henry, Thadeus Private	18	3/21/1861 Raleigh, North Carolina, Volunteer	Wake County, North Carolina, Laborer	Co. K, 14th North Carolina Infantry	7/3/1863 Gettysburg, Pennsylvania	Died of Chronic Diarrhea, 3/5/1865
Herden, William, Private Not Listed On Monument	Unk	Unknown	Unknown	Co. K, 21st Virginia Cavalry	11/12/1864, Nineveh, Virginia	Died of Acute Dysentery, 1/5/1865
Herl, John Private	25	6/4/1861, Camp Moore, Louisiana	Unknown	Co. K, 5th Louisiana Infantry	5/5/1864, Wilderness, Virginia	Died of Unknown Causes, 2/27/1865
Herndon, George W. Private	Unk	7/27/1861 Union Mills, Virginia	Unknown	Co. K, 6th Alabama Infantry	7/2/1863 Gettysburg, Pennsylvania	Died of Unknown Causes, 11/14/1863
Herndon, John W. Private	Unk	5/1/1864 Franklin, Alabama	Henry County, Alabama	Co. K, 6th Alabama Infantry	3/25/1865, Fort Stedman, Near Petersburg, Virginia	Died of Unknown Causes, 5/10/1865
Herndon, William G. Private	Unk	3/1/1863 Chester Station, Virginia, Conscript	Unknown	Co. I, 7th Virginia Infantry	4/6/1865 Harper's Farm, Virginia	Died of Inflammation of the Lungs (Pneumonia), 6/12/1865
Herring, Alexander Private	31	7/4/1862 Turkey, North Carolina, Volunteer	Duplin County, North Carolina, Farmer	Co. G, 61st North Carolina Infantry	8/27/1863, Morris Island, South Carolina	Died of Chronic Diarrhea, 12/26/1863
Herring, Lewis Corporal	Unk	3/4/1862 Albany, Georgia	Dougherty County, Georgia	Co. K, 51st Georgia Infantry	7/5/1863, Cashtown, Pennsylvania	Died of Chronic Diarrhea, 12/8/1863
Hersey, George Private	Unk	Unknown, South Carolina Conscript	Unknown	Co. F, 1st South Carolina Artillery	3/6/1865, Bennettsville, South Carolina	Died of Scurvy 5/9/1865
Hester, Joseph B. Private	Unk	10/1/1863, Rapidan Station, Virginia	Unknown	Co. M, 55th Georgia Infantry	8/19/1864, Globe Tavern, Near Weldon Railroad, Virginia	Died of Chronic Diarrhea, 3/23/1865

Name & Rank	Age	Enlisted & Age	Residence	Unit	Captured	Date and Cause of Death
Hester, L. J. Private	Unk	4/30/1863 Marion, Virginia	Smyth County, Virginia	Co. F, 23rd Virginia Infantry	9/19/1864, Winchester, Virginia	Died of Remittent Fever, 2/2/1865
Hester, Thomas Private	Unk	5/8/1862 Macon, Georgia	Hancock County, Georgia	Co. E, 15th Georgia Infantry	7/3/1863, Gettysburg, Pennsylvania	Died of Chronic Diarrhea, 12/31/1863
Hewett, James H. Private	Unk	2/18/1863 Fort Caswell, North Carolina	Brunswick County, North Carolina	Co. K, 36th North Carolina Heavy Artillery	1/13/1865, Fort Fisher, North Carolina	Died of Consumption, 2/27/1865
Hewitt, John Private	Unk	Unknown	Unknown	Co. E, 8th Virginia Infantry	Unknown	Unable to Locate
Hibberts, Cornelius Private	23	7/29/1861 Cherokee, North Carolina	Cherokee, North Carolina	Co. H, Walker's Battalion, Thomas Legion, North Carolina Infantry	9/19/1864, Winchester, Virginia	Died of Pneumonia, 2/14/1865
Hickmen, Henry Private Not Listed On Monument	24	2/19/1862 Smithville, North Carolina, Volunteer	Shallotte, North Carolina, Farmer	Co. K, 36th North Carolina Heavy Artillery	1/15/1865, Fort Fisher, North Carolina, Gunshot Wound Right Arm, Arm Amputated	Died of Pyaemia, Bacterial Disease of the Blood, 2/7/1865
Hicks, Augustus Private	21	8/5/1861, Wake County, North Carolina	Wake County, North Carolina	Co. I, 1st North Carolina Infantry	5/12/1864, Spotsylvania Court House, Virginia	Died of Unknown Causes, 8/21/1864
Hicks, George M. Private	38	3/3/1862 Union Hill, North Carolina, Volunteer	Franklin County, North Carolina, Farmer	Co. G, 47th North Carolina Infantry	7/3/1863, Gettysburg, Pennsylvania	Died of Chronic Diarrhea, 2/25/1865
Hicks, John O. Private	Unk	5/23/1863 Richmond, Virginia	Henrico County, Virginia	Co. B, James City Virginia Artillery	4/6/1865, Burkesville, Virginia	Died of Acute Diarrhea, 5/23/1865
Hicks, John S. Private	Unk	3/15/1862 Kittrell's, Granville County, North Carolina, Volunteer	Granville County, North Carolina	Co. G, 23rd North Carolina Infantry	7/1/1863, Gettysburg, Pennsylvania	Died of Unknown Causes, 7/27/1864

Name & Rank	Age	Enlisted & Age	Residence	Unit	Captured	Date and Cause of Death
Hicks, Richard L. Private	23	5/15/1861 Camp Fair, New Madrid, Missouri	Unknown	Co. G, 6th Tennessee Infantry	1/9/1863, Stone's River, Tennessee	Died of Chronic Diarrhea, 2/3/1864
Hide, R. H. See: Hyde, Reuben H.				Co. K, 11th South Carolina Rifles		
Hiers, William J. Private	Unk	12/6/1861 Colleton, South Carolina	Colleton County, South Carolina	Co. K, 11th South Carolina Infantry	2/20/1865, Town Creek, Near Fort Anderson, North Carolina	Died of Pneumonia, 3/22/1865
Higgins, Joseph W. Private Not Listed On Monument	37	3/8/1862, Johnston County, North Carolina	Johnston County, North Carolina, Farmer	Co. D, 47th North Carolina Infantry	7/3/1863, Gettysburg, Pennsylvania, Gunshot Wound Left Leg, Fractured Femur	Died of Wounds, 12/30/1863
Hightower, A. T. Private	Unk	Unknown	Unknown	Co. E, 2nd Georgia Infantry	Unknown	Unable to Locate
Hightower, John L. Private	25	2/27/1862 Vernon, Louisiana	Vernon Parish, Louisiana	Co. H, 12th Louisiana Infantry	5/16/1863, Champion Hill, Tennessee	Died of Chronic Diarrhea, 12/12/1863
Hightower, P. Private	Unk	4/1/1863 Vicksburg, Mississippi	Unknown	Co. F, 62nd Tennessee Infantry	5/17/ 1863, Big Black Bridge, Near Vicksburg, Mississippi	Died of Unknown Causes 11/29/1863
Higins, Joseph W. Private	37	3/18/1862 Johnson's County, North Carolina	Johnson's County, North Carolina, Farmer	Co. K, 47th North Carolina Infantry	7/3/1863, Gettysburg, Pennsylvania, Gunshot Wound Left Leg, Facture Left Femur	Died of Wounds, 12/30/1863
Hill, Daniel J. Private	Unk	1/10/1864, Fort Caswell, North Carolina	Brunswick County, North Carolina	Co. D, 40th Regiment, 3rd North Carolina Light Artillery	1/15/1865, Fort Fisher, North Carolina	Died of Pneumonia, 2/9/1865
Hill, J. F. Private	Unk	Unknown	Unknown	Co. I, 7th Alabama Infantry	7/4/1863, South Mountain, Maryland	Died of Unknown Causes 11/3/1863

Name & Rank	Age	Enlisted & Age	Residence	Unit	Captured	Date and Cause of Death
Hill, James W. Private	Unk	7/6/1861, S. P. Cave, Botetourt County, Virginia	Unknown	Co. K, 57th Virginia Infantry	7/3/1863 Gettysburg, Pennsylvania	Died of Unknown Causes, 12/22/1863
Hill, McDuffie Private	30	7/30/1861 Edgecombe County, North Carolina, Volunteer	Edgecombe County, North Carolina, Farmer	Co. C, 8th North Carolina Rangers	9/30/1864 Chapin's Farm, Virginia, Gunshot Wound in Both Forearms	Died of Chronic Diarrhea, 6/5/1865
Hill, R. A. Private	Unk	Unknown	Unknown	Enright's Partisan Rangers	Unknown	Unable to Locate
Hill, S. E. Private	Unk	5/1/1864 Athens, Georgia	Limestone County, Georgia	Co. I, 38th Georgia Infantry	9/22/1864, Fisher's Hill, Virginia	Died of Chronic Diarrhea, 10/24/1864
Hill, Thomas Private	Unk	1/1/1863 Camp Palmer, South Carolina	Unknown	Co. K, 7th South Carolina Cavalry	10/7/1864, Darbytown Road Near Richmond, Virginia	Died of Debility 4/7/1865
Hill, Thomas N. Private	Unk	12/9/1862 Camp Frausdale, Tennessee	Unknown	Co. B, 44th Tennessee Infantry	4/2/1865 Petersburg, Virginia	Died of Apoplexy (Stroke) 6/14/1865
Hill, William H. Private	Unk	1/1/1863 Hampton, Arkansas	Unknown	Co. A, 4th Arkansas Infantry	12/16/1864. Near Nashville, Tennessee	Died Inflammation of Pericardium (Lining Around Heart) 2/25/1865
Hill, William R. Private	Unk	10/3/1862 Morristown, Tennessee	Hamblen County, Tennessee	Co. G, 61st Tennessee Mounted Infantry	5/17/1863, Big Black Bridge, Near Vicksburg, Mississippi	Died of Unknown Causes Date Unknown
Hill, William T. Private	Unk	Unknown	Unknown	Co. E, 1st Tennessee Cavalry	10/28/1864, Jefferson County, Tennessee	Died of Pneumonia 5/17/1865
Hill, Willis W. Private	21	11/4/1861 Randolph County, North Carolina, Volunteer	Randolph County, North Carolina, Farmer	Co. H, 38th North Carolina Infantry	7/14/1863, Falling Waters, Maryland	Died of Chronic Diarrhea, 12/24/1863

Name & Rank	Age	Enlisted & Age	Residence	Unit	Captured	Date and Cause of Death
Hilliard, E. Private	45	4/3/1864 Camp Holmes, Raleigh, North Carolina	Wake County, North Carolina	Co. E, 8th North Carolina Infantry	9/30/1864. Fort Harrison, Virginia	Died of Chronic Diarrhea, 5/2/1865
Hilliard, James Private	Unk	6/1/1861 Bond's Store, Virginia	Unknown	Carter's Company of Virginia Light Artillery	7/5/1863, Waterloo, Pennsylvania	Died of Chronic Diarrhea, 12/18/1863
Hilliard, John W. Corporal	18	5/7/1861 New Prospect, Virginia	King and Queen County, Virginia, Sailor	Co. C, 26th Virginia Cavalry	6/17/1864, Near Petersburg, Virginia	Died of Unknown Causes 10/26/1864
Hilton, Riley H. Private	Unk	Unknown	Unknown	Co. A, 24th Virginia Infantry	4/6/1865, Farmville, Virginia	Died of Acute Diarrhea 6/1/1865
Hines, Coleman Private	Unk	4/10/1862 Sewell's Point, Norfolk, Virginia	Chesapeake County, Virginia	Co. I, 41st Virginia Infantry	6/22/1864, Near Petersburg, Virginia	Died of Scurvy 6/1/1865
Hines, Henry L. Private	25	3/15/1862 Lincolnton, Lincoln County, North Carolina, Volunteer	Lincoln County, North Carolina	Co. D, 1st North Carolina Infantry	5/12/1864, Spotsylvania Court House, Virginia	Died of Unknown Causes 8/5/1864
Hines, John H. Private	Unk	3/15/1862 Sandy Level, Virginia	Unknown	Co. E, 57th Virginia Infantry	7/3/1863, Gettysburg, Pennsylvania	Died of Unknown Causes 10/20/1863
Hines, John E. Private	Unk	3/15/1862 Prince Edward County, Virginia, Conscript	Prince Edward County, Virginia	Co. C, 18th Virginia Infantry	4/6/1865, Farmville, Virginia	Died of Dysentery, 6/11/1865
Hines, Sherwood Private	23	7/1/1862 Greene County, North Carolina, Volunteer	Greene County, North Carolina	Co. E, 61st North Carolina Infantry	8/27/1863, Morris Island, South Carolina	Died of Unknown Causes, 12/15/1863
Hinkle, George Washington Private Not Listed On Monument	29	6/25/1861, Lee County, Virginia	Lee County, Virginia	Co. K, 48th Virginia Infantry	7/3/1863, Waterloo, Gettysburg, Pennsylvania	Died of Consumption, 4/19/1864

Name & Rank	Age	Enlisted & Age	Residence	Unit	Captured	Date and Cause of Death
Hinscoe, J. See Insco, James				Co. I, 55th North Carolina Infantry		
Hinson, Bythel Private Not Listed On Monument	18	3/6/1862, Fort Johnston, Brunswick County, North Carolina	Columbus County, North Carolina	Co. D, 20th North Carolina Infantry	7/1/1863, Gettysburg, Pennsylvania	Date and Cause of Death Unknown
Hinton, Daniel C. Corporal	Unk	8/24/1861 Hartwell, Hart County, Georgia	Hart County, Georgia	Co. B, 24th Georgia Infantry	7/2/1863, Gettysburg, Pennsylvania	Died of Chronic Diarrhea, 2/28/1865
Hipps, William Private	Unk	2/14/1863 Decatur, Georgia	Richmond County, Georgia	Co. G, 3rd Georgia Infantry	7/23/1863 Manassas Gap, Virginia, Wounded	Died of Wounds, 10/23/1863
Hires, A. Private	Unk	4/26/1864 Savannah, Georgia	Stewart County, Georgia	Co. I, 1st Georgia Reserve Infantry	12/21/1864, Savannah, Georgia	Died of Unknown Causes, 6/21/1865
Hires, J. F. Private	Unk	4/26/1864 Savannah, Georgia	Stewart County, Georgia	Co. I, Symon's 1st Georgia Reserve Infantry	12/21/1864, Near Savannah, Georgia	Died of Unknown Causes, 2/27/1865
Hivley, Thomas J. Private Not Listed On Monument	21	5/14/1861, Warm Springs, Virginia	Hot Springs, Bath County, Virginia	Co. G, 11th Virginia Cavalry	10/14/1863, Catlet Station, Virginia	Died of Chronic Diarrhea & Dropsy, 4/14/1864
Hix, John S. Private	34	4/5/1862 Wilkesboro, North Carolina, Volunteer	Wilkes County, North Carolina	Co. F, 52nd North Carolina Infantry	7/14/1863, Falling Waters, Maryland	Died of Unknown Causes 1/13/1864
Hixson, William A. Private	Unk	10/17/1862 Paris, Loudon County, Virginia	Fauquier County, Virginia	Co. A, 6th Virginia Cavalry	12/29/1863. Middleburg, Virginia	Died of Chronic Diarrhea 10/27/1864

Name & Rank	Age	Enlisted & Age	Residence	Unit	Captured	Date and Cause of Death
Hodge, A. Private	Unk	4/15/1864 Camp Mercer, Georgia	Unknown	Clinch's Battery Georgia Light Artillery	12/13/1864. Fort McAllister, Georgia	Died of Pneumonia 2/25/1865
Hodge, George Private	Unk	10/7/1862 Putnam County, Virginia	Putnam County, Virginia	Co. I, 14th Virginia Cavalry	7/4/1863 Harrisburg, Gettysburg, Pennsylvania	Died of Dropsy 2/13/1865
Hodges, George T. Private	Unk	7/17/1861 Dunnsville, Virginia	Unknown	Co. D, 55th Virginia Infantry	7/14/1863, Falling Waters, Maryland	Died of Bronchitis 10/18/1863
Hodges, Junius B. Private	18	6/8/1861 Collin's Farm, Virginia	Nansemond County, Virginia, Student	Co. B, 16th Virginia Infantry	10/27/1864, Boyton Plank Road or Burgess' Mill, Virginia	Died of Pneumonia 3/17/1865
Hodges, Nathan H. First Sergeant	32	4/20/1861 Portsmouth, Virginia	Norfolk County, Virginia, Carpenter	Co. A, 3rd Virginia Infantry	7/2/1863, Gettysburg, Pennsylvania	Died of Unknown Causes 1/18/1864
Hodges, Peter Private	Unk	3/6/1862 Franklin County, Virginia	Franklin County, Virginia	Co. B, 57th Virginia Infantry	4/1/1865 Five Forks, Virginia	Died of Acute Dysentery 4/28/1865
Hoffman, T. L. Private Not Listed On Monument	Unk	4/20/63 Lewisburg, Virginia	Greenbrier County, West Virginia	Bryan's Battery, Virginia Artillery	9/19/1864 Winchester, Virginia	Died of Chronic Dysentery 1/29/1865
Hofler, Charles Private	19	2/20/1862 Gatesville, North Carolina, Volunteer	Gates County, North Carolina	Co. C, 2nd North Carolina Cavalry	8/17/1864, Deep Bottom, Virginia	Died of Unknown Causes, 10/15/1864
Hogan, John A. Private	Unk	5/1/1862 White Sulphur Springs, West Virginia	Greenbrier County, West Virginia	Co. C, 22nd Virginia Infantry	9/19/1864, Winchester, Virginia	Died of Pneumonia, 12/27/1864

Name & Rank	Age	Enlisted & Age	Residence	Unit	Captured	Date and Cause of Death
Hoggard, L. Private Not Listed On Monument	Unk	Unknown	Unknown	Co. G, 68th North Carolina Infantry	1/26/1864, Near Plymouth, North Carolina	Died of Intermittent Fever, 7/3/1864
Hogpade, W. Private	Unk	Unknown	Unknown	McLaughlin's Virginia Battery	Unknown	Unable to Locate
Holbrooks, John F. Private Not Listed On Monument	21	7/7/1862 Newton, North Carolina	Lincoln County, North Carolina	Co. E, 57th North Carolina Infantry	11/7/1863, Rappahannock Station, Virginia, Joined US Service 1/24/1864	Died of Bronchitis & Ulcer of Throat, 3/24/1864
Holder, Lemuel Sergeant	22	5/28/1861 Wake County, North Carolina	Wake County, North Carolina	Co. I, 6th North Carolina Infantry	7/6/1863, Waynesboro, Virginia	Died of Unknown Causes, 3/2/1864
Holdsclaw, James H. Private	37	6/14/1861 Rowan County, North Carolina	Rowan County, North Carolina	Co. B, 4th North Carolina Infantry	9/27/1864, Mount Cedar, Virginia	Died of Acute Dysentery, 12/17/1864
Holdsworth, George H. Private	21	5/4/1861 Petersburg, Virginia	Chesterfield County, Virginia, Printer	Co. K, 12th Virginia Infantry	6/12/1864, Near Petersburg, Virginia	Died of Unknown Causes, 9/24/1864
Holland, James R. Private	Unk	5/5/1862 Suffolk, Virginia	Isle of Wight County, Virginia	Co. A, 14th Virginia Infantry	7/14/1863, Suffolk, Virginia	Died of Unknown Causes, 12/22/1863
Holland, Marion L. Private	Unk	8/12/1862 Statesville, Gaston County, North Carolina, Conscript	Gaston County, North Carolina,	Co. H, 37th North Carolina Infantry	5/23/1864, North Anna River, Virginia	Died of Unknown Causes, 8/20/1864
Holland, Matthew Private	18	6/18/1861 Godwin's Point, Virginia	Nansemond County, Virginia, Farmer and Oysterman	Co. F, 3rd Virginia Infantry	7/3/1863, Gettysburg, Pennsylvania	Died of Chronic Diarrhea, 2/2/1865

Name & Rank	Age	Enlisted & Age	Residence	Unit	Captured	Date and Cause of Death
Holliday, James Private	22	8/7/1862 Abington, Kentucky	Unknown	Co. G, 4th Kentucky Cavalry	5/27/1863, Floyd County, Kentucky	Died of Unknown Causes 3/3/1864
Holliker, Monroe See: Hurlocker, Monroe				Co. A, 52nd North Carolina Infantry		
Holloway, James Private	Unk	11/4/1863 Camp Holmes, Raleigh, North Carolina	Wake County, North Carolina	Co. A, 37th North Carolina Infantry	5/12/1864, Spotsylvania Court House, Virginia	Died of Unknown Causes, 8/25/1864
Holloway, John M. Private	21	7/15/1861 Lenoir County, North Carolina, Volunteer	Caldwell County, North Carolina	Co. F, 26th North Carolina Infantry	7/14/1863, Williamsport, Maryland	Died of Chronic Diarrhea & Gangrene of Lungs, 10/18/1863
Holmes, Abner B. Private	Unk	7/3/1861 Glennville, Alabama	Unknown	Co. H, 15th Alabama Infantry	7/3/1863, Gettysburg, Pennsylvania	Died of Chronic Diarrhea, 1/8/1863
Holmes, Charles A. Private Not Listed On Monument	19	3/4/1862, Middleburg, Virginia	Farqure County, Virginia	Co. A, 7th Virginia Cavalry	8/12/1863, Hopewell, Virginia	Died of Unknown Causes, 11/20/1863
Holmes, John W. Private	Unk	5/3/1862, Mount Polk, Alabama	Unknown	Co. K, 48th Alabama Infantry	9/3/1863, Port Royal, Virginia	Died of Unknown Causes, 12/26/1863
Holmes, John W. Private Not Listed On Monument	Unk	Unknown	Unknown	Co. A, 2nd Maryland Cavalry	10/15/1863, Martinsburg, Virginia	Died of Unknown Causes, 7/12/1864
Holmes, W. J. Private	Unk	3/13/1862 Floyd County, Georgia	Floyd County, Georgia	Co. E, 1st Georgia Cavalry	5/29/1863, Mill Spring, Kentucky	Died of Chronic Diarrhea, 10/24/1864

Name & Rank	Age	Enlisted & Age	Residence	Unit	Captured	Date and Cause of Death
Holsinger, Abraham Private	Unk	3/1/1863 Winchester, Virginia	Frederick County, Virginia	Co. H, 12th Virginia Cavalry	9/14/1863, Near Culpepper Court House, Virginia	Died of Chronic Diarrhea, 12/3/1863
Holt, Ballard P. Sergeant	Unk	3/8/1863 Henry County, Virginia	Henry County, Virginia	Co. H, 24th Virginia Cavalry	12/13/1863, Charles City Court House, Virginia	Died of Unknown Causes 6/27/1864
Holt, Jacob Private	Unk	1/27/1864 Petersburg, Virginia	Chesterfield County, Virginia	Co. I, 8th North Carolina Infantry	9/30/1864, Chaffin's Farm, Near Fort Harrison, Virginia	Died of Scurvy 4/30/1865
Holyfield, Isaac Private	17	5/27/1864 Camp Holmes, Raleigh, North Carolina, Volunteer	Webb's Ford, Rutherford County, North Carolina, Farmer	Co. D, 2nd North Carolina Junior Reserves	Unknown	Died Date and Cause Unknown
Holyfield, John Corporal Not Listed On Monument	Unk	6/1/1861, Hobson, North Carolina	Unknown	Co. H, 21st North Carolina Infantry	7/3/1863, Gettysburg, Pennsylvania, Wounded in Leg	Died of Unknown Causes, 1/26/1865
Holyfield, William P. Private Not Listed On Monument	18	9/3/1861 Marion, North Carolina, Volunteer	McDowell County, North Carolina, Farmer	Co. H, 35th North Carolina Infantry	3/25/1865, Fort Stedman, Near Petersburg, Virginia	Died of Chronic Diarrhea 7/14/1865
Hondershet, M. Private	Unk	Unknown	Unknown	Co. F, 18th Virginia Infantry	Unknown	Unable to Locate
Hood, B. B. Private	Unk	11/1/1864 Sugar Loaf, North Carolina, Volunteer	Unknown	Co. B, 3rd North Carolina Junior Reserves	12/25/1864, Fort Fisher, North Carolina	Died of Scurvy, 4/24/1865
Hood, Robert L. Private	40	4/30/1862 Charlotte, North Carolina, Volunteer	Mecklenburg County, North Carolina	Co. B, 53rd North Carolina Infantry	7/5/1863, Gettysburg, Pennsylvania	Died of Scurvy, 3/30/1865

Name & Rank	Age	Enlisted & Age	Residence	Unit	Captured	Date and Cause of Death
Hood, Sidney H. Private	25	3/15/1862 Lenoir County, North Carolina, Volunteer	Caldwell County, North Carolina	Co. F, 26th North Carolina Infantry	10/14/1863, Bristoe Station, Virginia	Died of Chronic Diarrhea 3/26/1865
Hood, William W. Private	19	9/9/1861, Sampson County, North Carolina	Johnston County, North Carolina	Co. H, 20th North Carolina Infantry	7/1/1863 Gettysburg, Pennsylvania	Died of Chronic Diarrhea & Scurvy 3/30/1865
Hooker, Lorenzo H. Private	Unk	11/4/1861 Camp Trousdale, Tennessee	Russellville, Kentucky	Co. F, 41st Tennessee Infantry	5/12/1863, Raymond, Mississippi	Died of Unknown Causes, 3/31/1864
Hooks, Andrew Private	28	2/24/1862 Wadesboro, North Carolina, Volunteer	Anson County, North Carolina, Farmer	Co. H, 43rd North Carolina Infantry	5/16/1864, Near Drewry's Bluff, Virginia	Died of Unknown Causes, 10/21/1864
Hooper, John R. Private	Unk	2/15/1862 Pope County, Arkansas	Pope County, Arkansas	Co. G, 1st Battalion Arkansas Cavalry	5/17/ 1863, Big Black Bridge, Near Vicksburg, Mississippi	Died of Chronic Diarrhea & Pneumonia 11/24/1863
Hooser, G. Private	Unk	Unknown	Unknown	Co. B, 3rd North Carolina Junior Reserves	12/25/1864, Fort Fisher, North Carolina	Died of Scurvy, 5/10/1865
Hopkins, Reuben H. Private	Unk	4/1/1862 Franklin County, Virginia	Franklin County, Virginia	Co. D, 58th Virginia Infantry	9/19/1864, Winchester, Virginia	Died of Acute Diarrhea, 12/5/1864
Hopper, James E. Private	18	2/26/1862 Cove Creek, Missouri	Fleming County, Kentucky, Farmer	Co. G, 2nd Missouri Cavalry	3/7/1864, Guine's Mills, Mississippi	Died of Pneumonia, 2/25/1865
Horn, John H. Private	38	3/19/1862 Rockbridge County, Virginia	Rockbridge County, Virginia	Co. B, 27th Virginia Infantry	7/5/1863, Gettysburg, Pennsylvania	Died of Chronic Diarrhea, 10/30/1863
Horne, Robert R. Private	Unk	7/22/1861 Camp Adams, Virginia	Unknown	Co. I, 15th Virginia Infantry	4/6/1865, Burkesville, Virginia	Died of Chronic Diarrhea, 6/7/1865
Horner, Charles A. Private	Unk	Unknown	Unknown	Co. H, 7th Virginia Cavalry	8/12/1863, Hopewell, Virginia	Died of Unknown Causes 11/1/1863

Name & Rank	Age	Enlisted & Age	Residence	Unit	Captured	Date and Cause of Death
Hornsby, Daniel H. Private	Unk	11/2/1863 Albany, Georgia	Dougherty County, Georgia	Co. K, 28th Battalion Georgia Siege Artillery	12/20/1864, Savannah, Georgia	Died of Scurvy 6/17/1865
Horsely, Raisin Private	Unk	Unknown	Unknown	Co. F, 38th North Carolina Infantry	4/3/1865, Appomattox, Virginia	Died of Pneumonia, 5/30/1865
Horton, George R. Private	25	Unknown	Warren County, North Carolina	Co. K, 12th North Carolina Infantry	10/19/1864, Cedar Creek or Strasburg, Virginia	Died of Chronic Diarrhea & Scurvy 5/5/1865
Hosh, J. F. Private	Unk	Unknown	Unknown	Co. B, Phillip's Georgia Legion	Unknown	Unable to Locate
Houck, D. D. S. Corporal	Unk	4/11/1862 Coles Island, South Carolina	Jasper County, South Carolina	Co. F, 25th South Carolina Infantry	6/16/1864, Petersburg, Virginia	Died of Unknown Causes, 8/6/1864
House, Francis M. Private	Unk	2/16/1863 Atlanta, Georgia	Fulton County, Georgia	Co. A, 64th Georgia Infantry	8/16/1864, Deep Bottom, Virginia	Died of Typhoid Fever, 2/2/1865
House, James J. Private	Unk	2/9/1863 Strugeonville, Virginia	Brunswick County, Virginia	Co. E, 56th Virginia Infantry	7/3/1863, Gettysburg, Pennsylvania	Died of Chronic Diarrhea, 1/24/1864
Houser, John Sergeant	30	7/4/1862 Lincolnton, North Carolina, Volunteer	Lincolnton, Lincoln County, North Carolina	Co. G, 57th North Carolina Infantry	7/5/1863, Gettysburg, Pennsylvania	Died of Chronic Diarrhea, 12/1/1863
Houston, Lewis Private	31	2/17/1863 Jacksonville, Florida	Duval County, Florida	Co. D, 11th Florida Infantry	9/9/1864, Near Petersburg, Virginia	Date and Cause of Death Unknown
Houston, Robert H. Private Not Listed On Monument	Unk	9/20/1862, St. John's Bluff, Florida	Unknown	Co. A, 10th Florida Infantry	9/10/1864, Petersburg, Virginia	Died of Unknown Causes 4/29/1865

Name & Rank	Age	Enlisted & Age	Residence	Unit	Captured	Date and Cause of Death
Hovis, B. Monroe Private	Unk	Lincolnton, North Carolina, Volunteer	Lincolnton County, North Carolina	Co. F, 11th North Carolina Infantry	7/3/1863, Gettysburg, Pennsylvania	Died of Unknown Causes, 5/8/1864
Howard, Calvin Seaman	Unk	Unknown	Unknown	Confederate States Naval Battalion	Unknown	Unable to Locate
Howard, George W. Private	Unk	7/8/1861 Griffin, Georgia	Early County, Georgia	Co. G, 13th Georgia Infantry	7/5/1863, Waterloo, Pennsylvania	Died of Unknown Causes, 11/2/1863
Howard, William A. Private	19	7/1/1861 Taylorsville, Virginia, Volunteer	Orange County, North Carolina	Co. G, 44th North Carolina Infantry	4/3/1865, Sutherland Station, Virginia	Died of Pneumonia, 6/24/1865
Howard, William W. Sergeant	18	3/11/1862 Edgecombe County, North Carolina, Volunteer	Edgecombe County, North Carolina	Co. B, 33rd North Carolina Infantry	7/1/1863 Gettysburg, Pennsylvania, Wounded	Died of Gastritis, 2/14/1865
Howe, Samuel S. Corporal	Unk	9/25/1862 Martinsburg, Virginia	Berkeley County, Virginia	Co. E, 4th Virginia Infantry	Unknown	Died of Unknown Causes, 8/16/1864
Howell, Elijah Private	Unk	3/4/1862 Waresboro, Georgia	Ware County, Georgia	Co. B, 50th Georgia Infantry	7/23/1863, Manassas Gap, Virginia	Died of Chronic Diarrhea 10/16/1863
Howell, James Lewis Private	Unk	6/26/1861 Gauley Bridge, West Virginia	Unknown	Co. C. 60th Virginia Infantry	9/25/1864, Staunton, Virginia, Wounded	Died of Anasaica, Edema, Swelling of Skin, 1/24/1865
Howell, Lorenzo D. Private	Unk	3/13/1862 Newbern, Virginia	Montgomery County, Virginia	Co. C, 4th Virginia Infantry	5/5/1864, Wilderness, Virginia	Died of Unknown Causes, 8/21/1864
Howell, Robert P. Private	17	6/27/1861 Alamance County, North Carolina, Volunteer	Yancy County, North Carolina	Co. E, 6th North Carolina Infantry	7/2/1863, Gettysburg, Pennsylvania	Died of Unknown Causes, 12/29/1864
Howren, Adam C. Private	21	4/30/1862 Camp Leon, Florida	Leon County, Florida	Co. E, 5th Florida Infantry	4/6/1865, High Bridge, Virginia	Died of Unknown Causes, 5/22/1865

Name & Rank	Age	Enlisted & Age	Residence	Unit	Captured	Date and Cause of Death
Hoyal, David Private	22	8/7/1862 Greeneville, Tennessee	Greene County, Tennessee	Co. E, 16th Battalion Tennessee Cavalry	5/26/63, Stagall's Ferry, Kentucky	Died of Unknown Causes, 8/13/1864
Hubbard, James M. Private	Unk	10/20/1862 Leetown, Virginia	Frederick County, Virginia	Co. D, 3rd Virginia Cavalry	7/3/1863, Gettysburg, Pennsylvania	Died of Unknown Causes, 8/28/1864
Hubbard, John L. Private	Unk	5/15/1862 Newnan, Georgia	Coweta County, Georgia	Co. F, Cavalry Battalion, Phillip's Georgia Legion	5/21/1864, Milford Station, Virginia	Died of Chronic Diarrhea, 1/19/1865
Hubbard, William A. Private	21	4/24/1861 Prospect Depot, Virginia	Unknown, Farmer	Co. D. 18th Virginia Infantry	7/3/1863, Gettysburg, Pennsylvania	Died of Acute Diarrhea, 12/27/1864
Huckstep, Ira Private	Unk	2/20/1862 Richmond, Virginia	Henrico County, Virginia	Co. G. 22nd Battalion Virginia Artillery	7/14/1863, Falling Waters, Maryland	Died of Chronic Diarrhea, 11/30/1863
Hudgins, James H. Seaman	Unk	Unknown	Unknown	Confederate States Navy	Unknown	Unable to Locate
Hudgins, James H. Private	18	9/2/1861 Rutherford County, North Carolina, Volunteer	Rutherford County, North Carolina, Farmer	Co. C, 34th North Carolina Infantry	8/1/1863, Brandy Station, Near Culpepper Court House, Virginia	Died of Unknown Causes, 2/14/1864
Hudgins, John B. Private	53	6/19/1863 Granville County, North Carolina, Substitute	Pitt County, North Carolina, Farmer	Co. B, 16th North Carolina Infantry	4/2/1865, Hatcher's Run, Virginia	Died of Chronic Dysentery, 6/6/1865
Hudson, Benajah Private	41	9/5/1863 Sampson County, North Carolina, Volunteer	Sampson County, North Carolina	Co. A, 36th North Carolina Heavy Artillery	1/15/1865, Fort Fisher, North Carolina	Died of Chronic Diarrhea, 5/26/1865
Hudson, Wyatt Private	Unk	10/11863 Bravard, North Carolina, Volunteer	Transylvania County, North Carolina	Co. C, 6th North Carolina Cavalry	10/12/1864, Below Kinston, North Carolina	Died of Pneumonia, 2/24/1865

Name & Rank	Age	Enlisted & Age	Residence	Unit	Captured	Date and Cause of Death
Huff, Ferdinand Alex Private	27	5/14/1861 Floyd Court House, Virginia	Floyd County, Virginia	Co. A. 24th Virginia Infantry	4/6/1865 Burkesville, Virginia	Died of Acute Dysentery, 6/26/1865
Huffins, Daniel Private	36	12/20/1862, Guilford County, North Carolina, Volunteer	Guilford County, North Carolina, Farmer	Co. A, 53rd North Carolina Infantry	9/22/1864, Fisher's Hill, Virginia	Died of Consumption, 2/24/1865
Huffman, T. L. See: Hoffman, T. L.				Bryan's Virginia Battery		
Huffman, W. R. Private	Unk	4/11/1862 Cole's Island, South Carolina	Jasper County, South Carolina	Co. F, 25th South Carolina Infantry	6/16/1864, Petersburg, Virginia	Died of Unknown Causes, 9/14/1864
Hugan, J. W. See: Higins, Joseph W.				Co. K, 47th North Carolina Infantry		
Hughes, Aaron Private	19	6/20/1861 Windsor, North Carolina, Volunteer	Bertie County, North Carolina, Farmer	Co. F, 5th North Carolina Infantry	5/20/1864 Spotsylvania Court House, Virginia	Died of Acute Dysentery, 6/28/1864
Hughes, George H. Private	Unk	4/1/1862 Orange County, Virginia	Orange County, Virginia	Co. I, 6th Virginia Cavalry	10/9/1864, Fisher's Hill, Virginia	Died of Acute Dysentery, 2/10/1865
Hughes, Henry B. Private	42	5/26/1864 Camp Instruction, South Carolina, Conscript	Unknown	Co. B, 1st South Carolina Artillery	3/11/1865, Fayetteville, North Carolina	Died of Unknown Causes, 4/19/1865
Hughes, James Private	28	5/15/1861 Gloucester Point, Virginia	Gloucester County, Virginia, Clerk	Co. A, 5th Virginia Cavalry	11/25/1863, Greenville, North Carolina	Died of Unknown Causes, 2/19/1864
Hughes, John B. Sergeant	24	9/19/1862 Luka, Mississippi	Tishomingo County, Mississippi	Co. K, 1st Mississippi Infantry	12/16/1864, Nashville, Tennessee, Wounded	Died of Remittent Fever, 5/241865

Name & Rank	Age	Enlisted & Age	Residence	Unit	Captured	Date and Cause of Death
Hughes, Richard Private Not Listed On Monument	Unk	4/1/1862, Orange County, Virginia	Orange County, Virginia	Co. I, 6th Virginia Cavalry	6/15/1863, Winchester, Virginia	Died of Unknown Causes, ?/?/1863
Hughes, Saunders D. Private	Unk	4/15/1862 Tomotley, South Carolina	Beaufort County, South Carolina	Co. E, 14th South Carolina Infantry	7/3/1863, Gettysburg, Pennsylvania, Shell Wound in Left Thigh, Amputated Leg 1/10/1864	Died of Unknown Causes, 2/16/1864
Hughes, Samuel P. Private	23	5/1/1861 Massies Mill, Virginia	Nelson County, Virginia, Farmer	Co. G. 19th Virginia Infantry	7/3/1863, Gettysburg, Pennsylvania	Died of Chronic Diarrhea, 1/22/1864
Hughs, Joseph S. Private	Unk	12/29/1863 Pocotaligo, South Carolina	Jasper County, South Carolina	Co. C, 19th Battalion South Carolina Cavalry	3/5/1865, Florence, South Carolina	Died of Unknown Causes, 4/25/1865
Hull, P. T. Private	Unk	Unknown	Unknown	Co. D, 22nd Virginia Infantry	Unknown	Unable to Locate
Humphrey, Daniel Private	17	9/6/1861 Onslow County, North Carolina, Volunteer	Onslow County, North Carolina, Farmer	Co. A, 35th North Carolina Infantry	2/23/1864, Near Plymouth, North Carolina	Died of Pneumonia, 2/11/1865
Humphrey, John Private	19	3/3/1862 Wilmington, North Carolina, Volunteer	New Hanover County, North Carolina, Farmer	Co. G, 51st North Carolina Infantry	5/16/1864, Near Drewry's Bluff, Virginia	Died of Acute Dysentery, 3/5/1865
Humphrey, Joseph R. Private	Unk	3/9/1863 Orange County, Virginia	Orange County, Virginia	Co. H, 38th Virginia Infantry	7/21/1863, Chester's Gap, Virginia	Died of Unknown Causes, 9/5/1863
Humphreys, Elliott Private	37	2/28/1863 Rockingham County, North Carolina, Conscript	Rockingham County, North Carolina	Co. C, 13th North Carolina Infantry	5/6/1864, Wilderness, Virginia,	Died of Pneumonia, 11/8/1864
Humphreys, T. J. Private	Unk	8/12/1864 Camp Holmes, North Carolina	Warren County, North Carolina	Co. K, 12th North Carolina Infantry	9/22/1864 Fisher's Hill, Virginia	Died of Typhoid Fever, 12/21/1864

Name & Rank	Age	Enlisted & Age	Residence	Unit	Captured	Date and Cause of Death
Hunnings, William W. Private Not Listed On Monument	21	9/28/1861, Craven County, North Carolina	Newbern, North Carolina, Farmer	Co. D, 40th Regiment, 3rd North Carolina Light Artillery	1/15/1865, Fort Fisher, North Carolina, Severely Wounded in Groin	Died of Wounds, 2/14/1865
Hunsucker, Jonas Private	37	3/31/1863 Newton, North Carolina, Volunteer	Catawba County, North Carolina	Co. E, 32nd North Carolina Infantry	5/10/1864, Wilderness, Virginia	Died of Unknown Causes, 8/27/1864
Hunt, Charles Private	Unk	Unknown	Unknown	Co. G, 60th Tennessee Mounted Infantry	10/28/1864, Jefferson County, Tennessee	Died of Chronic Diarrhea, 4/22/1865
Hunt, Elam J. Private	42	2/22/1862 Guilford County, North Carolina, Volunteer	Guilford County, North Carolina	Co. E, 2nd North Carolina Infantry	7/14/1863, Falling Waters, Maryland	Died of Smallpox, 2/7/1864
Hunt, L. S. Private	Unk	5/1/1864 Columbia, South Carolina, Volunteered with consent of parents	Richland County, South Carolina	Co. B, 3rd South Carolina Infantry	10/19/1864, Cedar Creek or Strasburg, Virginia	Died of Scurvy, 5/26/1865
Hunt, Samuel G. Private	50	8/19/1862 Richmond County, North Carolina, Substitute for James Greene	Wake County, North Carolina	Co. I, 1st North Carolina Infantry	5/12/1864, Spotsylvania Court House, Virginia	Died of Unknown Causes, 9/9/1864
Hunt, Thomas H. Corporal	Unk	3/20/1863 Tallahassee, Florida	Leon County, Florida	Co. I, 11th Florida Infantry	4/6/1865, Burkesville, Virginia	Died of Unknown Causes, 4/28/1865
Hunter, Benjamin E. Private	17	6/10/1861 Helena, Arkansas	Phillips County, Arkansas	Co. G, 2nd Arkansas Infantry	12/18/1864, Franklin, Tennessee, Wounded Left Leg	Died of Scurvy, 4/19/1865
Hunter, Benjamin T. Private Not Listed On Monument	Unk	6/6/1861, Telfair County, Georgia	Telfair County, Georgia	Co. H, 20th Georgia Infantry	7/3/1863, Gettysburg, Pennsylvania	Died of Scurvy, 5/31/1864

Name & Rank	Age	Enlisted & Age	Residence	Unit	Captured	Date and Cause of Death
Hunter, Henry C. Private	24	9/16/1861 Mecklenburg County, North Carolina, Volunteer	Mecklenburg County, North Carolina, Farmer	Co. C, 37th North Carolina Infantry	8/12/1864, Deep Bottom, Virginia	Died of Pneumonia, 3/8/1865
Hunter, Hugh B. Private Not Listed On Monument	29	5/7/1863 Mecklenburg County, North Carolina, Conscript	Mecklenburg County, North Carolina, Farmer	Co. H, 35th North Carolina Infantry	6/17/1864, Petersburg, Virginia	Died of Unknown Causes, 7/1/1864
Hunter, Jacob Private	Unk	6/25/1864 James Island, South Carolina	Charleston District, South Carolina	Co. B, Lucas South Carolina Battalion, Heavy Artillery	3/16/1865, Averasboro, North Carolina	Died of Typhoid/ Pneumonia 4/17/1865
Hunter, John Private	Unk	4/18/1862 Giles Court House, Virginia	Giles County, Virginia	Co. H, 36th Virginia Infantry	9/19/1864, Winchester, Virginia	Died of Chronic Diarrhea, 2/21/1865
Hunter, John H. Sergeant Not Listed On Monument	23	2/10/1862, Charlotte, Mecklenburg County, North Carolina, Volunteer	Mecklenburg County, North Carolina, Farmer	Co. B, 43rd North Carolina Infantry	9/19/1864, Winchester, Virginia, Gunshot Wound of Spine	Died of Wounds, 2/6/1865
Hurlocker, Monroe Private	30	3/28/1862 Concord, North Carolina, Volunteer	Cabarrus County, North Carolina	Co. A, 52nd North Carolina Infantry	5/6/1864 Near Spotsylvania Court House, Virginia	Died of Unknown Causes, 9/7/1864
Hursey, G. A. Private	Unk	6/25/1861 Mobile, Alabama	Mobile, Alabama, Clerk	Co. H, 8th Alabama Infantry	7/2/1863, Gettysburg, Pennsylvania	Died of Smallpox, 11/19/1863
Hurst, William A. Private	Unk	Unknown	Unknown	Co. H, 10th Georgia Infantry	7/5/1863, Gettysburg, Pennsylvania	Died of Unknown Causes, 11/19/1863

Name & Rank	Age	Enlisted & Age	Residence	Unit	Captured	Date and Cause of Death
Hurt, William Private Not Listed On Monument	Unk	12/28/1862 Saintsville, Kentucky	Unknown	Co. I, 5th Kentucky Mounted Infantry	5/17/1863, Perry County, Kentucky	Died of Chronic Diarrhea, 1/17/1865
Huskey, James Private Not Listed On Monument	Unk	3/1/1862 Brunswick, Virginia	Brunswick County, Virginia	Coleman's Company Virginia Heavy Artillery	4/7/1865, Amelia Court House, Virginia	Died of Typhoid Fever, 6/10/1865
Hutchinson, Henry Private	Unk	7/27/1863 Abbeville, South Carolina	Unknown	Co. C, 6th South Carolina Cavalry	6/11/1864, Travillian's Station, Virginia	Died of Chronic Diarrhea, 1/9/1865
Hutchinson, Thomas Private	Unk	10/24/1864 Essex County, Virginia	Essex County, Virginia	Co. I, 26th Virginia Infantry	3/30/1865, Hatcher's Run, Virginia	Died of Chronic Diarrhea, 5/21/1865
Hutchison, James L. Private	26	7/16/1861, Centreville, Virginia	Fairfax County, Virginia	Co. G, 8th Virginia Infantry	7/3/1863, Gettysburg, Pennsylvania	Died of Chronic Diarrhea, 3/31/1865
Hyatt, Lafayette R. A. Private	Unk	4/5/1863 Waynesville, North Carolina	Haywood County, North Carolina	Co. E, 1st Regiment North Carolina Legion	9/19/1864, Winchester, Virginia	Died of Typhoid Fever, 1/15/1865
Hyde, Reuben H. Sergeant	19	7/20/1861 Camp Pickens, Anderson District, South Carolina	Anderson District, South Carolina	Co. G, Orr's Regiment, 1st South Carolina Rifles	7/14/1863, Falling Waters, Maryland	Died of Chronic Diarrhea, 11/3/1863
Hyde, Samuel L. Private	23	6/15/1861 Corinth, Mississippi	Alcorn County, Mississippi	Co. D, 20th Mississippi Infantry	5/18/1863, Near Baldwin's Ferry, Big Black Bridge, Mississippi	Died of Unknown Causes, 9/2/1864
Hylton, Jeremiah H. Private	18	3/8/1862 Floyd Court House, Virginia	Floyd County, Virginia	Co. B, 42nd Virginia Infantry	7/4/1863, South Mountain, Maryland	Died of Smallpox, 1/6/1864

Name	Age	Enlisted	Residence	Unit	Captured	Date and Cause of Death
Ingles, George A. Private	Unk	5/1/1862 White Sulphur Springs, Virginia	Monroe County, West Virginia	Co. F, 22nd Virginia Infantry	9/19/1864, Winchester, Virginia	Died of Hepatitis 12/31/1864
Ingold, Eli Private Not Listed On Monument	Unk	Unknown	Guilford County, North Carolina	Co. A, 15th North Carolina Infantry	4/3/1865, Petersburg, Virginia	Died of Scorbutus (Scurvy), 7/5/1865
Ingold, Jesse A. Private	38	4/7/1862 Guilford County, North Carolina, Substitute	Guilford County, North Carolina, Peddlar	Co. A, 53rd North Carolina Infantry	7/14/1863, Falling Waters, Maryland	Died of Chronic Diarrhea, 12/10/1863
Ingram, John Sergeant	Unk	3/4/1862 Sandersville, Georgia	Washington County, Georgia	Co. C, 49th Georgia Infantry	5/6/1864, Wilderness, Virginia	Died of Dropsy, Hepatic 9/24/1864
Ingram, William Private	Unk	9/7/1862, Place Unknown	Unknown	Co. K, 18th North Carolina Infantry	7/3/1863 Gettysburg, Pennsylvania	Died of Chronic Diarrhea 11/3/1863
Inman, Alexander Private	40	10/5/1863 Brunswick County, North Carolina	Lumberton, Robison County, North Carolina	Co. E, 40th North Carolina Light Artillery	1/15/1865, Fort Fisher, North Carolina	Died of Pneumonia, 3/9/1865
Inman, James H. Private	41	4/7/1862 Petersburg, Virginia	Chesterfield County, Virginia	Co. K, 5th Virginia Cavalry	10/10/1863 Mitchell's Ford, Brandy Station, Virginia	Died of Unknown Causes 9/15/1864
Inscoe, B. B. Private	Unk	9/15/1864 Camp Holmes, Raleigh, North Carolina	Wake County, North Carolina	Co. K, 12th North Carolina Infantry	10/19/1864, Bell Grove, Cedar Creek or Strasburg, Virginia	Died of Chronic Diarrhea 11/30/1864
Inscoe, Henry Private	29	3/24/1862 Warrenton, North Carolina, Volunteer	Halifax County, North Carolina	Co. K, 12th North Carolina Infantry	9/19/1864, Winchester, Virginia	Died of Chronic Diarrhea 11/7/1864
Inscoe, James W. Private Not Listed On Monument	17	9/15/1862, Camp Holmes, Raleigh, Volunteer	Greenville County, North Carolina	Co. I, 55th North Carolina Infantry	7/14/1863, Falling Waters, Maryland	Died of Smallpox 12/28/1863

Name	Age	Enlisted	Residence	Unit	Captured	Date and Cause of Death
Inscoe, J. S. Private Not Listed On Monument	Unk	9/18/1864 Camp Holmes, Raleigh, North Carolina	Warren County, North Carolina	Co. K, 12th North Carolina Infantry	10/19/1864, Bell Grove, Cedar Creek or Strasburg, Virginia	Died of Chronic Diarrhea 11/7/1864
Ipock, Albert Sergeant	27	1/23/1862 Craven County, North Carolina, Volunteer	Craven County, North Carolina	Co. E, 40th North Carolina Light Artillery	1/15/1865, Fort Fisher, North Carolina	Died of Heart Disease, 2/18/1865
Irick, W. M. Private	Unk	3/9/1863, C. C. Parish, South Carolina	Parish County, South Carolina	Co. E, 5th South Carolina Cavalry	12/1/1864 Stony Creek, North Carolina	Died of Pneumonia, 1/29/1865
Irwin, William P. Private	Unk	2/11/1863 Fosterville, Tennessee	Rutherford County, Tennessee	Co. E, 3rd Alabama Cavalry	6/27/1863, Shelbyville, Tennessee	Died of Smallpox, 11/1/1863
Isbell, Robert G. Private	Unk	7/14/1861 Camesville, Georgia	Franklin County, Georgia	Co. B, 15th Georgia Infantry	9/29/1864, Near Fort Harrison, Virginia	Died of Acute Dysentery, 12/10/1864
Isdel, James T. Private	Unk	7/9/1862 Camp Brown, Butler, Georgia	Taylor County, Georgia	Co. C, 59th Georgia Infantry	7/4/1863 Cashtown, Gettysburg, Pennsylvania, Gunshot Wound Left Thigh	Died of Wounds 7/12/1863
Isham, Nathan Private	Unk	Unknown	Unknown	Co. A, 15th North Carolina Cavalry	12/4/1864 Hertford County, North Carolina	Died of Chronic Diarrhea 1/6/1865
Isler, Dewitt C. Private Not Listed On Monument	Unk	4/26/1862 Camp Leon, Tallahassee, Florida	Leon County, Florida	Co. C, 5th Florida Infantry	9/10/1864 Petersburg, Virginia	Died of Chronic Diarrhea & Scurvy 3/10/1865
Isley, John Private	22	7/15/1862 Raleigh, North Carolina, Conscript	Alamance County, North Carolina	Co. E, 1st North Carolina Infantry	5/12/1864 Spotsylvania Court House, Virginia	Date and Cause of Death Unknown

Name	Age	Enlisted	Residence	Unit	Captured	Date and Cause of Death
Ivey, W. L. Private	38	7/15/1862 Halifax County, North Carolina, Volunteer	Halifax County, North Carolina	Co. A, 30th North Carolina Infantry	11/7/1863, Kelly's Ford, Rappahannock Station, Virginia	Died of Chronic Diarrhea, 1/26/1865

Name	Age	Enlisted	Residence	Unit	Captured	Date and Cause of Death
Jack, John H. Private	18	4/9/1862 Shenandoah, Virginia	Bath County, Virginia, Farmer	Co. K, 52nd North Carolina Infantry	7/3/1863 Cashtown, Gettysburg, Pennsylvania	Died of Unknown Causes 3/27/1864
Jackson, David Private	Unk	9/25/1862 Fordtown, Tennessee	Unknown	Co. E, 60th Tennessee Mounted Infantry	5/17/1863, Big Black Bridge, Near Vicksburg, Mississippi	Died of Unknown Causes 10/?/1863
Jackson, Henry Private	Unk	8/16/1862 Lebanon, Virginia	Russell County, Virginia	Co. B, 16th Virginia Cavalry	11/12/1864 Nineveh, Virginia	Died of Chronic Dysentery, 1/24/1865
Jackson, J. A. Private	Unk	Unknown	Unknown	Co. B, 7th South Carolina Cavalry	Unknown	Unable to Locate
Jackson, John M. Private	Unk	2/12/1862 Danbury, North Carolina	Stokes County, North Carolina	Co. G, 22nd North Carolina Infantry	5/25/1864 Mechanicsville, Virginia	Died of Unknown Causes, 6/27/1864
Jackson, Lyndhurst Private	Unk	1/1/1863 Nottoway Court House, Virginia	Nottoway County, Virginia	Co. B, 3rd Virginia Cavalry	4/6/1865 Deedhansville, Virginia	Died of Chronic Diarrhea, 6/24/1865
Jackson, Peter Private	Unk	Unknown	Unknown	Stiles Georgia Artillery	Unknown	Unable to Locate
Jackson, Thomas R. Private	22	2/28/1862 Cove Creek, Missouri	Unknown	Co. K, 1st Missouri Cavalry	5/17/1863, Big Black Bridge, Near Vicksburg, Mississippi	Died of Unknown Causes 9/18/1863
Jackson, William Private	Unk	5/5/1862 Suffolk, Virginia	Isle of Wight County, Virginia	Co. A, 14th Virginia Infantry	7/3/1863 Gettysburg, Pennsylvania	Died of Chronic Diarrhea 11/10/1863

Name	Age	Enlisted	Residence	Unit	Captured	Date and Cause of Death
Jackson, William C. Private	36	5/12/1861 Lombardy Grove, Virginia	Unknown	Co. F, 14th Virginia Infantry	5/10/1864, Near Petersburg, Virginia	Died of Chronic Diarrhea 1/27/1865
James, Andrew F. Corporal	21	8/31/1861 Spartanburg Court House, South Carolina	Spartanburg District, South Carolina	Co. B, 13th South Carolina Infantry	5/12/1864, Spotsylvania Court House, Virginia, Gunshot Wound Left side of Face and Neck.	Died of Unknown Causes, 10/22/1864
James, George T. Private	Unk	3/13/1862 Fredericksburg Virginia	Spotsylvania County, Virginia	Co. M, 55th Virginia Infantry	4/6/1865, Prince Edward County, Virginia	Died of Chronic Diarrhea 6/2/1865
James, Jeter Private	20	5/22/1861 Kilmarnock, Virginia	Lancaster County, Virginia	Co. H, 40th Virginia Infantry	5/6/1864, Wilderness, Virginia	Died of Unknown Causes, 8/6/1864
James, John M. Private	23	3/20/1862 Danbury, Stokes County, North Carolina	Stokes County, North Carolina, Farmer	Co. H, 53rd North Carolina Infantry	7/5/1863 Waterloo, Gettysburg, Pennsylvania	Died of Unknown Causes. 3/9/1864
James, Mitchell T. Private	19	4/18/1861 Marion, Virginia	Smyth County, Virginia, Farmer	Co. D, 4th Virginia Infantry	7/3/1863 Gettysburg, Pennsylvania	Died of Unknown Causes, 2/13/1864
Jameson, William R. D. Private	Unk	7/8/1861 Bristol, Tennessee	Sullivan County, Tennessee	Co. F, 37th North Carolina Infantry	5/12/1864 Spotsylvania Court House, Virginia, Gun Shot Wound Left Thigh	Died of Typhoid Fever 10/26/1864
Jamison, James W. Corporal	25	3/7/1862 Charlotte, North Carolina, Volunteer	Mecklenburg County, North Carolina	Co. E, 11th North Carolina Infantry	10/27/1864 Near Petersburg, Virginia	Died Inflammation of the Lungs (Pneumonia) 3/7/1865
Janes, John P. See: Jaynes, John P.				Co. B, 54th North Carolina Infantry		

Name	Age	Enlisted	Residence	Unit	Captured	Date and Cause of Death
Jarrell, Judson G. Private Not Listed On Monument	Unk	4/27/1861, Standardsville, Virginia	Unknown	Co. F, 7th Virginia Infantry	5/21/1864, Milford Station, Virginia	Died of Unknown Causes, 7/7/1864
Jarrett, J. E. Private	Unk	5/9/1864 Camp Vance, Raleigh, North Carolina	Wake County, North Carolina	Co. A, 2nd North Carolina Infantry	9/19/1864, Winchester, Virginia	Died of Chronic Diarrhea 5/29/1865
Jarvis, Bryant Private	Unk	7/15/1862 Raleigh, North Carolina, Conscript	Davidson County, North Carolina	Co. A, 2nd North Carolina Infantry	10/14/1863, Bristoe Station, Virginia	Died of Unknown Causes, 3/17/1864
Jarvis, Foster Sergeant	26	6/25/1861 Beaufort County, North Carolina	Hyde County, North Carolina	Co. I, 4th North Carolina Infantry	7/3/1863 Gettysburg, Pennsylvania	Died of Unknown Causes, 2/21/1864
Jaynes, John P. Private	23	10/6/1863 Morganton, North Carolina	Burke County, North Carolina	Co. B, 54th North Carolina Infantry	9/22/1864 Fisher's Hill, Virginia	Died of Scurvy, 3/29/1865
Jefcoat, S. F. Private	Unk	5/12/1862 Troy, Alabama	Pike County, Alabama	Co. G, 59th Alabama Infantry	5/25/1865, Hatchers Run, Near Richmond, Virginia	Died of Scurvy, 3/26/1865
Jeffreys, Thomas Sergeant	32	2/12/1862 Raleigh, North Carolina	Wake County, North Carolina	Co. I, 3rd North Carolina Cavalry	5/31/1864 Hanover Court House, Virginia	Died of Intermittent Fever, 7/17/1864
Jelks, Robert Private	37	Unknown	Unknown	Co. B, 44th Virginia Battalion Infantry	4/6/1865 Amelia Court House, Virginia	Died of Chronic Diarrhea & Scurvy 5/12/1865
Jenkins, Andrew B. Private	29	8/12/1862 Statesville, North Carolina, Conscript	Mecklenburg County, North Carolina	Co. H, 37th North Carolina Infantry	6/22/1864 Petersburg, Virginia	Died of Unknown Causes, 8/10/1864
Jenkins, Benjamin A. Corporal	33	5/10/1862 Cherryville, Cleveland County, North Carolina	Rutherford County, North Carolina, Farmer	Co. F, 56th North Carolina Infantry	3/25/1865, Fort Stedman, Near Petersburg, Virginia	Died of Chronic Diarrhea 6/15/1865

Name	Age	Enlisted	Residence	Unit	Captured	Date and Cause of Death
Jenkins, Timothy P. Private Not Listed On Monument	24	2/21/1862 Concord, North Carolina, Volunteer	Cabarrus County, North Carolina	Co. C, 33rd North Carolina Infantry	5/6/1864 Wilderness, Virginia	Died of Chronic Diarrhea, 8/9/1864
Jernigan, Joseph J. Private	24	7/16/1862 Raleigh, North Carolina, Conscript	Johnson County, North Carolina, Farmer	Co. D, 5th North Carolina Infantry	7/3/1863 Gettysburg, Pennsylvania	Died of Unknown Causes, 1/4/1864
Jessey, John Private	Unk	5/1/1864 Wytheville, Virginia	Wythe County, Virginia	Co. G, 37th Battalion Virginia Cavalry	9/23/1864, Cedar Creek or Strasburg, Virginia	Died of Chronic Diarrhea, 3/2/1865
Jett, Granville Private	Unk	9/7/1862 Jackson, Breathitt County, Kentucky	Unknown	Co. B, 5th Kentucky Mounted Infantry	6/6/1863, Perry County, Kentucky	Died of Unknown Causes, 3/1/1864
Jobe, Enoch Private	34	9/25/1862 Fordtown, Tennessee	Unknown	Co. E, 60th Tennessee Mounted Infantry	5/17/1863, Big Black Bridge, Near Vicksburg, Mississippi	Died of Chronic Diarrhea 1/25/1864
Johns, T. H. Private	23	9/28/1862 Richos Bluff, Sumterville, Florida	Unknown	Co. E, 10th Florida Infantry	9/20/1864 Petersburg, Virginia	Died of Pneumonia 3/2/1865
Johnson, Alex H. Private	Unk	5/21/1862 Chesterfield, South Carolina	Unknown	Co. A, 1st South Carolina Infantry	8/26/1863, Morris Island, South Carolina	Died of Typhoid Fever, 12/14/1864
Johnson, Eli Private	28	6/5/1861 Asheboro, North Carolina, Volunteer	Randolph County, North Carolina	Co. I, 22nd North Carolina Infantry	7/14/1863, Falling Waters, Maryland	Died of Unknown Causes, 12/30/1863
Johnson, Elias Private	23	3/1/1862 Nashville, North Carolina, Volunteer	Wake County, North Carolina	Co. H, 32nd North Carolina Infantry	5/10/1864, Wilderness, Virginia	Died of Unknown Causes, 9/7/1864
Johnson, F. M. Private	16	5/10/1862 Gadsden, Alabama	Etowah County, Alabama, Farmer	Co. G, 48th Alabama Infantry	7/3/1863 Gettysburg, Pennsylvania	Died of Unknown Causes, 11/8/1863

Name	Age	Enlisted	Residence	Unit	Captured	Date and Cause of Death
Johnson, Francis Private	Unk	7/18/1861 Botetourt, Virginia	Unknown	Co. K, 57th Virginia Infantry	4/4/1865, Five Forks, Virginia	Died of Chronic Dysentery, 6/19/1865
Johnson, George Private Not Listed On Monument	Unk	3/21/1862 Newton, North Carolina, Volunteer	Catawba County, North Carolina	Co. F, 23rd North Carolina Infantry	7/1/1863 Gettysburg, Pennsylvania	Died of Unknown Causes, 1/30/1864
Johnson, George W. Private	23	5/9/1861 Lewisburg, Virginia	Greenbrier County, West Virginia, Hotel Keeper	Co. E, 27th Virginia Infantry	5/20/1864 Spotsylvania Court House, Virginia	Died of Unknown Causes, 10/20/1864
Johnson, Green B. Private	Unk	5/28/1863 Quincy, Florida	Unknown	Co. D, 64th Georgia Infantry	8/17/1864, Deep Bottom, Virginia	Died of Pneumonia, 4/8/1865
Johnson, J. H. Private Not Listed On Monument	Unk	1/12/1864 Greenville, South Carolina	Greenville District, South Carolina	Co. E, Hampton's South Carolina Legion	4/3/1865, Richmond, Virginia, Captured in Hospital	Died of Chronic Diarrhea, 5/10/1865
Johnson, James S. Private	Unk	8/12/1862 Lake City, Florida	Columbia County, Florida	Co. G, 10th Florida Infantry	8/21/1864, Globe Tavern, Near Weldon Railroad, Virginia	Died of Unknown Causes, 6/3/1865
Johnson, John B. Private	17	4/12/1862 Battery Island, South Carolina	Unknown	Co. C, 25th South Carolina Infantry	1/15/1865, Fort Fisher, North Carolina, Wounded Bowels and Right Groin	Died of Wounds, 4/8/1865
Johnson, John M. Sergeant	Unk	8/14/1862 Lake City, Florida	Columbia County, Florida	Co. G, 10th Florida Infantry	8/21/1864, Globe Tavern, Near Weldon Railroad, Virginia	Died of Scurvy, 4/11865
Johnson, John W. Private	Unk	8/1/1863 Mobile, Alabama	Mobile County, Alabama	Co. E, 3rd Alabama Cavalry	10/7/1863, Farmington, Tennessee	Died of Chronic Diarrhea, 5/13/1865
Johnson, John W. Private	18	4/20/1861 Rappahannock County, Virginia	Rappahannock County, Virginia	Co. E, 7th Virginia Infantry	7/3/1863, Gettysburg, Pennsylvania	Died of Unknown Causes, 6/1/1864

Name	Age	Enlisted	Residence	Unit	Captured	Date and Cause of Death
Johnson, Josiah Private	Unk	7/15/1862 Raleigh, North Carolina, Conscript	Chatham County, North Carolina	Co. A, 5th North Carolina Infantry	5/12/1864, Spotsylvania Court House, Virginia	Died of Unknown Causes, 6/4/1864
Johnson, J. M. Private	Unk	3/16/1863 Atlanta, Georgia	Fulton County, Georgia	Co. E, 64th Georgia Infantry	4/6/1865, Prince Edward County, Virginia	Died of Acute Dysentery 4/7/1865
Johnson, J. W. Corporal	Unk	8/3/1863 Macon, Georgia	Bibb County, Georgia	Co. F, 28th Battalion, Georgia Siege Artillery	4/6/1865, Archer's Farm, Virginia	Died of Chronic Diarrhea 5/7/1865
Johnson, Philip Private	Unk	5/28/1863 Atlanta, Georgia	Fulton County, Georgia	Co. H, 64th North Carolina Infantry	8/11/1864, New Market, Virginia	Died of Unknown Causes, 10/18/1864
Johnson, Richard M. Private	Unk	5/1/1863 Grace Church, Virginia	Unknown	Co. G, 6th Alabama Infantry	5/12/1864, Spotsylvania Court House, Virginia	Died of Unknown Causes, 7/21/1864
Johnson, Samuel C. Private	Unk	5/1/1862 Macon, Georgia	Bibb County, Georgia	Co. B, 2nd Battalion Georgia Infantry	7/23/1863, Manassas Gap, Virginia	Died of Chronic Diarrhea, 12/12/1863
Johnson, Samuel N. Private Not Listed On Monument	16	3/4/1862, St. Marks, Florida	Unknown	Co. G, 5th Florida Infantry	6/24/1864, Petersburg, Virginia	Died of Chronic Diarrhea, 5/27/1865
Johnson, Samuel N. Sergeant	31	6/27/1862 Camp Martin, North Carolina	Wilkes County, North Carolina	Co. B, 5th North Carolina Cavalry	7/31/1863, Irvine, Kentucky	Died of Scurvy at Fort Delaware, De., 4/12/1865
Johnson, William B. Private	19	5/10/1861 Sampson County, North Carolina	Sampson County, North Carolina, Apprentice	Co. H, 20th North Carolina Infantry	7/2/1863, Gettysburg, Pennsylvania	Died of Chronic Dysentery, 2/14/1864
Johnson, William D. Private	Unk	10/6/1863 Richmond, Virginia, Substitute	Henrico County, Virginia	Co. E, 18th Virginia Infantry	4/6/1865, Prince Edward County, Virginia	Died of Chronic Dysentery, 6/17/1865

Name	Age	Enlisted	Residence	Unit	Captured	Date and Cause of Death
Johnson, William D. Private	Unk	1/1/1862, 1/29/1864, Charleston, South Carolina	Charleston County, South Carolina	Co. E, 26th South Carolina Infantry	4/1/1865, Southside Railroad, Virginia	Died of Chronic Diarrhea, 5/14/1865
Johnson, Willie Private	49	1/15/1863 Petersburg, Virginia, Substitute for Sgt. H. L. Leggett	Edgecombe County, North Carolina	Co. I, 15th North Carolina Infantry	10/14/1863, Bristoe Station, Virginia	Died of Unknown Causes, 11/15/1863
Johnson, W. H. Private	Unk	2/12/1863 Pocotaligo, South Carolina	Jasper County, South Carolina	Co. E, Hampton Legion South Carolina Infantry	Unknown	Date and Cause of Death Unknown
Jones, Andrew Sergeant	Unk	Unknown	Unknown	Co. E, 43rd Tennessee Infantry	5/17/1863, Big Black Bridge, Near Vicksburg, Mississippi	Died of Unknown Causes, 4/7/1864
Jones, Benoni M. Private	Unk	7/8/1861 Griffin, Georgia	Pike County, Georgia	Co. E, 14th Georgia Infantry	7/5/1863, Waterloo, Pennsylvania, Gunshot Wound Left Side of Face	Died of Chronic Diarrhea, 11/25/1863
Jones, Council B. Private	18	2/15/1862 Kenansville, North Carolina	Duplin County, North Carolina	Co. C, 2nd North Carolina Cavalry	5/8/1864, Wilderness, Virginia	Died of Unknown Causes, 7/20/1864
Jones, Charles Private	Unk	8/20/1863 Luallatown, North Carolina	Unknown	Co. F, 1st Thomas Regiment North Carolina Legion	9/19/1864, Winchester, Virginia,	Died of Chronic Diarrhea, 2/10/1865
Jones, Henry Coleman Private	Unk	11/4/1863 Halifax County, Virginia	Unknown	Confederate State Army, 1st Regiment Engineer Troops	4/3/1865 Amelia Court House, Virginia	Died of Unknown Causes, 5/10/1865
Jones, F. P. Private	Unk	Unknown	Unknown	Co. C, 4th Georgia Infantry	Unknown	Unable to Locate
Jones, George M. Private	Unk	6/30/1863 Lewisburg, Virginia	Greenbrier County, West Virginia	Co. A, 26th Battalion Virginia Infantry	6/3/1864 Gaines Farm, Virginia	Died of Unknown Causes, 8/26/1864

Name	Age	Enlisted	Residence	Unit	Captured	Date and Cause of Death
Jones, James A. Private	Unk	3/14/1862 Murfreesboro, North Carolina	Northampton County, North Carolina	Co. D, 54th North Carolina Infantry	11/7/1863, Kelly's Ford, Rappahannock Station, Virginia	Died of Unknown Causes, 2/23/1864
Jones, Jesse Corporal	Unk	11/3/1862 Dardenville, Arkansas	Unknown	Co. H, 21st North Carolina Infantry	5/19/1863, Big Black Bridge, Near Vicksburg, Mississippi	Died of Chronic Diarrhea, 11/2/1863
Jones, John E. Private	19	9/28/1862 Chatham County, North Carolina, Conscript	Chatham County, North Carolina	Co. E, 26th North Carolina Infantry	10/14/1863, Bristoe Station, Virginia	Died of Chronic Diarrhea, 2/25/1865
Jones, John H. Private	Unk	5/24/1861 Orange County Court House, Virginia	Unknown	Co. B, 12th Alabama Infantry	5/8/1864, Spotsylvania Court House, Virginia	Died of Chronic Diarrhea, 6/7/1864
Jones, John P. Corporal Not Listed On Monument	23	9/28/1862 Trenton, North Carolina, Volunteer	Jones County, North Carolina	Co. G, 2nd North Carolina Infantry	11/17/1863, Rappahannock Station, Virginia	Died of Smallpox, 4/13/1864
Jones, John W. Private	30	9/1/1862 Raleigh, North Carolina, Conscript	Rockingham County, North Carolina	Co. H, 45th North Carolina Infantry	7/5/1863, Gettysburg, Pennsylvania	Died of Unknown Causes, 8/8/1864
Jones, Lafayette B. Private	19	4/15/1861 New Orleans, Louisiana	Springfield, Louisiana	Co. A, 1st Louisiana Infantry	5/12/1864, Wilderness, Virginia	Died of Unknown Causes, 2/10/1865
Jones, Lawson Private	Unk	3/1/1862 Farmer's Fork, Virginia	Unknown	Co. D, 40th Virginia Infantry	7/14/1863, Falling Waters, Maryland	Died of Unknown Causes, 4/7/1864
Jones, Lewis A. Sergeant	Unk	5/11/1862 West Point, Virginia	Unknown	Co. E, 53rd Virginia Infantry	7/3/1863, Gettysburg, Pennsylvania	Died of Chronic Diarrhea, 1/3/1864
Jones, M. E. Private	Unk	Unknown	Unknown	Co. G, 11th Georgia Cavalry	12/4/1864 Waynesboro, Virginia	Died of Chronic Diarrhea, 4/27/1865

Name	Age	Enlisted	Residence	Unit	Captured	Date and Cause of Death
Jones, Matthew Private	18	6/24/1861 Duplin County, North Carolina, Volunteer	Duplin County, North Carolina	Co. B, 3rd North Carolina Infantry	7/3/1863, Gettysburg, Pennsylvania, Wounded	Date and Cause of Death Unknown
Jones, Peter D. Private	Unk	Unknown	Unknown	Co. D, 4th North Carolina Infantry	5/12/1864 Spotsylvania Court House, Virginia	Died of Unknown Causes 6/20/1864
Jones, R. H. Private	Unk	1/28/1862 Jacksonville, North Carolina	Onslow County, North Carolina	Co. B, 3rd North Carolina Cavalry	12/17/1863, Greenville, North Carolina	Died of Acute Diarrhea, 1/18/1865
Jones, Samuel Private	Unk	4/17/1862, Fort Dilliard, North Carolina	Unknown	Co. F, 57th Virginia Infantry	7/3/1863, Gettysburg, Pennsylvania	Died of Unknown Causes, 8/2/1864
Jones, Thomas E. Private	Unk	10/1/1862 Morrisville, Virginia	Fauquier County, Virginia	Co. I, 11th Virginia Infantry	9/14/1863, Near Culpepper, Virginia	Died of Chronic Diarrhea, 11/21/1863
Jones, Thomas Jefferson Private	Unk	6/20/1861 Clarksville, Virginia	Unknown	Co. I, 11th Virginia Infantry	7/3/1863, Gettysburg, Pennsylvania	Died of Unknown Causes, 3/7/1864
Jones, Thomas J. Sergeant	Unk	6/11/1861 Fort Ganes, Georgia	Clay County, Georgia	Co. D, 9th Georgia Infantry	7/3/1863, Gettysburg, Pennsylvania	Died of Unknown Causes, 11/9/1863
Jones, Thomas P. Private	17	1/28/1863 Montgomery County, Virginia	McDonald Mills, Montgomery County, Virginia, Student	Co. F, 14th Virginia Cavalry	11/12/1864, Near Nineveh, Virginia	Died of Typhoid Fever, 2/10/1865
Jones, William Private	Unk	2/15/1862 Danville, Arkansas	Yell County, Arkansas	Co. E, 21st Georgia Infantry	5/17/1863, Big Black Bridge, Near Vicksburg, Mississippi	Died of Smallpox, 1/12/1864
Jones, William Private	Unk	10/23/1863 Columbia, South Carolina	Richland County, South Carolina	Co. I, 23th South Carolina Infantry	6/17/1864, Petersburg, Virginia	Died of Chronic Diarrhea, 10/27/1864

Name	Age	Enlisted	Residence	Unit	Captured	Date and Cause of Death
Jones, William Private	Unk	4/14/1862 Rude's Hill, Virginia	Unknown	Co. K, 2nd Virginia Infantry	5/12/1864, Spotsylvania Court House, Virginia	Died of Unknown Causes, 5/24/1864
Jones, William L. Private	Unk	8/1/1863 Butler County, Alabama	Butler County, Alabama	Co. D, 61st Virginia Infantry	4/2/1865, Petersburg, Virginia	Died of Acute Diarrhea, 5/24/1865
Jones, William L. Private	Unk	3/5/1863 Lake City, Florida	Columbia County, Florida	Co. E, 9th Florida Infantry	9/10/1864, Petersburg, Virginia	Died of Unknown Causes, 6/10/1865
Jones, William L. Private Not Listed On Monument	Unk	8/19/1861 Sydnorsville, Franklin County, Virginia	Franklin County, Virginia	Co. G, 57nd Virginia Infantry	7/5/1863, Gettysburg, Pennsylvania	Died of Unknown Causes, 7/15/1864
Jordan, Elijah Private	18	4/27/1861 Fort Valley, Georgia	Houston County, Georgia, Painter	Co. E, 3rd Georgia Infantry	7/3/1863, Gettysburg, Pennsylvania, Gunshot Wound Right Thigh	Died of Smallpox, 9/9/1864
Jordan, J. J. Sergeant	Unk	12/21/1862 Chesterfield District, South Carolina	Chesterfield District, South Carolina	Co. F, 26th South Carolina Infantry	5/22/1864, North Anna River, Virginia, Gunshot Wound Right Thigh	Died of Wounds, 5/23/1864
Jordan, Jasper G. Sergeant	Unk	Unknown	Unknown	Co. I, 3rd Georgia Infantry	7/5/1863 Gettysburg, Pennsylvania, Wounded	Died of Unknown Causes, 10/1/1864
Jordan, Richard A. Private	Unk	4/18/1861, Lexington, Virginia	Rockbridge County, Virginia	Co. H, 27th Virginia Infantry	7/3/1863, Gettysburg, Pennsylvania	Died of Chronic Diarrhea, 2/4/1864
Jordan, W. J. Sergeant	Unk	3/4/1861 Charleston, South Carolina	Charleston County, South Carolina	Co. B, 26th South Carolina Infantry	6/24/1864, Petersburg, Virginia	Died of Acute Diarrhea, 12/30/1864
Joyner, John S. Private	30	7/15/1862 Nash County, North Carolina, Conscript	Nash County, North Carolina	Co. D, 4th North Carolina Infantry	7/3/1863, Gettysburg, Pennsylvania	Died of Smallpox, 12/30/1863

Name	Age	Enlisted	Residence	Unit	Captured	Date and Cause of Death
Joyner, Joseph R. Private	38	2/26/1862 Camp Leon, Tallahassee, Florida	Leon County, Florida	Co. K, 5th Florida Infantry	7/3/1863, Gettysburg, Pennsylvania	Died of Smallpox, 10/31/1863
Justice, John M. Private	33	1/20/1863 Upshur County, Texas	Upshur County, Texas	Co. K, 7th Texas Infantry	12/17/1864, Franklin, Tennessee	Died of Chronic Diarrhea, 6/10/1865
Justus, J. F. Private	Unk	1/10/1862 Columbia, South Carolina	Richland County, South Carolina	Co. D, 22nd South Carolina Infantry	6/3/1864, Near Bermuda Hundred, Virginia	Died of Acute Dysentery, 8/27/1864
Justus, Soloman Private	Unk	6/15/1864 Camp Vance, North Carolina	Burke County, North Carolina	Co. B, 3rd North Carolina Junior Reserves	12/25/1864, Fort Fisher, North Carolina	Died of Frost Bite, 3/10/1865

Name	Age	Enlisted	Residence	Unit	Captured	Date and Cause of Death
Kainey, R. G. Private	Unk	Unknown	Unknown	Co. A, 15th Virginia Infantry	Unknown	Unable to Locate
Kale, Coatsworth Private	18	6/20/1861 Alamance County, North Carolina	Alamance County, North Carolina	Co. D, 6th North Carolina Infantry	11/7/1863, Kelly's Ford, Rappahannock Station, Virginia	Died of Chronic Dysentery, 2/15/1865
Kanady, Robert J. Private	Unk	9/17/1861 Eastville, Alabama	Chilton County, Alabama	Co. E, 13th Alabama Infantry	5/12/1864, Spotsylvania Court House, Virginia	Died of Chronic Diarrhea, 10/267/1864
Keton, William H. Private	Unk	4/10/1863 Linden, Tennessee	Perry County, Tennessee	Co. B, 10th Tennessee Cavalry	7/7/1863 Patriot, Tennessee	Died of Acute Dysentery, 6/22/1865
Kee, James F. W. Private Not Listed On Monument	28	5/30/1861, Halifax County, North Carolina	Gates County, North Carolina	Co. H, 5th North Carolina Infantry	7/2/1863, Gettysburg, Pennsylvania	Died of Smallpox, 1/3/1864

Name	Age	Enlisted	Residence	Unit	Captured	Date and Cause of Death
Keen, William Private	28	5/30/1861 Weldon, North Carolina, Volunteer	Halifax County, North Carolina	Co. E, 13th North Carolina Infantry	7/3/1863, Gettysburg, Pennsylvania	Died of Smallpox, 1/3/1864
Kegley, Daniel Private	Unk	2/24/64 Narrows, Virginia	Giles County, Virginia	Co. B, 60th Virginia Infantry	9/19/1864, Winchester, Virginia	Died of Chronic Dysentery, 12/30/1864
Keith, T. E. Private	30	7/6/1861 Randolph County, Alabama	Randolph County, Alabama	Co. C, 13th Alabama Infantry	5/12/1864, Spotsylvania Court House, Virginia	Died of Acute Dysentery, 7/30/1864
Keller, John J. Private	18	2/11/1863 Caldwell County, North Carolina, Volunteer	Caldwell County, North Carolina	Co. E, 11th North Carolina Infantry	7/3/1863, Gettysburg, Pennsylvania, Wounded	Died of Smallpox, 12/21/1863
Keller, L. S. Private Not Listed On Monument	Unk	Unknown	Unknown	Co. A, 3rd North Carolina Junior Reserve Infantry	12/25/1864, Near Fort Fisher, North Carolina	Died of Meningitis, Inflammation of Brain, 6/29/1865
Keller, Thomas S. Private	Unk	Unknown	Unknown	Co. K, 1st Virginia Infantry	Unknown	Unable to Locate
Keller, Y. Alex Private	Unk	1/22/1862 Columbia, South Carolina	Richland County, South Carolina	Co. D, 22nd South Carolina Infantry	7/30/1864, Petersburg, Virginia, Wounded Head and Back	Died of Scurvy, 4/13/1865
Kelley, J. B. See Kelly, Preston				Co. C, 47th North Carolina Infantry		
Kelley, John H. Private Not Listed On Monument	26	4/18/1861 Harrisburg, Virginia	Unknown	Co. G, 10th Virginia Infantry	7/3/1863, Gettysburg, Pennsylvania	Died of Chronic Diarrhea, 4/6/1865

Name	Age	Enlisted	Residence	Unit	Captured	Date and Cause of Death
Kelley, Joseph H. Private	Unk	4/18/1861 Harrisburg, Virginia	Unknown	Co. B, 10th Virginia Infantry	5/12/1864, Spotsylvania Court House, Virginia	Date and Cause of Death Unknown
Kelley, Silas G. Private Not Listed On Monument	35	7/1/1861, Pittsylvania County, Virginia	Pittsylvania County, Virginia	Co. H, 21st Virginia Infantry	10/19/1864, Cedar Creek or Strasburg, Virginia	Died of Chronic Diarrhea & Scurvy, 4/6/1865
Kelly, David W. Private Not Listed On Monument	Unk	3/1/1862, New Camp Lamb, North Carolina, Substitute	Chatham County, North Carolina	Co. H, 30th North Carolina Infantry	9/19/1864, Chambersburg, Pennsylvania	Died of Unknown Causes, 7/13/1864
Kelly, Preston Private	45	1/18/1862 Raleigh, North Carolina	Wake County, North Carolina	Co. C, 47th North Carolina Infantry	10/27/1864, Burgess' Mill, Near Petersburg, Virginia	Died Intermittent Fever, 1/11/1865
Kelly, J. W. Private	Unk	8/4/1862 Brookhaven, Mississippi	Lincoln County, Mississippi	Co. G, 13th Mississippi Infantry	10/19/1864, Cedar Creek or Strasburg, Virginia	Died of Unknown Causes, 3/20/1865
Kelly, William D Private	Unk	6/18/1861 East Bend, North Carolina	Yadkin County, North Carolina	Co. E, 28th North Carolina Infantry	7/3/1863, Gettysburg, Pennsylvania	Died of Unknown Causes, 3/10/1864
Kelton, W. P. Private	Unk	Unknown	Unknown	Co. B, 22nd Battalion Virginia Infantry	Unknown	Unable to Locate
Kemp, Joseph Private	Unk	9/7/1864, Raleigh, North Carolina	Unknown	Co. A, 32nd North Carolina Infantry	3/25/1865, Fort Stedman, Near Petersburg, Virginia	Died of Pneumonia, 4/8/1865
Kendrick, James A. Private	Unk	3/4/1862 Srarkville, Georgia	Unknown	Co. B, 51st Georgia Infantry	4/6/1865, High Bridge, Virginia	Died of Unknown Causes, 6/6/1865

Name	Age	Enlisted	Residence	Unit	Captured	Date and Cause of Death
Kenerly, A. M. Private	26	7/5/1862 Salisbury, North Carolina	Irdell County, North Carolina	Co. A, 57th North Carolina Infantry	11/7/1863, Kelly's Ford, Rappahannock Station, Virginia	Died of Unknown Causes, 1/15/1864
Kenneday, Charles B. Private	25	3/12/1862 Davidson County, North Carolina	Davidson County, North Carolina, Farmer	Co. A, 10th Battalion North Carolina Heavy Artillery	12/7/1864, Near Savannah, Georgia	Died of Chronic Diarrhea, 4/7/1865
Kenneday, George See Cannaday, George				Co. C, 45th North Carolina Infantry		
Kennedy, Robert Seaman	Unk	Unknown	Unknown	Confederate States Navy	Unknown	Unable to Locate
Kerley, Elisha Private Not Listed On Monument	29	10/22/1862, Camp Holmes, Raleigh, North Carolina, Conscript	Alexander County, North Carolina	Co. F, 32nd North Carolina Infantry	5/10/1864, Wilderness, Virginia	Died of Unknown Causes, 10/22/1864
Kerns, Thomas A. Private	18	9/3/1861 Mecklenburg County, North Carolina, Volunteer	Mecklenburg County, North Carolina, Farmer	Co. H, 35th North Carolina Infantry	3/25/1865, Fort Stedman, Near Petersburg, Virginia	Died of Pneumonia, 6/26/1865
Kerr, James McD. Private Not Listed On Monument	Unk	7/6/1861, Rich Mountain, Virginia	Unknown	Co. H, 25th Virginia Infantry	7/4/1863, Gettysburg, Pennsylvania, Wounded in Back	Died of Chronic Diarrhea, 11/5/1863
Kesler, John Private	Unk	5/4/1862 Suffolk, Virginia	Isle of Wight County, Virginia	Co. H, 52rd Virginia Infantry	7/3/1863, Gettysburg, Pennsylvania, Wounded in Side	Died of Chronic Diarrhea & Erysipelas, 1/5/1864
Ketchum, James F. Sergeant	18	3/15/1862 Wilmington, North Carolina	New Hanover County, North Carolina, Student	Co. A, 51st North Carolina Infantry	9/30/1864, Fort Harrison, Virginia	Died of Pneumonia, 3/19/1865

313

Name	Age	Enlisted	Residence	Unit	Captured	Date and Cause of Death
Keys, William L. Private	26	4/7/1862 Petersburg, Virginia	Chesterfield County, Virginia	Co. K, 5th Virginia Cavalry	10/10/1863, Mitchell's Ford, Brandy Station, Virginia	Died of Hepatitis, 3/21/1865
Kidd, B. F. Private	26	8/14/1862 Place Unknown, Conscript	Surry County, North Carolina	Co. C, 21st North Carolina Infantry	7/3/1863, Gettysburg, Pennsylvania	Died of Chronic Diarrhea, 11/131863
Kilbey, John M. Private	Unk	8/24/1861 Hewassee, Torons County, Georgia	Torons County, Georgia	Co. D, 24th Georgia Infantry	4/6/1865, Burkesville, Virginia	Died of Tetanus, 5/10/1865
Kilby, John S. Private	Unk	7/1/1862 Anderson, South Carolina	Anderson County, South Carolina	Co. C, 7th South Carolina Infantry	5/23/1864, North Anna River, Virginia	Died of Typhoid Fever, 1/29/1865
Killebrew, J. J. Private	Unk	5/6/1862 Buena Vista, Georgia	Marion County, Georgia	Co. G, 59th Georgia Infantry	5/12/1864, Mine Run, Virginia	Died of Chronic Diarrhea, 10/26/1864
Killebrew, Jeremiah Private	Unk	9/13/1861 Camp McDonald, Georgia	Glasscock County, Georgia	Co. B, 22nd Georgia Infantry	8/16/1864, Deep Bottom, Virginia	Died of Chronic Diarrhea, 11/10/1864
Killian, John A. Private	17	6/22/1861 Garysburg, North Carolina, Volunteer	Lincoln County, North Carolina	Co. K, 23rd North Carolina Infantry	7/3/1863, Gettysburg, Pennsylvania	Died of Chronic Diarrhea, 11/11863
Killpatrick, Columbus L. Private	Unk	9/19/1861 Dalton, Georgia	Whitfield County, Georgia	Co. G, 60th Georgia Infantry	10/19/1864, Cedar Creek or Strasburg, Virginia	Died of Chronic Diarrhea, 4/7/1865
Kilpatrick, William A. Sergeant Not Listed On Monument	26	9/9/1861 Rowan, North Carolina, Volunteer	Rowan County, North Carolina, Merchant	Co. D, 34th North Carolina Infantry	7/14/1863, Falling Waters, Maryland	Died of Dysentery, 2/22/1864
Kilpatrick, William J. Private	Unk	4/20/1861 Greenville, North Carolina	Pitt County, North Carolina	Co. C, 27th North Carolina Infantry	10/14/1863, Bristow Station, Virginia	Died of Unknown Causes, 3/1/1864

Name	Age	Enlisted	Residence	Unit	Captured	Date and Cause of Death
Kimble, Louis F. Private	Unk	7/3/1863 Richmond, Virginia	Henrico County, Virginia	Co. F, 1st Maryland Cavalry	7/23/1863, Aimsville, Virginia	Died of Unknown Causes, 2/21/1864
Kindle, Rueben A. Private	27	8/8/1862 Camp Hill, Stanly County, North Carolina, Conscript	Stanly County, North Carolina	Co. F, 5th North Carolina Infantry	8/15/1863, Hagertown, Maryland	Died of Chronic Diarrhea, 2/14/1865
King, Allen D. Private	Unk	7/15/1862 Clinton, North Carolina	Sampson County, North Carolina	Co. C, 5th North Carolina Infantry	9/22/1863, Near Madison Court House, Virginia	Died of Chronic Diarrhea, 1/9/1864
King, B. H. Private	Unk	3/17/1864 Cedar Creek, Florida	Unknown	Co. G, 5th Georgia Cavalry	11/16/1864, Bear Creek Station, Georgia	Died of Unknown Causes, 3/16/1865
King, Bernard H. Private Not Listed On Monument	Unk	5/8/1861, Haymarket, Virginia	Prince William County, Virginia	Co. C, 8th Virginia Cavalry	8/25/1864, William Howlett's House, Virginia	Died of Chronic Diarrhea, 3/15/1865
King, David D. Sergeant	25	6/17/1861 Fayetteville, North Carolina	Cumberland County, North Carolina	Co. C, 3rd North Carolina Infantry	7/3/1863, Gettysburg, Pennsylvania	Died of Smallpox, 12/4/1863
King, Eli M. Private	25	4/13/1862 Camp Mangum, Wake County, North Carolina	Wake County, North Carolina, Farmer	Co. H, 47th North Carolina Infantry	7/5/1863, Gettysburg, Pennsylvania	Died of Chronic Diarrhea, 2/28/1865
King, Howell Private Not Listed On Monument	35	2/26/1863, Randolph County, North Carolina, Conscript	Randolph County, North Carolina	Co. E, 4th North Carolina Infantry	10/19/1864, Cedar Creek or Strasburg, Pennsylvania	Died of Chronic Diarrhea, 1/27/1865
King, James Private	18	6/20/1861 Goldsboro, North Carolina, Volunteer	Wayne County, North Carolina Farmer	Co. C, 2nd North Carolina Infantry	7/3/1863, Gettysburg, Pennsylvania	Died of Pneumonia, 10/21/1863

Name	Age	Enlisted	Residence	Unit	Captured	Date and Cause of Death
King, James W. Private	Unk	11/24/1862 Near Madison Court House, Virginia	Madison County, Virginia	Co. D, 44th Virginia Infantry	5/12/1864, Spotsylvania Court House, Virginia	Died of Unknown Causes, 9/1/1864
King, Joel J. Private	Unk	12/5/1861 Camp Hampton, South Carolina	Lancaster County, South Carolina	Co. A, 3rd Battalion South Carolina Infantry	5/23/1864, Hanover Junction, Virginia	Died of Unknown Causes, 4/24/1865
King, John Private	28	4/1/1864 Wake County, North Carolina, Conscript	Wake County, North Carolina	Co. H, 30th North Carolina Infantry	4/6/1865, Farmville, Virginia	Died of Chronic Diarrhea, 5/29/1865
King, Solomon Private	Unk	4/15/1864 Raleigh, North Carolina	Wake County, North Carolina	Co. H, 47th North Carolina Infantry	10/27/1864, Burgess' Mill, Near Petersburg, Virginia	Died of Chronic Diarrhea, 5/23/1865
King, W. H. Private	41	9/14/1863 Camp Holmes, North Carolina, Conscript	Wake County, North Carolina	Co. H, 30th North Carolina Infantry	5/17/1864, Near Spotsylvania Court House, Virginia	Died of Unknown Causes, 6/30/1864
King, William H. Private Not Listed On Monument	51	8/19/1861, Crabtree, North Carolina, Substitute	Unknown	Co. D, 26th North Carolina Infantry	5/24/1864, North Anna River, Virginia	Died of Unknown Causes, 7/9/1864
Kingry, Peter J. Private	Unk	2/1/1863 Giles Court House, Virginia	Giles County, Virginia	Co. H, 36th Virginia Infantry	9/19/1864, Winchester, Virginia	Died of Acute Dysentery, 2/1/1865
Kinley, William Private	38	9/14/1863 Raleigh, North Carolina, Conscript	Lincoln County, North Carolina	Co. G, 12th North Carolina Infantry	10/19/1864, Cedar Creek, Virginia	Died of Scurvy, 2/1/1865
Kinston, M. See: Mincey, Kinchen				Co. B, 11th North Carolina Infantry		

Name	Age	Enlisted	Residence	Unit	Captured	Date and Cause of Death
Kinzer, William T. Sergeant Not Listed On Monument	Unk	7/16/1861 Blacksburg, Virginia	Montgomery County, Virginia	Co. L, 4th Virginia Infantry	5/12/1864, Near Spotsylvania Court House, Virginia	Died of Unknown Causes, 7/15/1864
Kirby, Lafayette Private	Unk	2/17/1863 Charleston, South Carolina	Charleston County, South Carolina	Co. K, 27th South Carolina Infantry	5/9/1864, Near Petersburg, Virginia	Died of Typhoid Fever, 4/11/1865
Kirk, George E. Private	31	3/25/1862 Albemarle County, North Carolina, Volunteer	Stanley County, North Carolina	Co. I, 52nd North Carolina Infantry	7/14/1863, Falling Waters, Maryland	Died of Unknown Causes, 3/13/1864
Kirk, William H. Private	Unk	Unknown	Unknown	Quarter Master Department	Unknown	Unable to Locate
Kirkland, Stephen H. Private	18	8/16/1861 Warren County, North Carolina	Warren County, North Carolina	Co. B, 30th North Carolina Infantry	11/7/1863, Kelly's Ford, Rappahannock, Virginia	Died of Unknown Causes, 8/11/1864
Kirkman, Wiley P. Private	20	6/10/1861 Matthews, North Carolina, Volunteer	Mecklenburg County, North Carolina	Co. B, 30th North Carolina Infantry	7/5/1863, Gettysburg, Pennsylvania	Died of Scurvy, 3/10/1865
Kirkpatrick, William H. Sergeant	Unk	9/5/1861 Athens, Georgia	Limestone County, Georgia	Co. D, Cobb's Legion, Georgia Infantry	8/18/1864, Front Royal, Virginia	Died of Chronic Diarrhea, 11/1/1864
Kiser, Tandy Private	27	7/25/1863 Danbury, North Carolina, Conscript	Stokes County, North Carolina	Co. G, 21st North Carolina Infantry	10/19/1864, Cedar Creek or Strasburg, Virginia	Died of Remittent Fever, 11/1/1864

Name	Age	Enlisted	Residence	Unit	Captured	Date and Cause of Death
Kissiah, John H. M. Private	18	12/20/1861 Chesterfield District, South Carolina	Chesterfield District, South Carolina	Co. E, 21st South Carolina Infantry	7/10/1863, Morris Island, South Carolina	Died of Unknown Causes, 2/3/1864
Kitchen, Ransom Private	Unk	4/18/1864 Camp of Instruction, Talladega, Alabama	Talladega County, Alabama	Co. I, 12th Alabama Infantry	5/5/1864, Wilderness, Virginia	Died of Unknown Causes, 7/1/1864
Kitchen, William W. Private Not Listed On Monument	Unk	4/18/1864 Camp of Instruction, Talladega, Alabama	Talladega County, Alabama	Co. G, 12th Alabama Infantry	5/8/1864, Wilderness, Virginia	Died of Unknown Causes, 7/4/1864
Kitchens, Hugh Sergeant	Unk	3/4/1862 Starkville, Georgia	Unknown	Co. B, 51st Georgia Infantry	7/3/1863, Gettysburg, Pennsylvania	Died of Chronic Diarrhea, 1/5/1864
Kitchens, Jordan Private	19	3/4/1862 Gibson, Georgia	Glascock County, Georgia	Co. A, 48th Georgia Infantry	7/1/1863, Gettysburg, Pennsylvania	Died of Pneumonia, 11/7/1863
Kittle, J. B. Private	Unk	7/2/1863 Rowan County, North Carolina	Rowan County, North Carolina	Co. K, 54th North Carolina Infantry	11/7/1863, Rappahannock, Virginia	Died of Unknown Causes, 11/13/1863
Kivett, Alexander L. Sergeant	17	5/13/1862 Petersburg, Virginia	Randolph County, North Carolina	Co. H, 36th Virginia Infantry	7/2/1863, Gettysburg, Pennsylvania	Died of Smallpox, 12/30/1863
Kivett, John W. Jr. Private	24	7/25/1863 Randolph County, North Carolina, Volunteer	Randolph County, North Carolina	Co. M, 22nd North Carolina Infantry	7/14/1863, Falling Waters, Maryland	Died of Chronic Diarrhea, 4/8/1864

318

Name	Age	Enlisted	Residence	Unit	Captured	Date and Cause of Death
Knight, C. C. Private	Unk	Unknown	Spalding County, Georgia	Co. C, 13th Georgia Infantry	7/5/1863, Waterloo, Gettysburg, Pennsylvania	Died of Smallpox, 2/10/1864
Knight, George W. Private	30	5/1/1862 South Mills, North Carolina, Vollunteer	Northampton County, North Carolina	Co. D, 32th North Carolina Infantry	7/5/1863, Gettysburg, Pennsylvania, Wounded	Died of Smallpox 11/22/1863
Knight, Jacob F. Private Not Listed On Monument	Unk	6/1/1861 Luray, Page County, Virginia	Page County, Virginia	Co. H, 33rd Virginia Infantry	9/23/1864 Cedar Creek or Strasburg, Virginia	Died of Unknown Causes, 5/11/1865
Knight, Joel Private	Unk	6/1/1861 Luray, Page County, Virginia	Page County, Virginia	Co. H, 33rd Virginia Infantry	9/23/1864 Cedar Creek or Strasburg, Virginia	Died of Dropsy, 5/11/1865
Knight, Samuel D. Sergeant	23	3/3/1862 Greensboro, North Carolina, Volunteer	Guilford County, North Carolina, Farmer	Co. C, 45th North Carolina Infantry	10/19/1864 Cedar Creek or Strasburg, Virginia	Died of Debility (Feebleness), 12/30/1864
Knight, Thomas 2nd Lieutenant	28	7/15/1862, Kentucky	Unknown	Co. H, 2nd Regiment Kentucky Cavalry	7/18/1863, Hickman Bridge, Harrisburg, Kentucky	Died of Chronic Diarrhea, 10/27/1864
Knox, John D. Sergeant	34	4/29/1862 Sarepta, Mississippi	Calhoun County, Mississippi	Co. F, 42nd Mississippi Infantry	5/24/1864, North Anna River, Virginia	Died of Unknown Causes, 9/16/1864
Knuckles, Benjamin L. Private	Unk	Unknown	Unknown	Co. ?, Stiles Battery, Georgia Artillery	Unknown	Unable to Locate

Name	Age	Enlisted	Residence	Unit	Captured	Date and Cause of Death
Koiner, Martin Diller Private Not Listed On Monument	19	3/13/1862, Camp Alleghany, Virginia, Conscript	Augusta County, Virginia	Co. B, 52nd Virginia Infantry	7/9/1863, Washington County, Maryland	Died of Chronic Diarrhea, 10/29/1863
Koone, Noah Private	Unk	9/22/1863 Camp Vance, North Carolina	Burke County, North Carolina	Co. C, 34th North Carolina Infantry	3/25/1865, Fort Stedman, Near Petersburg, Virginia	Died of Rheumatism. 5/26/1865
Kornegay, Dudley Private	35	2/12/1863 Duplin County, North Carolina	Duplin County, North Carolina	Co. A, 43rd North Carolina Infantry	4/6/1865, Near Petersburg, Virginia	Died of Acute Dysentery, 6/7/1865
Kornegay, Marshall Private	17	1/26/1864 Fort Caswell, North Carolina, Volunteer	Mount Olive, Duplin County, North Carolina, Student	Co. A, 36th North Carolina Heavy Artillery	1/15/1865, Fort Fisher, North Carolina	Died of Pneumonia, 3/28/1865
Kriminger, George G. Private Not Listed On Monument	22	9/7/1861 Concord, North Carolina	Cabarrus County, North Carolina, Farmer	Co. C, 33rd North Carolina Infantry	5/12/1864, Spotsylvania Court House, Virginia	Died of Unknown Causes, 7/2/1864
Kroger, James M. Private Not Listed On Monument	Unk	5/22/1861, Spoon Creek, Virginia	Unknown	Co. H, 42nd Virginia Infantry	7/4/1863, South Mountain, Maryland	Died of Smallpox, 12/14/1863
Kyser, Malachi Private	Unk	10/18/1863 Butler County, Alabama	Butler County, Alabama	Co. D, 61st Alabama Infantry	4/2/1865, Petersburg, Virginia	Died of Unknown Causes, 5/30/1865

Name	Age	Enlisted	Residence	Unit	Captured	Date and Cause of Death
Lackey, George W. Corporal	17	5/8/1861 Marion, North Carolina, Volunteer	McDowell County, North Carolina	Co. B, 43rd North Carolina Infantry	7/3/1863, Gettysburg, Pennsylvania	Died of Chronic Diarrhea, 10/18/1863
Lacy, W. Private	Unk	Unknown	Unknown	Co. A, 8th Virginia Infantry	Unknown	Unable to Locate
Laffoon, John G. Private	Unk	2/14/1863 Camp Lee, Prince Edward County, Virginia	Prince Edward County, Virginia	Co. D, 18th Virginia Infantry	7/3/1863, Gettysburg, Pennsylvania	Died of Chronic Diarrhea, 2/11/1864
Lagervist, Abraham I. J. Private	Unk	5/17/1861 Macon, Georgia	Bibb County, Georgia	Co. E, 2nd Battalion Georgia Infantry	7/2/1863, Gettysburg, Pennsylvania	Died of Smallpox, 12/25/1863
Lake, Robert H. Sergeant	Unk	4/10/1861, Cahaba, Alabama	Dallas County, Alabama	Co. F, 5th Alabama Infantry	7/5/1863, Waterloo, Gettysburg, Pennsylvania	Died of Unknown Causes, 7/24/1864
Lake, Washington Private	18	8/20/1863 Monroe County, Virginia	Monroe County, Virginia, Farmer	Co. D, 8th Virginia Cavalry	3/30/1863, Mount Pleasant, West Virginia	Died of Chronic Diarrhea, 11/20/1863
Lamb, John Private	32	7/8/1862 Piney Woods, North Carolina, Volunteer	New Hanover County, North Carolina, Farmer	Co. G, 61st North Carolina Infantry	10/7/1864, Darbytown Road, Virginia	Died of Chronic Dysentery, 1/12/1865
Lamb, Robert Corporal	Unk	5/9/1862 Myersville, South Carolina	Unknown	Co. H, 25th South Carolina Infantry	5/9/1864, Near Petersburg, Virginia	Died of Chronic Diarrhea. 2/15/1865

Name	Age	Enlisted	Residence	Unit	Captured	Date and Cause of Death
Lamb, William Private	31	12/3/1861 Fernandina, Florida	Nassau County, Florida	Co. B, 10th Florida Infantry	8/21/1864, Globe Tavern, Near Weldon Railroad, Virginia	Died of Unknown Causes, 4/9/1865
Lamb, William B. Private	21	7/18/1861 Washington, North Carolina	Beaufort County, North Carolina	Co. G, 61st North Carolina Infantry	9/7/1863, Washington County, North Carolina	Died of Chronic Dysentery, 2/3/1865
Lambert, John A. Private	Unk	1/19/1863, Chaffin's Bluff, Virginia	Unknown	Captain Tacitus Allen's Company, Virginia Heavy Artillery	4/6/1865, Harper's Farm, Virginia	Died of Pneumonia, 5/27/1865
Lampert, James F. Private	Unk	5/3/1863 Dublin, Virginia	Pulaski County, Virginia	Co. G, 36th Virginia Infantry	9/19/1864, Winchester, Virginia	Died of Consumption, 1/30/1865
Lancaster, L. L. Private	28	10/9/1861 Enfield, North Carolina, Volunteer	Wilson County, North Carolina	Co. K, 36th North Carolina Heavy Artillery	1/15/1865, Fort Fisher, North Carolina	Died of Typhoid Fever/ Pneumonia 6/5/1865
Lane, Bryant Private	Unk	8/1/1863 Atlanta, Georgia	Fulton County, Georgia	Co. H, 64th Georgia Infantry	8/10/1864, Deep Bottom, Virginia	Died of Pneumonia, 1/30/1865
Lane, J. P. Private	Unk	4/26/1864 Chaffin's Farm, Virginia	Unknown	Co. D, 35th Virginia Infantry	4/6/1865, Burkesville, Virginia	Died of Rubeola (Measles), 6/22/1865
Lane, J. T. Private	Unk	5/1/1862 Savannah, Georgia	Stewart County, Georgia	Co. H, 64th Georgia Infantry	11/?/1864, No Location Given	Died Date and Cause Unknown

Name	Age	Enlisted	Residence	Unit	Captured	Date and Cause of Death
Lane, W. H. C. Private	Unk	9/1/1862 Cahaba, Alabama	Dallas County, Alabama	Co. A, 6th Alabama Infantry	10/19/1864, Cedar Creek or Strasburg, Virginia	Died of Pneumonia, 5/1/1865
Lane, Willam Private	30	5/13/1862 Goldsboro, North Carolina	Green County, North Carolina	Co. A, 3rd North Carolina Infantry	7/3/1863, Gettysburg, Pennsylvania, Wounded	Died Date and Cause Unknown
Lane, Willam Private	22	4/28/1862 Perquimans County, North Carolina, Volunteer	Perquimans County, North Carolina	Co. F, 11th North Carolina Infantry	7/3/1863, Gettysburg, Pennsylvania	Died of Acute Diarrhea, 10/15/1864
Lanford, Daniel A. Private	Unk	2/10/1863 Spartanburg, South Carolina	Spartanburg District, South Carolina	Co. A, Holcombe's South Carolina Legion Infantry	4/1/1865, Five Forks, Virginia	Died of Pneumonia, 5/29/1865
Lang, Lemuel Coporal	34	3/5/1862 Tallahassee, Florida	Leon County, Florida	Co. F, 5th Florida Infantry	7/4/1863, Gettysburg, Pennsylvania, Wounded Left Hip and Thigh	Died of Unknown Causes, 9/9/1864
Langston, Kindred Private	24	7/3/1862 Murfreesboro, North Carolina	Hertford County, North Carolina	Co. D, 4th North Carolina Cavalry	6/21/1863, Upperville, Virginia, Injured Back and Right Thigh in Fall of Horse	Died of Unknown Causes, 5/6/1864
Lanier, Bias D. Sergeant	21	10/30/1861 Harnett County, North Carolina, Volunteer	Harnett County, North Carolina	Co. I, 31st North Carolina Infantry	9/30/1864, Fort Harrison, Virginia	Died of Chronic Dysentery, 12/25/1864
Lankford, Jerome L. Private	18	5/6/1862 Shelby, North Carolina	Cleveland County, North Carolina, Farmer	Co. D, 55th North Carolina Infantry	7/1/1863, Gettysburg, Pennsylvania	Died of Chronic Diarrhea, 12/17/1863
Lankin, W. H. Private	Unk	Unknown	Unknown	Co. C, 9th Virginia Infantry	Unknown	Unable to Locate

Name	Age	Enlisted	Residence	Unit	Captured	Date and Cause of Death
Lantz, Jacob Private	Unk	Unknown	Unknown	Co. E, 57th North Carolina Infantry	11/7/1863, Kelly's Ford, Rappahannock Station, Virginia	Died of Unknown Causes, 4/29/1864
Lascas, A. M. Private	Unk	Unknown	Unknown	Co. C, 52nd Georgia Infantry	Unknown	Unable to Locate
Lasley, Charles A. Private	17	6/25/1861 Russell County, Virginia	Russell County, Virginia	Co. K, 48th Virginia Infantry	7/3/1863, Gettysburg, Pennsylvania	Died of Smallpox, 2/25/1864
Lassiter, William N. Private	Unk	7/1/1862 Hertford County, North Carolina, Conscript	Hertford County, North Carolina	Co. H, 33rd North Carolina Infantry	5/8/1864, Mine Run, Virginia	Died of Pneumonia, 8/18/1864
Lathan, John H. L. Private Not Listed On Monument	Unk	9/15/1864, Columbia, South Carolina	Richland County, South Carolina	Co. I, 17th South Carolina Infantry	4/2/1865, Petersburg, Virginia	Died of Typhoid Fever, 7/17/1865
Laughter, John R. Private	Unk	9/15/1863 Garysburg, Henderson County, North Carolina	Henderson County, North Carolina	Co. A, 25th North Carolina Infantry	4/2/1865, Petersburg, Virginia	Died of Chronic Diarrhea, 6/10/1865
Lawhorn, Alexander Private	17	8/26/1864 Carrolton, Mississippi	Pickens County, Alabama	Co. G, 11th Mississippi Infantry	3/25/1865, Hatchers Run, Near Richmond, Virginia	Died of Rubeola (Measles), 1/7/1865
Lawrence, Theodore J. Private	Unk	8/23/1862 Enterprise, Mississippi	Clarke County, Mississippi	Co. G, 11th Mississippi Infantry	5/16/1863, Champion Hill, Near Vicksburg, Mississippi	Died of Unknown Causes, 3/15/1864
Lawrence, Henry C. 1st Lieutenant	Unk	5/15/1862 Ashville, North Carolina, Conscript	Buncombe County, North Carolina	Co. D, 60th North Carolina Infantry	11/25/1863, Missionary Ridge, Tennessee	Died of Unknown Causes, 8/1/1864
Lawson, A. T. Private	Unk	Unknown	Unknown	Co. K, 50th Virginia Infantry	5/12/1864, Spotsylvania Court House, Virginia	Died of Unknown Causes, 8/7/1864

Name	Age	Enlisted	Residence	Unit	Captured	Date and Cause of Death
Lax, William Private	Unk	9/1/1862 Catawba County, Virginia	Catawba County, Virginia	Co. K, 26th Virginia Infantry	3/29/1865, Hatchers Run, Near Richmond, Virginia	Died of Acute Dysentery, 5/11/1865
Layman, Nathaniel Private	Unk	4/1/1864, Pisgah Church, Orange County, Virginia	Orange County, Virginia	Co. E, 2nd Virginia Infantry	9/22/1864, Fisher's Hill, Virginia	Died of Erysipelas, (Bacterial Infection of the Skin), 4/9/1865
Layton, John M. Private	Unk	1/22/1864, Columbia, South Carolina	Richland County, South Carolina	Co. H, 1st South Carolina Infantry	4/20/1865, Near Petersburg, Virginia	Died of Congestive Chill, 5/11/1865
Lazenby, Reason S. Private	Unk	7/30/1864, Camp Vance, North Carolina	Burke County, North Carolina	Co. G, 3rd North Carolina Junior Reserves	12/25/1864, Fort Fisher, North Carolina	Died of Typhoid Fever, 1/29/1865
Leach, Peter T. Private	Unk	7/30/1861 Salem, Virginia	Roanoke County, Virginia	Co. K, 26th Virginia Infantry	7/3/1863, Gettysburg, Pennsylvania, Gunshot Wound of Arm, Compound Fracture	Date and Cause of Death Unknown
Leak, William C. Private	Unk	1/20/1864, Mount Pleasant, South Carolina	Charleston District, South Carolina	Co. F, 22nd South Carolina Infantry	3/25/1865, Fort Stedman, Near Petersburg, Virginia	Died of Neuralgia of Head, 5/24/1865
Leake, P. F. Private Not Listed On Monument	Unk	2/26/1863, Richmond, Virginia	Henrico County, Virginia	Co. H, 24th Virginia Cavalry	12/13/1863, Charles City Court House, Virginia	Died of Unknown Causes, 7/8/1864
Leavister, John C. Private	Unk	10/31/1864, Franklin County, North Carolina	Franklin County, North Carolina	Co. F, 47th North Carolina Infantry	4/3/1865, Appomattox, Virginia	Died of Measles, 5/31/1865
Leavitt, Wyndham H. Sergeant	21	5/7/1861 Gloucester Court House, Virginia	Gloucester County, Virginia, Farmer	Co. A, 5th Virginia Cavalry	9/24/1864, Luray, Virginia	Date and Cause of Death Unknown

Name	Age	Enlisted	Residence	Unit	Captured	Date and Cause of Death
Ledbetter, John W. Private	27	7/1/1862 Rutherford County, North Carolina, Volunteer	Rutherford County, North Carolina	Co. C, 34th North Carolina Infantry	7/14/1863, Falling Waters, Maryland	Died of Chronic Diarrhea, 12/28/1864
Lee, Rufus Charles Private	Unk	7/4/1861 Camp Barksdale, Near Union City, Mississippi	Unknown	Co. H, 13th Mississippi Infantry	4/6/1865, Harper's Farm, Virginia	Died of Pneumonia, 5/28/1865
Lee, J. C. Private	Unk	6/19/1864, Camp Vance, North Carolina	Burke County, North Carolina	Co. G, 3rd North Carolina Junior Reserves	12/25/1864, Fort Fisher, North Carolina	Died of Unknown Causes, 1/17/1865
Lee, James H. Private	Unk	4/30/1862, Clinton, Alabama	Greene County, Alabama	Co. C, 43rd Alabama Infantry	7/30/1864, Petersburg, Virginia	Died of Inflammation Of Lungs (Pneumonia), 8/23/1865
Lee, Jesse J. Corporal	17	9/14/1862, Rogersville, Tennessee	Hawkins County, Tennessee	Co. I, 60th Tennessee Mounted Infantry	5/17/ 1863, Big Black Bridge, Near Vicksburg, Mississippi	Died of Chronic Dysentery, 12/25/1864
Lee, John T. Private	31	7/12/1862 Raleigh, North Carolina	Orange County, North Carolina	Co. D, 60th North Carolina Infantry	5/14/1864, Drewry's Bluff, Virginia	Died of Unknown Causes, 6/10/1865
Lee, John Thomas Private Not Listed On Monument	31	7/15/1862, Orange County, North Carolina	Orange County, North Carolina	Co. D, 56th North Carolina Infantry	5/22/1864, Drewry's Bluff, Virginia	Died of Unknown Causes, 6/19/1864
Lee, Joseph Thomas Private	Unk	12/17/1861 Barmbridge, Georgia	Decatur, County, Georgia	Co. I, 31st Georgia Infantry	5/20/1864, Spotsylvania Court House, Virginia	Died of Unknown Causes, 6/24/1864
Lee, Moses Allen Private Not Listed On Monument	Unk	10/16/1864, Camp Holmes, North Carolina	Johnston County, North Carolina	Co. E, 24th North Carolina Infantry	4/1/1865, Petersburg, Virginia	Died of Typhoid Fever, 7/8/1865

Name	Age	Enlisted	Residence	Unit	Captured	Date and Cause of Death
Lee, Nelson H. Private	22	1/24/1862, Craven County, North Carolina, Volunteer	Swift Creek, Craven County, North Carolina	Co. D, 40th North Carolina Light Artillery	1/15/1865, Fort Fisher, North Carolina	Died of Pneumonia, 1/30/1865
Leeman, James A. Private Not Listed On Monument	Unk	5/8/1863, Newton County, Georgia	Newton County, Georgia	Co. H, 3rd Georgia Infantry	7/2/1863, Gettysburg, Pennsylvania, Wounded, Left Ankle	Died of Unknown Causes, 2/28/1865
Leeper, P. Lewis Sergeant	Unk	10/4/1862, Warensburg, Tennessee	Greene County, Tennessee	Co. I, 61st Tennessee Mounted Infantry	5/17/ 1863, Big Black Bridge, Near Vicksburg, Mississippi	Died of Unknown Causes, 2/1/1864
Leffel, John M. Sergeant	24	5/10/1861 Newcastle, Virginia	Craig County, Virginia, Farmer	Co. C, 28th Virginia Infantry	7/3/1863, Gettysburg, Pennsylvania	Died of Unknown Causes, 8/25/1864
Lettwich, William B. Private	Unk	5/17/1863 Bedford, Virginia	Unknown	Co. C, 28th Virginia Infantry	4/3/1865, Richmond, Virginia	Died of Pneumonia, 5/25/1865
Legare, Solomon E. Private Not Listed On Monument	Unk	11/10/1861, John's Island, South Carolina	Charleston District, South Carolina	Co. D, 6th South Carolina Cavalry	11/7/1864, Petersburg, Virginia	Died of Chronic Diarrhea, 7/22/1865
Leman, Leaman B. Private Not Listed On Monument	20	8/20/1861, Ridgeville, South Carolina	Dorchester District, South Carolina	Co. G, 11th South Carolina Infantry	1/15/1865, Fort Fisher, North Carolina	Died of Chronic Diarrhea & Typhoid Fever, 3/10/1865
Lemons, John A. Private	Unk	10/24/1864 New Market, Virginia	Shenandoah County, Virginia, Shoemaker	Co. E, 45th North Carolina Infantry	4/6/1865, Burksville, Virginia	Died of Chronic Diarrhea, 5/10/1865

Name	Age	Enlisted	Residence	Unit	Captured	Date and Cause of Death
Lemons, Van M. Private	23	12/29/1861 Springfield, Green County, Missouri	Perry, Worth County, Missouri	Co. H, 1st Missouri Cavalry	5/17/ 1863, Big Black Bridge, Near Vicksburg, Mississippi	Died of Unknown Causes, 2/1/1864
Lemox, William Private	Unk	9/1/1864 Albany, Georgia	Dougherty County, Georgia	Co. A, 8th Georgia Cavalry	10/27/1864, Cousen's Farm, Near Petersburg, Virginia	Died of Acute Diarrhea, 5/10/1865
Leneave, Francis E. Private	23	5/28/1861, Meherrin, Virginia	Prince Edward County, Virginia	Co. K, 21st Virginia Infantry	9/23/1864, Cedar Creek or Strasburg, Virginia	Died of Erysipelas, 1/31/1865
Lentoe, L. Private	Unk	Unknown	Unknown	Co. C, 28th South Carolina Infantry	Unknown	Unable to Locate
Leonard, Caleb Private	23	1/24/1862, Lincolnton, Lincoln County, North Carolina, Volunteer	Lincoln County, North Carolina	Co. B, 23rd North Carolina Infantry	5/10/1864, Spotsylvania Court House, Virginia	Died of Unknown Causes, 6/29/1864
Leonard, David Private	Unk	11/1/1862 Haynesville, Tennessee	Unknown	Co. B, 60th Tennessee Mounted Infantry	5/17/ 1863, Big Black Bridge, Near Vicksburg, Mississippi	Died of Chronic Diarrhea, 11/21/1863
Leonard, John Private	Unk	8/7/1864 Camp Holmes, North Carolina	Warren County, North Carolina	Co. K, 12th North Carolina Infantry	9/19/1864, Winchester, Virginia	Died of Chronic Diarrhea, 1/20/1865
Leonard, J. J. Jr. Private	Unk	3/25/1861 Franklin County, North Carolina	Franklin County, North Carolina	Co. K, 12th North Carolina Infantry	6/18/1864, Near Petersburg, Virginia	Died of Unknown Causes, 11/1/1864
Leonard, J. M. Private	Unk	Unknown	Unknown	Co. D, 26th Alabama Infantry	Unknown	Unable to Locate
Leonard, William Private	26	9/14/1862 Rogersville, Tennessee	Hawkins County, Tennessee	Co. B, 60th Tennessee Mounted Infantry	5/17/ 1863, Big Black Bridge, Near Vicksburg, Mississippi	Died of Chronic Dysentery, 12/31/1863

Name	Age	Enlisted	Residence	Unit	Captured	Date and Cause of Death
Leslie, Larkin Private	Unk	Unknown	Unknown	Co. F, 51st Alabama Partisan Rangers	6/27/1863, Shelbyville, Tennessee	Died of Pneumonia, 12/1/1863
Lessley, Alexander C. Private Not Listed On Monument	43	8/10/1863, Augusta, Virginia	Northern District, Augusta County, Virginia, Laborer	Co. G, 25th Virginia Infantry	5/15/1864, Wilderness, Virginia	Died of Intermittent Fever, 10/26/1864
Lester, John H. Private	Unk	4/16/1864 Macon, Georgia	Bibb County, Georgia	Co. I, 7th Georgia Cavalry	6/11/1864, Travillian's Station, Virginia	Died of Chronic Diarrhea, 10/26/1864
Lester, John J. Private Not Listed On Monument	18	10/19/1861, Chester Springs, Virginia	Unknown	Co. C, 6th Virginia Cavalry	5/12/1864, Hanover Court House, Virginia	Died of Unknown Causes, 7/5/1864
Lett, Green H. Private	Unk	10/31/1864 Camp Holmes, North Carolina	Wake County, North Carolina	Co. H, 46th North Carolina Infantry	3/25/1865, Fort Stedman, Near Petersburg, Virginia	Died of Pneumonia, 6/18/1865
Lewallan, Dawson Private Not Listed On Monument	19	12/4/1861, Asheboro, Randolph County, North Carolina	Randolph County, North Carolina	Co. F, 2nd Battalion North Carolina Infantry	5/10/1864, Near Spotsylvania Court House, Virginia	Died of Unknown Causes, 7/12/1864
Lewis, David C. Private	Unk	3/27/1862 Lebanon, Virginia	Russell County, Virginia	Co. G, 29th Virginia Infantry	4/6/1865, Farmville, Virginia	Died of Acute Diarrhea, 6/22/1865
Lewis, Edward T. Private	19	7/31/1861 Fredericksburg Virginia	Spotsylvania, Virginia, Laborer	Co. I, 30th Virginia Infantry	4/6/1865, Farmville, Virginia	Died of Acute Dysentery, 6/16/1865
Lewis, James A. Private	28	10/31/1864 Camp Holmes, North Carolina, Conscript	Iredell County, North Carolina	Co. C, 4th North Carolina Infantry	7/3/1863, Gettysburg, Pennsylvania	Died of Unknown Causes, 3/10/1865

Name	Age	Enlisted	Residence	Unit	Captured	Date and Cause of Death
Lewis, John M. Private	Unk	10/21/1862 Pittsboro, North Carolina	Chatham County, North Carolina	Co. D, 61st North Carolina Infantry	9/30/1864, Chaffin's Farm or Fort Harrison, Virginia	Died of Intermittent Fever, 4/3/1865
Lewis, James M. Private	Unk	5/8/1862, Macon, Georgia	Bibb County, Georgia	Co. B, 59th Georgia Infantry	7/11/1863, Hagerstown, Pennsylvania, Wounded	Died of Pneumonia, 3/13/1865
Lewis, Joseph J. Private	Unk	9/7/1862, Quitman, Georgia	Brooks County, Georgia	Co. B, 59th Georgia Infantry	5/12/1864, Wilderness, Virginia	Died of Unknown Causes, 7/29/1864
Lewis, Posey Private Not Listed On Monument	Unk	7/1/1863, Spartanburg, South Carolina	Spartanburg District, South Carolina	Co. I, 27th South Carolina Infantry	6/24/1864, Petersburg, Virginia	Died of Unknown Causes, 7/15/1864
Lewis, Thomas B. Private	20	3/4/1862, Long Island, Alabama	Jackson County, Alabama	Co. D, 6th Alabama Infantry	7/5/1863, South Mountain, Maryland, Gunshot Wound of Face	Died of Unknown Causes, 11/5/1863
Lewis, Thomas M. Private Not Listed On Monument	28	8/10/1862 Statesville, North Carolina, Conscript	Iredell County, North Carolina	Co. C, 4th North Carolina Infantry	7/3/1863, Gettysburg, Pennsylvania	Died of Chronic Diarrhea, 3/4/1864
Lewis, Thomas W. Private	28	3/6/1862, Fort Caswell, North Carolina, Volunteer	Brunswick County, North Carolina	Co. K, 36th North Carolina Heavy Artillery	1/15/1865, Fort Fisher, North Carolina, Severe Gunshot Wound Right Side	Died of Wounds, 5/5/1865
Liles, Dennis A. Private	24	9/16/1861 Union County, North Carolina	Union County, North Carolina, Farmer	Co. K, 12th North Carolina Infantry	3/25/1865, Fort Stedman, Near Petersburg, Virginia	Died of Chronic Diarrhea, 6/4/1865
Liles, Kinchen Private	18	6/1/1861, Still Hope, Nash County, North Carolina, Volunteer	Nash County, North Carolina, Farmer	Co. E, 7th North Carolina Infantry	7/3/1863, Gettysburg, Pennsylvania	Died of Unknown Causes, 8/25/1864

Name	Age	Enlisted	Residence	Unit	Captured	Date and Cause of Death
Lilley, Isaac Private	Unk	5/1/1864 Christiansburg Virginia	Montgomery County, Virginia	Co. C, 36th Virginia Infantry	9/19/1864, Winchester, Virginia	Died of Pneumonia, 3/2/1865
Limerick, William A. Private	24	5/10/1861, Stafford County, Virginia	Stafford County, Virginia, Laborer	Co. A, 47th Virginia Infantry	7/14/1863, Falling Waters, Maryland	Died of Unknown Causes, 1/3/1864
Linch, William Private	Unk	Unknown	Unknown	Co. B, 18th North Carolina Infantry	Unknown	Unable to Locate
Lindsey, James Private	Unk	2/10/1863 Newberry, South Carolina	Newberry County, South Carolina	Co. E, 3rd South Carolina Infantry	10/19/1864, Cedar Creek or Strasburg, Virginia	Died of Unknown Causes, 1/4/1865
Link, Silas Private	Unk	8/28/1863 Halifax County, Virginia	Halifax County, Virginia	Co. I, 18th Virginia Infantry	4/6/1865, Harper's Farm, Virginia	Died of Acute Dysentery, 6/7/1865
Little, George B. Private	Unk	8/17/1862 Dalton, Georgia	Paulding County, Georgia	Co. C, 7th Georgia Infantry	7/3/1863, Gettysburg, Pennsylvania	Died of Typhoid Fever, 11/15/1863
Little, Jacob Private	Unk	6/1/1864, Richmond, Virginia	Union County, North Carolina	Co. B, 43rd North Carolina Infantry	9/19/1864, Winchester, Virginia	Died of Pneumonia, 1/12/1865
Little, John C. Private	Unk	Unknown	Unknown	Co. C, 23rd Virginia Infantry	Unknown	Unable to Locate
Little, Madison Private	Unk	11/21/1864, Petersburg, Virginia	Chesterfield County, Virginia	Co. H, 16th Mississippi Infantry	4/2/1865, Richmond & Danville Railroad, Virginia	Died of Chronic Diarrhea, 5/26/1865

Name	Age	Enlisted	Residence	Unit	Captured	Date and Cause of Death
Littleton, Early Private	Unk	7/8/1862 Jacksonville, North Carolina	Onslow County, North Carolina	Co. H, 3rd North Carolina Cavalry	12/17/1863, Greenville, North Carolina	Died of Chronic Diarrhea, 9/8/1864
Livingston, Gallen Private	26	10/3/1862, Morristown, Tennessee	Hamblen County, Tennessee	Co. G, 61st Tennessee Mounted Infantry	5/16/1863, Big Black Bridge, Near Vicksburg, Mississippi	Died of Unknown Causes, 2/7/1864
Lloyd, Nathaniel C. Private	23	12/6/1861, Marengo County, Alabama	Marengo County, Alabama	Co. F, 3rd Alabama Cavalry	6/27/1863, Shelbyville, Tennessee	Died Date and Cause Unknown
Loftin, Martin Private	Unk	10/1/1864, Camp Holmes, North Carolina	Mecklenburg County, North Carolina	Co. E, 11th North Carolina Infantry	10/27/1864, Boyton Plank Road or Burgess' Mill, Virginia	Died of Typhoid Fever, 2/12/1865
Logan, George W. Private	22	9/27/1861 Marion, Alabama	Perry County, Alabama	Co. A, 8th Alabama Infantry	7/3/1863, Gettysburg, Pennsylvania, Wounded in Left Side of Chest	Died of Unknown Causes, 12/27/1863
Long, Thomas Private	21	3/29/1862, X-Roads, Cleveland County, North Carolina Volunteer	Cleveland County, North Carolina, Farmer	Co. F, 55th North Carolina Infantry	7/1/1863, Gettysburg, Pennsylvania	Died of Unknown Causes, 1/6/1864
Long, William C. Private	Unk	2/25/1862, Place Unknown	Unknown	Co. F, 11th Georgia Infantry	7/3/1863, Gettysburg, Pennsylvania	Died of Smallpox, 11/5/1863
Long, William L. Corporal	19	7/8/1862, Pfafftown, Forsyth County, North Carolina, Conscript	Forsyth County, North Carolina	Co. I, 33rd North Carolina Infantry	7/3/1863, Gettysburg, Pennsylvania	Died of Unknown Causes, 11/1/1863
Longmire, L. A. Private	Unk	8/8/1861, Pickensville, Alabama	Pickens County, Alabama	Co. H, 5th Alabama Infantry	7/5/1863 Waterloo, Gettysburg, Pennsylvania	Died of Unknown Causes, 11/4/1863

Name	Age	Enlisted	Residence	Unit	Captured	Date and Cause of Death
Lotspeich, Henry D. Private	Unk	3/14/1862, Loachapoka, Alabama	Lee County, Alabama	Co. H, 5th Alabama Infantry	5/6/1864, Spotsylvania Court House, Virginia	Died of Unknown Causes, 8/8/1864
Lott, Robert E. Private	24	6/4/1861, Camp Moore, Louisiana	New Orleans, Louisiana, Clerk	Co. F, 5th Louisiana Infantry	5/5/1864, Spotsylvania Court House, Virginia	Died of Unknown Causes, 8/5/1864
Lough, Washington Private	22	4/23/1863, Randolph, Virginia	Braxton County, Virginia	Co. G, 25th Virginia Infantry	5/5/1864, Wilderness, Virginia	Died of Unknown Causes, 8/8/1864
Love, Albert G. Sergeant	34	2/28/1862, Graham, North Carolina Volunteer	Alamance County, North Carolina, Blacksmith	Co. K, 47h North Carolina Infantry	7/3/1863, Gettysburg, Pennsylvania	Died of Chronic Diarrhea & Scurvy, 3/20/1865
Lovegrove, W. H. Private Not Listed On Monument	Unk	6/5/1861, Petersburg, Virginia	Chesterfield County, Virginia	Co. C, 5th Virginia Cavalry	9/24/1864, Luray, Virginia	Died of Bronchitis, 2/2/1865
Lovelace, Henry R. Private	Unk	11/10/1861, Caswell, North Carolina Conscript	Caswell County, North Carolina	Co. G, 22nd North Carolina Infantry	5/23/1864, North Anna River, Virginia	Died of Pneumonia, 2/2/1865
Lovelace, Willis G. Private	18	5/6/1862, Shelby, North Carolina Volunteer	Cleveland County, North Carolina, Farmer	Co. D, 55th North Carolina Infantry	7/1/1863, Gettysburg, Pennsylvania	Died of Unknown Causes, 9/13/1864
Lovelace, William Private	28	5/6/1862, Shelby, North Carolina Volunteer	Cleveland County, North Carolina, Farmer	Co. D, 55th North Carolina Infantry	7/14/1863, Falling Waters, Maryland	Died of Unknown Causes, 3/8/1864
Lovett, Joshua T. Private	Unk	7/23/1864, White Marsh Island, Georgia	Chatham County, Georgia	Co. E, 1st (Symon's) Georgia Reserve Infantry	12/13/1864, Fort McAllister, Georgia, Gunshot Wound Left Forearm	Date & Cause of Death Unknown

Name	Age	Enlisted	Residence	Unit	Captured	Date and Cause of Death
Lovett, William Private Not Listed On Monument	26	5/3/1861, Elizabethtown, North Carolina, Volunteer	Bladen County, North Carolina, Laborer	Co. B, 18th North Carolina Infantry	7/21/1863, Chester Gap, Virginia	Died of Unknown Causes, 5/1/1864
Loving, Talioferro Private	Unk	10/14/1863, Caroline, Virginia	Caroline County, Virginia	Co. G, 17th Virginia Infantry	5/15/1864, Near Drury's Bluff, Virginia	Died of Bronchitis, 6/6/1865
Loving, V. B. Private	Unk	10/8/1862, Kanauha, Virginia	Unknown	Co. H, 22nd Virginia Infantry	6/3/1864, Gaines's Mill, Virginia	Died of Unknown Causes, 7/20/1864
Low, James H. Private	Unk	12/24/1861, Charleston, South Carolina	Laurens, South Carolina	Co. B, Holcombe's Spartanburg Legion, South Carolina	4/2/1865, Five Forks, Virginia	Died of Chronic Diarrhea, 6/7/1865
Lowder, Archibald C. Private	28	4/28/1862, Albemarle County, North Carolina Volunteer	Stanly County, North Carolina, Farmer	Co. D, 52nd North Carolina Infantry	10/14/1863, Bristoe Station, Virginia	Died of Unknown Causes, 9/16/1864
Lowe, James M. Private	20	11/10/1861, Statesville, North Carolina Conscript	Alexander County, North Carolina	Co. B, 37th North Carolina Infantry	7/5/1863, Gettysburg, Pennsylvania	Died of Debility, 2/7/1864
Lowery, Peter S. Private	Unk	8/19/1862, Coffee, Alabama	Coffee County, Alabama	Co. E, 5th Alabama Infantry	7/1/1863, Gettysburg, Pennsylvania	Died of Chronic Diarrhea, 1/24/1864
Lowrimore, H. L. Private	32	12/20/1861, Camp Harllee, Britton's Neck, South Carolina	Unknown	Co. I, 21st South Carolina Infantry	6/24/1864, Near Petersburg, Virginia	Died of Unknown Causes, 10/22/1864
Loyard, J. A. Private	Unk	Unknown	Unknown	Co. A, 1st Louisiana Infantry	Unknown	Unable to Locate
Loyd, Richard B. Corporal	Unk	2/25/1862, Camp Stephens, Georgia	Meriweather County, Georgia	Co. F, 28th Georgia Infantry	9/7/1863, Morris Island, South Carolina	Died of Pneumonia, 1/8/1864

Name	Age	Enlisted	Residence	Unit	Captured	Date and Cause of Death
Lucas, David D. Private	Unk	Unknown	Unknown	Co. C, 23rd Virginia Infantry	9/19/1864, Winchester, Virginia	Died of Acute Dysentery, 1/23/1865
Lucas, John Private	19	8/20/1861, Ridgeway Depot, Fairfield District, South Carolina	Fairfield District, South Carolina	Co. C, 12th South Carolina Infantry	7/14/1863, Falling Waters, Maryland	Died of Unknown Causes, 1/31/1864
Lucas, P. D. Private	Unk	Unknown	Unknown	Co. B, 16th North Carolina Infantry	5/6/1864, Wilderness, Virginia	Died of Chronic Diarrhea, 7/27/1865
Lucky, Levin McL. Private	21	6/4/1861, Camp Moore, Louisiana	Orleans Parish, Louisiana	Co. C, 12th Louisiana Infantry	5/16/1863, Champion Hill, Tennessee	Died Dropsy of Lungs, 10/22/1863
Ludlum, Benjamin Corporal	39	2/19/1862, Smithville, Brunswick County, North Carolina, Volunteer	Brunswick County, North Carolina	Co. K, 36th North Carolina Heavy Artillery	1/15/1865, Fort Fisher, North Carolina	Died of Pneumonia, 3/16/1865
Luke, James P. Private	19	4/17/1861, Suffolk, Virginia	Isle of Wight County, Virginia	Co. H, 16th Virginia Infantry	10/27/1864. Near Petersburg, Virginia	Died of Acute Dysentery, 12/3/1864
Lumsden, William M. Private	Unk	1/15/1863, Richmond, Virginia, Volunteer	Henrico County, Virginia	Goochland Virginia Light Artillery	4/6/1865, Sailor's Creek, Virginia	Died of Chronic Dysentery, 6/10/1865
Lunsford, E. M. Private	24	8/29/1861, Ashville, North Carolina Volunteer	McDowell County, North Carolina	Co. B, 1st North Carolina Cavalry	7/11/1863, Funkstown, Maryland	Died of Unknown Causes, 1/24/1864
Lunsford, John L. Private	29	10/12/1861, King George Court House, Virginia	King George County, Virginia	Co. I, 9th Virginia Cavalry	7/4/1863, Gettysburg, Pennsylvania	Died of Chronic Diarrhea, 12/21/1863

Name	Age	Enlisted	Residence	Unit	Captured	Date and Cause of Death
Lupton, John D. Private	18	3/1/1863, Craven County, North Carolina, Substitute	Craven County, North Carolina	Co. D, 40th Regiment, 3rd North Carolina Light Artillery	1/15/1865, Fort Fisher, North Carolina	Died of Chronic Diarrhea, 6/29/1865
Luter, Sandy Private	17	3/1/1863, Wake County, North Carolina Volunteer	Wake County, North Carolina	Co. F, 6th North Carolina Infantry	7/3/1863, Gettysburg, Pennsylvania	Died of Chronic Diarrhea, 3/4/1864
Luther, Riley Private	24	3/12/1862, Asheboro, North Carolina Volunteer	Randolph County, North Carolina, Blacksmith	Co. I, 46th North Carolina Infantry	3/31/1865, Hatchers Run, Near Richmond, Virginia	Died of Debility, 4/30/1865
Ludwick, Daniel Private	23	3/16/1862, Concord, North Carolina Volunteer	Cabarrus County, North Carolina	Co. A, 20th North Carolina Infantry	7/3/1863, Gettysburg, Pennsylvania	Died of Unknown Causes, 1/2/1864
Lyall, Asberry Private	Unk	8/1/1862, Statesville, North Carolina Conscript	Ash County, North Carolina	Co. H, 23rd North Carolina Infantry	7/1/1863, Gettysburg, Pennsylvania	Died of Dysentery, 12/26/1863
Lyday, William H. Private	Unk	7/12/1862, Hendersonville North Carolina	Henderson County, North Carolina	Co. D, 65th North Carolina Infantry	6/22/1864, Jackson's Mills, North Carolina	Died of Scurvy, 5/7/1865
Leyden, Joseph Private	Unk	Unknown	Unknown	Co. E, 66th North Carolina Infantry	7/8/1863, Place Unknown	Died of Congestive Chills, 5/1/1864
Lyerly, John T. Private	20	7/7/1862, Salisbury, North Carolina, Volunteer	Iredell County, North Carolina	Co. B, 57th North Carolina Infantry	7/5/1863, Gettysburg, Pennsylvania	Died of Intermittent Fever, 12/14/1863
Lyles, William M. Private	Unk	11/6/1861, Dahlonega, Georgia	Lumpkin County, Georgia	Co. B, 15th Battalion, Lucas, South Carolina, Heavy Artillery	3/16/1865, Averasboro, North Carolina	Died of Congestive Intermittent Fever, 4/4/1865
Lynch, Christopher Private	Unk	3/3/1862, Rocky Mount, Virginia	Franklin County, Virginia	Co. H, 22nd Virginia Infantry	7/3/1863, Gettysburg, Pennsylvania	Died of Unknown Causes, 12/20/1863

Name	Age	Enlisted	Residence	Unit	Captured	Date and Cause of Death
Lyons, Allen Private Not Listed On Monument	Unk	10/15/1863, Wilkesboro, North Carolina, Volunteer	Union County, North Carolina	Co. F, 37th North Carolina Infantry	5/6/1864, Near Spotsylvania Court House, Virginia	Died of Chronic Diarrhea, 7/2/1864

Name	Age	Enlisted	Residence	Unit	Captured	Date and Cause of Death
Maberry, Alexander Private	28	4/25/1862, Wilkes County, North Carolina	Iredell County, North Carolina, Farmer	Co. G, 54th North Carolina Infantry	11/7/1863, Kelly's Ford, Rappahannock Station, Virginia	Died of Unknown Causes, 4/20/1864
Maberry, Foster Private Not Listed On Monument	Unk	12/17/1861, Unionville, South Carolina	Union County, South Carolina	Co. B, 18th South Carolina Infantry	7/30/1864, Petersburg, Virginia	Died of Chronic Diarrhea, 10/23/1864
Maberry, Isaac See: Mayberry, Isaac				Co. I, 26th North Carolina Infantry		
Mabery, Daniel S. Private	Unk	12/9/1862, Macon County, Georgia	Macon County, Georgia	Co. C, 12th Georgia Infantry	4/2/1865, Petersburg, Virginia	Died of Measles, 6/27/1865
Mabry, Solomon Private	24	8/8/1862, Stanley County, North Carolina, Conscript	Stanley County, North Carolina	Co. F, 5th North Carolina Infantry	7/3/1863, Gettysburg, Pennsylvania, Wounded Right Foot	Died of Smallpox, 1/18/1864
Mack, Jacob Private	Unk	Unknown	Unknown	Co. I, 27th South Carolina Infantry	6/18/1864, Near Petersburg, Virginia	Died of Unknown Causes, 9/10/1864
Mack, John W. Private	Unk	12/17/1861, Skidaway Island, Georgia	Chatham County, Georgia	Co. C, 60th Georgia Infantry	5/23/1864, North Anna River, Virginia	Died of Acute Diarrhea, 12/27/1864

337

Name	Age	Enlisted	Residence	Unit	Captured	Date and Cause of Death
Macon, Isaac Private	Unk	8/21/1864, Raleigh, North Carolina, Conscript	Wake County, North Carolina	Co. I, 3rd North Carolina Infantry	9/19/1864, Winchester, Virginia	Died of Chronic Diarrhea, 10/11/1864
Maddox, J. W. Private Not Listed On Monument	Unk	4/8/1863, Macon, Georgia	Bibb County, Georgia	Co. B, 64th Georgia Infantry	8/17/1864, Deep Bottom, Virginia	Died of Chronic Diarrhea & Scurvy, 2/11/1865
Maddox, Thomas Private	Unk	Unknown	Unknown	Stiles Georgia Artillery	Unknown	Unable to Locate
Madison, G. F. Private	Unk	Unknown	Unknown	Co. F, 1st South Carolina Infantry	Unknown	Unable to Locate
Madison, James M. Private	Unk	5/23/1861, Clarksville, Tennessee	Montgomery County, Tennessee	Co. H, 14th Tennessee Infantry	7/1/1863, Gettysburg, Pennsylvania	Died of Unknown Causes, 1/18/1864
Madison, Robert G. Private	41	7/23/1861, Acquia Creek, Virginia	Caroline County, Virginia, Farmer	Co. K, 47th Virginia Infantry	7/14/1863, Falling Waters, Maryland	Died of Unknown Causes, 11/23/1863
Maffett, Jacob Private Not Listed On Monument	Unk	10/24/1864, Columbia, South Carolina	Richland County, South Carolina	Co. H, Holcombe's South Carolina Legion	4/2/1865, Five Forks, Virginia	Died of Chronic Diarrhea, 5/1/1865
Magee, W. G. 1st Sergeant	26	4/5/1862, Westville, Mississippi	Toccopola, Mississippi, Student	Co. A, 39th Mississippi Infantry	7/9/1863, Port Hudson, Mississippi	Died of Chronic Diarrhea, 5/7/1864

Name	Age	Enlisted	Residence	Unit	Captured	Date and Cause of Death
Mahon, S. H. Private See Mann, Samuel H.				Co. F, 20th South Carolina Infantry		
Majors, J. F. Private	Unk	Unknown	Unknown	Co. ?, 42nd Virginia Infantry	9/25/1864, Harrisburg, Pennsylvania	Died of Chronic Dysentery, 2/21/1865
Malcom, John Private	26	4/1/1863, Pocahontas, Virginia	Tazewell County, Virginia, Farmer	Co. G. 19th Virginia Cavalry	5/5/1863, Harrison County, Virginia	Died of Rheumatism, 3/12/1864
Malloy, L. N. Private	Unk	8/31/1862, Randolph, Alabama	Bibb County, Alabama	Co. F, 59th Alabama Infantry	6/17/1864, Petersburg, Virginia	Died of Unknown Causes, 8/8/1864
Malloy, William W. Sergeant Not Listed On Monument	29	7/18/1862, Columbus, Georgia	Muscogee County, Georgia	Co. D, 7th Confederate States Cavalry	6/22/1864, Jacksonville, North Carolina	Died of Scorbutus (Scurvy), 2/25/1865
Maloney, Clem H. Private	25	8/1/1862, Camp Lee, Richmond, Virginia	Prince Edward County, Virginia	Co. K. 18th Virginia Infantry	7/3/1863, Gettysburg, Pennsylvania, Severely Wounded in Left Thigh	Died of Gangrene from Gunshot Wound, Date of Death Unknown
Maness, Alexander Captain	52	Unknown	Unknown	Co. D. 21st Virginia Infantry	10/10/1863, Scott County, Virginia	Died of Chronic Diarrhea, 8/1/1864
Maness, Lewis W. Private Not Listed On Monument	27	3/14/1863 Wilmington, North Carolina	New Hanover County, North Carolina	Co. K, 10th North Carolina Heavy Artillery	1/15/1865. Fort Fisher, North Carolina, Gunshot Wound Left Side and Lung	Died of Wounds, 2/15/1865

Name	Age	Enlisted	Residence	Unit	Captured	Date and Cause of Death
Mankins, Joel Private	24	6/22/1861, Wytheville, Virginia	Patrick County, Virnia, Farmer	Co. K. 50th Virginia Infantry	7/5/1863, Cashtown, Pennsylvania	Died of Smallpox, 11/20/1863
Mann, John Private See Munn, John				Co. E. 15th Alabama Infantry		
Mann, Joseph H. Private	24	9/29/1864, Maryville, Tennessee	Blount County, Tennessee	Co. C, Walker's Battalion, Thomas' Legion, North Carolina and Tennessee Volunteers	9/19/1864, Winchester, Virginia	Died of Chronic Dysentery 1/21/1865
Mann, Samuel H. Private	Unk	12/29/1861, Anderson, South Carolina	Anderson County, South Carolina	Co. F, 20th South Carolina Infantry	10/19/1864, Cedar Creek or Strasburg, Virginia	Died of Chronic Diarrhea, 2/21/1865
Mann, William Private	27	4/2/62, Hamilton, North Carolina, Volunteer	Tyrrell County, North Carolina, Farmer	Co. H, 17th North Carolina Infantry	2/11/1865, Near Fort Fisher, North Carolina	Died of Chronic Diarrhea, 4/20/1865
Manring, Leander Private	Unk	9/10/1864, Danbury, Virginia	Unknown	Co. F, 21st North Carolina Infantry	10/19/1864, Cedar Creek, Virginia	Died Disease of Heart, 3/20/1865
Mantin, Allen See: Martin, Allen				Co. A, 2nd North Carolina Infantry		
Mappin, James W. Private	Unk	12/17/1863, Macon, Georgia	Putnam County, Georgia	Co. G, 12th Georgia Infantry	5/10/1864, Spotsylvania Court House, Virginia	Died of Unknown Causes, 8/2/1864
Marable, William M. Private	28	6/7/1861, Moffett's Mills, North Carolina	Lurenburg, Virginia	Co. C, 10th North Carolina Infantry	7/7/1863, Williamsport, Virginia	Died of Chronic Diarrhea, 1/21/1864

Name	Age	Enlisted	Residence	Unit	Captured	Date and Cause of Death
Marks, Henry Private	22	7/15/1862, Raleigh, North Carolina, Conscript	Northampton County, North Carolina	Co. A, 15th North Carolina Infantry	10/20/1863, Bristoe Station, Virginia	Died of Chronic Diarrhea, 1/10/1864
Markes, Joseph Private	44	8/19/1863, Brunswick County, North Carolina	Edgecombe County, North Carolina	Co. A, 36th North Carolina Heavy Artillery	1/15/1865, Fort Fisher, North Carolina, Severely Wounded in Back of Head	Died of Wounds, 4/5/1865
Marks, William Private	18	8/17/1862, Jonesboro, Tennessee	Washington County, Tennessee	Co. A, 60th Tennessee Mounted Infantry	5/17/1863, Big Black Bridge, Near Vicksburg, Mississippi	Died of Unknown Causes, 1/8/1864
Marrs, John Sergeant	Unk	2/1/1862, Franklin County, Tennessee	Franklin County, Tennessee	Co. C, 1st Arkansas Infantry	5/17/1863, Big Black Bridge, Near Vicksburg, Mississippi	Died of Unknown Causes, 12/27/1863
Marsh, Isaac Private	Unk	5/13/1861, Fayetteville, North Carolina	Cumberland County, North Carolina	Co. C, 15th Battalion, South Carolina Heavy Artillery	Unknown	Date and Cause of Death Unknown
Marsh, W. P. Private	Unk	5/5/1862, Grahamville, South Carolina	Jasper County, South Carolina	Co. A, 48th Georgia Infantry	7/3/1863, Gettysburg, Pennsylvania	Died of Smallpox, 12/27/1863
Marshall, C. C. Private	Unk	Unknown	Unknown	Co. E, 40th North Carolina Infantry	Unknown	Unable to Locate
Marshall, George W. Private Not Listed On Monument	17	3/22/1862, Forsyth County, North Carolina	Forsyth County, North Carolina	Co. D, 53rd North Carolina Infantry	7/2/1863, Gettysburg, Pennsylvania	Died of Chronic Diarrhea, 4/7/1864
Marshall, Josephus Private	28	7/4/1862, Winston, North Carolina	Forsyth County, North Carolina	Co. D, 57th North Carolina Infantry	11/7/1863, Rappahannock Station, Virginia	Died of Unknown Causes, 12/24/1863

Name	Age	Enlisted	Residence	Unit	Captured	Date and Cause of Death
Marshall, Laurister Sergeant	23	3/27/1862, Surry County, North Carolina, Volunteer	Surry County, North Carolina, Farmer	Co. E, 53rd North Carolina Infantry	7/3/1863 Gettysburg, Pennsylvania	Date and Cause of Death Unknown
Martin, Allen Private	22	8/9/1862, Raleigh, North Carolina, Conscript	Montgomery County, North Carolina	Co. A, 2nd North Carolina Infantry	7/12/1863, Hagerstown, Maryland	Died of Unknown Causes, 2/9/1864
Martin, George W. Private	Unk	4/15/1861, Edge District, South Carolina	Edge District, South Carolina	Co. M, 7th South Carolina Infantry	5/23/1864, North Anna River, Virginia	Died of Unknown Causes, 9/14/1864
Martin, Franklin Private	Unk	10/4/1862, Warrenburg, Tennessee	Unknown	Co. I, 61st Tennessee Mounted Infantry	5/16/ 1863, Big Black Bridge, Near Vicksburg, Mississippi	Died of Chronic Diarrhea, 12/4/1863
Martin, Irvin J. Private	28	4/12/1862, Battery Island, South Carolina	Unknown	Co. C, 25th South Carolina Infantry	2/20/1865, Near Town Creek, North Carolina	Died of Pneumonia, 5/9/1865
Martin, J. O. Private	Unk	3/7/1863, Columbia, South Carolina	Richland County, South Carolina	Co. K, Holcombe's South Carolina Legion	5/7/1864, Stony Creek, Virginia	Died of Unknown Causes, 8/20/1864
Martin, James See Martin, Franklin				Co. I, 61st Tennessee Mounted Infantry		
Martin, James J. Private	Unk	10/4/1862, Knoxville, Tennessee	Knox County, Tennessee	Co. B, 44th Tennessee Infantry	6/17/1864, Near Petersburg, Virginia, Wounded Left Leg, Leg Amputated	Died of Unknown Causes, 9/9/1864
Martin, James M. Private	Unk	6/30/1861, Camp Pryor. Prince William County, Virginia	Campbell County, Virginia	Co. H, 24th Virginia Infantry	5/12/1864, On the Turnpike Between Petersburg and Richmond, Virginia	Died of Unknown Causes, 8/1/1864

Name	Age	Enlisted	Residence	Unit	Captured	Date and Cause of Death
Martin, John Private	50	7/17/1864, Camp Lee, Floyd County Court House, Virginia, Conscript	Franklin County, Virginia, Farmer	Co. C, 57th Virginia Infantry	4/1/1865, Five Forks, Virginia	Died of Chronic Diarrhea, 5/20/1865
Martin, Joseph J. Private	26	6/19/1861, Camp Moore, Louisiana	Livingston, Louisiana, Farmer	Co. G, 8th Louisiana Infantry	11/7/1863, Kelly's Ford, Rappahannock Station, Virginia	Died of Unknown Causes, 12/27/1863
Martin, Moses Private	23	8/20/1861, Ridgeville, South Carolina	Dorchester District, South Carolina	Co. G, 11th South Carolina Infantry	10/7/1864, Darby Town Road Near Richmond, Virginia	Died of Chronic Diarrhea, 4/13/1865
Martin, M. G. Private	Unk	7/1/1863, Columbia, South Carolina	Richland County, South Carolina	Co. G, 3rd South Carolina Infantry	5/23/1864, North Anna River, Virginia	Died of Chronic Diarrhea, 2/24/1865
Martin, William J. Private	24	6/14/1861, Jamestown, Virginia	Franklin County, Virginia, Farmer	Co. K, 53rd Virginia Infantry	7/4/1863, Gettysburg, Pennsylvania	Died Debility & Bronchitis, 1/8/1864
Martin, William Q. Corporal Not Listed On Monument	29	2/27/1862, Lincoln County, Georgia	Elbert County, Georgia	Co. G, 15th Georgia Battalion Infantry	7/3/1863, Gettysburg, Pennsylvania	Died of Smallpox, 5/1/1864
Martindale, Jesse Private	21	5/1/1861, Luka, Tishomingo, Mississippi	Tishomingo, County, Mississippi	Co. K, 2nd Mississippi Infantry	4/3/1865, Richmond, Virginia	Died of Chronic Diarrhea, 5/8/1865
Marton, J. A. Private	Unk	Unknown	Unknown	Co. A, 7th South Carolina Cavalry	Unknown	Unable to Locate
Mason, James T. Private	28	7/8/1862, Raleigh, North Carolina, Conscript	Grandville County, North Carolina	Co. E, 23rd North Carolina Infantry	7/3/1863, Gettysburg, Pennsylvania, Gunshot, Wound Arm & Shoulder	Died of Acute Diarrhea, 1/8/1864
Mason, John K. Private	Unk	7/13/1861, Sydnorsville, Virginia	Unknown	Co. G, 57th Virginia Infantry	7/3/1863, Gettysburg, Pennsylvania	Died of Unknown Causes, 2/9/1864

Name	Age	Enlisted	Residence	Unit	Captured	Date and Cause of Death
Mason, John R. Private	Unk	5/24/1864, Petersburg, Virginia	Chesterfield County, Virginia	Co. A, 13th Battalion Virginia Light Artillery	6/9/1864, Petersburg, Virginia	Died of Unknown Causes, 7/31/1864
Mason, William L. Private	Unk	1/28/1863, Camp Gregg, Virginia	Unknown	Co. E, 22nd Battalion Virginia Infantry	7/14/1863, Falling Waters, Maryland	Died of Unknown Causes, 12/23/1863
Mason, William M. Private	25	4/29/1861, Winchester, Franklin County, Tennessee	Franklin County, Tennessee	Co. F, 1st Tennessee Infantry	4/3/1865, Dinwiddie Court House, Virginia	Died of Chronic Diarrhea, 4/26/1865
Massey, Peyton H. Corporal	Unk	5/2/1862, Franklin County, North Carolina, Volunteer	Franklin County, North Carolina	Co. B, 47th North Carolina Infantry	7/5/1863, Gettysburg, Pennsylvania	Died of Typhoid/ Pneumonia, 1/11/1864
Mastin, George Private	Unk	4/1/1864, Essex County, Virginia	Essex County, Virginia	Co. E, 9th Virginia Cavalry	6/10/1864, Spotsylvania Court House, Virginia	Died of Unknown Causes, 5/11/1865
Matheny, George M. Corporal	Unk	8/14/1862, Statesville, North Carolina, Conscript	Iredell County, North Carolina	Co. G, 18th North Carolina Infantry	5/12/1864, Spotsylvania Court House, Virginia	Died of Unknown Causes, 9/16/1864
Matheny, William Ballard P. Private	Unk	3/7/1863, Braxton County, Virginia	Braxton County, Virginia	Co. B, 36th Battalion Virginia Cavalry	7/5/1863, Waterloo, Gettysburg, Pennsylvania	Died of Unknown Causes, 12/29/1863
Mathews, J. L. Private See: Maffett, Jacob				Co. H, Holcombe's South Carolina Legion		
Mathews, Spencer G. Private	47	3/3/1862, Bedford, Virginia	Unknown, Stone Mason	Co. G, 28th Virginia Infantry	7/3/1863, Gettysburg, Pennsylvania	Date and Cause of Death Unknown

Name	Age	Enlisted	Residence	Unit	Captured	Date and Cause of Death
Mathews, William H. Private	21	7/4/1862, Kinston, North Carolina, Volunteer	Forsyth County, North Carolina	Co. G, 18th North Carolina Infantry	11/7/1863, Kelly's Ford, Rappahannock Station, Virginia	Died of Unknown Causes, 8/12/1864
Mathews, W. P. P. Corporal See Matheny, William Ballard P.				Co. B, 36th Battalion Virginia Cavalry		
Mathias, Cornelius Private	24	5/8/1861, Petersburg, Virginia	Chesterfield County, Virginia	Co. B, 12th Virginia Infantry	8/19/1864, Globe Tavern, Near Weldon Railroad, Virginia	Died of Scurvy, 4/6/1865
Mathis, Jeff Private	Unk	4/?/1861, Ridgeville, South Carolina	Dorchester District, South Carolina	Co. I, 12th South Carolina Infantry	5/23/1864, North Anna River, Virginia	Died of Scurvy, 4/17/1865
Mathis, John W. Private	Unk	5/18/1862, Richmond, Virginia	Butts County, Virginia	Co. D, 6th Georgia Infantry	8/19/1864, Globe Tavern, Near Weldon Railroad, Virginia	Died of Scurvy, 3/11/1865
Mathews, George W. Private	Unk	Unknown	Unknown	Co. A, Mosby's Regiment, Partisan Rangers, Virginia Cavalry	9/27/1863, Manassas Junction, Virginia	Died of Scurvy, 9/11/1864
Matthews, Nathan Private	19	9/10/1861, Jonesboro, North Carolina, Volunteer	Moore County, North Carolina	Co. G, 18th North Carolina Infantry	7/3/1863, Gettysburg, Pennsylvania	Died of Unknown Causes, 9/16/1864
Matthews, William H. Private Not Listed On Monument	24	7/24/1862, Forsyth County, North Carolina	Forsyth County, North Carolina	Co. D, 57th North Carolina Infantry	11/7/1863, Rappahannock Station, Virginia	Died of Unknown Causes, 8/12/1864

Name	Age	Enlisted	Residence	Unit	Captured	Date and Cause of Death
Mattison, George F. Private Not Listed On Monument	Unk	12/16/1863, Columbia, South Carolina	Richland County, South Carolina	Co. F, 1st South Carolina Infantry	5/23/1864, Hanover Junction, Virginia	Died of Unknown Causes, 8/13/1864
Mattox, Aaron Private	Unk	Unknown	Unknown	Co. G, 29th Georgia Infantry	7/22/1864, Near Atlanta, Georgia	Died of Acute Dysentery 5/30/1865
Mattox, Samuel Private	60	8/26/1861, Lightwood Knot Springs, Camden, South Carolina	Kershaw District, South Carolina	Co. D, 15th South Carolina Infantry	2/27/1865, Lynch's Creek, South Carolina	Died of Unknown Causes, 6/2/1865
Maurice, William N. Private	Unk	Unknown	Unknown	Co. E, 1st Virginia Engineers	Unknown	Unable to Locate
Maxwell, Alexander T. Private	24	9/15/1862, Raleigh, North Carolina, Conscript	Sampson County, North Carolina	Co. D, 2nd North Carolina Infantry	11/7/1863, Kelly's Ford, Rappahannock Station, Virginia	Died of Unknown Causes, 1/6/1864
May, Jonathan Private	Unk	5/1/1864, Raleigh, North Carolina	Wake County, North Carolina	Co. F, 27th North Carolina Infantry	5/12/1864, Spotsylvania Court House, Virginia	Died of Unknown Causes, 8/18/1864
May, Levi S. Private	Unk	5/1/1862, Fayetteville, Georgia	Fayette County, Georgia	Co. C, 53rd Georgia Infantry	7/3/1863, Gettysburg, Pennsylvania	Died of Chronic Diarrhea, 11/17/1863
Mayberry, Foster Private See Maberry, Foster				Co. B, 18th South Carolina Infantry		
Mayberry, Isaac S. Private	22	7/26/1862, Caldwell County, North Carolina	Chatham County, North Carolina	Co. I, 26th North Carolina Infantry	7/14/1863, Falling Waters, Maryland	Died of Unknown Causes, 1/19/1864

Name	Age	Enlisted	Residence	Unit	Captured	Date and Cause of Death
Maynard, J. Private	Unk	Unknown	Unknown	Co. K, 25th North Carolina Infantry	Unknown	Unable to Locate
Maynard, William Private	Unk	Unknown	Unknown	Co. A, 2nd Arkansas Infantry	6/27/1863, Shelbyville, Tennessee	Died of Intermittent Fever, Date Unknown
Mayo, Edward J. Sergeant	20	5/29/1861, Goldsboro, North Carolina, Volunteer	Wayne County, North Carolina	Co. D, 2nd North Carolina Infantry	4/6/1865, Burkesville, Virginia	Died of Chronic Dysentery 6/21/1865
Mayo, James G. Private	Unk	9/22/1862, Jackson, Mississippi	Madison County, Mississippi	Co. E, 26th Mississippi Infantry	4/2/1865, Hatcher's Run, Virginia	Died of Chronic Diarrhea, 6/30/1865
Mays, James A. Private	Unk	Unknown	Unknown	Co. A, 15th Battalion North Carolina Infantry	4/6/1865, Burke, North Carolina	Died of Scurvy 5/26/1865
Mays, M. D. Private	Unk	11/17/1862, Morristown, Tennessee	Hamblen County, Tennessee	Co. C, 61st Tennessee Mounted Infantry	7/4/1863, Vicksburg, Mississippi	Died of Smallpox, 11/20/1863
Mays, William P. Private	28	6/8/1861, Lynchburg, Virginia	Franklin County, Virginia	Co. B, 2nd Virginia Cavalry	7/3/1863, Gettysburg, Pennsylvania	Died of Unknown Causes 5/12/1864
McAlister, A. M. Private Not Listed On Monument	31	3/14/1863, Charlotte, North Carolina, Volunteer	Gaston County, North Carolina	Co. H, 49th North Carolina Infantry	5/31/1864, Drewry's Bluff, Virginia, Gunshot Wound	Died of Unknown Causes, 7/10/1864
McAllister, James M. Private	Unk	2/8/1864, Chaffin's Bluff, Virginia	Unknown	Allen's Company Virginia Heavy Artillery	4/6/1865, Harper's Farm, Virginia	Died of Measles, 6/23/1865
McArthur, James R. Private	30	1/27/1862, Greenville, North Carolina, Volunteer	Pitt County, North Carolina, Farmer	Co. D, 44th North Carolina Infantry	10/27/1865, Near Petersburg, Virginia	Died of Chronic Diarrhea, 1/19/1865

Name	Age	Enlisted	Residence	Unit	Captured	Date and Cause of Death
McArthur, Peter Private	Unk	8/21/1864, Wilmington, North Carolina	New Hanover County, North Carolina	Co. I, 3rd North Carolina Junior Reserves	12/25/1864, Fort Fisher, North Carolina	Died of Pneumonia 1/21/1865
McBride, Jeremiah Private	Unk	3/15/1864, Narrows, Virginia	Giles County, Virginia	Co. I, 60th Virginia Infantry	9/19/1864, Winchester, Virginia	Died of Pneumonia, 11/22/1864
McBride, Jesse Private	Unk	3/27/1864, Henry County, Virginia	Henry County, Virginia	Co. F, 42nd Virginia Infantry	5/12/1864 Spotsylvania Court House, Virginia	Died of Unknown Causes 6/29/1864
McCabe, John W. Private	Unk	10/8/1861, Galveston, Texas	Galveston County, Texas	Co. A, 25th South Carolina Infantry	8/21/1864, Globe Tavern, Weldon Railroad, North Carolina	Died of Acute Diarrhea, 12/19/1864
McCall, John C. See McCual, John C.				Co. H, 52nd North Carolina Infantry		
McCalla, Matthew Private	Unk	5/10/1862, Meriweather County, Georgia	Meriweather County, Georgia	Co. H, 60th Georgia Infantry	9/19/1864, Winchester, Virginia	Died of Typhoid Fever, 11/12/1864
McCan, Alfred P. Private	Unk	10/3/1863, Raleigh, North Carolina	Wake County, North Carolina	Co. F, 5th North Carolina Infantry	11/7/1863, Kelly's Ford, Rappahannock Station, Virginia	Died of Unknown Causes, 12/27/1863
McCarter, Philip Private	Unk	11/1/1863, Raleigh, North Carolina	Wake County, North Carolina	Co. H, 21st North Carolina Infantry	2/3/1864, New Berne, North Carolina	Died of Unknown Causes, 3/2/1864
McCarty, John Private	48	5/26/1861, Camp Moore, New Orleans, Louisiana	Born Ireland, New Orleans, Louisiana, Overseer	Co. I, 8th Louisiana Infantry	5/5/1864 Wilderness, Virginia	Died of Unknown Causes, 8/18/1864

Name	Age	Enlisted	Residence	Unit	Captured	Date and Cause of Death
McCaskill, Alexander Private	25	8/17/1861, Luka, Alabama	Tishomingo, County, Mississippi	Co. C, Jeff Davis Legion Mississippi Cavalry	8/1/1863, Brandy Station, Virginia	Died of Unknown Causes, 9/13/1863
McCauley, Robert W. Private	30	5/3/1862, Richmond, Virginia	Henrico County, Virginia	Co. F, 56th Virginia Infantry	7/3/1863, Gettysburg, Pennsylvania, Wounded Left Elbow	Died of Chronic Diarrhea, 8/19/1864
McClain, Joseph W. Private Not Listed On Monument	27	5/14/1862, Grenada, Mississippi	Unknown, Mechanic	Co. D, 42nd Mississippi Infantry	7/3/1863, Gettysburg, Pennsylvania	Died of Chronic Diarrhea & Scurvy, 11/15/1863
McClanahan, James T. Corporal	Unk	5/3/1862, Warrenton, Virginia	Fauquier County, Virginia	Co. K, 8th Virginia Infantry	8/1/1863, Brandy Station, Virginia	Died of Chronic Diarrhea, 2/15/1864
McClean, J. W. See: McClain, Joseph W.				Co. D, 47th Mississippi Infantry		
McClennan, Thomas Private	Unk	Unknown	Unknown	Co. K, 1st Virginia Mounted Guard	Unknown	Unable to Locate
McClelland, Patrick H. See McLelland, Patrick H.				Co. B, 41st Virginia Infantry		
McClimans, John P. Private	Unk	Date and Location Unknown, Conscript	Unknown	Co. F, 1st South Carolina Artillery	3/16/1865, Smith's Ferry, State Unknown	Died of Chronic Diarrhea, 5/9/1865
McClintic, Robert M. Sergeant	29	5/3/1862, White Sulphur Springs, Virginia	Lewisburg, Greenbrier County, West Virginia, Farmer	Co. A, 14th Virginia Cavalry	11/12/1864, Nineveh, Virginia	Died of Acute Dysentery, 12/15/1864

Name	Age	Enlisted	Residence	Unit	Captured	Date and Cause of Death
McClurg, Robert S. Private	Unk	8/12/1861, Resaca, Georgia	Gordon County, Georgia	Co. G, 28th Georgia Infantry	9/30/1864, Fort Harrison, Virginia	Died of Debility, 3/13/1865
McCombs, Cyrus Q. Private	Unk	2/15/1865, Mecklenburg County, North Carolina	Mecklenburg County, North Carolina	Co. H, 35th North Carolina Infantry	4/3/1865, Appomattox, Virginia	Died of Chronic Diarrhea, 5/20/1865
McCook, B. Franklin Private	Unk	8/15/1861, Sparta, Georgia	Washington County, Georgia	Co. E, 15th Georgia Infantry	7/3/1863, Gettysburg, Pennsylvania	Died of Smallpox, 12/4/1863
McCorkle, Lafayette Sergeant	Unk	5/3/1861, Decatur, Tennessee	Meigs County, Tennessee	Co. I, 3rd Tennessee Mounted Infantry	5/17/1863, Big Black River, Near Vicksburg, Mississippi	Died of Unknown Causes, 1/15/1864
McCoy, Daniel Private	Unk	Unknown	Elizabeth City, Pasquotank County, North Carolina	Co. H, 56th North Carolina Infantry	12/1/1863, Camden County, North Carolina	Died of Smallpox, 2/22/1864
McCoy, John L. Private	Unk	5/1/1861 Talladega, Alabama	Talladega County, Alabama	Co. B, 5th Alabama Infantry	7/5/1863, Gettysburg, Pennsylvania	Died of Chronic Diarrhea, 12/28/1863
McCoy, Joseph W. Private	Unk	11/21/1862, Elkton, Tennessee	Unknown	Co. I, 3rd Tennessee Mounted Infantry	5/12/1863, Raymond, Mississippi, Wounded	Died of Chronic Diarrhea, 5/5/1864
McCrary, Jacob D. Private	26	1/1/1863, Zollicoffer, Tennessee, Conscript	Maury County, Tennessee	Co. E, 63rd Tennessee Infantry	5/14/1864, Fort Darling, Virginia	Died of Unknown Causes, 7/26/1864
McCual, John C. Sergeant	28	3/25/1862, Sharon Station, North Carolina, Volunteer	Lincoln County, North Carolina	Co. H, 52nd North Carolina Infantry	10/27/1865, Near Petersburg, Virginia	Died of Pneumonia, 3/6/1865
McDade, George B. Corporal	29	6/28/1861, Panola, Mississippi	Panola County, Mississippi	Captain Hoole's Company Mississippi Light Artillery	5/22/1863, Near Vicksburg, Mississippi	Died of Chronic Diarrhea, 11/24/1863

Name	Age	Enlisted	Residence	Unit	Captured	Date and Cause of Death
McDaniel, Alexander Private	30	9/22/1862, Chatham County, North Carolina, Volunteer	Chatham County, North Carolina, Farmer	Co. D, 61st North Carolina Infantry	8/24/1863, Morris Island, South Carolina, Wound Left Ankle	Died of Wounds, 11/10/1863
McDaniel, John W. Private	27	5/28/1861, Bartersville, Chatham County, North Carolina, Volunteer	Chatham County, North Carolina	Co. E, 26th North Carolina Infantry	7/5/1863, Gettysburg, Pennsylvania	Died of Chronic Diarrhea, 11/13/1863
McDonald, Henry C Sergeant Not Listed On Monument	Unk	6/1/1861, Griffin, Georgia	Spalding County, Georgia	Co. D, 2nd Battalion Georgia Infantry	7/2/1863, Gettysburg, Pennsylvania	Died of Dysentery, 7/8/1864
McDonald, Howell G. Private	21	8/1/1861, Bartersville, North Carolina, Volunteer	Montgomery County, North Carolina	Co. E, 28th North Carolina Infantry	6/22/1864, Near Petersburg, Virginia	Died of Chronic Diarrhea, 4/20/1865
McDonald, John C. Private	Unk	6/1/1864, Tazewell County, Virginia	Tazewell County, Virginia	Co. I, 16th Virginia Cavalry	7/10/1864, Frederick, Maryland	Died of Chronic Diarrhea, 11/23/1864
McDonald, Kenneth A. Sergeant Not Listed On Monument	28	3/5/1862 Summerville, North Carolina	Unknown	Co. D, 3rd North Carolina Cavalry	3/13/1865, Murkison's Factory, Near Fayetteville, North Carolina	Died of Chronic Diarrhea, 6/15/1865
McDonald, Franklin M. Private	Unk	4/23/1864, Petersburg, Virginia	Chesterfield County, Virginia	Co. F, 51st North Carolina Infantry	6/14/1864, Cold Harbor, Virginia	Died of Chronic Diarrhea, 10/27/1864
McDonald, Virgil A. Private	23	7/5/1861, Dalton, Georgia	Murray County, Georgia	Co. I, 11th Georgia Infantry	7/3/1863, Gettysburg, Pennsylvania	Died of Bronchitis, 1/31/1865
McDow, F. M. Color Sergeant	Unk	10/21/1861, Jekyll Island, Georgia	Glynn County, Georgia	Co. C, 61st Georgia Infantry	5/12/1864, Wilderness, Virginia	Died of Unknown Causes, 8/3/1864

Name	Age	Enlisted	Residence	Unit	Captured	Date and Cause of Death
McDrew, John See McDrue, John				Co. E, 1st South Carolina Infantry		
McDrue, John Private	35	5/8/1861, Nashville, Virginia	Unknown	Co. E, 1st South Carolina Infantry	3/16/1865, Averasboro, North Carolina	Died of Chronic Diarrhea, 5/29/1865
McEwen, T. M. R. Private	Unk	7/27/1862, Jefferson, North Carolina, Volunteer	Chatham County, North Carolina	Co. A, 1st North Carolina Cavalry	7/3/1863, Gettysburg, Pennsylvania	Died of Unknown Causes, 6/25/1864
McFarland, A. Corporal	Unk	3/4/1863, Chesterfield District, South Carolina	Chesterfield District, South Carolina	Co. E, 21st South Carolina Infantry	6/24/1864, Near Petersburg, Virginia	Died of Unknown Causes, 8/24/1864
McFarland, Duncan B. Landsman	Unk	Unknown	Unknown	Confederate States Navy	Unknown	Unable to Locate
McGalliard, James A. Corporal	33	7/27/1862, Marion, North Carolina, Volunteer	Burke County, North Carolina, Farmer	Co. B, 54th North Carolina Infantry	11/7/1863, Rappahannock Station, Virginia	Died of Unknown Causes, 1/9/1864
McGee, Paschal A. See McGeehee, Paschal A.				Co. G, 7th North Carolina Infantry		
McGee, Robert S. Private	Unk	7/8/1862, Mitchell County, North Carolina, Volunteer	Mitchell County, North Carolina	Co. E, 6th North Carolina Infantry	11/7/1863, Rappahannock Station, Virginia	Died of Pneumonia, 4/23/1865
McGeehee, Paschal A. Sergeant	30	7/27/1862, Cedar Fork, North Carolina, Volunteer	Wake County, North Carolina, Farmer	Co. G, 7th North Carolina Infantry	7/3/1863, Gettysburg, Pennsylvania	Died of Unknown Causes, 1/4/1864

Name	Age	Enlisted	Residence	Unit	Captured	Date and Cause of Death
McGhee, William Private	Unk	Unknown	Unknown	Co. H, 24th Virginia Cavalry	Unknown	Unable to Locate
McGilbert, Taylor Private Not Listed On Monument	23	6/24/1861, Williamston, North Carolina	Wake County, North Carolina	Co. H, 1st North Carolina Infantry	5/12/1864, Spotsylvania Court House, Virginia	Died of Unknown Causes, 8/10/1864
McGinn, Robert F. Private	30	5/15/1862, Charlotte, North Carolina, Volunteer	Mecklenburg County, North Carolina	Co. A, 11th North Carolina Infantry	7/14/1863, Falling Waters, Maryland	Died of Unknown Causes, 2/2/1864
McGinnis, Sidney A. Private	27	3/1/1863, Charlotte, North Carolina, Volunteer	Mecklenburg County, North Carolina	Co. A, 11th North Carolina Infantry	7/3/1863, Gettysburg, Pennsylvania	Died of Unknown Causes, 2/15/1864
McGlaughlin, Hugh P. See: McLaughlin, Hugh P.				Co. I, 25th Virginia Infantry		
McGougan, A. Private	Unk	4/3/1863, Camp Canty, South Carolina	Unknown	Co. F, 7th Battalion, South Carolina Infantry	8/21/1864, Globe Tavern, Weldon Railroad, Virginia	Died of Chronic Diarrhea, 1/1/1865
McGowan, Andrew M. Private	23	4/22/1861, Covington, Virginia	Alleghany County, Virginia, Laborer	Co. A, Alleghany Virginia Light Artillery	8/27/1864, Staunton, Virginia	Died of Consumption, 2/17/1865
McGray, John W. Private	Unk	6/1/1864, Carroll, Virginia	Carroll County, Virginia	Co. F, 25th Virginia Cavalry	7/6/1864, Harper's Ferry, Virginia	Died of Chronic Diarrhea, 10/27/1864
McGragan, A. See McGougan, A.				Co. F, 7th Battalion, South Carolina Infantry		

Name	Age	Enlisted	Residence	Unit	Captured	Date and Cause of Death
McGrady, James B. Private	Unk	7/21/1864, Petersburg, Virginia	Chesterfield County, Virginia	Co. F, Holcombe's South Carolina Legion	11/6/1864, Petersburg, Virginia	Died of Consumption, 4/6/1865
McGrady, John Private Not Listed On Monument	Unk	12/19/1864, Petersburg, Virginia	Chesterfield County, Virginia	Co. F, 52nd North Carolina Infantry	4/2/1865, Petersburg, Virginia	Died of Inflammation of the Lungs (Pneumonia), 6/27/1865
McGrtty, John See McGrady, John				Co. F, 57th North Carolina Infantry		
McGuinis, Elisha L. Private	30	9/23/1862, Smithville, Tennessee	DeKalb County, Tennessee	Co. A, 16th Tennessee Infantry	6/28/1863, Hillsboro, Tennessee	Died of Variola (Smallpox), 11/15/1863
McIntosh, Daniel J. Private	20	7/11/1861, Taylorville, North Carolina, Volunteer	Wake County, North Carolina, Farmer	Co. K, 7th North Carolina Infantry	7/3/1863, Gettysburg, Pennsylvania	Died of Unknown Causes, 8/15/1864
McIntosh, R. See McInturff, Hyram L.				Co. C, 33rd Virginia Infantry		
McIntosh, W. F. Seaman	Unk	Unknown	Unknown	Naval Battalion	Unknown	Unable to Locate
McInturff, Hyram L. Private	Unk	1/26/1863, Winder, Virginia	Unknown	Co. C, 33rd Virginia Infantry	7/5/1863, Chambersburg, Pennsylvania	Died of Chronic Diarrhea, 11/14/1863
McIver, John K. Captain	Unk	4/13/1861, Darlington District, South Carolina	Darlington District, South Carolina	Co. F, 8th South Carolina Infantry	7/14/1863, Williamsport, Wounded in Head	Died of Compression of Brain from Gunshot Wound, 10/15/1863

Name	Age	Enlisted	Residence	Unit	Captured	Date and Cause of Death
McKee, William A. Private	Unk	Unknown	Unknown	Co. D, 11th Mississippi Infantry	12/10/1864, Savannah, Georgia	Died of Chronic Diarrhea, 2/15/1865
McKeel, William Henry Private	Unk	6/4/1863, Coward's Bridge, North Carolina	Unknown	Co. D, 67th North Carolina Infantry	6/22/1864, Jackson's Mill's, North Carolina	Died of Unknown Causes, 9/9/1864
McKenna, Micheal J. Corporal	28	6/19/1861, Camp Moore, New Orleans, Louisiana	Born Ireland, Barkeeper	Co. E, 8th Louisiana Infantry	11/8/1863, Rappahannock Station, Virginia	Died of Chronic Dysentery, 10/20/1864
McKenny, R. See: McKinney, Richard				Co. G, 60th Tennessee Mounted Infantry		
McKinney, Richard Private	Unk	Unknown	Unknown	Co. G, 60th Tennessee Mounted Infantry	5/17/1863, Big Black River Bridge, Mississippi	Died of Smallpox, 1/5/1864
McKinny, W. H. Seaman	Unk	Unknown	Unknown	Confederate States Navy	Unknown	Unable to locate
McKinnon, Hosea Private	22	5/30/1861, Rockingham, North Carolina, Volunteer	Richmond County, North Carolina	Co. D, 23rd North Carolina Infantry	7/3/1863, Gettysburg, Pennsylvania	Died of Chronic Diarrhea, 2/16/1864
McKinnon, Kenneth B. Private	18	5/15/1863, Robeson County, North Carolina	Robeson County, North Carolina	Co. D, 1st Battalion North Carolina Heavy Artillery	1/15/1865, Fort Fisher, North Carolina, Severe Gunshot Wound of Right Arm, Fractured Humerous	Died of Wounds, 3/26/1865
McKinnon, William Private	25	6/6/1861, Carthage, North Carolina, Volunteer	Moore County, North Carolina	Co. H, 26th North Carolina Infantry	7/5/1863, Gettysburg, Pennsylvania	Died of Chronic Diarrhea, 12/6/1863

Name	Age	Enlisted	Residence	Unit	Captured	Date and Cause of Death
McKnight, Hardin Private	Unk	10/24/1862, Pocahontas, Arkansas	Randolph County, Arkansas	Co. B, 21st Arkansas Infantry	5/17/1863, Big Black River Bridge, Mississippi	Died of Chronic Diarrhea and Double Pneumonia, 1/26/1864
McKnight, John W. Private	22	3/22/1862, Forsyth County, North Carolina	Forsyth County, North Carolina, Farmer	Co. H, 26th North Carolina Infantry	7/3/1863, Gettysburg, Pennsylvania, Gunshot Wound Right Hip	Died of Unknown Causes, 5/25/1864
McLaughlin, Hugh P. Corporal	21	5/18/1861, Huntersville, Virginia	Pocahontas County, Virginia, Farmer	Co. I, 25th Virginia Infantry	5/17/1864, Spotsylvania, Virginia	Died of Unknown Causes, Date Unknown
McLaughlin, Richard Johnson Private Not Listed On Monument	20	5/18/1861, Sutton, Virginia	Braxton County, Virginia, Farmer	Co. C, 25th Virginia Infantry	5/15/1864, Wilderness, Virginia	Died of Inflammation of Lungs (Pneumonia), 7/21/1864
McLelland, Patrick H. Private	Unk	5/3/1862, Manchester, Virginia	Chesterfield County, Virginia	Co. B, 41st Virginia Infantry	8/19/1864, Globe Tavern, Weldon Railroad, North Carolina	Died of Pneumonia, 3/9/1865
McLeod, Edward Private	Unk	4/5/1863, Macon, Georgia	Bibb County, Georgia	Co. G, 64th Georgia Infantry	8/17/1864, Deep Bottom, Virginia	Died of Chronic Diarrhea, 2/1/1865
McLean, Albert A. Private	18	5/9/1862, New Hanover County, North Carolina	Lumberton, North Carolina, Farm Laborer	Co. D, 1st Battalion North Carolina Heavy Artillery	1/15/1865, Fort Fisher, North Carolina	Died of Chronic Diarrhea, 5/1/1865
McLean, Hugh C. Private	22	5/30/1861, Rockingham, North Carolina, Volunteer	Richmond County, North Carolina	Co. D, 23rd North Carolina Infantry	7/3/1863, Gettysburg, Pennsylvania	Died of Unknown Causes, 1/13/1864
McLean, Joseph E. Private	27	5/6/1862, Greensboro, North Carolina, Volunteer	Richmond County, North Carolina, Farmer	Co. B, 27th North Carolina Infantry	3/25/1865, Fort Stedman, Near Petersburg, Virginia	Died of Acute Diarrhea, 5/31/1865

Name	Age	Enlisted	Residence	Unit	Captured	Date and Cause of Death
McLellan, Alexander Private	20	5/18/1861, Lumberton, North Carolina, Volunteer	Marion, Robeson County, North Carolina, Farmer	Co. B, 27th North Carolina Infantry	5/12/1864 Spotsylvania Court House, Virginia	Died of Unknown Causes 7/19/1864
McLendon, J. Miller Private	20	1/13/1862, Darlington District, South Carolina	Darlington District, South Carolina	Co. A, 21st South Carolina Infantry	7/10/1863, Morris Island, South Carolina	Died of Unknown Causes 1/25/1864
McLucas, Andrew Private Not Listed On Monument	Unk	5/1/1862, Fayetteville, Georgia	Fayette County, Georgia	Co. C, 53th Georgia Infantry	7/3/1863, Gettysburg, Pennsylvania, Wounded	Date and Causes of Death Unknown
McMaley, Alexander Private	Unk	5/5/1861, Leesburg, Virginia	Loudoun County, Virginia	Fauquier Virginia Light Artillery	6/18/1863, Loudoun County, Virginia	Died of Chronic Diarrhea, 11/15/1863
McMeekin, William B. Private	Unk	8/28/1861, Alston, South Carolina	Fairfield County, South Carolina	Co. F, 12th South Carolina Infantry	8/17/1864, Deep Bottom, Virginia	Died of Chronic Diarrhea, 1/16/1865
McMillan, Daniel Sergeant	21	11/9/1861, Cumberland County, North Carolina, Volunteer	Robeson County, North Carolina, Farmer	Co. B, 27th North Carolina Infantry	7/14/1863, Falling Waters, Maryland	Died of Unknown Causes, 3/14/1864
McMillan, William J. Private	21	7/9/1864, Robeson County, North Carolina	Lumberton, Robeson County, North Carolina	Co. D, 1st Battalion North Carolina Heavy Artillery	1/15/1865, Fort Fisher, North Carolina	Died of Unknown Causes, 6/7/1865
McMillan, Pleasant Private	Unk	11/9/1861, Morganton, North Carolina, Volunteer	Wilkes County, North Carolina	Co. D, 11th North Carolina Infantry	4/2/1865, Petersburg, Virginia	Died of Pneumonia, 6/23/1865
McMordie, Abraham J. Private	Unk	8/20/1861, Danville, Kentucky	Boyle County, Kentucky	Co. I, 7th Kentucky Cavalry	7/19/1863, Buffington, Ohio	Died of Chronic Diarrhea, 4/30/1865

Name	Age	Enlisted	Residence	Unit	Captured	Date and Cause of Death
McMurray, Alexander Private Not Listed On Monument	22	4/10/1862, Blountsville, Alabama	Blount County, Alabama	Co. F, 48th Alabama Infantry	7/4/1863, Gettysburg, Pennsylvania	Died of Chronic Diarrhea & Scurvy, 2/1/1865
McNeill, Archibald A. Private	Unk	10/29/1864, Camp Holmes, North Carolina	Robeson County, North Carolina	Co. G, 24th North Carolina Infantry	3/25/1865, Fort Stedman, Near Petersburg, Virginia	Died of Acute Diarrhea, 5/7/1865
McNeill, Neely E. Private	Unk	8/15/1862, Dale County, Alabama	Dale County, Alabama	Co. H, 15th Alabama Infantry	7/1/1863, Gettysburg, Pennsylvania	Died of Chronic Diarrhea, 12/2/1863
McNew, Isaac Private	Unk	4/20/1863, Reedy Creek, Virginia	Pocahontas County, Virginia, Farmer	Co. C, 13th Battalion Virginia Light Artillery	4/6/1865, High Bridge, Virginia	Died of Unknown Causes, 6/28/1865
McPherson, John W. Sergeant	21	4/29/1862, Moore County, North Carolina, Volunteer	Moore County, North Carolina, Farmer	Co. E, 56th North Carolina Infantry	5/20/1864, Between Petersburg & Richmond, Virginia	Died of Pneumonia, 3/31/1865
McRacken, Lindsay Private Not Listed On Monument	Unk	2/4/1864, Raleigh, North Carolina	Wake County, North Carolina	Co. D, 2nd North Carolina Battalion	5/20/1864 Spotsylvania Court House, Virginia	Died of Remittent Fever, 7/15/1864
McRea, T. R. Private	Unk	7/1/1862, Americus, Georgia	Sumter County, Georgia	Co. B, 11th Battalion Georgia Artillery	Unknown	Date and Cause of Death Unknown
McSwain, Oliver Private Not Listed On Monument	18	5/12/1862, Shelby, North Carolina, Volunteer	Cleveland County, North Carolina, Farmer	Co. D, 55th North Carolina Infantry	7/14/1863, Falling Waters, Maryland	Died of Unknown Causes, 6/13/1864
McVay, Lancaster Private	Unk	3/1/1862, Washington, Arkansas	Hempstead County, Arkansas	Co. E, 20th Arkansas Infantry	5/17/ 1863, Big Black River, Near Vicksburg, Mississippi	Died of Chronic Diarrhea, 1/10/1864

358

Name	Age	Enlisted	Residence	Unit	Captured	Date and Cause of Death
Meadow, Stephen G. Private Not Listed On Monument	Unk	Unknown	Unknown	Co. G, 28th Virginia Infantry	4/6/1865, Farmville, Virginia	Died of Typhoid Fever, 5/4/1865
Meadows, Cornelius Private	23	2/29/1862, Granville County, North Carolina, Volunteer	Granville County, North Carolina, Farmer	Co. I, 46th North Carolina Infantry	8/25/1864, Reams Station, Virginia	Died of Pneumonia, 1/22/1865
Meadows, Milus Private	Unk	3/4/1862, Crawfordville, Georgia	Taliaferro County, Georgia	Co. D, 49th Georgia Infantry	7/2/1863, Gettysburg, Pennsylvania	Died of Smallpox, 10/31/1863
Meadows, W. T. Private See Meador, William T.				Co. E, 45th North Carolina Infantry		
Meador, William T. Private	Unk	3/10/1864, Orange County Court House, Virginia	Orange County, Virginia	Co. E, 45th North Carolina Infantry	5/10/1864, Spotsylvania Court House, Virginia	Died of Unknown Causes, 8/6/1864
Mealler, William L. Private	Unk	10/28/1861, Halifax County Court House, Virginia,	Halifax County, Virginia	Co. K, 3rd Virginia Cavalry	Unknown	Died of Chronic Dysentery, 11/26/1863
Meares, John H. Private	Unk	4/20/1864, Kinston, North Carolina	Lenoir County, North Carolina	Co. K, 54th North Carolina Infantry	4/6/1865, Gill Mills, Kentucky	Died of Acute Dysentery, 5/14/1865
Medlin, Archibald H Private	46	4/11/1863, Franklin County, North Carolina	Wake County, North Carolina	Co. B, 47th North Carolina Infantry	7/14/1863, Falling Waters, Maryland	Died of Smallpox, 12/20/1863
Medlin, Garison Private	21	4/5/1862, Kinston, North Carolina, Volunteer	Union County, North Carolina	Co. D, 37th North Carolina Infantry	5/12/1864, Spotsylvania Court House, Virginia	Died of Typhoid Fever, 12/29/1864

Name	Age	Enlisted	Residence	Unit	Captured	Date and Cause of Death
Medlin, Joseph Private	19	9/301862, Morristown, Tennessee	Hamblen County, Tennessee	Co. H, 60th Tennessee Mounted Infantry	5/17/ 1863, Big Black Bridge, Near Vicksburg, Mississippi	Died of Unknown Causes, 12/27/1863
Medlock, Stephen Private	Unk	Unknown	Lee County, Virginia	Co. E, 50th Virginia Infantry	11/17/1863, Rappahannock, Virginia	Died of Smallpox, 1/13/1864
Meggs, Joseph Private	24	5/30/1861 South Mills, North Carolina, Volunteer	Camden County, North Carolina	Co. H, 32nd North Carolina Infantry	5/10/1864, Mine Run, Virginia	Died of Chronic Diarrhea, 3/18/1865
Mellichamp, E. A. Private	Unk	Unknown	Unknown	Confederate States Engineer Corps	12/13/1864, Fort McAllister, Georgia	Died of Bronchitis, 5/25/1865
Melton, A. J. Corporal	Unk	5/15/1862 Jacksonville, North Carolina	Onslow County, North Carolina	Co. H, 3rd North Carolina Cavalry	4/30/1864, Swansboro, North Carolina	Died of Pneumonia, 3/19/1865
Melton, Alexander Private Not Listed On Monument	Unk	2/1/1864, Wilmington, North Carolina	New Hanover County, North Carolina	Co. K, 42nd North Carolina Infantry	3/10/1865, Wise Forks, Near Kinston, North Carolina	Died of Rubeola (Measles), 6/7/1865
Melton, Elijah S. Private	21	5/15/1862 Jacksonville, North Carolina	Onslow County, North Carolina	Co. H, 3rd North Carolina Cavalry	4/30/1864, Swansboro, North Carolina	Died of Scurvy, 3/19/1865
Melton, William Private	20	4/20/1861, Columbus County, North Carolina, Volunteer	Polk County, North Carolina	Co. D, 16th North Carolina Infantry	5/24/1864, North Anna River, Virginia	Died of Unknown Causes, 10/23/1864

Name	Age	Enlisted	Residence	Unit	Captured	Date and Cause of Death
Menude, John A. Corporal Not Listed On Monument	Unk	3/17/1862, Charleston, South Carolina	Charleston County, South Carolina	Co. I, 27th South Carolina Infantry	6/24/1864, Near Petersburg, Virginia	Died of Chronic Diarrhea, 10/25/1864
Mercer, Christopher C. Private Not Listed On Monument	38	2/19/1863, Fort Caswell, North Carolina	Lumberton, Robeson County, North Carolina, Farmer	Co. K, 40th North Carolina Light Artillery	1/15/1865, Fort Fisher, North Carolina	Died of Pneumonia, 2/7/1865
Mercer, James M. Private	22	5/13/1862, Wilson County, North Carolina	Wilson County, North Carolina, Farmer	Co. A, 55th North Carolina Infantry	7/1/1863, Gettysburg, Pennsylvania	Died of Unknown Causes, 11/24/1863
Mercer, John Private	Unk	1/26/1864, Georgetown, South Carolina	Georgetown County, South Carolina	Co. E, 7th Georgia Cavalry	6/11/1864, Louisa Court House, Virginia	Died of Unknown Causes, 8/6/1864
Mercer, John J. N. Private Not Listed On Monument	27	7/2/1862, Place Unknown	Wilson County, North Carolina	Co. E, 55th North Carolina Infantry	7/1/1863, Gettysburg, Pennsylvania	Died of Smallpox, 11/24/1863
Mercer, Robert R. Private	Unk	9/9/1864, Edgecombe County, North Carolina	Edgecombe County, North Carolina	Co. D, 40th North Carolina Artillery	1/15/1865, Fort Fisher, North Carolina	Died of Pneumonia, 3/11/1865
Merrit, James Private	Unk	10/2/1864, Richmond, Virginia	Henrico County, Virginia	Co. E, 59th Virginia Infantry	4/3/1865, Southland Station, Virginia	Died of Intermittent Fever, 6/29/1865

Name	Age	Enlisted	Residence	Unit	Captured	Date and Cause of Death
Merritt, James H. Private Not Listed On Monument	Unk	12/28/1862, New Market, Virginia	Shenandoah County, Virginia	Co. D, 11th Virginia Infantry	5/5/1864, Wilderness, Virginia	Died of Chronic Diarrhea, 8/30/1864
Merritt, William L. F. Private	22	7/16/1862, Franklin County, North Carolina, Conscript	Franklin County, North Carolina	Co. K, 44th North Carolina Infantry	10/14/1863, Bristoe Station, Virginia	Died of Unknown Causes, 3/11/1864
Michie, Hugh W. Corporal	Unk	Unknown	Unknown	Co. C, 1st Virginia Reserve Infantry	Unknown	Unable to Locate
Middleton, S. T. B. Private	20	9/21/1861, Rusk, Cherokee County, Texas	Cherokee County, Texas	Co. E, 7th Texas Infantry	5/12/1863, Raymond, Mississippi Near Vicksburg	Died of Chronic Diarrhea, 1/10/1864
Milan, W. H. Private	Unk	11/21/1863, Mount Pleasant, South Carolina	Charleston District, South Carolina	Co. F, 22nd South Carolina Infantry	6/2/1864, Near Bermuda Hundred, Virginia	Died of Chronic Diarrhea, 2/23/1865
Milam, Wiley B. Private	19	8/12/1861, Campbellton, Campbell County, Georgia	Campbell County, Georgia	Co. K, 35th Georgia Infantry	7/3/1863, Gettysburg, Pennsylvania	Died of Smallpox, 11/17/1863
Milam, William Private	Unk	2/9/1864, Camp Elzey, Virginia	Unknown	Co. E, 7th South Carolina Cavalry	1/30/1865, Chickahominy, Virginia, Wound In Side	Died of Pneumonia, 4/23/1865
Miles, A. Monroe Private	Unk	5/6/1862 Tallapoosa, Alabama	Tallapoosa County, Alabama	Co. B, 5th Alabama Infantry	5/6/1864, Wilderness, Virginia	Died of Unknown Causes, 7/30/1864
Miller, Amos Private	26	7/15/1862, Raleigh, North Carolina, Conscript	Davidson County, North Carolina	Co. F, 15th North Carolina Infantry	10/14/1863, Bristoe Station, Virginia	Died of Unknown Causes, 3/13/1864

Name	Age	Enlisted	Residence	Unit	Captured	Date and Cause of Death
Miller, Amos J. Private	26	4/27/1864 Charleston, South Carolina, Conscript	Harnett County, North Carolina	Co. B, 15th Battalion South Carolina Heavy Artillery	3/6/1865, Cheraw, South Carolina	Died of Remittent Fever, 5/19/1865
Miller, Alexander Private Not Listed On Monument	Unk	9/17/1861, Atlanta, Georgia	Campbell County, Georgia	Co. C, 35th Georgia Infantry	7/14/1863, Falling Waters, Maryland	Died of Unknown Causes, 2/19/1864
Miller, B. F. Private	Unk	10/20/1862, Camp Rippon, Virginia	Unknown	Co. C, 6th Virginia Cavalry	7/4/1863, Millerstown, Pennsylvania	Died of Unknown Causes, 3/19/1864
Miller, Frederick A. Private Not Listed On Monument	Unk	2/1/1863, Smyth County, Virginia	Smyth County, Virginia	Co. E, 23rd Battalion Virginia Infantry	6/2/1864, Cold Harbor, Virginia	Died of Unknown Causes, 7/15/1864
Miller, Isaac W. Private	25	6/24/1861, Colerain, North Carolina, Volunteer	Bertie County, North Carolina	Co. F, 5th North Carolina Infantry	7/3/1863, Gettysburg, Pennsylvania	Died of Smallpox, 11/22/1863
Miller, James L. Private	Unk	10/16/1861, Sulphur Spring, Tennessee	Washington County, Tennessee	Co. B, 43rd Tennessee Infantry	9/23/1864, Cedar Creek or Strasburg, Virginia	Died of Typhoid Fever, 12/4/1864
Miller, James Private	22	3/2/1862, Reidsville, North Carolina, Volunteer	Rockingham County, North Carolina, Farmer	Co. F, 45th North Carolina Infantry	Date Unknown, Near Petersburg, Virginia	Died of Typhoid Fever, 9/6/1863
Miller, John C. Private	Unk	8/30/1862, Richmond, Virginia	Henrico County, Virginia	Co. C, 2nd Battalion Maryland Infantry	8/19/1864, Globe Tavern, Near Weldon Railroad, Virginia	Died on Parole, 4/?/1865
Miller, John W. Private Not Listed On Monument	36	2/25/1863, Rockingham County, North Carolina, Volunteer	Rockingham County, North Carolina	Co. F, 45th North Carolina Infantry	5/10/1864, Spotsylvania Court House, Virginia	Died of Chronic Diarrhea 11/3/1864

Name	Age	Enlisted	Residence	Unit	Captured	Date and Cause of Death
Miller, Robert J. Private	32	2/15/1862, Kenansville, North Carolina	Duplin County, North Carolina, Farmer	Co. F, 51st North Carolina Infantry	6/1/1864, Cold Harbor, Virginia	Died of Chronic Diarrhea, 10/22/1864
Miller, Samuel D. Private Not Listed On Monument	Unk	3/25/1864, Mossy Creek, Tennessee, Conscript	Jefferson County, Tennessee	Co. D, 7th Tennessee Infantry	6/4/1864 Talapatomoy Creek, Cold Harbor, Virginia	Died of Unknown Causes, 7/15/1864
Miller, Thomas Private	Unk	7/1/1862 Forsyth County, North Carolina, Conscript	Forsyth County, North Carolina	Co. H, 33rd North Carolina Infantry	7/14/1863, Falling Waters, Maryland	Died of Unknown Causes, 1/25/1864
Miller, Wesley H. Private	19	2/25/1863, Camp Near Kinston, North Carolina, Volunteer	Rockingham County, North Carolina	Co. F, 45th North Carolina Infantry	3/25/1865, Fort Stedman, Near Petersburg, Virginia	Died of Rubeola (Measles), 6/29/1865
Miller, W. M. Private Not Listed On Monument	Unk	Unknown	Unknown	Co. K, 3rd Virginia Cavalry	7/4/1863, Gettysburg, Pennsylvania	Date and Cause of Death Unknown
Milling, John A. Private	18	2/10/1864, Richmond, Virginia	Yorkville District, South Carolina	Co. C, 23rd North Carolina Infantry	5/12/1864, Spotsylvania Court House, Virginia	Died of Unknown Causes, 6/30/1864
Mills, Charles M. Private	25	7/8/1862, Salisbury, Alamance County, North Carolina, Volunteer	Iredell County, North Carolina	Co. H, 57th North Carolina Infantry	11/7/1863, Rappahannock Station, Virginia	Died of Acute Dysentery, 12/3/1864
Mills, John Private	19	4/20/1862, Greenville, North Carolina	Cleveland County, North Carolina, Farmer	Co. E, 55th North Carolina Infantry	7/4/1863, Gettysburg, Pennsylvania	Died of Unknown Causes, 2/22/1864

Name	Age	Enlisted	Residence	Unit	Captured	Date and Cause of Death
Mills, William D. Private Not Listed On Monument	Unk	10/31/1864, Camp Holmes, Raleigh, North Carolina	Robeson County, North Carolina	Co. D, 18th North Carolina Infantry	4/2/1865, Petersburg, Virginia	Died of Chronic Diarrhea, 7/20/1865
Milton, Alexander See Melton, Alexander				Co. K, 42nd North Carolina Infantry		
Mims, Cyrilo P. Private	Unk	12/1/1863, Sullivan's Island, South Carolina	Charleston District, South Carolina	Co. A, 18th South Carolina Infantry	6/16/1864, Near Petersburg, Virginia	Died of Unknown Causes, 9/10/1864
Mimms, B. A. Private	26	1/19/1862, Wake County, North Carolina,	Wake County, North Carolina	Co. I, 47th North Carolina Infantry	7/3/1863, Gettysburg, Pennsylvania	Died of Smallpox, 11/28/1863
Mincey, Kinchen Private Not Listed On Monument	Unk	2/11/1863 Burke County, North Carolina, Conscript	Burke County, North Carolina	Co. B, 11th North Carolina Infantry	10/27/1864, Burgess' Mill, Near Petersburg, Virginia	Died of Chronic Dysentery 4/23/1865
Minix, Elijah Private Not Listed On Monument	Unk	9/19/1864 Camp Watts, Georgia	Crawford County, Georgia	Co. K, 45th Georgia Infantry	3/25/1865, Petersburg, Virginia	Died of Rubeola (Measles), 6/4/1865
Minix, James Private	Unk	9/19/1864 Camp Watts, Georgia	Crawford County, Georgia	Co. K, 45th Georgia Infantry	3/25/1864, Near Petersburg, Virginia	Died of Unknown Causes, 6/5/1864

Name	Age	Enlisted	Residence	Unit	Captured	Date and Cause of Death
Minor, James A. Private	Unk	2/25/1862, Bedford County, Virginia	Bedford County, Virginia	Co. C, 20th Battalion Virginia Heavy Artillery	4/6/1865, Burkeville, Virginia	Died of Typhoid Fever 5/20/1865
Minor, T. A. Private	Unk	8/9/1864, Savannah, Georgia	Stewart County, Georgia	Co. C, 12th Battalion Georgia Light Artillery	3/25/1864, Near Petersburg, Virginia	Died of Unknown Causes, 6/26/1864
Mirac, Cornelius Private	39	3/11/1862, Love's Store, Holt, North Carolina	Chatham County, North Carolina, Farmer	Co. E, 44th North Carolina Infantry	10/14/1863, Bristoe Station, Virginia	Died of Smallpox, 12/27/1863
Mires, A. W. Private Not Listed On Monument	25	4/13/1863, Tazewell, Tennessee	Claiborne County, Tennessee	Co. A, 63rd Tennessee Infantry	5/16/1863, Cumberland Gap, Clayborne County, Tennessee	Died of Scurvy, 9/16/1864
Mitchel, William Iverson Private Not Listed On Monument	Unk	11/3/1864, Camp Stokes, North Carolina	Unknown	Co. E, 32nd North Carolina Infantry	3/25/1865, Fort Stedman, Near Petersburg, Virginia	Died of Acute Diarrhea, 5/3/1865
Mitchell, Alexander M. Private	30	5/2/1862, Franklin County, North Carolina, Volunteer	Franklin County, North Carolina, Farmer	Co. F, 47th North Carolina Infantry	7/2/1863, Gettysburg, Pennsylvania	Died of Unknown Causes, 1/23/1864
Mitchell, John C. Private	34	5/4/1862, Camp McIntosh, North Carolina, Volunteer	Wake County, North Carolina	Co. I, 1st North Carolina Infantry	5/12/1864, Spotsylvania Court House, Virginia	Died of Unknown Causes, 6/24/1864
Mitchell, John T. Private	Unk	11/2/1863 Columbus, Georgia	Muscogee County, Georgia	Co. B, 28th Battalion Georgia Siege Artillery	3/16/1865, Bentonville, North Carolina	Died of Scurvy, 5/28/1865

Name	Age	Enlisted	Residence	Unit	Captured	Date and Cause of Death
Mitchell, Joseph S. Sergeant	Unk	6/1/1861, Lancaster Court House, Virginia	Lancaster County, Virginia	Co. F, 47th Virginia Infantry	7/14/1863, Falling Waters, Maryland	Died of Chronic Diarrhea, 12/2/1863
Mitchell, Pinkney Private	34	9/24/1863, Camp Holmes, Raleigh, North Carolina, Conscript	Rockingham County, North Carolina	Co. G, 14th North Carolina Infantry	9/19/1864, Winchester, Virginia, Wounded, Left Forearm, Grape Shot	Died of Scurvy, 6/11/1865
Mitchell, William A. Private	Unk	Unknown	Unknown	South Carolina Artillery	Unknown	Unable to Locate
Mitchell, William J. Private	20	4/1/1862, Bertie County, North Carolina	Bertie County, North Carolina	Co. E, 32nd North Carolina Infantry	9/19/1864, Winchester, Virginia	Died of Acute Diarrhea, 5/4/1865
Mitchell, William P. Private Not Listed On Monument	Unk	5/14/1861 Petersburg, Virginia	Chesterfield County, Virginia	Co. K, 16th Virginia Infantry	Date & Place of Capture Unknown	Died of Debility, 5/18/1865
Mitchum, Benjamin F. Private	Unk	4/20/1863, Atlanta, Georgia	Fulton County, Georgia	Co. K, 64th Georgia Infantry	8/17/1864, Deep Bottom, Virginia	Died of Chronic Diarrhea, 1/29/1865
Mize, John Private	19	7/8/1862, Raleigh, North Carolina, Conscript	Granville County, North Carolina	Co. B, 23rd North Carolina Infantry	5/12/1864, Spotsylvania Court House, Virginia	Died of Unknown Causes 10/2/1864
Mobley, W. V. Private	27	3/3/1862, New Wilmington, Hanover County, North Carolina, Volunteer	Duplin County, North Carolina	Co. E, 30th North Carolina Infantry	9/19/1864, Winchester, Virginia	Died of Consumption, 2/12/1865
Monday, Isaac Private	19	7/6/1862, Salisbury, Alamance County, North Carolina, Volunteer	Davie County, North Carolina	Co. H, 57th North Carolina Infantry	11/7/1863, Rappahannock Station, Virginia	Died of Smallpox, 1/25/1864

Name	Age	Enlisted	Residence	Unit	Captured	Date and Cause of Death
Money, John Grey Private Not Listed On Monument	45	7/16/1863 Camp Bellton, Florida	Unknown	Co. F, 11th Florida Infantry	4/7/1865 Burkesville, Virginia	Died of Chronic Diarrhea, 5/22/1865
Monroe, G. D. Private	Unk	Unknown	Unknown	Confederate States Navy	Unknown	Unable to Locate
Monroe, John P. Private	15	9/20/1862, Strydert's Mill, Virginia	Unknown	Co. A, 4th Virginia Cavalry	7/18/1863, Ashby's Gap, Virginia	Died of Erysipelas & Chronic Diarrhea, 12/10/1863
Monroe, Thomas Private	33	6/4/1863, Fort Caswell, North Carolina	Cumberland County, North Carolina	Co. E, 40th North Carolina Artillery	1/15/1865, Fort Fisher, North Carolina	Died of Chronic Dysentery, 1/30/1865
Munroe, William A. Private Not Listed On Monument	38	4/7/1862, Stafford County, Virginia	Stafford County, Virginia, Farmer	Co. A, 47th Virginia Infantry	7/5/1863, Greencastle, Pennsylvania	Died of Unknown Causes, 11/15/1863
Monroe, William D. Private Not Listed On Monument	Unk	7/24/1861, Habersham County, Georgia	Habersham County, Georgia	Co. G, 16th Georgia Infantry	7/3/1863, Gettysburg, Pennsylvania	Died of Smallpox, 11/7/1863
Montgomery, George L. Private	Unk	11/18/1864, Camp Stokes, North Carolina	Unknown	Co. B, 57th North Carolina Infantry	3/25/1864, Fort Stedman, Near Petersburg, Virginia	Died From Inflammation of Lungs (Pneumonia), 6/2/1865
Montgomery, Joel Private	Unk	9/13/1862, Caustin Bluff, Georgia	Unknown	Co. E, 1st Georgia Infantry	12/11/1864, Chatham County, Georgia	Died of Typhoid Fever, 2/19/1865
Mondy, S. S. Private	Unk	Unknown	Unknown	Co. O, 7th Georgia Cavalry	Unknown	Unable to Locate

Name	Age	Enlisted	Residence	Unit	Captured	Date and Cause of Death
Moody, James P. Private Not Listed On Monument	Unk	5/1/1862, Newman, Georgia	Coweta County, Georgia	Co. A, 12th Battalion Georgia Light Artillery	7/16/1863, James Island, South Carolina	Died of Unknown Causes, 9/16/1864
Mooney, George W. Private	18	3/26/1862, Shelby, North Carolina, Volunteer	Cleveland County, North Carolina, Farmer	Co. D, 55th North Carolina Infantry	7/1/1863, Gettysburg, Pennsylvania	Died of Unknown Causes, 12/28/1863
Moore, Benjamin J. Private	17	12/25/1861, Bennettsville, South Carolina	Bennettsville District, South Carolina	Co. E, 21st South Carolina Infantry	7/10/1863, Morris Island, South Carolina	Date and Cause of Death Unknown
Moore, George W. Jr. Private	30	4/11/1861, Lillington, North Carolina, Volunteer	New Hanover County, North Carolina	Co. C, 1st North Carolina Cavalry	7/3/1863, Gettysburg, Pennsylvania	Died of Unknown Causes, 8/18/1864
Moore, James Alex Private Not Listed On Monument	45	8/28/1863, Campbell County, Virginia	Campbell County, Virginia	Co. I, 2nd Virginia Cavalry	5/15/1864, Caroline County, Virginia	Died of Unknown Causes, 7/5/1864
Moore, James H. Private	39	4/27/1861, Concord Depot, Virginia	Campbell County, Virginia	Co. A, 11th Virginia Cavalry	4/1/1865, Five Forks, Virginia	Died of Acute Diarrhea, 6/17/1865
Moore, James R. Private	Unk	6/1/1864, Kenansville, North Carolina	Duplin County, North Carolina	Co. E, 5th North Carolina Infantry	9/19/1864, Winchester, Virginia	Died of Pneumonia, 3/15/1865
Moore, Joseph L. Private	20	Unknown	Iredell County, North Carolina	Co. C, 18th North Carolina Infantry	6/6/1864, Wilderness, Virginia	Date and Cause of Death Unknown
Moore, Larry H. Private	Unk	10/18/1864, Camp Holmes, Raleigh, North Carolina	Wake County, North Carolina	Co. A, 24th North Carolina Infantry	4/2/1865, Five Forks, Virginia	Died of Chronic Diarrhea, 5/18/1865

Name	Age	Enlisted	Residence	Unit	Captured	Date and Cause of Death
Moore, Lemuel Private Not Listed On Monument	Unk	10/20/1863, Granville County, North Carolina	Granville County, North Carolina	Co. K, 28th North Carolina Infantry	5/6/1864, Wilderness, Virginia	Died of Acute Dysentery, 7/20/1864
Moore, Peter P. Sergeant	20	6/15/1861, Brookhaven, Mississippi	Lincoln County, Mississippi, Student	Co. G, 21st Mississippi Infantry	10/19/1864, Cedar Creek or Strasburg, Virginia	Died of Chronic Diarrhea & Scurvy, 5/18/1865
Moore, Robert M. Private	Unk	10/2/1862, Mossy Creek, Tennessee	Jefferson County, Tennessee	Co. F, 61st Tennessee Mounted Infantry	5/17/1863, Big Black Bridge, Near Vicksburg, Mississippi	Died of Chronic Diarrhea & Scurvy, 12/22/1863
Moore, Thomas F. Private	Unk	4/27/1862, Richmond, Virginia	Henrico County, Virginia	Co. K, 4th Virginia Cavalry	7/3/1863, Gettysburg, Pennsylvania	Died of Unknown Causes, 8/19/1864
Moore, Thomas J. Private Not Listed On Monument	Unk	1/1/1863, New Market, Virginia	Shenandoah County, Virginia	Co. C, 35th Virginia Cavalry	12/29/1863, Aldie, Loudon County, Virginia	Died of Acute Dysentery, 7/5/1864
Moore, Walter J. Private	17	5/21/1861 Thomasville, North Carolina	Davidson County, North Carolina, Artist	Co. D, 14th North Carolina Infantry	7/3/1863, Gettysburg, Pennsylvania	Died of Smallpox, 6/13/1864
Moore, William Private	Unk	4/16/1863, Richmond County, North Carolina	Richmond County, North Carolina	Co. F, 52nd North Carolina Infantry	7/5/1863, Gettysburg, Pennsylvania	Died of Chronic Diarrhea, 9/20/1863
Moreland, Joseph F. Private	Unk	2/25/1862, Gilmer, Georgia	Gilmer County, Georgia	Co. F, 60th Georgia Infantry	7/4/1863, Gettysburg, Pennsylvania	Died of Chronic Diarrhea, 6/14/1864
Morgan, Ezekiel L. Private	Unk	9/29/1863, Camp Randolph, Decatur, Georgia	DeKalb County, Georgia	Thompson's Georgia Light Artillery	3/9/1865, Fayetteville, North Carolina	Died of Unknown Causes, 4/29/1865
Morgan, Eli S. Private	Unk	Unknown	Unknown	Co. K, 34th North Carolina Infantry	3/30/1865, Hatchers Run, Near Richmond, Virginia	Died of Pneumonia, 4/25/1865

Name	Age	Enlisted	Residence	Unit	Captured	Date and Cause of Death
Morgan, Martin Private	29	5/1/1862, Albemarle, North Carolina, Volunteer	Stanly County, North Carolina	Co. I, 52nd North Carolina Infantry	7/5/1863, Gettysburg, Pennsylvania	Died of Chronic Diarrhea, 9/14/1864
Morgan, Martin Private Not Listed On Monument	Unk	5/18/1861 Chuckatuck, Virginia, Conscript	Suffolk County, Virginia	Co. D, 9th Virginia Infantry	7/3/1863, Gettysburg, Pennsylvania	Died of Smallpox, 11/2/1863
Morrill, J. Private	Unk	Unknown	Unknown	Co. A, 23rd Virginia Infantry	Unknown	Unable to Locate
Morris, C. H. Private	Unk	1/7/1862, Camp Hampton, South Carolina	Lancaster County, South Carolina	Co. H, Holcombe Legion, South Carolina Infantry	11/6/1864, Near Petersburg, Virginia	Died of Epilepsy, 4/18/1865
Morris, Cornelius Private	33	4/27/1863, Asheville, North Carolina	Buncombe County, North Carolina	Co. K, 11th North Carolina Infantry	7/14/1863, Falling Waters, Maryland, Wounded In Right Elbow	Died of Catarrh & Chronic Diarrhea, 12/10/1863
Morris, David P. Private	42	8/15/1861, Jonesboro, North Carolina, Conscript	Moore County, North Carolina	Co. H, 30th North Carolina Infantry	4/6/1865, High Bridge, Virginia	Died of Chronic Diarrhea, 5/3/1865
Morris, Edwin Private	Unk	3/9/1864 Camp Howard, Hanover Junction, Virginia	Hanover County, Virginia	Co. E, 1st Maryland Cavalry	5/27/1864, Hanover Junction or Pollard's Farm, Virginia	Died of Unknown Causes, 8/9/1864
Morris, George A. Private	Unk	Unknown	Unknown	Co. E, 31st Louisiana Infantry	Unknown	Unable to Locate
Morris, Henry C. Private	20	10/8/1862, Littletown, Virginia	Unknown	Co. D, 8th Virginia Cavalry	7/3/1864, Littletown, Virginia	Date and Cause of Death Unknown

Name	Age	Enlisted	Residence	Unit	Captured	Date and Cause of Death
Morris, George W. Private	19	1/20/1863, Camp Holmes, Raleigh, North Carolina, Conscript	Wake County, North Carolina	Co. D, 26th North Carolina Infantry	10/14/1863, Bristoe Station, Virginia	Died of Chronic Diarrhea, 1/10/1864
Morris, Horatio E. Private	26	7/3/1862 St. John's, Murfreesboro, North Carolina	Hertford County, North Carolina, Farmer	Co. D, 4th North Carolina Cavalry	7/3/1863, Gettysburg, Pennsylvania	Died of Chronic Diarrhea & Pneumonia, 2/19/1864
Morris, James Private	Unk	9/1/1861, Camp Mitchell, Virginia	Unknown	Co. F, 49th Virginia Infantry	7/5/1863, Waterloo, Gettysburg, Pennsylvania	Died of Chronic Diarrhea, 12/26/1863
Morris, James K. P. Private	Unk	3/4/1863, Concord Depot, Virginia	Unknown	Co. D, 20th Battalion Virginia Heavy Artillery	4/6/1865, Farmville, Virginia	Died of Acute Diarrhea, 5/27/1865
Morris, John W. Private	Unk	3/27/1862, Richmond, Virginia	Bedford County, Virginia, Farmer	Co. C, 14th Virginia Infantry	7/3/1863, Gettysburg, Pennsylvania	Died of Unknown Causes, 12/26/1863
Morris, L. Private	Unk	Unknown	Unknown	Co. F, 3th North Carolina Infantry	Unknown	Unable to Locate
Moris, Lockey Private Not Listed On Monument	Unk	7/25/1863, Raleigh, North Carolina, Conscript	Moore County, North Carolina	Co. L, 21st North Carolina Infantry	7/5/1863, Waterloo, Gettysburg, Pennsylvania	Died of Chronic Diarrhea & Purpura, 10/30/1863
Morris, Monroe Private	27	10/27/1861, Franklin, North Carolina	Buncombe County, North Carolina	Co. K, 11th North Carolina Infantry	7/3/1863, Gettysburg, Pennsylvania	Died of Unknown Causes, 2/2/1864
Morris, Richard H. Private	Unk	6/6/1861 Hicksford, Virginia	Greensville County, Virginia, Printer	Co. K, 12th Virginia Infantry	10/27/1864, Boyton Plank Road or Burgess' Mill, Virginia	Died of Chronic Dysentery, 7/9/1865
Morris, William A. Private	23	5/10/1861, Lynchburg, Virginia	Franklin County, Virginia	Captain Shoemaker's Lynchburg, Virginia Horse Artillery	9/13/1863, Near Culpepper, Virginia	Died of Unknown Causes, 1/25/1865

Name	Age	Enlisted	Residence	Unit	Captured	Date and Cause of Death
Moriss, Jordan T. Private Not Listed On Monument	22	10/3/1862, Cabell County, Virginia	Cabell County, Virginia	Co. D, 8th Virginia Cavalry	3/28/1863, Hurricane Bridge, Virginia, Wounded	Died of Acute Dysentery, 1/28/1865
Morisett, T. S. Private	Unk	Unknown	Unknown	Co. F, 66th North Carolina Infantry	8/5/1863, Near Camden County, North Carolina	Died of Smallpox, 1/20/1864
Morrow, John V. Private	Unk	10/15/1863, Camp Vance, North Carolina	Wake County, North Carolina	Co. K, 16th North Carolina Infantry	5/24/1864, Jericho Ford, North Anna, Virginia	Died of Chronic Dysentery, 9/12/1864
Morse, Alexander Private	Unk	8/9/1863 Hixford, Virginia,	Unknown	Co. H, 8th Virginia Infantry	4/6/1865, Amelia Court House, Virginia	Died of Measles, 6/23/1865
Moss, Alexander Private	Unk	4/27/1862, Halifax, Virginia	Halifax County, Virginia	Co. D, 1st Virginia Infantry	4/2/1865, Hatcher's Run, Virginia	Died of Acute Diarrhea, 4/25/1865
Moss, Benson Private Not Listed On Monument	Unk	3/1/1863, Camp No. 38, Elberton, Georgia	Elbert County, Georgia	Co. F, 38th Georgia Infantry	7/5/1863, Gettysburg, Pennsylvania	Died of Unknown Causes, 7/1/1864
Moss, William S. Private	Unk	4/27/1862, Richmond, Virginia	Henrico County, Virginia	Co. K, 4th Virginia Cavalry	7/3/1863, Gettysburg, Pennsylvania	Died of Chronic Diarrhea, 12/24/1863
Motsinger, A. Frank Private	Unk	8/8/1862, Davidson County, North Carolina, Conscript	Davidson County, North Carolina	Co. K, 48th North Carolina Infantry	10/1/1864, Petersburg, Virginia	Died of Pneumonia, 3/5/1865
Mozingo, James Private	Unk	4/13/1863, Fredericksburg Virginia	Spotsylvania County, Virginia	Co. F, 15th Virginia Infantry	9/13/1863, Near Culpepper, Virginia	Died of Unknown Causes, 10/20/1864

Name	Age	Enlisted	Residence	Unit	Captured	Date and Cause of Death
Mullomy, James Private	30	6/3/1861, New Orleans, Louisiana	Orleans Parish, Louisiana	Co. B, 14th Louisiana Infantry	11/7/1863, Rappahannock Station, Virginia	Died of Unknown Causes, 11/17/1863
Munn, John Private	Unk	8/15/1862, Westville, Alabama	Unknown	Co. E. 15th Alabama Infantry	5/6/1865, Richmond, Virginia, Captured In Hospital After Lee's Surrender	Died of Chronic Diarrhea, 7/9/1865
Murdock, A. W. Sergeant	Unk	3/4/1862, Georgetown, Quitman County, Georgia	Quitman County, Georgia	Co. G, 51st Georgia Infantry	7/3/1863, Gettysburg, Pennsylvania	Died of Smallpox, 11/2/1863
Murphy, Ezekiel Private	21	3/1/1862, Reidsville, North Carolina, Volunteer	Rockingham County, North Carolina, Farmer	Co. H, 45th North Carolina Infantry	7/4/1863, Gettysburg, Pennsylvania, Wounded	Died of Chronic Diarrhea, 11/9/1863
Murphy, J. W. Private Not Listed On Monument	Unk	6/4/1861, Camp Moore, Louisiana	New Orleans, Louisiana	Co. E, 6th Louisiana Infantry	5/5/1864, Mine Run, Virginia	Died of Unknown Causes, 7/1/1864
Murphy, Madison J. Private	19	8/29/1861 Union Court House, South Carolina	Union County, South Carolina	Co. F, 15th South Carolina Infantry	6/17/1864, Near Cedar Creek or Strasburg, Virginia	Died of Chronic Diarrhea 12/9/1864
Murphy, Madison James Private	Unk	5/22/1861, Spoon Creek, Virginia	Unknown	Co. H, 42nd Virginia Infantry	5/12/1864, Spotsylvania Court House, Virginia	Died of Unknown Causes, 8/27/1864
Murphy, William P. Corporal	33	2/15/1862, Cooks, Franklin County, North Carolina, Volunteer	Cooks, Franklin County, North Carolina, Farmer	Co. K, 44th North Carolina Infantry	10/14/1863, Bristoe Station, Virginia	Died of Chronic Diarrhea, 1/1/1864
Murray, James M. Private	19	6/20/1861, Alamance County, North Carolina	Orange County, North Carolina, Farmer	Co. K, 6th North Carolina Infantry	11/7/1863, Rappahannock Station, Virginia	Died of Chronic Dysentery, 2/19/1865

Name	Age	Enlisted	Residence	Unit	Captured	Date and Cause of Death
Murray, James Sergeant	Unk	3/18/1862, Fort Pillow, Tennessee	Unknown	Co. E, 1st Battalion Confederate Infantry	4/2/1865, Hatcher's Run, Virginia	Died of Typhoid Fever, 4/19/1865
Murray, Robert A. Private	Unk	9/3/1861 White Plains, Alabama	Calhoun County, Alabama	Co. C, 5th Alabama Infantry	7/3/1863, Gettysburg, Pennsylvania	Died of Unknown Causes, 2/22/1864
Murray, Samuel Private	Unk	5/21/1863, Camp Holmes, North Carolina	Wake County, North Carolina	Co. A, 51st North Carolina Infantry	9/30/1864, Fort Harrison, Virginia	Died of Acute Diarrhea, 12/27/1864
Murray, Samuel Private	24	5/3/1863 Nashville, Nash County, North Carolina, Volunteer	Nash County, North Carolina, Mechanic	Co. A, 47th North Carolina Infantry	7/14/1863, Falling Waters, Maryland	Date and Cause of Death Unknown
Murray, W. D. Private Not Listed On Monument	Unk	8/31/1864, McDowell County, North Carolina	McDowell County, North Carolina	Co. A, 49th North Carolina Infantry	4/2/*1865,* Five Forks, Virginia	Died of Pneumonia, 5/17/1865
Murrell, J. S. Private	Unk	Unknown	Unknown	Co. D, 11th Virginia Infantry	5/12/1864, Spotsylvania Court House, Virginia	Date and Cause of Death Unknown
Music, J. M. Private	20	8/1/1862, Carrollton, Georgia	Carroll, Georgia, Farmer	Co. B, Claiborne's Partisan Rangers, 7th Confederate Cavalry	8/20/1864, Deep Bottom, Petersburg, Virginia	Died of Unknown Causes, 9/8/1864
Myers, Andrew J. Private	29	2/22/1862, Oak Grove, North Carolina, Volunteer	Union County, North Carolina	Co. H, 7th North Carolina Infantry	7/3/1863, Gettysburg, Pennsylvania	Died of Unknown Causes, 3/10/1864
Myers, Daniel M. Private	10	3/24/1863, Augusta County, Virginia	Augusta County, Virginia	Co. E, 62nd Virginia Infantry	5/11/1863, Buchanan, Virginia	Died of Typhoid Fever, 12/4/1863

Name	Age	Enlisted	Residence	Unit	Captured	Date and Cause of Death
Myers, Jacob H. Private	23	6/4/1861, Brownsburg, Virginia	6th District, Rockbridge County, Virginia, Farmer	Co. H, 25th Virginia Infantry	5/5/1864, Mine Run, Virginia	Died of Unknown Causes, 6/24/1864
Myrick, Cornelius Private See Mirac, Cornelius				Co. E, 44th North Carolina Infantry		
Myrick, William W. Private	38	4/24/1862, Camp Saunders, Warren County, North Carolina	Warren County, North Carolina	Co. B, 30th North Carolina Infantry	7/4/1863, South Mountain, Maryland	Died of Smallpox, 2/6/1864

Name	Age	Enlisted	Residence	Unit	Captured	Date and Cause of Death
Nailand, William Private	18	9/2/1861, Rutherford County, North Carolina, Volunteer	Rutherford County, North Carolina, Farmer	Co. C, 34th North Carolina Infantry	7/14/1863, Falling Waters, Maryland	Date and Cause of Death Unknown
Nance, J. D. Private	20	7/15/1862, Granville County, North Carolina, Volunteer	Granville County, North Carolina	Co. I, 5th North Carolina Infantry	7/12/1863, Hagerstown, Maryland	Died of Chronic Diarrhea, 10/26/1863
Nance, Shedrack Private	27	5/29/1861, Charlotte, North Carolina, Volunteer	Orange County, North Carolina, Farmer	Co. G, 6th North Carolina Infantry	7/3/1863, Gettysburg, Pennsylvania	Died of Pneumonia, 11/15/1863
Nanny, William W. Private	16	7/6/1862, Salisbury, Alamance County, North Carolina, Substitute	Iredell County, North Carolina	Co. H, 57th North Carolina Infantry	11/7/1863, Rappahannock Station, Virginia	Died of Smallpox, 2/18/1864
Narron, John G. Private	Unk	9/15/1864, Camp Holmes, North Carolina, Volunteer	Mecklenburg County, North Carolina	Co. E, 11th North Carolina Infantry	10/27/1864, Boyton Plank Road or Burgess' Mill, Virginia	Died of Strangulated Inguinal Hernia, 11/23/1864

Name	Age	Enlisted	Residence	Unit	Captured	Date and Cause of Death
Nash, Frederick Sergeant	17	8/20/1863, Battery Bolles, Fort Fisher, North Carolina	Fayetteville, North Carolina	Co. G, 18th North Carolina Infantry	5/12/1864, Spotsylvania Court House, Virginia	Died of Unknown Causes, 8/2/1864
Nead, Benjamin Private See Nead, Franklin				Co. C, 6th Tennessee Infantry		
Nead, Franklin Private	19	9/20/1862, Washington County, Tennessee	Washington County, Tennessee	Co. C, 60th Tennessee Mounted Infantry	5/17/ 1863, Big Black Bridge, Near Vicksburg, Mississippi	Died of Chronic Diarrhea & Scurvy, 11/4/1863
Neese, Godfrey R. Private Not Listed On Monument	Unk	9/5/1861, Columbia, South Carolina	Richland County, South Carolina	Co. G, 27th South Carolina Infantry	6/18/1864, Near Petersburg, Virginia	Died of Scurvy, 3/14/1865
Neff, William Private	Unk	3/1/1864, New River, Virginia	Unknown	Co. A, 36th Virginia Infantry	9/19/1864, Winchester, Virginia	Died From Inflammation of Lungs (Pneumonia), 4/19/1865
Nelson, Ervin Private Not Listed On Monument	38	12/25/1861, Bennettsville, South Carolina	Columbia, Richland County, South Carolina	Co. F, 21st South Carolina Infantry	7/10/1863, Morris Island, South Carolina	Date and Cause of Death Unknown
Nelson, J. Private	Unk	Unknown	Unknown	Co. F, 21st North Carolina Infantry	Unknown	Died of Smallpox, 11/21/1863
Nelson, Jesse Private	Unk	5/15/1863, Decatur, Georgia	DeKalb County, Georgia	Co. F, 60th Georgia Infantry	5/20/1864, Spotsylvania Court House, Virginia	Died of Unknown Causes, 2/26/1865

Name	Age	Enlisted	Residence	Unit	Captured	Date and Cause of Death
Nelson, John Wesley Private Not Listed On Monument	22	6/10/1861, Mathews, North Carolina, Volunteer	Chatham County, North Carolina	Co. G, 26th North Carolina Infantry	7/4/1863, Gettysburg, Pennsylvania	Died of Unknown Causes, 4/1/1864
Nelson, Leander Private	Unk	2/15/1864, Abingdon, Virginia	Washington County, Virginia	Co. C, 13th Battalion Virginia Light Artillery	4/6/1865, Burkeville, Virginia	Died of Chronic Diarrhea, 5/25/1865
Nelson, Thomas J. Private	Unk	2/3/1864, Greenville, South Carolina	Greenville District, South Carolina	Co. K, 7th South Carolina Cavalry	4/6/1865, Burkeville, Virginia	Died of Chronic Dysentery 5/20/1865
Nelson, W. Private See: Nailand, William				Co. C, 34th North Carolina Infantry		
Nelson, Washington R. Private	18	6/10/1861 Mathews, North Carolina, Volunteer	Mecklenburg County, North Carolina	Co. G, 26th North Carolina Infantry	7/5/1863, Gettysburg, Pennsylvania	Date and Cause of Death Unknown
Nelson, William R. Private	19	9/14/1861, Boone, North Carolina, Volunteer	Watauga County, North Carolina, Farmer	Co. B, 37th North Carolina Infantry	7/5/1863, Gettysburg, Pennsylvania	Died of Unknown Causes, 12/23/1863
Nesmith, Samuel Private	Unk	7/1/1863, Georgetown, South Carolina	Georgetown County, South Carolina	Co. A, 7th South Carolina Cavalry	4/6/1865, Farmville, Virginia	Died of Acute Diarrhea, 5/16/1865
Nevitt, John E. Private	Unk	10/7/1861, Camp Field, Virginia	Unknown	Co. A, 6th Virginia Cavalry	6/9/1863, Beverley Ford, Near Culpepper Court House, Virginia	Died of Chronic Diarrhea, 9/7/1864
Newberry, Blount Absalom Private	Unk	10/4/1861, Columbus, Georgia	Muscogee County, Georgia	Co. A, 31st Georgia Infantry	7/7/1863, Washington County, Maryland	Died of Chronic Diarrhea & Variola (Smallpox), 12/11/1863

Name	Age	Enlisted	Residence	Unit	Captured	Date and Cause of Death
Newby, Asa Thomas Private Not Listed On Monument	18	3/14/1862, Aspen Grove, Virginia	Prince Edward County, Virginia	Co. D, 18th Virginia Infantry	4/6/1865, Farmville, Virginia	Died of Scurvy, 6/22/1865
Newby, Isaac Private	Unk	Date Unknown, Pittsylvania County, Virginia	Pittsylvania County, Virginia	Co. I, 18th Virginia Infantry	Unknown	Date and Cause of Death Unknown
Newcomb, John Private	Unk	7/1/1864 Howlett's House, Manarin, Virginia	Unknown	Co. C, 56th Virginia Infantry	8/25/1864, William Howlett's House, Virginia	Died of Typhoid Fever, 2/12/1865
Newcomer, Henry Private	23	4/28/1861, New Orleans, Louisiana	Orleans Parish, Louisiana, Farmer	Co. B, 1st Louisiana Infantry	7/3/1863, Gettysburg, Pennsylvania	Died of Unknown Causes, 11/19/1863
Newlin, William J. Private	Unk	5/21/1863, Camp Cheatham, Tennessee	Hickman County, Tennessee	Co. B, 3rd Tennessee Mounted Infantry	5/12/ 1863, Raymond, Mississippi	Died of Unknown Causes, 11/28/1863
Newman, Caleb W. Private Not Listed On Monument	Unk	2/16/1863, Camp, Virginia	Unknown	Captain C. W. Fry's Company, Carter's Battalion, Virginia Light Artillery	7/4/1863, Gettysburg, Pennsylvania	Died of Unknown Causes, 11/4/1863
Newman, Callohill M. Private	Unk	7/26/1861, Jamestown, Virginia	James City County, Virginia	Co. B, 14th Virginia Infantry	7/3/1863, Gettysburg, Pennsylvania	Died of Unknown Causes, 8/21/1864
Newman, Drury W. Private	21	8/23/1861, Camp Moore, Louisiana	New Orleans, Louisiana	Co. C, 12th Louisiana Infantry	5/16/1863, Champion Hill, Tennessee	Died of Unknown Causes, 2/15/1864
Newsmith, Samuel Private See: Nesmith, Samuel				Co. A, 7th South Carolina Cavalry		

Name	Age	Enlisted	Residence	Unit	Captured	Date and Cause of Death
Newsom, Eli Private	30	7/8/1862, Murfreesboro, North Carolina	Hertford County, North Carolina, Farmer	Co. D, 4th North Carolina Cavalry	7/3/1863, Gettysburg, Pennsylvania	Died of Smallpox & Pneumonia, 12/23/1863
Newton, Ebenezer G. Private	45	9/20/1863, Cleveland County, North Carolina, Conscript	Cleveland County, North Carolina	Co. F, 56th North Carolina Infantry	6/17/1864, Near Petersburg, Virginia	Died of Acute Diarrhea, 8/18/1864
Newton, John Private	Unk	1/24/1864, Camp Holmes, North Carolina	Wake County, North Carolina	Co. I, 23rd North Carolina Infantry	3/25/1865, Fort Stedman, Near Petersburg, Virginia	Died of Unknown Causes, 5/8/1865
Newton, N. J. Private	Unk	Unknown	Unknown	Co. D, 50th Virginia Infantry	11/7/1863, Rappahannock, Virginia	Date and Cause of Death Unknown
Newton, William J. Private Name Not On Monument	Unk	2/9/1863 Buckingham, Virginia	Nelson County, Virginia	Co. E, 56th Virginia Infantry	7/3/1863, Gettysburg, Pennsylvania	Died of Smallpox, 11/11/1863
Niblet, Caleb Private	23	9/10/1861 Camp Clark, Gilmer, Texas	Upshur County, Texas	Co. B, 7th Texas Infantry	5/12/1863, Raymond, Mississippi	Died of Unknown Causes, 2/20/1864
Nickles, Henry B. Private	Unk	2/20/1864 Abb. Court House, South Carolina	Unknown	Co. F, Holcombe's South Carolina Legion Infantry	11/6/1864, Petersburg, Virginia	Died of Chronic Diarrhea, 12/13/1864
Nicholson, Richard J. Private	18	Unknown	Unknown	Co. E, Confederate States Marine Corp, CS Ironclad Savannah	1/15/1865, Fort Fisher, North Carolina	Died of Pneumonia, 2/8/1865
Nixon, Samuel W. 2nd Lieutenant	21	6/12/1861, Weldon, Halifax County, North Carolina	Gates County, North Carolina, Student	Co. B, 5th North Carolina Infantry	7/2/1863, Gettysburg, Pennsylvania	Died of Smallpox, 11/3/1863

Name	Age	Enlisted	Residence	Unit	Captured	Date and Cause of Death
Nixon, Sidney Private	35	3/17/1862 Camp Mangum, North Carolina, Volunteer	Lincoln County, North Carolina, Farmer	Co. G, 52nd North Carolina Infantry	10/27/1864 Near Petersburg, Virginia	Died of Dropsy, 2/8/1865
Nobles, Bryant Private	19	7/1/1861, Columbus County, North Carolina	Columbus County, North Carolina, Farmer	Co. K, 20th North Carolina Infantry	7/1/1863, Gettysburg, Pennsylvania	Died of Scorbutus (Scurvy), 2/8/1865
Nobles, William F. Private	Unk	8/26/1861, Frog Level Depot, Newberry District, South Carolina	Newberry District, South Carolina	Co. G, 13th South Carolina Infantry	3/31/1865, Hatcher's Run, Virginia	Died of Rubeola (measles), 6/25/1865
Noblit, James Private	Unk	10/6/1863, Camp Vance, North Carolina	Wake County, North Carolina	Co. K, 22nd North Carolina Infantry	5/6/1864, Wilderness, Virginia	Died of Unknown Causes, 8/17/1864
Noe, Joseph Jr. Private Not Listed On Monument	42	9/30/1862, Morristown, Tennessee	Hamblen County, Tennessee	Co. H, 60th Tennessee Mounted Infantry	5/17/ 1863, Big Black Bridge, Near Vicksburg, Mississippi	Died of Chronic Diarrhea, 4/17/1864
Norris, James W. Corporal	Unk	2/28/1862, Hogansville, Georgia	Troup County, Georgia	Co. D, 35th Georgia Infantry	3/24/1864, Mulford Station, Virginia	Died of Unknown Causes, 9/24/1864
Norris, Thomas Ship's Cook	Unk	Unknown	Unknown	Confederate States Navy	Unknown	Date and Cause of Death Unknown
Norwood, George W. Private	17	9/10/1862, Raleigh, North Carolina, Substitute	Chatham County, North Carolina	Co. G, 26th North Carolina Infantry	10/27/1864, Boyton Plank Road or Burgess' Mill, Virginia	Died of Chronic Diarrhea, 3/28/1865
Norwood, Joseph B. Private	24	6/17/1861, Oak Hill, North Carolina, Volunteer	Grandville County, North Carolina	Co. I, 23rd North Carolina Infantry	7/1/1863, Gettysburg, Pennsylvania	Died of Chronic Diarrhea, 1/28/1864
Norwood, Thomas S. Private	28	3/17/1862 Camp Mangum, North Carolina, Volunteer	Lincoln County, North Carolina, Farmer	Co. G, 52nd North Carolina Infantry	10/27/1864, Boyton Plank Road or Burgess' Mill, Virginia	Died of Acute Dysentery, 1/23/1865

Name	Age	Enlisted	Residence	Unit	Captured	Date and Cause of Death
Nosler, Harry B. Private	Unk	4/10/1862, Giles County, Virginia	Giles County, Virginia	Co. B, 23rd Virginia Infantry	9/19/1864, Winchester, Virginia	Died of Rubeola (measles), 2/17/1865
Nuckols, Benjamin J. Private Not Listed On Monument	Unk	6/6/1861, Goochland Court House, Virginia	Goochland County, Virginia	Captain Guy's Company, Goochland Light Artillery, Virginia	4/6/1865, Sailor's Creek, Virginia	Died of Chronic Diarrhea, 5/15/1865
Nuckols, Nathan W. Private	Unk	9/25/1863, Kinston, North Carolina	Lenoir County, North Carolina	Co. K, 57th Virginia Infantry	4/2/1865, Five Forks, Virginia	Died of Debility, 6/12/1865
Nungazer, Gary Sergeant Not Listed On Monument	Unk	9/22/1862, Waynesville, Georgia	Brantley County, Georgia	Co. G, 7th Georgia Cavalry	5/12/1864, Spotsylvania Court House, Virginia	Died of Unknown Causes, 7/12/1864
Nunneller, J. T. Private	Unk	Unknown	Unknown	Co. A, Garnett's Artillery Battalion	Unknown	Unable to Locate

Name	Age	Enlisted	Residence	Unit	Captured	Date and Cause of Death
Oberly, Zachariah Private	Unk	4/17/1864, Camp Vance, Yadkin County, North Carolina	Yadkin County, North Carolina	Co. E, 5th North Carolina Infantry	10/19/1864, Cedar Creek or Strasburg, Virginia	Died of Chronic Diarrhea, 5/14/1865
Ochiltree, William Private	Unk	10/18/1864, New Market, Virginia	Shenandoah County, Virginia	Co. C, 5th Virginia Infantry	4/14/1865, High Bridge, Virginia	Died of Chronic Diarrhea, 5/25/1865
Odom, David M. Private Not Listed On Monument	Unk	9/10/1863, Nashville, North Carolina	Nash County, North Carolina	Co. F, 32nd North Carolina Infantry	5/10/1864, Near Mine Run, Virginia	Died of Unknown Causes, 7/3/1864

Name	Age	Enlisted	Residence	Unit	Captured	Date and Cause of Death
Odom, W. H. Private	31	5/10/1862 Wadesboro, North Carolina	Anson County, North Carolina	Co. A, 4th North Carolina Cavalry	3/5/1865, Anson County, North Carolina	Died of Pneumonia, 5/12/1865
Odom, William G. Private	Unk	10/1/1861 Augusta, Georgia	Richmond County, Georgia	Co. C, 38th Georgia Infantry	7/5/1863, Gettysburg, Pennsylvania	Died of Chronic Diarrhea, 1/11/1864
Ogden, Daines S. Corporal	29	9/18/1861 Fort Johnson, South Carolina	Unknown	Co. E, 1st South Carolina Infantry	9/30/1864, Chaffin's Farm, Virginia, Gunshot Wound Abdomen & Right Arm	Died of Acute Diarrhea, 5/28/1865
Oliphant, Thomas Sergeant	30	6/7/1861, Camp Moore, New Orleans, Louisiana	Orleans Parish, Louisiana	Co. E, 7th Louisiana Infantry	11/7/1863, Rappahannock Station, Virginia	Died of Unknown Causes, 12/23/1863
Olive, Henderson Private	Unk	2/11/1863, Raleigh, North Carolina	Wake County, North Carolina	Co. I, 3rd North Carolina Cavalry	4/3/1865, Amelia Court House, Virginia	Died of Chronic Diarrhea, 6/5/1865
Oliver, Cornelius Private	Unk	10/18/1864, Camp Holmes, Raleigh, North Carolina	Wake County, North Carolina	Co. A, 24th North Carolina Infantry	3/25/1865, Fort Stedman, Near Petersburg, Virginia	Died of Unknown Causes, 6/27/1865
Oliver, H. C. Private	Unk	Unknown	Unknown	Co. F, 15th South Carolina Militia Infantry	Unknown	Unable to Locate
Olmstead, James W. Private	17	5/21/1864, Camp Holmes, Raleigh, North Carolina	Wake County, North Carolina	Co. B, 1st North Carolina Junior Reserves	12/12/1864, Hamilton, North Carolina	Died of Unknown Causes, 3/6/1865
Oneill, David R. Private	Unk	Unknown	Unknown	Co. A, 66th North Carolina Infantry	2/20/1864, Near Fairfield, North Carolina	Died of Unknown Causes, 6/22/1864
Orange, E. C. Private	Unk	4/27/1862, Richmond, Virginia	Henrico County, Virginia, Blacksmith	Co. K, 4th Virginia Cavalry	7/3/1863, Gettysburg, Pennsylvania	Died of Chronic Diarrhea, 2/27/1865

Name	Age	Enlisted	Residence	Unit	Captured	Date and Cause of Death
Organ, James Private	22	3/4/1862, Milliken's Bend, Louisiana	Madison, Louisiana, Carpenter	Co. E, 8th Louisiana Infantry	3/20/1865, Petersburg, Virginia	Date and Cause of Death Unknown
Orr, N. C. H. Private	19	2/1/1862, Charlotte, North Carolina, Volunteer	Mecklenburg County, North Carolina	Co. A, 11th North Carolina Infantry	10/14/1863, Bristoe Station, Virginia	Died of Unknown Causes, 9/29/1864
Osborne, J. Private	Unk	Unknown	Unknown	Co. B, 2nd North Carolina Infantry	7/4/1863, Gettysburg, Pennsylvania, Wounded in Side	Died of Smallpox, 2/17/1864
Ostwalt, Francis Private	38	2/26/1862, Statesville, North Carolina, Volunteer	Iredell County, North Carolina	Co. E, 11th North Carolina Infantry	7/3/1863, Gettysburg, Pennsylvania	Died of Smallpox, 12/30/1863
Overbey, Warren Private	19	5/14/1861, South Boston, Virginia	Unknown, Farmer	Co. K, 14th Virginia Infantry	7/3/1863, Gettysburg, Pennsylvania	Died of Unknown Causes, 12/23/1863
Overcash, P. A. Private	23	7/7/1862, Salisbury, North Carolina, Volunteer	Rowan County, North Carolina	Co. B, 57th North Carolina Infantry	7/5/1863, Gettysburg, Pennsylvania	Died of Smallpox, 11/26/1863
Overman, William Private	45	6/10/1861, Matthews, North Carolina Volunteer	Chatham County, North Carolina	Co. G, 26th North Carolina Infantry	8/15/1863, Charlestown, Virginia	Died of Unknown Causes, 2/21/1864
Overstreet, Benjamin F. Private	19	3/1/1862, Bedford, Virginia	Bedford County, Farmer	Co. G, 28th Virginia Infantry	7/3/1863, Gettysburg, Pennsylvania	Died of Unknown Causes, 1/13/1864
Overton, Asa Private	32	7/15/1862, Raleigh, North Carolina, Conscript	Wake County, North Carolina	Co. I, 5th North Carolina Infantry	5/12/1864, Spotsylvania Court House, Virginia, Severely Wounded	Died of Wounds, 7/17/1864
Overton, James B. Private	44	5/30/1861, Camden County, North Carolina, Volunteer	Camden County, North Carolina	Co. B, 32nd North Carolina Infantry	5/10/1864, Near Mine Run, Virginia	Died of Unknown Causes, 7/27/1864

Name	Age	Enlisted	Residence	Unit	Captured	Date and Cause of Death
Owen, A. W. Corporal	Unk	4/20/1861, Homer, Georgia	Banks County, Georgia	Co. A, 2nd Georgia Infantry	7/3/1863, Gettysburg, Pennsylvania	Died of Unknown Causes, 1/27/1864
Owen, George F. Private	26	5/14/1862, Davidson County, North Carolina	Davidson County, North Carolina, Farmer	Co. A, 54th North Carolina Infantry	11/7/1863, Rappahannock, Virginia	Died of Unknown Causes, 2/15/1864
Owen, George F. Private Not Listed On Monument	Unk	2/8/1865, Chesterfield, Virginia	Chesterfield County, Virginia	Captain N. Penick's Co., Richardson's Battalion Virginia Light Artillery	4/5/1865, Amelia County, Virginia	Died of Unknown Causes, 6/13/1865
Owen, William C. Private	Unk	3/14/1862, Petersburg, Virginia	Chesterfield County, Virginia	Co. A, 9th Virginia Infantry	4/1/1865, Five Forks, Virginia	Died of Chronic Dysentery, 5/15/1865
Owens, Andrew J. Private	Unk	4/9/1864, Macon, Georgia	Morgan County, Georgia	Co. D, 3rd Georgia Infantry	4/3/1865, Richmond Hospital, Virginia	Died of Phthisis Pulmonalis (tuberculosis) & Chronic Diarrhea, 5/8/1865
Owens, Francis M. Private	Unk	5/10/1861, Camp Harris, Tennessee	Unknown	Co. K, 1st Tennessee Infantry	9/3/1864, Jonesboro, Georgia	Died of Dropsy, 5/25/1865
Owens, G. M. Private	Unk	4/12/1864, Petersburg, Virginia	Chesterfield County, Virginia	Co. B, 8th North Carolina Infantry	8/1/1864, Cold Harbor, Virginia	Died of Unknown Causes, 8/5/1864
Owens, Henry C. Private	Unk	Unknown	Unknown	Co. C, 13th Alabama Infantry	5/12/1864, Spotsylvania Court House, Virginia	Died of Unknown Causes, 6/18/1864
Owens, John C. Private	26	4/5/1862, Wilkesboro, North Carolina, Volunteer	Wilkes County, North Carolina, Farmer	Co. F, 52nd North Carolina Infantry	10/27/1864, Burgess' Mill, Near Petersburg, Virginia	Died of Acute Dysentery, 8/5/1864

Name	Age	Enlisted	Residence	Unit	Captured	Date and Cause of Death
Owens, William Private	Unk	6/11/1861, King George Court House, Virginia	King George County, Virginia	Co. B, 47th Virginia Infantry	7/14/1863, Falling Waters, Maryland	Died of Unknown Causes, 8/251864
Owens, William F. Private	35	9/23/1864, Camp Holmes, Rowan County, North Carolina, Conscript	Beaufort County, North Carolina	Co. G, 33rd North Carolina Infantry	4/2/1865, Petersburg, Virginia	Died of Remittent Fever, 6/13/1865
Owens, William H. Private	20	7/1/1861, Davie County, North Carolina	Davie County, North Carolina	Co. G, 4th North Carolina Cavalry	5/5/1864, Currituck County, North Carolina	Died of Pneumonia, 4/18/1865
Oxley, R. A. Private	Unk	7/4/1863, Calhoun County, Georgia	Calhoun County, Georgia	Co. E, 51st Georgia Infantry	7/5/1863, Greencastle, Gettysburg, Pennsylvania	Died of Chronic Diarrhea, 11/6/1863

Name	Age	Enlisted	Residence	Unit	Captured	Date and Cause of Death
Pace, James A. Private	Unk	3/10/1862, Marion, South Carolina	Marion District, South Carolina	Co. I, 21st South Carolina Infantry	7/10/1863, Morris Island, South Carolina	Died of Unknown Causes, 12/23/1863
Pack, Tyree Private	Unk	Unknown	Unknown	Co. K, 50th Virginia Infantry	5/12/1864, Spotsylvania Court House, Virginia	Died of Typhoid Fever, 8/9/1864
Packard, William Private	Unk	11/15/1862, Place Unknown	Fairfax County, Virginia	Co. A, 7th Virginia Cavalry	8/3/1863, Salem, Virginia	Died of Typhoid Fever, 11/9/1863
Padgett, Andrew Private	32	3/29/62, Columbus, County, North Carolina	Rutherford County, North Carolina, Farmer	Co. I, 54th North Carolina Infantry	11/7/1863, Rappahannock Station, Virginia	Died of Unknown Causes, 2/19/1864
Padgett, Daniel Private	Unk	11/18/1861, Colleton, South Carolina	Colleton County, South Carolina	Co. K, 11th South Carolina Infantry	8/21/1864, Globe Tavern, Near Weldon Railroad, North Carolina	Died of Pneumonia, 3/15/1865

Name	Age	Enlisted	Residence	Unit	Captured	Date and Cause of Death
Padgett, Francis Private	Unk	3/20/1862, Colleton, South Carolina	Colleton County, South Carolina	Co. K, 11th South Carolina Infantry	8/21/1864, Globe Tavern, Near Weldon Railroad, North Carolina	Died of Acute Dysentery, 12/28/1864
Paine, Edgar Private	Unk	Unknown	Unknown	Co. B, 67th North Carolina Infantry	10/31/1864, Plymouth, North Carolina	Died of Pleuritis, 3/5/1865
Palmer, George Pierce Private	Unk	8/201861, Camp Griffin, South Carolina	Unknown	Co. B, Hampton's South Carolina Legion	9/30/1864, Chaffin's Farm or Fort Harrison, Virginia	Died of Acute Dysentery, 11/21/1864
Palmer, George R. Private	Unk	7/18/1861, Urbana, Virginia	Middlesex County, Virginia	Co. C, 55th Virginia Infantry	7/5/1863, Gettysburg, Pennsylvania, Left Behind to Care For Wounded	Died of Chronic Diarrhea, 12/6/1863
Palmer, J. L. Corporal	Unk	5/19/1864, Quitman, Georgia	Brooks County, Georgia	Co. E, 1st Symon's Georgia Reserve	12/13/1864, Fort McAllister, Georgia	Died of Unknown Causes, 2/19/1865
Palmer, J. W. Private	32	6/17/1862, Anderson District, South Carolina	Anderson District, South Carolina	Co. D, 6th South Carolina Cavalry	12/10/1864, Armstrong Mill, Virginia	Died of Pneumonia, 6/7/1865
Pankey, Peter L. Private	26	4/3/1864, Orange Court House, Virginia. Conscript	Orange County, Virginia	Co. H, 2nd Virginia Cavalry	5/28/1864, Hall's Shop, Near Cold Harbor, Virginia	Died of Unknown Causes, 7/28/1864
Pannell, William P. Private	Unk	4/4/1864, Near Orange Court House, Virginia	Orange County, Virginia	Co. I, 38th North Carolina Infantry	3/25/1865, Fort Stedman, Near Petersburg, Virginia	Died of Typhoid Fever, 5/19/1865
Pannill, John H. Private	18	4/17/61, Gordonsville, Virginia	Orange County, Virginia, Student	Co. C, 13th Virginia Infantry	10/19/1864, Cedar Creek or Strasburg, Virginia	Died of Chronic Diarrhea, 4/6/1865
Parham, A. J. See Parham, Edmund. J.				Co. F, 3rd Tennessee Infantry		
Parham, Edmund. J. Private	Unk	9/20/1861 Bowling Green, Tennessee	Warren County, Tennessee	Co. F, 3rd Tennessee Infantry	5/12/1863 Raymond, Fort Donelson, Mississippi	Died of Chronic Diarrhea, 11/24/1863

Name	Age	Enlisted	Residence	Unit	Captured	Date and Cause of Death
Paris, James M. Private	Unk	7/15/1862, Hendersonville North Carolina	Henderson County, North Carolina	Co. D, 6th North Carolina Cavalry	6/22/1864, Jackson's Mills, Near Kinston, North Carolina	Died of Chronic Dysentery, 1/25/1865
Parish, C. P. Corporal	Unk	5/8/1864, Savannah, Georgia	Stewart County, Georgia	Co. D, Symon's Georgia Reserves	12/13/1864, Fort McAllister, Georgia	Died of Chronic Diarrhea, 2/22/1865
Parish, Hey D. Private	19	7/14/1862, Raleigh, North Carolina, Volunteer	Chatham County, North Carolina, Farmer	Co. C, 56th North Carolina Infantry	8/21/1864, Globe Tavern, Near Weldon Railroad, Virginia	Died of Acute Dysentery 1/5/1865
Park, John Sergeant	44	1/4/1863, Hampshire, Virginia	Hampshire County, West Virginia	Co. B, 18th Virginia Cavalry	9/11/1863, Hardie County, Virginia	Died of Unknown Causes, 4/13/1864
Parker, Amos D. Private	Unk	6/18/1863, Coward's Bridge, North Carolina	Unknown	Co. D, 67th North Carolina Infantry	6/22/1864, Jackson's Mills, Near Kinston, North Carolina	Died of Typhoid Fever, 2/3/1865
Parker, Calvin Private	32	12/20/1861, Cheraw District, South Carolina	Cheraw District, South Carolina	Co. D, 21st South Carolina Infantry	7/10/1863, Morris Island, South Carolina	Died of Paralysis, 4/21/1865
Parker, Daniel W. Private	Unk	8/16/1861, Morganton, North Carolina, Volunteer	Burke County, North Carolina	Co. E, 6th North Carolina Infantry	11/7/1863, Rappahannock Station, Virginia	Died of Acute Diarrhea, 1/5/1865
Parker, Esquire Private	20	6/28/1862, Poplar Spring, Hall County, Georgia	Hall County, Georgia, Farmer	Co. I, 24th Georgia Infantry	7/2/1863, Gettysburg, Pennsylvania	Died of Smallpox, 11/13/1863
Parker, Franklin Private Not Listed On Monument	28	3/4/1862, Greensboro, North Carolina, Substitute	Guilford County, North Carolina, Farmer	Co. B, 45th North Carolina Infantry	10/20/1864, Cedar Creek or Strasburg, Virginia	Died of Remittent Fever, 11/15/1864
Parker, George Private	Unk	3/18/1863, Camp Finnegan, Florida	Unknown	Co. C, 10th Florida Infantry	9/10/1864, Petersburg, Virginia	Died of Unknown Causes, 2/25/1865

Name	Age	Enlisted	Residence	Unit	Captured	Date and Cause of Death
Parker, Henry K. Private	Unk	11/1/1861, Bentonville, Arkansas	Benton County, Arkansas	Co. C, 15th Arkansas Infantry	5/17/1863, Big Black Bridge, Near Vicksburg, Mississippi	Died of Bronchitis & Diarrhea, 2/23/1864
Parker, John M. Private	18	10/29/1863, Kelly's Ford, Virginia, Conscript	Rockingham County, North Carolina	Co. B, 45th North Carolina Infantry	12/3/1863, Mine Run, Virginia	Died of Smallpox, 8/6/1864
Parker, Owen Sergeant	Unk	3/28/1863, Madison, Florida	Madison County, Florida	Co. G, 11th Florida Infantry	9/10/1864, Near Petersburg, Virginia	Died of Phthisis, 1/14/1865
Parker, Sampson S. Private	20	5/27/1862, Troy, North Carolina	Montgomery County, North Carolina	Co. C, 23rd North Carolina Infantry	7/1/1863, Gettysburg, Pennsylvania	Died of Unknown Causes, 2/24/1864
Parker, Sherod N. Private	Unk	8/1/1863, Butler County, Alabama	Butler County, Alabama	Co. D, 61st Alabama Infantry	10/23/1864, Cedar Creek or Strasburg, Virginia	Died of Catarrh, Inflammation of the Mucous Membranes, 4/30/1865
Parker, William A. Private	Unk	5/10/1862, Meriweather County, Georgia	Meriweather County, Georgia	Co. A, 60th Georgia Infantry	5/20/1864, Spotsylvania Court House, Virginia	Died of Chronic Diarrhea, 3/14/1865
Parkerson, George W. Private	28	7/18/1861, Fort Boykin, Virginia	Isle of Wight, Virginia, Farmer	Co. I, 3rd Virginia Infantry	7/3/1863, Gettysburg, Pennsylvania	Died of Unknown Causes, 8/20/1864
Parkerson, Malachi M. Private Not Listed On Monument	Unk	9/21/1863, Macon, Georgia	Bibb County, Georgia	Co. H, 12th Georgia Infantry	4/2/1865, Petersburg, Virginia	Died of Measles, 6/30/1865
Parks, A. L. Private	Unk	10/7/1861, Burke County, North Carolina	Burke County, North Carolina	Co. B, 11th North Carolina Infantry	4/2/1865, Petersburg, Virginia	Died of Pneumonia, 4/15/1865
Parks, William A. Private	31	3/13/1862, Salisbury, North Carolina	Rowan County, North Carolina	Co. D, 10th Regiment, 2nd North Carolina Artillery	4/5/1865, Amelia Court House, Virginia	Died of Typhoid Fever, 6/17/1865
Parks, William H. Private	22	2/2/1862, Hamilton, North Carolina, Volunteer	Halifax County, North Carolina	Co. D, 43rd North Carolina Infantry	10/19/1864, Cedar Creek or Strasburg, Virginia	Date and Cause of Death Unknown

Name	Age	Enlisted	Residence	Unit	Captured	Date and Cause of Death
Parnell, William D. Private	18	7/27/1861, Selma, Alabama	Dallas County, Alabama	Captain Montgomery's, Jeff Davis Alabama, Light Artillery	5/5/1864, Wilderness, Virginia	Died of Chronic Diarrhea, 10/25/1864
Parr, Alfred B. Corporal	Unk	Unknown	Unknown	Co. B, 1st Alabama Infantry	Unknown	Unable to Locate
Parrish, Doctor H. Private	18	5/1/1861, Orange County, North Carolina, Volunteer	Orange County, North Carolina,	Co. B, 6th North Carolina Infantry	11/7/1863, Kelly's Ford, Rappahannock, Virginia	Died of Chronic Dysentery, 3/3/1865
Parrish, James A. Private	Unk	4/1/1862, Aberdeen, Mississippi	Toccopola, Mississippi, Student	Co. C, 43rd Mississippi Infantry	5/18/1863, Chickasaw Bayou, Mississippi	Died of Unknown Causes, 3/20/1864
Parrish, John E. Private	35	3/24/1863, Baldwin, Florida	Duval County, Florida	Co. G, 9th Florida Infantry	9/9/1864, Near Petersburg, Virginia	Died of Unknown Causes, 4/4/1865
Parrish, William Private	56	Unknown	Unknown	Co. C, 44th Virginia Infantry	4/6/1865, Jetersville, Virginia	Died of Chronic Diarrhea, 6/30/1865
Parrish, William A. Private	Unk	4/7/1863, Chaffin's Bluff, Virginia	Unknown	Captain Allen's Virginia Heavy Artillery	4/6/1865, Harper's Farm, Virginia	Died of Pneumonia, 6/23/1865
Parrish, William S. Private Not Listed On Monument	36	5/27/1861, Camp Allegheny, Virginia	Pittsylvania County, Virginia	Co. E, 6th Virginia Cavalry	10/17/1863, Brandy Station, Virginia	Died of Unknown Causes, 7/13/1864
Parrott, Augustus Private	Unk	1/17/1862, Savannah, Georgia	Stewart County, Georgia	Co. E, 31st Georgia Infantry	7/4/1863, South Mountain, Maryland	Died of Scurvy, 4/4/1865
Parrott, Loyd A. Private	36	9/26/1862, Henderson's Mills, Green County, Tennessee	Green County, Tennessee	Co. D, 61st Tennessee Mounted Infantry	5/17/1863, Big Black Bridge, Near Vicksburg, Mississippi	Died of Unknown Causes, 1/15/1864
Parsons, Dawson S. Private	Unk	1/22/1863 Fredericksburg Virginia	Unknown	Co. G. 19th Virginia Infantry	4/6/1865 Farmsville, Virginia	Died of Acute Diarrhea, 5/25/1865

Name	Age	Enlisted	Residence	Unit	Captured	Date and Cause of Death
Parten, Elisha Private Not Listed On Monument	18	Fort Caswell, Brunswick County, North Carolina, 6/25/1863	Heathsville, Halifax County, North Carolina, Farm Laborer	Co. F, 36th North Carolina Heavy Artillery	1/15/1865, Fort Fisher, North Carolina, Gunshot Wound To Left Thigh, Fractured Femur	Left Leg Amputated, Died of Wounds, 2/8/1865
Partin, Stephen Private	Unk	5/5/1862, Bethesda, Georgia	Unknown	Co. B, 61st Georgia Infantry	7/4/1863, South Mountain, Maryland	Died of Unknown Causes, 11/10/1863
Parting, Henry Private	18	6/23/1863, Halifax County, North Carolina, Conscript	Halifax County, North Carolina	Co. A, 30th North Carolina Infantry	11/7/1863, Kelly's Ford, Rappahannock Station, Virginia	Died of Smallpox, 12/28/1863
Passmore, James P. Private	Unk	4/23/1862, Macon County, Georgia	Bibb County, Georgia	Co. A, 10th Georgia Infantry	8/16/1864, Deep Bottom, Petersburg, Virginia	Died of Acute Diarrhea, 10/16/1864
Pate, Bernard C. Private	Unk	8/4/1861, Trousdale, Tennessee	Trousdale County, Tennessee	Co. I, 3rd Tennessee Infantry	5/12/1863, Raymond, Fort Donellson, Mississippi	Died of Unknown Causes, 4/6/1864
Patterson, Elijah S. Sergeant	25	2/27/1862, Ashville, North Carolina, Volunteer	Buncombe County, North Carolina	Co. G, 1st North Carolina Cavalry	9/13/1863, Culpepper, Virginia	Died of Unknown Causes, 3/14/1864
Patterson, Franklin C. Private	20	10/10/1862, North East, North Carolina	Alexander County, North Carolina	Co. H, 56th North Carolina Infantry	5/14/1864, Near Fort Darling, Virginia	Died of Unknown Causes, 6/6/1864
Patterson, Joseph T. M. Private	Unk	3/12/1864, Decatur, Georgia	Muscogee County, Georgia	Co. E, 12th Georgia Infantry	5/6/1864, Wilderness, Virginia	Died of Unknown Causes, 6/2/1864
Patton, James F. Private	20	3/1/1863, Salem, Virginia	Roanoke County, Virginia	Co. H. 14th Virginia Cavalry	11/12/1864, Near Nineveh, Virginia	Died of Chronic Diarrhea, 3/10/1865
Paul, Edgar H. Private See: Paine, Edgar				Co. B, 67th North Carolina Infantry		

Name	Age	Enlisted	Residence	Unit	Captured	Date and Cause of Death
Paul, Jeremiah Private	Unk	1/4/1865, Macon, Georgia	Bibb County, Georgia	Co. G, 7th Georgia Infantry	4/6/1865, Farmville, Virginia	Died of Chronic Diarrhea, 5/31/1865
Paul, John Private	47	3/8/1862, Richmond County, North Carolina, Volunteer	Richmond County, North Carolina, Farmer	Co. E, 52nd North Carolina Infantry	7/14/1863, Falling Waters, Maryland	Died of Chronic Diarrhea, 10/11/1863
Paulk, George R. Sergeant Not Listed On Monument	42	3/4/1862, Irwinville, Georgia	Irwin County, Georgia	Co. F, 49th Georgia Infantry	5/6/1864, Mine Run, Virginia	Died of Chronic Diarrhea, 5/17/1865
Paxton, Samuel A. Private Not Listed On Monument	44	3/7/1862, Lexington, Virginia	Rockbridge County, Virginia	Captain Pogue's Company, Virginia, Rockbridge Light Artillery	7/3/1863, Gettysburg, Pennsylvania, Gunshot Wound of Face	Died of Wounds, 10/15/1863
Payne, Levi Private	Unk	11/1/1864, Camp Lee, Prince Edward County, Virginia	Prince Edward County, Virginia	Co. C, 29th Virginia Infantry	4/4/1863, Jetersville, Virginia	Died of Acute Diarrhea, 5/17/1865
Payne, Lewis Private Not Listed On Monument	19	3/7/1862, Stafford County, Virginia	Stafford County, Virginia, Laborer	Co. I, 47th Virginia Infantry	7/5/1863, Chambersburg, Pennsylvania	Died of Smallpox, 12/8/1863
Payne, S. Private	Unk	Unknown	Unknown	Co. I, 42nd Virginia Infantry	Unknown	Unable to Locate
Payne, Thomas Henry 1st Sergeant	Unk	4/19/1861, Harper's Ferry, Virginia	Fauquier County, Virginia	Co. A, 7th Virginia Cavalry	7/21/1863, Chester Gap, Virginia	Died of Unknown Causes, 1/27/1864
Payne, Thomas J. Private	17	4/5/1862, Alexander County, North Carolina	Caldwell County, North Carolina, Farmer	Co. H, 55th North Carolina Infantry	7/1/1863, Gettysburg, Pennsylvania	Died of Dysentery, 12/8/1863

Name	Age	Enlisted	Residence	Unit	Captured	Date and Cause of Death
Payne, William B. Corporal	Unk	9/24/1861, Hall and Gwinnett Counties, Georgia	Unknown	Co. H, 35th Georgia Infantry	7/3/1863, Gettysburg, Pennsylvania	Died of Smallpox, 11/10/1863
Payne, William R. Private	21	11/15/1861, Camp Wilkes, North Carolina, Volunteer	Caldwell County, North Carolina	Co. F, 26th North Carolina Infantry	7/14/1863, Falling Waters, Maryland	Died of Unknown Causes, 3/16/1864
Payton, Lawrence R. Private	27	Unknown	Hartford County, Kentucky	Co. F, Duke's, 2nd Kentucky Cavalry	6/25/1863, Harkin River, Ohio	Shot in Chest and Killed by Sergeant of the Guard, 3/20/1864
Pearce, James Private	21	4/21/1861 Carrolton, Mississippi	Pickens County, Alabama	Co. K, 11th Mississippi Infantry	5/5/1864, Mine Run, Virginia	Died of Unknown Causes, 9/7/1864
Pearman, C. C. Private	Unk	7/13/1861, Hart County, Georgia	Hart County, Georgia	Co. H, 15th Georgia Infantry	7/2/1863, Gettysburg, Pennsylvania	Died of Chronic Diarrhea, 12/20/1863
Pearman, Sandy H. Private	Unk	12/15/1862, Charles City Court House, Virginia	Charles County, Virginia	Co. K, 53rd Virginia Infantry	6/15/1864, Charles City Court House, Virginia	Died of Unknown Causes, 8/14/1864
Pearson, Moses Private	Unk	3/5/1862, Darby Town Road near Richmond, Virginia	Henrico County, Virginia	Co. F, 18th Mississippi Infantry	4/6/1865, Farmville, Virginia	Died of Pneumonia, 5/22/1865
Pearson, Solomon Private	17	6/10/1861, Holly Springs, North Carolina, Volunteer	Wake County, North Carolina	Co. D, 26th North Carolina Infantry	7/3/1863, Gettysburg, Pennsylvania	Died of Unknown Causes, 10/?/1863
Pearson, Thomas S. Sergeant	27	4/24/1862, Camp Wilkes, North Carolina, Volunteer	Wilkes County, North Carolina	Co. B, 55th North Carolina Infantry	7/1/1863, Gettysburg, Pennsylvania	Died of Unknown Causes, 12/26/1863
Pearson, William H. Sergeant	26	4/29/1862, Wilson County, North Carolina, Volunteer	Wilson County, North Carolina, Farmer	Co. B, 55th North Carolina Infantry	7/1/1863, Gettysburg, Pennsylvania	Died of Chronic Dysentery, 3/30/1865
Peden, William N. Private	27	7/15/1862, Raleigh, North Carolina Conscript	Johnston County, North Carolina	Co. C, 1st North Carolina Infantry	10/31/1864, Plymouth, North Carolina	Died of Pneumonia, 2/11/1865

Name	Age	Enlisted	Residence	Unit	Captured	Date and Cause of Death
Peed, James O. Private	Unk	10/1/1862, King George County, Virginia	King George County, Virginia	Co. I, 9th Virginia Cavalry	9/13/1863, Culpepper, Virginia, Wounded in Thigh	Died of Wounds, 12/22/1863
Peeding, Monroe Private	26	2/26/1862, Smithfield, North Carolina	Johnston County, North Carolina	Co. C, 5th North Carolina Infantry	7/1/1863, Gettysburg, Pennsylvania	Died of Smallpox, 11/27/1863
Peel, Thomas Private	Unk	3/19/1862, Suffolk, Virginia	Isle of Wight County, Virginia	Co. I, 61st Virginia Infantry	8/19/1864, Globe Tavern, Near Weldon Railroad, Near Petersburg, Virginia	Died of Chronic Diarrhea, 10/27/1864
Peele, William E. Private	21	7/7/1862, Windsor, North Carolina	Bertie County, North Carolina	Co. F, 4th North Carolina Cavalry	1/26/1864, Near Plymouth, North Carolina	Died of Enterilis, 8/6/1864
Pemberton, A. F. Private	26	3/18/1861, Rome, Georgia	Floyd County, Georgia	Co. H, 8th Georgia Infantry	Unknown	Date and Cause of Death Unknown
Pender, Andrew Private	28	9/15/1862, Raleigh, North Carolina, Volunteer	Orange County, North Carolina	Co. E, 31st North Carolina Infantry	6/16/1864, Petersburg, Virginia	Died of Chronic Diarrhea, 2/15/1865
Pender, Thomas R. Private Name Not On Monument	42	8/20/1863, Alamance County, North Carolina, Conscript	Alamance County, North Carolina	Co. A, 2nd North Carolina Infantry	11/7/1863, Kelly's Ford, Rappahannock Station, Virginia	Died of Diphtheria, 1/5/1864
Pender, William Private	32	2/24/1862, Hillsboro, County, North Carolina	Orange County, North Carolina	Co. F, 6th North Carolina Infantry	11/7/1863, Rappahannock Station, Virginia	Died of Unknown Causes, 1/6/1864
Pendergrass, J. R. Private	28	9/23/1862, Camp Holmes, North Carolina, Conscript	Wilkes County, North Carolina	Co. C, 30th North Carolina Infantry	11/7/1863, Rappahannock Station, Virginia	Died of Unknown Causes, 8/29/1864
Pendergrast, Jeremiah Private Name Not On Monument	Unk	5/10/1861, New Orleans, Louisiana	Born in Ireland, Painter	Co. B, 5th Louisiana Infantry	5/5/1863, Spotsylvania Court House, Virginia	Died of Unknown Causes, 7/15/1864

Name	Age	Enlisted	Residence	Unit	Captured	Date and Cause of Death
Pendleton, James L. S. Corporal	24	5/31/1861, Camp Gary, Virginia	Spotsylvania, Virginia, Farmer	Co. D, 30th Virginia Infantry	4/1/1865, Five Forks, Virginia	Died of Pneumonia, 4/21/1865
Pendry, John H. Private	30	3/22/1862, Winston, North Carolina	Forsyth County, North Carolina	Co. K, 52nd North Carolina Infantry	7/5/1863, Gettysburg, Pennsylvania	Died of Chronic Pneumonia, 11/10/1863
Penland, William N. Corporal	Unk	1/15/1862, Newport, Tennessee	Cocke County, Tennessee	Co. F, 5th Tennessee Cavalry	8/15/1864, Dalton, Georgia	Died of Pneumonia, 4/20/1865
Pennel, Thomas H. Private	25	3/15/1862, Lenoir County, North Carolina	Caldwell County, North Carolina	Co. I, 26th North Carolina Infantry	7/12/1864, Williamsport, Maryland	Died of Chronic Diarrhea, 2/18/1865
Penninger, William A. Corporal	30	7/5/1862, Salisbury, North Carolina	Rowan County, North Carolina	Co. K, 57th North Carolina Infantry	2/6/1865, Petersburg, Virginia	Died of Inflammation of the Lungs (Pneumonia), 4/19/1865
Penny, James S. Private	18	2/25/1864, Columbus County, North Carolina	Columbus County, North Carolina	Co. D, 1st Battalion North Carolina Heavy Artillery	1/15/1865, Fort Fisher, North Carolina	Died of Pneumonia, 2/25/1865
Penry, Noah Private	Unk	9/8/1863, Morganton, North Carolina	Mecklenburg County, North Carolina	Co. K, 42nd North Carolina Infantry	3/8/1865, Near Kinston, North Carolina	Died of Chronic Dysentery, 5/25/1865
Perdee, William Private Name Not On Monument	Unk	1/23/1864, Greensboro, Georgia	Greene County, Georgia	Co. G, 66th Georgia Infantry	12/17/1864, Franklin, Tennessee, Gunshot Wound Right Thigh	Died of Diarrhea & Scurvy, 7/4/1865
Perkins, Thomas M. Private	Unk	6/20/1861, Hermitage Camp, Virginia	Unknown	Co. E, 26th Virginia Infantry	Unknown	Died of Pneumonia, 2/27/1864
Permar, William Private	22	9/30/1863, Drewry's Bluff, Virginia, Conscript	Guilford County, North Carolina	Co. C, 45th North Carolina Infantry	9/19/1864, Winchester, Virginia	Died of Chronic Diarrhea, 5/20/1865

Name	Age	Enlisted	Residence	Unit	Captured	Date and Cause of Death
Pernett, Savory B. Private	Unk	8/19/1861 Camp Moore, Louisiana	Orleans Parish, Louisiana	Co. I, 12th Louisiana Infantry	5/16/1863, Champion Hill, Tennessee	Died of Unknown Causes, 10/?/1863
Perry, Samuel J. Private	Unk	11/6/1862, Chatham County, North Carolina	Chatham County, North Carolina	Co. D, 61st North Carolina Infantry	7/10/1863, Morris Island, South Carolina	Died of Typhoid Fever, 7/16/1864
Persinger, A. G. Private	Unk	3/1/1864, Salem, Virginia	Roanoke County, Virginia	Co. D, 5th Virginia Cavalry	5/11/1864, Hanover County, Virginia	Died of Unknown Causes, 8/21/1864
Perviance, David H. Private	17	2/18/1862, Clear Creek, North Carolina, Volunteer	Cabarrus County, North Carolina	Co. H, 7th North Carolina Infantry	7/2/1863, Gettysburg, Pennsylvania	Died of Unknown Causes, 11/21/1863
Peterson, Gaston M. Private	37	12/19/1862, Sampson County, North Carolina Volunteer	Sampson County, North Carolina	Co. A, 36th North Carolina Heavy Artillery	1/15/1865, Fort Fisher, North Carolina	Died of Pneumonia, 3/6/1865
Petterson, H. S. See: Tetterton, Hosea W.				Co. I, 61st North Carolina Infantry		
Pettigrew, William Private	Unk	Unknown	Unknown	Co. D, 13th Georgia Infantry	7/5/1863, Waterloo, Pennsylvania	Died of Smallpox 12/4/1863
Pettus, James G. Sergeant Major Name Not On Monument	18	5/31/1861, Harper's Ferry, Virginia	Louisa County, Virginia, Student	Co. D, 13th Virginia Infantry	9/19/1864, Winchester, Virginia	Died of Chronic Diarrhea, 2/22/1865
Pettus, Samuel Private	Unk	3/17/1862, Richmond, Virginia	Henrico County, Virginia	Captain Allen's Company, Virginia Heavy Artillery	Unknown	Date and Cause of Death Unknown
Pharr, Cicero H. Private	Unk	7/7/1862, Concord, North Carolina	Cabarrus County, North Carolina	Co. F, 57th North Carolina Infantry	11/7/1863, Rappahannock Station, Virginia	Died of Chronic Diarrhea, 2/20/1864

Name	Age	Enlisted	Residence	Unit	Captured	Date and Cause of Death
Phearoah, Jerry Private	Unk	8/24/1864, Montgomery, Alabama	Montgomery County, Alabama	Co. D, 12th Alabama Infantry	9/19/1864, Winchester, Virginia	Died of Acute Dysentery, 1/11/1865
Phelps, Britton Private	19	9/3/1862, Mocksville, North Carolina	Forsyth, County, North Carolina, Farmer	Co. G, 7th Confederate Cavalry	5/7/1864, Cypress Bridge, Virginia	Died of Chronic Diarrhea, 10/25/1864
Phendal, Thomas Private	Unk	9/10/1864, Botetourt, Virginia, Conscript	Unknown	Co. E, 52nd Virginia Infantry	9/23/1864, Fishers Hill, Virginia	Died of Chronic Diarrhea, 1/25/1865
Phillips, Charles Private	Unk	11/5/1863, Richmond, Virginia	Henrico County, Virginia	Co. D, 20th Battalion Virginia Heavy Artillery	4/6/1865, Farmville, Virginia	Died of Pneumonia, 5/25/1865
Phillips, John H. Private Name Not On Monument	Unk	Unknown	Unknown	Co. D, 16th Battalion North Carolina Cavalry	10/27/1864, Petersburg, Virginia	Died of Dysentery, 6/10/1865
Phillips, John W. Private	18	9/3/1862, Mocksville, North Carolina	Forsyth, County, North Carolina, Farmer	Co. G, 7th Confederate Cavalry	10/27/1864, Boyton Plank Road or Burgess' Mill, Virginia	Died of Acute Dysentery, 6/10/1865
Phillips, Levi W. Private	Unk	9/16/1861, Meriwether County, Georgia	Meriwether County, Georgia	Co. A, 60th Georgia Infantry	5/20/1864, Spotsylvania Court House, Virginia	Died of Unknown Causes, 10/221864
Phillips, Michael Private	22	4/20/1861, Portsmouth, Virginia	Norfolk County, Virginia	Co. G, 9th Virginia Infantry	7/3/1863, Gettysburg, Pennsylvania	Died of Pneumonia, 11/19/1863
Phillips, Peter Private	Unk	3/29/1862, Pickens, South Carolina	Pickens County, South Carolina	Co. E, 1st South Carolina Infantry	7/14/1863, Falling Waters, Maryland	Died of Chronic Diarrhea, 1/1/1864

Name	Age	Enlisted	Residence	Unit	Captured	Date and Cause of Death
Phillips, Richard Private	26	5/28/1861, Cartersville, North Carolina	Chatham County, North Carolina	Co. E, 26th North Carolina Infantry	10/14/1863, Bristoe Station, Virginia	Died of Chronic Dysentery, 10/26/1864
Phillips, Riley Private	Unk	10/31/1864, Place Unknown	Unknown	Co. C, 47th North Carolina Infantry	10/27/1864, Boyton Plank Road or Burgess' Mill, Virginia	Died of Measles, 3/14/1865
Phillips, William Private	23	6/5/1861, Monroe, North Carolina	Union County, North Carolina	Co. B, 26th North Carolina Infantry	7/5/1863, Gettysburg, Pennsylvania	Died of Unknown Causes, 11/27/1863
Phillips, William T. Sergeant	31	3/4/1862, Buena Vista, Georgia	Marion County, Georgia	Co. H, 46th Georgia Infantry	12/17/1864, Franklin, Tennessee, Wounded in Left Arm, Fractured Humerus	Died of Wounds, 4/19/1865
Philpot, John P. Private	Unk	6/22/1861, Henry County, Virginia	Henry County, Virginia	Co. F, 42nd Virginia Infantry	7/5/1863, Gettysburg, Pennsylvania	Died of Chronic Diarrhea, 2/4/1864
Pickett, Washington E. Corporal Name Not On Monument	23	5/1/1861, Durham, Orange County, North Carolina, Volunteer	Orange County, North Carolina	Co. C, 6th North Carolina Infantry	11/7/1863, Rappahannock Station, Virginia	Died of Unknown Causes, 12/7/1864
Pickle, Peter Private	30	5/4/1863, Smyth County, Virginia	Smyth County, Virginia, Farmer	Co. K, 48th Virginia Infantry	9/19/1864, Winchester, Virginia	Died of Consumption, 1/24/1865
Pierce, Benjamin Private Not Listed On Monument	32	4/22/1862, Stump Sound, North Carolina, Volunteer	Carteret County, North Carolina, Farmer	Co. H, 55th North Carolina Infantry	7/1/1863, Gettysburg, Pennsylvania	Died of Dysentery, 12/8/1863
Pierce, James H. Private	Unk	8/26/181, Waresboro, Georgia	Ware County, Georgia	Co. K, 26th Georgia Infantry	5/6/1864, Wilderness, Virginia	Died of Scurvy, 2/25/1865

Name	Age	Enlisted	Residence	Unit	Captured	Date and Cause of Death
Pierce, Robert F. Private	20	7/22/1861, Camp Moore, Louisiana	Hickory, Louisiana, Farmer	Co. K, 10th Louisiana Infantry	7/5/1863, Gettysburg, Pennsylvania	Died of Unknown Causes, 9/2/1864
Pierce, W. J. C. Private	Unk	8/2/1861, Near Harrisburg, Texas	Unknown	Co. D, 5th Texas Infantry	7/3/1863, Gettysburg, Pennsylvania	Died of Unknown Causes, 9/2/1864
Pierson, Thomas B. Private	Unk	9/20/1861, Salem, Tennessee	Franklin County, Tennessee	Co. F, 1st Tennessee Infantry	9/29/1864, Near Fort Harrison, Virginia	Date and Cause of Death Unknown
Pigg, William P. Private	Unk	2/4/1863 Chesterfield District, South Carolina	Chesterfield District, South Carolina	Co. B, 26th South Carolina Infantry	4/1/1865, Petersburg, Virginia	Died of curvy, 6/19/1865
Piles, George J. Private	Unk	7/25/1864 Dublin, Virginia	Pulaski County, Virginia	Co. F, 26th Virginia Battalion Infantry	9/19/1864, Winchester, Virginia	Died of Pneumonia, 1/18/1865
Pilkenton, J. F. Private	Unk	Unknown	Unknown	Co. D, 61st Georgia Infantry	Unknown	Unable to Locate
Pilkenton, Isaac Private Not Listed On Monument	18	9/12/1862, Chatham County, North Carolina	Chatham County, North Carolina	Co. D, 61st North Carolina Infantry	8/26/1863, Morris Island, South Carolina	Died of Chronic Diarrhea, 1/11/1864
Pilkinton, Stephen R. Private Not Listed On Monument	23	5/30/1861, Northampton County, North Carolina	Johnston County, North Carolina, Farmer	Co. C, 5th North Carolina Infantry	5/17/1864, Spotsylvania Court House, Virginia	Died of Dysentery, 7/2/1864
Pillow, Samuel B. Private	Unk	2/26/1863, Petersburg, Virginia	Chesterfield County, Virginia	Co. I, 53rd Virginia Infantry	4/1/1865, Five Forks, Virginia	Died of Chronic Diarrhea, 4/28/1865

Name	Age	Enlisted	Residence	Unit	Captured	Date and Cause of Death
Pines, Andrew J. Private	Unk	3/12/1862, Gloucester Point, Virginia	Gloucester County, Virginia	Co. B, 26th Virginia Infantry	6/15/1864, Petersburg, Virginia	Died of Unknown Causes, 8/1/1864
Pinker, A. See: Rinica, Andrew				Co. H, 33rd Virginia Infantry		
Pinkston, A. S. Private	Unk	5/13/1863, Savannah, Georgia	Stewart County, Georgia	Co. E, 7th Georgia Cavalry	4/6/1865, Burkesville, Virginia	Died of Remittent Fever, 5/29/1865
Pinson, Cornelius F. Private	Unk	12/5/1861, Camp Hampton, South Carolina	Lancaster County, South Carolina	Co. A, 3rd Battalion, South Carolina Infantry	5/23/1864, North Anna River, Virginia	Died of Acute Diarrhea, 5/14/1865
Pinson, George W. Private	27	2/26/1863, Cleveland County, North Carolina, Conscript	Cleveland County, North Carolina	Co. B, 34th North Carolina Infantry	7/14/1863, Falling Waters, Maryland	Died of Unknown Causes, 3/8/1864
Pinson, J. Private	Unk	Unknown	Unknown	Co. A, 10th Tennessee Cavalry	5/23/1863, Humphries County, Tennessee	Died of Unknown Causes, 10/25/1863
Pippins, Milus B. Private	32	8/15/1862, Mecklenburg, County, North Carolina, Conscript	Mecklenburg, County, North Carolina	Co. C, 37th North Carolina Infantry	5/12/1864, Near Spotsylvania Court House, Virginia	Died of Unknown Causes, 8/4/1864
Pitchford, James Private Name Not On Monument	34	7/15/1862, Guilford County, North Carolina, Conscript	Guilford County, North Carolina	Co. A, 1st North Carolina Infantry	7/3/1863, Gettysburg, Pennsylvania	Died of Unknown Causes, 2/5/1865
Pitman, John W. Private	Unk	3/16/1862, Pocahontas, Arkansas	Randolph County, Arkansas	Co. K, 21st Arkansas Infantry	5/17/1863, Big Black Bridge, Near Vicksburg, Mississippi	Date and Cause of Death Unknown
Pitt, Aaron A. Sergeant	25	6/25/1861, Newbern, North Carolina, Volunteer	Edgecombe County, North Carolina	Co. I, 2nd North Carolina Infantry	11/7/1863, Rappahannock, Virginia	Died of Congestive, Remittent Fever, 11/9/1864

Name	Age	Enlisted	Residence	Unit	Captured	Date and Cause of Death
Pitt, Frank B. 1st Sergeant	25	1/20/1862, Tarboro, Edgecombe County, North Carolina	Edgecombe County, North Carolina, Farmer	Co. B, 44th North Carolina Infantry	10/14/1863, Bristoe Station, Virginia	Died of Chronic Diarrhea, 12/28/1863
Pittman, Henry Private	44	Brunswick County, North Carolina, 9/1/1863	Halifax County, North Carolina	Co. F, 36th North Carolina Heavy Artillery	1/15/1865 Fort Fisher, North Carolina	Died of Gangrene, 3/11/1865
Pittman, Robert M. Corporal	27	4/29/1862, Wilson County, North Carolina	Wilson County, North Carolina, Farmer	Co. A, 55th North Carolina Infantry	7/5/1863, Gettysburg, Pennsylvania	Died of Unknown Causes, 11/23/1863
Pitts, D. C. Private	Unk	Unknown	Unknown	Co. F, 51st Alabama Infantry	6/27/1863, Shelbyville, Tennessee	Died of Chronic Diarrhea, 11/17/1863
Plunkett, William P. Private	Unk	3/1/1862, Camp Moore, Louisiana	Orleans Parish, Louisiana	Co. A, 12th Louisiana Infantry	5/16/1863, Champion Hill, Tennessee	Died of Chronic Diarrhea, 3/2/1864
Plyler, Felt P. Private	Unk	11/24/1863, Marietta, Georgia	Cobb County, Georgia	Co. A, 4th South Carolina Cavalry	5/30/1864, Old Church, Near Cold Harbor, Virginia	Died of Chronic Diarrhea, 9/18/1864
Poe, John M. Private	Unk	8/3/1861, Marion County, Arkansas	Marion County, Arkansas	1st Battalion Arkansas Cavalry	5/17/1863, Big Black Bridge, Near Vicksburg, Mississippi	Died of Unknown Causes, 12/10/1863
Poe, Nauflet F. Private	Unk	4/1/1864, Orange County, North Carolina, Volunteer	Orange County, North Carolina	Co. G, 28th North Carolina Infantry	5/17/1864, Spotsylvania Court House, Virginia	Died of Chronic Diarrhea, 10/29/1864
Poe, Zaccheus Private	34	7/16/1862, Camp Holmes, Raleigh, North Carolina, Conscript	Montgomery County, North Carolina	Co. F, 14th North Carolina Infantry	11/7/1863, Kelly's Ford, Rappahannock Station, Virginia	Died of Consumption, 3/25/1865
Pollard, Cicero Private	Unk	6/12/1861, Chattooga County, Georgia	Chattooga County, Georgia	Co. B, 9th Georgia Infantry	8/16/1864, Deep Bottom Run, Virginia	Died of Chronic Dysentery, 1/23/1865

Name	Age	Enlisted	Residence	Unit	Captured	Date and Cause of Death
Pollock, Gladen H. Private	22	7/5/1861, Camp Boone, Kentucky	Unknown	Co. B, 3rd Kentucky Infantry	5/16/1863, Champion Hill, Tennessee	Date and Cause of Death Unknown
Pollock, Robert A. Private	30	3/20/1862, Blue Sulphur Springs, Virginia	Lewisburg, West Virginia, Farmer	Co. K, 14th Virginia Cavalry	11/12/1864, Near Nineveh, Virginia	Died of Typhoid Fever, 1/9/1864
Polson, James H. Private	25	12/20/1861, Cheraw, Chesterfield District, South Carolina	Chesterfield District, South Carolina	Co. D, 21st South Carolina Infantry	7/10/1863, Morris Island, South Carolina	Died of Unknown Causes, 1/9/1864
Ponder, James T. Private	25	4/30/1861, Okolono, Mississippi	Unknown, Farmer	Co. C, 11th Mississippi Infantry	10/1/1864, Petersburg, Virginia	Died of Chronic Diarrhea, 1/24/1864
Pool, Joshua B. Private	15	6/10/1863, Faurquier County, Virginia	Faurquier County, Virginia	Co. A, Mosby's Regiment of Virginia Cavalry	5/23/1864, Upperville, Virginia	Died of Acute Diarrhea, 11/4/1864
Pool, Joshua W. Private	Unk	8/4/1862, Wake County, North Carolina	Wake County, North Carolina	Co. A, 10th Battalion North Carolina Heavy Artillery	12/18/1864, Near Savannah, Georgia	Died Chronic Diarrhea, 5/9/1865
Poole, Hinton Private	27	5/16/1861, Wake County, North Carolina	Wake County, North Carolina, Farmer	Co. E, 14th North Carolina Infantry	7/2/1863, Gettysburg, Pennsylvania, Wounded	Died of Chronic Diarrhea, 5/1/1865
Poole, John C. Private	Unk	Unknown	Unknown	Blockade Runner Alliance	4/12/1864, Captured by USS Vermont	Date and Cause of Death Unknown
Poore, Thomas Private	22	6/5/1861, Mount Airy, North Carolina, Volunteer	Surry County, North Carolina	Co. I, 21st North Carolina Infantry	7/3/1863, Gettysburg, Pennsylvania	Died of Unknown Causes, 3/27/1864
Pope, John T. Private	Unk	Unknown	Unknown	Co. D, 67th North Carolina Infantry	6/22/1864, Jackson's Mills, Near Kinston, North Carolina	Died of Acute Dysentery, 1/23/1865

Name	Age	Enlisted	Residence	Unit	Captured	Date and Cause of Death
Pope, Thomas M. Private Name Not On Monument	37	3/10/1862, Apalachicola, Florida	Franklin County, Florida	Co. H, 5th Florida Infantry	5/17/1864, Spotsylvania Court House, Virginia	Died of Dysentery, 7/3/1864
Pope, William T. Private	Unk	7/15/1862, Camp Holmes, North Carolina	Wake County, North Carolina	Co. E, 47th North Carolina Infantry	10/27/1864, Burgess Mills, near Petersburg, Virginia	Died of Unknown Causes, 2/11/1865
Popwell, James Private	Unk	10/6/1864, Montgomery, Alabama	Montgomery County, Alabama	Co. A, 12th Alabama Infantry	4/2/1865, Petersburg, Virginia	Died of Pneumonia, 5/3/1865
Porter, John M. Private	18	4/22/1864, Camp Pendleton, Greenville, Virginia	Unknown	Co. G, 3rd Virginia Infantry	4/1/1865, Five Forks, Virginia	Died of Pneumonia, 5/1/1865
Porter, Joseph W. Private	Unk	10/9/1861, Enfield, North Carolina	Halifax County, North Carolina	Co. F, 36th North Carolina Heavy Artillery	1/15/1865, Fort Fisher, North Carolina	Died of Pneumonia, 2/15/1865
Porter, Laban Private	22	3/1/1862, Dallas, Texas	Dallas County, Texas	Co. D, 15th Texas Cavalry	7/15/1864, Covington, Georgia	Died of Chronic Diarrhea, 4/21/1865
Porter, Travis L. Private	20	5/18/1861, Bladen County, North Carolina	Bladen County, North Carolina	Co. H, 3rd North Carolina Infantry	7/3/1863, Gettysburg, Pennsylvania	Died of Smallpox, 12/23/1863
Porter, William Private	Unk	1/1/1864, New Market, Virginia	Shenandoah County, Virginia	Co. G, 12th Virginia Cavalry	7/?/1864, Deserted Regiment	Died of Chronic Diarrhea, 6/24/1865
Poteet, James H. Private	Unk	7/5/1862, Haysville, North Carolina	Clay County, North Carolina	Co. B, 6th North Carolina Cavalry	6/22/1864, Near Kinston, Wise Forks, North Carolina	Died of Unknown Causes, 8/24/1864
Porterfield, Alexander Private	Unk	5/27/1864, Camp Holmes, North Carolina	Wake County, North Carolina	Co. C, 3rd North Carolina Junior Reserves	12/25/1864, Fort Fisher, North Carolina	Died of Unknown Causes, 6/16/1865

Name	Age	Enlisted	Residence	Unit	Captured	Date and Cause of Death
Portress, William Private Name Not On Monument	Unk	10/15/1864, Richmond, Virginia, Conscript	Henrico County, Virginia	Co. F, 12th Virginia Infantry	10/27/1864, Burgess Mill, Near Petersburg, Virginia	Died of Unknown Causes, 6/24/1865
Potter, Gustavus C. Private	20	12/25/1861, Camp Price, Springfield, Missouri	Kentucky, Farmer	Co. K, 1st Missouri Cavalry	5/17/1863, Big Black Bridge, Near Vicksburg, Mississippi	Died of Chronic Diarrhea, 11/15/1863
Potter, James Private	30	7/8/1861, Washington, North Carolina, Volunteer	Beaufort County, North Carolina	Co. G, 2nd North Carolina Cavalry	7/5/1863, Green Castle, Pennsylvania	Died of Chronic Diarrhea, 2/12/1864
Potts, William T. Private	18	6/30/1863, Captain Sowes, North Carolina, volunteer	Lincoln County, North Carolina	Co. G, 52nd North Carolina Infantry	10/14/1863, Bristoe Station, Virginia	Died of Unknown Causes, 12/23/1863
Powell, Carroll Private	Unk	3/11/1863, Augusta, Georgia	Richmond County, Georgia	Co. C, 48th Georgia Infantry	6/26/1863, Katerville, Virginia	Died of Smallpox, 1/8/1864
Powell, George L. Private	19	6/29/1861, Polk County, Georgia	Polk County, Georgia	Co. D, 21st Georgia Infantry	7/3/1863, Gettysburg, Pennsylvania	Died of Unknown Causes, 11/8/1863
Powell, George W. Private	18	4/23/1861, Fair Bluff, Columbus County, North Carolina	Columbus County, North Carolina, laborer	Co. C, 20th North Carolina Infantry	7/5/1863, Waterloo, Gettysburg, Pennsylvania	Died of Unknown Causes, 8/11/1864
Powell, Henry H. Private	23	7/12/1863, Clarksville, North Carolina, Volunteer	Northampton County, North Carolina	Co. B, 1st North Carolina Cavalry	10/27/1864, Boyton Plank Road or Burgess' Mill, Virginia	Died of Chronic Diarrhea, 3/1/1865
Powell, J. A. Private	20	4/14/1861, Clinton, South Carolina	Laurens County, South Carolina	Co. I, 3rd South Carolina Infantry	5/23/1864, North Anna River, Virginia	Died of Unknown Causes, 8/13/1864

Name	Age	Enlisted	Residence	Unit	Captured	Date and Cause of Death
Powell, James M. Private	Unk	4/15/1861, Buena Vista, Georgia	Marion County, Georgia	Co. I, 2nd Georgia infantry	7/3/1863, Gettysburg, Pennsylvania	Died of Unknown Causes, 2/25/1864
Powell, James W. Private	Unk	5/1/1862, Sumpkin, Georgia	Stewart County, Georgia	Co. E, 31st Georgia Infantry	7/14/1863, Williamsport, Maryland	Died of Chronic Diarrhea & Pneumonia, 11/26/1863
Powell, Jesse A. Private	21	3/1/1862, Nashville, North Carolina	Nash County, North Carolina	Co. H, 32nd North Carolina Infantry	7/3/1863, Gettysburg, Pennsylvania	Died of Chronic Diarrhea, 12/26/1863
Powell, S. Pinkney Private	19	2/20/1863, Lenoir County, North Carolina, volunteer	Caldwell County, North Carolina	Co. F, 26th North Carolina Infantry	10/14/1863, Bristoe Station, Virginia	Died of Unknown Causes, 6/25/1864
Powell, T. W. Private	Unk	Unknown	Unknown	Co. B, 17th Virginia Infantry	Unknown	Unable to Locate
Powers, Alexander Private	Unk	10/17/1864, Rockingham, North Carolina	Richmond County, North Carolina	Co. F, 45th North Carolina Infantry	4/2/1865, Petersburg, Virginia	Died of Remittent Fever, 6/9/1865
Powers, David George Private Name Not On Monument	23	5/6/1862 Bladen County, North Carolina	Whiteville, Columbus County, North Carolina, Farmer	Co. K, 40th Carolina, 3rd North Carolina Artillery	1/15/1865, Fort Fisher, North Carolina, Wounded Left Leg	Left Leg Amputated, Died of "Pyaemia from Gunshot Wound" 2/12/1865
Powers, George D. Private Name Not On Monument	19	4/29/1862, New Hanover County, North Carolina	New Hanover County, North Carolina	Co. B, 1st North Carolina Artillery	3/19/1865, Bentonville, North Carolina	Died of Pneumonia, 5/24/1865
Powers, James T. Private	28	2/22/1862, Greensboro, North Carolina	Guilford County, North Carolina	Co. E, 22nd North Carolina Infantry	6/2/1864, Near Mechanicsville, Virginia	Died of Pneumonia, 2/11/1865

Name	Age	Enlisted	Residence	Unit	Captured	Date and Cause of Death
Powers, William C. Private	Unk	2/12/1863, Tapp K, Virginia	Unknown	Co. B, 9th Virginia Cavalry	9/13/1863, Near Culpepper, Virginia	Died of Unknown Causes, 9/14/1864
Prater, James Private	Unk	9/7/1862, Pocahontas, Arkansas	Randolph County, Arkansas	Co. D, 21st Arkansas Infantry	5/17/1863, Big Black Bridge, Near Vicksburg, Mississippi	Died of Smallpox, 2/28/1864
Pratt, James A. Private Not Listed On Monument	Unk	4/11/1862, Huger Barracks, Virginia	Henry County, Virginia	Co. F, 16th Virginia Infantry	10/27/1864, Burgess' Mill, Virginia	Died of Paralysis, 7/5/1865
Pratt, William R. Corporal	21	3/22/1862, Forsyth County, North Carolina	Forsyth County, North Carolina, Farmer	Co. K, 52nd North Carolina Infantry	7/3/1863, Gettysburg, Pennsylvania	Died of Unknown Causes, 3/6/1864
Prescott, John A. Private	Unk	11/16/1863, Camp Mercer, Georgia	Unknown	Clinche's Georgia Light Artillery Battery	12/3/1864, Fort McAllister, Georgia	Died of Unknown Causes, 5/18/1865
Prescott, William L. Private	Unk	9/2/1862, Coffee County, Alabama	Coffee County, Alabama	Co. F, 3rd Alabama Infantry	7/2/1863, Waterloo, Gettysburg, Pennsylvania, Wounded Right Hand	Date and Cause of Death Unknown
Pressler, Darlin Private	Unk	2/14/1862, Munroe County, North Carolina, Volunteer	Union County, North Carolina	Co. B, 26th North Carolina Infantry	10/14/1863, Bristoe Station, Virginia	Died of Chronic Diarrhea, 8/31/1864
Pressley, Lawson Private	Unk	10/30/1864, Petersburg, Virginia	Chesterfield County, Virginia	Co. H, 55th North Carolina Infantry	4/1/1865, Five Forks, Virginia	Died of Chronic Dysentery, 6/18/1865
Preston, Thomas P. Sergeant	Unk	3/4/1862, Thomas County, Georgia	Thomas County, Georgia	Co. E, 50th Georgia Infantry	7/4/1863, Cashtown, Pennsylvania	Died of Chronic Dysentery, 12/9/1863
Previance, David H. Private Name Not On Monument	17	2/18/1862, Clear Creek, North Carolina, Volunteer	Cabarrus County, North Carolina	Co. H, 7th North Carolina Infantry	7/2/1863, Gettysburg, Pennsylvania	Died of Unknown Causes, 11/28/1863

Name	Age	Enlisted	Residence	Unit	Captured	Date and Cause of Death
Pribble, John W. Private	Unk	2/25/1862, Bedford County, Virginia	Bedford County, Virginia	Co. C, 20th Battalion Virginia Heavy Artillery	4/6/1865, Farmville, Virginia	Died of Chronic Dysentery, 6/14/1865
Price, Andrew Gatewood Private Not Listed On Monument	Unk	3/1/1862, Huntersville, West Virginia	Pocahontas County, West Virginia	Co. G, 11th Virginia Cavalry	5/28/1864, Hall's Shop, Virginia	Died of Unknown Causes, 7/11/1864
Price, David Private	19	4/15/1862, Grayson County, Virginia	Grayson County, Virginia, Farmer	Co. D, 50th Virginia Infantry	7/14/1863, Falling Waters, Maryland	Died of Unknown Causes, 8/30/1863
Price, Henry W. Private	18	7/8/1862, Rutherford County, North Carolina, Volunteer	Rutherford County, North Carolina	Co. I, 56th North Carolina Infantry	3/25/1865, Fort Stedman, Near Petersburg, Virginia	Inflammation of Lungs (Pneumonia), 4/7/1865
Price, Jackson Private	47	12/13/1864, Wilson County, North Carolina, Substitute	Wilson County, North Carolina	Co. A, 55th North Carolina Infantry	7/14/1863, Falling Waters, Maryland	Died of Unknown Causes, 3/7/1864
Price, Needham Private	25	4/15/1863, Raleigh, North Carolina, Volunteer	Johnston County, North Carolina	Co. C, 24th North Carolina Infantry	4/2/1865, Petersburg, Virginia	Died of Chronic Diarrhea, 6/7/1865
Price, Thomas K. Private	Unk	5/5/1862, Charleston, South Carolina	Charleston County, South Carolina	Co. F, 1st South Carolina Infantry	8/14/1864, Deep Bottom, Virginia	Died of Chronic Diarrhea, 2/24/1865
Price, William F. Private	Unk	Unknown	Unknown	Stiles' Georgia Artillery	Unknown	Unable to Locate
Price, William R. Private	32	5/5/1862, Union County, North Carolina	Union County, North Carolina	Co. I, 53rd North Carolina Infantry	7/5/1863, Waterloo, Gettysburg, Pennsylvania	Died Chronic Diarrhea, 1/3/1864

Name	Age	Enlisted	Residence	Unit	Captured	Date and Cause of Death
Priddy, William B. Private	Unk	7/22/1862, Charlottesville Virginia	Albemarle County, Virginia	Co. H, 57th Virginia Infantry	Deserted Regiment, Captured Unknown Date	Died Chronic Diarrhea, 5/16/1865
Pridgen, Josiah J. Private	25	5/1/1862, Nash County, North Carolina, Volunteer	Nash County, North Carolina	Co. I, 30th North Carolina Infantry	11/7/1863, Kelly's Ford, Rappahannock, Virginia	Died of Unknown Causes, 11/26/1863
Prince, Joseph Private	Unk	Unknown	Unknown	Co. E, 16th Virginia Infantry	Unknown	Unable to Locate
Prison, Bartell Private	Unk	Unknown	Unknown	Co. D, 20th North Carolina Infantry	Unknown	Unable to Locate
Pritchett, N. C. Corporal	Unk	7/14/1861, Hartwell, Georgia	Hart County, Georgia	Co. C, 16th Georgia Infantry	7/2/1863, Gettysburg, Pennsylvania	Died of Unknown Causes, 9/5/1863
Pritt, James Private	Unk	12/3/1863, Washington, Virginia	Rappahannock County, Virginia	Co. G, 18th Virginia Cavalry	6/29/1863, McConnelsburg Virginia	Died of Unknown Causes, 2/27/1864
Proctor, A. M. Private	Unk	Unknown	Unknown	Co. F, 22nd Georgia Infantry	12/3/1864, Fort McAllister, Georgia	Died of Unknown Causes, 5/10/1865
Proctor, Granbury Private	32	2/28/1862, Nashville, North Carolina, Volunteer	Nash County, North Carolina, farmer	Co. D, 47th North Carolina Infantry	10/27/1864, Boyton Plank Road or Burgess' Mill, Virginia	Died of Chronic Diarrhea, 2/9/1865
Proffit, G. R. Private	Unk	8/29/1862, Goochland Court House, Virginia	Goochland County, Virginia	Captain Carter's Co., Virginia Light Artillery	7/5/1863, Waterloo, Gettysburg, Pennsylvania	Died of Unknown Causes, 1/15/1864
Propst, Joel A. Private	Unk	4/15/1862. Rudes Hill, Virginia	Unknown	Co. G, 2nd Virginia Infantry	5/20/1864, Spotsylvania Court House, Virginia	Died of Gastroenteritis 6/27/1864
Provence, John A. Private	18	10/2/1862, Mossy Creek, Tennessee	Jefferson County, Tennessee	Co. F, 61st Tennessee Mounted Infantry	5/17/1863, Big Black Bridge, Near Vicksburg, Mississippi	Died of Chronic Diarrhea & Scrofula, 1/9/1864

Name	Age	Enlisted	Residence	Unit	Captured	Date and Cause of Death
Pruitt, J. C. Private	Unk	Unknown	Unknown	Co. B, 3rd Georgia Cavalry	Unknown	Unable to Locate
Pruitt, M. Private	Unk	Unknown	Unknown	Co. E, 34th Virginia Infantry	Unknown	Unable to Locate
Pry, Robert O. Private	Unk	6/17/1862, Columbus, Georgia	Muscogee County, Georgia	Co. C, 7th Confederate Cavalry	8/19/1864, Deep Bottom, Virginia	Died of Chronic Diarrhea, 2/25/1865
Puett, S. E. Private	Unk	9/18/1862, Ivor, North Carolina	Southampton County, North Carolina	Co. F, 3rd North Carolina Cavalry	5/27/1864, North Anna or Near Hanover Junction, Virginia	Died of Unknown Causes, 7/27/1864
Puffenbarger, William Private	30	11/16/1861, Franklin, Virginia	Dry Run, Pendleton County, Virginia, Laborer	Co. K, 25th Virginia Infantry	7/5/1863, Waterloo, Gettysburg, Pennsylvania	Died of Debility, (Feebleness) 11/9/1863
Pugh, James H. Private	30	4/20/1861, Lexington, Virginia	Rockbridge County, Virginia, Farmer	Co. H, 4th Virginia Infantry	7 3/1863, Gettysburg, Pennsylvania	Died of Unknown Causes, 1/17/1864
Pugh, William Private	Unk	10/20/1863, Dublin, Virginia	Pulaski County, Virginia	Co. C, 4th Virginia Infantry	5/12/1863, Spotsylvania Court House, Virginia	Died of Unknown Causes, 7/29/1864
Pullen, Rufus Corporal	40	2/21/1862, Castalia, North Carolina	Nash County, North Carolina, Farmer	Co. D, 47th North Carolina Infantry	7/3/1863, Gettysburg, Pennsylvania	Died of Chronic Diarrhea, 6/16/1865
Pullin, George W. Sergeant	Unk	12/3/1862, Camp Washington, Virginia	Unknown	Co. G, 18th Virginia Infantry	6/29/1863, McConnellsburg Virginia	Died of Smallpox, 1/7/1864
Pullin, Henry O. Private	43	10/1/1863, Macon, Mississippi	Enterprise, Clarke County, Mississippi	Co. B, 4th Mississippi Infantry	12/22/1863, Columbia, Tennessee, Wounded by Gunshot Wound in Left Leg	Died of Hospital Gangrene, 5/3/1865

Name	Age	Enlisted	Residence	Unit	Captured	Date and Cause of Death
Pultz, Jacob Private	Unk	10/5/1862, Stryder's Mill, Virginia	Unknown	Co. C, 1st Virginia Cavalry	7/4/1863, Gettysburg, Pennsylvania, Left in Hospital	Died of Acute Rheumatism, 12/1/1863
Purcell, E. J. Private	Unk	Unknown	Unknown	Co. A, 5th Virginia Cavalry	Unknown	Died of Unknown Causes, 3/8/1865
Purgear, Benjamin J. Private	Unk	Unknown	Unknown	Invalid Corps	Unknown	Unable to Locate
Purgason, F. M. Private	32	9/1/1863, Drewry's Bluff, Virginia, Conscript	Rockingham County, North Carolina	Co. F, 45th North Carolina Infantry	7/5/1863, Gettysburg, Pennsylvania	Died of Chronic Dysentery, 1/20/1864
Pursur, Solomon Private	40	3/4/1863, Dublin, Laurens County, Georgia	Laurens County, Georgia	Co. G, 49th Georgia Infantry	6/28/1863, Hagerstown, Maryland	Died of Smallpox, 12/18/1863
Purviance, David H. See: Perviance, David H.				Co. H, 7th North Carolina Infantry		
Puryear, Rufus A. Private	Unk	5/14/1861, Boydton, Virginia	Mecklenburg County, Virginia	Co. A, 3rd Virginia Cavalry	10/11/1863, Raccoon Ford, Virginia	Died of Unknown Causes, 8/8/1864
Puryer, Giles Private	Unk	3/8/1862, Mecklenburg, Virginia	Mecklenburg County, Virginia	Co. B, 34th Virginia Infantry	3/31/1865, Hatcher's Run. Virginia	Died of Chronic Diarrhea, 5/22/1865
Putnam, Arthur Corporal	34	8/14/1862, Raleigh, North Carolina, Conscript	Cleveland County, North Carolina	Co. C, 15th North Carolina Infantry	4/2/1865, Hatcher's Run. Virginia	Died of Chronic Dysentery, 5/10/1865
Putnam, Perry G. Sr. Private	39	2/28/1862, Shelby, Cleveland County, North Carolina, Conscript	Cleveland County, North Carolina	Co. H, 34th North Carolina Infantry	7/14/1863, Falling Waters, Maryland	Died of Unknown Causes, 8/18/1864

410

Name	Age	Enlisted	Residence	Unit	Captured	Date and Cause of Death
Pyles, N. M. Private	Unk	1/20/1864, Mount Pleasant, North Carolina	Charleston District, South Carolina	Co. G, 27th South Carolina Infantry	6/24/1864, Near Petersburg, Virginia	Died of Unknown Causes, 7/30/1864

Name	Age	Enlisted	Residence	Unit	Captured	Date and Cause of Death
Quick, John B. Private Not Listed On Monument	33	12/25/1861, Bennettsville, South Carolina	Bennettsville, Marlboro District, South Carolina, Laborer	Co. F, 21st South Carolina Infantry	1/15/1865, Fort Fisher, North Carolina, Severe Gunshot Wound Left Forearm	Died of Wounds, 3/9/1865
Quinn, John W. Private	Unk	2/1/1863, Duplin County, North Carolina	Duplin County, North Carolina	Co. C, 66th North Carolina Infantry	3/10/1865, Wilmington Road, Kinston, North Carolina	Died of Pneumonia, 5/21/1865
Quesenberry, Richard D. Private	Unk	10/24/1861, Fort Lowery, Richmond County, Virginia	Stony Hill, Virginia	Co. K, 9th Virginia Cavalry	6/30/1863, Hanover, Pennsylvania	Died of Unknown Causes, 12/10/1863
Quisenbury, R. H. See: Quesenberry, Richard D.				Co. K, 9th Virginia Cavalry		

Name	Age	Enlisted	Residence	Unit	Captured	Date and Cause of Death
Rackley, Hardy Private	Unk	5/16/1862, Warsaw, North Carolina	Sampson County, North Carolina	Co. C, 5th North Carolina Cavalry	7/12/1863, Hagerstown, Pennsylvania	Died of Unknown Causes, 1/20/1864
Radford, Calvin Private Not Listed On Monument	24	5/6/1864, Quitman, Georgia	Brooks County, Georgia	Co. E, 1st Georgia Infantry	12/13/1864, Fort McAllister, Georgia	Died of Chronic Diarrhea and General Debility, 5/21/1865
Rafer, Calvin Private	Unk	Unknown	Unknown	Co. A, 35th North Carolina Infantry	Unknown	Unable to Locate

Name	Age	Enlisted	Residence	Unit	Captured	Date and Cause of Death
Ragsdale, William Private	Unk	5/14/1862, Boonesville, Mississippi	Jacinto, Mississippi, Farmer	Co. E, 42nd Mississippi Infantry	7/14/1863, Falling Waters, Maryland	Died of Unknown Causes, 9/28/1863
Rainwater, P. J. Private	Unk	3/1/1863, Coosahatchie, South Carolina	Beaufort District, South Carolina	Co. G, 27th South Carolina Infantry	6/24/1864, Near Petersburg, Virginia	Died of Unknown Causes, 7/19/1864
Rambo, James Sergeant	Unk	5/6/1864, Quitman, Georgia	Brooks County, Georgia	Co. E, 1st Georgia Infantry Reserves	12/13/1864, Fort McAllister, Georgia	Died of Unknown Causes, 2/13/1865
Rambo, Thomas M. Corporal	26	6/10/1861, Athens, Alabama	Limestone County, Alabama	Co. H, 9th Alabama Infantry	7/1/1863, Gettysburg, Pennsylvania	Died of Chronic Diarrhea, 2/4/1864
Rampy, J. P. Private	21	9/3/1861, Camp Butler, South Carolina	Unknown	Co. H, 14th South Carolina Infantry	8/1/1863, Brandy Station, Virginia	Died of Congestive, Remittent Fever, 1/13/1865
Rampey, J. R. Private	Unk	12/28/1861, Camp Hampton, South Carolina	Lancaster County, South Carolina	Co. F, Holcombe's Legion South Carolina Infantry	3/8/1864, Jarrett's Depot, Virginia	Died of Disease, 7/29/1864
Ramsey, James A. Private	21	9/9/1861, Camp Clark, North Carolina, Volunteer	Iredell County, North Carolina	Co. B, 2nd North Carolina Cavalry	4/3/1865, Amelia Court House, Virginia	Died of Acute Diarrhea, 6/1/1865
Ramsey, E. N. See: Ramsey, Jesse H.				Co. D, 24th Virginia Infantry		
Ramsey, Jesse H. Private	Unk	3/15/1863, Rocky Mount, Franklin County, Virginia	Franklin County, Virginia	Co. D, 24th Virginia Infantry	7/3/1863, Gettysburg, Pennsylvania	Died of Chronic Diarrhea, 1/17/1864
Ramsey, Warren Private	Unk	6/20/1861, Clarksville, Virginia	Mecklenburg County, North Carolina	Co. G, 14th Virginia Infantry	7/3/1863, Gettysburg, Pennsylvania	Died of Unknown Causes, 1/19/1864

Name	Age	Enlisted	Residence	Unit	Captured	Date and Cause of Death
Randolph, Matthew F. Private Not Listed On Monument	23	2/14/1862, Camp Price, Virginia, Volunteer	Green County, North Carolina	Co. A, 3rd North Carolina Infantry	5/12/1864, Spotsylvania Court House, Virginia	Died of Unknown Causes, 7/11/1864
Raney, James R. 1st Sergeant	27	5/20/1861, Lewisburg, North Carolina	Franklin County, North Carolina	Co. G, 15th North Carolina Infantry	10/14/1863, Bristoe Station, Virginia	Died of Acute Dysentery, 8/25/1864
Rankin, George W. Private	Unk	1/7/1862, Camp Hampton, South Carolina	Lancaster County, South Carolina	Co. H, Holcombe's Legion South Carolina Infantry	4/1/1865, Five Forks, Virginia	Died of Chronic Diarrhea, 4/23/1865
Raper, Calvin Private Not Listed On Monument	33	5/2/1862, Wilson County, North Carolina, Volunteer	Wilson County, North Carolina, Farmer	Co. B, 55th North Carolina Infantry	7/1/1863, Gettysburg, Pennsylvania	Died of Unknown Causes, 2/4/1864
Rasbury, John A. Private	Unk	1/13/1864, Kenansville, North Carolina	Duplin County, North Carolina	Co. F, 7th Confederate Cavalry	1/28/1864, Smith's Mill, Onslow County, North Carolina	Died of Pneumonia, 3/20/1865
Rash, Asa Private	21	10/15/1862, Wilkes County, North Carolina, Conscript	Wilkes County, North Carolina	Co. B, 55th North Carolina Infantry	7/1/1863, Gettysburg, Pennsylvania	Died of Unknown Causes, 11/4/1863
Rast, Thomas F. Private	Unk	4/13/1863, Orangeburg, South Carolina	Orangeburg District, South Carolina	Co. B, 20th South Carolina Infantry	10/19/1864, Cedar Creek or Strasburg, Virginia	Died of Pneumonia, 2/23/1865
Ratcliff, C. A. Private	Unk	Unknown	unknown	Co. L, 2nd Georgia Infantry	Unknown	Unable to Locate
Ray, J. C. Private	24	8/6/1861, Martin's Depot, South Carolina	Sawrens District, South Carolina	Co. A, 13th South Carolina Infantry	7/14/1863, Falling Waters, Maryland	Died of Unknown Causes, 9/28/1863

Name	Age	Enlisted	Residence	Unit	Captured	Date and Cause of Death
Ray, James Private	20	5/18/1861, Dover, Tennessee	Stewart County, Tennessee	Co. E, 14th Tennessee Infantry	7/14/1863, Falling Waters, Maryland	Died of Chronic Diarrhea, 3/10/1864
Ray, Ransom Private Not Listed On Monument	Unk	8/5/1862, Notasulga, Alabama	Lee County, Alabama	Co. L, 6th Alabama Infantry	5/6/1864, Spotsylvania Court House, Virginia	Died of Dysentery, 7/9/1864
Raysor, J. M. Private	Unk	2/22/1862, Pocotaligo, South Carolina	Jasper County, South Carolina	Co. G, 7th South Carolina Cavalry	11/10/1863, Spanish Wells, Virginia	Died of Typhoid Fever, 12/25/1864
Read, J. W. Private	Unk	Unknown	Unknown	Co. L, 2nd Georgia Infantry	9/8/1863, Place Unknown	Died of Typhoid Fever, 11/9/1863
Reamy, Robert G. Private Not Listed On Monument	26	3/18/1862, Montrose, Virginia	Westmoreland County, Virginia	Co. A, 15th Virginia Cavalry	9/14/1863, Near Culpepper, Virginia	Died of Diphtheria, 11/14/1863
Reamey, Robert L. Private	Unk	3/7/1862, Fort Lowry, Virginia	Unknown	Co. E, 55th Virginia Infantry	7/14/1863, Falling Waters, Maryland	Died of Chronic Dysentery, 9/20/1863
Reardon, Drury W. Private	24	8/16/1861, Fayetteville, North Carolina, Volunteer	Cumberland County, North Carolina	Co. D, 2nd North Carolina Cavalry	7/3/1863, Gettysburg, Pennsylvania	Died of Chronic Diarrhea, 2/15/1865
Reaves, George D. Private	Unk	10/15/1864, Richmond, Virginia	Henrico County, Virginia	Co. C, 59th Virginia Infantry	4/6/1865, Farmville, Virginia	Died of Chronic Diarrhea, 5/20/1865
Rector, Caleb C. Corporal	Unk	7/24 1861, Union, Virginia	Floyd County, Virginia	Co. A, 6th Virginia Cavalry	6/11/1864, Louisa Court House, Virginia	Died of Unknown Causes, 8/16/1864

Name	Age	Enlisted	Residence	Unit	Captured	Date and Cause of Death
Redd, John W. Private	25	5/7/1861, New Prospect, Virginia	King and Queen County, Virginia, Farmer	Co. C, 26th Virginia Infantry	6/16/1864, Near Petersburg, Virginia	Died of Unknown Causes, 8/7/1864
Reddick, Julius A. Private	19	5/7/1863, Camp Holmes, North Carolina, Conscript	Wake County, North Carolina	Co. D, 7th North Carolina Infantry	8/25/60 1863, Shepherdstown, Virginia	Died of Acute Rheumatism and Chronic Diarrhea, 12/5/1863
Redman, W. Sergeant	19	3/20/1861, Iredell County, North Carolina	Iredell County, North Carolina, Farmer	Co. H, 54th North Carolina Infantry	11/7/1863, Rappahannock, Virginia	Died of Unknown Causes, 7/24/1864
Redman, William Corporal	37	8/1/1861, Camp Boone, Kentucky	Unknown	Co. I, 3rd Kentucky Mounted Infantry	5/16/1861, Champion Hill, Mississippi	Died of Typhoid Fever, 3/11/1863
Redwine, William R. Private	23	7/1/1861, Salisbury, North Carolina	Rowan County, North Carolina, Farmer	Co. F, 7th North Carolina Infantry	5/24/1864, North Anna, Virginia	Died of Chronic Diarrhea, 10/19/1864
Reece, Jonathan Private	27	9/20/1862, Haynesville, Greene County, Tennessee	Greene County, Tennessee	Co. C, 60th Tennessee Mounted Infantry	5/17/1863, Big Black Bridge, Near Vicksburg, Mississippi	Died of Unknown Causes, 10/23/1864
Reed, Thomas Corporal Not Listed On Monument	Unk	5/17/1861, Nashville, Tennessee	Davidson County, Tennessee	Co. A, 3rd Tennessee Infantry	5/17/1863, Raymond, Mississippi	Died of Smallpox, 1/31/1864
Reed, W. H. Private	Unk	Unknown	Unknown	Co. K, 26th Alabama Infantry	Unknown	Date and Cause of Death Unknown
Reed, William Private	Unk	11/10/1863, Dublin, Virginia	Pulaski County, Virginia	Co. A, 8th Virginia Infantry	4/6/1865, Farmville, Virginia	Died of Chronic Dysentery, 6/12/1865
Reel, Stanopher Private	Unk	7/15/1862, Hendersonville North Carolina	Henderson County, North Carolina	Co. D, 6th North Carolina Cavalry	6/22/1864, Jackson's Mills, North Carolina	Died of Pneumonia, 3/21/1865

Name	Age	Enlisted	Residence	Unit	Captured	Date and Cause of Death
Reese, Aaron Private	Unk	7/15/1862, Brevard, North Carolina	Transylvania County, North Carolina	Co. C, 6th North Carolina Cavalry	3/17/1865, Near Kinston, North Carolina	Died of Intermittent Fever, 6/8/1865
Reese, G. Private See: Neese, Godfrey				Co. G, 27th South Carolina Infantry		
Reeves, Jeremiah Harrison B. Private	Unk	7/8/1861. Griffin, Georgia	Upson County, Georgia	Co. D, 13th Georgia Infantry	7/5/1863, Gettysburg, Pennsylvania	Died of Chronic Diarrhea, 12/2/1863
Reeves, Marshall Private Not Listed On Monument	Unk	Unknown	Unknown	Morgan's Scouts, Confederate States Army	5/4/1863, Clinton County, Kentucky	Died of Unknown Causes, 11/19/1863
Reeves, N. A. Private	Unk	Unknown	Unknown	Morgan's Kentucky Scouts	Unknown	Unable to Locate
Reeves W. J. Private	Unk	Unknown	Unknown	Co. F, 41st Virginia Infantry	Unknown	Unable to Locate
Reeves, William J. Private	Unk	3/4/1862, Griffin, Georgia	Spalding County, Georgia	Co. E, 44th Georgia Infantry	7/3/1863, Gettysburg, Pennsylvania	Died of Smallpox, 12/25/1863
Register, Noel P. Private	Unk	9/18/1862, Pike County, Alabama	Pike County, Alabama	Co. B, 3rd Alabama Infantry	9/19/1864, Winchester, Virginia	Died of Typhoid Fever, 1/14/1865
Register, Robert M. Private	Unk	5/3/1862, Dublin, Georgia	Laurens County, Georgia	Co. H, 14th Georgia Infantry	6/29/1863. Hagerstown, Pennsylvania	Died of Unknown Causes, 11/26/1863

Name	Age	Enlisted	Residence	Unit	Captured	Date and Cause of Death
Rehburg, William Corporal	Unk	5/3/1862, Bainbridge, Georgia	Decatur County, Georgia	Co. A, 59th Georgia Infantry	8/14/1863, Deep Bottom, Virginia	Died of Scurvy, 3/13/1865
Reid, J. C. Private	Unk	Unknown	Unknown	Co. A, 3rd Tennessee Infantry	Unknown	Unable to Locate
Reid, Marcus R. Private	Unk	Unknown	Unknown	Co. E, 51st Alabama Infantry	10/7/1863, Farmington, Tennessee	Died of Unknown Causes, 3/28/1864
Reid, Robert E. Private	Unk	8/26/1864, Leetown, Virginia	Frederick County, Virginia	Co. C, 26th Virginia Infantry	9/19/1864, Winchester, Virginia	Died of Acute Diarrhea, 10/28/1864
Renn, James H. Corporal	28	7/30/1861, Henderson, North Carolina	Warren County, North Carolina, Farmer	Co. D, 8th North Carolina Infantry	9/30/1864, Fort Harrison, Virginia	Died of Acute Dysentery, 2/15/1865
Renfroe, David C. Corporal	26	4/26/1861, Talbotton, Georgia	Talbot County, Georgia	Co. A, 4th Georgia Infantry	5/6/1864, Wilderness, Virginia, Wounded	Died of Unknown Causes, 7/20/1864
Repass, Gordon Private	Unk	Unknown	Unknown	Co. K, 1st Virginia Infantry	Unknown	Unable to Locate
Repass, Richard F. Private	20	5/10/1861, Washington, North Carolina, Volunteer	Beaufort County, North Carolina	Co. I, 3rd North Carolina Infantry	2/10/1864, Near Washington, North Carolina	Died of Nostalgia, 10/28/1864
Revels, John J. Private	Unk	11/23/1864, Columbia, South Carolina	York District, South Carolina	Co. G, 18th South Carolina Infantry	3/25/1865, Fort Stedman, Near Petersburg, Virginia	Died of Measles, 5/26/1865
Reynolds, James W. Sergeant	20	12/28/1861, Springfield, Greene County, Missouri	Springfield, Greene County, Missouri Farmer	Co. F, 1st Missouri Cavalry	5/17/1863, Big Black Bridge, Near Vicksburg, Mississippi	Died of Chronic Diarrhea and Irritation of the Bladder, 1/27/1864

Name	Age	Enlisted	Residence	Unit	Captured	Date and Cause of Death
Reynolds, Joseph P. Private	27	5/10/1861, Jackson's River, Virginia	Alleghany County, Virginia, Farmer	Co. C, 27th Virginia Infantry	7/3/1863, Gettysburg, Pennsylvania	Died of Smallpox, 11/19/1863
Reynolds, John F. Private	Unk	4/7/1864, Dublin, Virginia	Craig County, Virginia	Co. I, 22nd Virginia Infantry	9/19/1864, Winchester, Virginia	Died of Acute Dysentery, 1/12/1865
Rheinaman, Henry Private Not Listed On Monument	19	6/1/1861, Corinth, Mississippi	Alcorn County, Mississippi	Co. I, 16th Mississippi Infantry	9/1/1863, U. S. Ford, Virginia	Died of Unknown Causes, 7/7/1864
Rheinhardt, John W. Private	Unk	10/11/1864, Camp Holmes, North Carolina	Wake County, North Carolina	Co. K, 37th North Carolina Infantry	4/1/1865, Petersburg, Virginia	Died of Pneumonia, 4/20/1865
Rhew, John W. Private	Unk	2/24/1862, Hillsboro, North Carolina, Volunteer	Orange County, North Carolina	Co. K, 2nd North Carolina Cavalry	4/3/1865, Aberdeen Church, Virginia	Died of Acute Diarrhea, 6/8/1865
Rhodes, Claudius Jasper Private	25	5/1/1861, Durham, Orange County, North Carolina, Volunteer	Orange County, North Carolina	Co. C, 6th North Carolina Infantry	2/6/1865, Near Petersburg, Virginia	Died of Consumption, 4/12/1865
Rhodes, John Private	Unk	9/15/1863, Camp Vance, North Carolina	Henderson County, North Carolina	Co. A, 25th North Carolina Infantry	3/25/1865, Fort Stedman, Near Petersburg, Virginia	Died of Measles, 6/10/1865
Rice, Francis W. Private	Unk	8/11/1863, Richmond, Virginia	Henrico County, Virginia	Co. D, 25th Battalion Virginia Infantry	4/6/1865, Farmville, Virginia	Died of Typhoid Fever, 6/11/1865
Rice, S. W. Private	Unk	7/23/1862, Bristol, Tennessee	Sullivan County, Tennessee	Captain Price's Co. Virginia Light Artillery	5/9/1864, Caroline County, Virginia	Died of Unknown Causes, 9/15/1864
Richards, Thomas W. Private	Unk	9/18/1863, Montgomery County, Alabama	Montgomery County, Alabama	Co. B, Love Battalion Alabama Infantry	6/10/1864, Spotsylvania, Virginia	Died of Unknown Causes, 9/10/1864

Name	Age	Enlisted	Residence	Unit	Captured	Date and Cause of Death
Richardson, Jesse Lieutenant	Unk	3/4 1862, Cleveland, Georgia	White County, Georgia	Co. B, 52nd Georgia Infantry	5/17/1863, Champion Hill, Tennessee	Died of Chronic Diarrhea, 5/23/1864
Richardson, Joseph Private	26	11/11/1863, Ashe County, North Carolina, Conscript	Ashe County, North Carolina	Co. H, 52nd North Carolina Infantry	7/14/1863, Falling Waters, Maryland	Died of Chronic Diarrhea, 4/5/1864
Richardson, Ruffin B. Private	21	7/10/1861, Halifax County, North Carolina, Volunteer	Johnston County, North Carolina	Co. C, 5th North Carolina Infantry	7/2/1863, Gettysburg, Pennsylvania	Died of Smallpox, 11/29/1863
Richardson, S. F. Private	Unk	5/13/1862, Laurens, South Carolina	Laurens County, South Carolina	Co. A, 3rd South Carolina Infantry	5/23/1864, North Anna River, Virginia	Died of Unknown Causes, 7/20/1864
Richardson, William Private	Unk	9/26/1862, Marion, South Carolina	Marion District, South Carolina	Captain Gregg's South Carolina Light Artillery	4/2/1865, Petersburg, Virginia	Died of Chronic Diarrhea, 4/21/1865
Richardson, William J. Private	29	3/10/1862, Richmond, Virginia	Richmond County, Virginia	Co. H, 23rd Virginia Infantry	4/6/1863, Harpers Farm, Virginia	Died of Typhoid Fever, 6/17/1865
Richie, Charles Private	28	5/29/1861, Charlotte, North Carolina, Volunteer	Mecklenburg County, North Carolina	Co. G, 6th North Carolina Infantry	7/3/1863, Gettysburg, Pennsylvania	Died of Erysipelas of Face, 12/12/1863
Ricks, John E. Private	Unk	4/1/1864, Camp Terrell, Virginia	Unknown	Co. H, 32nd North Carolina Infantry	5/10/1864, Wilderness, Virginia	Died of Unknown Causes, 8/5/1864
Riddlemoser, David Private	Unk	10/2/1862, Winchester, Virginia	Frederick County, Virginia	Co. D, 2nd Battalion Maryland Infantry	7/4/1863, Gettysburg, Pennsylvania	Died of Scurvy, 4/19/1864
Ridgeway, Abner C. Private	46	5/14/1862, Granada, Mississippi	Senatobia, South Carolina, Farmer	Co. B, 42nd Mississippi Infantry	7/5/1863, Greencastle, Pennsylvania, Wounded Right Thigh and Leg	Died of Wounds, 1/13/1864

Name	Age	Enlisted	Residence	Unit	Captured	Date and Cause of Death
Ridout, David C. Private	35	3/27/1862, Hicksford, Virginia, Conscript	Greensville County, Virginia	Co. F 12th Virginia Infantry	8/19/1864, Near Petersburg, Virginia, Wounded	Died of Unknown Causes, 1/8/1865
Ridout, William D. Private Not Listed On Monument	Unk	6/6/1861, Hicksford, Virginia	Greensville County, Virginia	Co. F, 12th Virginia Infantry	7/2/1863, Gettysburg, Pennsylvania	Died of Unknown Causes, 1/8/1864
Rieves, Henry Private	24	6/13/1861, Statesville, North Carolina, Volunteer	Iredell County, North Carolina	Co. H, 4th North Carolina Infantry	7/3/1863, Gettysburg, Pennsylvania	Died of Chronic Diarrhea, 10/26/1863
Riggs, Daniel Private	34	8/17/1862, Wake County, North Carolina, Conscript	Wake County, North Carolina	Co. I, 18th North Carolina Infantry	7/3/1863, Gettysburg, Pennsylvania	Died of Scurvy, 10/28/1863
Riggs, James Private	Unk	3/5/1862, S. Plains, Tennessee	Unknown	Co. H, 60th Tennessee Mounted Infantry	5/17/1863, Big Black, Mississippi	Died of Chronic Diarrhea, 2/21/1864
Rigsby, Robert H. Sergeant	Unk	6/3/1861, Lacy's Store, Goochland, Virginia	Goochland County, Virginia	Co. B, 44th Virginia Infantry	5/12/1864, Spotsylvania Courthouse, Virginia	Died of Unknown Causes, 7/28/1864
Riley, Henry Private	25	8/12/1862, Knoxville, Tennessee	Mill Springs, Kentucky	Co. C, 2nd Tennessee Cavalry	5/30/1863, Mill Springs, Kentucky	Died of Chronic Diarrhea, 4/27/1864
Rimmer, Wiley P. Private	Unk	5/1/1862, Smyth County, Virginia	Smyth County, Virginia	Co. E, 23rd Battalion Virginia Infantry	10/19/1864, Cedar Creek or Strasburg, Virginia	Died of Chronic Diarrhea, 1/20/1865
Rinica, Andrew Private	Unk	6/1/1861, Luray, Page County, Virginia	Page County, Virginia	Co. H, 33rd Virginia Infantry	7/6/1863, Fayetteville, Virginia	Died of Abscess of Throat, 12/6/1863
Ripps, C. Private	Unk	Unknown	Unknown	Co. I, 37th North Carolina Infantry	Unknown	Unable to Locate

Name	Age	Enlisted	Residence	Unit	Captured	Date and Cause of Death
Rippy, Calvin Private Not Listed On Monument	24	7/4/1862, Salisbury, North Carolina	Alamance County, North Carolina	Co. I, 57th North Carolina Infantry	7/5/1863, Gettysburg, Pennsylvania	Died of Chronic Diarrhea, 12/28/1863
Ritchey, Pleasant Private Not Listed On Monument	31	8/8/1862, Stanley County, North Carolina, Conscript	Stanley County, North Carolina, Farmer	Co. F, 5th North Carolina Infantry	5/12/1864, Spotsylvania Court House, Virginia	Died of Unknown Causes, 7/8/1864
Ritchie, George W. Private Not Listed On Monument	26	7/4/1862, Rowan County, North Carolina	Rowan County, North Carolina	Co. A, 57th North Carolina Infantry	11/7/1863, Rappahannock Station, Virginia	Died of Unknown Causes, 12/15/1863
Ritchie, William N. Private	29	7/7/1862, Concord, North Carolina	Cabarrus County, North Carolina, Farmer	Co. A, 57th North Carolina Infantry	7/5/1863, Gettysburg, Pennsylvania	Died of Unknown Causes, 3/21/1864
Roach, James R. Private	Unk	7/15/1862, Hendersonville North Carolina	Henderson County, North Carolina	Co. D, 6th North Carolina Cavalry	Jackson's Mills, Wise Forks, North Carolina	Died of Scurvy, 2/26/1865
Roach, Thomas N. Private	Unk	9/12/1862, Columbus, Kentucky	Hickman County, Kentucky	Co. A, 7th Kentucky Mounted Infantry	5/16/1863, Baker's Creek, Champion Hill, Tennessee	Died of Unknown Causes, 1/18/1864
Robbins, John B. Private	27	3/3/1862, Rutherford County, North Carolina, Volunteer	Rutherford County, North Carolina, Mechanic	Co. I, 56th North Carolina Infantry	3/25/1865, Fort Stedman, Near Petersburg, Virginia	Died of Chronic Dysentery, 6/15/1865
Robbins, J. S. Seaman	Unk	Unknown	Unknown	Co. H, CSS Palmetto	Unknown	Unable to Locate
Robbins, John Private	Unk	1/1/1863, Camp Catlett, Virginia	Unknown	Co. D, 9th Virginia Cavalry	8/16/1863, Rappahannock, Virginia	Died of Unknown Causes, 12/23/1863

Name	Age	Enlisted	Residence	Unit	Captured	Date and Cause of Death
Robins, John W. Private	Unk	Unknown	Unknown	Co. C, 1st Virginia Reserves	Unknown	Unable to Locate
Robinson, Thomas James Private	38	3/1/1862, Heathsville, Virginia	Unknown, Farmer	Co. F, 40th Virginia Infantry	7/14/1863, Falling Waters, Maryland	Died of Unknown Causes, 2/2/1864
Roberson, James A. Private	30	9/22/1862, Morganton, North Carolina, Conscript	Burke County, North Carolina	Co. E, 6th North Carolina Infantry	11/7/1863, Rappahannock, Virginia	Died of Chronic Diarrhea, 2/16/1865
Robeson, John L. Private	Unk	3/5/1864, Milford, North Carolina	Unknown	Co. I, 52nd North Carolina Infantry	4/2/1865, Petersburg, Virginia	Died of Chronic Diarrhea, 5/28/1865
Roberts, James Private	Unk	8/13/1863. Washington County, Virginia	Washington County, Virginia	Co. C, 22nd Virginia Cavalry	9/24/1864, Martinsburg, Virginia	Died of Measles, 4/14/1865
Roberts, John M. Sergeant Not Listed On Monument	Unk	3/4/1862, Macon, Georgia	Bibb County, Georgia	Co. A, 45th Georgia Infantry	4/3/1865, Petersburg, Virginia	Died of Double Pneumonia, 6/1/1865
Roberts, John Marion Private	24	12/27/1861, Springfield, Green County, Missouri	Cape Girardeau, Missouri, farmer	Co. H, 1st Missouri Cavalry	5/17/1863, Big Black Bridge, Near Vicksburg, Mississippi	Died of Unknown Causes, 10/?/1863
Roberts, John N. Sergeant	19	5/1/1861, Dallas, Gaston County, North Carolina	Gaston County, North Carolina	Co. M, 16th North Carolina Infantry	7/3/1863, Gettysburg, Pennsylvania	Died of Unknown Causes, 12/25/1863
Roberts, R. R. Private	Unk	5/11/1861, New Orleans, Louisiana	Orleans Parish, Louisiana	Co. C, 2nd Louisiana Infantry	5/12/1864, Wilderness, Virginia	Died of Unknown Causes, 8/24/1864
Roberts, Stephen Private	Unk	5/19/1862, Fredericksburg Virginia	Spotsylvania County, Virginia	Co. E, 16th Georgia Infantry	6/1/1864, Cold Harbor, Virginia	Died of Unknown Causes, 10/22/1864

Name	Age	Enlisted	Residence	Unit	Captured	Date and Cause of Death
Roberts, T. A. Private	Unk	Unknown	Unknown	Co. C, 11th Georgia Infantry	Unknown	Unable to Locate
Roberts Wilson A. Private	38	2/12/1862, Coosawhatchie Dawson's Bluff, South Carolina	Jasper County, South Carolina, Blacksmith	Co. F, 11th South Carolina Infantry	1/15/1865, Fort Fisher, North Carolina	Died of Consumption, 6/4/1865
Robertson, Isaac K. Private	Unk	4/22/1862, Marietta, Cobb County, Georgia	Cobb County, Georgia	Co. M, Phillips Georgia Legion Infantry	7/3/1863, Gettysburg, Pennsylvania	Died of Unknown Causes, 11/4/1864
Robertson, James W. Private	Unk	5/14/1861, Rome, Floyd County, Georgia	Floyd County, Georgia	Co. E, 8th Georgia Infantry	7/2/1863, Gettysburg, Pennsylvania	Died of Unknown Causes, 5/21/1864
Robertson, John H. Sergeant	Unk	Unknown	Unknown	Confederate States Navy, Naval Battalion	Unknown	Unable to Locate
Robins, John Private	Unk	1/1/1863, Camp Catlett, Virginia, Substitute	Unknown	Co. C, 9th Virginia Cavalry	8/13/1863, Rappahannock River, Virginia	Died of Unknown Causes, 12/23/1863
Robertson, Thomas H. Private	Unk	5/3/1862, Newton County, Georgia	Newton County, Georgia	Co. E, 53rd Georgia Infantry	5/6/1864, Mine Run, Virginia	Died of Unknown Causes, 6/26/1864
Robinson, Andrew J. Sergeant	Unk	7/7/1862, Newton, North Carolina	Catawba County, North Carolina	Co. E, 57th North Carolina Infantry	11/7/1863, Rappahannock Station, Virginia	Died of Chronic Dysentery, 1/28/1865
Robinson, D. S. Private	38	3/31/1863, Newton County, North Carolina, Volunteer	Newton County, North Carolina	Co. E, 32nd North Carolina Infantry	7/4/1863, South Mountain, Maryland	Died of Scurvy, 12/25/1863
Robinson, Gale C. Sergeant	Unk	Unknown	Unknown	Co. C, 35th Alabama Infantry	12/17/1864, Columbia, Tennessee, Gunshot Wound	Died of Chronic Diarrhea, 6/14/1865

Name	Age	Enlisted	Residence	Unit	Captured	Date and Cause of Death
Robinson, J. W. See: Robertson, James W.				Co. E, 8th Georgia Infantry		
Robinson, John W. Private	Unk	4/21/1862, Culpepper Court House, Virginia	Culpepper County, Virginia	Co. G, 2nd Virginia Cavalry	7/3/1863, Gettysburg, Pennsylvania	Died of Chronic Diarrhea, 12/25/1863
Robinson, Melbourn Private	Unk	9/12/1862, Place Unknown	Unknown	Co. A, 6th Virginia Cavalry	5/11/1864, Yellow Tavern, Henrico County, Virginia	Died of Unknown Causes, 7/22/1864
Robinson, Miles B. Private	41	2/7/1862, Monroe, North Carolina, Volunteer	Union County, North Carolina, Farmer	Co. B, 43rd North Carolina Infantry	3/25/1865, Fort Stedman, Near Petersburg, Virginia	Died of Chronic Diarrhea, 5/12/1865
Robinson, Nathaniel G. R. Private	Unk	5/14/1862, Sandersville, Georgia	Washington County, Georgia	Co. E, 12th Battalion Georgia Light Artillery	3/25/1865, Fort Stedman, Near Petersburg, Virginia	Died of Pneumonia, 5/27/1865
Robinson, Samuel S. Private	30	9/25/1861, Burnsville, North Carolina, Volunteer	Yancey County, North Carolina	Co. C, 16th North Carolina Infantry	5/25/1864, North Anna, Virginia	Died of Unknown Causes, 8/24/1864
Robinson, T. H. See: Robertson, Thomas H.				Co. E, 53rd Georgia Infantry		
Robinson, Thomas James Private Not Listed On Monument	38	3/1/1862, Heathsville, Virginia	Unknown, Farmer	Co. F, 40th Virginia Infantry	7/14/1863, Falling Waters, Maryland	Died of Unknown Causes, 2/2/1864
Robinson, William S. B. Private	Unk	11/18/1861, Columbia, South Carolina	Richland County, South Carolina	Co. A, 18th South Carolina Infantry	7/30/1864, Petersburg, Virginia	Died of Chronic Diarrhea, 10/28/1864

Name	Age	Enlisted	Residence	Unit	Captured	Date and Cause of Death
Robison, J. H. Private	Unk	5/15/1862, Newman, Georgia	Coweta County, Georgia	Co. F, Phillips Legion, Georgia Cavalry	8/1/1863, Brandy Station, Virginia	Died of Unknown Causes, 11/4/1863
Robuck, P. C. Private	Unk	5/16/1862, Waynesville, Georgia	Brantley County, Georgia	Co. K, 4th Georgia Cavalry	12/4/1864, Waynesville, Georgia	Died of Congestive Fever, 2/26/1865
Rodgers, D. F. See: Rogers, David F.				Co. K, 51st North Carolina Infantry		
Rodgers, John H. See: Rogers, John H.				Co. G, 22nd North Carolina Infantry		
Roe, John H. See: Rowe, John H.				45th Georgia Infantry		
Roe, William H. Private	Unk	11/20/1863, Camp Lee, Virginia	Prince Edward County, Virginia	Co. A, 40th Virginia Infantry	4/7/1865, Richmond, Virginia	Died of Congestive Chill, 4/20/1865
Rogers, A. B. Corporal	26	10/22/1861, Red Springs, Tennessee	Unknown	Co. E, 30th Tennessee Infantry	5/12/1863, Raymond, Mississippi	Died of Typhoid Fever, 10/18/1863
Rogers, Albert Private	20	9/27/1862, Jonesboro, Tennessee	Washington County, Tennessee	Co. F, 60th Tennessee Mounted Infantry	5/17/1863, Big Black Bridge, Near Vicksburg, Mississippi	Died of Chronic Diarrhea, 1/26/1864
Rogers, David F. Private	21	3/29/1862, Warsaw, North Carolina	Sampson County, North Carolina, Farmer	Co. K, 51st North Carolina Infantry	8/19/1864, Globe Tavern, Near Weldon Railroad, Virginia	Died of Acute Dysentery, 3/24/1865
Rogers, John H. Private	Unk	3/1/1864, Camp Holmes, North Carolina	Wake County, North Carolina	Co. G, 22nd North Carolina Infantry	5/23/1864, North Anna, Virginia	Died of Measles, 7/27/1864
Rogers, John J. Private	29	7/18/1861, Pittsboro, North Carolina, Volunteer	Chatham County, North Carolina	Co. C, 2nd North Carolina Cavalry	4/3/1865, Aberdeen, Ohio	Died of Disease of Heart, 5/8/1865

Name	Age	Enlisted	Residence	Unit	Captured	Date and Cause of Death
Rogers, John R. Corporal	21	7/8/1862, Salisbury, North Carolina	Alamance County, North Carolina	Co. I, 57th North Carolina Infantry	3/25/1865, Fort Stedman, Near Petersburg, Virginia	Died of Rubeola (measles), 6/8/1865
Rogers, John T. Private	22	5/10/1861, Newcastle, Virginia	Craig County, Virginia, Stage Driver	Co. C, 28th Virginia Infantry	7/3/1863, Gettysburg, Pennsylvania	Died of Chronic Diarrhea, 2/4/1864
Rogers, John W. Private	Unk	4/26/1863, Gatesville, North Carolina, Volunteer	Gates County, North Carolina	Co. D, 2nd North Carolina Cavalry	11/28/1864, Mine Run, Virginia	Died of Unknown Causes, 6/2/1865
Rogers, Josiah Private	Unk	7/11/1863, Columbia, South Carolina, Conscript	Richland County, South Carolina	Co. K, 1st South Carolina Infantry	4/3/1865, Richmond, Virginia	Died of Inflammation of Brain, 6/21/1865
Rogers, R. S. Private	Unk	Unknown	Unknown	Co. B, 11th Georgia Infantry	Unknown	Died of Erysipilas, 11/1/1863
Rogers, Thomas N. Private	Unk	2/27/1862, Camp Bartow, Milton County, Georgia	Milton County, Georgia	Co. B, 38th Georgia Infantry	5/22/1864, North Anna, Virginia	Died of Unknown Causes, 8/25/1865
Rollins, Thomas H. Private	Unk	Unknown	Unknown	Co. C, Cobb's Legion Georgia Infantry	8/26/1863, Armorsville, Virginia	Died of Unknown Causes, 9/16/1864
Rooper, T. L. Private	Unk	4/6/1863, Pickens, South Carolina	Pickens County, South Carolina	Co. D, 37th Battalion Virginia Cavalry	9/23/1863, Cedar Creek or Strasburg, Virginia	Died of Chronic Diarrhea, 3/1/1865
Roper, Amos W. Corporal	22	6/1/1861, Richmond County, North Carolina, Volunteer	Randolph County, North Carolina, Student	Co. F, 18th North Carolina Infantry	5/12/1864, Spotsylvania Court House, Virginia	Died of Unknown Causes, 8/4/1864
Roper, James W. Private	Unk	1/1/1864, Morganton, North Carolina	Burke County, North Carolina	Co. E, 6th North Carolina Cavalry	6/22/1864, Jackson's Mills, Near Kinston, North Carolina	Died of Unknown Causes, 8/9/1864

Name	Age	Enlisted	Residence	Unit	Captured	Date and Cause of Death
Rose, John H. Private	25	5/18/1863, Nash County, North Carolina, Volunteer	Nash County, North Carolina	Co. D, 47th North Carolina Infantry	7/14/1863, Falling Waters, Maryland	Died of Chronic Diarrhea, 6/30/1864
Rose, John W. A. Sergeant	23	7/5/1862, Salisbury, North Carolina, Volunteer	Rowan County, North Carolina	Co. C, 57th North Carolina Infantry	7/2/1863, Gettysburg, Pennsylvania	Died of Smallpox, 11/24/1863
Rose, William Quarter Master Sergeant	Unk	Unknown	Unknown	16th Battalion, North Carolina Cavalry	12/1/1864, Stony Creek, Virginia	Died of Unknown Causes, 1/24/1865
Ross, Frederick W. Private	Un k	7/1/1861, Cherokee County, Georgia	Cherokee County, Georgia	Co. D, 14th Georgia Infantry	Unknown	Date and Cause of Death Unknown
Ross, Henry Private	23	6/1/1861, Wilmington, North Carolina, Volunteer	New Hanover County, North Carolina	Co. E, 1st North Carolina Infantry	5/12/1864, Spotsylvania Court House, Virginia	Died of Unknown Causes, 9/16/1864
Ross, Thomas Private	Unk	Unknown	Unknown	Co. H, 36th North Carolina Heavy Artillery	1/15/1865, Fort Fisher, North Carolina	Died of Remittent Fever, 2/11/1865
Ross, William G. Private	Unk	8/1/1861, Grayson County, Virginia	Grayson County, Virginia	Co. E, 30th Virginia Sharp-Shooters	3/2/1865, Waynesboro, Virginia	Date and Cause of Death Unknown
Ross, William T. Private Not Listed On Monument	Unk	4/1/1863, Giles County, Virginia	Giles County, Virginia	Co. A, 30th Virginia Sharp-Shooters	9/19/1864, Winchester, Virginia	Died of Pneumonia, 3/18/1865
Rosselose, J. Private	Unk	Unknown	Unknown	Co. E, 37th Virginia Infantry	Unknown	Unable to Locate
Rosser, Montgomery Private	Unk	9/29/1863, Place Unknown, Conscript	Unknown	Co. E 10th Georgia Infantry	4/6/1865, Burkesville, Virginia	Died of Remittent Fever, 6/9/1865

Name	Age	Enlisted	Residence	Unit	Captured	Date and Cause of Death
Rothrock, J. H. Private	Unk	12/28/1861, Camp Hampton, South Carolina	Lancaster County, South Carolina	Co. F, Holcombe Legion South Carolina Infantry	5/8/1864, Jarrett's Depot, Virginia	Died of Pneumonia, 6/8/1864
Rountree, Merida Malone Sergeant Not Listed On Monument	Unk	5/8/1862, Tennille, Georgia	Washington County, Georgia	Co. D, 59th Georgia Infantry	7/5/1863, Gettysburg, Pennsylvania, Gunshot Wound of Right Thigh	Died of Chronic Diarrhea & Scurvy, 2/5/1865
Rountree, Thomas James Private	Unk	5/21/1861, Camp Cheatham, Tennessee	Hickman County, Tennessee	Co. F, 3rd Tennessee Infantry	5/12/1863, Raymond, Mississippi	Died of Unknown Causes, 2/12/1864
Rouse, Stephen Private	Unk	9/14/1861, Smyth County, Virginia	Smyth County, Virginia	Co. A, 23rd Battalion Virginia Infantry	9/19/1864, Winchester, Virginia	Died of Acute Dysentery, 2/15/1865
Rowe, D. G. Private Not Listed On Monument	Unk	6/20/1863, South Newport, Georgia	McIntosh County, Georgia	Co. B, 20th Georgia Cavalry	12/4/1864, Waynesboro, Macintosh County, Georgia	Died of Intermittent Fever, 7/3/1865
Rowe, John H. Private	Unk	3/4/1862, Milledgeville, Georgia	Baldwin County, Georgia	Co. G, 45th Georgia Infantry	7/14/1863, Falling Waters, Maryland	Died of Chronic Diarrhea, 5/5/1865
Rowell, Richard Private	Unk	6/6/1864, Savannah, Georgia	Stewart County, Georgia	Co. F, 1st Georgia Reserve	12/21/1864, Near Savannah, Georgia	Died of Consumption, 3/12/1865
Rowland, Robert M. Private	34	10/21/1864, Luray, Virginia	Botetourt County, Virginia	Co. C 14th Virginia Cavalry	11/12/1864, Nineveh, Virginia	Died of Unknown Causes, 5/29/1865
Rowland, William J. Private	22	3/4/1862, Johnson County, Georgia	Johnson County, Georgia	Co. F, 48th Georgia Infantry	7/3/1863, Gettysburg, Pennsylvania	Died of Typhoid Fever, 10/24/1863

Name	Age	Enlisted	Residence	Unit	Captured	Date and Cause of Death
Royston, Joseph Sergeant	Unk	10/4/1862, Zollicoffer, Tennessee	Maury County, Tennessee	Co. H, 61st Tennessee Mounted Infantry	5/17/ 1863, Big Black Bridge, Near Vicksburg, Mississippi	Died of Chronic Diarrhea, 11/2/1863
Rudder, John Private	Unk	4/7/1862, Halifax Court House, Virginia, Conscript	Halifax County, Virginia	Co. K, 3rd Virginia Infantry	4/3/1865, Richmond, Virginia	Died of Chronic Diarrhea, 5/12/1865
Ruis, William Private	Unk	4/26/1864, Savannah, Georgia	Stewart County, Georgia	Co. F, 1st Georgia Reserve	12/4/1864, Savannah, Georgia	Died of Chronic Diarrhea, 4/17/1865
Rule, Christian Private	Unk	2/3/1863, Richmond, Virginia	Henrico County, Virginia	Co. H, 2nd Virginia Cavalry	7/3/1863, Gettysburg, Pennsylvania	Died of Chronic Diarrhea & Scurvy, 12/10/1863
Rumage, E. R. Private	Unk	Unknown	Unknown	Co. C, 42nd North Carolina Infantry	3/10/1865, Wise Forks, Near Kinston, North Carolina	Died of Pneumonia, 5/31/1865
Rungan, Henry Private	18	10/1/1862, Newport, Tennessee	Cocke County, Tennessee	Co. I, 60th Tennessee Mounted Infantry	5/17/ 1863, Big Black Bridge, Near Vicksburg, Mississippi	Died of Typhoid Fever, 1/25/1865
Runion, H. See: Rungan, Henry				Co. I, 60th Tennessee Mounted Infantry		
Runyan, J. P. Private	23	5/5/1862, Shelby, North Carolina	Cleveland County, North Carolina	Co. G, 49th North Carolina Infantry	4/1/1865, Five Forks, Virginia	Died of Intermittent Fever, 6/22/1865
Rush, Andrew J. Private	Unk	2/10/1863, Lancaster, South Carolina	Lancaster County, South Carolina	Co. A, 1st South Carolina Infantry	9/7/1863, Morris Island, South Carolina	Died of Unknown Causes, 1/14/1864
Rushing, Jacob Private	Unk	4/1/1862, Franklin County, Mississippi	Unknown, Bridge Guard, Memphis Railroad	Co. D, 33rd Mississippi Infantry	5/16/1863, Champion Hill, Mississippi	Died of Unknown Causes, 2/17/1864
Russ, Edward Private	37	12/3/1862, Fort Fisher, North Carolina, Volunteer	New Hanover County, North Carolina	Co. E, 36th North Carolina Heavy Artillery	1/16/1865, Fort Caswell Hospital, Smithville, North Carolina	Died of Chronic Rheumatism, 6/19/1865

Name	Age	Enlisted	Residence	Unit	Captured	Date and Cause of Death
Russ, Samuel P. Corporal	Unk	3/18/1862, Hoffer's Creek, Virginia	Unknown	Co. D, Richardson's Battalion Virginia Light Artillery	4/2/1865, Hatcher's Run, Virginia	Died of Erysipilas, 5/11/1865
Russell, Calvin L. Private	Unk	8/?/1863, Place Unknown	Unknown	Co. E, Confederate Marine Corps.	1/15/1865, Fort Fisher, North Carolina	Died of Pneumonia, 4/16/1865
Russell, Ebenezer Private	22	11/15/1864, Waynesboro, Mississippi	Waynesboro, Mississippi, Farmer	Co. B, 13th Mississippi Infantry	4/6/1865, Harper's Farm, Virginia	Died of Chronic Diarrhea, 5/31/1865
Russell, Elijah A. Private	23	12/25/1862, Camp Mangum, North Carolina	Montgomery County, North Carolina	Co. K, 34th North Carolina Infantry	6/27/1862, Gaines' Mill, Virginia	Date and Causes of Death Unknown
Russell, Gilbert Sergeant	30	3/1/1862, Montgomery County, North Carolina, Volunteer	Montgomery County, North Carolina, Mechanic	Co. F, 44th North Carolina Infantry	10/27/1864, Near Petersburg, Virginia	Died of Typhoid Fever, 1/9/1865
Russell, William Private	22	3/1/1862, Troy, Montgomery County, North Carolina, Volunteer	Montgomery County, North Carolina, Farmer	Co. F, 44th North Carolina Infantry	10/27/1864, Near Petersburg, Virginia	Died of Chronic Dysentery, 12/20/1864
Rust, T. F. See: Rast, Thomas				Co. B, 20th South Carolina Infantry		
Rutter, B. Private	Unk	Unknown	Unknown	Co. D, 1st Virginia Reserves	Unknown	Unable to Locate
Ryals, William Private	Unk	3/4/1862, Homersville, Georgia	Clinich County, Georgia	Co. G, 50th Georgia Infantry	10/19/1864, Cedar Creek or Strasburg, Virginia	Died of Acute Diarrhea, 6/11/1865
Rydont, W. D. See: Ridout, David C.				Co. F 12th Virginia Infantry		

Name	Age	Enlisted	Residence	Unit	Captured	Date and Cause of Death
Ryland, Robert Private Name Not On Monument	27	4/10/1862, Fort Caswell, North Carolina, Volunteer	Brunswick County, North Carolina	Co. E, 36th North Carolina Heavy Artillery	1/15/1865, Fort Fisher, North Carolina, Wounded Left Lung	Died of Pyaemia From Gunshot Wound, 2/10/1865

Name	Age	Enlisted	Residence	Unit	Captured	Date and Cause of Death
Saint, G. Z. Private	Unk	Unknown	Unknown	Co. L, 59th Georgia Infantry	7/6/1863, Funkstown, Maryland	Died of Unknown Causes, 3/14/1865
Sampson, J. D. Private	Unk	Unknown	Unknown	Co. G, 11th Alabama Infantry	4/3/1865, After General Lee's Surrender, Richmond, Virginia	Died of Chronic Diarrhea, 6/12/1865
Sampson, T. D. Private Not Listed On Monument	Unk	7/3/1862, Calhoun, Georgia	Catoosa County, Georgia	Co. G, 11th Georgia Infantry	4/3/1865, Captured in Richmond Hospital, Virginia	Died of Chronic Diarrhea, 6/12/1865
Sanderford, Luther Private Not Listed On Monument	Unk	7/1/1862, Hertford County, North Carolina, Conscript	Hertford County, North Carolina	Co. H, 33rd North Carolina Infantry	7/14/1863, Falling Waters, Maryland	Died of Chronic Diarrhea, 2/5/1864
Sanders, Allen J. Private	33	3/8/1862, Farmer's Fork, Warsaw, Virginia	Richmond County, Virginia	Co. D, 40th Virginia Infantry	7/14/1863, Falling Waters, Maryland	Died of Unknown Causes, 9/14/1864
Sanders, Joseph F. Private	Unk	1/5/1863, Trousdale, Tennessee	Lawrence County, Tennessee	Co. F, 41st Tennessee Infantry	5/12/1863, Raymond, Mississippi	Died of Smallpox, 2/20/1864
Sanderson, Calvin Prisoners	28	6/25/1861, Duplin County, North Carolina, Volunteer	Duplin County, North Carolina	Co. B, 3rd North Carolina Infantry	7/5/1863, Waterloo, Gettysburg, Pennsylvania	Died of Acute Diarrhea, 12/28/1864

Name	Age	Enlisted	Residence	Unit	Captured	Date and Cause of Death
Sandifer, Levi J. Private	22	4/1/1862, Amite County, Mississippi	Amite County, Mississippi	Co. B, 33rd Mississippi Infantry	5/16/1863, Champion Hill, Tennessee	Died of Chronic Diarrhea, 1/26/1864
Sandridge, William Richard Private	Unk	9/28/1862, White Hall, Virginia, Conscript	Frederick County, Virginia	Co. I, 7th Virginia Infantry	4/6/1865, Harper's Farm, Virginia	Died of Chronic Diarrhea, 5/12/1865
Saniford, Luther See: Sanderford, Luther				Co. H, 33rd North Carolina Infantry		
Sargent, John Private	22	2/27/1861, Verona, Mississippi	Lee County, Mississippi, Farmer	Co. C, 2nd Mississippi Infantry	7/1/1863, Gettysburg, Pennsylvania	Died of Disease, 3/18/1864
Satterfield, Onslow J. Private	Unk	7/12/1861, Jamestown, Virginia	James City County, Virginia	Co. K, 14th Virginia Infantry	7/3/1863, Gettysburg, Pennsylvania	Died of Acute Dysentery, 2/10/1865
Saul, John William Private Not Listed On Monument	Unk	3/1/1864, Rocky Mount, Virginia	Franklin County, Virginia	Co. K, 42nd Virginia Infantry	5/12/1864, Spotsylvania Court House, Virginia	Died of Remittent Fever, 7/5/1864
Saunders, J. S. See: Sanders, Joseph F.				Co. F, 41st Tennessee Infantry		
Saunders, James Seaman	Unk	Unknown	Unknown	Confederate States Navy	Unknown	Unable to Locate
Saunders, John T. Private	Unk	7/10/1861, Sturgeonville, Virginia	Brunswick County, Virginia	Co. E, 56th Virginia Infantry	7/5/1863, Gettysburg, Pennsylvania	Died of Chronic Diarrhea, 1/31/1864
Savage, John H. Sergeant	24	12/17/1862, Richmond, Virginia	Richmond County, Virginia	Co. E, 1st Maryland Cavalry	6/12/1863, Newton, Virginia, Suspicion of Being a Spy	Died of Chronic Diarrhea, 11/5/1863

Name	Age	Enlisted	Residence	Unit	Captured	Date and Cause of Death
Sawyer, E. W. Private	Unk	Unknown	Unknown	Co. E, 66th North Carolina Infantry	8/18/1863, Big Black Bridge, Near Vicksburg, Mississippi	Died of Unknown Causes, 3/26/1864
Sawyers, James A. Private	Unk	10/26/1861, Fayetteville, Arkansas	Washington County, Arkansas	Co. D, 1st Battalion Arkansas Cavalry	5/17/1863, Big Black Bridge, Near Vicksburg, Mississippi	Died of Typhoid Fever, 11/24/1863
Sawyers, John H. Private	Unk	7/30/1861, Marion, Virginia	Smyth County, Virginia	Co. D, 4th Virginia Cavalry	7/3/1863, Gettysburg, Pennsylvania	Died of Smallpox, 11/14/1863
Sayers, J. H. Private See: Sawyers, John H.				Co. D, 4th Virginia Cavalry		
Saylor, J. F. Private	20	9/18/1862, Rheatown, Greene County, Tennessee	Greene County, Tennessee	Co. A, 61st Tennessee Mounted Infantry	5/17/1863, Big Black Bridge, Near Vicksburg, Mississippi	Died of Unknown Causes, 10/?/1863
Scaff, William Private	Unk	11/13/1863, Dublin, Virginia	Pulaski County, Virginia	Co. F, 8th Virginia Infantry	4/6/1865, Farmville, Virginia	Died of Chronic Diarrhea, 6/3/1865
Scarborough, James Private	Unk	6/7/1861, Hawkinsville, Georgia	Pulaski County, Georgia	Co. G, 8th Georgia Infantry	5/6/1864, Wilderness, Virginia	Died of Unknown Causes, 6/30/1864
Scarborough, Miles Private	29	7/17/1862, Wake County, North Carolina	Wake County, North Carolina	Co. I, 55th North Carolina Infantry	7/1/1863, Gettysburg, Pennsylvania	Died of Acute Diarrhea, 10/25/1864
Scarborough, Robert S. Private	Unk	8/13/1862, Prince George Court House, Virginia	Prince George County, Virginia	Co. K, 13th Virginia Cavalry	6/30/1863, Hanover, Pennsylvania	Died of Unknown Causes, 11/15/1863
Scarborough, Thomas B. Private	Unk	11/25/1863, Montgomery, Alabama	Montgomery County, Alabama	Co. G, 6th Alabama Infantry	5/12/1864, Spotsylvania Court House, Virginia	Died of Unknown Causes, 6/24/1864

Name	Age	Enlisted	Residence	Unit	Captured	Date and Cause of Death
Scarlet, S. H. Private	18	8/14/1862, Davidson County, North Carolina, Conscript	Davidson County, North Carolina	Co. G, 48th North Carolina Infantry	10/14/1863, Bristoe Station, Virginia	Died of Unknown Causes, 8/23/1864
Scates, Joel Henry Private	Unk	Unknown	Unknown	Co. I, 53rd Virginia Infantry	4/1/1865, Five Forks, Virginia	Died of Measles, 4/24/1865
Schultz, Henry Private	Unk	2/17/1864, Richmond, Virginia, Conscript	Henrico County, Virginia	Co. K, 14th Virginia Infantry	8/25/1864, Near Hewlett's House, Virginia	Died of Chronic Diarrhea, 2/4/1865
Scogin, John L. Private	Unk	5/9/1862, Dublin, Alabama	Montgomery County, Alabama	Co. C, 60th Alabama Infantry	3/31/1865, Hatcher's Run, Virginia	Died of Unknown Causes, 4/16/1865
Scogin, William H. 2nd Lieutenant	Unk	Unknown	Unknown	Co. E, 15th Alabama Infantry	7/14/1863, Falling Waters, Maryland	Died of Unknown Causes, 9/11/1863
Scott, F. Callaway Sergeant	Unk	5/15/1862, Camp Prichard, Georgia	Unknown	Co. C, Phillips Legion Georgia Infantry	7/2/1863, Gettysburg, Pennsylvania	Died of Unknown Causes, 12/23/1863
Scott, G. W. Private	Unk	12/26/1863, Charleston, South Carolina	Charleston County, South Carolina	Co. I, Holcomb's Legion South Carolina Infantry	5/7/1864, Stony Creek, Virginia	Died of Chronic Diarrhea, 8/1/1864
Scott, George W. Private Not Listed On Monument	Unk	2/20/1863, Columbia, South Carolina	Richland County, South Carolina	Co. E, 7th Battalion South Carolina Infantry	8/21/1864, Globe Tavern, Weldon Railroad, Virginia	Died of Chronic Diarrhea, 4/14/1865
Scott, J. W. C. Private	27	3/20/1862, Homer, Louisiana	Homer, Louisiana, Carpenter	Co. A, 9th Louisiana Infantry	11/7/1863, Rappahannock, Virginia	Died of Smallpox, 1/11/1864
Scott, John H. Private	Unk	10/1/1863, Camp Price, Georgia	Unknown	Co. C, 20th Battalion Georgia Cavalry	5/31/1864, Cold Harbor, Virginia	Died of Gastro-Enteritis & Diarrhea, 6/27/1864

Name	Age	Enlisted	Residence	Unit	Captured	Date and Cause of Death
Scott, John W. Private	Unk	6/15/1861, Young's Store, Franklin County, Virginia	Franklin County, Virginia	Co. B, 57th Virginia Infantry	1/12/1864, Washington, North Carolina	Died of Typhoid Fever, 2/3/1865
Scott, Rayford S. Private	Unk	5/1/1862, Jacksonville, North Carolina	Mecklenburg County, North Carolina	Co. H, 11th North Carolina Infantry	3/29/1865, Hatcher's Run, Virginia	Died of Erysipelas, Bacterial Infection of the Skin, 5/23/1865
Scott, W. Private	Unk	2/20/1863, Columbia, South Carolina	Richland County, South Carolina	Co. E, 7th South Carolina Infantry	8/21/1864, Globe Tavern, Near Weldon Railroad, Virginia	Died of Chronic Diarrhea, 4/14/1865
Scott, Walter Private	Unk	3/18/1862, Camp Pemberton, Virginia	Unknown	Co. C, 3rd Virginia Infantry	7/3/1863, Gettysburg, Pennsylvania	Died of Chronic Diarrhea, 1/23/1864
Scully, Charles J. Corporal	Unk	6/18/1861, Jamestown Island, Virginia	Unknown	Co. D, 14th Virginia Infantry	7/3/1863, Gettysburg, Pennsylvania	Died of Causes Unknown, 3/29/1865
Seachrist, Lindsay Private	23	3/8/1862, Salisbury, North Carolina	Rowan County, North Carolina	Co. I, 42nd North Carolina Infantry	6/18/1864, Near Petersburg, Virginia	Died of Scurvy, 5/9/1865
Seaford, Peter Private	26	8/13/1862, Camp Hill, North Carolina	Davie County, North Carolina	Co. G, 5th North Carolina Infantry	7/1/1863, Gettysburg, Pennsylvania	Died of Scurvy, 10/27/1863
Seales, B. W. Sergeant	32	5/3/1861, New Orleans, Louisiana	Orleans Parish, Louisiana, Cooper	Co. K, 6th Louisiana Infantry	5/5/1864, Mine Run, Virginia	Died of Causes Unknown, 10/22/1864
Sealy, W. Riley Private	Unk	3/6/1863, C. C. Perish, South Carolina	Unknown	Co. K, 20th South Carolina Infantry	10/19/1864, Cedar Creek or Strasburg, Virginia	Died of Typhoid Fever, 11/18/1864
Searbery B. W. Private	Unk	6/22/1861, Henry County, Virginia	Henry County, Virginia	Co. F, 42nd Virginia Infantry	5/12/1864, Near Spotsylvania Court House, Virginia	Died of Inflammation of Lungs (Pneumonia), 10/25/1864

Name	Age	Enlisted	Residence	Unit	Captured	Date and Cause of Death
Seargeant, Nathaniel R. Private	22	4/16/1861, Charlottesville Virginia	Albemarle County, Virginia	Co. A, 19th Virginia Infantry	4/6/1865, Harper's Farm, Virginia	Died of Erysipelas, Bacterial Infection of the Skin, 5/18/1865
Searles, Chesley Private	Unk	2/12/1863, Raleigh, North Carolina, Volunteer	Wake County, North Carolina	Co. E, 47th North Carolina Infantry	10/14/1863, Bristoe Station, Virginia	Died of Unknown Causes, 2/20/1864
Seat, William P. Private	20	3/1/1862, Vienna, Forsyth County, North Carolina	Forsyth County, North Carolina	Co. I, 33rd North Carolina Infantry	6/22/1864, Near Petersburg, Virginia	Died of Pneumonia-Typhoid Fever, 1/31/1865
Seaton, W. S. Private	Unk	Unknown	Unknown	Co. B, fifth Virginia Infantry	Unknown	Unable to Locate
Sechrist, Barkeley Private	Unk	Unknown	Unknown	Co. D 9th Virginia Infantry	Unknown	Unable to Locate
Sedberry, John A. Private	31	8/1/1861, Troy, North Carolina, Volunteer	Montgomery County, North Carolina	Co. E, 28th North Carolina Infantry	7/3/1863, Gettysburg, Pennsylvania	Died of Unknown Causes, 12/27/1863
Self, Lemuel S. Private	22	9/17/1861, Cleveland County, North Carolina	Cleveland County, North Carolina, Farmer	Co. F, 34th North Carolina Infantry	5/23/1864, North Anna, Virginia	Died of Unknown Causes, 10/3/1864
Self, Robert Private Not Listed On Monument	22	5/3/1862, Cleveland County, North Carolina	Cleveland County, North Carolina, Farmer	Co. E, 55th North Carolina Infantry	4/1/1865, Five Forks, Virginia	Died of Chronic Diarrhea, 7/4/1865
Sessoms, Sherwood Private	20	2/26/1862, Blockersville, North Carolina	Mitchell County, North Carolina	Co. A, 36th North Carolina Heavy Artillery	12/9/1864, Near Savannah, Georgia	Died of Pneumonia, 3/14/1865
Sessoms, William J. Private	32	2/26/1862, Fayetteville, North Carolina, Volunteer	Cumberland County, North Carolina	Company C, 36th North Carolina Heavy Artillery	1/15/1865, Fort Fisher, North Carolina, Severely Wounded Right Knee and Foot	Died of Wounds, 4/23/1865

Name	Age	Enlisted	Residence	Unit	Captured	Date and Cause of Death
Setser, Ervine Eli Private	34	9/23/1862, Camp French, North Carolina, Conscript	Caldwell County, North Carolina	Co. I, 26th North Carolina Infantry	7/14/1863, Falling Waters, Maryland	Died of Typhoid Fever, 11/3/1863
Setzer, Marcus E. Private	32	7/1/1862, Newton, North Carolina	Catawba County, North Carolina	Co. E, 57th North Carolina Infantry	11/7/1863, Rapidan Station, Virginia	Died of Scurvy, 3/21/1865
Sexton, Albert F. H. Sergeant	18	4/18/1861, Marion, Virginia	Smyth County, Virginia, Clerk	Co. D 4th Virginia Infantry	7/3/1863, Gettysburg, Pennsylvania	Died of Chronic Diarrhea, 12/4/1863
Sexton, Augustine G. Private Not Listed On Monument	Unk	4/15/1864, Wake County, North Carolina	Wake County, North Carolina	Co. C, 31st North Carolina Infantry	6/1/1864, Gaines Farm, Cold Harbor, Virginia	Died of Unknown Causes, 7/13/1864
Sharp, Thomas Private	27	6/19/1862, Tarboro, North Carolina, Volunteer	Wilson County, North Carolina, Farmer	Co. F, 7th Confederate Cavalry	12/12/1864, Hamilton, North Carolina	Died of Acute Dysentery, 4/22/1865
Sharpe, Thomas Private Not Listed On Monument	Unk	Unknown	Unknown	Co. B, 16th Battalion North Carolina Cavalry	12/12/1864, Hamilton, North Carolina	Died of Chronic Dysentery, 4/22/1865
Sharron, Drury Private	Unk	2/26/1862, Granville County, North Carolina	Granville County, North Carolina	Co. A, 44th North Carolina Infantry	10/27/1864, Near Petersburg, Virginia	Died of Congestive Intermittent Fever, 2/11/1865
Shaver, Henry S. Private	22	2/10/1864, Dublin, Virginia	Pulaski County, Virginia	Co. D, 5th Virginia Cavalry	5/11/1864, Yellow Tavern, Virginia	Died of Disease, 8/22/1864
Shaw, Benjamin A. Private	Unk	3/17/1862, Marion District, South Carolina	Marion District, South Carolina	Co. L, 21st South Carolina Infantry	7/10/1863, Morris Island, South Carolina	Died of Chronic Diarrhea, 11/2/1863

Name	Age	Enlisted	Residence	Unit	Captured	Date and Cause of Death
Shaw, Cornelius Private Not Listed On Monument	35	2/15/1862, Alamance County, North Carolina	Alamance County, North Carolina	Co. F, 6th North Carolina Infantry	11/7/1863, Rappahannock Station, Virginia	Died of Scurvy, 5/5/1865
Shaw, John A. Private	18	11/10/1862, Fayetteville, North Carolina	Cumberland County, North Carolina	Co. C, 36th North Carolina Heavy Artillery	1/15/1865, Fort Fisher, North Carolina	Died of Measles, 4/13/1865
Shaw, Stephen Private	Unk	3/1/1862, Columbus County, North Carolina	Columbus County, North Carolina	Co. K, 20th North Carolina Infantry	7/1/1863, Gettysburg, Pennsylvania	Died of Chronic Diarrhea, 11/28/1863
Shaw, W. E. Private	Unk	Unknown	Unknown	Co. F, 6th North Carolina Infantry	11/7/1863, Rappahannock, Virginia	Died of Unknown Causes, 5/5/1865
Shealey, W. Riley Private Not Listed On Monument	Unk	12/31/1861, Lexington District, South Carolina	Lexington District, South Carolina	Co. K, 20th South Carolina Infantry	10/19/1864, Cedar Creek or Strasburg, Virginia	Died of Typhoid Fever, 11/18/1864
Shearin, Landon T. Private	19	1/8/1862, Camp Wyatt, North Carolina	Warren County, North Carolina, Volunteer	Co. B, 30th North Carolina Infantry	7/3/1863, Gettysburg, Pennsylvania	Died of Pneumonia, 2/25/1865
Sheehan, Cornelius Private Not Listed On Monument	27	8/15/1861, Richmond, Virginia	Henrico County, Virginia	Co. F, 59th Virginia Infantry	6/18/1864, Near Petersburg, Virginia	Died of Chronic Dysentery, 7/31/1864
Sheely, Yerby Private	Unk	7/1/1862, Columbia, South Carolina, Conscript	Richland County, South Carolina	Co. C, 2nd South Carolina Infantry	8/1/1863, Brandy Station, Virginia	Died of Acute Diarrhea, 1/26/1865
Shehan, John Private	Unk	4/28/1864, Camden, South Carolina	Kershaw County, South Carolina	Co. D, 5th South Carolina Reserves	2/25/1865, Kershaw District, South Carolina	Died of Acute Diarrhea, 6/11/1865

Name	Age	Enlisted	Residence	Unit	Captured	Date and Cause of Death
Shehaw, C. Private	Unk	Unknown	Unknown	Co. F, 57th Virginia Infantry	Unknown	Date and Cause of Death Unknown
Shehorn, John See: Shehan, John				South Carolina Reserve		
Shell, S. B. Private	20	4/30/1861, Lenore County, North Carolina, Volunteer	Caldwell County, North Carolina	Co. A, 22nd North Carolina Infantry	7/14/1863, Williamsport, Maryland	Died of Unknown Causes, 12/24/1864
Shell, Thomas C. Private	25	3/4/1862, Aberdeen, Mississippi	Monroe County, Mississippi	Co. I, 11th Mississippi Infantry	7/14/1863, Falling Waters, Maryland	Died of Unknown Causes, 12/23/1863
Shelley, David Private	Unk	3/5/1864, Marion District, South Carolina	Marion District, South Carolina	Co. I, 21st South Carolina Infantry	5/9/1864, Near Petersburg, Virginia	Died of Unknown Causes, 10/4/1864
Shelton, James M. Private	Unk	4/21/1862, Abingdon, Virginia	Washington County, Virginia	Co. B, 37th Virginia Infantry	11/28/1863, Mine Run, Virginia	Died of Chronic Diarrhea, 1/2/1865
Shepard, Jackson L. Private Not Listed On Monument	23	7/1/1861, Onslow County, North Carolina	Onslow County, North Carolina	Co. G, 3rd North Carolina Infantry	7/3/1863, Gettysburg, Pennsylvania, Wounded	Died of Unknown Causes, 9/11/1864
Shepherd, Eli Private	17	3/25/1862, Richmond County, North Carolina	Richmond County, North Carolina	Co. E, 52nd North Carolina Infantry	7/14/1863, Falling Waters, Maryland	Died of Chronic Diarrhea, 1/4/1864
Shepherd, William H. Corporal	27	2/22/1862, Lick Creek, Brassfield, North Carolina	Wake County, North Carolina, Farmer	Co. I, 47th North Carolina Infantry	7/3/1863, Gettysburg, Pennsylvania	Died of Unknown Causes, 3/15/1864
Sheppard, C. L. Private	Unk	Unknown	Unknown	Georgia	Unknown	Unable to Locate

Name	Age	Enlisted	Residence	Unit	Captured	Date and Cause of Death
Sheppard, J. L. Private	23	7/1/1861, Jacksonville, North Carolina, Volunteer	Onslow County, North Carolina	Co. G, 3rd, North Carolina Infantry	7/3/1863, Gettysburg, Pennsylvania, Wounded	Died of Unknown Causes, 9/11/1864
Sheppard, James M. Private	Unk	3/4/1862, Talbottom, Georgia	Talbot County, Georgia	Co. E, 9th Georgia Infantry	7/3/1863, Gettysburg, Pennsylvania	Died of Smallpox, 11/9/1863
Sheron, Drury W. See: Sharron, Drury				Co. A, 44th, North Carolina Infantry		
Sherson. Lewis A. Private Not Listed On Monument	23	2/7/1862, Camp Gist, South Carolina	Unknown	Co. C, 2nd South Carolina Cavalry	7/14/1863, Williamsport, Maryland	Died of Chronic Diarrhea, 3/15/1865
Shields, C. W. Private	Unk	Unknown	Unknown	Co. F, 36th North Carolina Heavy Artillery	1/15/1865, Fort Fisher, North Carolina	Died of Chronic Diarrhea, 3/7/1865
Shimpock, Henry Private	35	8/8/1862, Raleigh, North Carolina, Conscript	Cabarrus County, North Carolina	Co. B, 5th, North Carolina Infantry	7/2/1863, Gettysburg, Pennsylvania	Died of Smallpox, 10/?/1863
Shipley, T. M. Private	22	9/27/1862, Blountville, Tennessee	Sullivan County, Tennessee	Co. E, 61st Tennessee Mounted Infantry	5/17/ 1863, Big Black Bridge, Near Vicksburg, Mississippi	Died of Unknown Causes, 9/11/1863
Shipman, J. K. P. Sergeant	16	5/20/1861, Asheville, North Carolina, Volunteer	Buncombe County, North Carolina	Co. C, 1st, North Carolina Cavalry	9/22/1863, Near Madison Court House, Virginia	Died of Chronic Diarrhea, 10/22/1864
Shirrell, John N. Private	Unk	9/15/1864, Lincoln County, North Carolina	Lincoln County, North Carolina	Co. K, 49th Carolina Infantry	4/1/1865, Petersburg, Virginia	Died of Congestive Intermittent Fever, 5/3/1865
Shoe, Nimrod Private	Unk	2/25/1864, Orange County Court House, North Carolina	Orange County, North Carolina	Co. C, 45th North Carolina Infantry	6/10/1864, Spotsylvania, Virginia	Died of Unknown Causes, 4/19/1865

Name	Age	Enlisted	Residence	Unit	Captured	Date and Cause of Death
Shoemaker, John Franklin Private	37	4/14/1862, Athens, Tennessee	McMinn County, Tennessee	Co. H, 59th Tennessee Infantry	5/17/1863, Big Black Bridge, Near Vicksburg, Mississippi	Died of Unknown Causes, 1/28/1865
Shoemaker, M. Private	Unk	10/1/1864, Camp Vance, North Carolina	Burke County, North Carolina	Co. A, 6th, North Carolina Infantry	10/19/1864, Cedar Creek or Strasburg, Virginia	Died of Chronic Diarrhea, 5/26/1865
Shoemate, S. M. Private See: Shumate, L. J.				Co. H, 42nd Virginia Infantry		
Shoemodder, W. Private	Unk	Unknown	Unknown	Co. D, 15th Georgia Infantry	Unknown	Died of Smallpox, 11/14/1863
Shoffutt, John H. Private	Unk	7/26/1861, Montgomery, Alabama	Montgomery County, Alabama	Co. E, 13th Alabama Infantry	7/5/1863, Greencastle, Pennsylvania, Wounded in Right Leg, Fractured Femur	Died of Wounds, 11/2/1863
Shots, Edward F. Private	37	6/1/1862, Place Unknown, Virginia, Conscript	Shenandoah County, Virginia	Co. A, 10th Virginia Infantry	7/5/1863, Falling Waters, Maryland	Died of Smallpox, 12/1/1863
Short, William F. 2nd Lieutenant	Unk	12/7/1861, Hickman County, Tennessee	Hickman County, Tennessee	Co. D, 48th Tennessee Infantry	10/29/1863, Hickman County, Tennessee	Died of Chronic Diarrhea, 8/7/1864
Shuler, Bennett Private	Unk	Unknown	Unknown	Co. D, 14th South Carolina Militia	3/1/1865, Columbia, South Carolina	Died of Chronic Diarrhea, 6/3/1865
Shuler, P. L. Private	Unk	5/28/1862, Lexington, South Carolina	Lexington District, South Carolina	Co. C, 20th South Carolina Infantry	10/19/1864, Cedar Creek or Strasburg, Virginia	Died of Pneumonia, 2/12/1865

Name	Age	Enlisted	Residence	Unit	Captured	Date and Cause of Death
Shumate, L. J. Private	Unk	2/18/1864, Henry County, Virginia	Unknown	Co. H, 42nd Virginia Infantry	5/12/1864, Spotsylvania Court House, Virginia	Died Typhoid Fever, 10/27/1864
Shurley, W. B. Private See: Sealy, W. Riley						
Sifford, John F. Private	37	3/21/1862, Lincoln County, North Carolina	Lincoln County, North Carolina, Farmer	Co. G, 52nd North Carolina Infantry	7/14/1863, Falling Waters, Maryland	Died of Unknown Causes, 2/20/1864
Sigler, S. Private	Unk	Unknown	Unknown	Unassigned	10/17/1864, Edinburgh, Virginia	Date and Cause of Death Unknown
Sigman. Benjamin Private Not Listed On Monument	30	7/7/1862, Newton, North Carolina	Catawba County, North Carolina	Co. E, 57th North Carolina Infantry	11/7/1863, Rappahannock Station, Virginia	Died of Unknown Causes, 7/14/1864
Sigmon, Elijah Private	Unk	3/26/1863, Lincolnton, North Carolina, Volunteer	Lincoln County, North Carolina	Co. I, 11th North Carolina Infantry	7/3/1863, Gettysburg, Pennsylvania	Died of Chronic Diarrhea, Pneumonia & Scurvy, 11/26/1863
Silcox, John Private	Unk	1/29/1864, Marianna, Jackson County, Florida	Jackson County, Florida	Co. A, 11th Florida Infantry	9/10/1864, Petersburg, Virginia	Died of Unknown Causes, 1/31/1865
Simmons, A. E. Private	Unk	2/1/1863, Onslow County, North Carolina	Onslow County, North Carolina	Co. A, 13th North Carolina Infantry	Place Unknown	Date and Cause of Death Unknown
Simmons, Archibald Private	30	7/16/1862, Raleigh, North Carolina, Conscript	Montgomery County, North Carolina	Co. F, 14th North Carolina Infantry	9/19/1864, Winchester, Virginia	Died of Acute Dysentery, 1/15/1865

Name	Age	Enlisted	Residence	Unit	Captured	Date and Cause of Death
Simmons, Christian Private	Unk	10/13/1862, Camp Near Bunker Hill, Virginia	Berkeley County, Virginia	Co. F, 25th Virginia Infantry	5/5/1864, Wilderness, Virginia	Died of Remittent Fever, 7/30/1864
Simmons, David Private	Unk	4/7/1864, Dublin, Virginia	Pulaski County, Virginia	Co. I, 22nd Virginia Infantry	6/5/1864, Gaines Farm, Virginia	Died of Unknown Causes, 8/22/1864
Simmons, Ephraim Private	20	9/1/1862, Francisco, Stokes County, North Carolina	Stokes County, North Carolina	Co. A, 2nd Battalion North Carolina Infantry	7/6/1863, Fairfield, Gettysburg, Pennsylvania	Died of Unknown Causes, 8/8/1864
Simmons, Jesse Private	Unk	7/24/1861, Salem, Virginia	Roanoke County, Virginia	Co. D, 5th Virginia Cavalry	5/11/1864, Spotsylvania, Hanover County, Virginia	Died of Intermittent Fever, 10/18/1864
Simmons, John E. Private	Unk	4/29/1862, Sumter County, Georgia	Sumter County, Georgia	Co. A, 12th Georgia Infantry	5/10/1864, Spotsylvania Court House, Virginia	Died of Unknown Causes, 6/13/1864
Simmons, M. L. Private	Unk	12/16/1862, Jackson County, Georgia	Jackson County, Georgia	Co. D, 7th Georgia Cavalry	10/27/1864, Near Petersburg, Virginia	Died of Measles, 4/8/1865
Simons, James W. See: Symons, James W.				Co. H, 6th Virginia Cavalry		
Simpson, Alexander T. Private	44	3/4/1862, Camilla Mitchell County, Georgia	Mitchell County, Georgia	Co. D, 51st Georgia Infantry	6/3/1864, Gaines Form, Virginia	Died of Unknown Causes, 6/18/1864
Simpson, James W. Sergeant	23	6/6/1861, New Hanover County, North Carolina, Volunteer	New Hanover County, North Carolina	Co. F, 3rd North Carolina Infantry	7/3/1863, Gettysburg, Pennsylvania, Wounded in Face	Died of Unknown Causes, 11/22/1863
Simpson, Thomas P. Private	Unk	2/17/1862, Little Rock, Arkansas	Pulaski County, Arkansas	Co. G, 20th Arkansas Infantry	5/16/1863, Champion Hill, Tennessee	Died of Unknown Causes, 10/?/1863

Name	Age	Enlisted	Residence	Unit	Captured	Date and Cause of Death
Sims, E. Private	Unk	4/3/1862, Bryan County, Georgia	Bryan County, Georgia	Co. K, 7th Georgia Cavalry	12/6/1864, Bryan County, Georgia	Died of Pneumonia, 2/17/1865
Sims, Thomas J. Private	18	10/2/1862, Mossy Creek, Tennessee	Jefferson County, Tennessee	Co. F, 61st Tennessee Mounted Infantry	5/17/1863, Big Black Bridge, Near Vicksburg, Mississippi	Died of Unknown Causes, 2/9/1864
Sipe, Sidney Private	Unk	7/1/1862, Newton, North Carolina	Catawba County, North Carolina	Co. E, 57th North Carolina Infantry	5/22/1864, Near Milford Station, Virginia	Died of Chronic Diarrhea, 5/30/1865
Sipples, John B. Private	19	9/15/1862, Harrison County, Kentucky	Harrison County, Kentucky	Co. H, 9th Kentucky Cavalry	5/14/1863, Grant County, Kentucky	Died of Unknown Causes, 7/25/1864
Sisk, Bartley Seyers Private	Unk	2/10/1863, Benton, Tennessee	Polk County, Tennessee	Co. H, 43rd Tennessee Infantry	5/17/1863, Big Black Bridge, Near Vicksburg, Mississippi	Died of Typhoid Fever, 12/11/1863
Skeen, James Private	25	8/8/1862, Davidson County, North Carolina, Conscript	Davidson County, North Carolina	Co. B, 48th North Carolina Infantry	10/14/1863, Bristoe Station, Virginia	Died of Inflammation of the Kidneys, 11/6/1864
Skelton, Andrew J. Private	Unk	11/28/1862, Fort Pemberton, South Carolina	Unknown	Co. B, 15th Battalion South Carolina Heavy Artillery	3/16/1865, Averasboro, North Carolina	Died of Chronic Dysentery, 5/7/1865
Skelton, J. T. Private	Unk	Unknown	Unknown	Co. C, 45th Georgia Infantry	Unknown	Unable to Locate
Skipper, Samuel T. Private	Unk	12/10/1862, Morris Island, South Carolina	Charleston District, South Carolina	Co. A, 21st South Carolina Infantry	7/10/1863, Morris Island, South Carolina	Died of Unknown Causes, 7/27/1864
Slayden, Joseph Private	Unk	1/29/1864, Bristol, Tennessee	Sullivan County, Tennessee	Co. I, 14th Tennessee Infantry	10/1/1864, Petersburg, Virginia	Died of Chronic Diarrhea, 11/7/1864

Name	Age	Enlisted	Residence	Unit	Captured	Date and Cause of Death
Sloan, Newton A. Private	Unk	9/7/1861, Quitman, Georgia	Brooks County, Georgia	Co. C, 61st Georgia Infantry	7/5/1863, South Mountain, Maryland	Died of Smallpox, 1/5/1864
Slough, Baxter A. Private	Unk	6/2/1863, Camp Paxton, Virginia	Unknown	Co. H, 4th Virginia Infantry	7/5/1863, Gettysburg, Pennsylvania	Died of Apoplexy (Stroke), 12/31/1864
Smart, Thomas R. Private	23	3/10/1862, Salisbury, North Carolina, Volunteer	Rowan County, North Carolina	Co. G, 6th North Carolina Infantry	11/7/1863, Rappahannock, Virginia	Died of Unknown Causes, 8/31/1864
Smith, A. Anderson Private	Unk	3/6/1863, Wilmington, North Carolina	New Hanover County, North Carolina	Co. G, 22nd South Carolina Infantry	4/3/1865, Sutherland Station, Virginia	Died of Debility, 4/29/1865
Smith, A. P. Private	Unk	Unknown	Unknown	Co. H, 45th North Carolina Infantry	Unknown	Unable to Locate
Smith, A. W. Private	Unk	3/10/1862, Madison Court House, Virginia	Madison County, Virginia	Co. C, 4th Virginia Cavalry	10/9/1864, Cedar Creek or Strasburg Virginia	Died of Pneumonia, 5/21/1865
Smith, Alvin Sergeant	22	9/21/1862, Livingston, Tennessee	Overton County, Tennessee	Co. F, 25th Tennessee Infantry	5/16/1864, Albemarle Sound, North Carolina	Died of Chronic Diarrhea, 8/1/1864
Smith, Benjamin Private	21	6/12/1861, Weldon, North Carolina, Volunteer	Gates County, North Carolina	Co. B, 5th North Carolina Infantry	5/20/1864, Spotsylvania Court House, Virginia	Died of Wounds, 5/27/1864
Smith, Charles Private	Unk	11/19/1862, Morristown, Tennessee	Hamblen County, Tennessee	Co. G, 61st Tennessee Mounted Infantry	5/17/ 1863, Big Black Bridge, Near Vicksburg, Mississippi	Died of Chronic Dysentery, 12/18/1864
Smith, Charles Private	Unk	6/15/1861, Young's Store, Virginia	Unknown	Co. B, 57th Virginia Infantry	6/12/1864, Washington, North Carolina	Died of Scurvy, 2/10/1865

Name	Age	Enlisted	Residence	Unit	Captured	Date and Cause of Death
Smith, David Private	18	12/14/1863, Fort Pender, North Carolina	Unknown	Co. H, 36th North Carolina Heavy Artillery	1/15/1865, Fort Fisher, North Carolina	Died of Chronic Diarrhea, 6/23/1865
Smith, David J. Sergeant	Unk	5/21/1861, Camp Cheatham, Tennessee	Hickman County, Tennessee	Co. B, 3rd Tennessee Infantry	5/22/1863, Raymond, Mississippi	Date and Cause of Death Unknown
Smith, DeWitt Clinton 2nd Lieutenant	33	7/22/1861, Creswell's Springs, North Carolina, Volunteer	Iredell County, North Carolina, Teacher	Co. I, 7th North Carolina Infantry	7/3/1863, Gettysburg, Pennsylvania	Died of Chronic Diarrhea, 2/21/1864
Smith, Edmund P. Corporal	28	5/5/1861, Albemarle, North Carolina, Volunteer	Stanley County, North Carolina	Co. K, 14th North Carolina Infantry	4/6/1865, Farmville, Virginia	Died of Chronic Diarrhea, 6/24/1865
Smith, Floyd Private	23	4/4/1862, Surry County, North Carolina, Volunteer	Surry County, North Carolina, Farmer	Co. E, 53rd North Carolina Infantry	8/15/1863, Martinsburg, Virginia	Died of Chronic Diarrhea, 12/22/1863
Smith, George Private Not Listed On Monument	34	8/8/1862, Statesville, North Carolina, Conscript	Iredell County, North Carolina	Co. H, 5th North Carolina Infantry	5/19/1864, Spotsylvania Court House, Virginia	Died of Chronic Diarrhea, 2/4/1865
Smith, George M. Private	Unk	9/25/1861, Mooresville, Alabama	Limestone County, Alabama	Co. I, 54th Alabama Infantry	5/16/1863, Baker's Creek, Champion Hill, Mississippi	Died of Unknown Causes, 6/27/1864
Smith, George W. Private	18	5/14/1862, Boonesville, Mississippi	Jacinto, Mississippi, Farmer	Co. E, 42nd Mississippi Infantry	5/23/1864, North Anna, Virginia	Died of Unknown Causes, 8/1/1864
Smith, Henry D. Private	19	6/23/1862, Concord, North Carolina, Volunteer	Cabarrus County, North Carolina	Co. H, 57th North Carolina Infantry	7/4/1863, South Mountain, Maryland	Died of Unknown Causes, 4/5/1864

Name	Age	Enlisted	Residence	Unit	Captured	Date and Cause of Death
Smith, Horace W. 2nd Lieutenant	31	4/29/1861, Buffalo Springs, Virginia	Unknown, Farmer	Co. I, 19th Virginia Infantry	7/3/1863, Gettysburg, Pennsylvania	Died of Unknown Causes, 8/10/1864
Smith, James Private	25	5/10/1862, Wayne County, North Carolina	Wayne County, North Carolina	Co. G, 55th North Carolina Infantry	7/1/1863, Gettysburg, Pennsylvania	Died of Chronic Diarrhea, 10/23/1863
Smith, James Private	17	10/3/1862, Morristown, Tennessee	Hamblen County, Tennessee	Co. G, 61st Tennessee Mounted Infantry	5/17/1863, Big Black Bridge, Near Vicksburg, Mississippi	Died of Chronic Diarrhea, 12/6/1863
Smith, James Private	22	11/21/1861, Spartanburg, South Carolina	Spartanburg District, South Carolina	Co. A, Holcombe's South Carolina Legion	4/1/1865, Five Forks, Virginia	Died of Acute Diarrhea, 6/16/1865
Smith, James W. Private Not Listed On Monument	20	9/10/1862, Staunton, Virginia	Augusta County, Virginia, Farmer	Co. G, 52nd Virginia Infantry	5/30/1864, Mechanicsville, Virginia	Died of Unknown Causes, 7/12/1864
Smith, Jesse D. Private	20	5/15/1862, Jacksonville, North Carolina	Onslow County, North Carolina	Co. H, 3rd North Carolina Cavalry	12/17/1863, Near Greenville, North Carolina	Died of Typhoid Fever, 9/5/1864
Smith, John B. Private	24	3/25/1862, Kinston, North Carolina	Lenoir County, North Carolina	Co. C, 35th North Carolina Infantry	6/17/1864, Petersburg, Virginia	Died of Chronic Diarrhea, 10/25/1864
Smith, John C. Private	Unk	5/15/1862, Madison, Georgia	Morgan County, Georgia	Co. G, Cobb's Legion Georgia Infantry	10/19/1864, Cedar Creek or Strasburg, Virginia	Died of Consumption, 6/10/1865
Smith, John L. Private	26	10/20/1861, Camp Wilkes, Chatham County, North Carolina, Volunteer	Chatham County, North Carolina	Co. E, 26th North Carolina Infantry	7/14/1863, Falling Waters, Maryland	Died of Unknown Causes, 2/28/1864

Name	Age	Enlisted	Residence	Unit	Captured	Date and Cause of Death
Smith, John S. Private	36	3/1/1863, Charlotte, North Carolina, Volunteer	Mecklenburg County, North Carolina	Co. A, 11th North Carolina Infantry	7/3/1863, Gettysburg, Pennsylvania, Gunshot Wound in Head	Died of Wounds, 7/15/1863
Smith, John S. Private	37	4/2/1863, Raleigh, North Carolina, Conscript	Anson County, North Carolina	Co. K, 30th North Carolina Infantry	5/8/1864, Mine Run, Virginia	Died of Chronic Diarrhea, 2/7/1865
Smith, Larkin G. Private Not Listed On Monument	28	2/26/1862, Bradly's Store, Cumberland County, North Carolina	Unknown	Co. C, 36th North Carolina Heavy Artillery	1/15/1865, Fort Fisher, North Carolina, Severely Wounded in Left Forearm and Wrist	Died of Pyemia, 2/15/1865, Amputated Left Forearm
Smith, Mathias H. Private	26	10/15/1863, Raleigh, North Carolina, Conscript	Cabarrus County, North Carolina	Co. A, 52nd North Carolina Infantry	7/5/1863, Gettysburg, Pennsylvania	Died of Chronic Diarrhea, 11/12/1863
Smith, Marion I. Private	Unk	12/15/1863, Orange County, Virginia	Unknown	Co. E, 44th North Carolina Infantry	10/27/1864, Near Petersburg, Virginia	Died of Debility, 2/26/1865
Smith, Peter H. Private	21	12/5/1861, St. Clair County, Missouri	Rockingham, Virginia, Farmer	Co. K, 1st Missouri Cavalry	5/16/1863, Champion Hill, Tennessee	Died of Unknown Causes, 3/31/1864
Smith, Samuel S. Private	Unk	9/15/1863, Greenbrier, Virginia	Greenbrier County, Virginia	Co. B, 46th Battalion Virginia Cavalry	10/8/1864, Fisher's Hill, Virginia	Died of Acute Diarrhea, 12/25/1864
Smith, Silas Private	60	4/10/1862, Alexander County, North Carolina, Substitute	Alexander County, North Carolina, Farmer	Co. H, 56th North Carolina Infantry	6/17/1864, Petersburg, Virginia	Died of Unknown Causes, 7/26/1864
Smith, Thaddeus Private	Unk	6/10/1861, Wayne County, North Carolina	Wayne County, North Carolina	Co. K, 27th North Carolina Infantry	3/31/1865, Hatcher's Run, Virginia	Died of Pneumonia, 5/20/1865

Name	Age	Enlisted	Residence	Unit	Captured	Date and Cause of Death
Smith, Thomas J. Private Not Listed On Monument	19	3/15/1862, Mecklenburg County, North Carolina	Mecklenburg County, North Carolina	Co. H, 11th North Carolina Infantry	7/14/1863, Falling Waters, Maryland	Date and Cause of Death Unknown
Smith, Virginius Sergeant	23	8/6/1861, Lynhawn Beach, Virginia	Unknown	Co. I, 15th Virginia Cavalry	5/12/1864, Near Ashland, Virginia	Died of Acute Diarrhea, 12/25/1864
Smith, W. C. Private	Unk	7/4/1863, McPherson-Ville, South Carolina	Hampton County, South Carolina	Co. C, 4th South Carolina Cavalry	5/28/1864, Haw's Shop, Virginia	Died of Unknown Causes, 8/29/1864
Smith, W. C. Private	Unk	6/1/1864, Raleigh, North Carolina	Wake County, North Carolina	Co. K, 32nd North Carolina Infantry	3/25/1865, Fort Stedman, Near Petersburg, Virginia	Died of Congestive Intermittent Fever, 4/25/1865
Smith, W. S. Private	Unk	Unknown	Unknown	Co. D, 30th Battalion Georgia Cavalry	Unknown	Unable to Locate
Smith, William Henry 1st Sergeant	17	5/14/1862, Granada, Mississippi	Flewellin's X-Roads, Desota County, Mississippi	Co. D, 42nd Mississippi Infantry	7/3/1863, Gettysburg, Pennsylvania	Died of Smallpox, 12/26/1863
Smith, Woody M. Private	19	5/15/1862, Pitt County, North Carolina, Volunteer	Pitt County, North Carolina	Co. D, 44th North Carolina Infantry	10/27/1864, Near Petersburg, Virginia	Died of Unknown Causes, 6/22/1865
Smithson, Ephraim Private	Unk	4/25/1861, Place Unknown	Larenburg County, Virginia	Co. B, 22nd Virginia Infantry	4/6/1865, Farmville, Virginia	Died of Chronic Dysentery, 6/9/1865
Smithson, Thomas Richard Private	Unk	8/11/1864, Nottoway County, Virginia	Lunenburg County, Virginia	Co. C, 18th Virginia Infantry	4/3/1865, Amelia Court House, Virginia	Died of Acute Diarrhea, 5/11/1865
Smothers, William C. Private	32	2/27/1862, Reidsville, North Carolina	Rockingham, North Carolina, Farmer	Co. E, 45th North Carolina Infantry	7/23/1863, Martinsburg, Virginia	Died of Inflammation of Lungs, 4/19/1865

Name	Age	Enlisted	Residence	Unit	Captured	Date and Cause of Death
Smyly, John Private	Unk	5/6/1862, Grahamville, South Carolina	Jasper County, South Carolina	Co. G, 4th South Carolina Cavalry	3/4/1865, Thompson's Bridge, North Carolina	Died of Chronic Diarrhea, 6/25/1865
Snyder, E. T. Private	Unk	Unknown	Unknown	Ordinance Department	Unknown	Unable to Locate
Snavely, John H. Private Not Listed On Monument	Unk	9/14/1861, Marion, Virginia	Smyth County, Virginia	Co. F, 23rd Battalion Virginia Infantry	9/19/1864, Winchester, Virginia	Died of Chronic Diarrhea, 3/1/1865
Snead, John W. Private	39	1/25/1862, St. John's Church, Lunenburg County, Virginia	Lunenburg County, Virginia	Lunenburg Virginia Heavy Artillery	4/6/1865, Harper's Farm, Virginia	Died of Chronic Diarrhea, 6/8/1865
Snedaker, William Private Not Listed On Monument	Unk	2/6/1862, Savannah, Georgia	Stewart County, Georgia	Co. F, 22nd Battalion Georgia Heavy Artillery	3/16/1865, Fayetteville, North Carolina	Died of Chronic Diarrhea, 7/4/1865
Snider, John Joe Private Not Listed On Monument	24	6/4/1861, Monterey, Virginia	Rockbridge Baths, Virginia, Farm Hand	Co. C, 25th Virginia Infantry	5/5/1864, Wilderness, Virginia	Died of Unknown Causes, 8/2/1864
Snider, Jonathan H. Private	31	11/29/1863, Davidson County, North Carolina	Davidson County, North Carolina	Co. K, 44th North Carolina Infantry	10/27/1864, Boydton Plank Road, Near Petersburg, Virginia	Died of Dropsy, 5/2/1865
Snider, Lewis W. Private	33	11/29/1863, Davidson County, North Carolina	Davidson County, North Carolina	Co. K, 44th North Carolina Infantry	10/14/1863, Bristoe Station, Virginia	Died of Catarrhus, 6/25/1864
Snipes, James K. Corporal	20	5/1/1862, Thomaston, Georgia	Upson County, Georgia	Co. A, 46th Georgia Infantry	12/17/1864, Franklin, Tennessee, Gunshot Wound of Right Thigh	Died of Pneumonia, 6/6/1865

Name	Age	Enlisted	Residence	Unit	Captured	Date and Cause of Death
Snipes, John W. Private	18	9/7/1863, Orange County, North Carolina	Orange County, North Carolina	Co. G, 28th North Carolina Infantry	5/12/1864, Wilderness, Virginia	Died of Unknown Causes, 6/27/1864
Snipes, Nelson Private	46	2/28/1862, Lumberton, North Carolina	Robeson County, North Carolina, Farmer	Co. E, 51st North Carolina Infantry	5/14/1864, Drury's Bluff, Virginia, Wounded	Died of Wounds, 5/28/1864
Snipes, Wiley T. Private	20	5/10/1862, Kinston, North Carolina	Forsyth County, North Carolina	Co. K, 52nd North Carolina Infantry	7/5/1863, Gettysburg, Pennsylvania	Died of Chronic Diarrhea, 12/18/1863
Snyder, J. Mc Private	24	4/23/1861, Brownsburg, Virginia	Rockbridge County, Virginia	Co. H, 25th North Carolina Infantry	5/5/1864, Wilderness, Virginia	Died of Intermittent Fever, 5/11/1865
Snyder, John Private Not Listed On Monument	Unk	10/1/1862, Bunker Hill, Virginia	Berkeley County, Virginia	Co. H, 2nd Virginia Infantry	5/12/1864, Spotsylvania Court House, Virginia, Wounded in Right Groin and Thigh	Died of Wounds, 6/1/1864
Sollis, D. Vaugh Private	36	9/4/1863, Camp Holmes, Raleigh, North Carolina, Conscript	Sampson County, North Carolina	Co. G, 30th North Carolina Infantry	11/7/1863, Kelly's Ford, Rappahannock Station, Virginia	Died of Unknown Causes, 1/23/1865
Sollis, John J. Private	18	3/27/1863, Camp Gregg, North Carolina	Sampson County, North Carolina	Co. D, 38th North Carolina Infantry	4/3/1865, Sutherland Station, Virginia	Died of Rubeola (Measles), 6/24/1865
Solomon, Thomas F. Private	23	2/1/1862, Salisbury, North Carolina, Volunteer	Stanley County, North Carolina	Co. C, 42nd North Carolina Infantry	6/1/1864, Gaines Farm, Virginia	Died of Chronic Diarrhea, 10/19/1864
Sorrell, John Private	Unk	Unknown	Unknown	Co. E, 1st Virginia Reserves	4/6/1865, Harper's Farm, Virginia	Died of Unknown Causes, 2/21/1864
Sorrells, Benjamin W. Private	Unk	3/4/1862, Monroe, Georgia	Walton County, Georgia	Co. C, 9th Georgia Infantry	7/4/1863, Gettysburg, Pennsylvania	Died of Unknown Causes, 2/21/1864

Name	Age	Enlisted	Residence	Unit	Captured	Date and Cause of Death
Southall, Stephen W. Private	Unk	4/29/1861, Suffolk, Virginia	Isle of Wight County, Virginia	Co. A, 19th Battalion Virginia Heavy Artillery	4/6/1865, Harper's Farm, Virginia	Died of Chronic Dysentery, 5/12/1865
Southern, Josephus See: Suthern, Josepus				Co. D, 7th Virginia Infantry		
Spady, S. G. Corporal	Unk	3/24/1863, Charleston, South Carolina	Charleston County, South Carolina	Co. A, 27th South Carolina Infantry	8/21/1864, Globe Tavern, Near Weldon Railroad, Virginia	Died of Acute Diarrhea, 12/8/1864
Spainhour, Solomon Private Not Listed On Monument	45	4/1/1864, Kinston, North Carolina	Lenoir County, North Carolina	Co. B, 6th North Carolina Infantry	4/22/1864, Fisher's Hill, Virginia	Died of Chronic Diarrhea & Scurvy, 2/27/1865
Spainhour, William Private	20	7/1/1862, Pfafftown, North Carolina, Conscript	Forsyth County, North Carolina	Co. C, 33rd North Carolina Infantry	7/14/1863, Falling Waters, Maryland	Died of Chronic Diarrhea, 12/10/1863
Spangler, Ananias Private	Unk	2/1/1863, Floyd Court House, Virginia	Floyd County, Virginia	Co. E, 17th Virginia Cavalry	Unknown	Died of Unknown Causes Date Unknown
Sparrow, Edward S. Corporal Not Listed On Monument	18	12/27/1862, Place Unknown	Unknown	Spencer's Co., 66th North Carolina Cavalry	2/20/1864, Fairfield, North Carolina	Died of Chronic Diarrhea & Scurvy, 2/31865
Spaugh, Julius E. Private	25	7/8/1862, Winston, North Carolina Conscript	Forsyth County, North Carolina	Co. K, 21st North Carolina Infantry	5/22/1864, North Anna River, Virginia	Died of Chronic Diarrhea, 11/11/1864
Speagle, Cain Private	Unk	8/19/1864, Camp Holmes, Raleigh, North Carolina	Lincoln County, North Carolina	Co. I, 11th North Carolina Infantry	10/27/1864, Burgess' Mills, Near Petersburg, Virginia	Died of Chronic Diarrhea, 1/25/1865
Spearman, William S. Private	Unk	5/31/1861, Atlanta, Georgia	Heard County, Georgia	Co. G, 7th Georgia Infantry	7/3/1863, Gettysburg, Pennsylvania	Died of Unknown Causes, 12/21/1863

Name	Age	Enlisted	Residence	Unit	Captured	Date and Cause of Death
Spears, George S. Private	35	8/29/1861, Union County Court House, South Carolina	Union County, South Carolina	Co. F, 15th South Carolina Infantry	10/19/1864, Cedar Creek or Strasburg, Virginia	Died of Chronic Diarrhea and Scurvy, 2/4/1865
Speer, Alex Private	19	4/5/1862, East Bend, North Carolina	Yadkin County, North Carolina	Co. F, 28th North Carolina Infantry	4/2/1865, Petersburg, Virginia	Died of Diphtheria, 5/8/1865
Speer, John D. Private	30	9/20/1862, Sullivan County, Tennessee	Sullivan County, Tennessee	Co. C, 66th Tennessee Infantry	5/17/1863, Big Black Bridge, Near Vicksburg, Mississippi	Died of Chronic Diarrhea, 11/1/1863
Spell, Samuel S. Private	24	3/4/1862, Dublin, Laurens County, Georgia	Johnson County, Georgia	Co. G, 49th Georgia Infantry	5/23/1864, Jericho Ford, Virginia	Died of Dysentery, 8/5/1864
Spencer, James F. Private	Unk	2/20/1864, Dublin, Virginia	Pulaski County, Virginia	Co. F, 4th Virginia Infantry	Unknown	Date and Cause of Death Unknown
Spencer, John M. Private	Unk	9/7/1863, Fauquier County, Virginia	Fauquier County, Virginia	Co. C, 43rd Battalion Virginia Cavalry	9/22/1863, Near Madison Court House, Virginia	Died of Chronic Diarrhea, 12/24/1863
Spencer, W. W. Private	Unk	2/23/1863, Baton Rouge, Louisiana	New Orleans, Louisiana, Mechanic	1st Co. Washington Battalion Louisiana Artillery	4/2/1865, Hatcher's Run, Virginia, Wounded	Died of Unknown Causes, 5/13/1865
Spitler, David F. Private	20	4/17/1861, Augusta County, Virginia	Augusta County, Virginia	Co. D, 5th Virginia Infantry	7/7/1863, Fairfield, Maryland	Died of Typhoid Fever & Dysentery, 3/14/1864
Spitter, E. B. See: Spitler, David F.				Co. D, 5th Virginia Infantry		
Spotts, Joseph B. Private	18	4/18/1861, Jefferson Court House, Virginia	Jefferson County, Virginia, Student	Co. A, 2nd Virginia Infantry	5/12/1864, Near Spotsylvania Court House, Virginia	Died of Unknown Causes, 6/4/1864
Sprail, Benjamin See: Spruill, Henry W.				Co. A, 32nd North Carolina Infantry		

Name	Age	Enlisted	Residence	Unit	Captured	Date and Cause of Death
Sprouse, H. H. Private	Unk	2/14/1863, Greenville, South Carolina	Greenville County, South Carolina	Co. A, 6th South Carolina Cavalry	12/1/1864, Stony Creek, Virginia	Died of Chronic Diarrhea, 4/15/1865
Spruill, Henry W. Private	28	10/4/1861, Norfolk, Virginia	Unknown	Co. A, 32nd North Carolina Infantry	Unknown	Died of Scurvy, 4/28/1865
Stabler, D. V. Private	Unk	8/19/1863, Sullivan's Island, South Carolina	Charleston District, South Carolina	Co. D, 20th South Carolina Infantry	10/19/1864, Cedar Creek or Strasburg, Virginia	Died of Congestive Intermittent Fever, 1/20/1865
Stacey, R. M. Private	17	1/7/1862, Camp Hampton, South Carolina	Lancaster County, South Carolina	Co. K, 18th South Carolina Infantry	7/30/1864, Petersburg, Virginia	Died of Chronic Diarrhea, 11/8/1864
Stafford, J. H. Private	Unk	Unknown	Unknown	Co. A, 42nd North Carolina Infantry	12/25/1864, Battery Anderson, Fort Fisher, North Carolina	Died of a Scurvy, 6/9/1865
Stafford, James T. Private	Unk	5/16/1861, King George County Court House, Virginia	King George County, Virginia	Co. C, 47th Virginia Infantry	6/13/1864, Westmoreland County, Virginia	Died of Chronic Diarrhea, 7/31/1864
Stafford, John 2nd Class Fireman	Unk	Unknown	Unknown	Confederate States Navy, CSS Albemarle	11/7/1864, Captured by North Atlantic Squadron	Date and Cause of Death Unknown
Stafford, John James Private	Unk	1/20/1862, Henderson Station, Tennessee	Unknown	Co. H, 55th Tennessee Infantry	5/17/1863, Big Black Bridge, Near Vicksburg, Mississippi	Died of Chronic Diarrhea, 11/10/1863
Stafford, Samuel H. Private	29	4/13/1864, Raleigh, North Carolina Conscript	Wake County, North Carolina	Co. I, 54th North Carolina Infantry	5/22/1864, Spotsylvania Court House, Virginia	Died of Unknown Causes, 7/27/1864
Stafford, Z. J. Private Not Listed On Monument	Unk	Unknown	Unknown	Co. I, 54th North Carolina Infantry	5/22/1864, Spotsylvania Court House, Virginia	Died of Unknown Causes, 7/3/1864

Name	Age	Enlisted	Residence	Unit	Captured	Date and Cause of Death
Stallings, J. G. Private	Unk	11/10/1864, Lenoir County, North Carolina	Lenoir County, North Carolina	Co. A, 22nd North Carolina Infantry	5/24/1864, Hanover, Virginia	Died of Unknown Causes, 7/22/1864
Stallings, Willis Private	Unk	3/17/1863, Choctaw County, Mississippi	Choctaw County, Mississippi	Co. B, 31st Mississippi Infantry	5/17/1863, Champion Hill, Tennessee	Died of Chronic Diarrhea, 11/7/1863
Stalls, Miles B. Private	35	9/16/1861, Tarboro, North Carolina, Volunteer	Martin County, North Carolina, Farmer	Co. B, 33rd North Carolina Infantry	6/17/1864, Riddle Shop, Petersburg, Virginia	Died of Unknown Causes, 7/22/1864
Stalmaker, R. Private	Unk	4/15/1861, Edgefield District, South Carolina	Edgefield District, South Carolina	Co. H, 7th South Carolina Infantry	5/8/1864, Spotsylvania, Virginia	Date and Cause of Death Unknown
Staly, A. M. Private	Unk	5/24/1864, Camp Holmes, North Carolina	Unknown	Co. B, 3rd North Carolina Junior Reserves	12/25/1864, Fort Fisher, North Carolina	Died of Unknown Causes, 2/13/1865
Stamper, Gilbert N. Private	25	6/10/1861, Statesville, North Carolina	Iredell County, North Carolina, Farmer	Co. A, 33rd North Carolina Infantry	7/2/1863, Gettysburg, Pennsylvania	Died of Scurvy, 3/18/1865
Stamy, William Private	31	9/22/1862, Burke County, North Carolina, Conscript	Burke County, North Carolina	Co. B, 6th North Carolina Infantry	11/7/1863, Rappahannock Station, Virginia	Died of Chronic Diarrhea, 1/23/1865
Stancel, L. M. Private	Unk	1/18/1862, Camp Hampton, Columbia, South Carolina	Richland County, South Carolina	Co. F, 22nd South Carolina Infantry	6/2/1864, Near Bermuda Hundred, Virginia	Died of Acute Diarrhea, 2/6/1865
Stancer, M. See: Stancel, L. M.				Co. F, 22nd South Carolina Infantry		
Standerfer, James Private	Unk	Unknown	Unknown	Co. B, 50th Virginia Infantry	5/12/1864, Spotsylvania Court House, Virginia	Died of Unknown Causes, 9/4/1864
Stanfield, William R. Private	Unk	5/21/1861, Camp Cheatham, Tennessee	Hickman County, Tennessee	Co. F, 3rd Tennessee Infantry	5/22/1863, Raymond, Mississippi	Died of Smallpox, 12/2/1863

Name	Age	Enlisted	Residence	Unit	Captured	Date and Cause of Death
Stanley, Atlas J. Private	18	3/8/1862, Chatham County, North Carolina, Volunteer	Chatham County, North Carolina	Co. E, 26th North Carolina Infantry	5/12/1864, Spotsylvania Court House, Virginia	Died of Unknown Causes, 6/24/1864
Stanly, Nathan W. Private	23	3/26/1862, Salisbury, North Carolina Volunteer	Davie County, North Carolina	Co. D, 42nd North Carolina Infantry	10/7/1864, Near Fort Harrison, Richmond, Virginia	Died of Pneumonia, 2/21/1865
Stansberry, William P. Private	26	9/25/1862, Morristown, Tennessee	Hamblen County, Tennessee	Co. H, 60th Tennessee Mounted Infantry	5/17/1863, Big Black Bridge, Near Vicksburg, Mississippi	Died of Unknown Causes, 10/?/1863
Stanton, Thomas Private	Unk	6/9/1864, Camp Vance, North Carolina	Burke County, North Carolina	Company G, 3rd North Carolina Junior Reserves	12/25/1864, Fort Fisher, North Carolina	Died of Typhoid Fever & Pneumonia, 1/22/1865
Stapleton, G. W. Private	Unk	Unknown	Unknown	Co. H, 50th Virginia Infantry	5/12/1864, Spotsylvania Court House, Virginia	Died of Acute Dysentery, 5/29/1864
Starcher, James Private	29	9/22/1862, Charleston, West Virginia	Jackson County, West Virginia	Co. B, 22nd Virginia Infantry	9/19/1864, Winchester, Virginia	Died of Chronic Diarrhea, 11/4/1864
Starley, James H. Landsman	Unk	Unknown	Unknown	Confederate States Navy	Unknown	Unable to Locate
Starnes, M. L. Private	Unk	2/14/1863, Monroe County, North Carolina, Volunteer	Union County, North Carolina	Co. B, 26th North Carolina Infantry	7/3/1863, Gettysburg, Pennsylvania	Died of Chronic Diarrhea, 1/11/1864
Statum, William Private	Unk	4/26/1861, Augusta, Georgia	Richmond County, Georgia	Co. G, 3rd Georgia Infantry	8/17/1864, Deep Bottom Run, Virginia	Died of Scurvy, 4/21/1865
Stawford, J. J. See: Stafford, John James				Co. H, 55th Tennessee Infantry		
Starnes, John L. Private	38	10/21/1862, Camp French, North Carolina, Conscript	Union County, North Carolina	Co. B, 52nd North Carolina Infantry	10/14/1863, Bristoe Station, Virginia	Died of Pneumonia, 4/17/1864

Name	Age	Enlisted	Residence	Unit	Captured	Date and Cause of Death
Steffey, B. F. Private	Unk	3/1/1863, Marion, Virginia	Smyth County, Virginia	Co. F, 23rd Battalion Virginia Infantry	9/19/1864, Winchester, Virginia	Died of Chronic Diarrhea, 1/24/1865
Steffey, Pleasant Private	35	7/2/1861, Nickelsville, Scott County, Virginia	Scott County, Virginia	Co. E, 48th Virginia Infantry	5/12/1864, Near Spotsylvania Court House, Virginia	Died of Chronic Dysentery
Stegall, Samuel N. Private	Unk	3/1/1862, Vernon, Louisiana	Vernon Parish, Louisiana	Co. M, 12th Louisiana Infantry	5/16/1863, Champion Hill, Tennessee	Died of Smallpox, 1/1/1864
Stephens, James A. Private	22	5/29/1861, Holly Springs, North Carolina, Volunteer	Wake County, North Carolina	Co. D, 26th North Carolina Infantry	10/14/1863, Bristoe Station, Virginia	Died of Smallpox, 12/25/1863
Stephens, Jesse Private	Unk	5/14/1862, Fort Boykin, Virginia	Smithfield, Isle of Wight County, Virginia	Co. E, 9th Virginia Infantry	7/3/1863, Gettysburg, Pennsylvania	Died of Smallpox, 2/26/1864
Stephens, John D. Private	Unk	6/22/1861, Carroll County, Georgia	Carroll County, Georgia	Co. I, 19th Georgia Infantry	9/30/1864, Fort Harrison, Virginia	Died of Chronic Diarrhea, 1/12/1865
Stephens, Reuben Private	29	12/25/1861, Bennettsville, South Carolina	Marlboro District, South Carolina	Co. F, 21st South Carolina Infantry	7/10/1863, Morris Island, South Carolina	Died of Pneumonia, 2/23/1864
Stephens, Theodore B. See: Stevens, Theodore B.				Co. K, 1st Missouri Cavalry		
Stevens, C. E. Private	Unk	7/1/1862, Busbayville, Georgia	Unknown	Co. G, 8th Georgia Cavalry	2/18/1865, Near Greenville, Virginia	Died of Chronic Diarrhea, 6/1/1865
Stevens, Simeon Private	Unk	2/1/1863, Columbia, South Carolina	Richland County, South Carolina	Co. I, Holcombe's Legion, South Carolina	11/6/1864, Petersburg, Virginia	Died of Typhoid Fever, 12/4/1864
Stevens, Theodore B. Private	Unk	12/25/1861, Springfield, Greene County, Missouri	Greene County, Missouri	Co. K, 1st Missouri Cavalry	5/17/1863, Champion Hill, Tennessee	Died of Chronic Diarrhea, 10/27/1863

Name	Age	Enlisted	Residence	Unit	Captured	Date and Cause of Death
Steward, Alexander Private	Unk	Unknown	Unknown	Co. A, 27th Georgia Infantry	9/7/1863, Morris Island, South Carolina	Died of Chronic Diarrhea, 1/29/1865
Steward, Ferd Private	Unk	1/1/1863, Williamsville, Virginia	Bath County, Virginia	Co. G, 18th Virginia Cavalry	7/3/1863, Gettysburg, Pennsylvania	Died of Unknown Causes, 2/10/1864
Stewart, Henry S. Private	Unk	4/20/1862, Sullivan County, Tennessee	Sullivan County, Tennessee	Co. C, 60th Tennessee Mounted Infantry	5/17/1863, Big Black Bridge, Near Vicksburg, Mississippi	Died of Unknown Causes, 1/9/1864
Stewart, John M. Private	Unk	Unknown	Unknown	Co. F, 36th Mississippi Infantry	12/17/1864, Franklin, Tennessee	Died of Scurvy, 6/22/1865
Stewart, S. A. See: Stuart, S. A.				Co. H, 15th North Carolina Infantry		
Stier, William Private	Unk	2/16/1864, Wentworth, Rockingham County, North Carolina	Rockingham County, North Carolina	Co. I, 13th North Carolina Infantry	5/6/1864, Wilderness, Virginia	Died of Unknown Causes, 6/22/1864
Stiff, George Private Not Listed On Monument	Unk	10/16/1864, Richmond, Virginia	Middlesex County, Virginia	Co. B, 19th Battalion Virginia Heavy Artillery	4/6/1865, Sailor's Creek, Virginia	Died of Chronic Diarrhea & Fever, 7/10/1865
Stilwell, Newell Private	Unk	6/24/1862, Dublin, Virginia	Pulaski County, Virginia	Co. H, 23rd Battalion Virginia Infantry	9/19/1864, Winchester, Virginia	Died of Chronic Diarrhea, 5/19/1865
Stocks, Christopher C. Private	45	5/4/1862, Monroe, Louisiana	Ouachita County, Louisiana	Co. G, 12th Louisiana Infantry	5/16/1863, Champion Hill, Tennessee	Died of Smallpox, 12/11/1863

Name	Age	Enlisted	Residence	Unit	Captured	Date and Cause of Death
Stocks, Henry Private	Unk	7/2/1863, Greenville, North Carolina	Pitt County, North Carolina	Co. B, 67th North Carolina Infantry	11/29/1863, Greenville, North Carolina	Died of Unknown Causes, 6/8/1864
Stogner, T. Private	Unk	4/6/1863, Bennettsville, South Carolina	Marlboro District, South Carolina	Co. F, 21st South Carolina Infantry	7/10/1863, Morris Island, South Carolina	Died of Unknown Causes, 3/26/1864
Stoker, Robert Private	39	7/29/61, Albemarle, North Carolina, Volunteer	Stanly County, North Carolina	Co. D, 28th North Carolina Infantry	7/4/1863, Gettysburg, Pennsylvania	Died of Unknown Causes, 12/23/1863
Stokes, Compton W. Sergeant	Unk	4/22/1862, Camp Lee, Florida	Unknown	Co. C, 7th Florida Infantry	1/4/1865, Murfreesboro, Tennessee, Wounded Right Leg	Died of Hospital Gangrene, 5/21/1865, Amputated Lower Right Leg
Stokes, L. H. Private	Unk	7/24/1864, Warren County, Virginia	Warren County, Virginia	Co. D, 23rd Virginia Cavalry	11/13/1864, Cedar Creek or Strasburg, Virginia	Died of Chronic Diarrhea, 4/27/1865
Stokes, Samuel B. Private	19	7/14/1862, Wilmington, North Carolina, Volunteer	Duplin County, North Carolina, Farmer	Co. G, 61st North Carolina Infantry	10/27/1864, Darbytown Road, Burgess' Mill, Virginia	Died of Unknown Causes, 1/26/1865
Stone, Alexander Private	30	2/19/1862, Charlotte, North Carolina, Volunteer	Mecklenburg County, North Carolina	Co. E, 11th North Carolina Infantry	7/4/1863, Gettysburg, Pennsylvania	Died of Syncope, 1/28/1864
Stone, James Private	Unk	5/?/1863, Place Unknown	Unknown	Co. I, 1st South Carolina Artillery	7/10/1863, Morris Island, South Carolina	Died of Unknown Causes, 3/8/1864
Stone, James R. Private	Unk	3/10/1862, Henry County, Virginia	Henry County, Virginia	Co. G, 42nd Virginia Infantry	5/12/1864, Spotsylvania Court House, Virginia	Died of Chronic Diarrhea, 8/4/1864
Stone, Marshall N. Private	Unk	9/15/1863, Verdierville, Virginia	Unknown	Co. A, 4th Virginia Cavalry	12/29/1863, Loudon County, Virginia	Died of Unknown Causes, 8/27/1864

Name	Age	Enlisted	Residence	Unit	Captured	Date and Cause of Death
Stone, William A. Private	39	3/10/1862, Franklin County, North Carolina, Volunteer	Franklin County, North Carolina	Co. G, 47th North Carolina Infantry	7/5/1863, Gettysburg, Pennsylvania	Died of Smallpox, 12/20/1863
Stone, William A. Private	Unk	2/11/1863, Charleston, South Carolina	Charleston County, South Carolina	Co. G, 27th South Carolina Infantry	6/24/1864, Near Petersburg, Virginia	Died of Unknown Causes, 8/6/1864
Stone, William J. Private	33	8/18/1862, Raleigh, North Carolina, Conscript	Davidson County, North Carolina	Co. I, 2nd North Carolina Infantry	11/7/1863, Kelly's Ford, Virginia	Died of Unknown Causes, 7/18/1864
Stough, Allison Private	39	9/28/1861, Concord, North Carolina, Volunteer	Cabarrus County, North Carolina, Farmer	Co. C, 33rd North Carolina Infantry	7/14/1863, Falling Waters, Maryland	Died of Unknown Causes, 3/4/1864
Stout, Delaney B. Private	Unk	Unknown	Unknown	Co. A, 1st Battalion Arkansas Cavalry	Unknown	Unable to Locate
Stowe, W. L. Private	Unk	7/1/1862, Newton, North Carolina	Catawba County, North Carolina	Co. E, 57th North Carolina Infantry	9/23/1864, Cedar Creek or Strasburg, Virginia	Died of Chronic Diarrhea, 1/23/1865
Stowe, Washington S. Private	24	6/15/1861, Concord, North Carolina, Volunteer	Cabarrus County, North Carolina	Co. F, 1st North Carolina Cavalry	9/22/1863, Near Madison County Court House, Virginia	Died of Chronic Diarrhea, 1/31/1865
Stowe, Wilson L. Private Not Listed On Monument	Unk	5/4/1863, Kinston, North Carolina	Union County, North Carolina	Co. B, 43rd North Carolina Infantry	5/30/1864, Hanover Junction, Virginia	Died of Unknown Causes, 6/16/1864
Strain, James A. Private	22	2/26/1862, Chapel Hill, North Carolina, Volunteer	Orange County, North Carolina	Co. G, 11th North Carolina Infantry	10/27/1864, Near Petersburg, Virginia	Died of Chronic Diarrhea, 3/29/1865
Stramby, Peter Private	22	6/4/1861, Camp Moore, New Orleans, Louisiana	Parish County, Louisiana	Co. E, 5th Louisiana Infantry	11/7/1863, Rappahannock Station, Virginia	Died of Unknown Causes, 3/2/1864

Name	Age	Enlisted	Residence	Unit	Captured	Date and Cause of Death
Strange, Francis M. Private	18	6/4/1861, Fork of Wilson, Virginia	Grayson County, Virginia, Laborer	Co. D, 50th Virginia Infantry	7/5/1863, Gettysburg, Pennsylvania	Died of Unknown Causes, 3/2/1864
Stribling, Robert H. Private Not Listed On Monument	Unk	10/1/1862, Morrisville, Virginia	Fauquier County, Virginia	Co. I, 11th Virginia Infantry	7/3/1863, Gettysburg, Pennsylvania	Died of Chronic Dysentery, 10/31/1863
Stribling, Segismund T. Sergeant	Unk	6/7/1861, Camp Moore, New Orleans, Louisiana	New Orleans, Louisiana, Clerk	Co. H, 7th Louisiana Infantry	5/11/1864, Spotsylvania Court House, Virginia	Died of Unknown Causes, 8/22/1864
Strickland, D. O. Private	19	6/28/1862, Anderson District, South Carolina	Unknown	Co. G, 6th South Carolina Cavalry	12/1/1864, Stony Creek, Virginia	Died of Chronic Diarrhea, 5/31/1865
Strickland, John R. Private	26	2/24/1862, Nashville, North Carolina	Nash County, North Carolina, Farmer	Co. A, 47th North Carolina Infantry	10/27/1864, Burgess' Mill, Near Petersburg, Virginia	Died of Remittent Fever, 12/7/1864
Strickland, Reddin Private	36	2/28/1863, Nash County, North Carolina, Volunteer	Nash County, North Carolina	Co. G, 47th North Carolina Infantry	10/27/1864, Burgess' Mill, Near Petersburg, Virginia	Died of Chronic Diarrhea, 5/30/1865
Stringfield, Chapman J. Sergeant	19	6/23/1861, Smithfield, Virginia	Isle of Wight, Virginia, Student	Co. I, 3rd Virginia Infantry	4/1/1865, Five Forks, Virginia	Died of Congestive Fever, 6/22/1865
Stroup, Hosea Private	35	5/5/1864, Lincoln County, North Carolina, Conscript	Lincoln County, North Carolina	Co. H, 52nd North Carolina Infantry	10/27/1864, Near Petersburg, Virginia	Died of Typhoid Fever, 12/5/1864
Stroup, Lafayette Private	20	7/6/1863, Lincoln County, Virginia	Lincoln County, Virginia	Co. H, 52nd North Carolina Infantry	7/14/1863, Falling Waters, Maryland	Died of Unknown Causes, 2/25/1864
Stroup, Robert Private	20	3/25/1862, Lincoln County, North Carolina, Volunteer	Lincoln County, Virginia	Co. H, 52nd North Carolina Infantry	7/14/1863, Falling Waters, Maryland	Died of Unknown Causes, 2/20/1864

Name	Age	Enlisted	Residence	Unit	Captured	Date and Cause of Death
Strukey, W. D. Private	Unk	2/28/1863, James Island, South Carolina	Charleston District, South Carolina	Co. H, 21st South Carolina Infantry	5/7/1864, Near Petersburg, Virginia	Died of Acute Dysentery, 1/22/1865
Stryker, Martin Private	25	4/19/1861, Norfolk, Virginia	Norfolk County, Virginia	Co., A, 6th Virginia Infantry	10/27/1864, Near Petersburg, Virginia	Died of Scurvy, 5/7/1865
Stuart, George F. Private	Unk	8/22/1863, Decatur, Georgia	DeKalb County, Georgia	Co. B, 7th South Carolina Cavalry	10/11/1864, Petersburg, Virginia	Died of Typhoid Fever, 12/26/1864
Stuart, S. A. Private	21	7/15/1862, Raleigh, North Carolina, Conscript	Davidson County, North Carolina	Co. H, 15th North Carolina Infantry	10/14/1863, Bristoe Station, Virginia	Died of Unknown Causes, 2/23/1864
Stubblefield, Wyatt Private	32	10/3/1862, Morristown, Tennessee	Granger County, Tennessee	Co. G, 61st Tennessee Mounted Infantry	Unknown	Date and Cause of Death Unknown
Stuckey, Wiley D. Private Not Listed On Monument	Unk	2/28/1863, James Island, South Carolina	Charleston District, South Carolina	Co. H, 21st South Carolina Infantry	5/9/1864, Near Petersburg, Virginia	Died of Acute Dysentery, 1/22/1865
Stump, Fleming S. Private Not Listed On Monument	31	4/5/1862, Camp Shenandoah, Virginia	Pendleton, County, West Virginia	Co. F, 25th Virginia Infantry	5/21/1864, Spotsylvania Court House, Virginia	Died of Unknown Causes, 7/4/1864
Sturdivant, Francis M. Private	34	5/14/1862, Granada, Mississippi	Hernando, Mississippi, Farmer	Co. C, 42nd Mississippi Infantry	7/23/1863, Front Royal, Virginia	Died of Unknown Causes, 3/5/1864
Sugden, Samuel H. Private	Unk	5/4/1861, New Orleans, Louisiana	New Orleans, Louisiana, Mechanic	Co. K, 1st Louisiana Infantry	5/23/1864, North Anna, Virginia	Died of Unknown Causes, 9/14/1864

Name	Age	Enlisted	Residence	Unit	Captured	Date and Cause of Death
Sugg, George W. Private	Unk	1/12/1864, Green County, North Carolina	Green County, North Carolina	Co. I, 40th North Carolina Artillery	3/19/1865, Bentonville, North Carolina	Died of Pneumonia, 5/28/1865
Suggs, George P. Private	Unk	4/20/1862, Bethesda, Georgia	Unknown	Co. F, 61st Georgia Infantry	5/24/1864, North Anna, Virginia	Died of Unknown Causes, 9/18/1864
Sullens, John F. Private	Unk	7/27/1862, Blountsville, Alabama	Blount County, Alabama	Co. C, 12th Alabama Cavalry	6/27/1863, Shelbyville, Tennessee	Died of Chronic Diarrhea & Typhoid Fever, 10/31/1863
Sullins, J. Private	Unk	8/1/1864, Christb., Virginia	Unknown	Co. D, 21st Virginia Cavalry	9/25/1864, Woodstock, Virginia	Died of Chronic Diarrhea, 2/25/1865
Sullivan, Adam Private	Unk	4/15/1862, Wilmington, North Carolina	New Hanover County, North Carolina	Co. C, 51st North Carolina Infantry	6/1/1864, Cold Harbor, Virginia	Died of Consumption, 10/18/1864
Sullivan, Dennis S. Private	Unk	6/8/1861, New Orleans, Louisiana	New Orleans, Louisiana, Porter	Co. K, 15th Louisiana Infantry	5/5/1864, Wilderness, Virginia	Died of Acute Dysentery, 7/28/1864
Sullivan, Jesse D. Private	23	7/1/1861, Wadesboro, North Carolina	Anson County, North Carolina	Co. K, 26th North Carolina Infantry	7/5/1863, Gettysburg, Pennsylvania, Wounded	Died of Chronic Diarrhea, 11/13/1863
Summers, Adolphus C. Private	Unk	7/26/1861, Olin, North Carolina, Volunteer	Iredell County, North Carolina, Farmer	Co. A, 33rd North Carolina Infantry	6/13/1864, Riddle Shop, White Oak Swamp, Virginia	Died of Unknown Cause, 6/13/1864
Summers, Hezekiah Private Not Listed On Monument	Unk	4/10/1864, Camp Holmes, Raleigh, North Carolina	Caswell County, North Carolina	Co. A, 13th North Carolina Infantry	5/23/1864, North Anna, Virginia	Died of Pneumonia, 4/16/1865
Summers, William A. Private	Unk	Unknown	Unknown	Co. C, 6th Battalion South Carolina Reserves	2/28/1865, Near Chesterfield, South Carolina	Died of Erysipelas, 5/11/1865

Name	Age	Enlisted	Residence	Unit	Captured	Date and Cause of Death
Surratt, Whitson H. Private	Unk	8/21/1864, Raleigh, North Carolina, Conscript	Wake County, North Carolina	Co. I, 3rd North Carolina Infantry	9/19/1864, Winchester, Virginia	Died of Typhoid Fever, 1/8/1865
Suther, David S. Private	Unk	7/8/1862, Concord, North Carolina, Conscript	Cabarrus County, North Carolina	Co. F, 23rd North Carolina Infantry	7/2/1863, Gettysburg, Pennsylvania	Died of Unknown Causes, 12/22/1863
Sutherland, James W. Private Not Listed On Monument	Unk	3/13/1862, Fredericksburg Virginia	Stafford County, Virginia	Co. M, 55th Virginia Infantry	5/6/1864, Wilderness, Virginia	Died of Inflammation of Lungs (Pneumonia), 7/13/1864
Sutherland, Robert Private	Unk	3/31/1862, Orange County, Virginia	Orange County, Virginia	Capt. Tailor's Co. Virginia Artillery	4/6/1865, Amelia County, Virginia	Died of Typhoid Fever, 6/29/1865
Suthern, Josephus Private	Unk	3/10/1862, Giles County Court House, Virginia	Giles County, Virginia	Co. D, 7th Virginia Infantry	4/6/1865, Harper's Farm, Virginia	Died of Dysentery, 6/24/1865
Sutton, Thomas J. Private	Unk	Unknown	Unknown	Co. H, 36th North Carolina Heavy Artillery	1/15/1865, Fort Fisher, North Carolina	Died of Rubeola (Measles), 2/10/1865
Swafford, Moses W. Private	Unk	2/25/1863, Hog Mountain, Georgia	Unknown	Co. H, 35th Georgia Infantry	7/3/1863, Gettysburg, Pennsylvania	Died of Chronic Diarrhea, 11/22/1863
Swains, T. N. Private	Unk	Unknown	Unknown	8th Louisiana Infantry	Unknown	Unable to Locate
Swan, W. H. Sergeant	Unk	4/30/1862, Haralson, Georgia	Haralson County, Georgia	Co. G, 53rd Georgia Infantry	10/19/1864, Cedar Creek or Strasburg, Virginia	Died of Acute Dysentery, 11/27/1864

Name	Age	Enlisted	Residence	Unit	Captured	Date and Cause of Death
Swanson, John Private	32	7/15/1861, Camp Near Bentonville, Arkansas	Benton County, Arkansas	Co. A, 15th Arkansas Infantry	5/10/1863, Champion Hill, Tennessee	Died of Smallpox, 12/24/1863
Swartz, John B. Private	Unk	7/15/1861, Leesburg, Virginia	Loudoun County, Virginia	Co. C, 8th Virginia Infantry	7/4/1863, Gettysburg, Pennsylvania	Died of Chronic Diarrhea, 3/10/1865
Sweeny, William Private	21	6/25/1861, Wytheville, Virginia	Wytheville County, Virginia	Co. B, 50th Virginia Infantry	5/12/1864, Spotsylvania Court House, Virginia	Died of Inflammation of Lungs (Pneumonia), 8/31/1864
Swicord, Thomas Sergeant	Unk	9/23/1863, Bainbridge, Decatur County, Georgia	Decatur County, Georgia	Co. B, 29th Battalion Georgia Cavalry	12/12/1864, Liberty County, Georgia	Died of Remittent Fever, 3/19/1865
Swiney, William See: Sweeny, William				Co. B, 50th Virginia Infantry		
Swing, Henry E. Private	28	3/11/1862, Guilford County, North Carolina, Volunteer	Guilford County, North Carolina, Farmer	Co. A, 53rd North Carolina Infantry	7/5/1863, Gettysburg, Pennsylvania	Died of Smallpox, 11/24/1863
Swinson, Elbert Private	Unk	10/16/1864, Camp Holmes, Raleigh, North Carolina	Wake County, North Carolina	Co. A, 38th North Carolina Infantry	4/8/1865, Petersburg, Virginia	Died of Inflammation of Lungs (Pneumonia), 4/19/1865
Switzer, James C. Private	Unk	8/4/1864, Dublin, Virginia	Pulaski County, Virginia	Co. F, 26th Battalion Virginia Infantry	9/22/1864, Fisher's Hill, Virginia	Died of Pneumonia, 2/7/1865
Sykes, John Private	Unk	7/4/1862, Enfield, North Carolina	Halifax County, North Carolina	Co. F, 7th Confederate Cavalry	1/28/1864, Smith's Mills, Onslow County, North Carolina	Died of Unknown Causes, 7/28/1864
Symons, James W. Private	Unk	3/7/1862, Camp Smith, Virginia	Unknown	Co. H, 6th Virginia Cavalry	8/18/1863, Markham Station, Maryland	Died of Unknown Causes, 8/9/1864

Name	Age	Enlisted	Residence	Unit	Captured	Date and Cause of Death
Talbert, Milton See: Tolbert, Milton				Co. F, 44th North Carolina Infantry		
Talbert, T. J. Private	Unk	5/11/1861, New Orleans, Louisiana	Parish County, Louisiana	Co. A, 2nd Louisiana Infantry	5/20/1864, Spotsylvania Court House, Virginia	Died of Unknown Causes, 10/21/1864
Taliaferro, Charles Private	22	4/1/1861, Columbia, Georgia	Coweta County, Georgia	Co. E, 14th Georgia Infantry	5/12/1864, Spotsylvania Court House, Virginia, Wounded	Died of Unknown Causes, 7/17/1864
Taliaferro, Morgan O. Private	Unk	4/22/1861, New Orleans, Louisiana	Parish County, Louisiana	Co. A, 1st Louisiana Infantry	7/9/1864, Frederick City, Monocacy, Maryland, Gunshot Wound Left Side	Died of Smallpox, 3/15/1865
Talley, Charles Private	37	10/1/1862, Newport, Tennessee	Cocke County, Tennessee	Co. H, 60th Tennessee Mounted Infantry	5/17/1863, Big Black Bridge, Near Vicksburg, Mississippi	Died of Unknown Causes, 9/12/1864
Talley, Robert B. Corporal	Unk	7/26/1861, Fork Church, Louisa County, Virginia	Louisa County, Virginia	Co. F, 56th Virginia Infantry	8/25/1864, Near Howlett's House, Virginia	Died of Typhoid Fever, 11/18/1864
Tally, John Private	Unk	3/1/1862, Heathsville, Virginia	Unknown	Co. A, 40th Virginia Infantry	6/27/1863, Mercerville, Maryland	Died of Chronic Diarrhea, 10/31/1863
Tankersley, Jackson D. W. Private	Unk	10/26/1861, Fayetteville, Arkansas	Washington County, Arkansas	Co. D, 1st Battalion Arkansas Cavalry	5/17/1863, Big Black Bridge, Near Vicksburg, Mississippi	Died of Chronic Diarrhea, 11/29/1863
Tannerhill, D. M. See: Tannihill, D. M.				Co. C, 3rd Louisiana Infantry		

Name	Age	Enlisted	Residence	Unit	Captured	Date and Cause of Death
Tannihill, D. M. Private	Unk	Unknown	Unknown	Co. C, 3rd Louisiana Infantry	5/20/1863, Snyder's Bluff, Virginia	Died of Ascites (Abdominal Dropsy), 3/7/1864
Tarpley, F. W. 1st Sergeant	Unk	5/2/1862, McDonough, Georgia	Henry County, Georgia	Co. F, 53rd Georgia Infantry	4/3/1865, Richmond, Virginia	Died of Chronic Dysentery, 5/3/1865
Tate, Charles Private	Unk	Unknown	Unknown	Co. D, 2nd North Carolina Infantry	Unknown	Unable to Locate
Tate, Nathan G. Private	Unk	7/26/1861, Fork Church, Louisa County, Virginia	Unknown	Co. F, 56th Virginia Infantry	8/25/1864, Near Howlett's House, Virginia	Died of Gangrene, 3/4/1865
Tatom, N. Gray See: Tatum, Nicholas Gray				Co. D, 53rd North Carolina Infantry		
Tatum, Nicholas Gray Private	18	10/7/1862, Bladen County, North Carolina, Conscript	Bladen County, North Carolina	Co. D, 53rd North Carolina Infantry	7/5/1863, Gettysburg, Pennsylvania	Died of Smallpox, 12/10/1863
Taylor, Alfred A. Private	23	6/1/1861, Dogwood Grove, North Carolina, Volunteer	New Hanover County, North Carolina	Co. K, 3rd North Carolina Infantry	5/10/1864, Spotsylvania Court House, Virginia	Died of Unknown Causes, 8/8/1864
Taylor, Benjamin B. Private	Unk	7/29/1862, Florence, South Carolina	Florence County, South Carolina	Co. H, 23rd South Carolina Infantry	4/1/1865, Five Forks, Virginia	Died of Chronic Dysentery, 6/28/1865
Taylor, Benoni Private	Unk	Unknown	Unknown	Co. I, 1st Virginia Reserves	4/3/1865, Richmond, Virginia	Died of Ammonia, 6/14/1865
Taylor, C. J. Private	Unk	Unknown	Unknown	Co. A, 2nd Battalion Virginia Infantry	Unknown	Unable to Locate

Name	Age	Enlisted	Residence	Unit	Captured	Date and Cause of Death
Taylor, C. M. Private	19	8/17/1861, Luka, Mississippi	Kemper County, Mississippi	Co. C, Jeff Davis Legion Mississippi Cavalry	6/21/1863, Upperville, Virginia, Wounded	Died of Smallpox, 12/5/1863
Taylor, Charles Private	Unk	Unknown	Unknown	Co. B, 2nd Mississippi Infantry	7/3/1863, Gettysburg, Pennsylvania	Died of Chronic Diarrhea and Scurvy, 10/22/1863
Taylor, Columbus W. Private Not Listed On Monument	Unk	7/1/1861, Crawfordsville Georgia	Taliaferro County, Georgia	Co. D, 15th Georgia Infantry	7/5/1863, Gettysburg, Pennsylvania	Died of Unknown Causes, 10/14/1863
Taylor, David Corporal	Unk	6/24/1861, Independence, Virginia	Grayson County, Virginia	Co. K, 51st Virginia Infantry	3/2/1865, Waynesboro, Virginia	Died of Scurvy, 4/25/1865
Taylor, David F. Private	Unk	3/1/1862, Washington, Arkansas	Hempstead County, Arkansas	Co. A, 20th Arkansas Infantry	5/17/1863, Big Black Bridge, Near Vicksburg, Mississippi	Died of Chronic Diarrhea, 11/20/1863
Taylor, F. C. Private	Unk	Unknown	Unknown	Co. B, 2nd Virginia Cavalry	Unknown	Unable to Locate
Taylor, Henry Private	36	3/29/1862, Fredericksburg Virginia	Caroline County, Virginia, Manager	Co. H, 47th Virginia Infantry	5/23/1864, Milford, Virginia	Died of Chronic Dysentery, 1/28/1865
Taylor, Henry E. Private	22	11/1/1862, Brandy Station, Virginia, Volunteer	Northampton County, North Carolina	Co. H, 2nd North Carolina Cavalry	9/23/1863, Near Madison Court House, Virginia	Died of Unknown Causes, 6/22/1864
Taylor, James H. 1st Sergeant	22	6/25/1861, Near Aberdeen, Mississippi	Monroe County, Mississippi	Co. B, 20th Mississippi Infantry	5/16/1863, Edwards Depot, Brownsville, Virginia	Died of Unknown Causes, 8/22/1864
Taylor, James W. Private	Unk	10/26/1863, Laurinburg County, Virginia	Laurinburg County, Virginia	Co. I, 59th Virginia Infantry	4/6/1865, Harper's Farm, Virginia	Died of Unknown Causes, 5/18/1865

Name	Age	Enlisted	Residence	Unit	Captured	Date and Cause of Death
Taylor, Joseph W. Private	23	12/16/1863, Surry County, North Carolina	Surry County, North Carolina	Co. E, 53rd North Carolina Infantry	9/22/1864, Fisher's Hill, Virginia	Died of Chronic Diarrhea, 1/22/1865
Taylor, McGilbert Private	23	6/24/1861, Williamston, North Carolina	Martin County, North Carolina	Co. H, 1st North Carolina Infantry	5/12/1864, Spotsylvania Court House, Virginia	Died of Unknown Causes, 8/10/1864
Taylor, Reuben Private	Unk	3/29/1862, Lewisburg, Virginia	Greenbrier County, West Virginia	Co. H, 26th Battalion Virginia Infantry	9/19/1864, Winchester, Virginia	Died of Chronic Diarrhea, 1/14/1865
Taylor, Robert J. Private	Unk	6/22/1861, Tanner's Store, Virginia	Unknown	Co. B, 56th Virginia Infantry	4/1/1864, Chaffin's Farm, Virginia	Died of Chronic Diarrhea, 6/3/1865
Taylor, Samuel F. Private	Unk	4/20/1862, York County, Virginia	York County, Virginia	Jones' Co., Pamunkey, Virginia Heavy Artillery	4/6/1865, Harper's Farm, Virginia	Died of Chronic Diarrhea, 4/25/1865
Teague, Loss L. Private	19	5/20/1862, Asheville, North Carolina	Buncombe County, North Carolina	Co. G, 1st North Carolina Cavalry	8/1/1863, Brandy Station, Virginia	Died of Unknown Causes, 12/26/1863
Temple, James F. Private	Unk	10/11/1864, Brunswick County, Virginia	Brunswick County, Virginia	Co. D, 12th Virginia Infantry	4/7/1865, Amelia Court House, Virginia	Died of Pneumonia, 5/6/1865
Templeton, W. A. Private	Unk	9/1/1863, Thunderbolt, Richmond County, Georgia	Richmond County, Georgia	Co. F, 22nd Battalion Georgia Heavy Artillery	12/13/1864, Fort McAllister, Georgia	Died of Pneumonia, 4/8/1865
Terrel, Mahlon Syrell Sergeant	Unk	4/27/1861, Richmond, Virginia	Henrico County, Virginia	Co. K, 1st Virginia Artillery	7/3/1863, Gettysburg, Pennsylvania	Died of Unknown Causes, 2/1/1864
Terrell, James M. Private	20	8/1/1861, Warrenton, North Carolina, Volunteer	Warren County, North Carolina	Co. F, 12th North Carolina Infantry	7/5/1863, Hagerstown, Maryland	Died of Typhoid Fever, 11/26/1863

Name	Age	Enlisted	Residence	Unit	Captured	Date and Cause of Death
Terrill, William See: Ferrell, William				Co. C, 52nd North Carolina Infantry		
Terry, Edward G. Private	18	9/23/1861, Beaufort County, North Carolina	Beaufort County, North Carolina	Co. G, 36th North Carolina Heavy Artillery	9/8/1863, Topsail Inlet, Cape Fear River, North Carolina	Died of Smallpox, 1/3/1864
Terry, Stephen Private	17	9/11/1862, Jackson, Kentucky	Jackson County, Kentucky	Co. A, fifth Kentucky Mounted Infantry	5/16/1863, Champion Hill, Tennessee	Died of Smallpox, 1/22/1864
Terry, Thomas Private	19	9/11/1862, Jackson, Breathett County, Kentucky	Breathett County, Kentucky	Co. A, 5th Kentucky Mounted Infantry	5/16/1863, Champion Hill, Tennessee	Died of Chronic Diarrhea, 12/21/1863
Terry, W. B. Private	Unk	Unknown	Unknown	Co. D, 2nd Florida Infantry	Unknown	Unable to Locate
Tessenear, Jackson Name Not On Monument	37	2/12/1863, Rutherford County, North Carolina, Volunteer	Rutherford County, North Carolina, Farmer	Co. I, 56th North Carolina Infantry	5/20/1864, Drewry's Love, Virginia, Gunshot Wound Left Thigh	Died of Unknown Causes, 7/14/1864
Tetterton, Hosea Private	40	11/6/1861, Washington, North Carolina, Volunteer	Hunter's Bridge, Beaufort County, North Carolina, Farmer	Co. B, 61st North Carolina Infantry	9/10/1864, Near Petersburg, Virginia	Died of Remittent Fever, 11/26/1864
Tetterton, James H. Private	20	11/4/1861, Martin County, North Carolina, Volunteer	Martin County, North Carolina, Farmer	Co. H, 61st North Carolina Infantry	4/14/1864, Nansemond River, Virginia, Gunshot Wound Right Knee & Left Thigh	Died of Pneumonia, 3/5/1865
Tew, Sampson M. Private	20	5/10/1861, Sampson County, North Carolina, Volunteer	Sampson County, North Carolina, Farmer	Co. H, 20th North Carolina Infantry	7/1/1863, Gettysburg, Pennsylvania	Died of Chronic Diarrhea, 1/15/1864

Name	Age	Enlisted	Residence	Unit	Captured	Date and Cause of Death
Tezmier, Jackson See: Tessenear, Jackson				Co. I, 56th North Carolina Infantry		
Thacker, James M. Private	Unk	7/22/1861, Forsyth County, Georgia	Forsyth County, Georgia	Co. D, 2nd Battalion North Carolina Infantry	7/3/1863, Gettysburg, Pennsylvania	Died of Unknown Causes, 8/11/1864
Thacker, James M. Private Name Not On Monument	Unk	7/22/1861, Place Unknown	Unknown	Co. E, 21st Georgia Infantry	7/3/1863, Gettysburg, Pennsylvania	Died of Unknown Causes, 8/11/1864
Thaker, Camel Private	Unk	Unknown	Unknown	Semmes Artillery	4/6/1865, Harper's Farm, Virginia	Died of Unknown Causes, 5/24/1865
Thatch, Stephen Private	26	1/23/1862, Windsor, North Carolina, Volunteer	Bertie County, North Carolina	Co. C, 11th North Carolina Infantry	1/27/1864, Near Plymouth, North Carolina	Died of Chronic Diarrhea, 3/5/1865
Thomas, Benjamin Private	31	9/15/1862, Guilford County, North Carolina, Conscript	Guilford County, North Carolina	Co. A, 1st North Carolina Infantry	5/5/1864, Wilderness, Virginia	Died of Unknown Causes, 7/31/1864
Thomas, Charles W. Private	Unk	6/22/1861, Tanner's Store, Mecklenburg County, Virginia	Mecklenburg County, Virginia	Co. B, 56th Virginia Infantry	4/6/1865, Farmville, Virginia	Died of Pneumonia, 4/25/1865
Thomas, David L. Private	Unk	11/23/1864, Petersburg, Virginia	Chesterfield County, Virginia	Captain Gregg's Co., South Carolina Light Artillery	4/2/1865, Petersburg, Virginia	Died of Acute Diarrhea, 6/10/1865
Thomas, Fendall See: Thomas, Phendal				Co. E, 52nd Virginia Infantry		
Thomas, J. D. Private	Unk	Unknown	Unknown	Co. I, 60th Tennessee Mounted Infantry	Unknown	Unable to Locate

Name	Age	Enlisted	Residence	Unit	Captured	Date and Cause of Death
Thomas, John P. Private	Unk	6/2/1861, Lynchburg, Virginia	Franklin County, Virginia	Co. G, 24th Virginia Infantry	7/3/1863, Gettysburg, Pennsylvania	Died of Unknown Causes, 9/12/1864
Thomas, John P. Private	Unk	3/16/1864, Kinston, North Carolina	Anson County, North Carolina	Co. H, 43rd North Carolina Infantry	4/2/1865, Petersburg, Virginia	Died of Pneumonia, 5/3/1865
Thomas, Phendal F. Private Name Not On Monument	Unk	9/10/1864, Botetourt, Virginia	Botetourt County, Virginia	Co. E, 52nd Virginia Infantry	9/23/1864, Fisher's Hill, Cedar Creek or Strasburg, Virginia	Died of Chronic Diarrhea, 1/25/1865
Thomas, Oliver Private	Unk	4/21/1862, Marion, South Carolina	Marion District, South Carolina	Co. F, 27th South Carolina Infantry	8/21/1864, Globe Tavern, Near Weldon Railroad, Virginia	Died of Chronic Diarrhea, 2/5/1865
Thomas, William P. C. Private	Unk	5/10/1863, Palmyra, Virginia	Fluvanna County, Virginia	Co. E, 18th Virginia Infantry	7/3/1863, Gettysburg, Pennsylvania	Died of Unknown Causes, 9/13/1864
Thomas, W. R. Private	28	Unknown	Unknown	Co. E, 6th North Carolina Cavalry	6/6/1863, Simpson's Ford, Kentucky	Died of Chronic Diarrhea & Scurvy, 3/16/1865
Thomas, W. R. Private	Unk	4/1/1864, Indian Creek, Virginia	Unknown	Co. C, Wise Legion, Virginia Light Artillery	10/19/1864, Cedar Creek or Strasburg, Virginia	Died of Pneumonia, 4/4/1865
Thomason, James B. Private	Unk	4/1/1864, Columbia, South Carolina	Richland County, South Carolina	Co. F, Hampton's Legion South Carolina Mounted Infantry	4/6/1865, Burkesville, Virginia	Died of Acute Dysentery, 5/30/1865
Thomason, Joseph R. Private	Unk	1/15/1863, Mecklenburg County, Virginia	Mecklenburg County, Virginia	Captain Coleman's Virginia Heavy Artillery	Unknown	Died of Chronic Diarrhea, 5/27/1865
Thomason, Simeon Private	Unk	Unknown	Unknown	Co. C, 2nd Battalion Georgia Infantry	Unknown	Unable to Locate

Name	Age	Enlisted	Residence	Unit	Captured	Date and Cause of Death
Thompson, Armistead Private	Unk	6/22/1861, Dransesville, Virginia	Fairfax County, Virginia	Co. L, 8th Virginia Infantry	7/4/1863, Gettysburg, Pennsylvania	Died of Inflammation of the Lungs (Pneumonia), 11/23/1864
Thompson, George Winton Private	19	9/1/1864, Troy, Montgomery County, North Carolina	Alamance County, North Carolina	Co. B, 44th North Carolina Infantry	Unknown	Died of Chronic Diarrhea, 1/17/1865
Thompson, J. M. Private	Unk	1/15/1864, Goochland, Virginia	Goochland County, Virginia	Co. F, 4th Virginia Cavalry	3/14/1865, Ashland, Virginia	Died of Pneumonia, 6/4/1865
Thompson, James L. Private	Unk	5/13/1862, Camp Brown, Georgia	Taylor County, Georgia	Co. H, 50th Georgia Infantry	10/19/1864, Cedar Creek or Strasburg, Virginia	Died of Chronic Diarrhea, 1/9/1865
Thompson, John Private	19	3/22/1862, Camp Lowes, Lincoln County, North Carolina, Volunteer	Lincoln County, North Carolina, Volunteer	Co. G, 52nd North Carolina Infantry	7/3/1863, Gettysburg, Pennsylvania	Died of Chronic Diarrhea, 12/24/1863
Thompson, Josiah Private	27	5/1/1862, Wayne County, North Carolina, Volunteer	Wayne County, North Carolina, Farmer	Co. G, 55th North Carolina Infantry	7/1/1863, Gettysburg, Pennsylvania	Died of Unknown Causes, 1/25/1864
Thompson, O. Private	Unk	8/24/1861, Place Unknown	Banks County, Georgia	Co. A, 24th Georgia Infantry	7/12/1863, Hagerstown, Maryland	Died of Bronchitis & Diarrhea, 10/31/1863
Thompson, Oliver N. Private	22	7/15/1862, Alamance County, North Carolina	Alamance County, North Carolina	Co. B, 1st North Carolina Infantry	7/3/1863, Gettysburg, Pennsylvania, Wounded	Died of Chronic Diarrhea, 1/26/1864
Thompson, Richard C. Private	Unk	7/17/1861, Jamestown, Virginia	James City County, Virginia	Co. F, 14th Virginia Infantry	7/3/1863, Gettysburg, Pennsylvania	Died of Unknown Causes, 2/17/1864
Thompson, Samuel D. Private	25	12/20/1861, Camp Harlee, Mecklenburg County, Virginia	Mecklenburg County, Virginia	Co. D, 21st South Carolina Infantry	7/10/1863, Morris Island, South Carolina	Died of Unknown Causes, 11/5/1863

Name	Age	Enlisted	Residence	Unit	Captured	Date and Cause of Death
Thompson, Sydney A. Sergeant Name Not On Monument	18	7/5/1862, Fort Caswell, North Carolina, Volunteer	Caswell County, North Carolina	Co. H, 56th North Carolina Infantry	5/14/1864, Near Fort Darling, Virginia	Died of Pneumonia, 7/15/1864
Thompson, William S. Private	21	5/1/1861, Marshall, Texas	Harrison County, Texas	Co. D, 7th Texas Infantry	5/12/1863, Raymond, Mississippi	Died of Unknown Causes, 1/28/1864
Thornburry, James W. See: Thornbery, James W.				Co. K, 28th Battalion Georgia Siege Artillery		
Thornbery, James W. Private	Unk	11/2/1863, Albany, Georgia	Dougherty County, Georgia	Co. K, 28th Battalion Georgia Siege Artillery	12/21/1864, Savannah, Georgia	Died of Chronic Diarrhea, 2/15/1865
Thorner, M. D. See: Koiner, Martin Diller				Co. B, 52nd Virginia Infantry		
Thoroughgood Paul Private	Unk	4/24/1862, Currituck County Court House, North Carolina	Currituck County, North Carolina	Co. G, 4th North Carolina Cavalry	10/14/1863, Newberry Bridge, North Carolina	Died of Pneumonia & Shot by Guard, 4/27/1864
Thorpe, Hanson H. Private	Unk	4/9/1864, Orange County Court House, Virginia	Orange County, Virginia	Co. F, 52nd North Carolina Infantry	10/27/1864, Burgess' Mill, Virginia	Died of Unknown Causes, 2/9/1865
Threts, H. See: Fritts, Henry				Co. B, 49th North Carolina Infantry		
Thrower, Newbern N. Private	18	2/24/1863, Stokes County, North Carolina	Stokes County, North Carolina	Co. A, 2nd Battalion North Carolina Infantry	3/25/1865, Fort Stedman, Near Petersburg, Virginia	Died of Pneumonia, 5/31/1865

Name	Age	Enlisted	Residence	Unit	Captured	Date and Cause of Death
Thrower, Wesley P. Private	23	8/6/1861, Forestville, North Carolina, Volunteer	Wake County, North Carolina	Co. I, 1st North Carolina Infantry	7/3/1863, Gettysburg, Pennsylvania	Died of Chronic Diarrhea, 11/17/1863
Tice, W. E. Private	Unk	7/24/1861, Clarksville, Georgia	Habersham County, Georgia	Co. E, 16th Georgia Infantry	7/2/1863, Gettysburg, Pennsylvania	Died of Smallpox, 12/28/1863
Tilghman, George D. See: Tillman, George D.				Co. K, 44th Virginia Infantry		
Tiller, Gilmore Private	Unk	3/4/1862, Clarke County, Georgia	Clarke County, Georgia	Co. C, 44th Georgia Infantry	5/20/1864, Spotsylvania Court House, Virginia	Died of Acute Dysentery, 3/23/1865
Tillett, Jonathan Private	Unk	Unknown	Unknown	Co. B, 68th North Carolina Infantry	4/17/1864, Indian Ridge Road, North Carolina	Died of Remittent Fever, 7/29/1864
Tilley, John R. Private Name Not On Monument	19	2/13/1862, Wake County, North Carolina, Volunteer	Wake County, North Carolina	Co. D, 30th North Carolina Infantry	11/7/1863, Kelly's Ford, Rappahannock Station, Virginia	Died of Chronic Diarrhea & Scurvy, 1/25/1865
Tillison, John J. See: Tillotson, Jeff J.				Co. C, Holcombe's Legion, South Carolina Infantry		
Tillman, George D. Private	16	6/11/1861, Bledsoe's Store, Fluvanna County, Virginia	Fluvanna County, Virginia	Co. K, 44th Virginia Infantry	5/12/1864, Spotsylvania Court House, Virginia	Died of Chronic Diarrhea, 5/26/1864
Tillman, Jeremiah M. Private	34	7/15/1862, Raleigh, North Carolina, Conscript	Peddlar's Hill, Chatham County, North Carolina, Shoemaker	Co. A, 5th North Carolina Infantry	5/12/1864, Spotsylvania Court House, Virginia	Died of Unknown Causes, 7/15/1862

Name	Age	Enlisted	Residence	Unit	Captured	Date and Cause of Death
Tillotson, Jeff J. Private	Unk	10/30/1863, Spartanburg District, South Carolina	Spartanburg District, South Carolina	Co. C, Holcombe's Legion, South Carolina Infantry	4/1/1865, Five Forks, Virginia	Died of Chronic Dysentery & Intermittent Fever, 6/6/1865
Timmons, John Private	Unk	11/1/1863, Montgomery County, Alabama	Montgomery County, Alabama	Co. B, 61st Alabama Infantry	4/2/1865, Petersburg, Virginia	Died of Acute Dysentery, 5/1/1865
Timmons, William J. Private	42	1/1/1862, Camp Harlee, Georgetown, South Carolina	Georgetown County, South Carolina	Co. I, 25th South Carolina Infantry	9/7/1863, Morris Island, South Carolina	Died of Erysipilas, 11/19/1863
Tindale, Samuel B. Private	Unk	Unknown	Unknown	Co. A, 7th Florida Infantry	7/22/1864, Near Atlanta, Georgia	Died of Consumption, 4/8/1865
Tinder, Arthur Private	Unk	8/17/1864, Orange County, Virginia	Orange County, Virginia	Co. C, 13th Virginia Infantry	10/19/1864, Cedar Creek or Strasburg, Virginia	Died of Pneumonia, 5/14/1865
Todd, J. T. Private	Unk	Unknown	Unknown	Co. F, 14th South Carolina Infantry	Unknown	Unable to Locate
Todd, Julius J. Sergeant	19	12/3/1863, Fernandina, Florida	Nassau County, Florida	Co. B, 10th Florida Infantry	4/3/1865, Richmond, Virginia	Died of Chronic Diarrhea, 5/16/1865
Tolly, Samuel See: Tolbert, Samuel S				Co. E, 22nd South Carolina Infantry		
Tolbert, Milton Private	20	3/1/1862, Troy, Montgomery County, North Carolina, Volunteer	Montgomery County, North Carolina, Farmer	Co. F, 44th North Carolina Infantry	10/27/1864, Near Petersburg, Virginia	Died of Inflammation of the Stomach, 12/13/1864
Tolbert, Samuel S. Private	Unk	1/7/1864, Sullivan's Island, South Carolina	Charleston District, South Carolina	Co. E, 22nd South Carolina Infantry	7/30/1864, Petersburg, Virginia, Wounded Left Side	Died of Chronic Diarrhea, 9/16/1864

Name	Age	Enlisted	Residence	Unit	Captured	Date and Cause of Death
Tolston, Joseph Private	23	7/20/1862, Edgecombe County, North Carolina	Edgecombe County, North Carolina, Farmer	Co. C, 8th North Carolina Infantry	5/31/1864, Cold Harbor, Virginia	Died of Tonsillitis, 4/25/1865
Tomberlin, Josiah G. Private	20	5/5/1862, Union County, North Carolina, Volunteer	Union County, North Carolina	Co. I, 53rd North Carolina Infantry	7/5/1863, Gettysburg, Pennsylvania	Died of Smallpox, 12/31/1863
Tomlinson, H. N. Private	19	11/4/1861, Randolph County, North Carolina, Volunteer	Randolph County, North Carolina, Farmer	Co. H, 38th North Carolina Infantry	7/5/1863, Gettysburg, Pennsylvania	Died of Unknown Causes, 12/26/1863
Tomlinson, Morrison Private	21	2/14/1862, Black Creek, North Carolina	Wilson County, North Carolina, Farmer	Co. C, 43rd North Carolina Infantry	7/5/1863, Gettysburg, Pennsylvania	Died of Chronic Diarrhea, 1/11/1864
Tompkins, J. A. Private	Unk	8/ /1863, Fredericksburg, Virginia	Spotsylvania County, Virginia	Co. I, 5th Virginia Cavalry	5/11/1864, Hanover County, Virginia	Died Unknown Causes 6/5/1864
Tompkins, John A. Private	Unk	5/15/1862, Louisville, Georgia	Jefferson County, Georgia	Co. E, 48th Georgia Infantry	7/3/1863, Gettysburg, Pennsylvania, Gunshot Wound of Right Shoulder and Chest	Died of Smallpox, 12/24/1864
Tompkins, M. D. Private	30	10/19/1862, Scott's Hill, North Carolina	Unknown	Captain A. F. Newkirk's Co., 3rd North Carolina Cavalry	11/7/1864, King's Crossing, Near Reams Station, Virginia	Died Unknown Causes, 3/31/1865
Tompson, William B. Private	Unk	6/10/1863, Fauquier County, Virginia	Fauquier County, Virginia	Co. B, Mosby's Regiment, Virginia Cavalry	11/20/1863, Near Middleburg, Loudon County, Virginia	Died of Chronic Diarrhea, 7/30/1864
Toward, John Private	Unk	Unknown	Unknown	Co. H, 2nd Tennessee Infantry	Unknown	Unable to Locate
Towery, Bartlett Private	Unk	4/20/1864, Camp Holmes, Raleigh, North Carolina	Wake County, North Carolina	Co. F, 34th North Carolina Infantry	4/3/1865, Sutherland Station, Virginia	Died of Pneumonia, 5/14/1865

Name	Age	Enlisted	Residence	Unit	Captured	Date and Cause of Death
Townsend, Steven B. F. Private	38	3/4/1862, Irwinville, Georgia	Irwin County, Georgia	Co. F, 49th Georgia Infantry	7/2/1863, Gettysburg, Pennsylvania	Died of Smallpox, 11/3/1863
Trail, George P. Private Name Not On Monument	Unk	1/20/1864, Charleston, South Carolina	Spartanburg District, South Carolina	Co. A, Holcombe's Legion, South Carolina Infantry	4/1/1865, Five Forks, South Carolina	Died of Chronic Diarrhea, 7/2/1865
Trainer, Arthur Private Name Not On Monument	Unk	Unknown	Unknown	Co. G, 61st North Carolina Infantry	8/26/1863, Morris Island, South Carolina	Died of Unknown Causes, 11/1/1864
Trainer, James Private	Unk	Unknown	Fulton County, Georgia	Co. B, 19th Georgia Infantry	8/19/1864, Globe Tavern, Near Weldon Railroad, Virginia	Died of Acute Dysentery, 3/4/1865
Trammel, Andrew Private Not Listed On Monument	Unk	6/20/1861, Bachelor's Hall, Virginia	Unknown	Co. I, 57th Virginia Infantry	7/3/1863, Gettysburg, Pennsylvania	Died of Chronic Diarrhea, 11/1/1863
Trammel, J. F. Private	Unk	4/5/1864, Dallas County, Alabama	Dallas County, Alabama	Co. E, 12th Alabama Infantry	5/13/1864, Spotsylvania Court House, Virginia	Died of Unknown Causes, 6/23/1864
Trammell, John E. Private Not Listed On Monument	Unk	6/22/1861, Dranesville, Virginia	Fairfax County, Virginia	Co. G, 8th Virginia Infantry	Deserted Regiment 8/31/1863	Died of Apoplexy 6/21/1865
Traylor, John W. Private	Unk	2/26/1862, Columbia County, Arkansas	Columbia County, Arkansas	Co. B, Dockery's 19th Arkansas Infantry	5/17/ 1863, Big Black Bridge, Near Vicksburg, Mississippi	Died of Chronic Diarrhea, 11/2/1863

Name	Age	Enlisted	Residence	Unit	Captured	Date and Cause of Death
Traywick, Henry S. Private	Unk	7/1/1862, Anson County, North Carolina, Conscript	Anson County, North Carolina	Co. E, 33rd North Carolina Infantry	7/14/1863, Following Waters, Maryland	Died of Chronic Diarrhea, 1/28/1864
Tredaway, James Corporal	Unk	3/4/1863, Camilla, Mitchell County, Georgia	Mitchell County, Georgia	Co. C, 51st Georgia Infantry	7/3/1863, Gettysburg, Pennsylvania	Died of Chronic Bronchitis, 1/19/1864
Tremmel, A. Private	26	8/12/1862, Camp Watts, Alabama	Tallapoosa County, Alabama, Farmer	Co. I, 8th Alabama Infantry	7/2/1863, Gettysburg, Pennsylvania, Wounded	Died of Smallpox, 12/6/1863
Trent, James L. Private	Unk	9/27/1863, Richmond County, North Carolina, Conscript	Richmond County, North Carolina	Co. G, 18th North Carolina Infantry	5/22/1864, Jericho Ford, Virginia	Date and Cause of Death Unknown
Trice, Thomas Private	Unk	3/7/1863, King & Queen Court House, Virginia	King & Queen County, Virginia	Co. E, 24th Virginia Cavalry	3/11/1864, King & Queen County, Virginia	Died of Unknown Causes, 8/4/1864
Trinnell, John Private	Unk	Unknown	Unknown	Co. H, 8th Virginia Infantry	Unknown	Unable to Locate
Tripp, Furnifold Private Name Not On Monument	Unk	7/10/1863, Pitt County, North Carolina	Pitt County, North Carolina	Co. G, 8th North Carolina Infantry	6/1/1864, Cold Harbor, Virginia	Died of Unknown Causes, 7/6/1864
Tripp, Thomas N. Private	Unk	12/1/1861, Dover, Pope County, Arkansas	Pope County, Arkansas	Co. I, 21st Arkansas Infantry	5/16/1863, Champion Hill, Tennessee	Died of Unknown Causes, 1/9/1864
Troublefield, Marcus Private	Unk	5/15/1864, Camp Vance, North Carolina	Burke County, North Carolina	Co. F, 3rd North Carolina Junior Reserves	12/25/1864, Fort Fisher, North Carolina	Died of Remittent Fever, 2/13/1865
Troutman, Daniel O. Private	29	2/27/1862, Rowan County, North Carolina	Rowan County, North Carolina	Co. D, 1st North Carolina Artillery	4/5/1865, Burkesville, Virginia	Died of Chronic Diarrhea, 4/25/1865

Name	Age	Enlisted	Residence	Unit	Captured	Date and Cause of Death
Troxler, Daniel Private	31	7/15/1862, Guilford County, North Carolina	Guilford County, North Carolina	Co. A, 1st North Carolina Infantry	5/5/1864, Wilderness, Virginia	Died of Pneumonia, 10/25/1864
Truman, Robert H. Private	Unk	3/3/1862, Henrico, Virginia	Henrico County, Virginia	Co. F, 25th Battalion Virginia Infantry	4/6/1865, Prince Edward County, Virginia	Died of Acute Dysentery, 5/5/1865
Tubman, Richard Private	Unk	Unknown	Unknown	Co. C, 1st Maryland Cavalry	7/5/1863, Cashtown, Pennsylvania	Died of Unknown Causes, 11/15/1863
Tuck, Richard W. Private	Ubk	1/24/1862, Richmond, Virginia	Henrico County, Virginia	Co. D, 25th Battalion Virginia Infantry	4/6/1865, Burkesville, Virginia	Died of Chronic Diarrhea, 6/14/1865
Tucker, Arthur Private	20	1/27/1862, Greenville, North Carolina, Volunteer	Pitt County, North Carolina, Farmer	Co. I, 44th North Carolina Infantry	10/14/1863, Bristoe Station, Virginia	Died of Unknown Causes, 6/23/1864
Tucker, C. W. Private	Unk	Unknown	Unknown	Co. B, 1st Virginia Cavalry	Unknown	Unable to Locate
Tucker, J. W. Private	Unk	8/12/1861, Richmond, Virginia	Henrico County, Virginia	Co. H, 13th Georgia Infantry	10/19/1864, Cedar Creek or Strasburg, Virginia	Died of Chronic Dysentery, 11/25/1864
Tucker, Leroy C. Private	Unk	Unknown	Unknown	Co. C, 7th Alabama Cavalry	6/27/1863, Shelbyville, Tennessee	Died of Chronic Diarrhea, 2/3/1864
Tucker, Lewis R. Private	23	9/2/1862, Raleigh, North Carolina, Conscript	Anson County, North Carolina	Co. H, 43rd North Carolina Infantry	3/25/1865, Fort Stedman, Near Petersburg, Virginia	Died of Inflammation of Lungs (Pneumonia), 4/19/1865
Tuggle, Charles M. Captain	Unk	3/18/1863, Hog Mountain, Hall County, Georgia	Unknown	Co. H, 35th Georgia Infantry	7/2/1863, Gettysburg, Pennsylvania	Died of Disease, 10/12/1864
Trune, William K. Private	Unk	8/25/1864, Place Unknown	Unknown	Co. F, 53rd Virginia Infantry	4/1/1865, Five Forks, Virginia	Died of Chronic Dysentery, 5/2/1865

Name	Age	Enlisted	Residence	Unit	Captured	Date and Cause of Death
Turnipseed, Henry W. Private Name Not On Monument	18	5/4/1861, Raleigh, Mississippi	Smith County, Mississippi	Co. H, 16th Mississippi Infantry	4/21/1864, Globe Tavern, Near Weldon Railroad, Virginia	Died of Chronic Diarrhea, 2/20/1865
Turley, James S. Private	23	7/1/1862, Camp Perry, Virginia	Unknown	Co. H, 29th Virginia Infantry	4/3/1865, Richmond, Virginia, Hospital	Died of Pneumonia, 6/2/1865
Turner, Charles H. Private	21	6/15/1861, Manassas, Virginia	Prince William County, Virginia, Farmer	Co. H, 11th Virginia Infantry	7/3/1863, Gettysburg, Pennsylvania	Died of Chronic Diarrhea, 1/10/1865
Turner, J. C. Private	Unk	Unknown	Unknown	Co. K, 5th North Carolina Infantry	4/3/1865, Richmond, Virginia, After Lee's Surrender	Died of General Debility & Dropsy, 7/4/1865
Turner, James J. Private	26	4/8/1862, Atlanta, Georgia	Fulton County, Georgia	Co. G, Cobb's Legion, Georgia infantry	12/12/1864, Sussex Court House, Virginia	Died of Unknown Causes, 1/20/1865
Turner, James P. Private	Unk	1/28/1864, Yorkville, South Carolina	York County, South Carolina	Co. F, 17th South Carolina Infantry	3/25/1865, Fort Stedman, Near Petersburg, Virginia	Died of Scurvy, 6/17/1865
Turner, Joel A. Private	Unk	4/15/1861, Pittsboro, North Carolina	Chatham County, North Carolina	Co. F, 13th Virginia Cavalry	7/12/1863, Hagerstown, Maryland	Died of Unknown Causes, 9/9/1863
Turner, John Private	Unk	10/4/1862, Zollicoffer, Tennessee	Maury County, Tennessee	Co. I, 61st Tennessee Mounted Infantry	5/16/1863, Big Black Bridge, Near Vicksburg, Mississippi	Died of Unknown Causes, 1/13/1864
Turner, John A. Private	Unk	6/20/1863, Mocksville, North Carolina	Davie County, North Carolina	Co. M, 7th Confederate Cavalry	3/5/1864, Suffolk, Virginia	Died of Phthisis (Wasting Away), 2/13/1865
Turner, Martin L. Private	30	10/22/1862, Winchester, Virginia	Louisa County, Virginia, Farmer	Co. D, 44th Virginia Infantry	5/12/1864, Spotsylvania Court House, Virginia	Died of Dysentery, 9/17/1864

Name	Age	Enlisted	Residence	Unit	Captured	Date and Cause of Death
Turner, Samuel Private	19	10/4/1862, Zollicoffer, Tennessee	Maury County, Tennessee	Co. K, 61st Tennessee Mounted Infantry	5/16/ 1863, Big Black Bridge, Near Vicksburg, Mississippi	Died of Scurvy, 3/10/1865
Turner, William Private	23	3/17/1862, Henry Court House, Virginia	Henry County, Virginia	Co. H, 24th Virginia Infantry	4/1/1865, Five Forks, Virginia	Died of Chronic Dysentery, 6/5/1865
Turner, William R. Private	Unk	3/10/1863, Albany, Georgia	Dougherty County, Georgia	Co F, 64th Georgia Infantry	8/17/1864, Deep Bottom, Virginia	Died of Typhoid Fever, 12/22/1864
Turpin, Matthew W. Private	22	11/26/1862, Camp Trousdale, Tennessee	Unknown	Co. K, 41st Tennessee Infantry	5/17/1863, Raymond, Mississippi	Died of Chronic Bronchitis & Diarrhea, 1/28/1864
Tusson, René Sergeant	Unk	6/4/1861, Camp Moore, New Orleans, Louisiana	Parish County, Louisiana	Co. A, 5th Louisiana Infantry	5/12/1864, Spotsylvania Court House, Virginia	Died of Unknown Causes, 8/27/1864
Tuten, Redding G. Sergeant Name Not on Monument	18	6/25/1861, Beaufort County, North Carolina, Volunteer	Beaufort County, North Carolina	Co. I, 4th North Carolina Infantry	9/19/1864, Winchester, Virginia	Died of Chronic Diarrhea, 2/3/1865
Tye, Henry M. Private	Unk	4/15/1862, Quitman County, Georgia	Quitman County, Georgia	Co. G, 51st Georgia Infantry	6/3/1864, Gaines Farm, Virginia	Died of Unknown Causes, 6/26/1864
Tyler, J. R. Private	Unk	Unknown	Unknown	Co. B, 4th North Carolina Infantry	Unknown	Unable to Locate
Tyner, John G. Private	Unk	3/2/1862, Darlington District, South Carolina	Darlington District, South Carolina	Co. G, 21st South Carolina Infantry	7/10/1863, Morris Island, South Carolina	Died of Unknown Causes, 1/9/1864

Name	Age	Enlisted	Residence	Unit	Captured	Date and Cause of Death
Umbarger, John Private	Unk	5/3/1862, Bland County, Virginia	Bland County, Virginia	Co. G, 36th Virginia Infantry	9/19/1864, Winchester, Virginia	Died of Chronic Diarrhea, 1/7/1865
Umbarger, Stephen Private	Unk	Unknown	Unknown	Co. K, 1st Virginia Infantry	4/5/1865, Amelia Court House, Virginia	Died of Chronic Diarrhea, 5/26/1865
Underdown, John W. Private	18	7/15/1861, Lenoir County, North Carolina, Volunteer	Caldwell County, North Carolina	Co. F, 26th North Carolina Infantry	7/5/1863, Gettysburg, Pennsylvania, Wounded	Died of Chronic Diarrhea, 4/19/1864
Underwood, John W. See: Underdown, John W.				Co. F, 26th North Carolina Infantry		
Unknown	Unk	Unknown	Unknown	Unknown	Unknown	Unknown
Upchurch, Daniel Private	Unk	2/13/1864, Rutherford County, North Carolina	Rutherford County, North Carolina	Co. I, 34th North Carolina Infantry	5/23/1864, North Anna, Virginia	Died of Unknown Causes, 6/14/1864
Upchurch, Jasper N. Corporal	19	8/11/1862, Louisburg, North Carolina, Volunteer	Franklin County, North Carolina	Co. E, 1st North Carolina Cavalry	4/3/1865, Petersburg, Virginia	Died of Pneumonia, 4/18/1865
Upchurch, John W. Private	22	5/2/1862, Franklin County, North Carolina, Volunteer	Franklin County, North Carolina	Co. B, 47th North Carolina Infantry	10/27/1864, Near Petersburg, Virginia	Died of Acute Diarrhea, 12/31/1864
Updyke, Ammon W. Private	Unk	4/21/1862, Suffolk, Virginia	Isle of Wight County, Virginia	Co. I, 53rd Virginia Infantry	4/2/1865, Five Forks, Virginia	Died of Acute Dysentery, 5/27/1865
Ury, Jacob Private Name Not On Monument	31	6/23/1862, Concord, North Carolina, Volunteer	Cabarrus County, North Carolina	Co. H, 57th North Carolina Infantry	11/7/1863, Rappahannock Station, Virginia	Died of Chronic Diarrhea, 6/10/1864

Name	Age	Enlisted	Residence	Unit	Captured	Date and Cause of Death
Uzzell, Benjamin Private	18	2/8/1864, Franklin County, North Carolina, Volunteer	Franklin County, North Carolina	Co. G, 47th North Carolina Infantry	10/27/1864, Near Petersburg, Virginia	Died of Pneumonia, 4/30/1865
Uzzell, James E. Sergeant	16	3/29/1862, Franklin County, North Carolina, Volunteer	Franklin County, North Carolina, Student	Co. G, 47th North Carolina Infantry	10/27/1864, Near Petersburg, Virginia	Died of Pneumonia, 3/8/1865
Uzzell, William Gray Private	Unk	6/20/1861, Wilson County Court House, North Carolina	Wilson County, North Carolina	Co. G, 5th North Carolina Infantry	7/5/1863, Gettysburg, Pennsylvania	Died of Chronic Diarrhea and Scurvy, 11/28/1863
Name	Age	Enlisted	Residence	Unit	Captured	Date and Cause of Death
Vail, John Calvin Private Name Not On Monument	33	3/24/1861, Antioch, Alabama	Clarke County, Alabama	Co. E, 5th Alabama Infantry	7/2/1863, Gettysburg, Pennsylvania	Died of Chronic Diarrhea & Scurvy, 2/28/1865
Vandeventer, James Private	Unk	5/20/1861, Williamsburg, Virginia	York County, Virginia	Co. F, 1st Richmond Howitzers, Virginia Artillery	7/3/1863, Gettysburg, Pennsylvania	Died of Chronic Diarrhea, 9/1/1864
VanDyke, William R. Private	20	3/29/1862, X-Roads, Cleveland County, North Carolina, Volunteer	Gaston County, North Carolina, Farmer	Co. C, 55th North Carolina Infantry	7/4/1863, Gettysburg, Pennsylvania	Died of Smallpox, 1/3/1864
Vanhook, James Private	18	2/14/1863, Caroline County, Virginia Volunteer	Orange County, North Carolina, Volunteer	Co. B, 6th North Carolina Infantry	11/7/1863, Rappahannock Station, Virginia	Died of Chronic Diarrhea, 2/16/1865
VanHorn, John L. Private Name Not On Monument	Unk	3/1/1864, Orange County Court House, North Carolina	Orange County, North Carolina	Co. A, 32nd North Carolina Infantry	5/10/1864, Mine Run, Virginia	Died of Unknown Causes, 7/4/1864

Name	Age	Enlisted	Residence	Unit	Captured	Date and Cause of Death
VanHorn, Washington Sergeant	21	5/31/1861, Gillmor County Court House, Virginia	Gillmor County, Virginia	Co. D, 31st Virginia Infantry	7/5/1863, Waterloo, Gettysburg, Pennsylvania, Wounded	Died of Unknown Causes, 6/19/1864
Vann, Edward W. Private	Unk	4/10/1863, Madison Court House, Florida	Madison County, Florida	Co. G, 11th Florida Infantry	9/10/1864, Petersburg, Virginia	Died of Chronic Diarrhea, 10/26/1864
Varn, T. J. Private	Unk	1/15/1864, Camp Mercer, Georgia	Unknown	Captain Clinch's Battery, Georgia Light Artillery	12/13/1864, Fort McAllister, Georgia	Died of Dropsy & Scurvy, 6/6/1865
Varn, W. T. Private	Unk	Unknown	Unknown	Co. H, 6th Georgia Reserves	3/19/1865, Near Goldsboro, North Carolina	Died of Congestive Intermittent Fever, 4/9/1865
Varner, Albert See: Varner, Rankin A.				Co. H, 52nd North Carolina Infantry		
Varner, Nathan Private	Unk	4/1/1864, Greensboro, North Carolina	Guilford County, North Carolina	Co. G, 46th North Carolina Infantry	3/31/1865, Hatcher's Run, Virginia	Died of Pneumonia, 4/25/1865
Varner, Rankin A. Private	Unk	3/9/1864, Lincolnton, Lincoln County, North Carolina	Lincoln County, North Carolina	Co. H, 52nd North Carolina Infantry	10/24/1864, Near Petersburg, Virginia	Died of Scurvy, 4/7/1865
Varnier, Robert Private	Unk	Unknown	Unknown	Co. C, 9th Virginia Infantry	4/1/1865, Five Forks, Virginia	Died of Pneumonia, 4/28/1865
Vaughan, David Private	Unk	11/10/1862, Giles County, Tennessee	Giles County, Tennessee	Co. G, 3rd Tennessee Infantry	5/12/1863, Raymond, Mississippi	Died of Phthisis Pulmonalis (Tuberculosis), 11/14/1863
Vaughan, David Private	Unk	4/1/1864, Greenville, South Carolina	Greenville District, South Carolina	Co. F, Hampton's Legion, South Carolina Mounted Infantry	4/6/1865, Burkesville, Virginia	Died of Chronic Diarrhea, 6/30/1865

Name	Age	Enlisted	Residence	Unit	Captured	Date and Cause of Death
Vaughan, N. H. Private	Unk	1/20/1864, Lunenburg Court House, Virginia	Lunenburg County, Virginia	Co. G, 9th Virginia Cavalry	10/14/1864, Petersburg, Virginia	Died of Typhoid Fever, 1/10/1865
Vaughan, Stephen Private	28	5/1/1862, Camp Davis, North Carolina	Anson County, North Carolina	Co. K, 43rd North Carolina Infantry	10/19/1864, Cedar Creek or Strasburg, Virginia	Died of Chronic Dysentery, 2/17/1865
Vaughn, George W. Private	Unk	3/4/1862, Dahlonega, Georgia	Lumpkin County, Georgia	Co. E, Phillip's Legion, Georgia Infantry	7/5/1863, Gettysburg, Pennsylvania	Died of Chronic Diarrhea, 11/14/1863
Vaughn, J. Private	Unk	Unknown	Unknown	Co. H, 10th Kentucky Infantry	Unknown	Unable to Locate
Veach, George W. Private Name Not On Monument	Unk	10/1/1863, Salisbury, North Carolina	Rowan County, North Carolina	Co. D, 42nd North Carolina Infantry	3/10/1865, Wise Forks, Near Kinston, North Carolina	Died of Chronic Diarrhea, 7/2/1865
Veasey, James H. Sergeant	Unk	3/1/1862, Montgomery, Alabama	Montgomery County, Alabama	Co. I, 8th Confederate Cavalry	6/27/1863, Shelbyville, Tennessee	Died of Unknown Causes, 10/?/1863
Verser, Cicero A. Sergeant	23	4/23/1861, Farmville, Virginia	Prince Edward County, Virginia, Clerk	Co. C, 18th Virginia Infantry	7/4/1863, Gettysburg, Pennsylvania	Died of Unknown Causes, 3/27/1864
Verser, John A. Sergeant	Unk	9/1/1862, Richmond, Virginia	Henrico County, Virginia	Co. D, 25th Battalion Virginia Infantry	4/6/1865, Nottoway, Virginia	Died of Acute Diarrhea, 5/14/1865
Vest, Alexander Private Name Not On Monument	27	7/8/1862, Pfafftown, North Carolina, Conscript	Forsyth County, North Carolina	Co. I, 33rd North Carolina Infantry	5/12/1864, Near Spotsylvania Court House, Virginia	Died of Acute Diarrhea, 6/17/1864

Name	Age	Enlisted	Residence	Unit	Captured	Date and Cause of Death
Vestal. Henry T. Private	23	3/6/1862, Chatham County, North Carolina	Chatham County, North Carolina	Co. G, 26th North Carolina Infantry	7/14/1863, Falling Waters, Maryland	Died of Pneumonia, 12/26/1863
Via, Dillard Private	Unk	Unknown	Unknown	Co. H, 57th Virginia Infantry	4/2/1865, Hatcher's Run, Virginia	Died of Acute Diarrhea, 5/31/1865
Vick, Andrew J. Sergeant	Unk	8/21/1862, Camp Ruffin, Virginia	Unknown	Co. A, 13th Virginia Cavalry	10/17/1863, Brandy Station, Virginia	Died of Typhoid Fever, 1/26/1865
Vicker, A. Private	Unk	Unknown	Unknown	Co. B, 61st Virginia Infantry	10/27/1864, Near Petersburg, Virginia	Died of Inflammation of Lungs (Pneumonia), 4/10/1865
Vie, W. T. Private	Unk	Unknown	Unknown	Stiles Georgia Artillery	Unknown	Unable to Locate
Vincent, John J. Private	37	11/1/1862, Macon, Mississippi	Macon, Mississippi, Farmer	Co. F, 11th Mississippi Infantry	7/14/1863, Falling Waters, Maryland	Died of Smallpox, 12/29/1863
Vogler, Augustus E. N. Private	32	7/4/1862, Winston, North Carolina	Forsyth County, North Carolina	Co. D, 57th North Carolina Infantry	7/5/1863, Gettysburg, Pennsylvania	Died of Chronic Diarrhea, 3/22/1865
Vogler, John E. Private	32	9/1/1862, Mocksville, North Carolina	Forsyth County, North Carolina	Co. G, 7th Confederate Cavalry	9/30/1864, Fort Harrison, Virginia	Date and Cause of Death Unknown

Name	Age	Enlisted	Residence	Unit	Captured	Date and Cause of Death
Wadall, A. See: Weddele, Ahab A.				Co. A, 24th Virginia Infantry		

Name	Age	Enlisted	Residence	Unit	Captured	Date and Cause of Death
Waddell, George W. Private Name Not On Monument	19	9/28/1861, Camp Butler, South Carolina	Unknown	Co. E, 14th South Carolina Infantry	5/24/1862, North Anna, Virginia	Died of Chronic Diarrhea & Scurvy, 2/4/1865
Waddle, John M. Private	20	9/5/1863, Spotsylvania Court House, Virginia	Spotsylvania County, Virginia	Co. C, 5th Virginia Cavalry	12/21/1864, Lacey Springs, Virginia	Died of Pneumonia, 3/3/1865
Weddele, Ahab A. Private	26	5/4/1861, Floyd County Court House, Virginia	Floyd County, Virginia, Farmer	Co. A, 24th Virginia Infantry	7/6/1863, Gettysburg, Pennsylvania	Died of Typhoid Fever, 3/7/1864
Wade, Jesse L. Private	Unk	Unknown	Unknown	Co. A, 36th Virginia Infantry	9/19/1864, Winchester, Virginia	Died of Chronic Diarrhea, 3/3/1865
Wade, John V. Corporal	32	3/8/1862, Richmond County, North Carolina	Richmond County, North Carolina, Farmer	Co. E, 52nd Battalion North Carolina Infantry	7/5/1863, Gettysburg, Pennsylvania	Died of Chronic Diarrhea, 2/2/1864
Wade, Mat G. Private	Unk	3/21/1862, Charlottesville, Virginia	Albemarle County, Virginia	Captain Carrington's Co., Virginia Light Artillery	10/19/1864, Cedar Creek or Strasburg, Virginia	Died of Chronic Diarrhea, 12/5/1864
Wade, W. E. Private	Unk	Unknown	Unknown	Gilmore's	Unknown	Unable to Locate
Wagner, Alexander Private	Unk	9/?/1862, Wilkesboro, North Carolina	Wilkes County, North Carolina	Co. F, 26th North Carolina Infantry	3/25/1865, Fort Stedman, Near Petersburg, Virginia	Died of Inflammation of Lungs (Pneumonia), 4/9/1865
Wagner, George W. Private	Unk	2/1/1864, Botetourt County, Virginia	Botetourt County, Virginia	Co. K, 60th Virginia Infantry	9/19/1864, Winchester, Virginia	Died of Pneumonia, 11/8/1864
Wagner, William Private	33	7/15/1862, Raleigh, North Carolina	Wake County, North Carolina	Co. H, 15th North Carolina Infantry	10/14/1863, Bristoe Station, Virginia	Died of Unknown Causes, 12/24/1863

Name	Age	Enlisted	Residence	Unit	Captured	Date and Cause of Death
Wagner, William F. Private	31	7/4/1862, Catawba County, North Carolina	Catawba County, North Carolina, Blacksmith	Co. E, 57th North Carolina Infantry	11/7/1863, Rappahannock Station, Virginia	Died of Chronic Diarrhea, 1/13/1864
Waisner, William N. Private	25	3/1/1862, Montgomery County, North Carolina, Volunteer	Montgomery County, North Carolina, Farmer	Co. F, 44th North Carolina Infantry	10/27/1864, Near Petersburg, Virginia	Died of Pneumonia, 1/20/1865
Waits, Beaufort Private	Unk	1/7/1862, Camp Hampton, South Carolina	Lancaster County, South Carolina	Co. H, Holcombe's Legion South Carolina Infantry	4/1/1865, Five Forks, Virginia	Died of Unknown Causes, 4/24/1865
Waits, Drayton Private Name Not On Monument	Unk	1/7/1862, Camp Hampton, South Carolina	Lancaster County, South Carolina	Co. H, Holcombe's Legion, South Carolina Infantry	4/1/1865, Five Forks, Virginia	Died of Acute Dysentery, 4/24/1865
Wakefield, Martin L. Private	Unk	8/26/1862, North Market, Alabama	Unknown	Co. K, Captain Russel's 4th Alabama Cavalry	6/27/1863, Shelbyville, Tennessee	Died of Unknown Causes, 2/25/1864
Walden, Alex J. Private	33	4/4/1862, Manchester, North Carolina	Chatham County, North Carolina, Farmer	Co. C, 54th North Carolina Infantry	6/7/1864, Cold Harbor, Virginia	Died of Scurvy, 3/2/1865
Walden, George P. Private	Unk	3/5/1862, Jacksonville, Alabama	Calhoun County, Alabama	Co. G, 10th Alabama Infantry	7/5/1863, Gettysburg, Pennsylvania, Gunshot Wound Right Arm	Died of Unknown Causes, 1/12/1864
Waldridge, Thomas D. Private	Unk	9/12/1862, Bedford County, Virginia	Bedford County, Virginia	Co. F, 18th Virginia Infantry	4/6/1865, High Bridge, Virginia	Died of Chronic Diarrhea, 6/9/1865
Waldron, J. Private	47	Unknown	Unknown	Co. G, 50th Virginia Infantry	4/3/1865, After Lee's Surrender, Richmond, Virginia, Hospital	Died of Gunshot Wound of Left Hip, 6/13/1865

Name	Age	Enlisted	Residence	Unit	Captured	Date and Cause of Death
Waldrop, Theron D. Private	Unk	5/18/1864, Camp Vance, North Carolina	Burke County, North Carolina	Co. C, 34th North Carolina Infantry	4/3/1865, Amelia Court House, Virginia	Died of Chronic Dysentery, 5/28/1865
Walker, Alexander W. Private	20	5/22/1861, Louisville, North Carolina, Volunteer	Rockingham, North Carolina	Co. K, 13th North Carolina Infantry	7/4/1863, Gettysburg, Pennsylvania	Died of Chronic Diarrhea, 11/27/1863
Walker, David B. Private	Unk	6/15/1862, Macon, Georgia	Bibb County, Georgia	Co. D, 59th Georgia Infantry	7/4/1863, Gettysburg, Pennsylvania	Died of Unknown Causes, 12/29/1863
Walker, David Private	19	3/1/1862, Reidsville, North Carolina, Volunteer	Rockingham, North Carolina, Farmer	Co. H, 45th North Carolina Infantry	7/5/1863, Gettysburg, Pennsylvania	Died of Unknown Causes, 1/26/1864
Walker, Francis M. Corporal	Unk	1/14/1862, Camp Brooks, South Carolina	Unknown	Co. B, 3rd South Carolina Infantry	5/23/1864, Hanover Junction, Virginia	Died of Acute Diarrhea, 10/29/1864
Walker, James Private	30	4/19/1861, Fishersville, Virginia	Augusta County, Virginia, Blacksmith	Co. H, 5th Virginia Infantry	9/22/1864, Waynesboro, Virginia	Died of Acute Diarrhea, 11/14/1864
Walker, Jefferson H. Private	32	7/8/1862, Salisbury, North Carolina	Alamance County, North Carolina	Co. I, 57th North Carolina Infantry	11/7/1863, Rappahannock Station, Virginia	Died of Unknown Causes, 12/29/1863
Walker, John Private	26	3/2/1863, Guilford County, North Carolina, Conscript	Guilford County, North Carolina	Co. G, 22nd North Carolina Infantry	7/3/1863, Gettysburg, Pennsylvania	Died of Unknown Causes, 12/25/1864
Walker, John H. Private	18	6/6/1861, Yanceyville, North Carolina	Caswell County, North Carolina	Co. H, 6th North Carolina Infantry	11/7/1863, Rappahannock Station, Virginia	Died of Remittent Fever, 2/22/1865
Walker, Robert Private	33	3/19/1862, Milton, North Carolina, Volunteer	Virginia County, North Carolina, Farmer	Co. I, 45th North Carolina Infantry	5/10/1864, Spotsylvania Court House, Virginia	Died of Unknown Causes, 9/6/1864

Name	Age	Enlisted	Residence	Unit	Captured	Date and Cause of Death
Walker, Robert Private Name Not On Monument	Unk	1/17/1864, Decatur, Georgia	DeKalb County, Georgia	Co. B, 29th Battalion Georgia Cavalry	12/13/1864, Dorchester, Liberty County, Georgia	Died of Remittent Fever, 7/2/1865
Walker, S. P. Private	Unk	Unknown	Unknown	Co. B, 19th Arkansas Infantry	5/16/1863, Champion Hill, Tennessee	Died of Unknown Causes, 3/18/1864
Walker, Thomas G. Sergeant	Unk	3/12/1862, Craig Court House, Virginia	Craig County, Virginia	Co. B, 28th Virginia Infantry	7/3/1863, Gettysburg, Pennsylvania	Died of Erysipelas of Face & Chronic Diarrhea, 1/6/1864
Walker, W. G. Private	Unk	Unknown	Unknown	Co. C, 15th South Carolina Infantry	Unknown	Unable to Locate
Walker, W. H. Seaman	Unk	Unknown	Unknown	Naval Battalion	Unknown	Unable to Locate
Walker, William Private	Unk	5/6/1861, Knoxville, Tennessee	Knox County, Tennessee	Co. A, 3rd Tennessee Mounted Infantry	5/17/1863, Big Black River, Near Vicksburg, Mississippi	Died of Chronic Diarrhea, 11/8/1863
Walker, William Private	Unk	2/28/1862, Goldsboro, North Carolina	Wayne County, North Carolina	Co. C, 52nd North Carolina Infantry	7/5/1863, Gettysburg, Pennsylvania, Gunshot Wound Right Leg	Died of Chronic Diarrhea, 1/27/1865
Walker, William A. Private	19	7/8/1862, Salisbury, North Carolina, Volunteer	Davie County, North Carolina	Co. H, 57th North Carolina Infantry	7/5/1863, Chambersburg Hospital, Virginia	Died of Chronic Diarrhea, 12/61863
Walker, William W. Sergeant	34	2/27/1862, Guilford County, North Carolina	Guilford County, North Carolina, Farmer	Co. F, 54th North Carolina Infantry	11/7/1863, Rappahannock Station, Virginia	Died of Pneumonia, 6/22/1864
Walker, Zebedee P. Private	Unk	4/22/1861, Pittsylvania Court House, Virginia	Pittsylvania County, Virginia	Co. I, 53rd Virginia Infantry	5/12/1864, Spotsylvania Court House, Virginia	Died of Chronic Diarrhea, 8/20/1864

Name	Age	Enlisted	Residence	Unit	Captured	Date and Cause of Death
Walls, Arthur Private	Unk	7/13/1862, Jackson County, Georgia	Jackson County, Georgia	Co. B, 16th Georgia Infantry	6/1/1864, Gaines Mills, Virginia	Died of Unknown Causes, 8/25/1864
Wall, John B. Private	34	5/17/1861, Clarksville, Tennessee	Montgomery County, Tennessee	Co. B, 14th Tennessee Infantry	5/5/1864, Wilderness, Virginia	Died of Erysipelas, 1/30/1865
Wall, John Richard Francis Private	18	2/20/1863, Stokes County, North Carolina	Stokes County, North Carolina	Co. D, 52nd North Carolina Infantry	7/14/1863, Falling Waters, Maryland	Died of Dropsy, 6/27/1864
Wall, Marcellus Henry Private	25	5/14/1862, Grenada, Mississippi	Chulahoma, Mississippi, Farmer	Co. D, 42nd Mississippi Infantry	7/14/1863, Falling Waters, Maryland	Died of Unknown Causes, 9/14/1864
Wall, W. D. Corporal	Unk	2/3/1862, Georgetown, South Carolina	Georgetown County, South Carolina	Co. F, 4th South Carolina Cavalry	5/28/1864, Hall's Shop, Virginia	Died of Unknown Causes, 9/6/1864
Wall, William A. Private	Unk	10/16/1864, Camp Holmes, Raleigh, North Carolina	Wake County, North Carolina	Co. C, 24th North Carolina Infantry	3/25/1865, Fort Stedman, Near Petersburg, Virginia	Died of Phthisis Pulmonalis (Tuberculosis), 5/25/1865
Wallace, George P. Private	22	6/2/1863, Culpepper Court House, Virginia	Albemarle County, Virginia	Co. F, 10th Virginia Cavalry	10/11/1863, Raccoon Ford, Brandy Station, Virginia, Wounded	Shot to Death by Point Lookout Guard, 1/27/1864
Wallace, Henry Private	42	9/27/1862, Winter's Gap, Tennessee	Anderson County, Tennessee	Co. K, Thomas' Legion, North Carolina & Tennessee Infantry	9/19/1864, Winchester, Virginia	Died of Chronic Diarrhea, 6/1/1865
Wallace, James Private	34	6/10/1861, Camp Anderson, Statesville, Iredell County, North Carolina	Iredell County, North Carolina	Co. K, 4th North Carolina Infantry	Unknown	Died of Scurvy, 3/21/1865

Name	Age	Enlisted	Residence	Unit	Captured	Date and Cause of Death
Wallace, James K. Private	26	1/20/1863, Camp Holmes, Raleigh, North Carolina	Wake County, North Carolina	Co. D, 26th North Carolina Infantry	7/14/1863, Falling Waters, Maryland	Died of Debility, 1/19/1864
Wallace, Rich H. Private Name Not On Monument	27	12/27/1864, Petersburg, Virginia	Wilkes County, North Carolina, Blacksmith	Co. F, 52nd North Carolina Infantry	4/2/1865, Petersburg, Virginia	Died of Chronic Diarrhea, 7/6/1865
Wallace, R. W. See: Waters, Rufus W.				Co. G, 22nd Virginia Infantry		
Wallace, William W. Corporal Name Not On Monument	Unk	3/10/1862, Blacksburg, Virginia	Montgomery County, Virginia	Co. L, 4th Virginia Infantry	5/12/1864, Near Spotsylvania, Virginia	Died of Unknown Causes, 7/5/1864
Waller, James W. Private	45	9/2/1863, Edgecombe County, North Carolina, Conscript	Tarboro, Edgecombe County, North Carolina, Farmer	Co. D, 40th North Carolina Artillery	1/15/1865, Fort Fisher, North Carolina	Died of Pneumonia, 2/24/1865
Waller, Woodley H. Private	Unk	6/4/1861, Republican Grove, Virginia	Halifax County, North Carolina	Co. F, 38th Virginia Infantry	7/3/1863, Gettysburg, Pennsylvania	Died of Unknown Causes, 9/3/1864
Waller, William A. Private	Unk	8/1/1863, Butler County, Alabama	Butler County, Alabama	Co. D, 61st Alabama Infantry	4/2/1865, Petersburg, Virginia	Died of Unknown Causes, 5/13/1865
Waller, William H. Corporal	Unk	6/15/1861, Eatonton, Georgia	Putnam County, Georgia	Co. G, 12th Georgia Infantry	7/3/1863, Gettysburg, Pennsylvania	Died of Unknown Causes, 4/1/1864
Walsh, Samuel Private	Unk	12/10/1863, Wilkes County, North Carolina	Wilkes County, North Carolina	Co. K, 53rd North Carolina Infantry	9/19/1864, Winchester, Virginia	Died of Pneumonia, 2/28/1865

Name	Age	Enlisted	Residence	Unit	Captured	Date and Cause of Death
Walters, Isaac Private	Unk	4/26/1862, Gates County, North Carolina, Volunteer	Gates County, North Carolina	Co. C, 2nd North Carolina Cavalry	6/30/1863, Hanover Junction, Pennsylvania	Died of Chronic Diarrhea, 12/28/1863
Walters, Thomas B. Private	Unk	9/1/1863, Hager Hill, Kentucky	Unknown	Co. I, 5th Kentucky Mounted Infantry	6/20/1863, Irvine, Kentucky	Died of Chronic Diarrhea & Pneumonia, 11/22/1863
Ward, Austin Private	Unk	3/1/1862, Atlanta, Georgia	Fulton County, Georgia	Co. C, 21st Georgia Infantry	7/3/1863, Gettysburg, Pennsylvania	Died of Smallpox, 12/10/1863
Ward, Daniel Private Name Not On Monument	Unk	5/5/1862, Wilmington, North Carolina	New Hanover County, North Carolina	Co. G, 51st North Carolina Infantry	5/19/1864, Near Drewry's Bluff, Virginia	Died of Unknown Causes, 1864
Ward, James M. Private	18	3/8/1862, Hillsboro, North Carolina, Volunteer	Orange County, North Carolina, Farmer	Co. G, 44th North Carolina Infantry	10/27/1864, Near Petersburg, Virginia	Died of Chronic Diarrhea, 2/19/1865
Ward, John Private	Unk	9/7/1864, Camp Holmes, Raleigh, North Carolina	Wake County, North Carolina	Co. A, 32nd North Carolina Infantry	10/19/1864, Cedar Creek or Strasburg, Virginia	Died of Chronic Dysentery, 3/16/1865
Ward, William C. Private	Unk	2/15/1864, Windsor, North Carolina	Bertie County, North Carolina	Co. C, 11th North Carolina Infantry	10/27/1864, Near Petersburg, Virginia	Died of Unknown Causes, 3/18/1865
Wardell, John M. See: Waddle, John M.				Co. C, 5th Virginia Cavalry		
Warlick, Maxwell H. Private Name Not On Monument	18	2/28/1863, Fredericksburg, Virginia	Catawba County, North Carolina, Farmer	Co. F, 23rd North Carolina Infantry	7/1/1863, Gettysburg, Pennsylvania	Died of Chronic Diarrhea, 4/18/1864
Warner, C. J. Private	31	9/3/1862, Mocksville, North Carolina	Forsyth County, North Carolina, Laborer	Co. G, 7th Confederate Cavalry	9/30/1864, Fort Harrison, Virginia	Died of Chronic Diarrhea, 12/31/1864

Name	Age	Enlisted	Residence	Unit	Captured	Date and Cause of Death
Warner, Emery Private	18	8/24/1862, Orange County Court House, North Carolina, Volunteer	Cleveland County, North Carolina	Co. F, 34th North Carolina Infantry	7/14/1863, Falling Waters, Maryland	Died of Unknown Causes, 9/7/1863
Warner, John H. Sergeant Not Listed On Monument	Unk	3/12/1862, Carthage, Moore County, North Carolina	Moore County, North Carolina	Co. H, 26th North Carolina Infantry	4/3/1865, Appomattox River, Virginia	Died of Chronic Diarrhea, 7/9/1865
Warnock, Jesse K. Corporal Name Not On Monument	Unk	4/3/1862, Bryan County, Georgia	Bryan County, Georgia	Co. H, 7th Georgia Cavalry	6/11/1864, Louisa Court House, Virginia	Died of Unknown Causes, 7/9/1864
Warren, Emery See: Warner, Emery				Co. F, 34th North Carolina Infantry		
Warren, Henry Private	31	11/1/1863, Germanton, North Carolina	Stokes County, North Carolina	Co. G 21st North Carolina Infantry	9/22/1864, Fisher's Hill, Virginia	Died of Chronic Diarrhea, 1/29/1865
Warren, James W. S. Private	Unk	7/8/1861, Griffin, Georgia	Spalding County, Georgia	Co. 13th Georgia Infantry	7/5/1863, Waterloo, Gettysburg, Pennsylvania	Died of Pneumonia, 12/3/1863
Warren, Malcolm Private Name Not On Monument	Unk	12/16/1863, Camp Near Orange Court House, Virginia	Sampson County, North Carolina	Co. C, 38th North Carolina Infantry	4/3/1865, Sutherlands Station, Virginia	Died of Pneumonia, 7/6/1865
Warren, Richard Private	28	7/25/1862, Danbury, North Carolina, Conscript	Stokes County, North Carolina	Co. G, 21st North Carolina Infantry	9/22/1864, Fisher's Hill, Virginia	Died of Typhoid Fever, 1/2/1865

Name	Age	Enlisted	Residence	Unit	Captured	Date and Cause of Death
Warwick, John J. Private	Unk	2/25/1862, Lillington, Kinston, North Carolina	Harnett County, North Carolina, Farmer	Co. H, 50th North Carolina Infantry	3/8/1865, Near Fayetteville, North Carolina	Died of Inflammation of the Lungs (Pneumonia), 4/10/1865
Washburn, John Jacob Private	1 9	5/18/1863, Marion, North Carolina, Volunteer	Mitchell County, North Carolina	Co. B, 22nd North Carolina Infantry	5/6/1864, Wilderness, Virginia	Died of Unknown Causes, 9/22/1864
Waters, Harrison Private	18	6/3/1861, Washington, North Carolina, Volunteer	Beaufort County, North Carolina	Co. E, 4th North Carolina Infantry	10/30/1863, Beaufort County, North Carolina	Died of Unknown Causes, 1/26/1864
Waters, John W. Private	Unk	7/1/1861, Prince William County, Virginia	Prince William County, Virginia	Co. B, 49th Virginia Infantry	9/14/1863, Dumfries, Virginia	Died of Unknown Causes, 8/11/1864
Waters, John R. Private	22	6/11/1861, Camp McDonald, Georgia	Unknown	Co. B, Phillip's Legion, Georgia Infantry	7/8/1863, Boonesboro, Maryland	Died of Chronic Dysentery & Smallpox, 1/12/1865
Waters, Rufus W. Private	Unk	1/31/1862, Gloucester Point, Virginia	Gloucester County, Virginia	Co. G, 22nd Virginia Infantry	6/4/1864, Cold Harbor, Virginia	Died of Scurvy, 6/12/1865
Waters, Thomas Private	Unk	10/24/1863, Raleigh, North Carolina	Wake County, North Carolina	Co. C, 18th North Carolina Infantry	5/12/1864, Spotsylvania Court House, Virginia	Date & Cause of Death Unknown
Waters, W. H. Private Name Not On Monument	Unk	Unknown	Unknown	Co. F, 8th Virginia Infantry	10/30/1863, Buford County, North Carolina	Died of Unknown Causes, 1/261864
Watkins, George W. Private	Unk	8/8/1864, Petersburg, Virginia	Chesterfield County, Virginia	Co. F, 16th Virginia Infantry	10/27/1864, Near Petersburg, Virginia	Died of Scurvy, 3/30/1865

Name	Age	Enlisted	Residence	Unit	Captured	Date and Cause of Death
Watkins, John Private	24	2/24/1862, Raleigh, North Carolina, Substitute	Wake County, North Carolina, Laborer	Co. E, 47th North Carolina Infantry	7/5/1863, Gettysburg, Pennsylvania, Gunshot Wound of Neck	Died of Chronic Dysentery, 2/8/1864
Watkins, John H. Private	Unk	Unknown	Unknown	No Regiment	3/10/1864, King and Queen County, Virginia	Died of Unknown Causes, 10/24/1864
Watkins, Joseph L. Private	26	4/28/1861, Tuskegee, Alabama	Tuskegee, Alabama, Farmer	Co. B, 4th Alabama Infantry	7/4/1863, Gettysburg, Pennsylvania	Died of Chronic Diarrhea, 11/22/1863
Watkins, Miniard E. Private	19	10/27/1862, Franklin County, North Carolina	Buncombe County, North Carolina	Co. K, 11th North Carolina Infantry	7/14/1863, Falling Waters, Maryland	Died of Chronic Diarrhea, 11/28/1863
Watkins, W. B. Private	Unk	5/8/1862, Butler, Georgia	Taylor County, Georgia	Co. C, 59th Georgia Infantry	7/4/1863, Cashtown, Pennsylvania	Died of Unknown Causes, 10/13/1864
Watkins, William B. Private	Unk	Unknown	Unknown	Co. E, 10th Battalion Virginia Heavy Artillery	4/6/1865, Amelia Court House, Virginia	Died of Chronic Dysentery, 5/10/1865
Watson, Apollas Private	21	9/20/1863, Winston, North Carolina, Conscript	Forsyth County, North Carolina	Co. D, 21st North Carolina Infantry	9/22/1864, Fisher's Hill, Virginia	Died of Acute Diarrhea, 1/14/1865
Watson, J. D. Private	Unk	2/9/1864, Notasulga, Alabama	Macon County, Alabama	Jeff Davis Alabama Artillery	10/19/1864, Cedar Creek or Strasburg, Virginia	Died of Pneumonia, 5/7/1865
Watson, William H. Private	Unk	3/7/1864, Macon, Georgia	Bibb County, Georgia	Captain Clinch's Battery, Georgia Light Artillery	12/13/1864, Fort McAllister, Georgia	Died of Chronic Diarrhea, 2/26/1865
Watts, John Private	Unk	11/20/1864, Burke County, Georgia	Wilkes County, North Carolina	Co. B, 11th North Carolina Infantry	4/2/1865, Hatcher's Run, Virginia	Died of Inflammation of Lungs (Pneumonia), 4/21/1865

Name	Age	Enlisted	Residence	Unit	Captured	Date and Cause of Death
Waugh, William J. Private	Unk	8/1/1863, Camp Hill, Statesville, North Carolina, Conscript	Iredell County, North Carolina	Co. C, 48th North Carolina Infantry	11/9/1863, Culpepper, Virginia	Died of Chronic Diarrhea, 3/3/1865
Waynefield, Thomas H. Private	Unk	Unknown	Unknown	Co. H, 19th Virginia Infantry	4/2/1865, Hatcher's Run, Virginia	Died of Inflammation of Bowels, 5/12/1865
Weaver, John Private	Unk	2/4/1864, Jefferson, North Carolina	Unknown	Co. A, 26th North Carolina Infantry	5/12/1864, Spotsylvania Court House, Virginia	Died of Unknown Causes, 5/20/1864
Webb, James W. Private	Unk	2/17/1864, Craig, Virginia	Craig County, Virginia	Co. G, 23rd Battalion Virginia Infantry	9/19/1864, Winchester, Virginia	Died of Chronic Dysentery, 11/7/1864
Webb, John Private	Unk	5/21/1861, Savannah, Georgia	Chatham County, Georgia	Co. B, 8th Georgia Infantry	7/5/1863, Gettysburg, Pennsylvania	Died of Unknown Causes, 3/13/1864
Webb, Joseph D. Private	18	6/24/1861, Williamston, North Carolina	Martin County, North Carolina	Co. H, 1st North Carolina Infantry	5/12/1864, Spotsylvania Court House, Virginia	Died of Erysipelas, 11/6/1864
Webb, Noah R. Private	20	10/30/1861, Richmond County, North Carolina, Substitute	Richmond County, North Carolina	Co. E, 30th North Carolina Infantry	5/6/1864, Mine Run, Virginia	Died of Unknown Causes, 6/17/1864
Weber, William H. Private	Unk	8/15/1863, Salem, Virginia	Roanoke County, Virginia	Co. B, 11th Virginia Infantry	4/1/1865, Five Forks, Virginia	Died of Measles, 6/13/1865
Webster, M. J. Private	33	9/13/1862, Pittsboro, North Carolina	Chatham County, North Carolina, Shoemaker	Co. D, 61st North Carolina Infantry	8/27/1863, Morris Island, South Carolina	Died of Chronic Diarrhea, 11/11/1863

Name	Age	Enlisted	Residence	Unit	Captured	Date and Cause of Death
Weeks, J. D. Corporal	Unk	1/13/1862, South Santee, South Carolina	Unknown	Co. D, 4th South Carolina Cavalry	6/11/1864, Louisa Court House, Virginia	Died of Unknown Causes, 7/24/1864
Weems, John A. Private	Unk	3/19/1862, Pickens Court House, South Carolina	Anderson District, South Carolina	Co. A, 1st South Carolina Rifles	7/14/1863, Falling Waters, Maryland	Died of Chronic Diarrhea, 1/27/1864
Wegner, William F. Private	Unk	7/1/1862, Newton, North Carolina	Catawba County, North Carolina	Co. E, 57th North Carolina Infantry	11/7/1863, Rappahannock Station, Virginia	Died of Chronic Diarrhea, 1/12/1864
Welch, Augustus Private	Unk	7/25/1861, Columbia County, Georgia	Columbia County, Georgia	Co. K, 16th Georgia Infantry	7/2/1863, Gettysburg, Pennsylvania	Died of Unknown Causes, 10/25/1863
Welch, Elisha A. Private	Unk	4/12/1864, Winston, Davidson County, North Carolina	Davidson County, North Carolina	Co. G, 7th Confederate Cavalry	9/30/1864, Fort Harrison, Virginia	Died of Consumption, 12/13/1864
Welch, W. H. Private	Unk	10/24/1864, Guilford County, North Carolina, Conscript	Guilford County, North Carolina	Co. K, 45th North Carolina Infantry	4/6/1865, Farmville, Virginia	Died of Chronic Diarrhea, 4/28/1865
Welchel, Charles C. Private Name Not On Monument	Unk	6/6/1861, Fairfax Station, Lynchburg, Virginia	Polk County, Tennessee	Co. D, 3rd Tennessee Mounted Infantry	5/17/ 1863, Big Black River, Near Vicksburg, Mississippi	Died of Smallpox, 12/23/1863
Wells, Henry H. Private	Unk	Unknown	Unknown	Smith's Battery Virginia Artillery	Unknown	Unable to Locate
Wells, James Private	Unk	Unknown	Unknown	Co. D, 7th South Carolina Cavalry	Unknown	Unable to Locate
Wells, John Private	19	9/26/1862, Henderson's Mills, Green County, Tennessee	Green County, Tennessee	Co. D, 61st Tennessee Mounted Infantry	5/17/ 1863, Big Black River, Near Vicksburg, Mississippi	Died of Unknown Causes, 2/1/1864

Name	Age	Enlisted	Residence	Unit	Captured	Date and Cause of Death
Wells, Latuna L. Private	Unk	10/19/1862, Richmond, Virginia	Henrico County, Virginia	Co. G, 59th Virginia Infantry	5/8/1864, Nottaway Bidge, Virginia	Died of Chronic Dysentery, 2/12/1865
Wells, W. Private	Unk	Unknown	Unknown	Co. K, 2nd North Carolina Infantry	7/3/1863, Gettysburg, Pennsylvania	Died of Smallpox, 2/24/1864
Welsh, John Private Name Not On Monument	Unk	6/4/1861, Camp Moore, New Orleans, Louisiana	Parish County, Louisiana	Co. A, 5th Louisiana Infantry	5/5/1864, Spotsylvania Court House, Virginia	Died of Unknown Causes, 7/4/1864
Wenberry, John E. Private	19	7/1/1861, Jacksonville, Onslow County, North Carolina, Volunteer	Onslow County, North Carolina	Co. F, 3rd North Carolina Infantry	6/10/1864, Spotsylvania Court House, Virginia	Died of Erysipelas, 8/26/1864
Werts, Henry M. Private	Unk	1/7/1862, Camp Hampton, South Carolina	Lancaster County, South Carolina	Co. H, Holcombe's Legion South Carolina infantry	4/1/1865, Five Forks, Virginia	Died of Typhoid Fever, 5/16/1865
Wescott, John W. Sergeant	27	7/18/1861, Smithville, North Carolina, Volunteer	Brunswick County, North Carolina	Co. C, 30th North Carolina Infantry	10/19/1864, Cedar Creek or Strasburg, Virginia	Died of Unknown Causes, 1/25/1865
West, Alexander Private	25	2/28/1862, Oxford, North Carolina, Conscript	Granville County, North Carolina	Co. I, 23rd North Carolina Infantry	5/11/1864, Near Spotsylvania, Virginia	Died of Chronic Diarrhea, 10/17/1864
West, Augustus F. Private	23	4/23/1861, Thomasville, North Carolina, Volunteer	Davidson County, North Carolina	Co. K, 14th North Carolina Infantry	10/19/1864, Cedar Creek or Strasburg, Virginia	Died of Cerebritis, Infection of the Brain, 2/4/1865
West, John W. Private	Unk	4/21/1861, Richmond, Virginia	Henrico County, Virginia	Co. K, 1st Virginia Artillery	7/5/1863, Waterloo, Gettysburg, Pennsylvania	Died of Chronic Diarrhea, 3/13/1864

Name	Age	Enlisted	Residence	Unit	Captured	Date and Cause of Death
West, Napoleon B. Corporal	Unk	11/1/1861, Halifax County Court House, Virginia	Halifax County, Virginia	Co. K, 3rd Virginia Infantry	7/3/1863, Gettysburg, Pennsylvania	Died of Chronic Dysentery, 3/2/1864
West, S. W. Private	28	3/2/1864, Greenville, South Carolina, Conscript	Spartanburg District, South Carolina, Farmer	Co. A, 3rd South Carolina Infantry	5/22/1864, North Anna, Virginia	Died of Unknown Causes, 6/24/1864
West, William M. Private	40	6/7/1863, Raleigh, North Carolina	Rowan County, North Carolina	Co. K, 30th North Carolina Infantry	10/19/1864, Cedar Creek or Strasburg, Virginia	Died of Pneumonia, 4/26/1865
Westbrook, Samuel D. Private	Unk	5/10/1862, Augusta, Georgia	Franklin County, Georgia	Co. B, 15th Georgia Infantry	7/2/1863, Gettysburg, Pennsylvania	Died of Smallpox, 12/9/1863
Westbrook, Y. J. Private	Unk	7/16/1862, Raleigh, North Carolina	Wake County, North Carolina	Co. D, 5th North Carolina Infantry	5/12/1864, Spotsylvania Court House, Virginia	Died of Unknown Causes, 10/9/1864
Westendorf, Charles Private	Unk	10/5/1863, Charleston, South Carolina	Charleston County, South Carolina	Co. A, 27th South Carolina Infantry	2/19/1865, Fort Anderson, North Carolina	Died of Erysipilas, 4/4/1865
Westmoreland, D. H. Private	Unk	5/16/1861, Crimea, Virginia	Rockbridge County, Virginia	Co. G, 53rd Virginia Infantry	7/3/1863, Gettysburg, Pennsylvania	Died of Unknown Causes, 2/11/1864
Westmoreland, John Private	Unk	2/15/1862, Prairie County, Arkansas	Prairie County, Arkansas	Co. G, 21st Arkansas Infantry	5/17/1863, Big Black River, Near Vicksburg, Mississippi	Died of Unknown Causes, 11/2/1863
Westmoreland, William M. Sergeant	Unk	12/1/1862, Stokes County, North Carolina	Stokes County, North Carolina	Co. D, 53rd North Carolina Infantry	7/5/1863, Gettysburg, Pennsylvania	Died of Unknown Causes, 3/13/1864
Weston, John M. Sergeant	Unk	Unknown	Unknown	Co. F, 67th North Carolina Infantry	3/27/1864, Near Washington, New Berne, North Carolina	Died of Chronic Diarrhea, 2/20/1865

Name	Age	Enlisted	Residence	Unit	Captured	Date and Cause of Death
Wetherford, Lemuel J. Private	Unk	9/1/1861, Hilton Head, South Carolina	Beaufort District, South Carolina	Co. C, 11th South Carolina Infantry	2/20/1865, Fort Anderson, North Carolina	Died of Pneumonia, 6/17/1865
Whaley, Braddock Private	19	1/28/1862, Duplin County, North Carolina	Duplin County, North Carolina	Co. A, 38th North Carolina Infantry	4/6/1865, Gill's Mill, Virginia	Died of Chronic Diarrhea, 6/19/1865
Whate, J. B. See: Whit, John B.				Co. B, 4th Virginia Cavalry		
Wheeler, Benjamin J. Private	20	5/5/1862, Charlottesville, Virginia	Albemarle County, Virginia	Captain Carrington's Co., Virginia Light Artillery	10/19/1864, Cedar Creek or Strasburg, Virginia	Died of Chronic Diarrhea, 5/18/1865
Wheeler, William J. Private	Unk	11/21/1863, Richmond, Virginia	Henrico County, Virginia	Co. E, 19th Battalion Virginia Heavy Artillery	4/6/1865, Burke's Farm, Virginia	Died of Chronic Dysentery, 5/28/1865
Whelan, William Landsman	Unk	Unknown	Unknown	Confederate States Navy	Unknown	Unable to Locate
Whetstone, William See: Whitstone, William				Captain Hart's Battalion, South Carolina Horse Artillery		
Whisenhunt, William M. Private	37	2/8/1863, Place in Virginia Unknown	Unknown	Co. E, 6th North Carolina Infantry	11/7/1863, Rappahannock Station, Virginia	Died of Typhoid Fever, 12/9/1863
Whit, John B. Private	Unk	1/23/1863, Halifax County, Virginia	Halifax County, Virginia	Co. B, 4th Virginia Cavalry	10/19/1864, Cedar Creek or Strasburg, Virginia	Died of Chronic Dysentery, 1/6/1865
Whitaker, Martin Private	Unk	10/14/1863, Raleigh, Wake County, North Carolina	Cleveland County, North Carolina	Co. I, 15th North Carolina Infantry	4/2/1865, Hatcher's Run, Virginia	Died of Measles, 6/27/1865

Name	Age	Enlisted	Residence	Unit	Captured	Date and Cause of Death
Whitaker, William Franklin Private	23	5/27/1861, Allegheny County, North Carolina	Allegheny County, North Carolina	Co. F, 22nd North Carolina Infantry	7/14/1863, Falling Waters, Maryland	Died of Unknown Causes, 1/24/1864
White, Archibald L. Private Not Listed On Monument	Unk	7/15/1861, Elberton County, Georgia	Elbert County, Georgia	Co. F, 15th Georgia Infantry	7/4/1863, Gettysburg, Pennsylvania	Died of Unknown Causes, 11/19/1863
White, Benjamin Private	Unk	7/7/1862, Trenton, North Carolina	Jones County, North Carolina	Captain Nethercutt's Co., 8th Battalion Partisan Rangers, North Carolina	8/4/1863, Cove Creek, North Carolina	Died of Unknown Causes, 9/25/1863
White, David Private	Unk	2/27/1862, Monroe, Louisiana	Ouachita Parish, Louisiana	Co. H, 12th Louisiana Infantry	6/15/1863, Baker's Creek or Champion Hill, Tennessee	Died of Debility, 12/11/1863
White, E. F. Private	18	11/25/1863, Mecklenburg County, North Carolina, Volunteer	Mecklenburg County, North Carolina	Co. H, 35th North Carolina Infantry	6/17/1864, Petersburg, Virginia	Date and Cause of Death Unknown
White, James Private	Unk	4/2/1862, Tazewell County, Virginia	Tazewell County, Virginia	Co. H, 29th Virginia Infantry	4/6/1865, Farmville, Virginia, Shot Right Hand and Left Chest	Died of Chronic Diarrhea, 5/19/1865
White, James F. Private	44	4/1/1862, Amite County, Mississippi	Pike County, Mississippi	Co. B, 33rd Mississippi Infantry	5/17/1863, Big Black River, Near Vicksburg, Mississippi	Died of Smallpox, 12/25/1863
White, John E. Private	29	7/30/1861, Gaston County, North Carolina	Gaston County, North Carolina	Co. B, 28th North Carolina Infantry	7/4/1863, Gettysburg, Pennsylvania	Died of Chronic Diarrhea, 11/3/1863
White, John H. 1st Sergeant	22	7/20/1861, Gloucester Point, Virginia	Gloucester County, Virginia	Co. B, 26th Virginia Infantry	6/15/1864, Petersburg, Virginia	Died of Unknown Causes, 10/23/1864

Name	Age	Enlisted	Residence	Unit	Captured	Date and Cause of Death
White, Luke H. Sergeant	Unk	7/15/1861, Elbert County, Georgia	Elbert County, Georgia	Co. F, 15th Georgia Infantry	7/3/1863, Gettysburg, Pennsylvania	Died of Smallpox, 11/19/1863
White, Matthew Private	Unk	7/12/1864, Thomas County, Georgia	Thomas County, Georgia	Co. E, 50th Georgia Infantry	10/19/1864, Cedar Creek or Strasburg, Virginia	Died of Chronic Diarrhea, 2/11/1865
White, P. S. Private	Unk	1/1/1863, Radfordville, Alabama	Unknown	Co. K, 8th Alabama Infantry	7/2/1863, Gettysburg, Pennsylvania	Died of Dropsy of Lungs, 11/11/1863
White, Swan Private	Unk	1/15/1864, Surrey County, North Carolina	Surrey County, North Carolina	Co. A, 26th North Carolina Infantry	5/12/1864, Spotsylvania Court House, Virginia	Died of Acute Diarrhea, 6/19/1864
White, Thomas J. Private	Unk	5/28/1861, Matthews County Court House, Virginia	Matthews County, Virginia	Co. D, 26th Virginia Infantry	5/8/1864, Nottoway Bridge, Virginia, Wounded	Died of Chronic Diarrhea, 2/27/1865
White, Van Buren Private	Unk	Unknown	Unknown	Co. H, 67th North Carolina Infantry	12/17/1863, Greenville, North Carolina	Died of Chronic Diarrhea, 2/19/1865
White, W. C. Private	21	6/1/1863, Forsyth County, North Carolina	Cleveland County, North Carolina	Co. D, 21st North Carolina Infantry	7/3/1863, Gettysburg, Pennsylvania	Died of Smallpox, 11/29/1863
Whitehead, James G. Private	Unk	12/18/1862, Wilson County, North Carolina	Wilson County, North Carolina	Co. H, 4th North Carolina Cavalry	7/4/1863, South Mountain, Maryland	Died of Smallpox, 11/22/1863
Whitehead, W. H. Private	Unk	2/18/1864, Henry County, Georgia, Conscript	Henry County, Georgia	Co. H, 51st Georgia Infantry	4/6/1865, High Bridge, Virginia	Died of Chronic Diarrhea, 6/10/1865
Whitehurst, R. Private	Unk	6/7/1864, Camp Holmes, Wake County, North Carolina	Wake County, North Carolina	Co. C, 2nd North Carolina Infantry	9/19/1864, Winchester, Virginia	Died of Chronic Diarrhea, 4/11/1865

Name	Age	Enlisted	Residence	Unit	Captured	Date and Cause of Death
Whitehurst, William M. Private	Unk	Unknown	Unknown	Co. I, 66th North Carolina Infantry	8/14/1863, Elizabeth City, North Carolina	Died of Unknown Causes, 1/13/1864
Whiteley, Joseph A. Private	41	3/1/1862, Alamance County, North Carolina	Alamance County, North Carolina	Co. F, 6th North Carolina Infantry	11/7/1863, Rappahannock Station, Virginia	Died of Chronic Diarrhea, 1/9/1864
Whitemore, John Wesley Private	Unk	4/15/1862, Conrad's Store, Virginia	Unknown	Co. B, 8th Virginia Infantry	4/6/1865, Farmville, Virginia	Died of Chronic Diarrhea, 5/3/1865
Whitesell, Eli Private Name Not On Monument	43	8/20/1863, Alamance County, North Carolina	Alamance County, North Carolina	Co. A, 2nd North Carolina Infantry	11/7/1863, Kelly's Ford, Rappahannock Station, Virginia	Died of Unknown Causes, 12/28/1863
Whitfield, George V. Private	21	7/22/1862, Nashville, North Carolina	Nash County, North Carolina	Co. H, 32nd North Carolina Infantry	5/10/1864, Mine Run, Virginia	Died of Unknown Causes, 10/22/1864
Whitley, Perry Private	40	2/24/1862, Nash County, North Carolina	Nash County, North Carolina, Farmer	Co. A, 47th North Carolina Infantry	10/27/1864, Burgess' Mill, Virginia	Died of Scurvy, 6/11/1865
Whitlock, Samuel H. Private	Unk	8/4/1864, Richmond, Virginia	Henrico County, Virginia	Co. G, 57th North Carolina Infantry	4/1/1865, Five Forks, Virginia	Died of Unknown Causes, 8/4/1865
Whitman, John B. Private Name Not On Monument	Unk	5/12/1864, Columbia, South Carolina	Richland County, South Carolina	Co. C, 13th South Carolina Infantry	5/23/1864, Spotsylvania Court House, Virginia	Died of Unknown Causes, 7/3/1864

Name	Age	Enlisted	Residence	Unit	Captured	Date and Cause of Death
Whitmer, John See: Whitemore, John Wesley				Co. B, 8th Virginia Infantry		
Whitney, John Private Name Not On Monument	45	Unknown	Unknown	22nd Battalion Georgia Heavy Artillery	12/9/1864, Near Savannah, Georgia	Died of Typhoid Fever, 6/30/1865
Whitsol, Eli Private	43	8/20/1863, Alamance County, North Carolina, Conscript	Alamance County, North Carolina	Co. A, 2nd North Carolina Infantry	11/7/1863, Kelly's Ford, Rappahannock Station, Virginia	Died of Unknown Causes, 12/28/1863
Whitstone, William Sergeant	Unk	6/26/1861, Richmond, Virginia	Henrico County, Virginia	Captain Hart's Co., South Carolina Course Artillery	9/19/1863, Stevensburg, Virginia, Gunshot Wound Left Shoulder	Died of Smallpox, 11/25/1863
Whitt, William David Private Not Listed On Monument	26	3/17/1862, Whitlock, Virginia	Augusta County, Virginia	Co. E, 23rd Virginia Infantry	9/21/1864, Harrisonburg, Virginia	Died of Chronic Diarrhea, 12/2/1864
Wibber, William H. See: Weber, William H.				Co. B, 11th Virginia Infantry		
Wickers, Matthew D. Private	24	2/26/1862, Oakland, North Carolina	Chatham County, North Carolina	Co. E, 44th North Carolina Infantry	10/14/1863, Bristoe Station, Virginia	Died of Unknown Causes, 8/23/1864
Wicks, Virgil Private	Unk	5/25/1861, Columbus County, Georgia	Muscogee County, Georgia	Co. B, 20th Georgia Infantry	7/3/1863, Gettysburg, Pennsylvania	Died of Smallpox, 1/14/1864

Name	Age	Enlisted	Residence	Unit	Captured	Date and Cause of Death
Wiggins, Jesse Private	Unk	6/1/1864, Camp Holmes, Raleigh, North Carolina	Wake County, North Carolina	Co. G, 32nd North Carolina Infantry	10/19/1864, Cedar Creek or Strasburg, Virginia	Died of Consumption, 4/14/1865
Wilborn, John Private	Unk	10/17/1863, Camp Holmes, Raleigh, North Carolina	Wake County, North Carolina	Co. H, 54th North Carolina Infantry	11/7/1863, Rappahannock Station, Virginia	Died of Unknown Causes, 9/8/1864
Wilburn, Edward G. Private	23	3/1/1862, Reidsville, North Carolina, Volunteer	Rockingham County, North Carolina, Trader	Co. H, 45th North Carolina Infantry	7/6/1863, Gettysburg, Pennsylvania	Died of Chronic Diarrhea, 10/16/1863
Wilcox, William Corporal	Unk	6/4/1861, Warsaw, Virginia	Richmond County, Virginia	Co. E, 40th Virginia Infantry	7/14/1863, Falling Waters, Maryland	Died of Scurvy, 4/3/1865
Wilder, Matthew Private	Unk	9/1/1863, Raleigh, North Carolina	Wake County, North Carolina	Co. F, 47th North Carolina Infantry	10/27/1864, Burchett's Mill, Near Petersburg, Virginia	Died of Chronic Dysentery, 2/6/1865
Wiler, A. Private	Unk	Unknown	Unknown	Co. E, 35th Georgia Infantry	Unknown	Unable to Locate
Wilkerson, John See: Wilkinson, John S.				Co. F, 7th North Carolina Infantry		
Wilkerson, Stephen A. Private	Unk	Unknown	Unknown	Co. B, 18th Virginia Infantry	4/6/1865, Harper's Farm, Virginia	Died of Pneumonia, 5/19/1865
Wilkerson, Uriah M. Private Name Not On Monument	38	2/8/1863, Orange County, North Carolina	Orange County, North Carolina, Farmer	Co. G, 27th North Carolina Infantry	10/14/1863, Bristoe Station, Virginia	Died of Chronic Diarrhea, 1/17/1864
Wilkes, Benjamin W. Private	Unk	9/1/1862, Chaffin's Bluff, Virginia	Unknown	Captain Allen's Co., Lunenburg Virginia Heavy Artillery	4/5/1865, Amelia Court House, Virginia	Died of Intermittent Fever, 5/29/1865

Name	Age	Enlisted	Residence	Unit	Captured	Date and Cause of Death
Wilkins, George W. Private	18	4/29/1862, Oxford, Mississippi	Colkoon County, Mississippi	Co. F, 42nd Mississippi Infantry	7/14/1863, Falling Waters, Maryland, Wounded Left Thigh	Died of Smallpox, 12/27/1863
Wilkins, Robert Y. Private	Unk	1/23/1864, Charleston, South Carolina	Charleston County, South Carolina	Co. A, Holcombe's Legion, South Carolina	4/1/1865, Five Forks, Virginia	Died of Chronic Diarrhea, 5/21/1865
Wilkinson, Edgar F. Private	Unk	Unknown	Unknown	Winder's South Carolina Artillery	Unknown	Unable to Locate
Wilkinson, Harris Private Name Not On Monument	Unk	5/7/1862, Orange County, North Carolina	Orange County, North Carolina	Co. D, 56th North Carolina Infantry	4/1/1865, Five Forks, Virginia	Died of Acute Diarrhea, 6/17/1865
Wilkinson, Henry C. Private	Unk	5/22/1862, Camp Hare, Virginia	Unknown	Co. D, 14th Virginia Infantry	7/3/1863, Gettysburg, Pennsylvania	Died of Diphtheria, 12/3/1863
Wilkinson, John S. Private	Unk	8/10/1861, Rowan County, North Carolina	Rowan County, North Carolina	Co. F, 7th North Carolina Infantry	7/14/1863, Falling Waters, Maryland	Died of Smallpox, 11/25/1863
Wilkinson, John Private	30	8/10/1861, Salisbury, North Carolina, Volunteer	Rowan County, North Carolina	Co. F, 7th North Carolina Infantry	7/3/1863, Gettysburg, Pennsylvania	Died of Smallpox, 11/30/1863
Wilkinson, W. M. Private	Unk	Unknown	Unknown	Co. G, 27th North Carolina Infantry	10/14/1863, Bristoe Station, Virginia	Died of Chronic Diarrhea, 1/17/1864
Willard, William Private	Unk	9/15/1864, Raleigh, North Carolina	Wake County, North Carolina	Co. G, 2nd Battalion North Carolina Infantry	10/19/1864, Cedar Creek or Strasburg, Virginia	Died of Unknown Causes, 5/11/1865
Williams, A. N. Corporal	Unk	4/25/1862, Stone Mountain, Georgia	DeKalb County, Georgia	Co. C, 12th Battalion, Georgia Light Artillery	9/22/1864, Harrisburg, Pennsylvania	Died of Scurvy, 2/23/1865

Name	Age	Enlisted	Residence	Unit	Captured	Date and Cause of Death
Williams, Aquilla Private	23	9/22/1862, Camp Holmes, Raleigh, North Carolina, Conscript	Wake County, North Carolina	Co. D, 26th North Carolina Infantry	7/14/1863, Falling Waters, Maryland	Died of Typhoid Fever, 11/3/1863
Williams, Asa Corporal	23	7/17/1861, Carthage, North Carolina, Volunteer	Moore County, North Carolina	Co. I, 2nd North Carolina Cavalry	2/7/1864, Rapidan River, Virginia	Died of Typhoid Fever, 3/20/1864
Williams, Benjamin Private	Unk	8/20/1864, Chatham County, North Carolina, Conscript	Chatham County, North Carolina	Co. G, 48th North Carolina Infantry	3/25/1865, Fort Stedman, Near Petersburg, Virginia	Died of Acute Bronchitis, 6/30/1865
Williams, David Private	33	7/22/1861, Cresswell's Springs, North Carolina	Iredell County, North Carolina, Farmer	Co. I, 7th North Carolina Infantry	7/3/1863, Gettysburg, Pennsylvania	Died of Unknown Causes, 1/8/1864
Williams, George W. Private	Unk	Unknown	Unknown	Co. G, 2nd Battalion Maryland Infantry	7/5/1863, Williamsport, Hagerstown, Pennsylvania	Died of Unknown Causes, 10/?/1863
Williams, George W. Private	17	8/12/1861, Lincolns Factory, North Carolina, Volunteer	Lincoln County, North Carolina	Co. D, 1st North Carolina Infantry	7/3/1863, Gettysburg, Pennsylvania	Died of Unknown Causes, 12/21/1863
Williams, Henry H. Private	Unk	2/26/1864, Camp Holmes, Raleigh, North Carolina	Rockingham County, North Carolina	Co. I, 13th North Carolina Infantry	4/8/1865, Appomattox Court House, Virginia	Died of Scurvy, 5/10/1865
Williams, J. B. Private	Unk	Unknown	Unknown	Co. D, 2nd North Carolina Infantry	Unknown	Unable to Locate
Williams, J. H. Private	Unk	Unknown	Unknown	Co. D, 56th North Carolina Infantry	4/6/1865, Five Forks, Virginia	Died of Acute Diarrhea, 6/17/1865
Williams, Jacob C. Private	28	11/21/1861, Cleveland County, North Carolina, Volunteer	Cleveland County, North Carolina, Farmer	Co. I, 38th North Carolina Infantry	4/3/1865, Appomattox Court House, Virginia	Died of Acute Diarrhea, 6/11/1865
Williams, James O. Private	Unk	1/9/1862, Columbia, South Carolina	Richland County, South Carolina	Co. E, 22nd South Carolina Infantry	6/17/1864, Near Petersburg, wilderness, Virginia	Died of Unknown Causes, 8/10/1864

Name	Age	Enlisted	Residence	Unit	Captured	Date and Cause of Death
Williams, John B. Private	22	8/10/1861, Laurel Spring, Ashe County, North Carolina, Volunteer	Ashe County, North Carolina	Co. A, 34th North Carolina Infantry	7/14/1863, Falling Waters, Maryland	Died of Unknown Causes, 8/15/1864
Williams, Nathan C. Private	Unk	9/1/1863, Raleigh, North Carolina	Wake County, North Carolina	Co. I, 30th North Carolina Infantry	11/7/1863, Kelly's Ford, Rappahannock Station, Virginia	Died of Unknown Causes, 12/28/1863
Williams, R. S. Private	Unk	Unknown	Unknown	Co. E, 25th Battalion Virginia Infantry	Unknown	Unable to Locate
Williams, William G. Private	28	3/28/1862, Camp McDonald, Georgia	Unknown	Co. C, 39th Georgia Infantry	6/1/1863, Cynthia, Kentucky	Died of Consumption, 1/1/1864
Williams, William R. Private	Unk	4/30/1863, Grayson County, Virginia	Grayson County, Virginia	Co. K, 51st Virginia Infantry	10/19/1864, Cedar Creek or Strasburg, Virginia	Died of Chronic Diarrhea, 6/26/1865
Williamson, Bride J. Private Name Not On Monument	Unk	4/27/1862, Marion District, South Carolina	Marion District, South Carolina	Co. L, 21st South Carolina Infantry	7/10/1863, Morris Island, South Carolina	Died of Chronic Diarrhea, 11/3/1863
Williamson, Hardy Private	Unk	3/1/1862, Philadelphia, Mississippi	Neshoba County, Mississippi	Co. D, 11th Mississippi Infantry	7/4/1863, Gettysburg, Pennsylvania, Wounded Right Leg	Leg Amputated, Died of Chronic Diarrhea, 2/18/1864
Williamson, James D. Corporal	38	3/23/1862, Lincoln County, North Carolina	Lincoln County, North Carolina, Tanner	Co. G, 52nd North Carolina Infantry	10/27/1864, Near Petersburg, Virginia	Died of Chronic Diarrhea, 12/27/1864
Williamson, John Sergeant	19	6/10/1861, Clinton, North Carolina, Volunteer	Sampson County, North Carolina	Co. I, 20th North Carolina Infantry	7/1/1863, Gettysburg, Pennsylvania	Died of Chronic Dysentery, 2/13/1865

Name	Age	Enlisted	Residence	Unit	Captured	Date and Cause of Death
Williamson, Thomas H. Private	Unk	4/14/1864, Bristol, Tennessee	Sullivan County, Tennessee	Co. A, 14th Tennessee Infantry	5/6/1864, Wilderness, Virginia	Died of Unknown Causes, 6/24/1864
Williford, Jason T. Private	18	4/4/1862, Mingo, Warsaw, North Carolina	Sampson County, North Carolina, Farmer	Co. K, 51st North Carolina Infantry	9/30/1864, Fort Harrison, Virginia	Died of Chronic Diarrhea, 2/11/1865
Willinson, Harry See: Williamson, Thomas H.				Co. A, 14th Tennessee Infantry		
Willis, Absalom Sergeant Name Not On Monument	18	3/8/1862, Rockingham, North Carolina, Volunteer	Rockingham, North Carolina, Farmer	Co. G, 45th North Carolina Infantry	5/10/1864, Spotsylvania Court House, Virginia	Died of Acute Dysentery, 7/7/1864
Willis, Elliott Sergeant Name Not On Monument	32	4/17/1861, Christiansburg, Virginia	Montgomery County, Virginia, Farmer	Co. G, 4th Virginia Infantry	5/12/1864, Spotsylvania Court House, Virginia	Died of Unknown Causes, 7/5/1864
Willis, Joseph G. Private	23	4/30/1861, Culpepper Court House, Virginia	Culpepper County, Virginia, Farmer	Co. C, 7th Virginia Infantry	5/21/1864, Milford, Virginia	Died of Unknown Causes, 6/24/1864
Willis, Samuel L. Private	Unk	3/24/1862, Pickensville, Alabama	Pickens County, Alabama	Co. H, 5th Alabama Infantry	7/5/1863, Greencastle, Pennsylvania	Died of Unknown Causes, 2/3/1864
Willis, Samuel O. Private	26	5/10/1862, Cleveland County, North Carolina, Volunteer	Cleveland County, North Carolina, Farmer	Co. F, 55th North Carolina Infantry	7/1/1863, Gettysburg, Pennsylvania	Died of Chronic Dysentery, 5/7/1865
Willoughby, Rayford Private	24	7/1/1861, Wadesboro, North Carolina, Volunteer	Anson County, North Carolina	Co. K, 26th North Carolina Infantry	10/14/1863, Bristoe Station, Virginia	Died of Unknown Causes, 2/29/1864

Name	Age	Enlisted	Residence	Unit	Captured	Date and Cause of Death
Willoughby, William Private	20	5/20/1861, Nashville, Tennessee	Davidson County, Tennessee	Co. A, 7th Tennessee Infantry	7/14/1863, Falling Waters, Maryland	Died of Unknown Causes, 1/22/1864
Wills, William S. Private	22	2/28/1862, Cove Creek, Arkansas	Boone County, Missouri, Farmer	Co. K, 1st Missouri Cavalry	5/16/1863, Champion Hill, Tennessee	Died of Chronic Diarrhea, 11/7/1863
Wilmoth, William J. Private	Unk	4/8/1862, Marietta, Georgia	Cobb County, Georgia	Co. L, Phillips Legion, Georgia Infantry	7/3/1863, Gettysburg, Pennsylvania	Died of Smallpox, 11/18/1863
Wilson, Benjamin C. Private	Unk	7/15/1861, Sparta, Georgia	Hancock County, Georgia	Co. E, 15th Georgia Infantry	7/2/1863, Gettysburg, Pennsylvania	Died of Smallpox, 11/5/1863
Wilson, C. S. See: Wilson, Thomas R.				Co. D, 42nd Virginia Infantry		
Wilson, George Private	24	3/21/1862, Charleston, South Carolina	Charleston County, South Carolina	Co. G, 18th South Carolina Infantry	4/3/1865, Petersburg, Virginia	Date and Cause of Death Unknown
Wilson, George W. E. Private	22	5/27/1861, Chestnut Fork, Bedford County, Virginia	Bedford County, Virginia	Co. F, 28th Virginia Infantry	7/3/1863, Gettysburg, Pennsylvania	Died of Unknown Causes, 1/23/1865
Wilson, Henry B. Corporal	Unk	8/1/1861, Brunswick County, Georgia	Glynn County, Georgia	Co. A, 26th Georgia Infantry	10/19/1864, Cedar Creek or Strasburg, Virginia	Died of Acute Dysentery, 12/21/1864
Wilson, Houston M. Private	Unk	1/1/1864, Franklin, North Carolina	Macon County, North Carolina	Co. G, 6th North Carolina Cavalry	6/22/1864, Jackson's Mill, Virginia	Died of Chronic Diarrhea, 4/20/1865
Wilson, J. G. Private	19	7/12/1862, Guilford County, North Carolina	Guilford County, North Carolina	Co. I, 5th North Carolina Cavalry	7/12/1863, Hagerstown, Pennsylvania, Detailed as Nurse	Died of Chronic Diarrhea, 4/3/1864

Name	Age	Enlisted	Residence	Unit	Captured	Date and Cause of Death
Wilson, James M. Private	Unk	8/12/1861, Camellia, Georgia	Mitchell County, Georgia	Co. E, 17th Georgia Infantry	6/1/1864, Gaines' Mill, Virginia	Died of Pneumonia, 2/21/1865
Wilson, Jefferson Jasper Private	21	5/26/1861, Corinth, Mississippi	Alcorn County, Mississippi	Co. C, 16th Mississippi Infantry	8/21/1864, Globe Tavern, Weldon Railroad, Virginia	Died of Acute Diarrhea, 10/19/1864
Wilson, John Sergeant	47	6/23/1862, Salisbury, North Carolina	Rowan County, North Carolina	Co. H, 57 North Carolina Infantry	11/7/1863, Rappahannock Station, Virginia	Died of Smallpox, 1/5/1864
Wilson, John 1st Sergeant	29	1/1/1862, Springfield, Missouri	Unknown, Farmer	Co. F, 3rd Battalion Missouri Cavalry	5/17/ 1863, Big Black River, Near Vicksburg, Mississippi	Died of Unknown Causes, 12/30/1863
Wilson, John Mark Private	Unk	3/6/1863, Harrisonburg, Virginia	Rockingham County, Virginia	Co. B, 10th Virginia Infantry	9/19/1864, Winchester, Virginia	Died of Acute Diarrhea, 10/28/1864
Wilson, John N. Sergeant	47	6/23/1862, Salisbury, North Carolina, Substitute	Union County, North Carolina	Co. H, 57th North Carolina Infantry	11/7/1863, Rappahannock Station, Virginia	Died of Smallpox, 1/4/1864
Wilson, John W. Private	Unk	8/9/1861, Fredericksburg, Virginia	Spotsylvania County, Virginia	Captain Cooper's Co., Braxton Battery, Virginia Light Artillery	9/23/1864, Strasburg, Virginia	Died of Unknown Causes, 1/27/1865
Wilson, Joseph Corporal	Unk	5/25/1861, Floyd Court House, Virginia	Floyd County, Virginia	Co. B, 42nd Virginia Infantry	5/12/1864, Near Spotsylvania Court House, Virginia	Died of Unknown Causes, 9/3/1864
Wilson, Martin V. Corporal Name Not On Monument	20	8/30/1862, Frederick County, Virginia	Unknown	Co. H, 11th Virginia Cavalry	9/19/1863, Cedar Creek or Strasburg, Virginia	Died of Chronic Diarrhea, 4/5/1865

Name	Age	Enlisted	Residence	Unit	Captured	Date and Cause of Death
Wilson, Robert L. Sergeant	30	3/4/1862, Charlotte, North Carolina, Volunteer	Mecklenburg County, North Carolina	Co. E, 11th North Carolina Infantry	10/27/1864, Near Petersburg, Virginia	Died of Unknown Causes, 4/10/1865
Wilson, Samuel Private	28	4/29/1861, Lexington, Virginia	Rockbridge County, Virginia, Farmer	Captain Archibald Graham's Co., Rockbridge Virginia Light Artillery	7/4/1863, Gettysburg, Pennsylvania	Died of Chronic Dysentery, 11/5/1863
Wilson, T. J. Corporal	21	4/14/1861, Columbia, South Carolina	Richland County, South Carolina	Co. C, 3rd South Carolina Infantry	5/22/1864, North Anna, Virginia	Died of Rheumatism, 2/28/1865
Wilson, Thomas Private	Unk	5/1/1862, Athens, Tennessee	McMinn County, Tennessee	Co. K, 59th Tennessee Mounted Infantry	5/17/1863, Big Black River, Near Vicksburg, Mississippi	Died of Unknown Causes, 12/26/1863
Wilson, Thomas Private	18	7/20/1863, Hillsboro, North Carolina, Volunteer	Person County, North Carolina	Co. E, 31st North Carolina Infantry	9/30/1864, Fort Harrison, Virginia	Died of Chronic Diarrhea, 1/18/1865
Wilson, Thomas R. Private	Unk	5/31/1861, Yellow Branch, Campbell County, Virginia	Campbell County, Virginia	Co. D, 42nd Virginia Infantry	7/4/1863, South Mountain, Maryland	Died of Smallpox, 12/15/1863
Wilson, W. W. Corporal	Unk	9/19/1861, Dalton, Georgia	Whitfield County, Georgia	Co. C, 60th Georgia Infantry	9/19/1864, Winchester, Virginia	Died of Chronic Dysentery, 3/2/1865
Wilzhel, W. See: Welchel, Charles C.				Co. D, 3rd Tennessee Mounted Infantry		
Winders, Horace Landsman	Unk	Unknown	Unknown	Confederate States Navy	Unknown	Unable to Locate
Winderweedle, Wright Private	Unk	Unknown	Unknown	Co. C, 6th Florida Infantry	7/22/1864, Near Atlanta, Georgia	Died of Epilepsy, 5/7/1865

Name	Age	Enlisted	Residence	Unit	Captured	Date and Cause of Death
Windson, James A. Private Name Not On Monument	Unk	1/18/1862, Bainbridge, Georgia	Webster County, Georgia	Co. I, 31st Georgia Infantry	3/25/1865, Fort Stedman, Near Petersburg, Virginia	Died of Chronic Diarrhea, 7/12/1865
Wincoff, David R. Private	28	8/17/1861, Concord, North Carolina, Volunteer	Cabarrus County, North Carolina	Co. H, 7th North Carolina Infantry	7/2/1863, Gettysburg, Pennsylvania	Died of Chronic Diarrhea, 1/11/1864
Wingate, James Private	36	3/14/1862, Charlotte, North Carolina, Volunteer	Mecklenburg County, North Carolina	Co. E, 11th North Carolina Infantry	7/4/1863, Gettysburg, Pennsylvania, Wounded	Died of Chronic Diarrhea & Scurvy, 12/29/1863
Winstead, Charles W. Private	Unk	3/1/1862, Heathsville, Virginia	Unknown	Co. F, 40th Virginia Infantry	7/14/1865, Falling Waters, Maryland	Died of Chronic Diarrhea, 11/21/1863
Winston, David C. Private	24	3/5/1862, Franklinton, North Carolina	Franklin County, North Carolina	Co. E, 15th North Carolina Infantry	10/14/1863, Bristoe Station, Virginia	Died of Chronic Diarrhea, 1/8/1864
Winston, Peyton D. Private	17	2/24/1863, Franklin, North Carolina, Volunteer	Franklin County, North Carolina	Co. I, 55th North Carolina Infantry	7/14/1865, Falling Waters, Maryland	Died of Chronic Dysentery, 1/23/1865
Winston, Rufus H. Private Name Not On Monument	36	2/9/1863, Franklin County, North Carolina, Volunteer	Franklin County, North Carolina, Farmer	Co. I, 55th North Carolina Infantry	7/1/1863, Gettysburg, Pennsylvania	Died of Chronic Diarrhea, 3/10/1864
Winters, Alfred A. Private	21	4/22/1862, Morganton, Burke County, North Carolina	Burke County, North Carolina, Farmer	Co. B, 54th North Carolina Infantry	6/27/1863, Hagerstown, Pennsylvania	Died of Chronic Diarrhea, 12/12/1863
Wise, Samuel A. Landsman	Unk	Unknown	Unknown	Confederate States Navy, Duty on CSS Arctic & CSS Neuse	Unknown	Unable to Locate
Wise, Stephen D. Private	Unk	7/13/1861, Glebe School House, Virginia	Unknown	Co. I, 61st Virginia Infantry	10/27/1864, Near Petersburg, Virginia	Died of Pneumonia, 4/16/1865

Point Lookout Prison Camp

Name	Age	Enlisted	Residence	Unit	Captured	Date and Cause of Death
Wishane, Pleasant Private	Unk	7/16/1864, Camp Holmes, Raleigh, North Carolina	Wake County, North Carolina	Co. C, 24th North Carolina Infantry	3/25/1865, Fort Stedman, Near Petersburg, Virginia	Died of Typhoid Fever, 6/1/1865
Wishon, Plesent See: Wishane, Pleasant				Co. C, 24th North Carolina Infantry		
Witherspoon, Lawson A. Private	Unk	3/10/1864, Camp Holmes, Raleigh, North Carolina	Wake County, North Carolina	Co. B, 32nd North Carolina Infantry	5/10/1864, Mine Run, Spotsylvania, Virginia	Died of Unknown Causes, 7/24/1864
Witte, Louis Private	23	5/23/1861, Fredericksburg, Virginia	Fredericksburg Virginia, Clerk	Co. C, 30th Virginia Infantry	3/16/1865, Chesterfield County, Virginia	Died of Unknown Causes, 4/25/1865
Witten, Benson Private	Unk	2/26/1862, Little Rock, Arkansas	Pulaski County, Arkansas	Co. I, 20th Arkansas Infantry	5/17/1863, Big Black River, Near Vicksburg, Mississippi	Died of Chronic Diarrhea, 11/9/1863
Wittenberg, W. W. Sergeant	Unk	9/25/1862, Bradley County, Tennessee	Unknown	Co. F, 62nd Tennessee Mounted Infantry	5/17/1863, Big Black River, Near Vicksburg, Mississippi	Died of Chronic Diarrhea, 1/10/1864
Wofford, Joseph H. Private	Unk	8/9/1864, Columbia, South Carolina	Richland County, South Carolina	Co. E, 18th South Carolina Infantry	4/3/1865, Petersburg, Virginia	Died of Chronic Diarrhea, 5/25/1865
Wolf, David Private	Unk	Unknown	Unknown	Co. F, 15th South Carolina Militia	2/28/1865, Near Chesterfield, South Carolina	Died of Scurvy, 4/17/1865
Wolf, M. R. Private	Unk	3/1/1863, Camp Radford, Montgomery County, Virginia	Montgomery County, Virginia	Co. A, 8th Virginia Cavalry	9/22/1864, Fisher's Hill, Virginia	Died of Inflammation of Lungs (Pneumonia), 10/27/1864
Wolfe, Robert B. Private	25	9/13/1861, Mecklenburg County, North Carolina, Volunteer	Mecklenburg County, North Carolina	Co. K, 30th North Carolina Infantry	11/7/1863, Rappahannock Station, Virginia	Died of Pneumonia, 3/1/1865

Name	Age	Enlisted	Residence	Unit	Captured	Date and Cause of Death
Womack, Benjamin T. Private	Unk	5/6/1861, Fort Powhatan, Virginia	Unknown	Co. C, 53rd Virginia Infantry	7/3/1863, Gettysburg, Pennsylvania	Died of Unknown Causes, 11/5/1863
Womack, James Rufus Private	19	9/10/1861, Jonesboro, North Carolina	Unknown	Co. H, 30th North Carolina Infantry	11/7/1863, Rappahannock Station, Virginia	Died of Chronic Diarrhea, 5/3/1865
Womble, John J. Private	Unk	Unknown	Unknown	Co. E, Confederate States Marine Corp	4/6/1865, Farmville, Virginia	Died of Unknown Causes, 5/17/1865
Wood, A. G. Private	Unk	Unknown	Unknown	Co. E, 11th Alabama Infantry	7/2/1863, Gettysburg, Pennsylvania	Died of Chronic Diarrhea, 11/17/1863
Wood, D. M. Private	Unk	3/9/1863, Greenville, South Carolina	Greenville District, South Carolina	Co. C, 22nd South Carolina Infantry	4/3/1865, Petersburg, Virginia	Died of Chronic Dysentery, 5/2/1865
Wood, Green B. C. Private	18	10/3/1863, Cleveland County, North Carolina, Volunteer	Cleveland County, North Carolina	Co. C, 15th North Carolina Infantry	4/2/1865, Hatcher's Run, Virginia	Died of Unknown Causes, 5/12/1865
Wood, George Corporal	33	4/28/1862, Jones County, North Carolina	Jones County, North Carolina, Farmer	Co. K, 61st North Carolina Infantry	10/7/1864, Darbytown Road, Burgess' Mill, Virginia	Died of Chronic Diarrhea, 2/23/1865
Wood, George C. Private	Unk	3/26/1863, Decatur, Georgia	DeKalb County, Georgia	Co. F, 22nd Battalion Georgia Heavy Artillery	12/13/1864, Fort McAllister, Georgia	Died of Pneumonia, 3/23/1865
Wood, James Private	Unk	3/28/1863, James Island, South Carolina	Charleston District, South Carolina	Co. G, 2nd South Carolina Artillery	3/4/1865, Cheraw, South Carolina	Died of Pneumonia, 5/30/1865
Wood, Leroy Private	Unk	2/2/1863, Gills Court House, Virginia	Unknown	Co. D, 30th Battalion Virginia Sharp Shooters	10/19/1864, Cedar Creek or Strasburg, Virginia	Died of Measles, 3/20/1865

Name	Age	Enlisted	Residence	Unit	Captured	Date and Cause of Death
Wood, Oliver Private	Unk	3/20/1864, Columbia, South Carolina	Richland County, South Carolina	Co. I, 13th South Carolina Infantry	3/31/1865, Hatcher's Run, Virginia	Died of Chronic Diarrhea, 6/10/1865
Wood, Perry Private	20	3/17/1862, Lincolnton, North Carolina, Volunteer	Lincoln County, North Carolina	Co. I, 11th North Carolina Infantry	10/27/1864, Burgess' Mill, Near Petersburg, Virginia	Died of Unknown Causes, 5/19/1865
Wood, Starling Private	47	2/27/1862, Franklin County, North Carolina, Volunteer	Franklin County, North Carolina, Farmer	Co. B, 47th North Carolina Infantry	7/5/1863, Gettysburg, Pennsylvania, Sick, Left as Nurse at Hospital	Died of Chronic Diarrhea, 12/26/1864
Wood, William A. Private	Unk	11/1/1862, Fredericksburg, Virginia	Spotsylvania County, Virginia	Co. G, 1st Virginia Infantry	Unknown	Died of Scurvy, 6/12/1865
Woodall, William C. Private	24	8/15/1862, Iredell County, North Carolina, Conscript	Mecklenburg County, North Carolina	Co. I, 37th North Carolina Infantry	7/14/1863, Falling Waters, Maryland	Died of Smallpox, 12/4/1863
Woodall, William W. Private	Unk	12/18/1863, Morton's Ford, Virginia	Unknown	Co. D, 42nd Virginia Infantry	5/12/1864, Spotsylvania, Virginia	Date & Cause of Death Unknown
Woodde, Henry B. Private	Unk	3/19/1864, Camp Vance, North Carolina	Burke County, North Carolina	Co. A, 34th North Carolina Infantry	5/24/1864, Hanover Junction, Virginia	Died of Gastroenteritis (Stomach Infection), 6/22/1864
Woodhall, W. W. See: Woodall, William W.				Co. D, 42nd Virginia Infantry		
Woods, J. L. Private	Unk	Unknown	Unknown	Co. H, 2nd Georgia Infantry	11/29/1864, Emanuel County, Georgia	Died of Chronic Diarrhea, 5/15/1865
Woods, James Private	28	9/22/1862, Wilkes County, North Carolina, Conscript	Unknown	Co. F, 52nd North Carolina Infantry	Unknown	Date & Cause of Death Unknown

Name	Age	Enlisted	Residence	Unit	Captured	Date and Cause of Death
Woods, Joseph Private	Unk	1/19/1863, Camp Winder, Virginia	Unknown	Co. A, 5th Virginia Infantry	7/3/1863, Gettysburg, Pennsylvania	Died of Congestive Intermittent Fever, 11/14/1864
Woodson, Tarleton S. Private	25	7/15/1861, Charlottesville, Virginia	Albemarle County, Virginia	Co. H, 1st Virginia Light Artillery	7/3/1863, Gettysburg, Pennsylvania	Died of Unknown Causes, 12/20/1863
Woodward, John G. Private	Unk	4/23/1861, Mobile, Alabama	Mobile County, Alabama	Co. E, 3rd Alabama Infantry	7/4/1863, Gettysburg, Pennsylvania	Date & Cause of Death Unknown
Woodward, Oden Private	Unk	3/4/1862, Navy Yard, Virginia	Unknown	Co. F, 41st Virginia Infantry	7/5/1863, Waterloo, Gettysburg, Pennsylvania	Died of Chronic Diarrhea & Fever, 12/10/1863
Woodward, Thomas W. Private	Unk	4/1/1864, Place Unknown	Unknown	Captain Carter's Co., Virginia Light Artillery	5/12/1864, Spotsylvania Court House, Virginia	Died of Inflammation of Lungs (Pneumonia), 11/2/1864
Woodward, William J. Corporal	Unk	5/11/1861, West Point, Virginia	Unknown	Co. B, 53rd Virginia Infantry	7/5/1863, Gettysburg, Pennsylvania	Died of Chronic Diarrhea, 4/18/1864
Wooddy, Henry B. See: Woodde, Henry B				Co. A, 34th North Carolina Infantry		
Woodyard, James Private	Unk	Unknown	Unknown	Virginia	Unknown	Unable to Locate
Woolen, George H. Private	23	4/28/1862, Greensboro, North Carolina, Volunteer	Guilford County, North Carolina	Co. B, 27th North Carolina Infantry	10/14/1863, Bristoe Station, Virginia	Died of Pneumonia, 9/18/1864
Woolly, James J. Private	Unk	8/12/1861, Camellia, Georgia	Unknown	Co. E, 17th Georgia Infantry	7/3/1863, Gettysburg, Pennsylvania	Died of Unknown Causes, 2/19/1864

Name	Age	Enlisted	Residence	Unit	Captured	Date and Cause of Death
Wooten, Benjamin F. Private	Unk	9/1/1863, Kinston, North Carolina	Lenoir County, North Carolina	Co. H, 7th Confederate Cavalry	9/30/1864, Fort Harrison, Virginia	Died of Erysipelas, 2/19/1865
Wooten, David A. Private Name Not On Monument	25	8/8/1862, Iredell County, North Carolina, Conscript	Iredell County, North Carolina	Co. H, 4th North Carolina Infantry	4/3/1865, Richmond, Virginia	Died of Chronic Diarrhea, 5/21/1865
Workman, Francis Private	Unk	9/6/1862, Wayne County, Virginia	Unknown	Co. E, 16th Virginia Cavalry	6/26/1863, Winchester, Virginia	Died of Chronic Diarrhea, 2/28/1865
Workman, James F. Private	22	5/8/1861, Corinth, Mississippi	Alcorn County, Mississippi	Co. F, 12th Mississippi Infantry	7/14/1863, Falling Waters, Maryland	Died of Unknown Causes, 3/6/1864
Worly, Robert K. Private	50	11/10/1864, Wilmington, North Carolina	Richmond County, North Carolina, Farmer	McNeill's Co. 8th North Carolina Senior Reserves	12/25/1864, Fort Fisher, North Carolina	Date & Cause of Death Unknown
Wright, Alfred G. Private	23	4/26/1861, Fredericksburg, Virginia	Spotsylvania County, Virginia	Co. A, 30th Virginia Infantry	3/31/1865, Dinwiddie Court House, Virginia	Died of Acute Dysentery, 6/22/1865
Wright, Alexander M. Private	Unk	4/30/1862, Louisa Court House, Virginia	Louisa County, Virginia	Co. A, 23rd Virginia Infantry	7/3/1863, Gettysburg, Pennsylvania	Died of Chronic Diarrhea, 12/26/1863
Wright, Bedford C. Private	Unk	6/30/1862, Chester, South Carolina	Unknown	Co. H, 7th Battalion South Carolina Infantry	Unknown	Date and Cause of Death Unknown
Wright, J. A. Private	Unk	Unknown	Unknown	Co. ?, 40th Virginia Infantry	Unknown	Date and Cause of Death Unknown

Name	Age	Enlisted	Residence	Unit	Captured	Date and Cause of Death
Wright, James Private	Unk	10/16/1864, Shenandoah, Virginia	Pendleton, County, West Virginia	Co. B, 6th North Carolina Infantry	10/19/1864, Cedar Creek or Strasburg, Virginia	Died of Unknown Causes, 12/17/1864
Wright, James W. Corporal	Unk	3/20/1863, Greenville, North Carolina	Pitt County, North Carolina	Co. C, 26th North Carolina Infantry	10/27/1864, Near Petersburg, Virginia	Died of Chronic Diarrhea, 1/31/1865
Wright, John H. Private Name Not On Monument	27	10/18/1862, Camp Holmes, Raleigh, North Carolina, Conscript	Forsyth County, North Carolina	Co. F, 32nd North Carolina Infantry	5/10/1864, Wilderness, Virginia	Died of Unknown Causes, 7/10/1864
Wright, John W. Private Name Not On Monument	20	9/5/1863, Camp Harmon, Virginia	Unknown	Co. F, 4th Virginia Infantry	7/3/1863, Gettysburg, Pennsylvania	Died of Diphtheria, 11/1/1863
Wright, M. Private	Unk	Unknown	Unknown	Co. A, 30th Virginia Infantry	9/19/1864, Winchester, Virginia	Died of Unknown Causes, 2/22/1865
Wright, Patrick H. Private	Unk	3/21/1862, Richmond, Virginia	Henrico County, Virginia	Co. A, 15th Virginia Infantry	4/6/1865, Harper's Farm, Virginia	Died of Chronic Diarrhea, 6/26/1865
Wright, Ralph Private	30	3/22/1863, Guilford County, North Carolina, Conscript	Guilford County, North Carolina	Co. K, 22nd North Carolina Infantry	5/23/1864, Hanover Junction, Virginia	Died of Scurvy, 4/1/1865
Wright, Thomas B. Private	Unk	4/29/1861, Lincoln County, Tennessee	Unknown	Co. K, 1st Tennessee Infantry	7/14/1863, Falling Waters, Maryland	Died of Unknown Causes, 11/30/1863

Name	Age	Enlisted	Residence	Unit	Captured	Date and Cause of Death
Wright, Thomas H. Private Name Not On Monument	Unk	5/7/1861, Gloucester Court House, Virginia	Gloucester County, Virginia	Co. A, 5th Virginia Cavalry	9/24/1864, Luray, Virginia	Died of Smallpox, 3/2/1865
Wright, William Private	Unk	3/15/1862, Amherst Court House, Virginia	Amherst County, Virginia	Co. I, 19th Virginia Infantry	7/3/1863, Gettysburg, Pennsylvania	Died of Pneumonia, 1/12/1864
Wright, Willis F. Private	28	8/29/1862, Raleigh, North Carolina, Conscript	Montgomery County, North Carolina	Co. A, 2nd North Carolina Infantry	11/7/1863, Kelly's Ford or Rappahannock Station, Virginia	Died of Unknown Causes, 8/18/1864
Wyatt, John L. Private	Unk	3/17/1862, Dallas, North Carolina, Volunteer	Gaston County, North Carolina	Co. M, 16th North Carolina Infantry	7/3/1863, Gettysburg, Pennsylvania	Died of Smallpox, 12/11/1863
Wyatt, Silas Private	25	8/13/1862, Camp Hill, North Carolina, Conscript	Northampton County, North Carolina	Co. G, 5th North Carolina Infantry	7/4/1863, Gettysburg, Pennsylvania	Died of Chronic Diarrhea, 1/19/1864
Wylie, John Private	Unk	4/28/1862, Marietta, Cobb County, Georgia	Cobb County, Georgia	Co. M, Phillip's Legion Georgia Infantry	7/2/1863, Gettysburg, Pennsylvania	Died of Smallpox, 11/17/1863
Wylie, Thomas H. Private	Unk	9/11/1863, Sam Jones Store, Virginia	Unknown	Co. E, 26th Battalion Virginia Infantry	6/3/1864, Gaines Farm, Virginia	Died of Chronic Dysentery, 8/22/1864
Wyrick, Absalom Private	30	7/15/1862, Guilford County, North Carolina, Conscript	Guilford County, North Carolina	Co. A, 1st North Carolina Infantry	5/30/1864, Mechanicsville, Virginia	Died of Chronic Diarrhea, 3/30/1865

Name	Age	Enlisted	Residence	Unit	Captured	Date and Cause of Death
Yarborough, James M. Private	Unk	12/11/1861, Sullivan's Island, South Carolina	Charleston District, South Carolina	Co. A, Butler's 1st South Carolina Infantry	7/7/1863, Morris Island, South Carolina	Died of Smallpox, 1/9/1864
Yarborough, Tiberas Z. Private	Unk	Unknown	Unknown	Co. E, 44th Virginia Infantry	4/6/1865, Farmville, Virginia	Died of Congestive Intermittent Fever, 5/8/1865
Yates, Calvin Private	Unk	10/10/1864, Harrisonburg, Virginia	Rockingham County, Virginia	Co. F, 21st North Carolina Infantry	10/21/1864, Fisher's Hill, Virginia	Died of Chronic Diarrhea, 1/25/1865
Yates, James W. Private	Unk	3/1/1863, Columbus County, North Carolina	Columbus County, North Carolina	Co. K, 20th North Carolina Infantry	7/1/1863, Gettysburg, Pennsylvania	Died of Unknown Causes, 11/3/1864
Yates, John Private	26	5/1/1861, Whiteville, North Carolina	Columbus County, North Carolina	Co. K, 20th North Carolina Infantry	7/1/1863, Gettysburg, Pennsylvania, Wounded	Died of Epilepsy, 11/3/1864
Yaunt, Sylvanius Private	Unk	9/28/1864, Camp Holmes, Raleigh, North Carolina	Wake County, North Carolina	Co. C, 24th North Carolina Infantry	3/25/1865, Fort Stedman, Near Petersburg, Virginia	Died of Inflammation of the Brain, 6/25/1865
Yeargan, W. W. Private	Unk	4/29/1862, Cedar Bluff, Alabama	Cherokee County, Alabama	Co. H, 48th Alabama Infantry	7/5/1863, Cashtown, Pennsylvania	Died of Chronic Diarrhea, 11/13/1863
Yearkey, George P. Private	Unk	9/4/1862, Mill Point, Virginia	Unknown	Co. B, 36th Battalion Virginia Cavalry	7/5/1863, Waterloo, South Mountain, Maryland	Date and Cause of Death Unknown

Name	Age	Enlisted	Residence	Unit	Captured	Date and Cause of Death
Yeatman, Milton H. Private	21	5/22/1861, Warsaw, Virginia	Richmond County, Virginia, Farmer	Co. B, 40th Virginia Infantry	7/18/1863, North Mountain, West Virginia	Date and Cause of Death Unknown
Yeatman, William W. Private Name Not On Monument	Unk	6/19/1861, Camp Ruggles, Warsaw, Virginia	Richmond County, Virginia	Co. B, 40th Virginia Infantry	7/14/1863, Falling Waters, Maryland	Died of Chronic Diarrhea, 12/31/1863
Yeldell, John Private	Unk	6/6/1861, Greenville, Butler County, Alabama	Butler County, Alabama	Co. G, 9th Alabama Infantry	7/3/1863, Gettysburg, Pennsylvania	Died of Unknown Causes, 12/?/1863
Yeonge, Joseph S. Private	Unk	1/20/1862, Camp Hampton, South Carolina	Lancaster County, South Carolina	Co. B, 4th South Carolina Cavalry	6/11/1864, Louisa Court House, Virginia	Died of Inflammation of Lungs (Pneumonia), 7/26/1864
Yonas, John Private	Unk	9/20/1862, Rogersville, Tennessee	Hawkins County, Tennessee	Co. B, 60th Tennessee Mounted Infantry	5/17/1863, Big Black River, Near Vicksburg, Mississippi	Died of Unknown Causes, 2/2/1864
York, Daniel Private	Unk	Unknown	Unknown	Co. D, 50th Virginia Infantry	5/12/1864, Spotsylvania Court House, Virginia	Died of Unknown Causes, 9/26/1864
York, E. I. Private	20	3/13/1862, Yadkin County, North Carolina	Yadkin County, North Carolina, Farmer	Co. A, 54th North Carolina Infantry	11/7/1863, Rappahannock Station, Virginia	Died of Typhoid Fever, 2/29/1864
Yost, Levi Private	24	8/13/1862, Camp Hill, North Carolina, Conscript	Northampton County, North Carolina	Co. G, 5th North Carolina Infantry	7/3/1863, Gettysburg, Pennsylvania	Died of Scurvy, 8/23/1864
Young, Charles Private	Unk	4/30/1862, Cedar Bluff, Alabama	Cherokee County, Alabama	Co. E, 47th Alabama Infantry	9/17/1863, Chickamauga, Georgia	Died of Chronic Diarrhea, 12/20/1864

Name	Age	Enlisted	Residence	Unit	Captured	Date and Cause of Death
Young, Francis M. Private	17	5/1/1864, Illegible Court House, South Carolina	Unknown	Co. B, 15th South Carolina Infantry	10/19/1864, Cedar Creek or Strasburg, Virginia	Died of Remittent Fever, 12/9/1864
Young, J. S. See: Yeonge, Joseph S.				Co. B, 4th South Carolina Cavalry		
Young, Jasper N. Private	Unk	9/17/1861, Atlanta, Georgia	Fulton County, Georgia	Co. C, 35th Georgia Infantry	7/3/1863, Gettysburg, Pennsylvania	Died of Scurvy, 3/14/1865
Young, James H. Corporal Name Not On Monument	22	1/10/1862, Raleigh, North Carolina, Volunteer	Wake County, North Carolina	Co. I, 1st North Carolina Infantry	5/12/1864, Spotsylvania Court House, Virginia, Wounded	Died of Unknown Causes, 7/7/1864
Young, Jesse H. Private	19	5/1/1861, Burnsville, North Carolina	Yancey County, North Carolina	Co. C, 16th North Carolina Infantry	7/14/1863, Falling Waters, Maryland	Died of Chronic Diarrhea, 12/18/1863
Young, John Private	Unk	9/6/1862, Statesville, North Carolina, Conscript	Catawba County, North Carolina	Co. A, 23rd North Carolina Infantry	7/1/1863, Gettysburg, Pennsylvania	Died of Chronic Diarrhea, 11/6/1863
Young, Simeon T. Private	21	5/29/1861, Holly Spring, North Carolina, Volunteer	Wake County, North Carolina	Co. D, 26th North Carolina Infantry	7/3/1863, Gettysburg, Pennsylvania	Died of Unknown Causes, 8/16/1864
Young, Thomas Private	Unk	3/26/1863, Madison Court House, Florida	Unknown	Co. E, 11th Florida Infantry	8/21/1864, Globe Tavern, Weldon Railroad, Virginia	Died of Unknown Causes, 9/11/1864

Name	Age	Enlisted	Residence	Unit	Captured	Date and Cause of Death
Young, W. A. Private	17	6/1/1861, Stokes County, North Carolina	Stokes County, North Carolina	Co. H, 22nd North Carolina Infantry	7/14/1863, Falling Waters, Maryland	Died of Chronic Diarrhea, 3/2/1864
Young, William Private	21	9/23/1862, Boone's Creek, Tennessee	Unknown	Co. D, 60th Tennessee Mounted Infantry	5/17/1863, Big Black River, Near Vicksburg, Mississippi	Died of Chronic Diarrhea, 11/18/1863
Young, William G. Private Name Not On Monument	Unk	10/19/1863, Chattanooga, Georgia	Walker County, Georgia	Co. B, 5th Georgia Infantry	11/17/1864, Goldsboro, North Carolina	Died of Pneumonia, 4/5/1865
Youngue, S. W. Private	Unk	3/8/1862, Talladega, Alabama	Talladega County, Alabama	Co. E, 10th Alabama Infantry	7/2/1863, Gettysburg, Pennsylvania	Died of Chronic Diarrhea & Scurvy, 2/18/1864

Name	Age	Enlisted	Residence	Unit	Captured	Date and Cause of Death
Zahler, J. M. Private	Unk	9/15/1863, Pocotaligo, South Carolina	Jasper County, South Carolina	Co. D, 4th South Carolina Cavalry	12/1/1864, Stony Creek, Virginia	Died of Chronic Dysentery, 6/4/1865
Zigler, Benjamin J. Private	22	3/13/1862, Stokes County, North Carolina, Volunteer	Stokes County, North Carolina, Farmer	Co. D, 52nd North Carolina Infantry	7/5/1863, Gettysburg, Pennsylvania	Died of Chronic Diarrhea, 12/10/1863
Zombro, James William Private	21	2/14/1862, Charlestown, Virginia	Jefferson County, Virginia	Co. B, 12th Virginia Cavalry	9/15/1863, Smithfield, Virginia	Died of Chronic Diarrhea, 12/20/1864

Civil War Medical Terminology

Disease	Meaning
Abcpsia	Blindness
Abscessus	A swollen, inflamed area of the body where pus gathers
Acute	Severe
Aegrotantem	Illness, sickness
Ague	Recurring fever and chills of malaria
Ambustio	A burn or scald
Anasaica	Generalized edema or generalized dropsy
Anchylosis	A stiffening of the joints
Aphonia	A lost of voice due to organic or psychological causes
Apoplexy	Stroke
Ascites	Accumulation of serous fluid in the abdominal cavity
Billious Fever	Any fever that exhibited the symptom of nausea or vomiting in addition to an increase in internal body temperature and strong diarrhea.
Bad Blood	Syphilis
Bilious fever	Fever caused by liver disorder
Black Death	Bubonic plague
Bloody Flux	Dysentery
Bright's Disease	Kidney disease
Catarrh	Inflammation of mucous membrane most commonly in the throat and nose, accompanied by an increased secretion mucous, sometimes accompanied by fever, or, rarely cerebral hemorrhage
Cephalalgia	Headache
Cerebritis	Infection of the brain
Chilblain	Swelling of the extremities caused by exposure to cold
Chin Cough	Whooping Cough
Chorea	Disease characterized by convulsions and contortions
Chronic	Continuing for a long period of time
Colica	Acute abdominal pains, caused by abnormal condition of the bowel
Congestiva	Excessive accumulation of blood in parts of the body
Congestion of the Brain	This disease consists of an accumalation of blood in the cerebral tissue. It is caused by any impediment to the return of blood from the brain, such as a tumor of the neck, smallpox, heart disease or an injury such as a fall were the victim has a contusion of his head.
Congestion of the Lungs	Pneumonia
Congestive Fever	Malaria
Conjunctivitis	Inflammation of the eye or eyelid
Consecutiva	Unrelated illness following another

Consumption	Tuberculosis
Continua	Without interruption
Contusion	A bruise or injury where the skin is not broken
Cramp Colic	Appendicitis
Crop Sickness	Overextended stomach
Croup	Laryngitis, diphtheria, or strep throat
Debilitas	Weakness or feebleness
Debility	Weakness or feebleness
Delirium Tremens	Hallucinations & seizures due to alcohol withdrawal
Diphtheria	Contagious disease of the throat
Dropsy of the Brain	Encephalitis, disease with acute onset of fever, headache, confusion, and sometimes seizures
Dropsy	Edema, an abnormal accumulation of fluid in the tissue spaces, cavities, or joint capsules of the body, causing swelling of the area.
Dysentery	Inflammation of intestinal membrane
Dyspepsia	Acid indigestion
Encephalitis	Swelling of the brain
Enteritis	Inflammation of the bowels
Erysipelas	An acute infectious disease of the mucous membranes characterized by the inflammation of the skin, accompanied by a fever.
Febris	Fever
Flux	Discharge of fluid from the body
Galloping Consumption	Pulmonary Tuberculosis
Gastroenteritis	Gastroenteritis is a condition that causes irritation and inflammation of the stomach and intestines.
Glandular Fever	Mononucleosis, A sore throat where the patient's tonsils become swollen and develop a whitish-yellow covering. The lymph nodes in the neck are frequently swollen and painful.
Green Sickness	Anemia, Disease of the blood characterized by weakness, or fatigue, general malaise, and sometimes poor concentration.
Gripe	Influenza
Hemophthis	Spitting of blood
Hemorrhia	Heavy Bleeding
Herpes	An inflammatory virus disease of the skin or mucous membranes
Incipt Hydrothorax	An abnormal amount of watery fluid in the pleural cavity
Inflammation of Lungs	Pneumonia
Intermittent	Stopping and Starting, usually referring to Intermittent Fever
Intermittent Fever	A malarial fever in which feverish periods lasting a few hours then alternate with periods in which the temperature is normal.
Jail Fever	Typhus. A bacterial disease spread by lice or fleas. It is characterized Abdominal pain, Headache, red rash and high fever.

530

Jaundice	yellowing of the skin due to liver dysfunction (hyperbilirubinemia)
Lithiasis	Abnormal concretion, usually composed of mineral salts, occurring within the human body
Lock Jaw	Tetanus, Prolonged muscle spasms that affect the jaw, chest, neck, back and abdominal muscles. Mortality rates reported vary from 48% to 73%.
Lumbago	A Back Ache
Lung Fever	Pneumonia
Lung Sickness	Tuberculosis
Mania	Insanity
Miasma	Poisonous vapors thought to infect the air
Morbi Cutis	A skin disease
Moribund	Approaching death; About to die
Morsal	Gangrene
Mortis	Death
Myelitis	Inflammation of the spine
Myocarditits	Inflammation of the heart muscles
Necrosis	Mortification of bones or tissue, usually skin
Nephritis	Inflammation of the kidneys
Nostalgia	Disease marked by homesickness, melancholia and loss of appetite
Ophthalmia	Relating to the Eyes
Orchitis	An inflammation of one or both testicles, most commonly associated with the virus that causes mumps.
Otalgia	Earache
Palsy	Paralysis or loss of muscle control
Paronychia	A painful, pus-producing inflammation at the end of a toe or finger
Parotitis	Mumps
Paroxysm	Convulsion
Phlegmon	Inflammation, especially of the connective tissues, leading to ulceration or abscess
Phthisis Pulmonalis	A wasting away of the body or any part as in tuberculosis
Pleurisy	Inflammation of the lung
Pleuritis	Pleurisy, inflammation of the lining of the pleural cavity surrounding the lungs. Characterized by a sharp, stabbing pain in the chest that gets worse with deep breathing, coughing, sneezing, or laughing.
Podagra	Gout
Pott's Disease	Tuberculosis of the spinal vertebrae
Pox	Syphilis
Pulmonalis	Relating to the heart
Putrid Fever	Typhus, so called from the decomposing and offensive state of the discharges and diseased textures of the body.
Purpura	Purpura is the appearance of red or purple discolorations on the skin that do not blanch on applying pressure. They are caused by bleeding underneath the skin.

Pyaemia	Widespread abscesses caused by pus-forming organisms in the blood
Qyotidiana	A fever occurring or returning daily
Remittent Fever	19th century term. A fever that drops, but does not altogether disappear. May be a misdiagnosis of typhoid fever.
Rickets	Disease of the skeletal system
Rheumatic Pericarditis	Inflammation and swelling of the pericardium (fibrous sac surrounding the heart) that occurs as a complication in people with rheumatism.
Rheumatism	Condition characterized by inflammation or pain in muscles, joints
Rubeola	Measles
Scarlet Fever	Disease characterized by a red rash and sore
Scorbutus	Scurvy
Screws	Rheumatism
Scrofula	Tuberculosis of the neck lymph nodes or lymphatic glands
Ship's Fever	Typhus
Softening of the Brain	Sudden impairment of neurological function, especially that resulting from a cerebral hemorrhage; a stroke.
Spotted Fever	Typhus, cerebrospinal meningitis fever
St. Vitus Dance	Nervous twitches, chorea
Sub-Laxatio	An incomplete dislocation
Syncope	Fainting, losing consciousness indicating a more serious illeness
Typhus	Disease transmitted especially by body lice and is marked by high fever, stupor alternating with delirium, intense headache, and a dark red rash
Variola	Smallpox
Venesection	Bleeding
Viper's Dance	St. Vitus' Dance, An abnormal involuntary movement disorder
Vulnus Incisum	Relating to a wound caused by a cut
Vulnus Punctum	Relating to a wound caused by a puncture
Vulnus Sclopeticum	Relating to a wound, typically a gunshot wound
Vulnus	Relating to a wound
Whitlow	A painful, pus-producing inflammation at the end of a toe or finger
Winter Fever	Pneumonia
Yellow Jack	Yellow Fever

Notes

Chapter 1,
pages 1-10:

1. *The Baltimore Police Commissioners—Writ of Habeas Corpus*, Baltimore Sun, 8/12/1861; *Fort Lafayette*, New York Evening Post, 12-2-1861; Francis Key Howard, *Fourteen Months in American Bastilles*, pages 8-9;

2. *Official Records of Union and Confederate Armies, Series II, Volume II*, page 19; Bulla, David W., *Abraham Lincoln and Press Suppression Reconsidered*, American Journalism Historians Association;

3. *Official Records of Union and Confederate Armies, Series II, Volume 1, Arrest of the Mayor, Marshal and Police Commissioners of Baltimore by Military Authorities* page 619-621; Francis Key Howard, *Fourteen Months in American Bastilles*, pages 2-3; *From Maryland*, New York Tribune 9/23/1861;

4. Francis Key Howard, *Fourteen Months in American Bastilles*, page 9;

5. *Official Records of Union and Confederate Armies, Series II, Volume 1*, page 627; *Official Records of Union and Confederate Armies, Series II, Volume V*, pages 216-217; Francis Key Howard, *Fourteen Months in American Bastilles*, page 44;

6. Francis Key Howard, *Fourteen Months in American Bastilles*, pages 13-14;

7. *Official Records of Union and Confederate Armies*, Series II, Volume II, page 156; Francis Key Howard, *Fourteen Months in American Bastilles*, page 60; *The Political Prisoners*, Baltimore Sun, February 6, 1862;

8. *Official Records of Union and Confederate Armies, Series II, Volume 1, William H. Seward to Lt. General Winfield Scott, 8/8/1861*, page 637; *Official Records, Series II, Volume 1*, page 641; *Official Records of Union and Confederate Armies, Series II, Volume II, Letter from Lt. General Winfield Scott*, pages 41-42; *The American Annual Cyclopedia and Register of Important Events of the Year 1861*, Pages 354-356, 360-361, New York: D. Appleton & Company, 443 & 445 Broadway, 1864;

9. *Official Records of Union and Confederate Armies, Series II, Volume I, Ex Parte John Merryman*, pages 577-585; Randall, James G., *Constitutional Problems under Lincoln*, page 121, University of Illinois Press, 1926/1964;

10. *Official Records of Union and Confederate Armies, Series II, Volume 1*, page 585;

11. Adams, Charles, *When In the Course of Human Events, Arguing the Case For Southern Secession*, pages 48-49, Bowman & Littlefield, Publishers, Inc., Lanham, Boulder, New York, Oxford;

12. Merryman indictment, *Baltimore Sun*, July 11, 1861;

13. *The Diary of George Templeton Strong, Volume III, The Civil War 1860-1865*, October 30, 1862, pages 268-269, Edited by Allan Nevins and Milton Halsey Thomas, Octagon Books, New York,1974;

14. *Important from Baltimore; Proclamation by Major General Dix*, New York Times, November 2, 1861; *Official Records of Union and Confederate Armies, Series II, Volume 1*, page 608; Sprague, Dean, *Freedom Under Lincoln*, pages 203-206, Houghton Mifflin Co Boston, The Riverside Press Cambridge, 1965; *Baltimore Sun, Local Matters*, 11/7/1861; *Baltimore American*, 11/6/1861; Baker, Jean H., *The Politics of Continuity: Maryland Political Parties from 1858 to 1870*, Baltimore, Md., pages 62-75, John Hopkins University Press, 1973;

15. *Official Records of Union and Confederate Armies*, Series II, Volume III, pages 5-6;

16. *Official Records of Union and Confederate Armies,* Series II, Volume 1, page 667, 668-669, 675; *Official Records of Union and Confederate Armies,* Series II, Volume III, pages 6-7, 7, 7-8, 9;

17. Sprague, Dean, *Freedom Under Lincoln,* pages 57-73, Houghton Mifflin Co Boston, The Riverside Press Cambridge, 1965;

18. McElry, John, *The Struggle for Missouri,* page 117, Washington, 1909; Rombauer, Robert, *The Union Cause in St. Louis in 1861,* page 262, St. Louis, 1909: Snead, Thomas Lowndes, *The Fight for Missouri,* pages 198, 200 New York, New York, Charles Scribner's Sons, 1888; Sprague,
Dean, *Freedom Under Lincoln,* pages 86-87, Houghton Mifflin Co Boston, The Riverside Press Cambridge, 1965; *Missouri Democrat,* 6/14/1861;

19. *Official Records of Union and Confederate Armies, Series II, Volume III,* pages 11-14;

20. Letter to Orville Browning, September 22, 1861;

21. Harrison, Lowell, H., *The Civil War in Kentucky*, Lexington, Kentucky, pages 7- 8; Lewis and Richard Collins, history of Kentucky, volume 1, page 87;

22. Harrison, Lowell, H., *The Civil War in Kentucky*, Lexington, Kentucky, page 11;

23. Harrison, Lowell, H., *The Civil War in Kentucky*, Lexington, Kentucky, page 80;

24. Harrison, Lowell, H., *The Civil War in Kentucky*, Lexington, Kentucky, pages 20-21;

25. Harrison, Lowell, H., *The Civil War in Kentucky*, Lexington, Kentucky, page 82-83;

26. Webb, Ross A., *Kentucky's Governor's,* page 94;

27. Webb, Ross A., *Kentucky's Governor's,* page 94;

28. Harrison, Lowell H., *The Kentucky Encyclopedia*, page 113;

Chapter 2,
pages 11-76:

1. Beitzell, Edwin W., *Point Lookout Prison Camp for Confederates,* page 103, St. Mary's County Historical Society, 1983;

2. Beitzell, Edwin W., *Point Lookout Prison Camp For Confederates,* page 19;

3. United States National Archives, War Records, Surgeon General's office, Letter Book number 31, June 2, 1862 to July 25, 1862, page 20; Annual Reports of Officers of the Quartermaster Department, 1863, Volume II, Page 357;

4. Beitzell, Edwin W., *Point Lookout Prison Camp For Confederates,* page 19, St. Mary's County Historical Society, 1983; Information about Sisters of Charity from Catholicism.org;

5. *Official Records of Union and Confederate Armies, Series II, Volume V,* page 669;

6. *Official Records of Union and Confederate Armies, Series II, Volume VI,* page 226; *Official Records of Union and Confederate Armies,* Series II, Volume VII, page 914;

7. *Official Records of Union and Confederate Armies, Series II, Volume V,* page 237;

8. *Official Records of Union and Confederate Armies,* Series II, Volume IV, pages 328-329, 770-771; Butler, Benjamin Franklin, *Autobiography and Personal Reminiscences of Major-General Benjamin Franklin Butler,* pages 370, 376, 437, 443, 542-546, 547, A. M. Thayer & Co., Publishers & Printers, Boston, 1892; Bland, T. A., *Life of Benjamin F. Butler,* pages 74-75, 96-100, 101-104, Lee and Shepard, Publisher, New York, 1879; Marshall, Jessie Ames, *Private and Official Correspondence of Gen. Benjamin F. Butler During the Period of the Civil War, Volume II,* June 1862-February 1863, pages 22, 72, 557, 558, 562, 569, The Plimpton Press, Norwood, Mass., 1917;

9. *Official Records of Union and Confederate Armies,* Series II, Volume V, pages 795-797;

10. *Official Records of Union and Confederate Armies,* Series II, Volume IV, pages 271, 329-330;

11. Miller, Edward A., *Lincoln's Abolitionist General: The Biography of David Hunter,* Columbia: University of South Carolina Press, 1997; *Letters and Proclamations of*

the President, Library of Congress, pages 2-3;

12. *Official Records of Union and Confederate Armies, Series II, Volume IV,* pages 836-837;

13. Speer, Lonnie R., *Portal of Hell, Military Prisons of the Civil War,* pages 109, Stackpole Books, Mechanicsburg, Pa., 1997; (Glattharr, Joseph T., *Forged in Battle, The Civil War Alliance of Black Soldiers and White Officers,* The Free Press, A Division of Macmillan, Inc., New York, 1990, page 160;

14. Fox, William F., *Regimental Losses in the American Civil War, 1861-1865,* pages 53-54; Glattharr, Joseph T., *Forged in Battle, The Civil War Alliance of Black Soldiers and White Officers,* The Free Press, A Division of Macmillan, Inc., New York, 1990, pages 123-130, 131-135;

15. *Official Records of Union and Confederate Armies,* Series II, Volume V, pages 940-941; *Official Records of Union and Confederate Armies,* Series II, Volume VI, pages 17-18, 226;

16. *Official Records of Union and Confederate Armies,* Series II, Volume IV, pages 266-268, articles 4, 6; *Official Records of Union and Confederate Armies,* Series II, Volume V, pages 670-682, Section VII, Subsection 130; *Official Records of Union and Confederate Armies,* Series II, Volume V, page 679, Section VII, Subsection 120;

17. *Official Records of Union and Confederate Armies,* Series II, Volume V, page 669; Volume VI, page 178, 315; Volume VII, pages 606-607; Saunders Jr., Charles W. *While In the Hands of the Enemy, Military Prisons of the Civil War,* pages 310-311;

18. *Southern Historical Society Papers,* Volume 1, No. 3, March 1876, page 147; Speer, Lonnie R., *Portal of Hell, Military Prisons of the Civil War,* page 115, Stackpole Books, Mechanicsburg, Pa., 1997;

19. Grigsby, Colonel Melvin, *The Smoked Yank,* page 137-138;

20. Boate, Edward Wellington, *Southern Historical Society Papers,* Volume X, 1882, No. 1, 31-32;

21. Urban, John W., *Battlefield and Prison Pen,* page 382;

22. Ould, Judge Robert, *Southern Historical Society Papers,* Volume I, No.3, March, 1876, pages 128-129;

23. Ould, Judge Robert, *Southern Historical Society Papers,* Volume I, No.3, March, 1876, pages 128-129;

24. *Official Records of Union and Confederate Armies,* Series II, Volume VII, page 891-892;

25. *Southern Historical Society Papers,* Volume I, No.3, March, 1876, page 136;

26. Beitzell, Edwin W., *Point Lookout Prison Camp For Confederates,* page 21, St. Mary's County Historical Society, 1983;

27. *Official Records of Union and Confederate Armies,* Series II, Volume VI, pages 368, 390;

28. *Official Records of Union and Confederate Armies,* Series II, Volume VI, page 132; Beitzell, Edwin W., *Point Lookout Prison Camp for Confederates,* page 23, St. Mary's County Historical Society, 1983;

29. *Official Records of Union and Confederate Armies,* Series II, Volume IV, pages 152-153;

30. Speer, Lonnie R., *Portals to Hell,* page 14; O. R., Series II, Volume 8, pages 767-768;

31. Thomas, Benjamin P. & Hyman, Harold M., *Stanton: The Life and Times of Lincoln's Secretary of War,* page 378;

32. Wells, James T., *Prison Experience, Southern Historical Society Papers,* Volume VIII, No. 7, July, 1879, page 327;

33. Holliday, B. T., *Account of My Capture,* University of Virginia Library, Charlottesville, Special Collections, page 17; Boatner III, Mark M., *The Civil War Dictionary,* page 760;

34. Loehr, Charles T., *Treatment of Prisoners, Southern Historical Society Papers,* Volume XVIII, Richmond, Virginia, January-December 1890, page 116;

35. Jones, George M., *In Prison at Point Lookout,* page 4;

36. Neese, George M., pages 333-334; Toney, Marcus B., page 96;
37. Loehr, Charles T., *Treatment of Prisoners, Southern Historical Society Papers*, Volume XVIII, Richmond, Virginia, January-December 1890, pages 115-116;
38. Wells, James T., *Prison Experience*, page 326;
39. *Official Records of Union and Confederate Armies*, Series II, Volume 6, page 577;
40. *Official Records of Union and Confederate Armies*, Series II, Volume 6, page 575;
41. King, John R., *My Experience In the Confederate Army and In Northern Prisons*, 27; *Official Records of Union and Confederate Armies*, Series II, Volume 6, page 579;
42. Toney, Marcus B., page 85;
43. Bietzell, Edwin, W. page 25; Holliday, B. T., 17; Neese, George M., 337; O. R., Series II,
Volume 8, page 1002;
44. Addison, Walter D., *Recollections of a Confederate Soldier*, page 1;
45. King, John R., *My Experience In the Confederate Army and In Northern Prisons*, pages 28-29;
46. Perkins, Alfred, *Diary of Capt. Robert E. Park*, page 99;
47. *Official Records of Union and Confederate Armies*, Series II, volume 7, pages 382-385;
48. *Official Records*, Series II, Volume 7, page 1; Harman, N. F., *Prison Experiences at Point Lookout*, page 400; Holliday, B. T., *Account of My Capture*, pages 16-17; Jones, George W., *In Prison at Point Lookout*, page 3; Keiley Anthony M., *In Vinculis Or, The Prisoner Of War*, page 70; King, John R., *My Experience In the Confederate Army and In Northern Prisons*, pages 27-28; Leon, L., *Diary Of A Tar Heel Confederate Soldier*, page 64; Loehr, Charles T., *Treatment of Prisoners, Southern Historical Society Papers*, Volume XVIII, Richmond, Virginia, January-December 1890, pages 116; Neese, George M., *Three Years In the Confederate Horse Artillery*, page 336; Peyton, George Q., *Stonewall Jackson's Foot Cavalry*, page 134; Rawlings, Benjamin Cason, *First Virginia Volunteer for the South*, page 84; Toney, Marcus B., *The Privations Of A Private*, page 88; Unknown Confederate Officer, *Letter of a Confederate Soldier, Southern Historical Society Papers*, Volume I, No. 4, March & April, 1876, page 258;
49. Leon, L., *Diary Of A Tar Heel Confederate Soldier*, page 64;
50. Toney, Marcus B., *The Privations of a Private*, page 88;
51. Loehr, Charles T., *Treatment of Prisoners*, page 118
52. Toney, Marcus B., *The Privations of a Private*, page 87;
53. Keiley Anthony M., *In Vinculis Or, The Prisoner Of War*, page 70;
54. Walker, Thad J., *Reminiscences of Point Lookout*, page 1;
55. Stamp, J. B., *Ten Months Experience in Northern Prisons.* page 8;
56. Peyton, George Q., *Stonewall Jackson's Foot Cavalry*, page 149;
57. King, John R., *My Experience In the Confederate Army and In Northern Prisons*, page 30;
58. Walker, Thad. J., *Reminiscences of Point Lookout*, page 1;
59. Keiley Anthony M., *In Vinculis Or, The Prisoner Of War*, pages 77-78;
60. King, John R., *My Experience In the Confederate Army and In Northern Prisons*, pages 27-28;
61. *Official Records of Union and Confederate Armies*, Series II, Volume 6, page 504;
62. *Official Records of Union and Confederate Armies*, Series II, Volume 6, Dr. William F. Swalm's report, pages 575-581;
63. *Official Records of Union and Confederate Armies*, Series II, Volume 6, Dr. William F. Swalm's report, page 580-581;
64. *Official Records of Union and Confederate Armies*, Series II, Volume 6, page 586;
65. *Official Records of Union and Confederate Armies*, Series II, Volume 6, page 741;
66. *Official Records of Union and Confederate Armies*, Series II, Volume 6, page 741;
67. *Official Records of Union and Confederate Armies*, Series II, Volume 6, Dr. William F.

Swalm's report, pages 577;

68. Loehr, Charles T., *Treatment of Prisoners, Southern Historical Society Papers*, Volume XVIII, January-December 1890, page 117;

69. Caison, Albert Stacey, *Experience at Johnson's Island and Point Lookout, Southern Historical Society Papers*, Volume XXIII, No. 6, page 162;

70. Keiley Anthony M., *In Vinculis Or, The Prisoner Of War: Being the Experience Of A Rebel In Two Federal Pens*, page 69;

71. Neese, George M., *Three years in the Confederate Horse Artillery, a Gunner in Chew's Battery, Stuart's Horse Artillery, Army of Northern Virginia*, 1911, page 345; Keiley Anthony M., *In Vinculis Or, The Prisoner Of War*, pages 68-69;

72. *Official Records of Union and Confederate Armies*, Series II, Volume 6, pages 577;

73. *Official Records of Union and Confederate Armies*, Series II, Volume 4, page 153;

74. Pallen, Montrose A., O. R., Series II, volume 6, page 718;

75. Miller, Gary, *Insects in the Civil War*, pages 1, 2;

76. Holliday, B. T., *Account of My Capture*, page 19;

77. Peyton, George Q., *Stonewall Jackson's Foot Cavalry*, pages 137, 140;

78. Peyton, George Q., *Stonewall Jackson's Foot Cavalry*, page 140;

79. Peyton, George Q., *Stonewall Jackson's Foot Cavalry*, page 145;

80. Wells, James T., *Prison Experience*, Southern Historical Society Papers, Volume VIII, No. 7, July, 1879, pages 328;

81. Holt, David, *A Mississippi Rebel in the Army of Northern Virginia*, page 326;

82. Malone, Bartlett Yancey, *The Diary of Bartlett Yancy Malone*, page 46;

83. Kerns, Josph M. papers, page 33, Traywick, Reverend J. B., *Prison Life at Point Lookout, Southern Historical Society Papers*, Volume XVIII, pages 432;

84. *Official Records of Union and Confederate Armies*, Series II, Volume VII, pages 150-152;

85. *Official Records of Union and Confederate Armies*, Series II, Volume IV, pages *152-153;* Speer, Lonnie R., *Portals to Hell*, page 14;

86. *Official Records of Union and Confederate Armies*, Series II, volume 6, Dr. William F. Swalm's report, page 578;

87. Neese, George M., *Three Years In the Confederate Horse Artillery,* Page 339;

88. Bowden, the Reverend Malachi, *My Life as a Yankee Captive*, page 97;

89. Jones, George, *In Prison at Point Lookout*, page 4;

90. Loehr, Charles T., *Treatment of Prisoners, Southern Historical Society Papers*, Volume XVIII, page 116;

91. Wells, James T., *Prison Experience, Southern Historical Society Papers*, Volume VIII, No. 8, August, page 394;

92. Holt, David, *A Mississippi Rebel in the Army of Northern Virginia*, page 323;

93. *Official Records of Union and Confederate Armies*, Series II, volume 6, Dr. William F. Swalm's report, page 578;

94. *Official Records of Union and Confederate Armies*, Series II, volume 6, Dr. William F. Swalm's report, page 581;

95. Bosworth, S. N., *Report of Vivid Prison Experiences,* page 472;

96. Neese, George M., *Three Years In the Confederate Horse Artillery*, page 349;

97. *Official Records of Union and Confederate Armies*, Series II, Volume 7, page 421;

98. Jones, George W., *In Prison at Point Lookout*, page 5;

99. Wells, James T., *Prison Experience*, page 394;

100. Jones, Freeman W, *War Talks of Confederate Veterans*, page 85;

101. *Official Records of Union and Confederate Armies*, Series II, volume 6, pages 764-768, 766;

102. Neese, George M., *Three Years In the Confederate Horse Artillery*, pages 339-340;

103. *Official Records of Union and Confederate Armies*, Series II, volume 7, page 75;

104. King, John R., *My Experience In the Confederate Army and In Northern Prisons*, page 38;

105. Toney, Marcus B., *The Privations of a Private,* page 87;

106. Keiley Anthony M., *In Vinculis Or, The Prisoner Of War,* page 90;

107. Loehr, Charles T., *Treatment of Prisoners, Southern Historical Society Papers,* Volume XVIII, page 117;

108. Hopkins, Luther, *Prison life at Point Lookout,* page 89; Whitehead, J. H., *Memories of the Battle of Gettysburg and Point Lookout Prison,* page 1;

109. Rose, Minnie Bowen, Editorial Director, *Diseases, Nursing Reference Library,* page 391;

110. *Official Records of Union and Confederate Armies,* Series II, volume 6, Dr. William F. Swalm's report, page 582;

111. Wells, James T., *Prison Experience, Southern Historical Society Papers,* Volume VIII, No. 8, August, page 395;

112. *Official Records of Union and Confederate Armies,* Series II, Volume 6, page 743, Report of Augustus M. Clark;

113. Addison, Walter D., *Recollections of a Confederate Soldier of the Prison-Pens of Point Lookout,Maryland, and Elmira, New York,* pages 4-5;

114. Rose, Minnie Bowen, Editorial Director, *Diseases, Nursing Reference Library,* pages 669-670;

115. Handy, Reverend I. W. K., *Southern Historical Society Papers,* Volume 1, April, 1876, page 271;

116. King, John A., *My Experience in the Confederate Army and In Northern Prisons,* page 37; Keiley Anthony M., *In Vinculis Or, The Prisoner Of War,* page 86;

117. Rose, Minnie Bowen, Editorial Director, *Diseases, Nursing Reference Library,* pages 332-333;

118. Loehr, Charles T., *Treatment of Prisoners, Southern Historical Society Papers,* Volume XVIII, page 117;

119. Rose, Minnie Bowen, Editorial Director, *Diseases, Nursing Reference Library,* pages 475-479;

120. *Official Records of Union and Confederate Armies,* Series II, volume 6 pages 578, 580;

121. *Official Records of Union and Confederate Armies,* Series II, volume 6, pages 473, 489;

122. Rose, Minnie Bowen, Editorial Director, *Diseases, Nursing Reference Library,* pages 864-865;

123. Holliday, B. T., *Account of My Capture,* page 21;

124. Hopkins, Luther, *Prison life at Point Lookout,* page 88;

125. Bowden, the Reverend Malachi, *My Life as a Yankee Captive,* page 97;

126. Rose, Minnie Bowen, Editorial Director, *Diseases, Nursing Reference Library,* page 330;

127. Neese, George M., *Three Years In the Confederate Horse Artillery,* pages 344-345;

128. Neese, George M., *Three Years In the Confederate Horse Artillery,* pages 345-346;

129. Unknown Confederate officer, *Southern Historical Society Papers,* volume 1, No. 4, April, 1876, page 257;

130. Hutt, Charles W., *The diary of Charles Warren Hutt,* entry for April 29, 1864,; Beitzell, Edwin W., *Point Lookout Prison Camp for Confederates,* page 73;

131. Peyton, George Q., *Stonewall Jackson's Foot Cavalry,* pages 149, 153, 154-155;

132. King, John R., *My Experience In the Confederate Army and In Northern Prisons,* page 40;

133. *Official Records of Union and Confederate Armies,* Series II, volume 6, Dr. William F. Swalm's report, page 578;

134. Neese, George M., *Three Years In the Confederate Horse Artillery,* pages 337-338; *Official Records,* Series II, volume 6, Dr. William F. Swalm's report, page 578;

135. Hutt, Charles Warren, *The Diary of Charles Warren Hutt,* page 72;

136. Keiley Anthony M., *In Vinculis or, The Prisoner Of War:* pages 72;

137. Hutt, Charles Warren, *The diary of Charles Warren Hutt,* pages 74;

138. *Official Records of Union and Confederate Armies,* Series II, volume 6, Dr. William F. Swalm's

report, page 578; *Official Records of Union and Confederate Armies,* Series II, Volume 6, page 742;

139. Keiley, Anthony M., *In Vinculis Or, The Prisoner Of War,* page 113;
140. Wells, James T., *Prison Experience,* page 395;
141. Jones, Freeman, W., *War Talks of Confederate Veterans,* page 85;
142. Neese, George M., *Three Years In the Confederate Horse Artillery,* page 340;
143. Hopkins, Luther, *Prison life at Point Lookout,* page 88; Peyton, George Q., *Stonewall Jackson's Foot Cavalry,* page 150;
144. *Official Records of Union and Confederate Armies,* series II, volume 6, pages 576, 579;
145. *Official Records of Union and Confederate Armies,* Series II, volume 6, page 742, 743;
146. Wells, James T., *Prison Experience, Southern Historical Society Papers,* Volume VIII, No. 8, August, page 393;
147. Holliday, B. T., *Account of My Capture,* page 18;
148. King, John R., *My Experience in the Confederate Army and In Northern Prisons,* page 28;
149. Loehr, Charles T., *Treatment of Prisoners,* page 118;
150. Harman, N. F., *Prison Experiences at Point Lookout, Md,* page 400;
151. Holliday, B. T., *Account of My Capture,* page 19; King, John R., *My Experience In the Confederate Army and In Northern Prisons,* page 36;
152. Bartlett Yancey Malone, *The Diary of Bartlett Yancy Malone,* page 55; George Q. Peyton, *Stonewall Jackson's Foot Cavalry,* page 146;
153. George Q. Peyton, *Stonewall Jackson's Foot Cavalry,* page 146;
154. Smith, Alfred Jefferson, *Civil War Diary of Alfred Jefferson Smith,* page 8;
155. George Q. Peyton, *Stonewall Jackson's Foot Cavalry,* pages 150-151;
156. William H. Haigh to Kate, May 24, 1863, William H. Haigh papers, Southern Historical Collection;
157. Wells, James T., *Prison Experience, Southern Historical Society Papers,* Volume VIII, No. 7, July, page 328;
158. Bartlett Yancey Malone, *The Diary of Bartlett Yancy Malone,* page 46;
159. George M. Neese, *Three Years in the Confederate Horse Artillery:* page 345;
160. Benson, Susan, *Berry Benson's Civil War Book,* page 94;
161. Elliott, James Carson, *The Southern Soldier Boy,* page 49;
162. Walker, Thad. J., *Reminiscences of Point Lookout,* page 2;
163. Neese, George M., *Three Years in the Confederate Horse Artillery,* page 350;
164. Holliday, B. T., *Account of My Capture,* page 19;
165. Berry, Susan, *Berry Benson's Civil War Book,* page 94;
166. Holt, David, *A Mississippi Rebel in the Army of Northern Virginia,* pages 323-324;
167. Wells, James T., *Prison Experience, Southern Historical Society Papers,* page 487;
168. Malone, Bartlett Yancey, *The Diary of Bartlett Yancy Malone,* page 47;
169. Peyton, George Q., *Stonewall Jackson's Foot Cavalry,* page 143;
170. King, John R., *My Experience In the Confederate Army and In Northern Prisons,* page 42;
171. Hopkins, Luther, *Prison life at Point Lookout,* page 88; Toney, Marcus B., *The Privations Of A Private* Pages 115-116;
172. Addison, Walter D., *Recollections of a Confederate Soldier of the Prison-Pens of Point Lookout, Maryland, and Elmira,* page 5;
173. Descendants of Point Lookout POW Organization webpage;
174. Leon, L., *Diary Of A Tar Heel Confederate Soldier,* page 66;
175. Keiley Anthony M., *In Vinculis Or, The Prisoner Of War,* pages 81-82;
176. *Official Records of Union and Confederate Armies,* Series II, volume 6, page 450;
177. Keiley Anthony M., *In Vinculis or, The Prisoner Of War,* pages 113-114;
178. Toney, Marcus B., *The Privations of a Private,* page 88;
179. Jones, George W., *In Prison at Point Lookout,* pages 3-4;

180. *Official Records of Union and Confederate Armies*, Series I, Volume 33, pages 268-269; Beitzell, Edwin W., *Point Lookout Prison Camp For Confederates*, pages 25-26;
181. *Official Records of Union and Confederate Armies*, Series I, Volume 37, part I, pages 71-73;
182. *Official Records of Union and Confederate Armies*, Series I, Volume 37, part I, pages 163-167;
183. Keiley Anthony M., *In Vinculis or, The Prisoner Of War*, pages 84-85;
184. Jones, George W., *In Prison at Point Lookout*, page 6;
185. Keiley Anthony M., *In Vinculis or, The Prisoner Of War*, pages 73-74;
186. Lake, Luther B., *Escape from Point Lookout Prison*, pages 93-96;
187. *Official Records of Union and Confederate Armies*, Volume 5, page 676, No. 77;
188. Davis, Jefferson, *The Papers of Jefferson Davis*, Volume 10, pages 484-486; Beitzell, Edwin W., *Point Lookout Prison Camp for Confederates*, page 50;
189. Beitzell, Edwin W., *Point Lookout Prison Camp for Confederates*, page 50;
190. Beitzell, Edwin W., *Point Lookout Prison Camp for Confederates*, page 52;
191 Beitzell, Edwin W., *Point Lookout Prison Camp for Confederates*, page 53;
192. *Official Records of Union and Confederate Navies*, Series I, volume 10, page 721;
193. *Official Records of Union and Confederate Navies*, Series I, volume 10, pages 721-722;
194. Beitzell, Edwin W., *Point Lookout Prison Camp for Confederates*, page 53;
195. *Official Records of the Union and Confederate Navies*, Series I, Volume 10, pages 281, 288;
196. Beitzell, Edwin W., *Point Lookout Prison Camp for Confederates*, page 54;
197. *Official Records of the Union and Confederate Armies*, Series II, volume 7, page 502;
198. Malone, Bartlett Yancey, *The Diary of Bartlett Yancy Malone*, page 49; Holliday, B. T., *Account of My Capture*, page 20;
199. Wells, James T., *Prison Experience, Southern Historical Society Papers*, Volume VIII, No. 8, August, page 394;
200. Wells, James T., *Prison Experience, Southern Historical Society Papers*, Volume VIII, No. 8, August, pages 396, 490;
201. Unknown prisoner at Point Lookout Prison Camp, 10/10/1864;
202. Wells, James T., *Prison Experience, Southern Historical Society Papers*, Volume VIII, No. 8, August, page 396;
203. Neese, George M., *Three Years in the Confederate Horse Artillery*, pages 353, 354;
204. Holliday, B. T., *Account of My Capture*, pages 21-22;
205. Elliott, James C., *The Southern Soldier Boy*, page 49;
206. Murphy, John Joseph Pledger, *Diary of John Joseph Pledger*, pages 2, 4;
207. Holliday, B. T., *Account of My Capture*, pages 21-22;
208. Neese, George M., *Three Years In the Confederate Horse Artillery*, page 355;
209. Loehr, Charles T., *Address before Pickett Camp Confederate Veterans, October 10, 1890*, pages 7-8;
210. Caison, Albert S., *Experience at Johnson's Island and Point Lookout*, pages 162-163;
211. Holliday, B. T., *Account of My Capture*, pages 22-23;
212. Traywick, J. B., *Prison Life at Point Lookout*, page 435;
213. Holliday, B. T., *Account of My Capture*, pages 22-23;

Chapter 3,
pages 77-80:

1. Speer, Lonnie R., *Portal of Hell, Military Prisons of the Civil War*, page 241; Horigan, Michael *Elmira: Death Camp of the North*, page 27;
2. Stanton, Edwin M, *Official Records*, Series II, Volume 4, page 48;
3. *Official Records*, Series II, Volume 3, page 157;
4. Dix, John A., *Official Records*, Series II, Volume 4, pages 266-268;

5. Boatner, Mark M., *The Civil War Dictionary*, page 620;

6. Speer, Lonnie R., *Portal of Hell, Military Prisons of the Civil War*, page 336;
7. *Official Records of Union and Confederate Armies*, Volume 7, pages 113-114;
8. *Official Records of Union and Confederate Armies*, Volume 7, page 113;
9. Williams T. Harry, *Lincoln and the Radicals*, pages 344-345, University of Wisconsin Press; 1960;
10. Senate Joint Resolution 97, Library of Congress, web page: http://memory.loc.gov/cgi-bin/ampage?collId=llsr&fileName=038/llsr038.db&recNum=105 ;
11. *New York Times*, October 2, 1864;
12. Richard N. Current, *The Lincoln Nobody Knows*, page 176;
13. *The Southern Historical Society Papers*, vol. 1, No. 4, April 1876, page 295; *The Confederate Veteran*, April 1907, page 163; Pratt, Fletcher, *Stanton: Lincoln's Secretary of War*, page 357;
14. Horigan, Michael, *Elmira: Death Camp of the North*, page 155;

Chapter 4,
pages 81-90:

1. *Official Records*, Series II, Volume 7, page 776; Saunders Jr., Charles W. *While in the Hands of the Enemy, Military Prisons of the Civil War*, pages 257-258; Hesseltine, Ph. D., William Best, *Civil War Prisons, A Study in War Psychology*, pages 221-225; Page, James Madison, *The True Story of Andersonville Prison: A Defense of Major Henry Wirz*, pages 105-106; Thomas, Benjamin P. & Hyman, Harold M., *Stanton: The Life and Times of Lincoln's Secretary of War*, page 599-605;
2. Page, James Madison, Second Lieutenant, Sixth Michigan cavalry, *The True Story of Andersonville Prison*, pages 102-103;
3. Pepper, Captain George W., *Personal recollections of Sherman's campaign in Georgia and the Carolinas*, pages 216-217;
4. Belknap, Charles E., *Recollections of the Bummer*, War Papers 28, January 5, 1898; Nichols, Major George Ward, *The Story of the Great March from the Diary of a Staff Officer*, pages 240-244;
5. Butler, Benjamin F., *Butler's Book: Autobiography and Personal Reminiscences of Major General Benjamin F. Butler*, page 610-611, A. M. Thayer & Co., Book Publishers, Boston, 1892;
6. *Official Records of Union and Confederate Armies*, Series II, volume 7, page 385;
7. Richard N. Current, *The Lincoln Nobody Knows*, page 176;
8. *Southern Historical Society Papers*, An Important Incident of the Shenandoah Valley Campaign, Volume XXX, page 229; Speer, Lonnie, *War of Vengeance*, page 131;
9. Bates, David Homer, *Lincoln in the Telegraph Office*, The Century Publishing Company, New York, 1907, pages 113-123;
10. Triebe, Richard H., *Point Lookout Prison Camp and Hospital*, page 16;

Bibliography

Primary Sources

Diaries, Papers, Letters and Recollections

Addison, Walter D., *Recollections of a Confederate Soldier of the Prison-Pens of Point Lookout, Maryland, and Elmira, New York,* Southern Historical Collection of the North Carolina Library, Chapel Hill.

Beckham, Elihu C., *A Good Story, Where I was and What I Saw During the Late War,* Melbourne Times, Arkansas, 9/6/1906

Belknap, Charles E., Military Order of the Loyal Legion of the United States, War Papers 28, January 5, 1898

Bernard, George S., *War Talks of Confederate Veterans,* Penn & Owen, Publishers, Petersburg, Virginia, 1892.

Boate, Edward Wellington, *Southern Historical Society Papers*, Volume X, 1882, No. 1, 25-32;

Bosworth, S. N., *Report of Vivid Prison Experiences, Southern Historical Society Papers*, Volume XVIII, No. 10, October, 1910, page 472;

Bowden, the Reverend Malachi, *My Life As A Yankee Captive*, pages 96-99, Beitzell, Edwin W., *Point Lookout Prison Camp For Confederates,* St. Mary's County Historical Society, 1983;

Caison, Albert Stacey, *Experience at Johnson's Island and Point Lookout, Southern Historical Society Papers*, Volume XXIII, 1895, No. 6, pages 159-165.

Cone, A. J., *Major Brady, Pt. Lookout's Provost Marshall, Confederate Veteran Magazine,* have 1912, Volume 20, page 524-525.

Haigh, William H., Letter to Kate, May 24, 1863, William H. Haigh papers, Southern Historical Collection, University of North Carolina;

Handy, Dr. I. W. K., *Treatment of Prisoners During the War, Southern Historical Society Papers*, Volume I, 1876, April, 270-273.

Harman, N. F., *Prison Experiences at Point Lookout, Md, Confederate Veteran Magazine,* Volume XV, No. 9, September,1907.

Holliday, B. T., *Account of My Capture,* Manuscript, Special Collections Library, University of Virginia.

Hopkins, Luther, *Prison life at Point Lookout*, pages 87-89, Beitzell, Edwin W., *Point Lookout Prison Camp For Confederates,* St. Mary's County Historical Society, 1983;

Hutt, Charles Warren, *The diary of Charles Warren Hutt*, pages 85-87, Edwin W., *Point Lookout Prison Camp For Confederates,* St. Mary's County Historical Society, 1983;

Jameson, James H., *A Civil War Collection From the VMI Archives,* Virginia Military Institute.

Jones, Freeman W, *War Talks of Confederate Veterans,* page 83-86, Penn & Owen, Publishers, Petersburg, Virginia, 1892.

Jones, George W., *In Prison at Point Lookout,* The Bivouac, Bivouac Books;

Jones, Rev. J. Williams, *Confederate View of the Treatment of Prisoners,* pages 256-258, Richmond, Southern Historical Society, 1876.

Kerns, Joseph M. papers, *Digital Southern Historical Collection, At the Louis Round Wilson Special Collections Library, University of North Carolina.*

King, John R., *My Experience In the Confederate Army and In Northern Prisons*, Stonewell Jackson Chapter, No. 1333, United Daughters Of the Confederacy, Clarksburg, West Virginia, 1917.

Lake, Luther B., *Escape from Point Lookout Prison*, pages 93-96, Beitzell, Edwin W., *Point Lookout Prison Camp For Confederates,* St. Mary's County Historical Society, 1983;

Loehr, Charles T., *Treatment of Prisoners, Southern Historical Society Papers*, Volume XVIII, Richmond, Virginia, January-December 1890, pages 114-120.

Malone, Bartlett Yancey, *The Diary of Bartlett Yancy Malone,* Published by the University of North Carolina, Chapel Hill, 1919.

Murphy, John Joseph Pledger, *Diary of John Joseph Pledger Murphy, Written While In A Union Prison (Point Lookout, Md) Being A Confederate Soldier—1865,* Posted on Ancestry.com by Sandy Clark, great granddaughter of John Joseph Pledger Murphy;

Nelson, Reverend George W., *Confederate View Of the Treatment of Prisoners, Southern Historical Society*, page 243-256, Richmond, Virginia, 1876;

Park, Robert E., *The Diary of Capt. Robert E. Park,* pages 99-101, Beitzell, Edwin W., *Point Lookout Prison Camp For Confederates,* St. Mary's County Historical Society, 1983;

Parkins, Alfred, page 99, *The Diary of Capt. Robert E. Park,* pages 99-101, Beitzell, Edwin W., *Point Lookout Prison Camp For Confederates,* St. Mary's County Historical Society, 1983;

Read, Thomas G., papers, *Read Family Correspondence*, Manuscripts of the American Civil War, University of Notre Dame, Rare Books and Special Collections, author George Rugg;

Robinson, John W., *Experiences in Camp Chase and Point Lookout, Confederate Veteran Magazine,* Volume XIV, No. 11, November 1906;

Seward, Simon, *War Talks of Confederate Veterans,* author George S. Bernard, Fenn & Owen, Publishers, Petersburg, Virginia, 1892;

Smith, Alfred Jefferson, *Civil War Diary of Alfred Jefferson Smith,* Chatahoochee Hills Historical Society, Georgia;

Stamp, J. B., *Ten Months Experience in Northern Prisons,* State of Alabama, Department of Archives and History, Montgomery, Alabama

Timberlake, W. L., *Point Lookout, Confederate Veteran Magazine,* Volume XXI, No. 12, December 1913;

Traywick, Reverend J. B., *Prison Life at Point Lookout, Southern Historical Society Papers,* Volume XVIII, pages 432-436;

Unknown author, *Letter of a Confederate Soldier, Southern Historical Society Papers,* Volume I, No. 4, March & April, 1876, pages 257-258;

Unknown author, *Confederate POW Tells of Yankees' Psychological Warfare During American Civil War* by Tom Martinscroft, Abroad in the Yard;

Walker, Thad. J., *Reminiscences of Point Lookout, The Bivouac Banner*, Volume V, Issue 1, Spring 2006;

Wells, James T., *Prison Experience, Southern Historical Society Papers*, Volume VIII, No. 7, July, 1879, pages 324-330, No. 8, August, 393-399, No. 10, October, 487-491;

Whitehead, J. H., *Memories of the Battle of Gettysburg and Point Lookout Prison,* Chatham and Pittsylvania County, Virginia and the Civil War, online;

Williams, Hiram Smith, *This War So Horrible, The Civil War Diary of Hiram Smith Williams,* Edited by Lewis N. Wynne and Robert A. Taylor, The University of Alabama Press, Tuscaloosa & London, 1993;

Published Primary Sources

Benson, Susan Williams, *Berry Benson's Civil War Book*, The University of Georgia Press, Athens, Georgia, 1992;

Billings, John D., *Hardtack and Coffee*, George M. Smith & Company, Boston,1887;

Butler, Benjamin Franklin, *Autobiography and Personal Reminiscences of Major-General Benjamin Franklin Butler, Butler's Book*, A. M. Thayer & Co., Publishers & Printers, Boston, 1892;

Davis, Jefferson C., *The Papers of Jefferson Davis, Oct. 1863-Aug. 1864*, Volume 10, Editors Lynda L. Crist, Kenneth H. Williams, Peggy L. Dillard, Louisiana State University Press, Baton Rouge, 1999;

Elliott, James Carson, *The Southern Soldier Boy: A Thousand Shots For the Confederacy*, Edwards & Broughton Printing Company, Raleigh, N. C., 1907.

Grigsby, Colonel Melvin, *The Smoked Yank*, Regan Printing Company, Chicago, Illinois, 1891;

Holt, David, *A Mississippi Rebel in the Army of Northern Virginia: The Civil War Memoirs of Private David Holt*, Louisiana State University Press, Baton Rouge, 1995.

Howard, Francis Key, *Fourteen Months in American Bastilles*, Published by Kelly, Hedian & Piet, Baltimore, 1863;

Keiley Anthony M., *In Vinculis Or, The Prisoner Of War: Being the Experience Of A Rebel In Two Federal Pens*, Blelock & Co., No. 19 Beekman Street, New York, 1866;

Leon, Lewis, *Diary Of A Tar Heel Confederate Soldier*, Stone Publishing Company, Charlotte, North Carolina, 1913.

Neese, George M., *Three Years In the Confederate Horse Artillery, A Gunner in Chew's Battery, Stuart's Horse Artillery, Army of Northern Virginia*, 1911;

Peyton, George Q., *Stonewall Jackson's Foot Cavalry, Company A, 13th Virginia Infantry*, Burd Street Press, Shippensburg, Pennsylvania, 2001;

Pollard, Edward A., *Observations In the North: Eight Months In Prison and On Parole*, C. W. Ayres, Corner Ninth and Main Streets, Richmond, Virginia, 1865.

Rawlings, Benjamin Cason, *First Virginia Volunteer for the South*, Author Byrd Barnette Tribble, Butternut and Blue, 1995;

Strong, George Templeton, *The Diary of George Templeton Strong, Volume III, The Civil War 1860-1865*, Edited by Allan Nevins and Milton Halsey Thomas, Octagon Books, New York, 1974;

Toney, Marcus B., *The Privations Of A Private*, Printed For the Author, Nashville, Tennessee, 1905;

Urban, John W., *Battlefield and Prison Pen, or Through the War, and Thrice a Prisoner in Rebel Dungeons*, Edgewood Publishing Company, 1882;

Published Secondary Sources

Adams, Charles, *When In the Course of Human Events, Arguing the Case For Southern Secession*, Bowman & Littlefield, Publishers, Inc., Lanham, Boulder, New York, Oxford, 2004;

Baker, Jean H. *The Politics of Continuity: Maryland Political Parties from 1858 to 1870*, Baltimore, Md., John Hopkins University Press, 1973;

Basler, Roy P., *Collected Works of Abraham Lincoln, volume 4*, University of Michigan Digital Library production services;

Bates, David Homer, *Lincoln in the Telegraph Office*, The Century Publishing Company, New York, 1907;

Beitzell, Edwin W., *Point Lookout Prison Camp for Confederates*, St. Mary's County Historical Society, 1983;

Billings, John Davis, *Hardtack and coffee: The Unwritten Story of Army Life*, R.R. Donnelley &

Sons Company, 1960;

Boatner III, Mark M., *The Civil War Dictionary,* Revised Edition, Vintage Books, A Division of Random House, Inc., New York, 1991;

Bland, T. A., *Life of Benjamin F. Butler,* Lee and Shepard, Publisher, New York, 1879;

Bulla, David W., *Abraham Lincoln and Press Suppression Reconsidered,* American Journalism Historians Association, 2009;

Current, Richard N., *The Lincoln Nobody Knows,* Hill and Wang Publishers, New York, 1958;

Crist, Lynda S well, ed., *The Papers of Jefferson Davis,* Volume 10, Baton Rouge, La., Louisiana State University Press, 1999;

Fox, William F., *Regimental Losses in the American Civil War, 1861-1865,* Albany Publishing Company, Albany, New York, 1889;

Glatthaar, Joseph T., *Forged in Battle, The Civil War Alliance of Black Soldiers and White Officers,* The Free Press, A Division of Macmillan, Inc., New York, 1990;

Harrison, Lowell, H. *The Civil War in Kentucky.* The University Press of Kentucky, Lexington, Kentucky. 1975; *The Kentucky Encyclopedia,* The University press of Kentucky, Lexington, Kentucky, 1992;

Hesseltine, Ph. D., William Best, *Civil War Prisons, A Study in War Psychology,* The Ohio State Press, Columbus, Ohio, 1930;

Holmes, Clay W., *The Elmira Prison Camp,* G. P. Putnam's Sons, The Knickerbocher Press, New York, 1912;

Horigan, Michael, Elmira: *Death Camp of the North,* Stackpole Books, Mechanicsburg, Pa., 2002;

Jones, Reverend J. William, *Confederate View of the Treatment of Prisoners,* Richmond, Southern Historical Society, Richmond, Virginia, 1876;

Marshall, Jessie Ames, *Private and Official Correspondence of Gen. Benjamin F. Butler During the Period of the Civil War, Volume II,* June 1862-February 1863, The Plimpton Press, Norwood, Mass., 1917;

McElry, John, *The Struggle for Missouri,* page 117, Washington, 1909;

Miller, Edward A., *Lincoln's Abolitionist General: The Biography of David Hunter,* Columbia: University of South Carolina Press, 1997;

Pickenpaugh, Roger, *Captives in Gray, The Civil War Prisons of the Union,* The University of Alabama Press, Tuscaloosa, 2009;

Randall, James G., *Constitutional Problems under Lincoln,* University of Illinois Press, 1926/1964;

Rose, Minnie Bowen, Editorial Director, *Diseases, Nursing Reference Library,* Springhouse Corporation, Springhouse, Pennsylvania, 1985;

Rombauer, Robert, *The Union Cause in St. Louis in 1861,* St. Louis, 1909;

Sangston, Lawrence, *Bastille's of the North: By a member of the Maryland Legislature of Baltimore,* Kelly, Hedian and Piett, 1863;

Saunders Jr., Charles W. *While In the Hands of the Enemy, Military Prisons of the Civil War,* Louisiana State University Press, Baton Rouge, Louisiana, 2005;

Shingleton, Royce Borden, *John Taylor Wood: Ghost of the Confederacy,* Athens, Georgia: University of Georgia Press, 1979;

Snead, Thomas Lowndes, *The Fight for Missouri,* 200 New York, New York, Charles Scribner's Sons, 1888;

Speer, Lonnie R., *Portal of Hell, Military Prisons of the Civil War,* Stackpole Books, Mechanicsburg, Pa., 1997; *War of Vengeance, Acts of Retaliation Against Civil War POWs,* Stackpole Books, 2002;

Sprague, Dean, *Freedom Under Lincoln,* Houghton Mifflin Co Boston, The Riverside Press Cambridge, 1965;

Thomas, Benjamin P. & Hyman, Harold M., *Stanton: The Life and Times of Lincoln's Secretary of War,* Alfred A. Knoff, New York, 1962;

The American Annual Cyclopedia and Register of Important Events of the Year 1861, New York: D. Appleton & Company, 443 & 445 Broadway, 1864;

Webb, Ross A., *Kentucky's Governors*, The University Press of Kentucky, Lexington, Kentucky, 2004;
Williams T. Harry, *Lincoln and the Radicals,* University of Wisconsin Press, 1960;

Manuscripts and Papers

Miller, Gary, *Insects in the Civil War,* Online;

Government Publications

United States National Archives, War Records, Surgeon General's office, Letter Book number 31, June 2, 1862 to July 25, 1862;
Annual Reports of Officers of the Quartermaster Department, 1863, Volume II;
War of the Rebellion, Official Records of the Union and Confederate Armies, Series II, Prisoners of War;
Letters and Proclamations of the President, Library of Congress;

Newspapers and Periodicals

Baltimore American,
Baltimore Sun,
Missouri Democrat,
New York Evening Post,
New York Times,

Index

<u>About The Author</u>

Richard H. Triebe is a freelance writer and historian published in multiple periodicals. He is the author of several historical novels and has done extensive research work regarding the Fort Fisher prisoners. Two of his books, *Fort Fisher to Elmira* and *Point Lookout Prison Camp and Hospital,* were awarded the coveted Jefferson Davis Historical Gold Medal Award for outstanding achievement for a literary work. His ground breaking research resulted in hundreds of names being added to the rolls of Confederate prisoners who died at both prisons. This list contains the names of the Confederate dead which include civilians, marines, sailors and soldiers.

Richard has an Associate's Degree in Marine Technology. He is a former Chicago police officer and was a Provost Marshal investigator in the United States Army. Richard is a member of the Coastal Carolina Writers Guild, a Brunswick Writers Forum panelist, and has appeared as a guest on several television shows, including *The Artist's Craft* hosted by Stacy Cochran and WWAY TV's *Book Corner* with Marcy Cuevas. He is a member of the Cape Fear Civil War Round Table, and has presented historical overviews of the battles of Fort Fisher to many local organizations. Richard is also presenting a PowerPoint talks about the northern prisons at Elmira, New York, and Point Lookout, Maryland. He and his wife, Barbara, live in Wilmington, North Carolina.

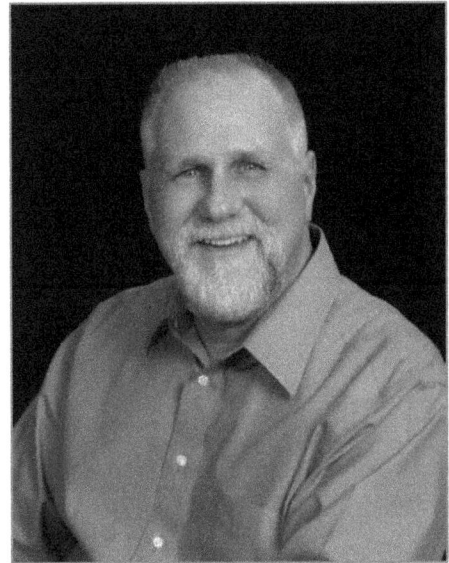

www.ingramcontent.com/pod-product-compliance
Lightning Source LLC
Chambersburg PA
CBHW062019090426
42811CB00005B/901